Fodor's 2015

WALT DISNEY WORLD

WELCOME TO WALT DISNEY WORLD

Orlando vacations are events that often become part of family legend. Kids and parents swap Disney or Universal stories for years, fondly reliving favorite moments such as the first Butterbeer in Hogsmeade, the "Be Our Guest" dance with Belle, or the final battle between Buzz Lightyear and Zurg. Beyond the Wizarding Worlds and Fantasylands, Orlando towns such as Mount Dora and Kissimmee lure travelers away from the parks with fascinating museums, great shopping, and freshwater lakes. Farther out is the out-of-this-world experience of the Kennedy Space Center.

TOP REASONS TO GO

★ **Walt Disney World:** Quite simply, the magic of the Disney parks touches all who visit.

★ **Universal Orlando:** Islands of Adventure and Universal Studios are high-energy fun.

★ **Sea World and Discovery Cove:** A tropical retreat with Shamu, dolphins, and seals.

★ **International Drive:** Bustling strip with attractions like Fun Spot and Wet 'n Wild.

★ **Downtown Orlando:** Top restaurants, theater, and music create a thriving scene.

★ **The Space Coast:** Kennedy Space Center—and 70 miles of white-sand beaches

Fodor's WALT DISNEY WORLD 2015

Publisher: Amanda D'Acierno, *Senior Vice President*

Editorial: Arabella Bowen, *Editor in Chief*; Linda Cabasin, *Editorial Director*

Design: Fabrizio La Rocca, *Vice President, Creative Director*; Tina Malaney, *Associate Art Director*; Chie Ushio, *Senior Designer*; Ann McBride, *Production Designer*

Photography: Melanie Marin, *Associate Director of Photography*; Jessica Parkhill and Jennifer Romains, *Researchers*

Maps: Rebecca Baer, *Senior Map Editor*; Mark Stroud, Moon Street Cartography and David Lindroth, *Cartographers*

Production: Linda Schmidt, *Managing Editor*; Evangelos Vasilakis, *Associate Managing Editor*; Angela L. McLean, *Senior Production Manager*

Sales: Jacqueline Lebow, *Sales Director*

Marketing & Publicity: Heather Dalton, *Marketing Director*; Katherine Punia, *Senior Publicist*

Business & Operations: Susan Livingston, *Vice President, Strategic Business Planning*; Sue Daulton, *Vice President, Operations*

Fodors.com: Megan Bell, *Executive Director, Revenue & Business Development*; Yasmin Marinaro, *Senior Director, Marketing & Partnerships*

Writers: Kate Bradshaw, Rona Gindin, Jennifer Greenhill-Taylor, Jennie Hess, Steve Master, Gary McKechnie

Editors: Perrie Hartz

Production Editor: Carrie Parker

ISBN 978-0-8041-4267-0

ISSN 1531-443X

SPECIAL SALES

This book is available at special discounts for bulk purchases for sales promotions or premiums. For more information, e-mail specialmarkets@randomhouse.com

PRINTED IN THE UNITED STATES OF AMERICA

10 9 8 7 6 5 4 3 2 1

CONTENTS

Fodor's Features

MAPS

ABOUT THIS GUIDE

Fodor's Recommendations

Everything in this guide is worth doing—we don't cover what isn't—but exceptional sights, hotels, and restaurants are recognized with additional accolades. **Fodor's**Choice★ indicates our top recommendations; and **Best Bets** call attention to notable hotels and restaurants in various categories. Care to nominate a new place? Visit Fodors.com/contact-us.

Trip Costs

We list prices wherever possible to help you budget well. Hotel and restaurant price categories from **$** to **$$$$** are noted alongside each recommendation. For hotels, we include the lowest cost of a standard double room in high season. For restaurants, we cite the average price of a main course at dinner or, if dinner isn't served, at lunch. For attractions, we always list adult admission fees; discounts are usually available for children, students, and senior citizens.

Hotels

Our local writers vet every hotel to recommend the best overnights in each price category, from budget to expensive. Unless otherwise specified, you can expect private bath, phone, and TV in your room. For expanded hotel reviews, facilities, and deals visit Fodors.com.

Restaurants

Unless we state otherwise, restaurants are open for lunch and dinner daily. We mention dress code only when there's a specific requirement and reservations only when they're essential or not accepted. To make restaurant reservations, visit Fodors.com.

Credit Cards

The hotels and restaurants in this guide typically accept credit cards. If not, we'll say so.

Top Picks

★ **Fodor's**Choice

Listings

- Address
- Branch address
- Telephone
- Fax
- Website
- E-mail
- Admission fee
- Open/closed times
- Subway
- Directions or Map coordinates

Hotels & Restaurants

- Hotel
- Number of rooms
- Meal plans
- Restaurant
- Reservations
- Dress code
- No credit cards
- Price

Other

- See also
- Take note
- Golf facilities

1

EXPERIENCE ORLANDO AND THE PARKS

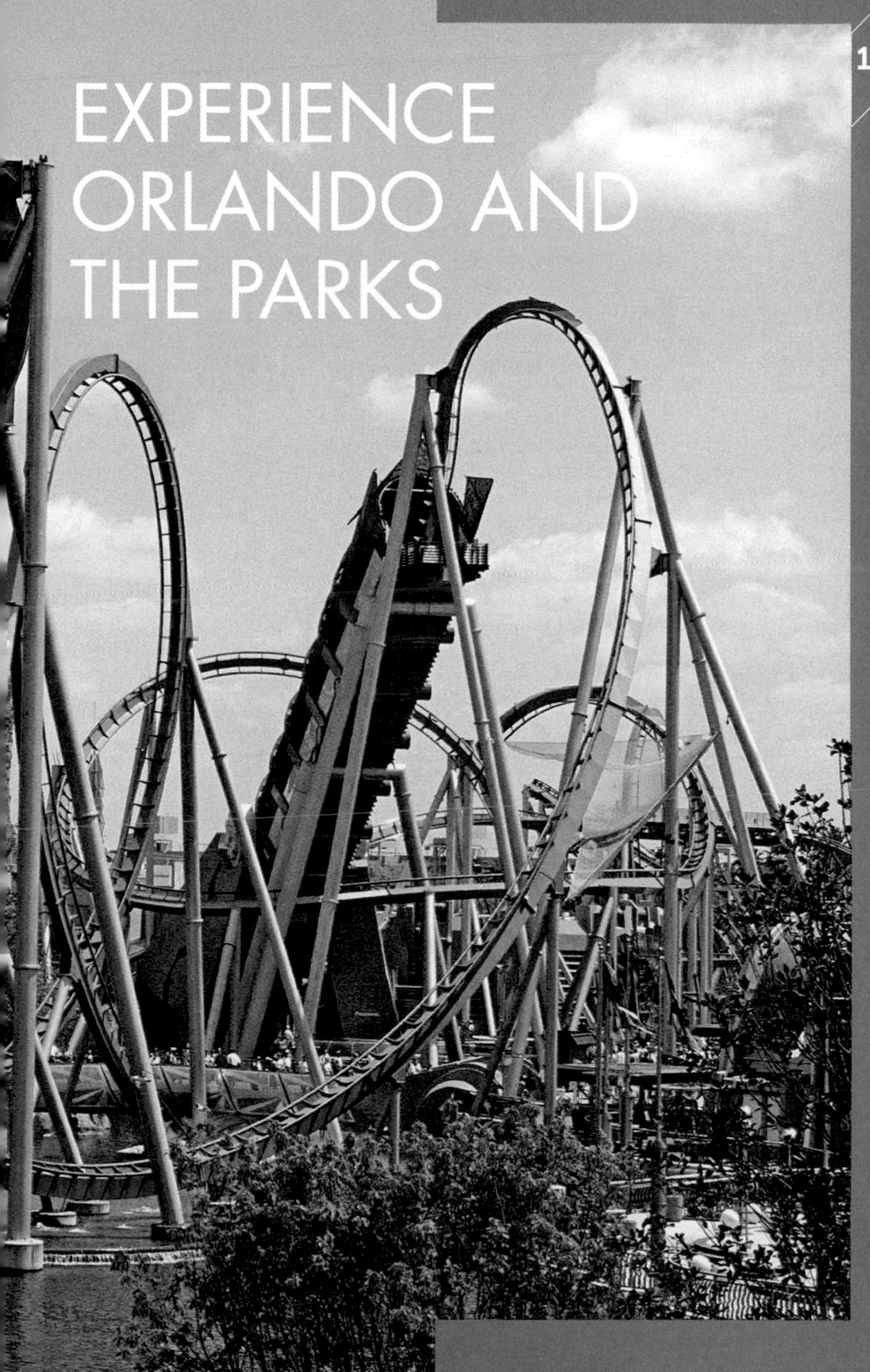

WHAT'S NEW IN THE PARKS

Visitors see Orlando as a shiny vacation kingdom bolstered by cartoon characters. Residents see it as a city on the rise, albeit one that's too reliant on a single industry—namely, tourism. Local officials have responded to these sentiments by courting and welcoming new industry to the area, and as a result, Orlando is becoming an increasingly sophisticated city.

Theme parks also are staying cutting-edge with interactive exhibits and attractions. Disney's new MyMagic+ Experience invites guests to manage their vacations by planning both online and with mobile tools; then they can use the new MagicBand wrist band for everything from park admission and hotel entry to FastPass+ attraction appointments and food and merchandise purchases.

Walt Disney World

The Magic Kingdom recently completed the final phase of the park's largest-ever expansion—to **Fantasyland,** with the opening of the Seven Dwarfs Mine Train family coaster. The redesign allows guests to visit not one, but three castles: the park's iconic and original Cinderella Castle, the new Beast's Castle that houses the lavish Be Our Guest Restaurant, and Prince Eric's castle where Under the Sea: Journey of the Little Mermaid features a voyage with Ariel. Fantasyland also boasts a double-the-fun Dumbo ride and a French cottage where Belle herself meets guests for a storybook "tale as old as time" in the Enchanted Tales with Belle attraction. The new Princess Fairytale Hall, with its richly appointed greeting rooms in the Castle Courtyard, offers photo ops with Cinderella, Rapunzel, and visiting princesses like Snow White. In Adventureland, an interactive quest, A Pirates Adventure: Treasures of the Seven Seas, sends guests on a treasure hunt throughout Adventureland.

At **Downtown Disney,** the AMC Theater multiplex now offers six dine-in theaters with premium and casual dining experiences. Downtown Disney West Side turned the former Virgin Megastore building into Splitsville, a bowling mega-hangout across from House of Blues. Splitsville's menu, including beef-fillet sliders and sushi, adds to the entertainment center's upscale vibe. Meanwhile, Downtown Disney is in the midst of a multiyear transformation into Disney Springs. When it's completed sometime in 2016, guests will find easier access with new parking garages, lots of new shopping, dining, and entertainment options, and open-air promenades along a waterfront. At the **Walt Disney World Speedway** just outside the Magic Kingdom, an upgraded Richard Petty driving experience offers an Exotics Course, where guests can ride in or drive "supercars" by Ferrari, Lamborghini, Audi, and Porsche. Epcot has its own thrill-a-minute custom-car adventure with the made-over, now-interactive Test Track by Chevrolet attraction.

Disney's luxury custom homes in the Golden Oaks community are built on ¼- to ¾-acre lots nestled beside the Magic Kingdom and Four Seasons.

Universal Orlando

Harry Potter became such a theme-park star at Islands of Adventure that Universal just opened its own Potter playland, **The Wizarding World of Harry Potter—Diagon Alley Live,** complete with a marquee ride based on the book series' Gringotts bank. And park guests can immerse themselves in Homer Simpson's hometown at the new **Springfield**-themed area. The Lard Lad donut shop and Moe's Tavern are

Come to Universal Studios to spend some quality time with your minions.

both there, offering Homer-friendly treats for all. **Transformers: The Ride 3-D** opened in 2013, an attraction packed with fast and furious explosions and attacks of an intergalactic battle between the Autobots and the Decepticons. Plus, Universal Studios introduced the daytime **Superstar Parade,** starring animated characters and street performers, and the evening film-and-firework extravaganza **Cinematic Spectacular: 100 Years of Movie Memories.**

SeaWorld, Discovery Cove, Aquatica

SeaWorld recently jumped into the fray with its new **Antarctica: Empire of the Penguin** attraction. And the park's **TurtleTrek,** which opened in 2012, takes you on the underwater journey of a sea turtle via 3-D film. But even before you get to the 360-degree domed theater, you walk past habitats filled with hundreds of freshwater and saltwater fish, gentle manatees, and more than a dozen sea turtles. At Discovery Cove, two recently added attractions bring nature close: the tropical rain-forest environment that is **Freshwater Oasis** provides face-to-face encounters with playful otters and curious marmoset monkeys, and **SeaVenture** lets you walk underwater through a reef filled with tropical fish and rays. Aquatica in 2014 was slated to open its new multislide thrill ride, **Ihu's Breakaway Falls,** named after a colorful gecko that serves as the water park's mascot.

WHAT'S WHERE

The following numbers refer to chapter

5 Walt Disney World Resort. Disney invites you to four attraction-packed theme parks: Magic Kingdom, Animal Kingdom, Epcot, and Hollywood Studios, as well as two water parks, Blizzard Beach and Typhoon Lagoon. The lively Downtown Disney area is full of restaurants, shops, and diversions like the House of Blues and Cirque du Soleil. What else? Only a 220-acre sports complex, myriad hotels, full-service spas, golf courses, character meals, dinner shows, a wedding pavilion, and other experiences that are the stuff of dreams.

6 Universal Orlando. Universal Studios brings movies to life, and Islands of Adventure delivers gravity-defying rides and special-effects surprises. Four on-site resorts offer themed accommodations. CityWalk is the nightlife hub with restaurants, bars, movies, and clubs, and Hard Rock Live is the big-ticket concert venue.

7 Wet 'n Wild. This long-popular water park in the heart of the International Drive corridor is more about big thrills than theming. With attraction names like Bomb Bay, Brain Wash, and The Storm, Wet 'n Wild promises a good time for adrenaline junkies of all ages.

8 SeaWorld Orlando and Discovery Cove. Marine life takes the stage at SeaWorld Orlando, where killer whales and other marine mammals perform in meticulously choreographed shows, and thrill seekers find their adrenaline rush on coaster and simulator attractions. Sister park Discovery Cove is a daylong, swim-with-the-dolphins beach escape. SeaWorld also invites you to a day of water play at Aquatica water park.

9 Orlando and Environs. Those who venture beyond the parks to Downtown Orlando, International Drive, Kissimmee, Winter Park, and Cape Canaveral discover new sights and experiences. Lunch with an astronaut or experience the g-forces of a space-shuttle liftoff at the Kennedy Space Center.

10 Tampa Bay Area. Tampa's Busch Gardens adventure park and nearby Ybor City are two great places to visit on Florida's west coast. But there's much more: culture vultures flock to St. Petersburg for concerts, major-league ball, and the Salvador Dalí Museum. Eco-adventurers veer north to the Nature Coast.

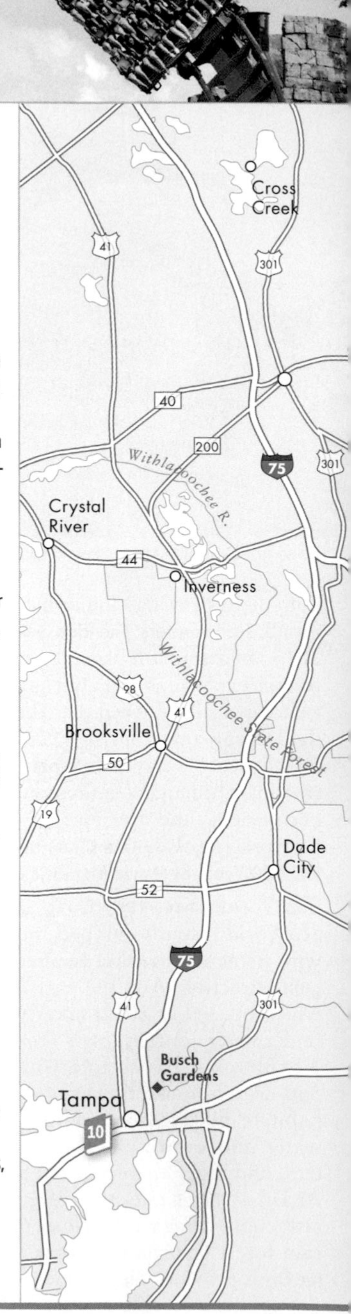

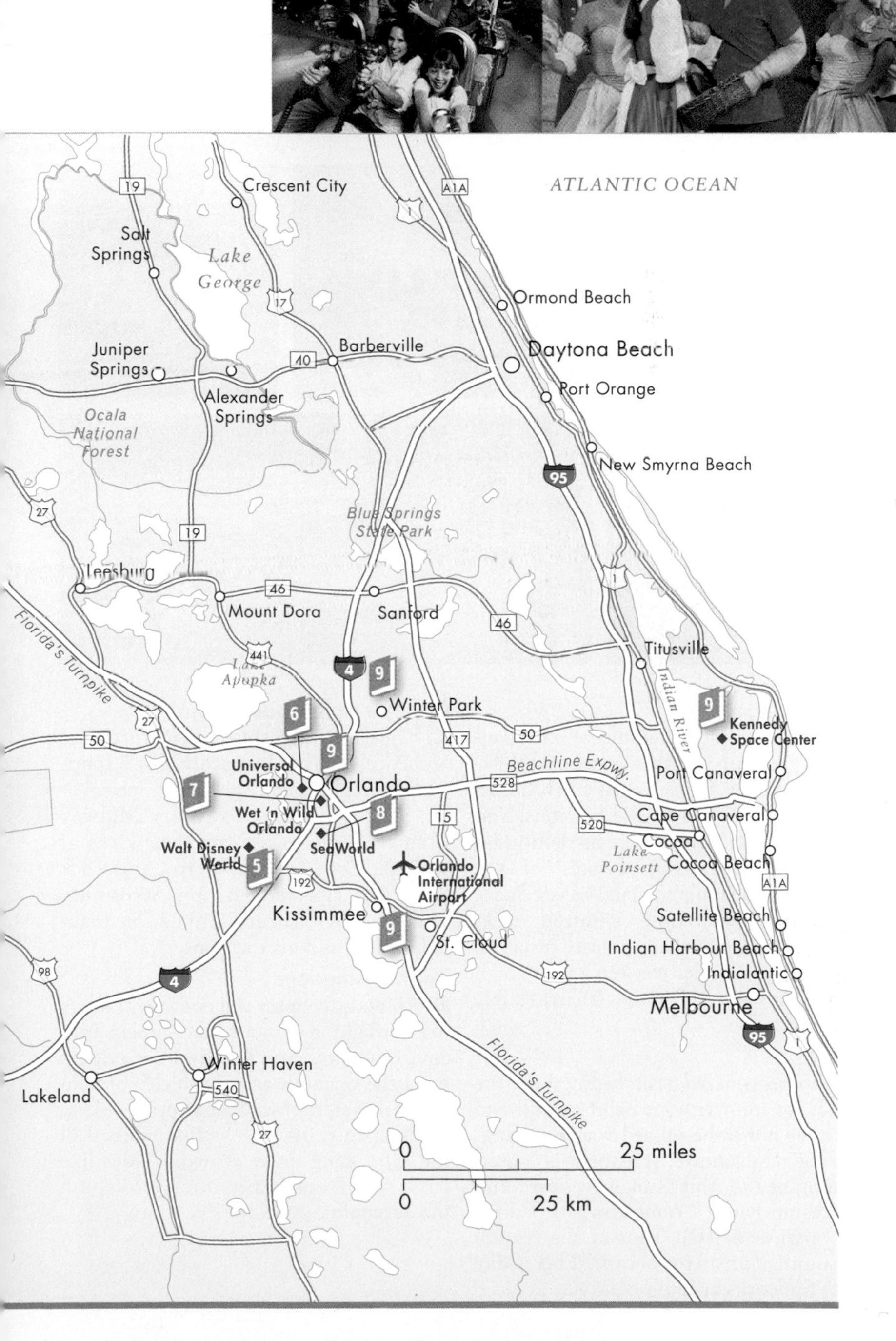
ATLANTIC OCEAN
Crescent City
Salt Springs
Lake George
Ormond Beach
Juniper Springs
Barberville
Daytona Beach
Alexander Springs
Port Orange
Ocala National Forest
New Smyrna Beach
Blue Springs State Park
Leesburg
Mount Dora
Sanford
Florida's Turnpike
Titusville
Lake Apopka
Winter Park
Indian River
Kennedy Space Center
Beachline Expwy.
Universal Orlando
Orlando
Port Canaveral
Wet 'n Wild Orlando
Cape Canaveral
Walt Disney World
SeaWorld
Cocoa
Lake Poinsett
Cocoa Beach
Orlando International Airport
Kissimmee
Satellite Beach
St. Cloud
Indian Harbour Beach
Indialantic
Melbourne
Winter Haven
Lakeland
0
25 miles
0
25 km

WALT DISNEY WORLD TOP ATTRACTIONS

A

B

C

D

Magic Kingdom

(A) Disney's most visited theme park welcomes you with a barbershop quartet serenade and the fragrance of fresh-baked cookies. Cinderella Castle beckons, and magical lands have classic attractions—from Adventureland's Pirates of the Caribbean to Tomorrowland's sleek Space Mountain. Wide-eyed children meet Mickey Mouse or their favorite princess, ride their first roller coaster, and fly high with Peter Pan and Dumbo. It's irresistible for adults, too.

Epcot

(B) Top reasons to visit begin with the hands-on Innoventions exhibits and end with the not-to-be-missed Soarin' "hang-gliding" adventure. History is entertaining at the American Adventure and Spaceship Earth. Count down to launch on Mission: SPACE. Dine at Via Napoli or another great restaurant. End a day with fireworks at IllumiNations.

Disney's Hollywood Studios

(C) Film- and TV-inspired adventures lure audiences to the American Idol Experience, Indiana Jones Epic Stunt Spectacular, Star Tours, and Toy Story Midway Mania! Thrill seekers get their kicks at Twilight Zone Tower of Terror and Rock 'n' Roller Coaster Starring Aerosmith. The Magic of Disney Animation highlights Walt and his cartoons.

Animal Kingdom

(D) Animals from several continents share the spotlight in habitats that mimic native environments. You'll see some critters from the open-air safari vehicles of Kilimanjaro Safaris; you'll spot others along landscaped trails. Shows like Festival of the Lion King draw crowds. Rides like DINOSAUR and Expedition Everest push the adrenaline envelope.

Universal Studios

(E) Universal is known for action, adventure, and a touch of irreverence. From Terminator 2: 3-D to Revenge of the Mummy, attractions score points with fans of contemporary film. City-street reproductions set the movie back-lot scene. Younger kids love Woody Woodpecker's Kid Zone.

Islands of Adventure

(F) The Wizarding World of Harry Potter packs in the crowds at this park, which is already known for such draws as the Amazing Adventures of Spider-Man and the Incredible Hulk Coaster. There's also whimsical Seuss Landing.

SeaWorld and Discovery Cove

(G) Lagoons are populated by all manner of sea creatures, and shows are well done. Kraken and Manta are first-rate coasters, and Shamu's Happy Harbor makes young kids gleeful. Discovery Cove lets you swim with dolphins.

I-Drive

(H) International Drive, 7 miles northeast of Disney, is a busy commercial strip with attractions like Ripley's Believe it or Not! Odditoruim, WonderWorks, Wet 'n Wild water park, and Fun Spot.

Kennedy Space Center

About an hour's drive east of Orlando, the center has exhibits about space exploration, interactive rides like the Shuttle Launch Experience, an astronaut memorial and a hall of fame, and an IMAX theater.

Busch Gardens Tampa

It's a 335-acre adventure park with free-roaming animals. It's an amusement park with six roller coasters. It's an entertainment venue with Broadway-style theater extravaganzas and 4-D movies. It's all in Tampa, just 84 miles southwest of Orlando.

IF YOU LIKE

Thrill Rides

Many people love high-speed launches and stomach-churning multiple inversions. Simulator rides that produce similar results are just as popular. Strap on your seat belt and prepare for liftoff!

■ **Roller Coasters.** Coaster fans can't get enough of the Incredible Hulk at Islands of Adventure, Manta at SeaWorld, and Rock 'n' Roller Coaster at Disney's Hollywood Studios. There's also Expedition Everest at Animal Kingdom, Space Mountain at Magic Kingdom, Hollywood Rip Ride Rockit at Universal Studios, and SheiKra at Busch Gardens.

■ **Simulators.** Soarin' at Epcot gives you the sensation of hang gliding over California. Wild Arctic at SeaWorld takes you on a virtual helicopter ride above polar ice caps. The Simpsons Ride at Universal Studios is a cartoonish romp, and the Amazing Adventures of Spider-Man at Islands of Adventure uses 3-D technology to the max for high-voltage thrills. At DisneyQuest, Innoventions at Epcot, and at WonderWorks you can "build," then ride, your own simulated roller coaster. Pretend you're an astronaut at Kennedy Space Center's Shuttle Launch Experience.

■ **Wet Rides.** Hot Florida days and wet thrill rides go together like burgers and fries. Cool off at Journey to Atlantis at SeaWorld; Popeye & Bluto's Bilge-Rat Barges and Dudley Do-Right's Ripsaw Falls at Islands of Adventure; Splash Mountain at the Magic Kingdom; and Kali River Rapids at Animal Kingdom.

■ **Waterslides.** Wedgie alert: get your bikini in a bunch on Humunga Kowabunga speed slide at Typhoon Lagoon, Summit Plummet at Blizzard Beach, Bomb Bay at Wet 'n Wild, and Dolphin Plunge at Aquatica.

Special Effects and Interactive Fun

Bubbles burst on your nose. A 3-D Michael Jackson dances off the big screen. Cartoons come to life. Aliens attack. Anything's possible when theme-park attractions throw special effects, animation magic, and hands-on action into the mix.

■ **Theater Shows.** If you get a kick out of special-effects surprises in 3-D films, these top shows should be on your itinerary: Shrek 4-D at Universal Studios; *It's Tough to Be a Bug!* at Animal Kingdom; Mickey's PhilharMagic at Magic Kingdom; *Captain EO* (with Michael Jackson) at Epcot; and Muppet*Vision 3-D at Hollywood Studios.

■ **Interactive Rides.** Competitive streak? These scored rides, complete with hands-on laser guns or spring-action shooters, are just the ticket: MEN IN BLACK: Alien Attack at Universal Studios; Toy Story Midway Mania! at Hollywood Studios; and Buzz Lightyear's Space Ranger Spin at Magic Kingdom.

■ **Audio-Animatronics.** Disney's Audio-Animatronics characters pop up in every park, and some of the figures can be quite convincing. Among the best: the wicked witch of the Great Movie Ride "Oz" sequence at Hollywood Studios; the President Obama figure at the Hall of Presidents and Captain Jack Sparrow of *Pirates of the Caribbean,* both at Magic Kingdom; and the monstrous yeti of Expedition Everest at Animal Kingdom.

■ **Cartoon Magic.** Animation brings characters to life on dozens of rides and attractions, from nutty Homer at Universal's The Simpsons Ride to wacky Mushu of the Disney film *Mulan* at the Magic of Disney Animation in Hollywood Studios.

Animal Antics

Alligators don't just hang out in Orlando's many large lakes—they also headline gator-wrestling shows and whole-chicken feeding frenzies at Gatorland. If reptiles aren't your thing, consider the options.

■ **Natural Habitats.** Frolic with dolphins and snorkel amid stingrays at Discovery Cove's Dolphin Lagoon and the Grand Reef. SeaWorld's Wild Arctic and other attractions feature many animals and fish in re-created environments. At Animal Kingdom you'll see Bengal tigers along the Maharajah Jungle Trek, lowland gorillas at Pangani Forest Exploration Trail, and Galápagos tortoises at Discovery Island Trails. Myombe Reserve at Busch Gardens is a rain-forest environment with gorillas and chimps.

■ **Safaris.** Kilimanjaro Safaris at Animal Kingdom is a bumpy adventure in open-air vehicles through African habitats. No 20-minute safari is the same, as the elephants, hippos, lions, zebras, and other animals are constantly on the move. At Busch Gardens the off-road Rhino Rally safari passes crocs, rhinos, and hippos.

■ **Performances.** SeaWorld is the top park in which to see animals trained to entertain. Shamu makes a huge splash in the show One Ocean. Sea lions, otters, and walruses astound you at the Clyde and Seamore Take Pirate Island dramedy. At the Pets Ahoy show, dogs, cats, parrots, and even a pig play for laughs.

■ **Critter Connections.** At Rafiki's Planet Watch in Animal Kingdom are exotic-animal encounters and a petting yard with animals from around the world. At SeaWorld, you can feed and pet dolphins at Key West and stroke rays at Stingray Lagoon.

Parades, Fireworks, and Shows

Lights, fireworks, action! You'll get your fill at Orlando's theme parks. The Magic Kingdom alone uses 683 pieces of pyro nightly for its dazzling 12-minute Wishes fireworks and music show. If you love a parade, find your section of curb and park it early.

■ **Daytime Pageants.** You can set your watch by the Magic Kingdom's daily 3 pm Disney Festival of Fantasy Parade. Mickey's Jammin' Jungle Parade is a safari of fun at Animal Kingdom. Universal's Superstar Parade boogies through the park with bubble machines, stunt performers, and popular characters like SpongeBob SquarePants.

■ **Nighttime Spectacles.** The Magic Kingdom's Wishes explodes almost nightly over Cinderella Castle, and the Main Street Electrical Parade with millions of twinkling lights charms crowds several times weekly along Main Street, U.S.A. Epcot's nightly IllumiNations combines music, flames, fireworks, and fountains in a 13-minute display of near-cosmic proportion. Get a seat early for Fantasmic! at Hollywood Studios, a 25-minute fireworks, laser, lights, and dancing-fountains show starring Sorcerer Mickey Mouse, which runs several times nightly during busy times and two or three times weekly in the off-season. Universal's Cinematic Spectacular—100 Years of Movie Memories gives a fireworks salute to a century of iconic films.

■ **Explosive Action.** The Eighth Voyage of Sindbad Stunt Show at Islands of Adventure juices up its story line with 25 minutes of physical stunt work, plus water explosions, flames, and fireworks. Indiana Jones Epic Stunt Spectacular! has dynamic action sequences straight from the film.

Car, boat, and motorcycle stunts take the stage at the Lights, Motors, Action! Extreme Stunt Show (both at Hollywood Studios).

Luxury Resorts

Orlando attracts millions of visitors each year, and it stands to reason that some are big spenders. Here are our favorite upscale lodging resorts that offer an array of amenities from first-rate service, fine food, and pampering spas to championship golf courses, attractive architecture, and a general ambience of luxury.

■ **Disney's Animal Kingdom Lodge.** One of the few places at Disney where the exotic animals strolling past your window are real. The soaring thatch-roofed lobby is breathtaking, and staff tell stories about their African homelands.

■ **Disney's Grand Floridian Resort & Spa.** A hotel in the Victorian style, complete with broad verandas, that allows guests to feel as though they've traveled back in time to an era when they were truly pampered.

■ **Loews Portofino Bay Hotel.** The hotel is as close to a clone of the Mediterranean town as you'll find; it's easy to imagine yourself in Italy, sunbathing in a formal Italian garden, drinking Campari, and enjoying la dolce vita, contemplating a fine Italian dinner or a visit to the restful spa.

■ **Ritz-Carlton Orlando Grande Lakes.** A golf course, a spa, and chef Norman Van Aken's signature restaurant are just some of the jewels set in this luxury chain.

■ **Waldorf Astoria Orlando.** Although it's not an exact copy of the famed Manhattan original, it's a thoroughly updated ode to Waldorf luxury, with a deluxe spa, fine restaurants, and a championship golf course.

Family- and Budget-Friendly Stays

Families flock to this theme-park-oriented area, which means that there are endless budget options that can accommodate the entire clan.

■ **All-Star Sports, Music, and Movies Resorts.** Each section of these sprawling resorts is geared to a particular interest, providing fun for kids and a break for parents' wallets. The Music resort pays homage to genres from Broadway show tunes to country, jazz, and rock and roll; the pools are shaped like a guitar and a piano. In the Movies resort, huge characters from classic Disney films frame each building. The Sports resort celebrates baseball, football, basketball, and more, and has a pool shaped like a baseball diamond.

■ **Best Western Lake Buena Vista Resort.** Close enough to Disney to watch the fireworks from your balcony, this hotel has something for every member of the family: free Wi-Fi, free shuttles to Disney and outlet malls, and a fun pool. Best of all, it's within walking distance of Downtown Disney's entertainment complex.

■ **Fort Wilderness Resort Campground.** This relatively unknown and inexpensive part of Disney World offers a unique glimpse of Florida wilderness, along with entertainment, such as the ridiculously funny Hoop-Dee-Doo Musical Revue, which makes the kid in all of us erupt with laughter. If you don't have a tent, staff will provide one and put it up!

■ **Nickelodeon Suites Resort.** SpongeBob and Co. are as familiar to kids as Mickey and Minnie, and this reasonably priced hotel complex is near Disney but allows for an escape to something completely different.

Foodie Experiences

The Orlando dining scene does not consist only of hamburgers and hot dogs. You can also find five-star dining and creative cuisine mixed in among the sea of food courts and fast-food chains.

■ **Boma.** African-inspired dishes like spiced roasted chicken and curried-coconut seafood stew are a hit with parents and kids at this casual and excellent buffet in the Animal Kingdom Lodge.

■ **Luma on Park.** Under the deft guidance of chef Brandon McGlamery, over-the-top delicious takes on creative American fare are served in a stylish see-and-be-seen space right on Winter Park's tony Park Avenue.

■ **Primo.** Melissa Kelly's farm-to-table ethos is in full effect at the Orlando outpost of the chef's famed Italian-organic Maine restaurant. Here produce is grown in the hotel garden, so diners can expect all of the dishes to be prepared with the freshest ingredients.

■ **The Ravenous Pig.** From a charcuterie platter on which every salami is made entirely from scratch to a small inventive menu that changes every day based on what's fresh in the market (plus the best burger in town), this comfortable Winter Park gastropub is worth the drive.

■ **Victoria & Albert's.** One of the plushest dining experiences in Florida, this Disney resort restaurant serves up modern American cuisine with a seven-course prix-fixe menu that changes daily.

Theme Restaurants

Part of the fun of Orlando is the over-the-top theme parks, and the restaurants to match. Here are our favorite restaurants where ambience and decor are just as prized as what is on the plate.

■ **Cuba Libre.** This expansive eatery on International Drive replicates the streets of Cuba, and if you close your eyes, sip a mojito, and snack on some *papas rellenas,* you'll almost feel like you're in Havana.

■ **50's Prime Time Café.** Head back in time at this replica of a kitschy, classic American diner in Disney's Hollywood Studios. Clips of sitcoms like *I Love Lucy* and the *Donna Reed Show* play in the background as you chow down on comfort-food favorites like meat loaf and fried chicken.

■ **Sci-Fi Dine-In Theater Restaurant.** Dine in at this (fake) drive-in, also at the Studios, where standard American fare like salads, sandwiches, and burgers are served to you as you sit in a faux convertible and watch movie clips from classic sci-fi flicks from the '50s and '60s.

■ **Taverna Opa.** Taverna Opa on International Drive takes Greek dining to a whole new level. While sampling excellent Mediterranean fare, you are entertained by a fire-eating belly dancer. If the spirit moves you, dance around the dining room with a slew of fellow guests.

■ **Three Broomsticks.** Harry Potter fans should look no farther than this fast-food restaurant designed to look like a tavern at the Wizarding World of Harry Potter attraction. Dining here feels like you're in the heart of Hogsmeade, rather than the heart of Islands of Adventure theme park.

SEASONAL AND HOLIDAY EVENTS

If you've been to Orlando and its parks and enjoyed the top attractions at least once, consider a special trip around one of the many festivals and events.

The year-end holiday season is particularly festive. Decorations go up and events begin around Thanksgiving and continue through early January. It pays to book a trip during the first few weeks of December, when there's a lull between Thanksgiving and Christmas crowds.

Winter

Candlelight Processional. Don't miss Epcot's nightly, included-with-admission Candlelight Processional, with celebrity narrators retelling the Christmas story accompanied by a choir and orchestra. Line up very early for the America Gardens Theatre event or snag reserved seating by purchasing the Candlelight lunch or dinner package. ✉ *World Showcase, America Gardens Theatre, Epcot* ☎ *407/939–3463.*

Grinchmas Wholiday Spectacular. At Islands of Adventure the season takes a curmudgeonly turn during Grinchmas, a stage show based on the popular Dr. Seuss book. You'll hear an original Mannheim Steamroller musical score and six songs by a cast including the Grinch and the Whos from Whoville. ✉ *Islands of Adventure.*

Mickey's Jingle Jungle Parade. Disney's Animal Kingdom unwraps Mickey's Jingle Jungle Parade for the holiday festivities. ✉ *Discovery Island, Animal Kingdom.*

Mickey's Very Merry Christmas Party. Mickey's Very Merry Christmas Party spreads holiday cheer at the Magic Kingdom during scheduled November and December evenings. It "snows" on Main Street, U.S.A. Hot cocoa and cookies, seasonal stage shows, and a holiday parade and fireworks add to the fun that's priced lower than one day's park admission. ✉ *Magic Kingdom.*

Osborne Family Spectacle of Dancing Lights. At Disney's Hollywood Studios you can see the long-running holiday-time Osborne Family Spectacle of Dancing Lights from mid-November through early January. It dazzles with millions of colorful holiday lights as manufactured snow falls over the park's Streets of America. ✉ *Streets of America, Disney's Hollywood Studios.*

The Polar Express Experience. The Wild Arctic attraction at SeaWorld becomes The Polar Express Experience from mid-November through early January. You can enjoy a multisensory ride past classic scenes from the popular film based on the Caldecott-medal-winning book *The Polar Express.* SeaWorld's Christmas Celebration lineup also includes shows starring sea lions, otters, Shamu, and even the Sesame Street gang. ✉ *SeaWorld.*

Walt Disney World Marathon. At least 40,000 athletes from around the globe lace up their running shoes each January during the Walt Disney World Marathon weekend. Donald, Mickey, and Goofy challenge racers to a half marathon, a full marathon, or both. There are also a 5K family fun run, a relay, kids' races, and a Health and Fitness Expo at ESPN Wide World of Sports Complex. In 2014, race officials added a 10K and the aptly named Dopey Challenge, in which participants run a 5K, 10K, half marathon, and marathon, totaling 48.6 miles. ✉ *Walt Disney World.*

Spring

Mardi Gras at Universal Studios. During Mardi Gras at Universal Studios, beads, stilt walkers, and floats keep the spirit of New Orleans alive on Saturday nights and

some Sundays from February through May. Popular live bands perform, and you can watch the parade and slurp up authentic New Orleans–style food and drinks. Included with park admission. ✉ *Universal Studios.*

Winter Park Sidewalk Art Festival. For more than 50 years, the juried Winter Park Sidewalk Art Festival has taken over Park Avenue and Central Park in posh Winter Park during the third weekend of March. More than 300,000 visitors typically show up to enjoy exhibits by 225 or more artists, nosh on curly fries and gyros, and listen to live music. Children can participate in art workshops. ✉ *Park Ave. and Central Park, Winter Park* 🌐 *www.wpsaf.org.*

Summer

City of Kissimmee July 4 Celebration. Kissimmee's Lakefront Park launches its own City of Kissimmee July 4 Celebration at 5 pm with live music and entertainment, food, and children's events and activities before the pyrotechnics. ✉ *Kissimmee.*

Fireworks at the Fountain. Downtown Orlando draws thousands to Lake Eola Park for the free July 4 Fireworks at the Fountain, which begins in the afternoon with games, food, and live entertainment. ✉ *Lake Eola Park, Downtown Orlando.*

A Sci-Fi 4th of July. A Sci-Fi 4th of July in the city of Celebration near Walt Disney World features a festival-themed costume contest tied to a science fiction theme, plus live music, games, and fireworks. ✉ *Celebration.*

Gay Days Orlando. In early June, Gay Days Orlando organizes DJ parties, pool parties, music, and events throughout the metro area and the theme parks for the gay, lesbian, bisexual, and transgendered community and their families and friends. ☎ *407/896–8431* 🌐 *www.gaydays.com.*

Fall

Epcot International Food & Wine Festival. For six weeks (late September through mid-November) the Epcot International Food & Wine Festival transforms the park into a food-and-wine wonderland with tasting seminars, culinary demonstrations, and a constant stream of celebrity chefs. Dine around the world at international marketplaces selling tasty bites, or splurge on wine schools and signature dinner events. ✉ *World Showcase, Epcot.*

Halloween Horror Nights. Blood-curdling screams are the night music of Halloween Horror Nights, the wildly popular fright-fest at Universal Studios. Chill-inducing haunted houses and scare zones populated by characters from your worst nightmares guarantee delicious terrors for less than the price of regular park admission. ✉ *Universal Studios* 🕒 *Select nights Sept. and Oct.*

Macy's Holiday Parade. The Macy's Holiday Parade at Universal Studios replicates the New York original with balloons, floats, and marching bands from across the country. Holiday shows in the park star Barney, the Blues Brothers, and other Universal celebs. ✉ *Universal Studios* 🌐 *www.universalorlando.com.*

Mickey's Not-So-Scary Halloween Party. Kids in costumes own the streets of the Magic Kingdom during their quest for treats (no tricks!) at Mickey's Not-So-Scary Halloween Party, a gently spooky celebration on scheduled evenings throughout September and October. Party tickets are priced below regular park admission, and it's easier to meet the characters and avoid ride queues. ✉ *Magic Kingdom.*

GREAT ITINERARIES

AWAY FROM THE THEME PARKS

If you're like most visitors to Orlando, you've come for a theme park (or two or three). But if you need a break from them, have people in your group who aren't interested in them, or have an extra day or two, know that it's easy to get out and explore Central Florida. A stay in Orlando puts you an hour from the eastern coast and 90 minutes from the Gulf of Mexico.

1 Day: Central Orlando Highlights

Head out midmorning. If it's rainy or hot and humid, visit the Mennello Museum of Folk Art northeast of Downtown in Loch Haven Park. If it's a nice day, however, explore the 50-acre Harry P. Leu Gardens, also northeast of Downtown Orlando. Arrive for one of the day's first guided tours (they start at 10) of the Leu House Museum.

■ TIP→ LYNX Bus 50 runs directly from Disney and I-Drive to Downtown Orlando.

Head southwest to Downtown's Lake Eola Park. Have a late lunch in the park's Relax Grill or at one of the many eateries nearby—maybe Wildside BBQ, popular for its outdoor seating and live music on weekends. Work off some calories in a swan-shape pedal boat. At this point, happy hour and the bars and clubs of Orange Avenue aren't far off. If you feel like dancing later, Firestone Live is a couple of blocks north; the Beacham and the Social are both on North Orange Avenue.

■ TIP→ The Orlando Science Center, in Loch Haven, is a kid-friendly alternative to the museum or gardens, and Hawkers or CityFish are good Downtown dinner bets.

1 Day: Shopping Highlights

If it's Saturday, head out early so you can start your spree at the Winter Park Farmers' Market, where there's free valet parking. There are also stalls that sell locally sourced foods—including breakfast—and crafts. Winter Park is just north of Downtown, at Exit 87 off Interstate 4.

■ TIP→ There's no need to rent a car if you're planning to visit only Winter Park; instead hop a LYNX bus from the main Orlando terminal.

Regardless of the day, Winter Park's shopping-and-dining drag, Park Avenue, beckons. Boutiques and galleries—including Ten Thousand Villages and Timothy's—line the east side, opposite an oak-shaded lawn. An alfresco lunch at a restaurant here will carry you through an afternoon of still more shopping.

Hop on Interstate 4 at the Fairbanks entrance, and head west about 8 miles to Exit 78 (Conroy Road) and the upscale Mall at Millenia. If you'd rather hunt for bargains, take Millenia Boulevard to Oak Ridge Road (at the intersection of International Drive) and its outlet malls—Festival Bay and Orlando Premium Outlets International Drive. Farther south, on International Drive at Vineland Avenue, is Orlando Premium Outlets Vineland Avenue.

■ TIP→ Nonshopping alternatives in Winter Park are the Charles Hosmer Morse Museum of American Art (though you can always spend at the museum's terrific gift shop) and the town's scenic boat tour. On I-Drive, you'll find Fun Spot, WonderWorks, and Ripley's.

You've spent the day shopping like a local, so you should spend the evening dining like one. Head to Sand Lake Road for a pick of places and cuisines—from Italian

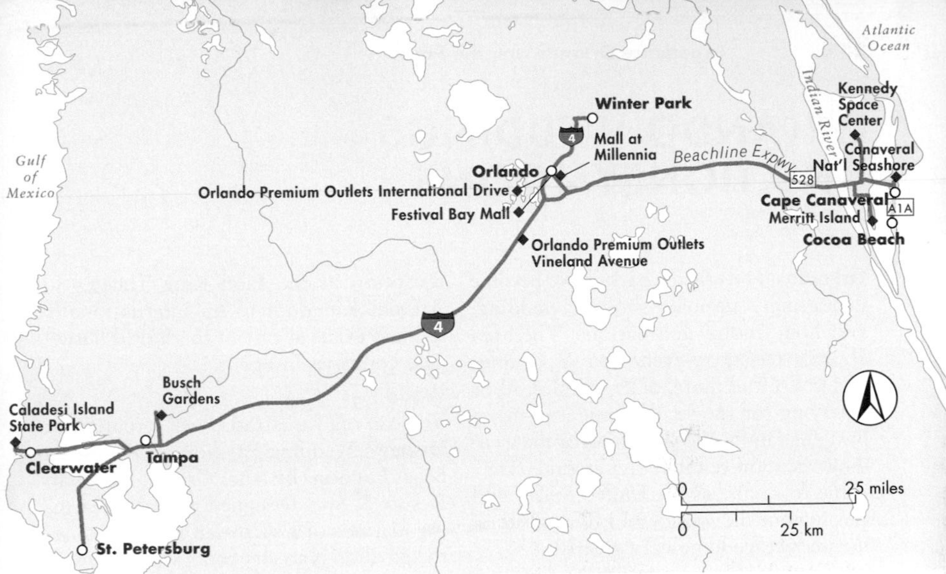

and Mediterranean to Thai and Hawaiian fusion. Splurge on a steak at Morton's The Steakhouse or go lighter—in terms of both your budget and the food—with seasonal fare at Seasons 52.

1 to 2 Days: The Space Coast

From Orlando, you can be at the Kennedy Space Center in a little over an hour on SR528 (the Beachline Expressway, a toll road), which makes it a good day trip. Several Orlando tour companies have trips for about $100 per person. Exhibits on American space travel here have enthralled visitors since 1968.

■ TIP→ An overlooked space-center alternative is the Valiant Air Command Warbird Museum in Titusville. Check out the military-aircraft memorabilia, and then buy a bomber jacket.

With an overnight stay, you can lounge on the blissful beaches of Canaveral National Seashore, catch a wave like surfing legend (and local hero) Kelly Slater, or explore the adjacent 140,000-acre Merritt Island National Wildlife Refuge.

There are also opportunities for horseback riding, hiking, bird-watching, and fishing. Cape Canaveral and Cocoa Beach make great bases, thanks to their coastal locations and selection of hotels, restaurants, outfitters, and other amenities.

1 to 3 Days: Tampa and St. Pete

Shamu enthusiasts can include a visit to Busch Gardens Tampa with their SeaWorld Orlando combo ticket (they're owned by the same company). The city is only about 90 minutes southwest on Interstate 4, so you can take in the theme park on a day trip. But many attractions make Tampa, St. Petersburg, and other coastal towns worthy of a car rental, exploration, and an overnight stay.

If you stay, spend an evening in Ybor City, Tampa's Cuban enclave and a nightlife mecca, particularly along 7th Avenue. In the morning, head to a beach in St. Pete or Clearwater. Spend the day sunbathing or make an afternoon visit to St. Pete's Salvador Dalí Museum.

■ TIP→ Dalí Museum docents conduct free tours and can explain how works by the Spanish surrealist ended up in Florida.

Alternatively (or in addition), you can take a Segway tour of St. Petersburg, catch a spring training or Buccaneers game, bike along Tampa's Bayshore Boulevard Trail or Clearwater's Pinellas Trail, or hunt for shells at Caladesi Island State Park.

ORLANDO WEDDINGS AND HONEYMOONS

Orlando and its theme parks have become increasingly popular shower, wedding, and honeymoon destinations. The area appeals to starry-eyed Gen Y couples and, more and more, older couples, some marrying for the second time and many bringing family and friends in for the wedding-vacation-reunion of a lifetime. They come from across the United States and throughout the world, and their ideas of the perfect wedding vary greatly.

One bride made an entrance in Cinderella's glass coach; her groom rode in on a white horse. A thrill-seeking couple took the free-fall plunge on the Twilight Zone Tower of Terror at Disney's Hollywood Studios. Two couples, on separate occasions, tied the knot in the middle of their Walt Disney World Marathon run, exchanging vows in front of Cinderella Castle at the Magic Kingdom. Moonlight on the Ritz-Carlton lawn set the scene for another couple's romantic vow exchange, and a rooftop Orlando wedding wowed yet another couple's guests with a 360-degree view of the Downtown skyline and scenic Lake Eola Park.

Prewedding Events

Showers and bachelor and bachelorette parties are easy to arrange in a city where there's so much to do. At Disney, the Mad Hatter can show up for a bridesmaids' tea event at the Grand Floridian. Parties can begin with dinner and a wine tasting at Hannibal's wine cellar in Winter Park before moving on to a local nightclub. Grooms who stay at Portofino Bay like to party at Universal CityWalk because no driving is required—a ferry will shuttle them back to the hotel.

For rehearsal dinners (or wedding receptions), Disney pulls out the stops to stage events ranging from an after-hours reception at the Lion King Theater in Animal Kingdom to an internationally themed event at one of the World Showcase countries in Epcot.

Weddings

You can opt for a traditional ceremony at Disney's Wedding Pavilion on the Seven Seas Lagoon by the Grand Floridian Resort & Spa. Designed with the charming features of a Victorian summerhouse, the pavilion is an airy room with a view of Cinderella Castle just across the lagoon. Alternatively, you can plan an informal beachside vow exchange at a lakeside Disney resort; a garden or gazebo ceremony; an over-the-top, Cinderella-style wedding; or a Broadway-themed blowout.

Downtown Orlando and historic Winter Park are popular wedding destinations, as well, says Lisa Stoner, owner of E Events (🌐 *www.eeventsdesign.com*). The Grand Bohemian Hotel stages amazing rooftop ceremonies. Stoner and her team have planned rooftop weddings and receptions at other Downtown buildings, including one with a panoramic view of the skyline and Lake Eola.

Other top wedding spots are Downtown's Orange County Regional History Center; the Mennello Museum of American Art in the city's Loch Haven area; and Casa Feliz, a historic Spanish home–museum in Winter Park.

According to Stoner, couples who hire E Events tend to have sophisticated tastes and like to hold the wedding ceremony and reception in one location, making Orlando the perfect choice. The area is rife with professional entertainers who are available for receptions. Theme-park musicians and other performers often contract out at reasonable prices, and there's a lot of diversity, from zydeco and

DID YOU KNOW?

Disney arranges wedding or vow-renewal ceremonies for about 1,500 couples a year. Packages range from $5,000 to $100,000 or more, with the average price tag at about $20,000 for 40 guests, according to Disney's Fairy Tale Weddings & Honeymoons.

salsa bands to groups that specialize in swing music.

Heather Snively, owner of Weddings Unique (🌐 *www.weddingsunique.com*), says Orlando attracts a lot of couples planning second marriages, couples with children, and those seeking a wedding reunion–minivacation. Resort hotels like the Ritz, Waldorf Astoria, and Portofino Bay at Universal feature romantic backdrops for the ceremony, plus smaller ballrooms ideal for receptions.

The hotels can also support activities ranging from spa parties to golf outings for those in the wedding party. Snively and her team plan up to 40 weddings a year from soup to nuts, working closely with in-house resort coordinators to smooth out every detail and with travel agents to make arrangements for guest travel.

Honeymoons

Central Florida resorts cater to honeymooners with special packages. Honeymoon suites with whirlpools and other amenities create the backdrop for romance that's enhanced with extras like champagne and chocolate-covered strawberries. Resort pools with cabanas, beaches, waterfalls, swaying palms, and poolside margarita delivery make the subtropical setting seem as exotic as a tropical island.

Disney's Fairy Tale Honeymoons division helps you customize a vacation package and even offers a Honeymoon Registry if your guests wish to contribute to your postwedding getaway rather than give a traditional gift. There are package deals to be had at Walt Disney World resorts and at Disney's Vero Beach Resort. Some couples make their wedding dreams or vow renewals come true at sea, where the honeymoon follows immediately.

Planning Tips

If you're dreaming about a Central Florida wedding, keep these tips from the experts in mind:

- If your budget can handle the expense, hire a reputable planner long before the big date. Though you'll pay a fee for your planner, he or she will be an advocate with barter power when dealing with vendors.
- For a destination wedding, build in plenty of time to book travel arrangements and accommodations for all who plan to attend.
- If your budget is tight, plan your Orlando wedding between Monday and Thursday during nonpeak season for the lowest hotel rates.
- Split the wedding-planning tasks with your partner. If the groom is focused more on the reception's music, food, and beverages, the bride can focus on, say, wedding flowers and photography.
- Let your wedding planner arrange romantic escapes from your guests, especially if you plan to wed *and* honeymoon in Orlando. If everyone's staying at the Gaylord Palms Resort or the Hard Rock Hotel, have your wedding planner book you a spa package at the Waldorf Astoria or Ritz-Carlton.
- Start your research by visiting several Orlando-area wedding-planner websites; Visit Orlando at 🌐 *www.visitorlando.com/weddings*; and Disney's Fairy Tale Weddings & Honeymoons at 🌐 *www.disneyweddings.disney.go.com*.

DISNEY CRUISES

More than a dozen years after Disney Cruise Line (DCL) first set sail with the *Disney Magic* and the *Disney Wonder,* it launched its third ship, *Disney Dream,* in 2011. In 2012, the line's fourth ship, *Disney Fantasy,* debuted, expanding the line's cruise-ship guest capacity to more than 13,000. Disney made waves with innovations aboard the *Fantasy* and *Dream,* from its shipboard AquaDuck waterslide coasters, the first of their kind in the industry, to virtual portholes in inside staterooms that provide real-time views from outside the ship. In 2013, the Magic debuted a full renovation that included a new grand atrium lobby, the three-story AquaDunk thrill ride, and Marvel character experiences for the kids.

The cruise line continues to offer its popular excursions from Port Canaveral, Florida, to the Bahamas as well as to eastern and western Caribbean destinations with stops that include Grand Cayman, San Juan, Cozumel, St. Maarten, and St. Thomas. All Caribbean and Bahamian cruises include at least one stop at Disney's gem of a private island, Castaway Cay. DCL also offers a lineup of sailings to the Mediterranean and Alaska, and new itineraries include departures from Miami. A big Disney plus: you can combine an ocean getaway with a stay at Walt Disney World for a seamless land-and-sea vacation. You check in just once: your room key at your Disney resort hotel doubles as your boarding pass at Disney's terminal at Port Canaveral and the key to your stateroom.

Cruise Packages

Packages include room, meals (there are extra charges at the exclusive restaurants though), and most shipboard activities, but not shore excursions or, generally, transportation to and from the ship. Prices vary greatly, depending on the package, the stateroom, the destination, the time of year, and which week you book. A Disney Cruise Line voyage starts at about $450 per person for three nights, $460 for four nights, $575 for five nights, and $910 for seven nights based on double occupancy and not including taxes and fees.

Booking early may help you secure a better rate, but also a bargain may be obtained by booking at the last minute on a ship that hasn't filled. **■TIP→ Dig for a discount on your Disney cruise with a travel agent who specializes in cruises. Find one at** 🌐 *www.travelsense.org.*

Disney Cruise Line. To book any Disney cruise or to check into vessels, staterooms, shore excursions, and more, contact the Disney Cruise Line. ☎ *800/370–0097* 🌐 *www.disneycruise.com.*

Staterooms

Disney Magic and *Disney Wonder* each have 875 staterooms, 73% of which have ocean-view rooms and 44% of which have private verandas. *Disney Dream* and *Fantasy* are larger ships, with 1,250 staterooms each—88% are outside rooms, and 901 staterooms and suites offer private verandas.

Cabins are ranked by category and range from standard inside staterooms (category 11 on the *Fantasy* and *Dream*; categories 11 and 12 on the *Magic* or *Wonder*; 169–184 square feet, sleeps three to four) to deluxe family staterooms with verandas (category 4 on all ships, 256–304 square feet, sleeps five). Luxurious concierge suites are top of the line, with every amenity from whirlpool bathtubs to walk-in closets.

Budget-minded cruisers are often tempted to stick with the least expensive option,

the inside stateroom, but this option lacks a valued amenity on Disney ships—the split bathroom. It features a vanity, sink, tub and shower in one area and a vanity, sink, and toilet in another—a real time-saver when it's time for you and your cabin mates to freshen up before excursions or evening dinners and shows.

Quite a few of the staterooms have a clever pull-down bunk-bed setup that saves space until bedtime and draws cheers from children. All rooms are elegantly appointed with natural wood furniture.

Disney does a commendable job of keeping rooms and much of the rest of the ship smoke-free while setting aside some deck, bar, and private veranda areas for smokers.

For Guests with Disabilities

Accessible staterooms for people with disabilities have ramps, handrails, fold-down shower seats, and handheld showerheads; special communications kits are available with phone alerts, amplifiers, and text typewriters. Assisted-listening systems are available in the ships' main theaters, and sign-language interpretation is offered for live performances on specified cruise dates.

Shore Excursions

At various ports of call, Disney offers between one and two dozen organized excursions, from snorkeling and diving to sightseeing and shopping. For example, at Grand Cayman you can visit a butterfly farm or sign up for a trip to Stingray City—not really a city, but a long sandbar where you can swim with hundreds of rays. During a stop at Cozumel you can explore the Mayan ruins of Tulum and strike a bargain for handcrafted Mexican hats, toys, and knickknacks. All activities are rated from "leisurely" to "strenuously active."

Adult Activities

Poolside games, wine tastings, and behind-the-scenes seminars are among the adults-only diversions. Each ship's spa is a don't-miss for those who need some pampering—book early!

For a romantic dinner, the intimate, adults-only **Palo** (*all ships*) offers sweeping ocean views. Expect a fantastic wine list and dishes such as grilled salmon with creamy risotto and grilled filet mignon with a port-wine reduction and Gorgonzola cheese sauce. Reserve early for this hot ticket. The champagne brunch is another great Palo dining event.

The decor in the *Dream*'s and *Fantasy*'s exclusive 80-seat restaurant, **Remy,** is a nod to the movie *Ratatouille,* and, of course, the cuisine is French inspired. The

THE PORT

Port Canaveral is the home port for DCL vessels and for Carnival Cruise Lines' *Sensation* (three- and four-night Bahamian cruises); Sunshine (five- and seven-night Caribbean cruises); and *Liberty* (Bahamian and Caribbean cruises), and for Royal Caribbean International's *Enchantment of the Seas* (three- and four-night Bahamian cruises); *Freedom of the Seas* (seven-night eastern- and western-Caribbean itineraries); and *Explorer of the Seas* (eastern-, western-, and southern Caribbean itineraries).

To learn more about all cruises departing from Port Canaveral, visit 🌐 *www.portcanaveral.com* and click on links to each cruise line, or contact a travel agent or cruise discounter.

DID YOU KNOW?

Mickey Mouse was the inspiration for the Disney ships' colors—black hull, white superstructure, yellow trim and lifeboats, and giant red funnels. The ships recall classic ocean liners of the 1930s, and when the captain hits the horn, it plays the first seven notes of "When You Wish Upon a Star."

eight or nine tasting dishes served each night might include Kurobata pork tenderloin and belly with corn ragout and wild turbot with lemon capers and spinach. Wine pairings are amazing; so are the pastries. Remy also has a champagne brunch. Book as far ahead of your trip as possible.

Children's Activities

On all four ships, there's nearly an entire deck reserved for kids. When you drop them off, use the onboard mobile phone service to stay in touch with the activities counselors. Babysitting is available on the *Wonder* for children ages 12 weeks old to 3 years old at **Flounder's Reef Nursery** for $9 per hour (two-hour minimum) and $8 an hour for each additional sibling. Disney also offers a groundbreaking online service, Babies Travel Lite, which lets parents order all of their baby's travel products, including diapers and formula, and have them shipped to their stateroom before the cruise begins. Similar services are offered at the Magic's, *Fantasy*'s, and *Dream*'s **It's a Small World Nursery.**

The well-run **Oceaneer Club** and **Oceaneer Lab** on each ship provide nonstop activities for kids ages 3–12. Little ones have a ball in the **Club** playroom designed to look like Captain Hook's pirate ship. They can scramble around on a rope bridge, watch a Disney movie, and make crafts at the **Toy Story Boot Camp** (*Magic* and *Dream*) or **Pixie Hollow** (*Fantasy*). Counselors customize activities to kids within different age groups.

At the high-tech **Lab,** there are science experiments, sports challenges, and karaoke jams. Disney revamped its kids' program approach so that children have more options to tailor their experiences to their interests.

Tweens (ages 11–14) chill out at a getaway called **Edge** on each Disney ship; older teens (14–17) have their own hangout at **Vibe.** They can tune in to music, watch plasma-screen TVs, play board and video games, or just hang out and meet new friends. Organized activities for teens include trivia games and evening dance parties. Internet message, photo, and video posting also are available.

Restaurants

Coordinators arrange for you to alternate restaurants each night so you can sample a variety of offerings. Disney offers early and late dinner seatings, too. Early ones are best for families with small children. Also, look into the Dine and Play option, where servers speed up the kids' service, and then the ship's activity counselors whisk youngsters off so older family members can relax. If you miss your seating altogether, you can always find a casual dining option.

At **Animator's Palate,** scenes featuring Disney characters change from black-and-white to Technicolor as the meal progresses on the *Magic* and *Wonder*; on the *Dream* and *Fantasy* diners are surrounded by an artist's studio where famous film scenes line the walls and fiber-optic "brush pillars" paint oversize ceiling "palettes" vibrant colors. Dining is slightly more formal at **Lumiere's,** on the *Magic,* where beef tenderloin, lamb shank, and other entrées are served French style in a classic ocean-liner-style dining room.

At **Triton's,** on the *Wonder,* seafood, roast duck, pasta, and other selections are served in an elegant, art deco, under-the-sea-theme dining room. The *Dream's* **Royal Palace** and the *Fantasy*'s **Royal Court** are inspired by Disney's princess films, with menus that may include crowned

rack of lamb, beef Wellington, and other royal dishes. At the Caribbean-themed **Parrot Cay** restaurant (*Wonder*) and the new Rio de Janeiro–themed **Carioca's** *(Magic)*, the mood is casual and festive. On the *Fantasy* and *Dream*, **Enchanted Garden** is the whimsical, more informal rotation restaurant. Character breakfasts are offered one morning on most seven-nights-or-longer sailings.

After-Dark Entertainment

During the **Pirates in the Caribbean** evening, swashbuckling servers dish up Caribbean and Bahamian taste treats, a cup of grog, and (on seven-night cruises) a pirate bandana for every dinner guest. After dinner, you head off to a deck party where Captain Hook, Mr. Smee, and others appear for some high-spirited action, dancing, and fireworks.

Lavish shows and variety acts entertain families every night of every cruise. The big hit on *Disney Wonder* is *Toy Story: The Musical,* a larger-than-life stage version of the film classic. The Golden Mickeys on the *Wonder* is a high-tech salute to the animation of Walt Disney in the form of a Hollywood-style awards ceremony. *Twice Charmed: An Original Twist on the Cinderella Story* is a Broadway-style production on *Disney Magic* that begins where the original Cinderella story ended.

Disney Dreams: An Enchanted Classic, on the *Magic* and *Wonder,* is a sweet bedtime story starring Peter Pan, Aladdin, Ariel, and other Disney characters. It combines animation, pyrotechnic, and laser features, snow effects, and mechanisms that let characters "fly" more convincingly. The *Dream* produces the first full-scale musical revue dedicated to Disney's famous animated villains in *Villains Tonight!* Two new shows are popular on the *Fantasy*: *Disney Wishes* and *Disney's Aladdin: A Musical Spectacle.* Each ship also has a **cinema** screening classic Disney films, and every guest has the opportunity to experience a show or film featuring digital 3-D enhancements.

There are also many things geared to adults. At the **Cove Café,** on all ships, you can enjoy gourmet coffee, watch TV, check email, and socialize. On the *Wonder,* the **Outlook Café** on Deck 10 has floor-to-ceiling windows with prime views. **After Hours,** the recently renovated nightlife district on the *Magic,* features **Fathoms** nightclub, O'Gill's Pub, and Keys, a piano bar. **Route 66,** the *Wonder*'s nightlife area, has the WaveBands dance club and the Cadillac Lounge piano bar. If you're looking for something more low key, check out **Diversions,** a sports pub on both ships.

On the *Dream,* Disney expands its nightlife offerings at the **District,** with lounges, a pub, a sky bar, and a nightclub. *Fantasy* cruisers can visit the trendy clubs of **Europa,** influenced by European nightspots, including a rollicking Irish pub and a French champagne bar. Movie fans can see first-run films at the ships' plush Buena Vista Theatre, where full-length features really pop with digital 3-D technology.

Castaway Cay

Disney has its own private Bahamian island, Castaway Cay, with white-sand beaches, towering palms, and swaying hammocks—it's a key stop on many Disney cruises. You can relax on the beach or join a snorkeling or parasailing excursion.

ORLANDO GOLF COURSES

The International Association of Golf Tour Operators has recognized Orlando as a top golf destination. There are more than 170 golf courses and 20 golf academies in the area. Sunny weather almost year-round doesn't hurt, and, though most of Florida is extremely flat, many of the courses feature hills that make them more challenging.

Resort hotels often let nonguests use their golf facilities. Some country clubs are affiliated with particular hotels, and their guests can play at preferred rates. **■TIP→ Twilight discounts often apply after 2 pm in busy seasons and after 3 pm the rest of the year; the discount is usually half off the normal rate.** Because golf is so incredibly popular, courses regularly raise rates.

In general, even public courses have dress codes, so call ahead for specifics and be sure to reserve tee times. Greens fees usually vary by season, and virtually all include mandatory cart rental, except for the few 9-hole walking courses.

GOLFPAC Travel. GOLFPAC Travel packages golf vacations and arranges tee times at nearly 80 Orlando courses. Rates vary based on hotel and course, and 60 to 90 days' advance notice is recommended to set up a vacation. ✉ *483 Montgomery Pl., Altamonte Springs* ☎ *407/260–2288, 888/848–8941* 🌐 *www.golfpactravel.com.*

Walt Disney World

Disney has four championship courses, plus a 9-hole walking course. Any guest at a WDW hotel who checks in specifically to play golf gets free cab rides to the course.

Greens Fees. Rates change frequently, so confirm when booking. Disney resort guests get a price break, and you should ask about twilight discount rates. If you plan to play only once, leave the gear at home—you can rent shoes, range balls, and clubs at any location.

Tee Times and Reservations. Tee times are available daily from dawn until dusk. You can book them up to 90 days in advance if you're staying at a WDW-owned hotel, 60 days ahead if you're staying elsewhere. You must cancel at least 24 hours out. For tee times and private lessons, call Disney's central World Golf reservations line. ☎ *407/939–4653*

The Lake Buena Vista. The Lake Buena Vista course winds among Downtown Disney–area town houses and villas. Greens are narrow, and hitting straight is important because errant balls risk ending up in someone's bedroom. Be prepared for the famous island green on the 7th. ✉ *Downtown Disney, Lake Buena Vista* ⛳ *18 holes, 6,745 yards, par 72.*

The Magnolia. The Magnolia, rated four stars by Golf Digest and certified by Audubon International as a Cooperative Wildlife Sanctuary, is long but forgiving, with extra-wide fairways. More than 1,500 magnolia trees line the course and water hazards can be found at 11 of the 18 holes. ✉ *Shades of Green, 1950 W. Magnolia-Palm Dr., Magic Kingdom Resort Area* ⛳ *18 holes, 7,516 yards, par 72.*

Oak Trail. Oak Trail is designed by Ron Garl to be fun for the entire family. It's noted for its small, undulating greens. ✉ *Shades of Green, 1950 W. Magnolia-Palm Dr., Magic Kingdom Resort Area* ⛳ *9 holes, 2,913 yards, par 36.*

Fodor's Choice **Four Seasons Golf Course.** Sculpted from some of the still-forested portions of the huge WDW acreage, the Tom Fazio–designed and

DID YOU KNOW?

Walt Disney World has 72 holes of golf on four championship courses as well as 9 more holes on a walking course. Golfers who stay at a Disney property can get free cab fare from the hotel to the course and back. Not ready for a serious round? Check out one of Disney's two miniature golf courses.

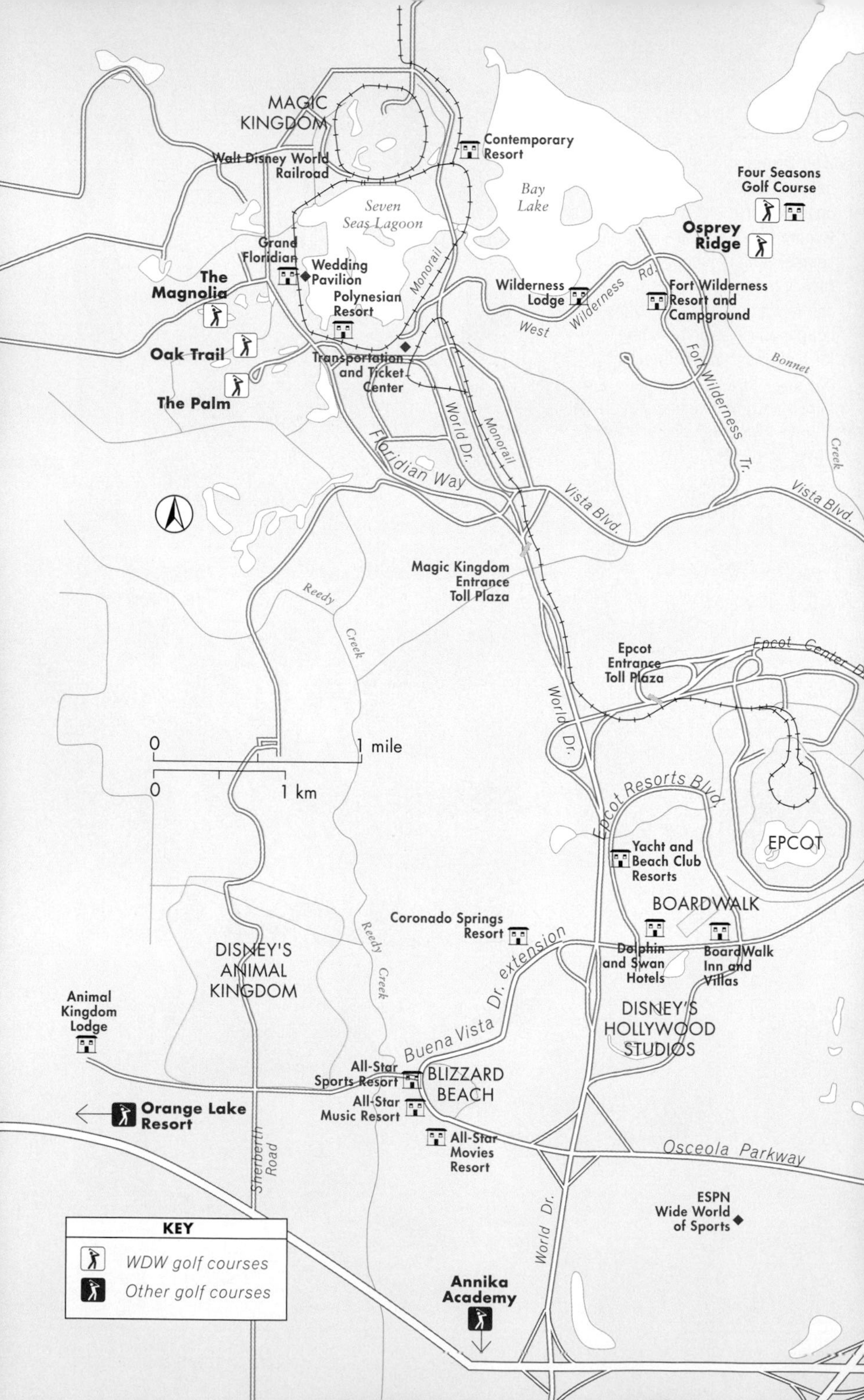

MAGIC KINGDOM
Walt Disney World Railroad
Contemporary Resort
Bay Lake
Seven Seas Lagoon
Four Seasons Golf Course
Osprey Ridge
Grand Floridian
Wedding Pavilion
The Magnolia
Polynesian Resort
Monorail
Wilderness Lodge
Fort Wilderness Resort and Campground
West Wilderness Rd.
Oak Trail
Transportation and Ticket Center
The Palm
Fort Wilderness Tr.
Bonnet Creek
World Dr.
Monorail
Floridian Way
Vista Blvd.
Vista Blvd.
Magic Kingdom Entrance Toll Plaza
Reedy Creek
Epcot Entrance Toll Plaza
Epcot Center Dr.
World Dr.
0
1 mile
0
1 km
Epcot Resorts Blvd.
EPCOT
Yacht and Beach Club Resorts
BOARDWALK
Coronado Springs Resort
Dolphin and Swan Hotels
BoardWalk Inn and Villas
Reedy Creek
DISNEY'S ANIMAL KINGDOM
Buena Vista Dr. extension
DISNEY'S HOLLYWOOD STUDIOS
Animal Kingdom Lodge
All-Star Sports Resort
BLIZZARD BEACH
All-Star Music Resort
Orange Lake Resort
All-Star Movies Resort
Osceola Parkway
Sherberth Road
World Dr.
ESPN Wide World of Sports
KEY
WDW golf courses
Other golf courses
Annika Academy

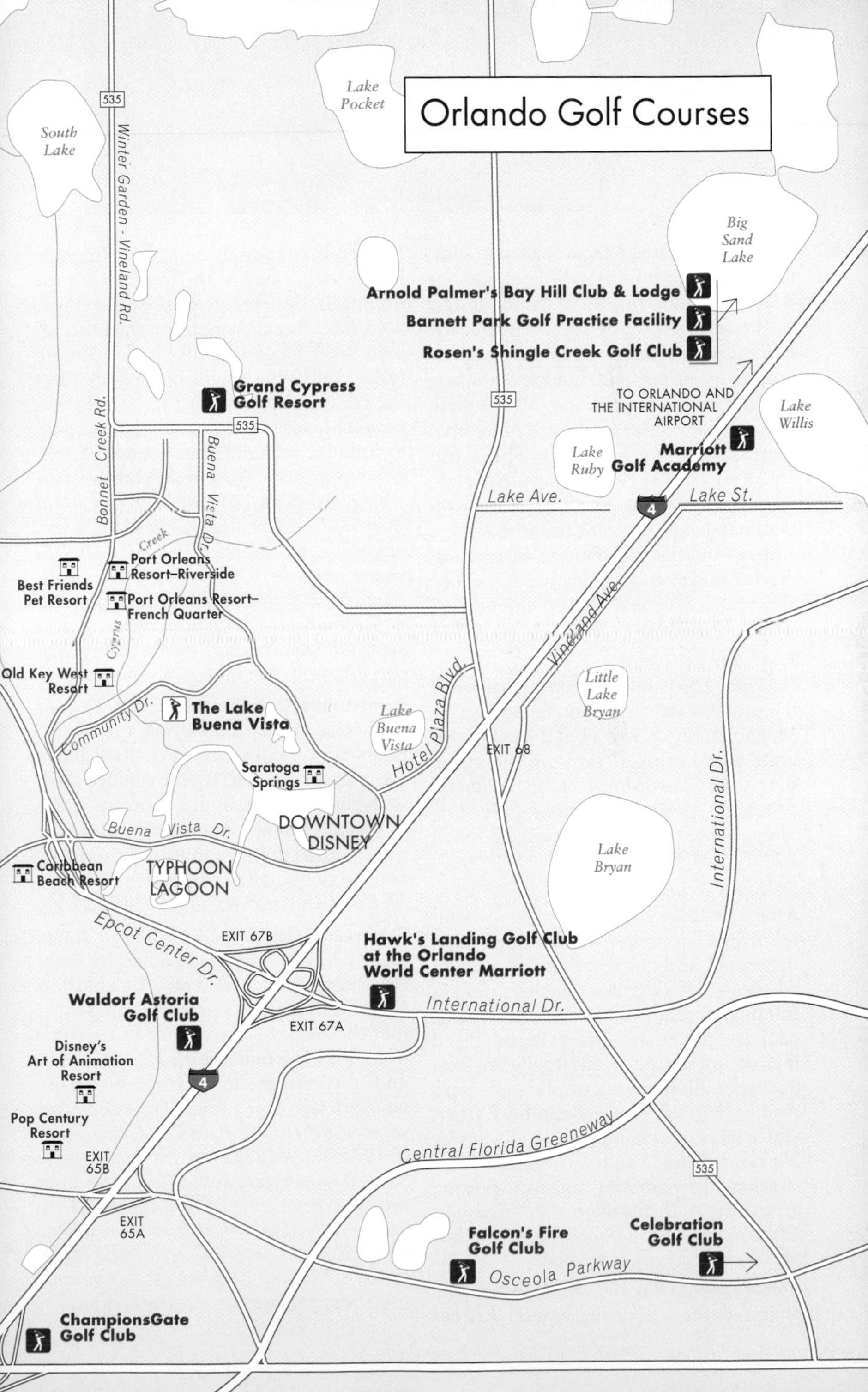

Orlando Golf Courses
South Lake
Lake Pocket
535
Winter Garden - Vineland Rd.
Big Sand Lake
Arnold Palmer's Bay Hill Club & Lodge
Barnett Park Golf Practice Facility
Rosen's Shingle Creek Golf Club
Grand Cypress Golf Resort
535
TO ORLANDO AND THE INTERNATIONAL AIRPORT
Lake Willis
Bonnet Creek Rd.
Buena Vista Dr.
Lake Ruby
Marriott Golf Academy
Lake Ave.
Lake St.
4
Creek
Port Orleans Resort–Riverside
Best Friends Pet Resort
Port Orleans Resort–French Quarter
Vineland Ave.
Cyprus
Old Key West Resort
Hotel Plaza Blvd.
Little Lake Bryan
Community Dr.
The Lake Buena Vista
Lake Buena Vista
EXIT 68
Saratoga Springs
International Dr.
Buena Vista Dr.
DOWNTOWN DISNEY
Caribbean Beach Resort
TYPHOON LAGOON
Lake Bryan
Epcot Center Dr.
EXIT 67B
Hawk's Landing Golf Club at the Orlando World Center Marriott
Waldorf Astoria Golf Club
International Dr.
EXIT 67A
Disney's Art of Animation Resort
Pop Century Resort
EXIT 65B
Central Florida Greeneway
535
EXIT 65A
Falcon's Fire Golf Club
Celebration Golf Club
Osceola Parkway
ChampionsGate Golf Club

recently renovated course opened in summer 2014 as part of the new Four Seasons Resort Orlando. Known to Disney golfers as the former Osprey Ridge course, the rebranded Four Seasons course has undergone contouring and bunker enhancement, including a new par-3 hole with deep bunkering, sand, and minimal greens. Tees and greens as much as 20 feet above the fairways keep competitive players from getting too comfortable. Amenities include luxury golf carts with GPS, a Cuban-American clubhouse restaurant, driving range, and putting green. ✉ *Four Seasons Golf Course, 10100 Dream Tree Blvd., Golden Oak* *18 holes, 6,968 yards, par 71.*

The Palm. The Palm has been confounding the pros for years. It's not as long as the Magnolia, nor as wide, but it has 9 water holes and a bunker featuring the iconic shape of Mickey Mouse's head. ✉ *Shades of Green, 1950 W. Magnolia-Palm Dr., Magic Kingdom Resort Area* *18 holes, 6,870 yards, par 72.*

Orlando Area

Annika Academy. Named for world-renowned pro golfer Annika Sorenstam (its owner and chief golf guru), Annika Academy offers golf instruction, fitness training, and nutrition counseling. Some package prices are steep. Personalized instruction starts at $150; higher-level packages allow guests to play golf with Annika herself. At the Reunion Resort, which has three championship courses by Nicklaus, Palmer, and Watson, the academy has its own driving range and putting green. ✉ *7450 Sparkling Ct., Reunion* ☎ *407/662–4653, 888/266–4522* 🌐 *www.theannikaacademy.com.*

Arnold Palmer's Bay Hill Club & Lodge. The course is the site of the annual Arnold Palmer Invitational, and the 18th hole is considered one of the toughest on the PGA tour. Courses are open only to those who have been invited by a member or who book lodging at the club's 70-room lodge. But with double-occupancy rates for rooms overlooking the course running as low as $346 for a double room in summer, including two rounds of golf, many consider staying at the club an interesting prospect. ✉ *9000 Bay Hill Blvd.* ☎ *407/876–2429, 888/422–9445* 🌐 *www.bayhill.com* *Greens fees included in resort package* *18 holes, 7,207 yards, par 72; 9 holes, 3,409 yards, par 36* ☞ *Restaurants, spa, salon, tennis, fitness center, heated pool, Golf Academy, private lessons, club rental.*

Barnett Park Golf Practice Facility. Besides having an attractive 18-hole disc (as in Frisbee) golf course, Barnett Park has a great asset: it's free. If you want to stick with traditional golf, just show up at the 159-acre Orange County park to use the net-enclosed driving range (with 10 pads) and the two small putting greens. ✉ *4801 W. Colonial Dr.* ☎ *407/836–6248* *Free.*

Celebration Golf Club. In addition to its great pedigree (it was designed by Robert Trent Jones Jr. and Sr.), Celebration Golf Club has the same thing going for it that the Disney-created town of Celebration has: it's 1 mile off the U.S. 192 strip and a 10-minute drive from Walt Disney World, yet it's lovely, wooded, and serene. ✉ *701 Golf Park Dr., Celebration* ☎ *407/566–4653* 🌐 *www.celebrationgolf.com* *Greens fees $49–$119, depending on time of yr, time of day, and whether you're a Florida or Celebration resident; daily discount rates begin at noon* *18 holes, 6,783 yards, par 72.* ☞ *Restaurant, pro shop, private lessons, club rental.*

ChampionsGate Golf Club. The two courses at ChampionsGate were designed by Greg Norman, and there's an on-site David Leadbetter Golf Academy. The 7,363-yard International has the feel of the best British Isles courses, whereas the 7,128-yard National course is designed in the style of the better domestic courses, with a number of par-3 holes with unusual bunkers. The club is less than 10 miles from Walt Disney World at Exit 58 on I–4. ✉ *1400 Masters Blvd., ChampionsGate* ☎ *407/787–4653 ChampionsGate, 407/787–3330 Leadbetter Academy, 888/633–5323 Leadbetter Academy* 🌐 *www.championsgategolf.com* *Greens fees $45–$142, depending on time of year and time of day. Golf lessons at Leadbetter Academy are $225 per hr and $1,750 per day for private lessons; group lessons are $275 for 2 hrs; a 3-day minischool is $975; a 3-day complete school is $3,000* *International: 18 holes, 7,363 yards, par 72. National: 18 holes, 7,128 yards, par 72* ☞ *Pro shop, restaurant, golf school, private lessons, club rental.*

Falcon's Fire Golf Club. Designed by Rees Jones, Falcon's Fire has strategically placed fairway bunkers that demand accuracy off the tee. This club is just off the Irlo Bronson Memorial Highway and is convenient to the hotels in the so-called Maingate area. ✉ *3200 Seralago Blvd., Kissimmee* ☎ *407/239–5445* 🌐 *www.falconsfire.com* *Greens fees $59–$124, $39 after 3:30 pm in summer* *18 holes, 7,015 yards, par 72* ☞ *Tee times 1–90 days in advance. Restaurant, private and group lessons, club rental, lockers, driving range, putting green.*

Marriott Golf Academy. The Marriott Golf Academy is an extensive-curriculum golf school and 9-hole golf course on the grounds of the corporation's biggest time-share complex, Marriott's Grande Vista. Here you can do anything from taking a one-hour, $119–$169 lesson with a certified instructor to immersing yourself in a three-day extravaganza ($999–$1,499) in which you learn more about golf technique than most nonfanatics would care to know. The Swing Studio offers high-tech teaching methods. The course, designed by Ron Garl, is geared to make you use every club in your bag—and perhaps a few you may elect to buy in the pro shop. You can also play the 18-hole course across the street at Marriott's Grande Pines Golf Club ($39–$124). ✉ *Marriott Grande Vista, 12001 Avenida Verde* ☎ *407/238–7677, 855/642–2369* 🌐 *www.marriottgolfacademy.com* *9 holes, 2,400 yards, par 32.*

Grand Cypress Golf Resort. Grand Cypress comprises three 9s: the North, South, and East courses, and the 18-hole New Course, fashioned after a Scottish glen. In addition, the Grand Cypress Academy of Golf, a 21-acre facility, has lessons and clinics. The North and South courses have fairways constructed on different levels, giving them added definition. The New Course, designed by Jack Nicklaus, was inspired by the Old Course at St. Andrews, and has deep bunkers, double greens, a snaking burn, and even an old stone bridge. ✉ *1 N. Jacaranda* ☎ *407/239–1909, 800/835–7377* 🌐 *www.grandcypress.com* *Greens fees $125–$175* *North: 9 holes, 3,521 yards, par 36. South: 9 holes, 3,472 yards, par 36. East: 9 holes, 3,434 yards, par 36. New: 18 holes, 6,773 yards, par 72.* ☞ *Tee times New Course 8–5; all others 7:30–5. Restaurant, club rental, shoe rental, locker room, driving range, putting green, free valet parking.*

Hawk's Landing Golf Club at the Orlando World Center Marriott. Originally designed by Joe Lee, The 220-acre Hawks' Landing course includes 15 water holes, lots of sand, and exotic landscaping. ✉ *Orlando World Center Marriott, 8701 World Center Dr.* ☎ *407/238–8660, 800/567–2623* 🌐 *www.golfhawkslanding.com* 🎫 *Greens fees $59–$144* 🏌 *18 holes, 6,602 yards, par 71* ☞ *Tee times 60 days in advance for public, 90 days in advance for World Center guests. Restaurants, private and group lessons at the resort's Bill Madonna Golf Academy, club and shoe rental.*

Orange Lake Resort. About five minutes from Walt Disney World's main entrance, Orange Lake has two 18-hole courses (the Legends and the Reserve), two 9-hole courses (Crane's Bend, Legends Walk), and pro instruction at the McCord Golf Academy (rates start at $65). The Legends is a signature Arnold Palmer–designed championship course; the Reserve was designed by Mike Dasher and has unique land and water challenges. Crane's Bend is family-friendly. Legend's Walk is an executive walker's course open until 9 pm nightly, where children 15 and younger play free with complimentary clubs. The signature hole for the entire group of courses is the Island Oak, No. 13, a 432-yard, par-4 hole in the Pines section (the back 9) of the Legends Course. ✉ *8505 W. Irlo Bronson Memorial Hwy., Kissimmee* ☎ *407/239–1050, 888/640–6522* 🌐 *www.golforangelake.com* 🎫 *Greens fees $35–$110 for resort guests; $60–$140 nonguests* 🏌 *The Legends: 18 holes, 7,072 yards, par 72. The Reserve: 18 holes, 6,670 yards, par 71. Crane's Bend: 9 holes, 1,901 yards, par 30. Legend's Walk: 9 holes, 1,581 yards, par 30* ☞ *Advance tee times preferred. Restaurant, private and group lessons, club rental, lighted driving range, putting green.*

Rosen's Shingle Creek Golf Club. Rosen's Shingle Creek Golf Club, designed by David Harman, lies alongside a lovely creek, the headwaters of the Everglades. The course is challenging yet playable, with dense stands of oak and pine trees and interconnected waterways. The golf carts even have GPS yardage systems. Universal Studios and the Orange County Convention Center are within a few minutes' drive. ✉ *9939 Universal Blvd.* ☎ *407/996–9933, 866/996–9933* 🌐 *www.shinglecreekgolf.com* 🎫 *Greens fees $79–$135* 🏌 *18 holes, 7,205 yards, par 72* ☞ *Tee times 7–dusk. Restaurant, club rental, shoe rental, driving range, putting green.*

Waldorf Astoria Golf Club. Rees Jones maintained natural elements while enhancing the land's existing contours when he designed Waldorf Astoria Golf Club. Majestic stands of pine and cypress line the fairways, and it winds through a scenic wetland preserve, with bunkers reminiscent of century-old hazards. It has a five-tee system for all playing levels. ✉ *14224 Bonnet Creek Resort La.* ☎ *407/597–3782, 888/924–6531* 🌐 *www.waldorfastoriagolfclub.com* 🎫 *$65–$195 (seasonal)* 🏌 *18 holes, 7,113 yards, par 72* ☞ *Tee times 7:30–6. Restaurant, club rental, shoe rental, locker room, driving range, putting green, free valet parking.*

ORLANDO SPORTS AND OUTDOOR ACTIVITIES

Tennis, anyone? Or maybe you'd rather surf, parasail, or drive a race car. You can take part in these activities and many more should you feel the need to stretch your legs and move around beyond the theme parks.

Disney is known for its championship golf courses, but if you'd rather swing a racquet, you'll be happy to know there are several lighted courts—both clay and hard—at five Disney resorts. Disney's Fort Wilderness is the place to saddle up for a ride through the woods, and the Contemporary Resort is number one for water sports, including parasailing.

Got a lead foot? Head over to the Richard Petty Driving Experience, where you can race a NASCAR-style stock car or ride shotgun with a pro. Anglers get hooked on fishing charters; runners and bikers get their adrenaline rush on trails across the property. If you'd rather be a spectator, take yourself out to a ball game at the ESPN Wide World of Sports Complex. Popcorn? Check. Hot dogs? Check. Does it get any better than this? For Disney recreation information, call ☎ *407/939–7529*.

MAGIC KINGDOM RESORT AREA

Auto Racing

Richard Petty Driving Experience. This experience lets you ride in or even drive a NASCAR-style stock car on a real racetrack, which is along the road that leads to the Magic Kingdom parking lot. Depending on what you're willing to spend, you can do everything from riding shotgun for three laps on the 1-mile track to taking driving lessons, culminating in your very own solo behind the wheel. The riding cost for three laps is $99; for eight laps, $449; 18 laps, $849; 30 laps, $1,299. The experience, priceless. The Speedway Challenge ($2,099) is a 50-lap program that includes tech talk with the crew chief, and the high-octane Racing Experience ($2,599) includes over-the-top perks. The Exotic Driving Experience puts you behind the wheel of a Ferrari, Lamborghini, or other "supercar" ($169 and up; $99 to ride with a pro driver). The Richard Petty organization has a second Central Florida location at the Daytona International Speedway, but prices differ, so check the website. ✉ *Walt Disney World Speedway, 3450 N. World Dr., Magic Kingdom Resort Area, Lake Buena Vista* ☎ *800/237–3889* 🌐 *www.drivepetty.com*.

Multisport

Fort Wilderness Resort. Fort Wilderness Resort offers a number of sporting activities. For 90 minutes you can get in some target shooting with an archery guide who oversees novice and expert marksmen (ages 6 and up). Nonresort guests are welcome to join campers, and the $39 fee includes use of the compound bow and arrows, plus instruction. You can book up to 180 days in advance.

Tame backwoods horseback trail rides from here begin at 8:30 am and continue through mid- to late afternoon. Children must be at least 9 years old and 48 inches tall to ride, and adults must weigh less than 250 pounds. Trail rides are $45 for 45 minutes; hours vary by season. You must check in 30 minutes prior to your ride, and reservations must be made at least one day ahead. Both horseback riding and the campground are open to nonresort guests.

On the Richard Petty Driving Experience, you get to ride in—or even drive—a NASCAR-style stock car.

Pick up rods and tackle at the **Fort Wilderness Bike Barn,** open daily 9–5, for fishing in the canals around Fort Wilderness Resort. Rod and reel with tackle is about $12.50 for the day. You must be at least 18 to rent here. ✉ *4510 N. Fort Wilderness Trail, Magic Kingdom, Lake Buena Vista* ☎ *407/939–7529 Archery, 407/824–2742 Bike Barn, 407/824–2832 Horseback riding.*

Spectator Sports

ESPN Wide World of Sports Complex. This complex is proof that Disney doesn't do anything unless it does it in a big way. The 220-acre facility, formerly Disney's Wide World of Sports Complex, is on the route to Animal Kingdom. It contains a 7,500-seat baseball stadium—housed in a giant stucco structure that, from the outside, looks like a Moroccan palace—a 5,000-seat field house, and a number of fan-oriented commercial ventures such as the ESPN Wide World of Sports Grill and shops that sell clothing and other items sanctioned by Major League Baseball, the NBA, and the NFL. During spring training the Atlanta Braves play here.

The complex also hosts more than 200 amateur and professional events each year, including big-ticket tennis tournaments. In all, some 30 spectator sports are represented among the annual events, including Harlem Globetrotters basketball games, baseball fantasy camps held in conjunction with the Braves at the start of spring training, and track events ranging from the Walt Disney World Marathon to Amateur Athletic Union (AAU) championships. The complex offers bowling, softball, basketball, and other games for group events ranging from family reunions to corporate picnics. ✉ *700 S. Victory Way, Kissimmee* ☎ *407/828–3267 events information* 🌐 *www.disneyworldsports.com.*

Water Sports

Sammy Duvall's Water Sports Centre. Thanks to Sammy Duvall's you can get a bird's-eye view of Disney while parasailing on Bay Lake. Flights with 450 feet of line last 8 to 10 minutes ($95); deluxe flights

with 600 feet of line last 10 to 12 minutes ($130). You must weigh at least 120 pounds, though lightweights can bulk up with the help of a lifeguard or family member and a tandem flight (without the tandem charge). But if you want to parasail with a partner from the get-go, tandem flights are $170; deluxe tandem flights are $195.

At the same location, you can try your skills at waterskiing, wakeboarding, and tubing. Up to five people can go on the ski boat, which includes equipment and an expert instructor and driver. For a group that large, instructors recommend booking two hours ($165 for the first hour and $135 for each additional hour); couples or smaller groups may want to try one hour, though half-hour rentals ($85) are available. ✉ *Contemporary Resort, Magic Kingdom Resort Area, Walt Disney World* ☎ *407/939–0754*.

SPORTS AND ACTIVITIES ELSEWHERE IN DISNEY

Biking

Paved trails take you past forests, lakes, wooded campgrounds, and resort villas. If you're 18 or older, you can rent bikes at multiple locations, but you must ride them in the area where you rent them.

Rental locations include Downtown Disney Marketplace (near the Rainforest Café) and nearly every moderate-to-deluxe Disney resort, including the BoardWalk Inn and other Epcot Resort Areahotels, Coronado Springs Resort near Disney's Hollywood Studios, Old Key West and Saratoga Springs near Downtown Disney, Animal Kingdom Lodge, Grand Floridian Resort, and the Fort Wilderness Bike Barn at Fort Wilderness Resort.

Most locations have children's bikes with training wheels and bikes with toddler seats. Surrey bikes are also an option. These look like old-fashioned carriages and are a great way to take your family on a sightseeing tour. The covered tops provide a rare commodity at Disney—shade.

Rates start at $9 an hour for regular bikes and go up to $20 to $25 per half hour for surrey bikes (depending on whether they have two, four, or six seats). Wear a helmet; it's free with each rental.

Boating

Disney has one of the nation's largest fleets of rental pleasure craft. There are marinas at the Caribbean Beach Resort, Contemporary Resort, Downtown Disney Marketplace, Fort Wilderness Resort, Grand Floridian, Old Key West Resort, Polynesian Resort, Port Orleans French Quarter and Riverside resorts, and the Wilderness Lodge.

You can rent 12-foot sailboats, catamarans, motor-powered pontoon boats, pedal boats, kayaks, canoes, and tiny two-passenger Sea Racers—a hit with children—for use on Bay Lake and the adjoining Seven Seas Lagoon, Crescent Lake at Epcot resorts, Lake Buena Vista, or Buena Vista Lagoon. You can also sail and water-ski on Bay Lake and the Seven Seas Lagoon; stop at the Fort Wilderness, Contemporary, Polynesian, or Grand Floridian marina to rent sailboats or sign up for waterskiing. Call ☎ *407/939–7529* for more information.

Fishing

Disney Fishing Excursions. You can sign up for two-hour catch-and-release excursions on regularly stocked Bay Lake and Seven Seas Lagoon. In fact, Bay Lake is so well stocked that locals joke that you can almost walk across the water on the

backs of the bass. Departing from the Fort Wilderness, Wilderness Lodge, Contemporary, Polynesian, Yacht & Beach Club, Saratoga Springs, Old Key West, Port Orleans Riverside, and Grand Floridian resort marinas, trips include boat, equipment, and a guide for up to five anglers. Similar charters depart at the same times from a Downtown Disney Marketplace dock by Lake Buena Vista. Your guide is happy to bait your hook, unhook your catches, and even snap pictures of you with your fish.

Two-hour trips for up to five people depart daily at 7, 10, and 1. The cost is $270 (per group) for morning departures and $235 at 1. Live bait and fishing equipment are included; a license is not required on Disney property. ☎ *407/939–2277.*

Ol' Man Island Fishin' Hole. You can fish inexpensively from a dock at Port Orleans–Riverside. Cane poles and bait are $15 per half hour for a family of up to six. You must rent equipment here to use the dock, and you're required to release any fish that you catch. The Fishing Hole is open daily 7–2:15. ✉ *Disney's Port Orleans, 1251 Riverside Dr., Downtown Disney Resort Area, Lake Buena Vista* 🌐 *www.disneyworld.com.*

Mini Golf

If mini golf is your game, Disney's Winter Summerland, next to Blizzard Beach, has 18 holes on its faux-snow "winter" course and 18 on its tropical "summer" course—sand castles and all. At the Fantasia Gardens 36-hole mini-golf course, adjacent to the Walt Disney World Swan, dancing hippos and broomsticks remind you of the classic animated film *Fantasia.* There's even a Fantasia Fairways challenge course, with sand traps, water hazards, and par-3 and par-4 holes up to 75 feet long for experienced golfers.

Running

The World has several scenic running trails from the Grand Floridian, Polynesian, and Contemporary in the Magic Kingdom area. At the Epcot resorts, you can get your heart rate up along the promenade that circles Crescent Lake past the BoardWalk and Yacht and Beach Club resorts. If you're staying at Port Orleans, you can work up a sweat on nearby trails; Coronado Springs guests run along the resort's 1-mile esplanade.

The roads that snake through Downtown Disney resorts are pleasant, and early in the morning traffic isn't too bad. At the Caribbean Beach Resort, there's a 1½-mile running promenade around Barefoot Bay. Fort Wilderness Campground has a woodsy 2-mile course with numerous exercise stations along the way.

Tennis

You can play tennis at several Disney hotels: Bay Lake Tower at Disney's Contemporary Resort (two hard courts), BoardWalk (two hard courts), Old Key West Resort (two hard courts), Saratoga Springs Resort & Spa (two Hydro-grid clay courts), and Yacht Club Resort (one hard court). Courts are available without charge on a first-come, first-served basis for resort and non–resort guests. All have lights, and most have lockers and racquets available to rent or borrow. At the Walt Disney World Swan and Dolphin hotels, you can get an hour-long private lesson on one of four courts for $90 from 7 am to 9 pm. Call ☎ *407/621–1991.*

DOING ORLANDO AND THE PARKS RIGHT

by Jennie Hess

You don't have to wish upon a star to make all your Orlando vacation dreams come true. Your trip will be memorable, whether you're traveling with small children, tweens, teens, or the whole gang of friends or family; whether you're on your honeymoon or flying solo.

Gather (or cyber-gather) all your travel companions together to create a wish list. Then, as you create your itinerary, consider everyone's needs and plan accordingly.

Got small children? Know their theme-park limits to prevent meltdowns, and factor in time away from crowded parks for a laid-back visit to smaller attractions. And, to avoid disappointments, don't wait to get to the parks to determine ride height restrictions.

Teens and tweens may want to head for some rides on their own. Determine theme-park meeting locations, and be sure everyone carries a cell phone in case they encounter longer ride lines and delays.

If the guys are planning to hit the links and the gals want a spa day, don't wait until you're in town to reserve a tee time or a facial-mani-pedi package.

What follows are suggestions (and a few quick tips) on how you can do Orlando and the parks right—regardless of who's in your group. For more planning tips and insights, check out Chapter 1.

Taumata Racer, Aquatica

Shamu's Happy Harbor play area, SeaWorld

FAMILIES WITH SMALL KIDS

Things will go more smoothly if you stick to routines. It's easier than you think. During naptime, for instance, you can relax on a bench while your toddler snoozes in her stroller and the rest of the family heads for a park attraction. Finding sights for wee ones is easy in the parks and outside.

Magic Kingdom. This is the top Disney destination for families with tots. Despite ongoing renovations, Fantasyland still has age-appropriate attractions. Tom Sawyer Island lets squirmy kids burn up some energy.

SeaWorld. Dolphins, whales, and other marine mammals mesmerize young children. Most shows are captivating, and Shamu's Happy Harbor is a wet, wonderful play area.

Typhoon Lagoon. It sets an idyllic water-park scene for families with small children. Ketchakiddie Creek is a favorite splash zone.

Orlando Science Center. Exhibits—many of them interactive—at this center near downtown Orlando let kids experience science and the world around them.

Downtown Disney Marketplace. A kiddie carousel, splash fountains, a LEGO Imagination Center, Bibbidi Bobbidi Boutique (think princess makeovers) are among the attractions for kids.

Pirates of the Caribbean, Magic Kingdom

FAMILIES WITH TWEENS

You and your tweens will have more fun together if you involve them in pre-trip planning. Let each child scope out best bets on Orlando- and theme-park Web sites, then gather to compare notes and create a rough itinerary. Here are a few suggestions to jumpstart the research.

Magic Kingdom. Who ever really outgrows this classic? Tweens love rides ending in "mountain"—Space, Splash, and Big Thunder. The Haunted Mansion and Pirates of the Caribbean are both cool.

Islands of Adventure. This theme-park will be a hit with tweens who love thrill rides and/or superheroes like Spider-Man. For muggle fans of J.K. Rowling's books, the Wizarding World of Harry Potter is a must-see.

Disney's Animal Kingdom. The exotic animals and safari are highlights, but so are scream-inducing Expedition Everest, DINOSAUR, and Kali River Rapids.

Aquatica. Orlando's newest water park has water-slide thrills and a tube slide through a Commerson's dolphin habitat.

Fun Spot. Tweens love the go-kart racetrack best, but the carnival-style rides and arcades are a big draw, too.

WonderWorks. Tweens can "build" their own coaster, and then ride it; lie on a bed of nails; and pilot a simulated fighter jet.

Incredible Hulk Coaster, Islands of Adventure

FAMILIES WITH TEENS

Let teens make their own "gotta do" list and head out on their own. (Chances are at least some of the sights below will make it to every list.) Stay in touch by texting updates and meeting for meals.

Disney's Hollywood Studios. Teens rave about The Twilight Zone Tower of Terror and Rock 'n' Roller Coaster Starring Aerosmith. Competing in Toy Story Midway Mania! and voting for contestants in The American Idol Experience are other cool options.

Islands of Adventure. Older kids are drawn to the action here—from the Amazing Adventures of Spider-Man to the Incredible Hulk Coaster.

Universal Studios. Teens love Hollywood Rip Ride Rockit, Revenge of the Mummy, and the irreverent The Simpsons Ride.

Blizzard Beach and Wet 'n Wild. Blizzard stands out for its wintry theme, mix of thrills, and laid-back "beach" scene. Wet 'n Wild has loud music and big-thrill slides.

Universal CityWalk. It gets high marks for trendy shopping, movie theaters, and concerts. The theatrics of Blue Man Group is a big teen draw around the corner.

Spa with Mom. Mother-daughter facials and pedicures make for a fun morning or afternoon at Orlando spas like the Buena Vista Palace or Disney's Grand Floridian.

Sleuths Mystery Dinner Show, Orlando

LARGE, MIXED GROUPS

Look into Disney's vacation-planning program, Grand Gatherings. Just remember that group members will be happier campers with some "me" time factored in. Here are some suggestions for shared and individual experiences.

Behind-the-Scenes Park Tours. Tours at SeaWorld, Magic Kingdom, Epcot, and Animal Kingdom are great shared experiences. Note that the more people you have on the expensive but oh-so-cool VIP tour at Universal, the better value it is.

Dinner shows. Some area favorites are Medieval Times in Kissimmee, Sleuths Mystery Dinner Show on I-Drive, Disney's Hoop-Dee-Doo Revue, and SeaWorld's Makahiki Luau.

Discovery Cove. Book a "beach" day here to share the experience of swimming with the dolphins. Meals and snacks are included.

Epcot. Everyone can fan out here to take in the attractions of Future World or World Showcase and then gather for dinner at a reserved table to share experiences.

Spa Visits and Golf Expeditions. These are perfect "breakaway" activities. And there are options for both at Disney and in the greater Orlando area.

Spring Training. In March, it's easy to arrange a group outing to a ballgame in one of several central Florida locations.

Cirque du Soleil – *La Nouba*

COUPLES

Let us count the ways to be romantic in Orlando . . . there are too many to list here. Even if the kids are along for the trip, you can carve out time together by using a hotel's sitter service or by packing the children off to a resort kids' club.

Victoria & Albert's. Splurge on a dinner fit for royalty at the Grand Floridian's elegant eatery, central Florida's only AAA Five-Diamond restaurant. Reserve months ahead.

Spa Treatments for Two. Top spas for couples pampering include those in the Ritz Carlton, Waldorf Astoria, Grand Floridian, Portofino Bay, Gaylord Palms, and Walt Disney World Dolphin.

Cirque du Soleil. Hold hands and share the wonder of the surreal show, *La Nouba*, at Downtown Disney West Side

Wekiwa Springs State Park. Escape here for a picnic and/or to rent a canoe and share quiet time on the river.

Islands of Adventure and CityWalk. Plan a wild and crazy evening of roller-coaster thrills and then belly up to the bar for a cheeseburger in paradise at Jimmy Buffet's Margaritaville.

Lake Eola. Paddle a swan-shaped boat together at this lake in downtown Orlando. Then share flatbread and sip champagne at Eola Wine Company across the street.

Disney's Animal Kingdom.

SINGLES (OR GROUPS OF FRIENDS)

It's nice to have a traveling companion, but there's an advantage to visiting on your own—you can cover a lot more territory. Single but traveling with friends? You still may want to split up to sample from your own play list.

Animal Kingdom. Animal-loving singles can linger longer at this park to watch behaviors of many exotic creatures. Rough it on the excellent new Wild Africa Trek for a fee.

Winter Park. On a day trip to this this town you can shop Park Avenue, take a scenic boat tour, and see the huge Tiffany collection at the Morse Museum of American Art.

Disney's Boardwalk. Let nostalgia take hold on a lakeside stroll. Or hop into a surrey or onto a bicycle built for two. Watch dueling pianos at Jellyrolls or a game at ESPN Club.

Run through the parks. Plan your visit in January and compete in the Walt Disney World Half- or Full Marathons—run both, and you'll go home with a Goofy medal as well as a Donald (half) and a Mickey (full)!

Tour new Worlds. Spend seven hours on Disney's Backstage Magic Tour of Magic Kingdom, Epcot, and Hollywood Studios. Or take one of SeaWorld's Spotlight tours into the penguin or dolphin backstage habitats.

2

PLANNING AN ORLANDO VACATION

ORLANDO TRANSPORTATION PLANNER

Getting Here

All the major and most discount airlines fly into **Orlando International Airport** (*MCO* ☎ *407/825–2001* 🌐 *www.orlandoairports.net*).

The **Beachline Expressway,** aka State Road 528, is a toll road that gets you from the airport to area attractions. Depending on the location of your hotel, follow it west, and either exit at SeaWorld for the International Drive (I-Drive) area or stay on it to Interstate 4, and head west for Disney and U.S. 192–Kissimmee or east for Universal and Downtown Orlando.

The **Central Florida Greenway** (☎ *407/690–5000* 🌐 *www.oocea.com* for toll info), **State Road 417,** also runs from the airport to Disney, but tolls are heftier.

Magical Express

If you're staying at a Disney hotel and flying on certain airlines, this free service will deliver your luggage from your home airport to your hotel (and back again) *and* shuttle you to and from your resort. You must book before departure (☎ *866/599–0951* 🌐 *www.disneysmagicalexpress.com*); have your flight information handy.

Getting Around

If you'll be on Disney property, you can use its buses, trams, boats, and monorails. If you're staying outside Disney—or want to visit a non-Disney attraction—options are cabs, shuttles (your hotel may have a free one), and rental cars. Some hotels have shuttles to and from Universal and SeaWorld, which don't have transit systems.

CABS, SHUTTLES, AND PUBLIC TRANSPORTATION

Many non-Disney hotels offer free airport shuttles. If yours doesn't, cabs from the airport to the Disney area run $55–$75. Try **Star Taxi** (☎ *407/857–9999*) or **Yellow Cab Co.** (☎ *407/422–2222*). **Town & Country Transportation** (☎ *407/828–3035*) charges $75 one-way for a town car. The **Mears Transportation Group** (☎ *407/423–5566* 🌐 *www.mearstransportation.com*) offers shuttle and charter services throughout the Orlando area.The **I-Ride Trolley** (☎ *407/248–9590* 🌐 *www.iridetrolley.com*) serves most attractions in the I-Drive area (including SeaWorld). It won't get you to Disney, but it does have a stop about a half mile from Universal. The **LYNX** (☎ *407/841–5969* 🌐 *www.golynx.com*) bus system provides service in Orlando.

CAR RENTAL

Rates vary seasonally and can begin as low as $30 a day or $149 a week for an economy car (excluding 6.5% rental-car tax). If you're staying on Disney property but want to rent a car for a day, you might get a better daily rate if you reserve for two or more days and then return the car early. (Just be sure there aren't any penalties for this.) ■ **TIP→ Gas stations near the airport are pricey.**

ROAD SERVICE

Dial *511 on your cell phone or 511 on a landline for traffic advisories (🌐 *www.fl511.com*). Dial *347 (*FHP) on your cell for the Florida Highway Patrol. Most Florida highways are also patrolled by Road Rangers, a free roadside service. The **AAA Car Care Center** (☎ *407/824–0976*) near the Magic Kingdom provides emergency services, including free towing on Disney property, even for non-AAA members. Office hours are weekdays 7–7, Saturday 7–4, but trucks run whenever the parks are open.

Transit Times and Costs

AIRPORT TO:	BY SHUTTLE (PER PERSON)	BY TAXI/CAR
Magic Kingdom	*30–45 mins; $36 round-trip (RT); $21 one way (OW)*	*35 mins; approx. $58 (taxi fare for up to 7 people)*
Downtown Disney	*30–45 mins; $36 RT; $21 OW*	*25–30 mins; approx. $51*
Animal Kingdom/Hollywood Studios	*30–45 mins; $36 RT; $21 OW*	*35 mins; approx. $58*
Universal	*30–40 mins; $32 RT; $19 OW*	*20 mins; approx. $45*
Kissimmee	*30–45 mins; $48 RT; $27 OW*	*30 mins; approx. $56*
I-Drive (midway)	*30–40 mins; $32 RT; $19 OW*	*20 mins; approx. $35*
Downtown Orlando	*30 mins; $31 RT; $20 OW*	*20 mins; approx. $34*
MAGIC KINGDOM TO:	**BY SHUTTLE**	**BY TAXI/CAR**
Downtown Disney	*N/A (use Disney transportation)*	*10–15 mins; approx. $18*
Animal Kingdom/Hollywood Studios	*N/A (use Disney transportation)*	*15 mins; approx. $17*
Universal	*25 mins; $20 RT*	*25 mins; approx. $43*
Kissimmee	*N/A*	*25–30 mins; approx. $28*
I-Drive (midway)	*N/A*	*30 mins; approx. $41*
Downtown Orlando	*N/A*	*40 mins; approx. $61*
UNIVERSAL TO:	**BY SHUTTLE**	**BY TAXI/CAR**
Magic Kingdom	*N/A*	*25 mins; approx. $43*
Downtown Disney	*N/A*	*20 mins; approx. $30*
Animal Kingdom/Hollywood Studios	*N/A*	*30 mins; approx. $17*
Kissimmee	*30 mins; $19 RT*	*25 mins; approx. $45*
I-Drive (midway)	*25 mins; $16 RT*	*5–10 mins; approx. $10*
Downtown Orlando	*N/A*	*10 mins; approx. $25*

Orlando Routes

Beachline Expressway: Toll road from the airport to I-Drive and Disney ($2.25). Also good for Universal, SeaWorld, and Space Coast.

Interstate 4: Main east–west highway between Tampa and Daytona; it follows a north–south track through Orlando, making for a little confusion. **■TIP→ Think north when I-4 signs say east (toward Daytona, say), and south when they say west (toward Tampa).**

Key exits:

–Exit 64B: Magic Kingdom/U.S. 192; *heavy* peak-season traffic near this exit

–Exit 65: Animal Kingdom, ESPN Wide World of Sports

–Exit 67: Epcot/Downtown Disney, Typhoon Lagoon, Universal; less-congested exit

–Exit 68: Downtown Disney, Typhoon Lagoon

–Exits 71 and 72: SeaWorld

–Exits 72, 74A, and 75A: I-Drive

–Exits 74B and 75A: Universal Orlando Resort

Semoran Boulevard: One of the main roads to Orlando and Winter Park from the airport. Heavily traveled but moves well; plenty of amenities.

Spacecoast Parkway or Irlo Bronson Memorial Highway (U.S. 192): Runs east–west to Kissimmee. Continues east to the coast at Melbourne. Crosses Interstate 4 at Exits 64A and 64B.

ORLANDO THEME PARKS PLANNER

Area Contacts

Florida Tourist Board: ☎ *850/488–5607* 🌐 *www.visitflorida.com*

Kennedy Space Center: ☎ *877/313–2610* 🌐 *www.kennedyspacecenter.com*

Kissimmee Visitors Bureau: ☎ *407/742–8000* 🌐 *www.experiencekissimmee.com*

Orlando Visitors Bureau: ☎ *407/363–5872 or 800/972–3304* 🌐 *www.visitorlando.com*

Space Coast: ☎ *877/572–3224 or 321/433–4470* 🌐 *www.visitspacecoast.com*

Visit Tampa Bay: ☎ *800/448–2672 or 813/223–1111* 🌐 *www.visittampabay.com*

Winter Park Welcome Center: ☎ *407/599–3399 or 407/644–8281* 🌐 *www.cityofwinterpark.org*

Disney Packages

Cruises. Disney Cruise Line ships have activities and amenities to thrill family members of all ages. From Florida's Port Canaveral you can sail to the Bahamas, the Caribbean, Canada, New England, Mexico, or the Panama Canal and even as far afield as Alaska and the Pacific Coast and the Mediterranean. Check out the website 🌐 *www.disneycruise.com*.

Fairy Tale Weddings and Honeymoons. Some 1,500 couples tie the knot at Disney World every year. At the Fairy Tale Wedding Pavilion and many other locations, the bride can ride in a Cinderella coach, have rings borne to the altar in a glass slipper, and spend time with Mickey and Minnie at the reception. Check out the interactive website 🌐 *www.disneyweddings.com*.

Magic Your Way Vacations. These packages bundle hotel, parks admission, and an array of add-on options—dining plans, airfare, Park Hopper passes, spa treatments—that make it easy to customize your trip. They can also offer good value for your money. Just do your homework so you'll know that, if you *aren't* interested in seeing Cirque du Soleil, it's best not to splurge on the deluxe plan, which includes tickets to this show. Also, be sure to determine how many park meals and snacks you'll truly need before investing in a dining plan. Check out the website 🌐 *www.disneyworld.com*.

Universal Packages

Vacation Package. Universal offers its own plans and ever-changing roster of deals to help you maximize value. Basic packages include hotel and park admission but can be expanded to include airfare; dining; rental cars; show tickets; spa treatments; admission to SeaWorld, Wet 'n Wild, Aquatica, Busch Gardens, and Discovery Cove; and a VIP treatment that lets you skip many theme-park lines. Note, though, that this last perk is free to guests of on-site hotels at Universal Resorts. Check out the website 🌐 *www.universalorlando.com*.

Parks Tickets

Per-day, per-person, at-the-gate admissions range from roughly $46 at Aquatica or Wet 'n Wild water parks, to about $95 at Universal, Disney, and SeaWorld. Discovery Cove runs between $169 without a dolphin swim to $399 with it, though prices vary seasonally. Combo ticket plans can save money, but be sure to weigh what they offer against your needs.

DISNEY

Magic Your Way: With this plan, the more days you stay, the greater your per-day savings. For instance, a one-day ticket costs about $95 for anyone age 10 and up, whereas a four-day ticket costs $199 (or just over $49 per day). There are also add-ons:

Park Hopper: This plan lets you move from park to park within a single day and adds $29 to the overall price of a ticket, no matter how many days your ticket covers. The flexibility is fantastic—you can spend the day at Animal Kingdom, for example, and then hit the Magic Kingdom for fireworks.

Water Parks Fun and More: With this $29-per-ticket add-on, you get admission to Typhoon Lagoon, Blizzard Beach, and other Disney attractions, including DisneyQuest, which is a huge draw for teens and preteens.

No Expiration: This add-on (prices vary) lets you use your ticket for more than one trip to Disney (for example, use five days of a seven-day Magic Your Way ticket on one visit and two days on another). Read the fine print on all the ticket packages, as blackout dates may apply.

UNIVERSAL, SEAWORLD, BUSCH GARDENS TAMPA

Universal Parks: A one-day Park to Park ticket is about $128 (ages 10 and up; if you want the expanded Harry Potter experience, a Park to Park ticket is mandatory); a four-day version is nearly $168 (a better per-day value at just under $42 a day). Add the Express Pass (prices vary) option to skirt ride lines; CityWalk Party Pass (roughly $12) for one-night venue access; CityWalk Party Pass and Movie ($15); and Length-of-Stay Wet 'n Wild pass (about $55).

SeaWorld and Busch Gardens Parks: There are various ticket plans for SeaWorld Orlando and Busch Gardens Tampa Bay, which are all run by one company.

Parks Planning Contacts

DISNEY

Central Reservations: ☎ *407/934-7639 (407/W-DISNEY)*

Dining: ☎ *407/939-3463 (407/WDW-DINE)*

Fairy Tale Weddings: ☎ *321/939-4610* 🌐 *www.disneyweddings.com*

Golf: ☎ *407/939-4653 (407/WDW-GOLF)*

Hotels: ☎ *407/939-7429*

Tickets: ☎ *407/939-1289*

Vacation Packages: ☎ *407/939-7675*

Website: 🌐 *www.disneyworld.com*

SEAWORLD

Discovery Cove: ☎ *888/800-5447* 🌐 *www.discoverycove.com*

SeaWorld: ☎ *888/800-5447* 🌐 *www.seaworld.com/orlando*

UNIVERSAL

Main Number: ☎ *407/363-8000*

Dining: ☎ *407/224-7554, 407/363-8000 for character meals*

Hotels: ☎ *888/273-1311*

Vacation Packages: ☎ *877/801-9720*

Website: 🌐 *www.universalorlando.com*

Disney *Magic Your Way* Price Chart

TICKET OPTIONS								
TICKET	1-DAY	2-DAY	3-DAY	4-DAY	5-DAY	6-DAY	7-DAY	10-DAY
BASE TICKET								
Ages 10–up	$94–$99	$188	$274	$294	$304	$314	$324	$354
Ages 3–9	$88–$93	$175	$255	$274	$284	$294	$304	$334
Base Ticket admits guest to one of the four major theme parks per day's use. Park choices are: Magic Kingdom, Epcot, Disney's Hollywood Studios, Disney's Animal Kingdom. 8- and 9-day tickets are also available.								
ADD: Park Hopper	$60	$60	$60	$60	$60	$60	$60	$60
Park Hopper option entitles guest to visit more than one theme park per day's use. Park choices are any combination of Magic Kingdom, Epcot, Disney's Hollywood Studios, Disney's Animal Kingdom.								
ADD: Water Parks Fun & More	$60 2 visits	$60 2 visits	$60 3 visits	$60 4 visits	$60 5 visits	$60 6 visits	$60 7 visits	$60 10 visits
Water Parks Fun & More option entitles guest to a specified number of visits to a choice of entertainment and recreation venues. Choices are Blizzard Beach, Typhoon Lagoon, DisneyQuest, Disney's Oak Trail golf course, and Wide World of Sports.								
ADD: Both	$86	$86	$86	$86	$86	$86	$86	$86
Adding both the *Park Hopper* and *Water Park* option entitles guests to all the privileges under both sepcific options above.								

MINOR PARKS AND ATTRACTIONS		
TICKET	AGES 10–UP	AGES 3–9
Typhoon Lagoon or Blizzard Beach 1-Day 1-Park	$53	$45
DisneyQuest 1-Day	$47	$40
Disney's ESPN Wide World of Sports	$16.50	$11.50
Cirque du Soleil's *La Nouba*	$78–$136	$69–$109
*All prices are subject to Florida sales tax		

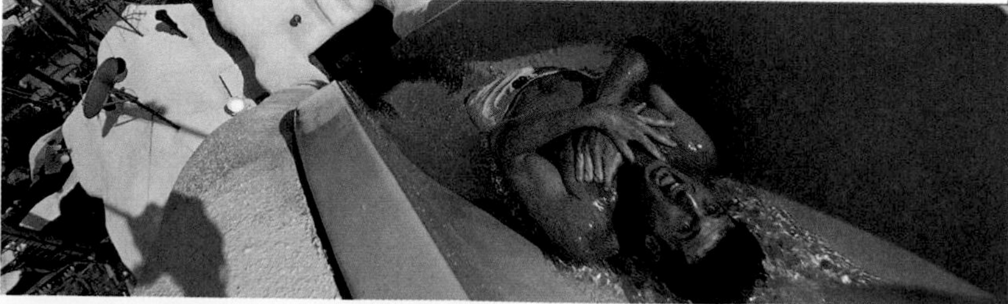

Get wet on the 12-story Summit Plummet at Disney's Blizzard Beach.

Universal Orlando Ticket Price Chart

TICKET OPTIONS				
TICKET	**1-DAY**	**2-DAY**	**3-DAY**	**4-DAY**
BASE TICKET				
Ages 10–up	$96	$135.99	$145.99	$155.99
Ages 3–9	$90	$125.99	$134.99	$143.99
Base Ticket admits guest to one park per day, either Universal Studios or Islands of Adventure.				
PARK-TO-PARK				
Ages 10–up	$136	$175.99	$185.99	$195.99
Ages 3–9	$130	$165.99	$174.99	$183.99
Park-to-Park Ticket allows guest to go back and forth between Universal Studios and Islands of Adventure; 7-day ticket available.				
ADD: CityWalk Party Pass	$12	Free	Free	Free
CityWalk Party Pass and Movie	$15	N/A	N/A	N/A
CityWalk Party Pass gives guest one-night access to CityWalk clubs and venues (some of which require you to be at least 21). CityWalk Party Pass and Movie adds to that a free movie at the AMC Universal Cineplex 20.				
ADD: Wet 'n Wild to Universal Orlando Base Ticket (2-day)	$171.74 for adults, $161.74 for kids.			
ADD: Wet 'n Wild to Part-to-Park ticket	$211.74 for adults, $201.74 for kids.			
ADD: Universal Express Pass	Prices vary greatly by options and season; check website for details.			
Gives guest access to much shorter lines at Universal Studios and Islands of Adventure rides. (Note that this pass is included in the room rate at Universal Resort hotels.)				
All prices are subject to Florida sales tax				

Universal Orlando.

Updated by Jennifer Greenhill Taylor

Say the words *dream vacation* to 10 people, and they'll picture 10 completely different experiences. But there's really only one way to make any dream vacation come true: careful planning. Figure out who's going, decide what everyone wants to do on this trip (and what can wait until the next one), and make reservations—all long before leaving home.

Start your planning by looking at the big picture and then moving on to the details. To guide you, we offer some answers to five questions—the ones most asked by people planning Orlando trips. Your own answers to these questions will form the backbone of your dream trip:

- What should we see and do?
- When should we go (and how long should we stay)?
- Where should we stay? (*see chapter 3, Where to Stay*)
- Where should we eat? (*see chapter 4, Where to Eat*)
- How much will we spend?

Really, though, the question to ask yourself before all others is: Who are we? The answer to that should inform the decisions you make about everything else. To help you in this endeavor, we give guidance specifically geared to several types of travelers: families with young kids; families with tweens; families with teens; couples; singles or groups of friends; and large, mixed groups (like family reunions).

Careful planning may be the backbone of a dream trip, but remember that a flexible spine is better than a rigid one. It's really not that hard—or that big a deal—to change segments of your itinerary as needed when you're on the ground. Be willing to indulge in downtime when someone in the group gets fussy; be prepared to alter plans when friends or relatives can't agree or the weather turns stormy.

So take a deep breath, plan away, go with the flow, and have a great trip!

WHAT SHOULD WE SEE AND DO?

FAMILIES WITH YOUNG KIDS

For a happy, low-stress trip, cater to your kids' desires. That doesn't mean buying or doing everything they want, but it does mean being mindful of their needs, schedules, and patience levels. Choose your parks wisely. Sure, Islands of Adventure's Seuss Landing is terrific for young kids, but most of the other rides at that park are geared to older kids. Water parks are fun, but height restrictions on the big slides can frustrate wannabe riders who don't make the cutoff.

■ TIP→ Even rides geared to young kids can have frightening sounds or darkness. Research attractions on YouTube, so you know what's what.

Get thee to the Magic Kingdom! There's absolutely no better spot for young kids than this wonderland, especially with the castles, rides, and experiences of the expanded Fantasyland. Everything about the kingdom lives up to its "magical" name: the horse-drawn carriages clopping down Main Street, U.S.A; the spires of Cinderella Castle and Beast's Castle; and the classic characters, from princesses to Mickey and Minnie, readily accessible and eager to share an autograph and a huge hug.

■ TIP→ Introduce young kids to giant versions of even beloved characters tentatively; some kids are intimidated at first.

Whichever parks you hit, bring or rent a stroller for the smaller members of your party. Your child may have plenty of energy and be a great walker on a normal day, but pounding the pavement under the hot sun for several hours takes its toll. These parks are big! Avert meltdowns by keeping a ready supply of snacks, water, and handheld games or activities. When kids are full and have things to do, they're less likely to get fussy while waiting in long lines.

■ TIP→ When the adults in your party want to hit grown-up rides, take advantage of Baby Swap.

Universal and Disney both offer this service on rides that are inappropriate for young children. Though each company handles it slightly differently, the gist is the same: one adult waits in line while the other watches the kids, and then the other adult gets to skip to the front of the line for his or her turn.

FAMILIES WITH TWEENS

Pick a theme park, any theme park. Even if they've outgrown Disney characters, your tweens will still love the thrills of Space Mountain at the Magic Kingdom, Rock 'n' Roller Coaster and Tower of Terror at Hollywood Studios, and Mission: SPACE at Epcot. Animal Kingdom combines exciting attractions like Kali River Rapids and Expedition Everest with the coolness factor of live lions, tigers, elephants, giraffes, and other animals on the Kilimanjaro Safaris.

More adventurous tweens will champ at the bit to prove their mettle on Islands of Adventure's monster roller coasters. And fans of the J. K. Rowling stories will adore the Wizarding World of Harry Potter, with its Dragon Challenge coasters, Hogwarts Castle and the new Diagon Alley, Hogwarts Express and Escape from Gringotts. SeaWorld is also

TIPS FOR SENIOR CITIZENS

People 65 and older who are vibrant and active are more likely to characterize themselves by family or interest (solo travelers, couples on a second—or third—honeymoon, or grandparents) than by age.

One good time to think of age is when it comes to discounts! Being older than 65 can mean perks such as reduced fares or specials on airfare, hotels, and restaurants. Two examples include the I-Ride Trolley, which cruises International Drive and offers a 25¢ fare for passengers age 65 and older; and the LYNX public transportation system, which offers various AdvantAge fares for passengers age 65 and older via the website 🌐 *www.golynx.com* or in person at the Downtown Orlando central depot.

You can find a wealth of senior discounts through AARP, formerly the American Association of Retired Persons, which, despite the name, does not require retirement to reap the benefits. Membership is open to anyone age 50 or older, costs only $16 a year, and entitles you to a wide variety of services and discounts. These are updated regularly on the AARP website 🌐 *www.aarp.org.*

a great choice for this age, and it combines theme-park attractions with educational opportunities (shh). In warm weather, water parks Blizzard Beach, Typhoon Lagoon, Wet 'n Wild, and Aquatica are huge draws. On a rainy day, DisneyQuest will satisfy any video-game fan, and create new ones of parents.

It's great fun to share your favorite big-deal rides with your kids, and at this age they can take advantage of just about everything—if they're ready, that is. Some tweens leap at the chance to ride up front in the Incredible Hulk Coaster; others are still frightened by Space Mountain. No need to rush into anything. The bigger rides will be there for you to enjoy together when your kids are older.

FAMILIES WITH TEENS

Universal Studios and Islands of Adventure are fantastic teen choices, with thrill rides like Incredible Hulk Coaster, Revenge of the Mummy, and Hollywood Rip Ride Rockit. Teens also love the late-night bustle of CityWalk, with its funky, neon-lighted stores, throngs of people, live music, and nightclubs that open their doors to younger patrons on teen nights. At Disney's Hollywood Studios, kids 14 and older can audition for the American Idol Experience, where the best singer of the day wins a chance to audition for the real *American Idol* TV show.

An Orlando vacation is a great time to give older teens some space. The bus and monorail system at Walt Disney World offers the opportunity for them to get around without relying on you for a ride. Just be sure you all keep your cell phones on, so you can keep in touch.

■ TIP→ Use cell phone–based GPS to pinpoint the location of your teens.

As much as you might be dying for family bonding time, at this age your teen may be happier if he or she can bring a friend. Before

Your theme-park vacation will be most successful if you combine thoughtful planning with flexibility and spontaneity. There's a lot to be said for having the wonder of a child!

offering an invitation, talk to the parents of the potential guest. Agree up front about expenses, who's paying, and how much supervision will be offered. Written permission—signed by the guest's parents and notarized—will be needed to fly. Such documentation, plus insurance info, will also be needed to get health care in the event of an emergency.

Of course, with freedom can come extravagance. Little things like arcade games or soft drinks and virgin cocktails ($1 to $5 each) add up in a hurry. Set a budget, and encourage your teens to stick to it.

■ TIP→ Giving teens prepaid debit cards helps both you and them stay on budget.

COUPLES

Believe it or not, there are plenty of opportunities for high-quality together time in the theme parks. Swimming with dolphins or tropical fish at Discovery Cove or Epcot is an unforgettable experience, especially when shared with the one you love. What's more romantic than a whirlwind trip around the world? It's possible at Epcot's World Showcase, where lunch in Paris and dinner in Mexico is no problem. And you can always grab on to each other for dear life on the Tower of Terror at Disney's Hollywood Studios or on the Incredible Hulk Coaster at Universal's Islands of Adventure.

Winter Park, just northeast of Orlando, is a great romantic getaway thanks to its Old South charm and its myriad boutiques, museums, and eateries. And on the scenic boat tour of the town's waterways you may just find yourselves holding hands.

After dark, stroll arm in arm through the Magic Kingdom, with all of Main Street, U.S.A, and Cinderella Castle lighted up and fireworks above. Later, go club-hopping into the wee hours at Downtown Disney or Universal's CityWalk.

SINGLES OR GROUPS OF FRIENDS

If you're a theme-park aficionado, oh my, are you in the right place. Even if you're not a big fan, the parks here are so good that you have to visit at least one.

■ TIP→ Use superfast-moving, single-rider lines to board crowded rides quicker. Rides with such lines include Animal Kingdom's Expedition Everest, Epcot's Test Track, Universal Studios' Revenge of the Mummy and Hollywood Rip Ride Rockit, Islands of Adventure's Amazing Adventures of Spider-Man and Incredible Hulk Coaster, and SeaWorld's Journey to Atlantis.

You non-theme-parkers are still in the right place. Orlando has all kinds of other options. Enjoy a blissful spa day at the Ritz-Carlton Orlando Grande Lakes or the Waldorf Astoria. Play golf at the Walt Disney World Resort, or tackle one of the dozens of other fantastic courses in and around Orlando. Shopping here is a treat, too, with many malls and outlets at your disposal.

In the evening you can head to Universal's CityWalk and make some memories with karaoke at the Rising Star or with a music show at Hard Rock Live. On Disney property you can stroll along the BoardWalk for Jellyrolls' dueling pianos and sing-alongs or head to Downtown Disney, where entertainment ranges from House of Blues to the cool retro bowling alley called Splitsville, a double-decker treat with food and live music. You can also hang with locals at Orlando institutions such as The Social or Wally's.

To make the trip truly memorable, push the envelope. Try racing NASCAR vehicles at the Richard Petty Driving Experience; call Bob's Balloons to see the Disney area by hot-air balloon; or let the Space Coast inspire you, and take to the skies yourself with Space Coast Skydiving.

LARGE GROUPS

Getting everyone to agree on what to do is tricky. Preschoolers are content on Dumbo, but older thrill seekers want faster-paced rides. Grandparents might rather play golf or swim laps than traipse around a water park. And those doing the planning may find themselves also doing the mediating—far more frustrating than fun.

Orlando offers some terrific things you can do as a large group. Behind-the-scenes or customized VIP theme-park tours, dinner shows, Cirque du Soleil, the Kennedy Space Center, and spring-training games are wonderful all-ages experiences. As for theme parks, Disney's Animal Kingdom, with its live mountain gorillas and safari ride, probably has the most universal appeal.

Be sure to schedule "apart time"; not every moment has to be a group hug. You can splinter into smaller groups during the day, so some can go shopping in Winter Park or at the outlet malls, some can hit the links,

TIPS FOR PEOPLE WITH DISABILITIES

The theme parks have many amenities and services for people with mobility issues or vision or hearing impairments. Park information centers can answer specific questions and dispense general information about this. Both Walt Disney World and Universal Studios offer free online or printed guidebooks that detail amenities and services (allow six weeks for delivery or pick one up at the front entrance).

Most hotels have been renovated to comply with the Americans with Disabilities Act (ADA). Outside Disney properties, however, the definition of accessibility may differ from hotel to hotel. Some places may be fully accessible by ADA standards for people with mobility problems—with things like roll-in showers, lift-assisted pool entry, or wheelchair-accessible buffets—but not for people with hearing or vision impairments, for example.

In most properties only elevators and room-number plaques are Braille equipped, though some employees are trained in assisting guests with visual impairments. Flashing or vibrating phones and alarms and closed-captioning are more common.

MOBILITY CONCERNS

Many theme-park attractions are accessible to guests with mobility issues. Note that in some you may be required to transfer to a wheelchair if you use an electronic convenience vehicle (ECV). In others, you must transfer from your wheelchair or ECV to the ride vehicle and must have a traveling companion who can assist you, if needed, as park staff are not allowed to do so.

Probably the most comfortable course is to bring your wheelchair from home. If your chair is wider than 24½ inches and longer than 32 inches (44 inches for ECVs), consult theme-park-attraction hosts and hostesses before getting in line. Also note that thefts of wheelchairs while their owners are inside attractions are rare but have been known to occur. Take the precautions you would in any public place.

Wheelchair rentals are available from area medical-supply companies, most of which will deliver to your hotel. You can also rent by the day in major theme parks.

VISION AND HEARING IMPAIRMENTS

Attractions in the parks typically have both a visual element that makes them appealing without sound and an audio element that conveys the charm even without the visuals.

Many attractions are equipped for assisted-listening, handheld-captioning, and other devices, which you can pick up (for a deposit but no fee) at Guest Relations (aka Guest Services) stations at park entrances. Some rides or shows also have closed-caption TV monitors and/or sign-language interpreters, though the latter are available only on certain days (check schedules at Guest Relations).

Service animals are permitted, unless a ride or special effect could spook or traumatize them. Large Braille maps are posted at centralized areas.

some can attack a theme park, and some can lounge by the pool. When you meet up for dinner, you'll all have stories to share.

WHEN SHOULD WE GO?

Let's be honest: there is no "empty" time at Orlando's theme parks. Crowds thin in January, after New Year's, and stay reasonable until around Presidents Day. From that point through Labor Day, though, crowds are either heavy (as in mid-February through early June and again in late August) or very heavy.

Things lighten up after Labor Day, but grow busy again around Columbus Day. After that, comes another light patch until right around Thanksgiving, which is huge in the parks. There's a slight lull in early December, right between Thanksgiving and Christmas vacations.

■TIP→ If your schedule demands that you go at a peak time, you can always get a break from the crowds by planning non-theme-park days. Visit the Kennedy Space Center early in the workweek, when you'll avoid both weekend crowds and late-week school field trips. Eschew Saturday theme-park madness in favor of a trip to charming Winter Park, where you can stroll a farmers' market between 7 am and 1 pm. Stick around to roam the grassy parks, visit the Morse Museum or Park Avenue's galleries, or maybe catch a matinee at the Winter Park Playhouse.

If you'd rather not venture far from the parks, you can escape the crowds by simply slipping back to your hotel for a spa treatment, a swim, a walk around the grounds, a paddleboat ride—many of Orlando's hotels offer such a variety of recreation options that they're practically theme parks themselves.

ORLANDO WEATHER

January and February can have a few cold days, with temps occasionally dropping to freezing at night. Spring is gorgeous: sunny and temperate. April and May can be nippy or warm enough for the water parks. Summer is hot and humid—water parks and swimming pools are the best ways to keep cool. Summertime crowds are thick and lines are long, but hours are extended. Late summer and fall comprise hurricane season, but late September through November, days are bright and beautiful and temperatures cooler.

CONSIDERATIONS FOR DIFFERENT TYPES OF TRAVELERS

As always, the makeup of your travel group will determine when it's best to go. In this case, however, it boils down to two types of travelers: those with school-age kids and those without them.

TRAVELING WITH KIDS

It's a dilemma: you want to plan a great vacation and avoid the crowds, but can you really rationalize taking the kids out of school to visit a theme park? It's a tough call, and the best plan is to consult with your child's teachers first. Ideally, they can advise you on the best time of the

Just saying "magic" and "Disney" in the same sentence brings to mind Cinderella Castle surrounded by dazzling fireworks.

school year to go and create a study plan to ensure your child's education isn't compromised during the trip.

For elementary-school kids there are ways of making the trip educational. For example, your child could write about the different countries featured at Epcot in lieu of a missed homework assignment, do a report on the animals of SeaWorld or Animal Kingdom, or prepare a talk about what he or she learned at the Kennedy Space Center.

■ **TIP→ To avoid crowds and meltdowns, families with young children should visit theme parks in the morning and evening. Leave the hot afternoons for naps and downtime at the hotel pool.**

Note that although it may be fine to take younger kids out of school for a few days, missing several days of middle or high school could set your child back for the rest of the semester. If you do go during school vacations like the rest of the world, all is not lost. Take advantage of Extra Magic Hours, FastPass+, or Universal's front-of-the-line privileges when you can; retreat to your hotel when you need to; and simply make peace with the crowds so you can enjoy your vacation.

TRAVELING WITHOUT KIDS

It's very simple: avoid crowds by avoiding school vacation times. If water parks aren't a priority, early January is a great time, specifically about two weeks after New Year's. Kids are back in school, and the Walt Disney World Marathon weekend is over, so those crowds are gone, and the weather can be spectacular. If you love water parks, go after Labor Day, when kids are back in school. It will still be hot enough to make the waterslides a joy.

ORLANDO THEME PARK ITINERARIES

The baseline is a day for every theme park you visit, plus two travel days. To have a rich, full experience in all six of the Disney and Universal theme parks, you'd need eight days. To include SeaWorld *or* one of the water parks *or* a non-theme-park attraction, add another day—for a total of nine days. Some find trying to see too many theme parks in a short time rather like eating too many sweets at a buffet. This is a vacation, not a marathon, so be sure to schedule free time.

If you're selective, though, you can have a great five- to seven-day trip, *including* two travel days. Families with young kids might spend full days at only a few theme parks. Those with tweens or teens might do two parks in a day but take in only the highlights. Singles, couples, or groups might take the full-day park-tour approach or mix the half-day park-highlights approach—perhaps with half days of downtime (rather than at other parks).

How long you stay might also affect your hotel choice. The longer and more varied the trip, the farther from the theme parks you can stay. The shorter the trip or the more time you plan to spend in the parks, the better off you are staying on or very near Disney or Universal property.

SAMPLE ITINERARIES

You should add two travel days to the following three- and five-day itineraries. These are our dream trips, but for best results, you really should create your own!

FAMILIES WITH YOUNG KIDS—3 Days

Day 1—Magic Kingdom early, with a nap or pool break back at the hotel, returning for the evening fireworks show or parade. **Day 2**—the whole family by the hotel pool or the kids busy in the hotel's children's program while Mom and Dad head to Downtown Disney or the BoardWalk. **Day 3**—Hollywood Studios through to the afternoon parade; back to the hotel for a nap and a swim before enjoying the Hoop-Dee-Doo Musical Revue dinner show.

Other Recommendations: Use Magical Express airport-transfer service; stay on Disney property; get the basic Disney meal plan; buy two-day Magic Your Way parks tickets (which you don't need to use on consecutive days). Work in a character meal on arrival or departure day. Take time to let the little ones rest and recharge.

FAMILIES WITH TWEENS—5 Days

Day 1—Magic Kingdom highlights in the morning; Epcot later in the day with dinner at World Showcase, followed by IllumiNations. **Day 2**—a day at Blizzard Beach, Typhoon Lagoon, or DisneyQuest. **Day 3**—Kids head to the hotel's kids' program; Mom and Dad rent a car and head to Winter Park or Downtown Orlando. **Day 4**—Islands of Adventure, with the Wizarding World of Harry Potter first thing. **Day 5**—SeaWorld or Kennedy Space Center.

Other Recommendations: Stay at a Disney or Lake Buena Vista property; skip the Disney or Universal meal plans. Add the Park Hopper option to the one-day Disney ticket, but skip the Water Parks and More option. Consider Universal's Express Pass.

ORLANDO THEME PARK ITINERARIES

FAMILIES WITH TEENS—3 Days

Day 1—a full day at Universal Studios. **Day 2**—teens spend time by the pool while Mom and Dad play golf or hit a spa; dinner together followed by an evening—together or apart—at CityWalk. **Day 3**—a full day at Islands of Adventure.

Other Recommendations: Take a shuttle or cab to and from the airport, and stay at a Universal property; do the Universal Meal Deal on theme-park days. Consider taking in Blue Man Group on the night out at CityWalk. Buy multiday Universal tickets online in advance to save; invest in Universal's Express Pass (note, though, that this is free if you stay at a Universal hotel except the new Cabana Bay).

SINGLES, COUPLES, OR GROUPS OF FRIENDS—3 Days

Day 1—morning at hotel pool or spa, lunch at the hotel, late-afternoon Magic Kingdom highlights and dinner at California Grill with a view of Castle fireworks. **Day 2**—take a balloon ride, golf a championship course, swim with dolphins at Discovery Cove or Epcot, or drive NASCAR-style at the Richard Petty Driving Experience. **Day 3**—full day at Animal Kingdom, Epcot, Universal Studios, or Islands of Adventure with dinner in Orlando or Winter Park.

Other Recommendations: If it's a special occasion, book a car service to and from the airport. Use shuttles or cabs the rest of the time.

Don't bother with park meal plans, but do splurge on a luxury hotel with lots of amenities (on or off theme-park property): Disney's Grand Floridian; Universal's Portofino Bay; Orlando's Ritz-Carlton, Waldorf Astoria, or Gaylord Palms.

Consider buying two-day Magic Your Way Disney tickets and getting Universal's Express Pass (free if staying at most on-site Universal hotels).

LARGE, MIXED GROUPS—2 to 5 Days

Large, mixed groups have the most flexibility. On any given day, there are bound to be some members heading to a theme park, some going out shopping or to play golf, and some relaxing by the pool or in a spa. Those who want to take in a theme park every day can do so (and will always have someone to go with), and those who don't will always have someone with whom to share the alternatives.

Just be sure to plan get-togethers: a meal or two, an evening (perhaps for a show), an afternoon—if not a full day—maybe at SeaWorld, a water park, or Kennedy Space Center.

Other Recommendations: Use the Magical Express service, opt for some version of the Disney meal plan, and stay on-site. Otherwise choose an all-suites hotel in a location that's convenient, regardless of who's doing what—perhaps a central I-Drive spot.

If group plans involve more than one day of sightseeing—say, one day in Winter Park and another at Kennedy Space Center, or a spring-training baseball game in the Tampa area—rent a van or charter a bus. Otherwise rely on in-park transportation, hotel shuttles, or cabs.

HOW MUCH WILL WE SPEND?

If you're traveling to Orlando, be prepared to spend and spend—and spend some more. Even if you get great deals on transportation and hotel, your credit-card balance will increase and cash will evaporate in the hot Orlando sun.

COSTS

First there are the usual vacation costs: pet boarding, airfare, trip insurance, ground transportation, lodging, and food. Then there are the vacation costs that you tend to take for granted but that add up: gratuities, souvenirs, and sundries (such as more sunscreen, bottled water, new batteries).

> **WORD OF MOUTH**
>
> "If you are going [to Disney World] at a busy time, pay attention to the extra magic hours for people staying at Disney resorts. If your kids are up to it, you can skip the middle of the day when everything is packed and hot, and stay in a park until midnight enjoying minimal lines." –KatieL

In Orlando you have to add another whole layer to the cost of a trip, starting with, of course, theme-park tickets. Although prices for these vary greatly depending on the park, the plan, and the ages of those in your group, you can peg admission at roughly $80 per day per person. For a family of four visiting three parks, that's more than $950.

What's more, costs for food and other items inside the parks are generally higher than elsewhere. For instance, a snack of churros and sodas can set a family of four back almost $25. To all this, add extras such as character meals, babysitting, cover charges, show tickets, greens fees, and spa treatments.

At this point you might begin to panic. Don't. Take your trip planning and budgeting step by step, and you'll soon find that there are lots of ways to make an Orlando vacation financially accessible.

BUDGETING

We can't stress enough the importance of creating a formal budget for a trip to Orlando and carrying it with you—so you'll be more likely to stick to it. If you do this for all your vacations, great. You're a step ahead. If you don't do this, have we got a plan for you!

THREE-STEP BUDGETING PLAN

Step 1: Create Your Dream Itinerary. First, go back through this chapter and answer the first four trip-planning questions. Your answers will enable you to create a wish list of theme parks and other sights and activities to enjoy (be sure to dream big). Slot these into a day-by-day itinerary to determine how long your dream trip should be and possibly even when to go. Having an itinerary can also help you figure out where to stay and eat.

Step 2: Create Your Dream Budget. Use your dream itinerary—and the decisions made because of it—to create your dream budget. In addition to

SAMPLE COSTS AT WALT DISNEY WORLD	
20 oz. bottle of water/soda $2.50–$4	1 GB digital memory card $17.95
Cup of coffee $2.19	Autograph book $6.95–$10.95
Cheeseburger $10	Plush character toys $12–$100
French fries $2.79	Commemorative pins $10–$100
Ice-cream treat $2.50–$4	Souvenir T-shirt $16–$35
Chicken nuggets $6	

2

calculating costs for parks tickets, other entertainments and activities, hotel, transportation, and food, be sure to include estimated daily totals for things like tips, souvenirs, and sundries. Also include kennel costs, trip insurance, and babysitting fees if applicable.

■ TIP→ Most of us lowball costs. To offset this, add in another 2% to 5% of the total budget. The percentage you use should depend on how well you generally police spending.

When you calculate the total cost of your trip, remember that at this point you're still dreaming big. Take a deep breath and move on to Step 3.

Step 3: Create Your Real Budget (and Itinerary). Okay. So your dream-vacation budget has, most likely, an astronomical total. Now it's time to bring everything back down to earth. This might mean spending more time researching discounts, lower rates, or package deals. It might also mean reassessing your priorities.

Perhaps you'll book a cheaper hotel so you can spend more days at Disney. Or maybe you'll splurge on lodging and take in fewer parks. You might move your trip up or back a month to get a lower airfare or plan a shorter trip to lower costs overall. Regardless, by making some adjustments you'll soon have a more realistic trip—in terms of both your budget and, no doubt, your itinerary.

SAVING MONEY

IN GENERAL

Shop around. Seem obvious? Not necessarily so. Did you know, for instance, that Internet prices aren't always the lowest? Travel agents may *still* be able to get you better deals, simply because it's their business to know their way around the reservations thicket. And online prices can be dramatically different from site to site—room costs alone can vary by as much as 200%. What's more, not all chains or carriers are represented on all sites. This is especially true of the smaller or discount airlines. You might also find the cheapest fare or best promotional room rate on an airline or hotel-chain website. Note also that you can sometimes get a better price if you call a hotel's local or toll-free number (if available) rather than a central reservations number.

Use aggregator sites to compare prices. Websites like Kayak.com, Mobissimo.com, and Travelgrove.com gather the best prices for airfares, hotels, and rental cars from many places. Most aggregators compare

TIPPING IN ORLANDO

Whether they carry bags, deliver food, or clean rooms, hospitality workers rely on tips to help them earn a living. Although you'll ultimately base tips on how involved the service is and how well it's performed, here are some guidelines:

In transit, tip airport skycaps and shuttle drivers $1 to $2 per bag and taxi drivers 15% to 20% of the fare. At hotels go with $1 to $2 per bag for bellhops, $1 or $2 per night per guest for housekeeping, $5 to $20 for special concierge service, and $1 to $2 for parking valets or doormen who hail cabs.

Tip the caddies 15% of the greens fee, and spa therapists and waitstaff in full-service restaurants 15% to 20% of the total bill (but check your bill first, as the tip may already be included). Tip bartenders and cocktail waitresses 10% to 15% of the total check.

the major online travel agent–booking engine sites such as Expedia, Travelocity, and Orbitz. They also look at some car-rental and airline websites. Some aggregators also compare such things as trip insurance or vacation packages.

■ TIP→ Booking directly with Disney rarely yields the lowest price. For everything but parks tickets and dining plans (whose prices are fixed), you'll get better deals with major online booking sites.

Investigate credit-card privileges. Even if your credit card doesn't give you frequent-flier miles for purchases, you may still be eligible for discounts on travel products or services. Visit the company's website to check on hotel deals or promotions. Disney also has its own Visa rewards card. Not only can you use the card for certain on-property discounts, but you can also earn the so-called Disney Dollars on your regular purchases, which you can later spend on a Disney vacation.

Have the best deals find you. On Expedia, Travelocity, and other sites you can sign up to receive emails the moment a fare to Orlando meets your price requirements. TravelZoo.com and FareCompare.com send emails alerting you to great deals on packages and airfares, respectively.

Consider what organizations you belong to. Are you a member of the American Dental Association or the American Bar Association? Are you U.S. military personnel? Even if you do nothing more than carry your membership card and pay yearly dues, you can take advantage of low rates that many organizations and unions negotiate with hotels and car-rental companies.

Look into group discounts. Depending on its size, your brood may qualify for rates normally offered to schools and corporations. Talk to group-sales professionals, and ask about discounts on flights as well as hotels (for multiroom blocks), theme parks, and shows.

ON THE THEME PARKS

Buy park tickets when you book your trip. This not only enables you to avoid any price increases that happen before you arrive, but also lets you take advantage of online discounts that parks like Universal and SeaWorld offer. For Discovery Cove, you must book well in advance, as attendance is limited to 1,000 people a day.

Save money with a multiday park pass. Theme-park admission can be pricey, but multiday packages are always available, and these often include additional benefits, such as early entry to the park.

Skip the theme parks on days you arrive and depart. It's not worth spending money for just a couple of hours in the parks. Instead, use those days to lounge around your hotel pool or to visit Downtown Disney, Disney's BoardWalk, or Universal CityWalk.

Don't sweat the wee ones. Babies and tots under three get into the parks for free—one less cost to worry about.

ON HOTELS

Watch out for the term "from" when pricing hotels. That baseline figure, although an effective come-on, might apply to an undesirable hotel. The minimally acceptable, midlevel options could be quite a hike up.

Always ask about packages and special rates. High-end hotel chains catering to business travelers are often busy only on weekdays; to fill rooms they often drop rates dramatically on weekends. And most hotels have special package deals or corporate rates.

Ask about incidental costs. Seemingly petty details such as surcharges on local phone calls, local occupancy taxes, early check-in fees, resort fees, energy surcharges, Internet fees, and parking fees can really add up. Some hotels tack on hidden gratuities, too.

ON MEALS

Stay at an all-suites hotel with in-room kitchens. Making some of your own meals will reduce your costs—as will bringing all of your own essentials.

Stock up at a supermarket on the way to the hotel. That's especially advisable if you're staying put for a while. You'll get better prices than at hotel shops.

Plan to have lunch at that fancy restaurant. Menus at lunch often vary only slightly from those at dinner, but prices at lunch can be much lower.

ON AIRFARE

Keep tabs on prices. To determine when to buy tickets, check out FareCompare.com, which has historical and current airfares, and Bing.com/travel, which uses Farecast technology to predict fare changes based on historical data. Unlike many other sites, AirfareWatchDog.com includes rates for budget airlines in its research.

Pick your days and times wisely. Look for departures on Tuesday, Wednesday, and Saturday, typically the cheapest days to travel. Flights on these days are often less crowded as well. Also check on prices for departures at different times of day.

Investigate flights to secondary airports. Flights to Daytona's airport, 45 minutes from Orlando, or to Sanford-Orlando, only 30 minutes away,

ORLANDO DISCOUNTS AND DEALS

DIS. Though Disney doesn't always publicize it, it does offer many of its own discounts and promotions, all of which the independent website DIS compiles and shares. The site also includes discounts and promotions for the Universal parks and properties. *www.wdwinfo.com/discounts.html*

Entertainment Travel Editions. Pick up local coupon books. This company has one for around $35 with discounts on rental cars, admission fees, and meals. *888/231–7283* *www.entertainment.com*

Mousesavers.com. This website aims to give the scoop on ways to score discounts on all things Disney: for the most part it doesn't offer specific discounts, but it does provide great advice on where you can ferret out your own. In a few cases, such as with its recommended non-Disney hotels, Mousesavers has negotiated added perks like free breakfasts. The site also lists many discounts for a long list of other Orlando parks and attractions, including all the biggies. *www.mousesavers.com*

Orlando/Orange County Convention and Visitors Bureau. The Orlando CVB sells park ticket plans and offers the free Magicard, which provides discounts for many attractions, restaurants, and stores. *407/363–5872 or 800/972–3304* *www.visitorlando.com/discounts-and-tickets*

Shades of Green Resort. If you're active-duty or retired military, National Guard, Army Reserve, a disabled veteran, foreign military stationed with U.S. armed forces, or a Department of Defense civilian with military ID, you can also stay at Disney's on-site Shades of Green Resort for a fraction of what it costs to stay at other Disney resorts. You can also buy up to three rooms so nonmilitary members of your party can stay with you.

Members of the military are eligible to purchase discounted and tax-free park tickets, including the Magic Your Way Stars and Stripes Pass. The resort's ticket office is open 8 am to 9 pm. (You can buy these tickets at the main entry gate, too, but tax will then be included.) Shades of Green sells heavily discounted tickets to Orlando's other attractions, including both Universal parks, SeaWorld, Busch Gardens, Kennedy Space Center, and Wet 'n Wild. Military personnel and their spouses can also buy tickets for a select number of nonmilitary guests. You do not need to stay at Shades of Green resort (but you *do* need to be staying at a Disney on-property resort) to qualify for any of its attractions' discounts. *407/824–1403* *www.shadesofgreen.org*

may be cheaper and have better availability, especially during high season. Area car-rental rates might also be lower.

Fly on a holiday. Just as the most expensive fares tend to be on the days or weekends at either side of a holiday, some of the least expensive are on the holiday itself, especially Christmas and Thanksgiving. Just be sure that the airfare cost savings isn't completely eaten up by hotel, car-rental, and other costs made more expensive by the holiday.

Ask about child and senior fares. Although it's rare to find discounts of any kind, it never hurts to ask.

ON CAR TRAVEL

Calculate the cost of a drive to Orlando. Input your route and the make and model of your car on AAA's fuel-cost calculator (🌐 *www.fuelcostcalculator.com*) and voilà! (The figures assume there are no traffic jams.) Use it to budget for a road trip and to compare that to the cost of flying. Check for the latest smartphone apps that do the same.

Find the cheapest gas. Gas prices are greatly influenced by state gas taxes. A website operated by the U.S. Environmental Protection Agency (🌐 *www.fueleconomy.gov*) gives national and regional average prices. Also helpful are sites like Gas Buddy (🌐 *www.gasbuddy.com*) and Gas Price Watch (🌐 *www.gaspricewatch.com*), which use consumer tips to rank prices in a particular area.

Decide whether you'll really need a rental car. If you're staying on Disney or Universal property, you most likely will not. If you'll be traveling, price out those trips by cab, then see if it pays to have a rental car. Don't forget the costs of gas and parking in your estimate.

Check out weekly rates and packages. Even if you want to rent a car for only five or six days, ask for the weekly rate; it may very well be cheaper than the daily rate for that period of time. Adding a car rental onto your air-hotel vacation package may be cheaper than renting a car separately.

Don't forget the locals. Price local companies as well as the majors. Avoiding the chains and renting through local agencies can save you big bucks, particularly in touristy areas like Florida, where competition is stiff. The potential downsides include limited counter office hours, infrequent shuttle service, limited car selection, and no guaranteed roadside assistance.

Ask about fees and surcharges. Most agencies impose a surcharge on drivers under age 25 (some won't rent to drivers under 25; for others the cutoff age is 21). Airports often add surcharges, which you can sometimes avoid by renting from an agency whose office is just off airport property. Don't assume that bringing the car back early will save you bucks. If you return your car before the minimum number of days (often five) specified in a weeklong contract, the weekly rate could revert to a much higher daily rate.

Check prices on different-size cars. Most of us assume that renting a compact car is less expensive than a standard-size model. But smaller cars are more popular with renters, so prices may be lower for the larger models. Check the fees. You may be pleasantly surprised.

Get smart about fuel. Pass on the option of paying the rental agency for a tank of gas rather than refueling the car yourself before you return it. In some cases the per-gallon rate is much higher than you'd pay at a gas station. Even if the per-gallon rate is lower, you'll be charged for an entire tank of gas whether you use it all or not (it's hard to work it so you can coast in on empty upon return). Plan to fill up the tank yourself, at a station away from the drop-off point, to get better prices. Check the average price of fuel as you drive around, and avoid filling up near the airport, as those stations are often the most expensive.

PACKING

In Orlando, casual, comfortable clothing is best. Men need a jacket and tie in only a handful of restaurants. ■ **TIP→ Restaurants with dress requirements are strict about enforcing them. If you plan to eat at a nicer place, check on dress codes so you aren't caught unprepared.**

It can get quite cool in December, January, and February. In general, though, be prepared for a range of temperatures in winter by packing clothing that you can layer.

In summer you'll want a sun hat and a rain poncho in case of sudden thunderstorms (or for watery theme-park rides). On hot summer days the perfect theme-park outfit begins with generous amounts of sunscreen, followed by shorts made of a breathable, quick-drying material, topped by a T-shirt or tank top. At any time of the year, pockets are useful for FastPass+ tickets, cell phones, and park maps.

PACKING TIPS

FOR KIDS

Give everyone his or her own bag. Individual suitcases (preferably different colors—red for one, blue for another, etc.—and preferably carry-on size, so you don't have to check bags and pay extra fees) help you find items in a hurry. This will make life easy at the airport, as even little kids are capable of toting around a mini Pullman—they often enjoy it.

Pack one communal carry-on. If logistics forces you to check luggage—despite hefty bag fees—packing a family bag of essentials saves heartache if some of your luggage is temporarily lost. Include an outfit for everyone, as well as prescriptions and other must-haves. A communal bag also simplifies car travel, giving quick access to overnight necessities for midway stops instead of having to unpack the whole car.

Consider creative carry-ons. Soft coolers that don't go beyond airline size limits make great carry-on luggage. Roomy and crushable, they're perfect for nonbreakable items (such as those extra outfits) and help you cut your food bill by becoming picnic baskets for snacks.

FOR CAR TRAVEL

Check the trunk. Trunks are prone to dampness—wetness from one big storm can remain in your trunk for long periods and then creep into luggage. Line the bottom of your trunk with a waterproof tarp or, better yet, with some kind of slightly elevated platform that allows air to circulate between the base of your trunk and the goods stored in it.

Separate your "getting there" and "there" clothes. If your Orlando trip involves a hotel stay or stays along the way, keep the clothing you plan to use once you arrive in one piece of luggage at the back of the trunk or under other bags. Put the clothing you need during the drive in lighter and smaller duffel bags or luggage stowed in an easy-to-reach place.

DID YOU KNOW?

You can get 400-foot-high, 360-degree, fair-weather views of the kingdom from the Characters in Flight helium balloon that's tethered in Downtown Disney's West Side. Mary Poppins has nothing on you!

Keep essential road-trip items handy. Pack the emergency kit last and in a place where it's easily accessible. Also keep books, electronic entertainment gadgetry, and the cell-phone charger handy.

Organize with plastic drawers. You can buy cheap, stackable plastic drawers at most department stores. Put a few of these in your trunk, filling one with books and maps and another with toiletries, and you'll have an efficient system for even the longest trip from home.

3

WHERE TO STAY

Updated by Jennifer Greenhill-Taylor

With tens of thousands of lodging choices available in the Orlando area, from tents to deluxe villas, there is no lack of variety in price or amenities. Narrowing down the possibilities can be part of the fun.

More than 50 million visitors come to the Orlando area each year, making it the most popular tourism destination on the planet. More upscale hotels are opening as visitors demand more luxurious surroundings, such as luxe linens, tasteful and refined decor, organic toiletries, or ergonomic chairs and work desks. But no matter what your budget or desires, lodging comes in such a wide range of prices, themes, color schemes, brands, meal plans, and guest-room amenities, you will have no problem finding something that fits.

Resorts on and off Disney property combine function with fantasy, as befits visitor expectations. Characters in costume perform for the kids, pools are pirates' caves with waterfalls, and some, like the Gaylord Palms, go so far as to re-create Florida landmarks under a gargantuan glass roof, giving visitors the illusion of having visited more of the state than they expected.

The area around the expanded Orange County Convention Center is going more upscale as the center draws more and more savvy conventioneers who bring their families along to visit the theme parks. Central Florida has weathered the tough economic times of the past few years so well, in fact, that prices are on the rise, and a wide range of new hotels are popping up.

Many hotels have joined the trend toward green lodging, bringing recycling, water conservation, and other environmentally conscious practices to the table. Best of all, the sheer number and variety of hotel rooms means you can still find relative bargains throughout the Orlando area, even on Disney property, by researching your trip well, calling the lodgings directly, negotiating packages and prices, and shopping wisely.

LODGING PLANNER

WHERE SHOULD WE STAY?

When it comes to Orlando lodging, no matter who you are and where you decide to stay, you should book months in advance (at least six months for hotels at Disney). This is particularly important for travel when rates are lowest, specifically early January to mid-February, late April to mid-June, and mid-August to early December.

Your choices include resorts on Disney property (most owned and operated by Disney), those on Universal property, and those not in or affiliated with either park. Each type of property merits consideration.

HOTELS ON DISNEY AND UNIVERSAL PROPERTY

If you're interested solely in attractions at Disney or Universal, **in-park hotels are best.** For starters, they offer such convenient transportation options that you probably won't need a rental car—a huge cost savings.

Walt Disney World's massive campus is tied together by a dizzying array of complimentary monorails, buses, and water taxis. All get you anywhere on the property you want to go. Universal provides complimentary shuttles and water taxis between its two theme parks and on-site hotels, though the hotels and parks are also within walking distance of one another.

Universal and Disney's on-site hotels also offer many special perks—some designed to save money, some designed to save time. Note that these perks don't necessarily extend to non-Disney-owned hotels on Disney property, so ask for those specifics before booking.

HOTELS OFF THEME-PARK PROPERTY

If you plan to visit several parks or go sightseeing elsewhere in Central Florida, consider off-site hotels. Those closest to Disney are clustered in a few areas: along I-Drive; in the U.S. 192 area and Kissimmee; and in the Downtown Disney–Lake Buena Vista Area, just off Interstate 4 Exit 68. I-Drive hotels such as the DoubleTree by Hilton at the Entrance to Universal Orlando and Hyatt Place Orlando/Universal are closest to Universal.

Nearly every hotel in these areas provides frequent (sometimes free) transportation to and from Disney or even Universal. In addition, there are some noteworthy and money-saving, if far-flung, options in the greater Orlando area. One suburban caveat: traffic on Interstate 4 in Orlando experiences typical freeway gridlock during morning (7–9) and evening (4–6) rush hours.

■ TIP→ Anyone can visit Disney hotels. To save money and still have on-site resort experiences, stay at a moderately priced hotel off-site and then visit the animals at the Animal Kingdom Lodge, say, or rent a boat at the Grand Floridian.

CONSIDERATIONS FOR DIFFERENT TYPES OF TRAVELERS

Whether you stay on theme-park property or off, prioritize your needs. A great spa is wonderful, but if you're running around with three young kids, will you actually use it? Do you want luxury or rustic simplicity? A splurge or a supersaver?

In addition, weigh what you get for the money. Sure, you might spend more on a room at a Disney or Universal resort than at an off-site property. But if staying at a cheaper off-site hotel means renting a car or spending a lot of money and time on cab rides, you might not ultimately be saving that much. Conversely, if you're planning to split your time between, say, Disney, Universal, and SeaWorld, you probably won't make full use of all of the Disney or Universal perks and might be better off shopping for a good-value, centrally located, off-site hotel with free theme-park shuttle service.

Finally, if you're traveling with children, be sure to mention their ages when you make reservations. Sometimes hotels have special features, such as rooms with bunk beds, just for families. Such things aren't necessarily offered up front, so be sure to ask.

■ TIP→ Regardless of whether you stay at hotels near the theme parks or at on-site resorts, it can take between 20 minutes and an hour to get to and from park entrances.

FAMILIES WITH YOUNG KIDS

If this is a Disney trip, stick with Disney hotels: the transportation system makes it simple to scoot back for a nap or some downtime at the pool.

Many Disney properties are designed to appeal to kids, some with great children's facilities and programs. At the value-priced Art of Animation Resort, young kids love the familiarity of *Finding Nemo, Little Mermaid,* and *Cars* themes everywhere. The Polynesian Resort's Never Land Club has an enchanting Peter Pan–themed clubhouse and youngsters-only dinner show. Parents rave about the Sand Castle Club at the Yacht and Beach Club resorts. What's more, most of these clubs are open from late afternoon until midnight, so parents can slip out for a romantic meal while the kids play games, do art projects, and enjoy a snack or dinner.

■ TIP→ Surprise kids with a wake-up call from Mickey while staying at a Disney resort.

If you do stay off-site, book a hotel geared to small children. The Nickelodeon Suites Resort, in Lake Buena Vista, offers suites whose separate kid-friendly bedrooms are decorated with images of cartoon characters. It also has live shows featuring Nick characters, a Nickelodeon-themed pool, and tons of kids' activities.

East of International Drive the connected JW Marriott and Ritz-Carlton Orlando, Grande Lakes resorts have rooms with adjoining kids' suites, complete with miniature furniture and toys. The Ritz also has a Kids Club with a play area and daily scheduled activities.

WHERE SHOULD WE STAY?

	VIBE	PROS	CONS
Disney	Thousands of rooms at every price; convenient to Disney parks; free transportation all over WDW complex.	Perks like early park entry and Magical Express, which lets you circumvent airport bag checks.	Without a rental car, you likely won't leave Disney. On-site buses, although free, can take a big bite of time out of your entertainment day; convenience comes at a price.
Universal	On-site hotels offer luxury, convenience, and value. There are less expensive options just outside the gates.	Central to Disney, Universal, SeaWorld, malls, and I–4; free water taxis to parks from on-site hotels.	Most on-site hotels are pricey; expect heavy rush-hour traffic during drives to and from other parks.
I-Drive	A hotel, convention center, and activities bonanza. A trolley runs from one end to the other.	Outlet malls provide bargains; world-class restaurants; the Orlando Eye lifts visitors up for a bird's-eye view; many hotels offer free park shuttles.	Transportation can be pricey, in cash and in time, as traffic is often heavy. Crime is up, especially after dark, although area hotels and businesses have increased security.
Kissimmee	It offers mom-and-pop motels and upscale choices, restaurants, and places to buy saltwater taffy.	It's just outside Disney, very close to Magic Kingdom. Lots of Old Florida charm and low prices.	Some of the older motels here are a little seedy. Petty crime in which tourists are victims is rare—but not unheard of.
Lake Buena Vista	Many hotel and restaurant chains here. Adjacent to WDW, which is where almost every guest in your hotel is headed.	Really close to WDW; plenty of dining and shopping options; easy access to I–4.	Heavy peak-hour traffic. As in all neighborhoods near Disney, a gallon of gas will cost 10%–15% more than elsewhere.
Central Orlando	Parts of town have the modern high-rises you'd expect. Other areas have oak tree–lined brick streets winding among small, cypress-ringed lakes.	Locally owned restaurants, trendy hotels, vibrant nightlife, and some quaint B&Bs. City buses serve the parks. There's good access to I–4.	You'll need to rent a car. And you will be part of the traffic headed to WDW. Expect the 25-mile drive to take at least 45 minutes.
Orlando International Airport	Mostly business and flight-crew hotels and car-rental outlets.	Great if you have an early flight or just want to shop in a mall. There's even a Hyatt on-site.	Watching planes, buses, taxis, and cars arrive and depart is all the entertainment you'll get.

Wherever you stay, inquire about child equipment. Most hotels—and certainly all owned by Disney—have amenities such as cribs. (Some hotels require you to reserve cribs in advance. Ask whether there will be an additional charge, and make sure the crib meets current child-safety standards.)

FAMILY WITH TWEENS

With tweens you don't really need a hotel that's superclose to a theme park, so your selection is greater. Even properties that seem adult-oriented have offerings that tweens love. The "lazy-river" pools at hotels including the Omni Orlando Resort at ChampionsGate and the JW Marriott, for instance, are generally big hits.

Many hotels also have supervised camp-style programs, with trained counselors and fun, active, outdoorsy things to do. These are great for arrival and departure days, when you probably don't want to schlep to a park, but you also don't want to hear the dreaded "I'm so bored."

Standouts are the Camp Holiday program at the Holiday Inn Resort Lake Buena Vista and the Camp Hyatt program at the Hyatt Regency Grand Cypress, near Downtown Disney. The latter is a top-class resort with sprawling grounds that abut Walt Disney World property, so it's perfect for families who want to be near the Mouse but prefer to take a break from Disney each night.

FAMILY WITH TEENS

A great hotel pool is a major boon for teens, who might not want to spend all of their time in the theme parks. Stormalong Bay, the pool complex shared by the Yacht and Beach Club, has it all: a lazy river, waterslide, sandy-bottom pool, and elevated tanning deck. This location is also surrounded by the shops, restaurants, and leisure activities of Disney's BoardWalk—a great place for teens to explore on their own.

Teens are usually partial to Universal's thrills, so the *South Pacific*–themed Loews Royal Pacific Resort here is also an excellent choice. It has a lagoon-style swimming pool with a sandy beach; "dive-in" movies on select nights; a fitness center with a whirlpool, steam room, and sauna; a nightly torch-lighting ceremony; and an authentic luau. The rock-and-roll-themed Hard Rock Hotel is also a great Universal option.

■ **TIP→ If at all possible, book more than one room. As they say, the family that sleeps together . . . hates each other in the morning.** Teens are used to having their own space; crabby moods stemming from cramped conditions can put a damper on the vacation. When booking, request connecting rooms—with a door linking your room to that of your teen—as opposed to adjoining rooms, which means only that your rooms are next to each other.

If booking more than one room is too pricey, look into accommodations at all-suites hotels or family suites at regular hotels. These larger quarters are often reasonably priced. Just be sure to check on the hotel's definition of "suite." Sometimes it's merely an L-shaped room with a sitting area (i.e., there's no door separating you from your teen). The key question is, "Do your suites have two separate rooms?"

SINGLES OR GROUPS OF FRIENDS

If you're traveling solo, you'll never feel lonely at a theme-park hotel. Consider one in Disney's BoardWalk area—perhaps the BoardWalk Inn and Villas, Disney's Yacht Club, or Disney's Beach Club. From here you're just steps from shopping, dining, and nightlife. Similarly, Universal hotels like the elegant Loews Portofino Bay Hotel are just a

DID YOU KNOW?

The All-Star Sports, Music, and Movies Resorts and the Art of Animation Resort all are thematically designed. Goofy is the pitcher in the baseball diamond–shaped pool at the Sports resort, a piano-shaped pool can be found at the Music resort, a huge Buzz Lightyear figure stands tall at the Movies resort, and Disney and Pixar animation classics star at Art of Animation.

DID YOU KNOW?

The spa at the Ritz-Carlton Orlando, Grande Lakes, is the largest in Orlando, with 40 treatment rooms.

BABYSITTING IN ORLANDO

If you're staying in a room, suite, or condo and need to rent baby equipment, such as a stroller, bassinet, high chair, or even pool toys, call **Orlando Crib Rental** (☏ *407/433–7770* 🌐 *www.orlandocribrental.com*) for swift delivery and fair rates. You can order online. The company also provides some concierge services, such as grocery or baby-supply delivery.

If you want to plan an adults-only evening, consider the **Kid's Nite Out** (☏ *407/828–0920 or 800/696–8105* 🌐 *www.kidsniteout.com*) program, which works with hotels throughout Orlando. It provides in-room babysitting for children ages 6 weeks to 12 years. Fees start at $16 an hour for one child, and increase by $2.50 for each additional child. There's a four-hour minimum, plus a transportation fee of $10 for the sitter to travel to your hotel room. The service also rents baby equipment, such as strollers and jogging carriages, and will babysit your pet, too.

When you make a reservation, you must provide a credit-card number. There's a 24-hour cancellation policy; if you cancel with less than 24 hours' notice, your credit card is charged the four-hour minimum fee ($64 for one child, higher rates for multiple children booked). The service recommends booking from two weeks to 90 days in advance.

blink away from the shopping and the hopping nightlife of CityWalk. Plus, Portofino has a spa.

If theme parks aren't your only interest, you can get your wow factor by staying at a hotel like the Gaylord Palms Resort. The interior of this place is like a Cecil B. DeMille movie—about Florida. Just walking around in the 4-acre atrium is an adventure, with indoor gardens evoking the Everglades and old St. Augustine. There's also a lot to do on-site, including dining, shopping, pampering yourself at the spa, or working out in the large fitness center.

COUPLES

Luxury properties such as the Ritz-Carlton Orlando, Grande Lakes spell romance. Ultraluxurious rooms, restaurants, and spa programs, plus a championship golf course, make this resort one of the best in the Orlando area. Another romantic option is Downtown's Grand Bohemian, with a rooftop pool, jazz in the Bösendorfer Lounge, and short-walk access to the new Dr. Phillips Center for the Performing Arts and the Amway Center's NBA games and world-class concerts.

If you and your sweetie are Disneyphiles, Disney's five-star Grand Floridian absolutely drips with Victorian romance, and the Animal Kingdom Lodge offers the delights of sunsets over the savanna and giraffes and zebras munching leaves just below your balcony. The Port Orleans Resort–French Quarter, in Downtown Disney, is a great, more affordable choice for couples.

LARGE GROUPS

All-suites properties are the logical choice. If you're coming mainly for the theme parks, stay on Disney or Universal grounds, as the many perks—especially those involving transportation—definitely make life easier. Some Disney properties with suites include the cabins at Fort Wilderness Resort, the Beach Club Villas, the BoardWalk Inn and Villas, the Bay Lake Tower at the Contemporary Resort, and the villas at Animal Kingdom. At the Universal properties, the new Cabana Bay has 1,800 rooms, half of them suites.

If you plan to spend time away from the parks or will be shuttling between Universal and Disney, consider reserving an apartment or condo. This works best for families who thrive on the chaos of communal living. (It also works better if you assign chores. This is a vacation for everyone, and it's just not fair if one or two people consistently do all the work.)

The only potential hang-up to the apartment-condo scenario is who gets the master suite. If it's a birthday, anniversary, or retirement event, the big room naturally goes to the guest(s) of honor. Otherwise, the decision isn't so straightforward. One solution: donate it to some of the kids. The suite will be plenty big for a slumber party, and you'll love the fact that their war-torn bathroom is blissfully out of sight.

If your family members tend to get in each other's hair, you're better off reserving a block of hotel rooms. Add a courtesy suite, and you have all the benefits of togetherness, plus a place to retreat to when you need it. Talk to a hotel agent to figure out how many people each room can accommodate comfortably, and how many rooms you'll need.

FACILITIES AND AMENITIES

All hotels and resorts in Central Florida have air-conditioning, and most have cable or satellite TV, coffeemakers, in-room irons, and ironing boards. Those in the moderate and expensive price ranges often have bathrobes and hair dryers. High-speed wireless access (Wi-Fi) is now common even at budget properties, but some hotels still charge a daily fee for Internet service. If being connected is important, it's best to ask. Most hotels, even the budget ones, have a pool, and many have fitness facilities and business centers. Ask whether the hotel charges a resort fee. Finding a week's worth of unexpected daily fees on your final bill can be a disconcerting surprise.

If a particular amenity is important to you, ask for it; many hotels will provide extras upon request. Double-check your bill at checkout, and if a charge seems unreasonable, this is the time to have it remedied. If you're traveling with pets, note the hotel's pet policies. Some hotels require substantial cleaning fees. A big note to smokers: most of the hotels and resorts in Central Florida are entirely smoke-free, meaning even smoking outdoors on hotel property is frowned upon or prohibited.

DISNEY AND UNIVERSAL RESORT PERKS

DISNEY PERKS

Extra Magic Hours. You get special early and late-night admission to certain Disney parks on specified days. Call ahead for details so you can plan your early- and late-visit strategies.

Free Parking. Parking is free for Disney hotel guests at Disney hotel and theme-park lots.

Magical Express. If you're staying at a select Disney hotel, this free airport service means you don't need to rent a car or think about finding a shuttle or taxi or worry about baggage handling.

At your hometown airport, you check your bags in and won't see them again till you get to your Disney hotel. At Orlando International Airport you're met by a Disney rep, who leads you to a coach that takes you to your hotel. Your luggage is delivered separately and usually arrives in your room an hour or two after you do. If your flight arrives before 5 am or after 10 pm, you will have to pick up your luggage and deliver it to the coach.

On departure, the process works in reverse (though only on some participating airlines, so check in advance). You get your boarding pass and check your bags at the hotel. At the airport you go directly to your gate, skipping check-in. You won't see your bags until you're in your hometown airport. Participating airlines include American, Delta, JetBlue, Southwest, and United.

Charging Privileges. You can charge most meals and purchases throughout Disney to your hotel room.

Package Delivery. Anything you purchase at Disney—at a park, a hotel, or in Downtown Disney—can be delivered to the gift shop of your Disney hotel for free.

Priority Reservations. Disney hotel guests get priority reservations at Disney restaurants and choice tee times at Disney golf courses up to 30 days in advance.

Guaranteed Entry. Disney theme parks sometimes reach capacity, but on-site guests can enter even when others would be turned away.

UNIVERSAL PERKS

Head-of-the-Line Access. Your hotel key (except Cabana Bay) lets you go directly to the head of the line for most Universal Orlando attractions. Unlike Disney's Fastpass program, you don't need to use this at a specific time; it's always good. Hotel guests also get early admission to the often-crowded Harry Potter attraction.

Priority Seating. Many of Universal's restaurants offer priority seating to those staying at on-site hotels.

Charging Privileges. You can charge most meals and purchases throughout Universal to your hotel room.

Delivery Services. If you buy something in the theme parks, you can have it sent directly to your room, so you don't have to carry it around.

Free Loaners. Some on-site hotels have a "Did You Forget?" closet that offers everything from kids' strollers to dog leashes to computer accessories. There's no fee for using this service.

ROOM RATES

In the Orlando area there's an inverse relationship between temperature and room rates. The hot and humid weather in late summer and fall brings lower prices and possibly hurricanes. Conversely, the balmy days of late February, March, and April attract lots of visitors; hotel owners charge accordingly. One note about hurricane season—it officially begins in June, but a hurricane in Florida before August is rare. Rates are often low from early January to mid-February, from late April to mid-June, and from mid-August to the third week in November.

Always call several places—availability and special deals can drive room rates at a $$$$ hotel down into the $$ range—and don't forget to ask whether you're eligible for a discount. You can always save by preparing a few meals in a room, suite, or villa with a kitchenette or kitchen. Websites will often offer a better room rate; so compare the prices offered on the Web and through the hotel's local or toll-free number (if one is available). Always ask about special packages or corporate rates. Don't be shy. Polite assertiveness can save you money.

The Disney Dining Plan: On-site Walt Disney World Hotels don't offer meal plans in their rates, but you can choose a Disney Dining Plan. It can be added to any on-site package, and many families swear by it. The plan saves you from having to carry around cash and—at least on the surface—masks the sting of coughing up nine bucks for a cheeseburger. To see if a Disney Dining Plan is right for your family, go to 🌐 *www.disneyworld.disney.go.com/dining* for more information.

RESERVATIONS

When booking by phone, expect a robot first, a sometimes protracted wait, then a real person who will be polite and helpful.

Walt Disney Travel Co. Packages can be arranged through the Walt Disney Travel Co. Guests can find planning tools on the website that allow them to customize vacation itineraries to suit interests as well as special needs based on age, height restrictions and medical needs. ☎ *407/939–5277* 🌐 *www.disneyworld.com.*

WDW Central Reservations Office. You can book many accommodations—Disney-owned hotels and some non-Disney-owned hotels—through the WDW Central Reservations Office. The website allows you to compare prices at the various on-site resorts. ☎ *407/934–7639* 🌐 *www.disneyworld.com.*

WDW Special Request Reservations. People with disabilities can call WDW Special Request Reservations, or check the website for specific needs. ☎ *407/824–4321, 407/TTY: 827–5141* 🌐 *www.disneyworld.com.*

WHAT IT COSTS

	$	$$	$$$	$$$$
FOR TWO PEOPLE	under $174	$175–$249	$250–$350	over $350

OUR REVIEWS

Prices: Prices in the hotel reviews are the lowest cost of a standard double room in high season, excluding taxes, service charges, and meal plans (except at all-inclusives). Prices for rentals are the lowest per-night cost for a one-bedroom unit in high season. Note that taxes in Central Florida can be as high as 12.5%.

Maps: *Throughout the chapter, you'll see mapping symbols and coordinates (✣ 3:F2) after property names or reviews. Maps are within the chapter. The first number after the ✣ symbol indicates the map number. After that is the property's coordinate on the map grid.*

WALT DISNEY WORLD

Disney-operated hotels are fantasies unto themselves. Each is designed according to a theme (quaint New England, the relaxed culture of the Polynesian Islands, an African safari village, and so on), and each offers the same perks: free transportation from the airport and to the parks, the option to charge all of your purchases to your room, special guest-only park-visiting times, and much more. If you stay on-site, you'll have better access to the parks and be more immersed in the Disney experience.

MAGIC KINGDOM RESORT AREA

Take I–4 Exit 62, 64B, or 65.

The ritzy hotels near the Magic Kingdom all lie on the monorail route and are only minutes away from the park. Fort Wilderness Resort and Campground, with RV and tent sites, is a bit farther away from the Magic Kingdom, and access to the parks is by bus or boat.

$$$$ RESORT **The Cabins at Disney's Fort Wilderness Resort.** The cabins in this 700-acre campground right across the lake from the Magic Kingdom don't exactly constitute roughing it, as they are small, air-conditioned log homes that accommodate four grown-ups and two youngsters. **Pros:** lots of traditional camping activities and a real campground community feel; you can save money by cooking, but you don't have to, as there is a three-meals-a-day restaurant and nightly barbecue; free Internet and Wi-Fi. **Cons:** shuttle to parks is free, but slow; pricey for what is really just a mobile home encased in logs; coin-op laundry is pricey, too. *Rooms from: $413* ✉ *4510 N. Fort Wildnerness Trail, Magic Kingdom Resort Area, Lake Buena Vista* ☎ *407/824–2900* 🌐 *www.disneyworld.disney.go.com/resorts* *421 cabins* *No meals* ✣ *1:C2.*

$ RESORT Fodor's Choice ★ **The Campsites at Disney's Fort Wilderness Resort.** One of the cheapest ways to stay on WDW property is in your own tent or RV, especially considering that some of the 799 sites in this 750-acre pine and cypress forest campground can accommodate up to 10 people. **Pros:** Disney's most economical lodging; pets allowed; free Wi-Fi, free parking. **Cons:** amount of walking to reach the store, restaurants, etc., can be a bit much; shuttle rides to Disney parks take a long time; the mosquitoes can be irritating, except in winter. *Rooms from: $85* ✉ *4510 N.*

BEST BETS FOR ORLANDO AND THE PARKS LODGING

Fodor's offers a selective listing of high-quality lodgings in every price range, both inside and outside the parks. Here are our top picks by price and experience. The best properties—those that provide a remarkable experience in their price range—are designated with the Fodor's Choice logo.

Fodor's Choice★

Best Western Lake Buena Vista Resort, $, p. 96

The Campsites at Disney's Fort Wilderness Resort, $, p. 85

Disney's All-Star Sports Resort, $, p. 92

Disney's Animal Kingdom Lodge, $$$$, p. 93

Disney's Coronado Springs Resort, $$$, p. 93

Disney's Grand Floridian Resort & Spa, $$$$, p. 90

Drury Inn & Suites Orlando, $, p. 99

Hyatt Regency Grand Cypress Resort, $$, p. 110

Loews Portofino Bay Hotel at Universal Orlando, $$$$, p. 99

Loews Royal Pacific Resort at Universal Orlando, $$$, p. 99

Meliá Orlando Suite Hotel at Celebration, $$, p. 103

Nickelodeon Suites Resort, $, p. 110

Residence Inn by Marriott Orlando at SeaWorld, $$, p. 107

Ritz-Carlton Orlando, Grande Lakes, $$$$, p. 108

Universal's Cabana Bay Beach Resort, $, p. 102

Waldorf Astoria Orlando, $$$, p. 111

By Price

$

Best Western Lake Buena Vista Resort, p. 96

The Campsites at Disney's Fort Wilderness Resort, p. 85

Disney's All-Star Resorts, p. 92

Disney's Art of Animation Resort, p. 91

Drury Inn & Suites Orlando, p. 99

Hyatt Place Orlando/Universal, p. 99

Nickelodeon Suites Resort, p. 110

Universal's Cabana Bay Beach Resort, p. 102

$$

Hyatt Regency Grand Cypress Resort, p. 110

Meliá Orlando Suite Hotel at Celebration, p. 103

Residence Inn by Marriott Orlando at SeaWorld, p. 107

$$$

Disney's Coronado Springs Resort, p. 93

Loews Royal Pacific Resort at Universal Orlando, p. 99

Waldorf Astoria Orlando, p. 111

$$$$

The Cabins at Disney's Fort Wilderness Resort, p. 85

Disney's Animal Kingdom Lodge, p. 93

Disney's Grand Floridian Resort & Spa, p. 90

Loews Portofino Bay Hotel at Universal Orlando, p. 99

Ritz-Carlton Orlando, Grande Lakes, p. 108

By Experience

MOST KID-FRIENDLY

Disney's All-Star Resorts, $, p. 92

Disney's Art of Animation Resort, $$, p. 91

Disney's Contemporary Resort, $$$$, p. 90

Nickelodeon Suites Resort, $, p. 110

BEST POOLS

Hyatt Regency Grand Cypress Resort, $$, p. 110

JW Marriott Orlando Grande Lakes, $$$$, p. 108

Loews Portofino Bay Hotel at Universal Orlando, $$$$, p. 99

Ritz-Carlton Orlando, Grande Lakes, $$$$, p. 108

BEST FOR BUSINESS

DoubleTree by Hilton at the Entrance to Universal Orlando, $, p. 98

Hilton Orlando, $$, p. 105

3

Hyatt Place Orlando/ Universal, $, p. 99

Hyatt Regency Orlando, $$, p. 106

Rosen Plaza Hotel, $$, p. 107

Westin Orlando Universal Boulevard, $$, p. 107

BEST SERVICE

JW Marriott Orlando Grande Lakes, $$$$, p. 108

Orlando World Center Marriott, $$$, p. 110

Ritz-Carlton Orlando, Grande Lakes, $$$$, p. 108

Waldorf Astoria Orlando, $$$$, p. 111

BEST NEW HOTELS

Aloft Orlando Downtown, $, p. 112

Avanti Resort, $, p. 104

Universal's Cabana Bay Beach Resort, $, p. 102

BEST-KEPT SECRET

CoCoKey Hotel & Water Resort, $, p. 104

The Florida Hotel & Conference Center, $, p. 113

Floridays Resort Orlando, $$, p. 105

Rosen Plaza Hotel, $, p. 107

Staybridge Suites Lake Buena Vista, $, p. 111

BEST FOR COUPLES

The Alfond Inn, $$, p. 114

Grand Bohemian Hotel, $$$, p. 113

Hyatt Regency Grand Cypress Resort, $$, p. 110

Loews Portofino Bay Hotel, $$$$, p. 99

Walt Disney World Dolphin, $$$, p. 96

BEST FOR MIXED GROUPS (I.E., MULTIGENERATION)

Caribe Royale, $, p. 109

Hard Rock Hotel, $$$$, p. 99

Holiday Inn Lake Buena Vista Downtown Disney, $, p. 97

JW Marriott Orlando Grande Lakes, $$$$, p. 108

Renaissance Orlando at SeaWorld, $$, p. 107

BEST FITNESS ROOM

Disney's Saratoga Springs Resort & Spa, $$$$, p. 94

Hard Rock Hotel, $$$$, p. 99

Hyatt Regency Orlando, $$, p. 106

Orlando World Center Marriott, $$$, p. 110

BEST DINING OPTIONS

Disney's Animal Kingdom Lodge, $$$$, p. 93

Disney's Grand Floridian, $$$$, p. 90

Loews Portofino Bay Hotel, $$$$, p. 99

Rosen Shingle Creek, $$, p. 109

Wyndham Grand Orlando Resort, Bonnet Creek, $$, p. 111

BEST VIEWS

Buena Vista Palace Hotel, $$, p. 97

Hyatt Regency Grand Cypress Resort, $$, p. 110

Orlando World Center Marriott, $$$, p. 110

Park Plaza, $$, p. 114

Rosen Shingle Creek, $$, p. 109

BEST BUDGET

Art of Animation Resort, $, p. 91

Avanti Resort, $, p. 104

The Campsites at Disney's Fort Wilderness Resort, $, p. 85

Drury Inn & Suites, $, p. 99

Staybridge Suites Lake Buena Vista, $, p. 111

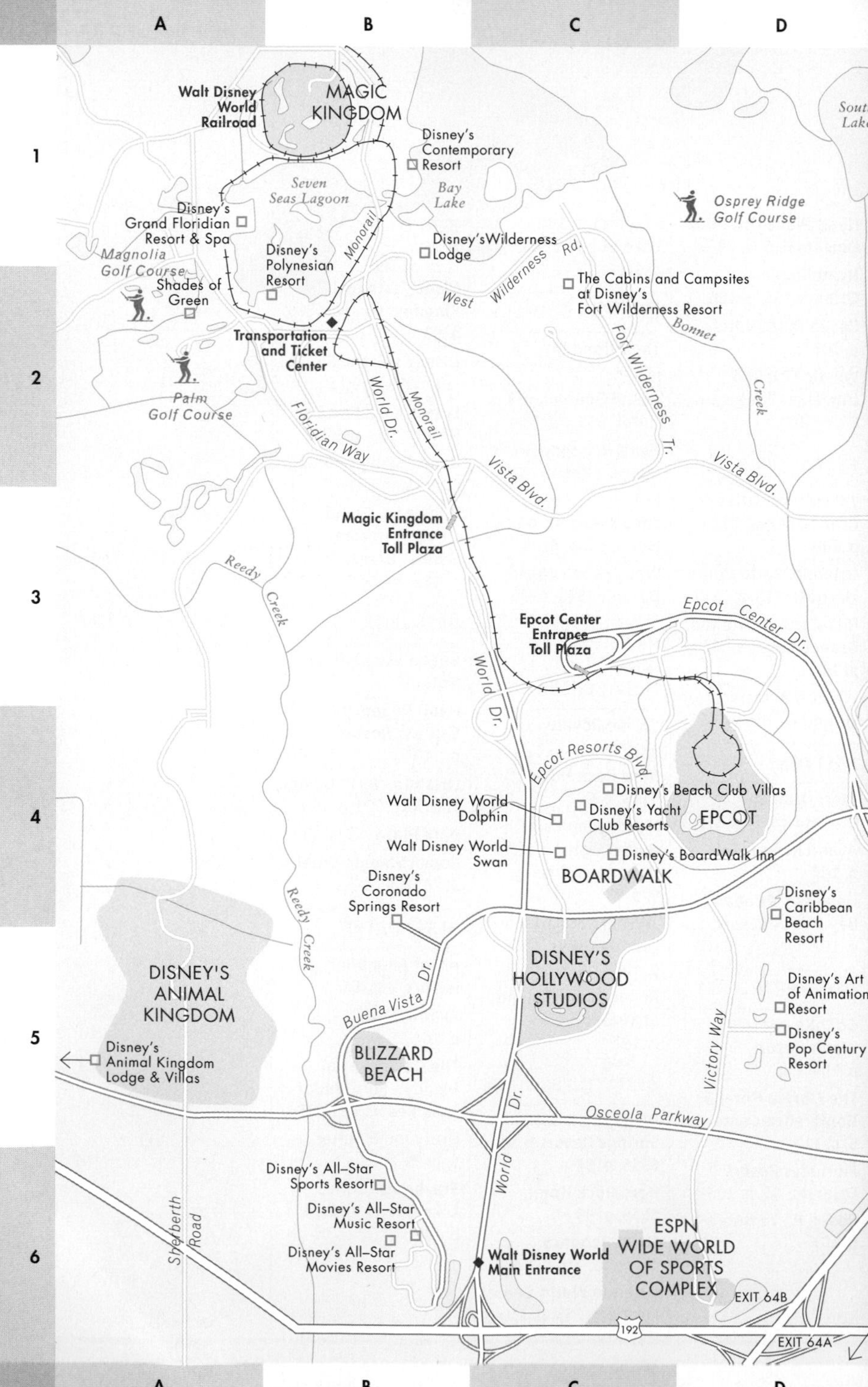
A
B
C
D
1
2
3
4
5
6
Walt Disney World Railroad
MAGIC KINGDOM
Disney's Contemporary Resort
South Lake
Seven Seas Lagoon
Bay Lake
Osprey Ridge Golf Course
Disney's Grand Floridian Resort & Spa
Magnolia Golf Course
Disney's Polynesian Resort
Monorail
Disney's Wilderness Lodge
West Wilderness Rd.
The Cabins and Campsites at Disney's Fort Wilderness Resort
Shades of Green
Transportation and Ticket Center
Bonnet Creek
Fort Wilderness Tr.
Palm Golf Course
World Dr.
Monorail
Floridian Way
Vista Blvd.
Vista Blvd.
Magic Kingdom Entrance Toll Plaza
Reedy Creek
Epcot Center Dr.
Epcot Center Entrance Toll Plaza
World Dr.
Epcot Resorts Blvd.
Disney's Beach Club Villas
Walt Disney World Dolphin
Disney's Yacht Club Resorts
EPCOT
Walt Disney World Swan
Disney's BoardWalk Inn
BOARDWALK
Disney's Coronado Springs Resort
Disney's Caribbean Beach Resort
Reedy Creek
DISNEY'S ANIMAL KINGDOM
DISNEY'S HOLLYWOOD STUDIOS
Disney's Art of Animation Resort
Buena Vista Dr.
Victory Way
Disney's Pop Century Resort
Disney's Animal Kingdom Lodge & Villas
BLIZZARD BEACH
Dr.
Osceola Parkway
Disney's All-Star Sports Resort
World
Disney's All-Star Music Resort
Sherberth Road
ESPN WIDE WORLD OF SPORTS COMPLEX
Disney's All-Star Movies Resort
Walt Disney World Main Entrance
EXIT 64B
192
EXIT 64A
A
B
C
D

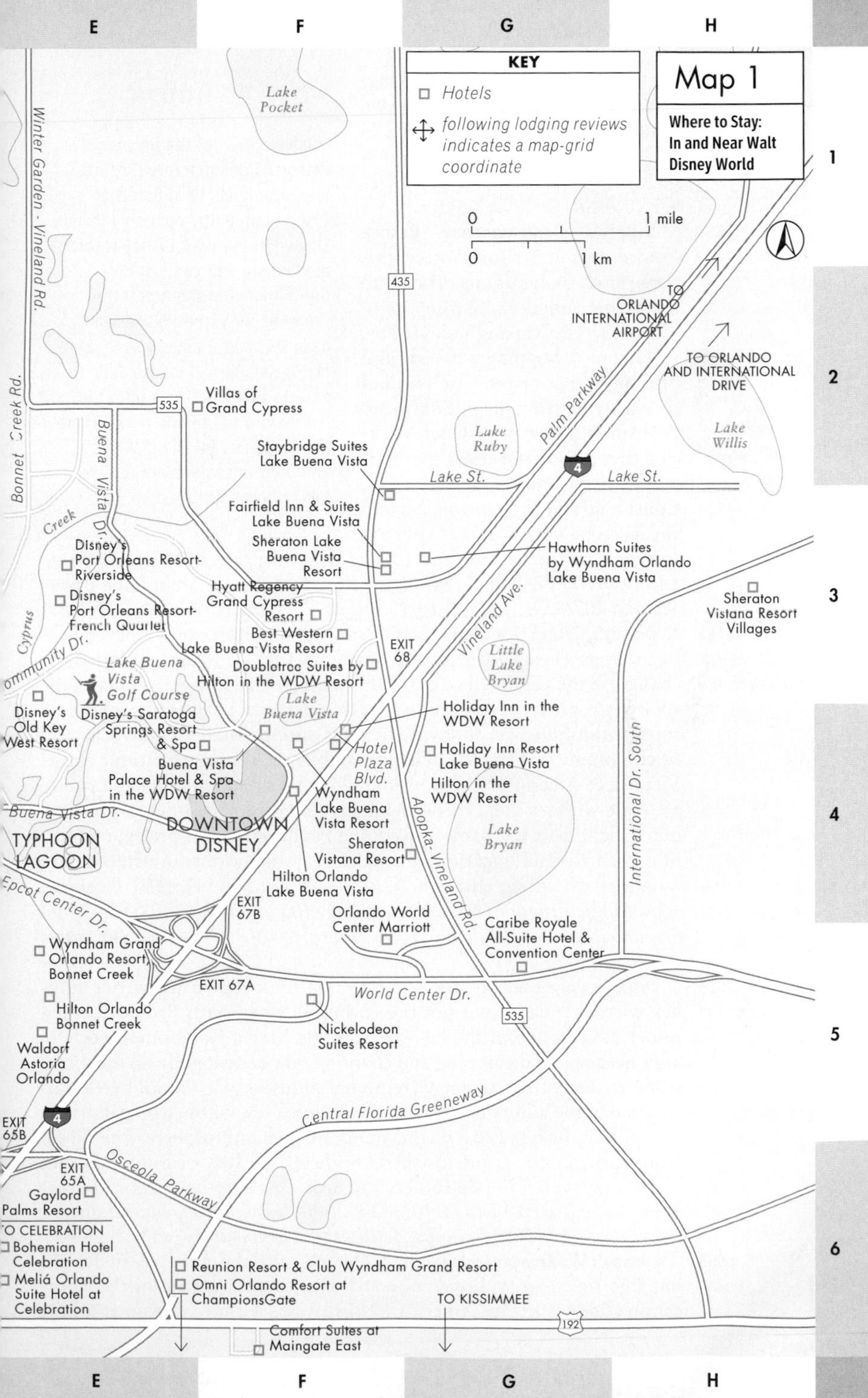

E
F
G
H
KEY
Hotels
following lodging reviews indicates a map-grid coordinate
Map 1
Where to Stay: In and Near Walt Disney World
1
0
1 mile
0
1 km
Lake Pocket
Winter Garden - Vineland Rd.
435
TO ORLANDO INTERNATIONAL AIRPORT
TO ORLANDO AND INTERNATIONAL DRIVE
2
Bonnet Creek Rd.
535
Villas of Grand Cypress
Palm Parkway
Lake Ruby
Lake Willis
Buena Vista Dr.
Staybridge Suites Lake Buena Vista
Lake St.
Lake St.
4
Creek
Fairfield Inn & Suites Lake Buena Vista
Disney's Port Orleans Resort-Riverside
Sheraton Lake Buena Vista Resort
Hawthorn Suites by Wyndham Orlando Lake Buena Vista
Hyatt Regency Grand Cypress Resort
Disney's Port Orleans Resort-French Quarter
Sheraton Vistana Resort Villages
3
Vineland Ave.
Best Western Lake Buena Vista Resort
Cypress
Community Dr.
EXIT 68
Little Lake Bryan
Lake Buena Vista Golf Course
Doubletree Suites by Hilton in the WDW Resort
Disney's Old Key West Resort
Disney's Saratoga Springs Resort & Spa
Lake Buena Vista
Holiday Inn in the WDW Resort
Hotel Plaza Blvd.
Holiday Inn Resort Lake Buena Vista
Buena Vista Palace Hotel & Spa in the WDW Resort
Hilton in the WDW Resort
Wyndham Lake Buena Vista Resort
International Dr. South
Buena Vista Dr.
4
DOWNTOWN DISNEY
TYPHOON LAGOON
Lake Bryan
Apopka-Vineland Rd.
Sheraton Vistana Resort
Hilton Orlando Lake Buena Vista
Epcot Center Dr.
EXIT 67B
Orlando World Center Marriott
Caribe Royale All-Suite Hotel & Convention Center
Wyndham Grand Orlando Resort, Bonnet Creek
EXIT 67A
World Center Dr.
Hilton Orlando Bonnet Creek
535
5
Nickelodeon Suites Resort
Waldorf Astoria Orlando
Central Florida Greenway
EXIT 65B
4
EXIT 65A
Osceola Parkway
Gaylord Palms Resort
TO CELEBRATION
Bohemian Hotel Celebration
6
Reunion Resort & Club Wyndham Grand Resort
Meliá Orlando Suite Hotel at Celebration
Omni Orlando Resort at ChampionsGate
TO KISSIMMEE
192
Comfort Suites at Maingate East
E
F
G
H

Fort Wilderness Trail, Magic Kingdom Resort Area, Lake Buena Vista ☎ 407/939–6244, 407/824–2742 ⊕ www.disneyworld.disney.go.com/resorts ⇌ 799 campsites 🍽 No meals ⊕ 1:C2.

WORD OF MOUTH

"I have stayed at the Polynesian [Resort], Contemporary [Resort], and BoardWalk [Inn] hotels in Disney, and in my opinion, I loved staying in the Walt Disney resort area where you can just hop onto the monorail at the hotel. The Contemporary and Polynesian have this and it takes you to the Magic Kingdom. It is also very easy to take the buses from the hotels to other theme parks. There are schedules for the pick-ups and drop-offs which are easy to follow." –jerseygrl

$$$$ RESORT **Disney's Contemporary Resort.** You're paying for location at this sleek, modern, luxury resort next to the Magic Kingdom, as the monorail runs right through the lobby, making park hopping a breeze, and offering quick respite for families seeking relief from the midday heat. **Pros:** monorail access; Chef Mickey's, the epicenter of character-meal world; health and wellness suites. **Cons:** a mix of conventioneers and vacationers means it can be too frenzied for the former and too staid for the latter. Ⓢ *Rooms from: $487 ✉ 4600 N. World Dr., Magic Kingdom Resort Area, Lake Buena Vista ☎ 407/824–1000 ⇌ 1,013 rooms, 25 suites 🍽 No meals ⊕ 1:B1.*

$$$$ RESORT Fodor's Choice ★ **Disney's Grand Floridian Resort & Spa.** On the shores of the Seven Seas Lagoon, so close to the Magic Kingdom that you can see the colors change on the Cinderella Castle, this red-roofed Victorian emulates the style of the great railroad resorts of the past with beautifully appointed rooms, rambling verandas, delicate, white-painted woodwork, and brick chimneys. **Pros:** old-Florida ambience; on the monorail route; Victoria & Albert's offers an evening-long experience in dining; if you're a couple with no kids, this is definitely the most romantic on-property hotel; right next to Disney's Wedding Pavillion. **Cons:** pricey; convention clientele and vacationing singles may be more comfortable than families with young children. Ⓢ *Rooms from: $655 ✉ 4401 Floridian Way, Magic Kingdom Resort Area, Lake Buena Vista ☎ 407/824–3000 ⊕ www.disneyworld.disney.go.com/resorts ⇌ 867 rooms, 90 suites 🍽 No meals ⊕ 1:A1.*

$$$$ RESORT **Disney's Polynesian Resort.** You may not think you're in Fiji, but families with kids can have fun pretending in this South Pacific–themed resort directly across the lagoon from the Magic Kingdom, especially after hearing the drumming and chanting that occasionally fill the three-story atrium of the Great Ceremonial House—aka the lobby—or, in the case of the adults in the party, downing a few of the tropical drinks available at the bar. **Pros:** on the monorail; great atmosphere; free Wi-Fi. **Cons:** pricey; not good for those bothered by lots of loud children. Ⓢ *Rooms from: $584 ✉ 1600 Seven Seas Dr., Magic Kingdom Resort Area, Lake Buena Vista ☎ 407/824–2000 ⊕ www.disneyworld.disney.go.com/resorts ⇌ 847 rooms, 5 suites 🍽 No meals ⊕ 1:B2.*

$$$$ RESORT **Disney's Wilderness Lodge.** The architects outdid themselves in designing this seven-story hotel modeled after majestic turn-of-the-20th-century lodges in the American Northwest, with a cavernous lobby,

supported by towering tree trunks, an 82-foot-high, fireplace made of rocks from the Grand Canyon, two 55-foot-tall hand-carved totem poles that pay homage to the region's Native American culture, all lighted by enormous tepee-shaped chandeliers. **Pros:** impressive architecture; boarding point for romantic cruises or free water taxi to Magic Kingdom; elegant dining options; children's activity center, free Wi-Fi. **Cons:** no direct bus to Magic Kingdom, no monorail. *Rooms from: $431 ✉ 901 Timberline Dr., Magic Kingdom Resort Area, Lake Buena Vista ☎ 407/824–3200 www.disneyworld.disney.go.com/resorts 727 rooms, 31 suites No meals ✣ 1:B1.*

3

EPCOT RESORT AREA

Take I–4 Exit 64B or 65.

From the Epcot resorts, you can walk or take a boat to the International Gateway entrance to Epcot, which deposits you right in the middle of the lands, or you can take the shuttle from your hotel or drive to the Future World (front) entrance.

$ RESORT **Disney's Art of Animation Resort.** This brightly colored three-story value resort is a kid's version of paradise: each of its four wings features images from *Finding Nemo, Cars, The Lion King,* or *The Little Mermaid,* and in-room linens and carpeting match the wing's theme. **Pros:** direct transportation to airport; free parking; images that kids adore; free Wi-Fi. **Cons:** can be crowded; standard rooms fill up fast. *Rooms from: $165 ✉ 1850 Animation Way, Epcot Resort Area, Lake Buena Vista ☎ 407/938–7000 www.disneyworld.disney.go.com/resorts 1,984 rooms, 1,120 suites No meals ✣ 1:D5.*

$$$$ RESORT **Disney's Beach Club Villas.** Each villa in this pale-turquoise-and-white waterfront area next to the Yacht and Beach Club Resorts has a separate living room, kitchen, and one or two bedrooms. **Pros:** short walk to the Disney BoardWalk area and Epcot; regular ferries to Epcot and Hollywood Studios; in-suite kitchens let you save money on meals; free Wi-Fi. **Cons:** can be noisy; not close to Magic or Animal Kingdoms. *Rooms from: $517 ✉ 1800 Epcot Resorts Blvd., Epcot Resort Area, Lake Buena Vista ☎ 407/934–8000 www.disneyworld.disney.go.com/resorts 576 units No meals ✣ 1:C4.*

$$$$ RESORT **Disney's BoardWalk Inn.** Harking back to Atlantic City in its heyday, the striking red and white hotel has a wood-floored lobby filled with potted palms and looks out on a classic waterfront promenade, where ferries and water taxis tootle about the bay, the smell of pretzels and popcorn hangs in the air, and hawkers call you to arcade games. **Pros:** casual, upscale atmosphere; lots of activities just outside the door, including Epcot; free Wi-Fi. **Cons:** pricey; long bus ride to Magic Kingdom; pool can get crowded; boat whistles can intrude if you have a waterfront room. *Rooms from: $518 ✉ 2101 Epcot Resorts Blvd., Epcot Resort Area, Lake Buena Vista ☎ 407/939–5100 www.disneyworld.disney.go.com/resorts 372 rooms No meals ✣ 1:C4.*

$$ RESORT **Disney's Caribbean Beach Resort.** A series of palm-studded "villages," awash in dizzying pastels and labeled with names straight from Pirates of the Caribbean, each with its own pool, form this Disney value resort.

Pros: plenty of on-site outdoor activities give the place a lush summer-camp feel; convenient to Epcot, Disney's Hollywood Studios, and Downtown Disney. **Cons:** you don't truly feel swept away to a tropical island; the beach is for sitting on, as the only swimmable waters are in the pools, not the lake; walks from your room to the beach or a restaurant can take up to 15 minutes. *Rooms from: $217 ✉ 900 Cayman Way, Epcot Resort Area, Lake Buena Vista ☎ 407/934–3400 ⊕ www.disneyworld.disney.go.com/resorts ➪ 2,112 rooms No meals ✥ 1:D4.*

$$$$ RESORT **Disney's Yacht Club and Beach Club Resorts.** These big Crescent Lake inns next door to Epcot seem straight out of a Cape Cod summer, with their nautical decor, waterfront locale, airy, light-filled rooms, rockingchair porches, and family-friendly water-based activities. **Pros:** location, location, location—it's easy to walk or hop a ferry to Epcot, the BoardWalk, or Hollywood Studios; free Wi-Fi. **Cons:** distances within the hotel—like from your room to the front desk—can seem vast; high noise factor. *Rooms from: $517 ✉ 1700 Epcot Resorts Blvd., Epcot Resort Area, Lake Buena Vista ☎ 407/934–8000 Beach Club, 407/934–7000 Yacht Club ⊕ www.disneyworld.disney.go.com/resorts ➪ 1,213 rooms, 112 suites No meals ✥ 1:C4.*

ANIMAL KINGDOM RESORT AREA

Take I–4 Exit 64B.

In the park's southwest corner, Disney's third resort area comprises a mix of high-end, moderate-range, and budget-price complexes.

$ RESORT **Disney's All-Star Movies Resort.** Kids will delight in recognizing the scenes and characters from favorite Disney movies that dot the landscape of this large, value-priced resort: Mickey, in his Sorcerer's Apprentice robes, commands the waters at the *Fantasia* pool, *101 Dalmatians* of all sizes scamper along railings, and a larger-than-life Woody cavorts with his *Toy Story* pals. **Pros:** familiar characters will amuse kids; free Wi-Fi; easy access to Animal Kingdom. **Cons:** at the opposite end of WDW from Magic Kingdom; no full-service restaurant. *Rooms from: $151 ✉ 1901 W. Buena Vista Dr., Animal Kingdom Resort Area, Lake Buena Vista ☎ 407/939–7000 ⊕ www.disneyworld.disney.go.com/resorts/ ➪ 1,920 rooms No meals ✥ 1:B6.*

$ RESORT FAMILY **Disney's All-Star Music Resort.** Music is everywhere in this colorful value-priced resort that looks like a Florida beach resort of the 1950s, with a guitar-shaped pool and balcony railings that resemble notated musical staffs. **Pros:** good value for family holidays; free Wi-Fi. **Cons:** suites have sleeper chair and sleeper ottoman; long way to Magic Kingdom. *Rooms from: $152 ✉ 1801 W. Buena Vista Dr., Animal Kingdom Resort Area, Lake Buena Vista ☎ 407/939–6000 ⊕ www.disneyworld.disney.go.com/resorts ➪ 1,704 rooms, 215 family suites No meals ✥ 1:B6.*

$ RESORT FAMILY Fodor's Choice ★ **Disney's All-Star Sports Resort.** Stay here if you want the quintessential Disney-with-your-kids experience, or if you're a couple to whom all that pitter-pattering of little feet is a reasonable tradeoff for a good deal on a room. **Pros:** unbeatable price for a Disney property; free Wi-Fi. **Cons:** no kids' clubs or programs, possibly because this is on the bottom tier

Disney's Animal Kingdom Lodge

of Disney hotels in terms of room rates; distances between rooms and on-site amenities can seem vast; furthest resort from Magic Kingdom means you'll spend time on the bus. *Rooms from: $145* *1701 W. Buena Vista Dr., Animal Kingdom Resort Area, Lake Buena Vista* *407/939–5000 Sports* *www.disneyworld.disney.go.com/resorts* *1,920 rooms* *No meals* *1:B6.*

$$$$ RESORT FAMILY Fodor's Choice ★ **Disney's Animal Kingdom Lodge.** Giraffes, zebras, and other wildlife roam three 11-acre savannas separated by the encircling arms of this grand hotel, designed to resemble a "kraal" or animal enclosure in Africa. **Pros:** extraordinary wildlife and cultural experiences; excellent on-site restaurants: Jiko, Boma, and Sanaa; breakfast buffet in Boma is a bargain. **Cons:** shuttle to parks other than Animal Kingdom can take more than an hour; guided savanna tours available only to guests on the concierge level, where the least expensive room is $100 a night higher than the least expensive rooms in other parts of the hotel. *Rooms from: $524* *2901 Osceola Pkwy., Animal Kingdom Resort Area, Lake Buena Vista* *407/938–3000* *www.disneyworld.disney.go.com/resorts* *972 rooms, 499 suites and villas* *No meals* *1:A5.*

$$$ RESORT Fodor's Choice ★ **Disney's Coronado Springs Resort.** Popular with convention-goers who love the huge meeting spaces, and with families who appreciate its casual Southwestern architecture; lively, Mexican-style food court; and elaborate swimming pool, colorful Coronado Springs Resort also offers a moderate price. **Pros:** great pool with a play-area arcade for kids and a bar for adults; lots of outdoor activities, free Wi-Fi. **Cons:** some accommodations are a long trek from the restaurants; standard rooms are on the small side; as in many Disney lakefront properties, the lake

is for looking at and boating on, not for swimming in. *Rooms from: $261 1000 W. Buena Vista Dr., Animal Kingdom Resort Area, Lake Buena Vista 407/939–1000 www.disneyworld.disney.go.com/resorts 1,917 rooms No meals 1:B4.*

DOWNTOWN DISNEY RESORT AREA

Take I–4 Exit 64B or 68.

The Downtown Disney–Lake Buena Vista resort area, east of Epcot, has a variety of inexpensive, mid-price, and upscale hotels—some Disney owned, others not—all of which offer shuttles to the Disney parks.

$$$$ RESORT **Disney's Old Key West Resort.** Villas and studios resembling turn-of-the-20th-century Key West houses have full kitchens, white and pastel clapboard siding, delicate ornamental woodwork, and private balconies that overlook the waterways and golf fairways winding through the grounds. **Pros:** quiet and romantic; full kitchens in villas; abundance of accommodations with whirlpool baths. **Cons:** long walks between rooms and restaurants, recreation facilities, bus stops. *Rooms from: $431 1510 N. Cove Rd., Downtown Disney Resort Area, Lake Buena Vista 407/827–7700 www.disneyworld.disney.go.com/resorts 761 units No meals 1:E3.*

$$ HOTEL **Disney's Port Orleans Resort–French Quarter.** Ornate Big Easy–style row houses with wrought iron–clad balconies cluster around magnolia-shaded squares in this relatively quiet resort, which appeals to couples more than families. **Pros:** authentic, or as authentic as Disney can make it, fun, New Orleans–style; moderate price; lots of water recreation options, including boat rentals; free Wi-Fi. **Cons:** even though there are fewer kids here, public areas can still be quite noisy; shuttle service is slow; food court is the only on-site dining option. *Rooms from: $227 1251 Riverside Dr., Downtown Disney Resort Area, Lake Buena Vista 407/934–5000 www.disneyworld.disney.go.com/resorts 1,008 rooms No meals 1:E3.*

$$ RESORT **Disney's Port Orleans Resort–Riverside.** Buildings in this family-friendly, moderately priced resort look like Southern plantation–style mansions (in the Magnolia Bend section) and rustic bayou dwellings (in the Alligator Bayou section), and you can usually pick which section you want. **Pros:** carriage rides; river cruises; lots of recreation options for kids. **Cons:** shuttle to parks can be slow; no shortage of extremely noisy youngsters. *Rooms from: $227 1251 Riverside Dr., Downtown Disney Resort Area, Lake Buena Vista 407/934–6000 www.disneyworld.disney.go.com/resorts 2,048 rooms No meals 1:E3.*

$$$$ RESORT **Disney's Saratoga Springs Resort & Spa.** This sprawling Disney Vacation Club property takes its inspiration from 19th-century horse-and-spa resorts in upstate New York, where hot springs and lakes ruled the landscape. **Pros:** water taxis whisk you to Downtown Disney; kitchens can shave down the food bill; in-room massage available; abundance of rooms with whirlpool baths. **Cons:** it's a fair hike from some accommodations to the restaurant and other facilities; no full-service restaurant. *Rooms from: $431 1960 Broadway, Downtown Disney Resort*

CLOSE UP

Top Spas

If you hit the ground running after arriving in Orlando, at some point you may need to shift your pace from "fast forward" to "pause." If so, head directly to one of Orlando's resort spas. The area has enough standout pampering palaces to indulge every theme park–weary parent, aching golfer, parched sunbather, and Disney princess.

Each of Orlando's resort spas is known for something special, whether it's the Balinese four-hand massage at the Mandara at Portofino Bay, or customized therapies at the Waldorf. Several spas draw on Florida's citrus-producing region to offer refreshing orange, grapefruit, and lime therapies. And you can go global with massage techniques from Japan, Thailand, Polynesia, and Sweden.

Families who want to stay together can even spa together at treatment centers specializing in youth facials, massages, and manicure/pedicure (aka mani/pedi) packages. The Ritz-Carlton Orlando treats kids like royalty with manicures, pedicures, and facials. Disney's Senses Spas at Saratoga Springs and the Grand Floridian offer Magical Manicures and Princess Pedicures.

Make your spa excursion special by planning enough time to use complimentary whirlpools, saunas, and steam rooms. Most spas offer free access to impressively equipped fitness centers and relaxation rooms stocked with herbal teas, fresh fruits, and other goodies. Book treatments early, and ask about gratuities—often 18% to 20%—which may or may not be included in your treatment or package.

TOP SPAS

Blue Harmony, Downtown Disney Resort Area

Portofino Bay Mandara Spa, Portofino Bay Resort, Universal Orlando

Ritz Carlton Orlando, Grande Lakes Spa, South Orlando

Senses Spa, Disney's Saratoga Springs Resort, Downtown Disney Resort Area

Senses Spa, Grand Floridian Resort, Magic Kingdom Resort Area

The Spa at Hilton Orlando, Downtown Disney Resort Area

The Spa at Rosen Centre, International Drive, Orlando

Area, Lake Buena Vista ☎ 407/934–7639 🌐 www.disneyworld.disney.go.com/resorts ⇨ 924 units 🍽 No meals ⊕ 1:F4.

OTHER ON-SITE DISNEY HOTELS

Although not operated by the Disney organization, the Swan and the Dolphin, just outside Epcot; Shades of Green, near the Magic Kingdom; and the hotels along Hotel Plaza Boulevard near Downtown Disney call themselves "official" Walt Disney World hotels. Whereas the Swan, Dolphin, and Shades of Green have the special privileges of on-site Disney hotels, such as free transportation to and from the parks and early park entry, the Downtown Disney resorts may use Disney transportation, but don't have all the same perks.

MAGIC KINGDOM RESORT AREA

Take I–4 Exit 62, 64B, or 65.

$ HOTEL **Shades of Green.** Operated by the U.S. Armed Forces Recreation Center, this resort in the heart of Disney is open only to active-duty and retired personnel from the armed forces, reserves, and National Guard; active civilian employees of the Department of Defense; widows or widowers of service members; disabled veterans; and Medal of Honor recipients. **Pros:** large standard rooms; on Disney's shuttle bus line; Army–Air Force Exchange store discounts deeply for people with military IDs. **Cons:** prices vary based on rank. *Rooms from: $125 1905 W. Magnolia Palm Dr., Magic Kingdom Resort Area, Lake Buena Vista 407/824–3600, 888/593–2242 www.shadesofgreen.org 585 rooms, 12 suites No meals 1:A2.*

EPCOT RESORT AREA

Take I–4 Exit 64B or 65.

$$$ RESORT **Walt Disney World Dolphin.** A pair of 56-foot-tall sea creatures bookend this 25-story glass pyramid, a luxe resort designed, like the adjoining Swan, by world-renowned architect Michael Graves. **Pros:** access to all facilities at the Swan; easy walk or boat ride to BoardWalk and Epcot; excellent on-site restaurants. **Cons:** daily self-parking fee; a daily resort fee covers Wi-Fi and Internet access, use of health club, and local phone calls; room-charge privileges stop at the front door and don't extend to the Disney parks. *Rooms from: $325 1500 Epcot Resorts Blvd., Epcot Resort Area, Lake Buena Vista 407/934–4000, 800/227–1500 www.swandolphin.com 1,509 rooms, 112 suites No meals 1:C4.*

$$$ RESORT **Walt Disney World Swan.** With Epcot and Hollywood Studios close by, guests here can hit the parks in the morning, return for a swim or nap on a hot afternoon, and go back to the parks refreshed and ready to play until the fireworks. **Pros:** charge privileges and access to all facilities at the Dolphin (but not inside Disney World); easy walk to BoardWalk; free boats to BoardWalk and Epcot; good on-site restaurants. **Cons:** long bus ride to Magic Kingdom; daily resort fee. *Rooms from: $274 1200 Epcot Resorts Blvd., Epcot Resort Area, Lake Buena Vista 407/934–3000, 800/325–3535 www.swandolphin.com 756 rooms, 55 suites No meals 1:C4.*

DOWNTOWN DISNEY RESORT AREA

Take I–4 Exit 68.

$ RESORT Fodor's Choice ★ **Best Western Lake Buena Vista Resort.** Only a few minutes' walk from Downtown Disney, this towering resort with its airy lobby offers luxury linens, flat-screen TVs, and, in many rooms, a bird's-eye view of the nightly Disney World fireworks. **Pros:** A quick walk takes you to

Downtown Disney; a $12 resort fee covers Wi-Fi, parking and other amenities, making it one of the best bargains on Hotel Row. **Cons:** inconvenient to Universal and Downtown Orlando; transportation to the parks can eat up time. *Rooms from: $129 2000 Hotel Plaza Blvd., Downtown Disney Resort Area, Lake Buena Vista 407/828–2424, 800/348–3765 www.lakebuenavistaresorthotel.com 325 rooms No meals 1:F3.*

$$ RESORT **Buena Vista Palace Hotel & Spa.** This large and amenity-filled hotel, just yards from Downtown Disney, caters to business and leisure guests and gets kudos as much for its on-site charms as for its location. **Pros:** easy walk to Downtown Disney; good restaurants and bars on-site; kids' activities; pool is heated; spa is large and luxurious. **Cons:** inconvenient to Universal and Downtown Orlando; daily resort fee for Wi-Fi and fitness center. *Rooms from: $189 1900 E. Buena Vista Dr., Downtown Disney Resort Area, Lake Buena Vista 407/827–2727 www.buenavistapalace.com 1,014 rooms No meals 1:F4.*

$$ HOTEL **DoubleTree Suites by Hilton in the WDW Resort.** Price and location make this all-suites, Hilton-owned hotel a good choice for families and business travelers, as there are amenities for both, and it's a quick, free bus ride to any of the Disney parks. **Pros:** family and business traveler amenities; restaurants on-site; adult pool and splash pad for kids, adults; free shuttle to Disney attractions; quick access to I–4. **Cons:** of the properties on Hotel Plaza Boulevard, this is the farthest away from Downtown Disney; inconvenient to Universal and Downtown Orlando; daily fee for parking, Wi-Fi. *Rooms from: $199 2305 Hotel Plaza Blvd., Downtown Disney Resort Area, Lake Buena Vista 407/934–1000, 800/222–8733 www.doubletreeguestsuites.com 229 units No meals 1:F3.*

$ HOTEL **Hilton Orlando Lake Buena Vista.** Although this hotel offers full service to business travelers, families are not neglected, with scheduled Disney character breakfasts every Sunday, and extended theme park hours. **Pros:** ergonomic work stations; 24-hour health club; character breakfasts; free transportation to Disney parks. **Cons:** pricey resort fee; parking and Wi-Fi fees; need a car to get to Universal and Downtown Orlando. *Rooms from: $109 1751 Hotel Plaza Blvd., Downtown Disney Resort Area, Lake Buena Vista 407/827–4000, 800/782–4414 reservations www.hilton.com 814 rooms, 27 suites No meals 1:F4.*

$ HOTEL **Holiday Inn Lake Buena Vista Downtown Disney.** The very modern lobby, with its glass-roofed atrium, muted colors, contemporary furnishings, and linen sheers over floor-to-ceiling windows, is typical of the hotel's low-key elegance; but elegance doesn't mean hidden charges, as this hotel specializes in free stuff: free Wi-Fi, no resort fee, free breakfast, and kids under 12 eat free breakfast lunch and dinner when with parents. **Pros:** walking distance to Downtown Disney; free transportation to all Disney parks; free Wi-Fi. **Cons:** no free shuttle to Universal or SeaWorld; daily parking fee; need a car to get to Orlando. *Rooms from: $108 1805 Hotel Plaza Blvd., Downtown Disney Resort Area, Lake Buena Vista 407/828–8888, 888/465–4329 www.hiorlando.com 323 rooms Breakfast 1:G4.*

$ RESORT **Wyndham Lake Buena Vista Resort.** Any hotel within a skip and a hop of Downtown Disney is a great draw, and one with a water-playground complex that can entice kids away from the Magic Kingdom during the midday heat is even better. **Pros:** good kids' programs; great views from some rooms; free shuttle to all Disney attractions. **Cons:** daily resort fee for parking, Wi-Fi, gym; inconvenient to Universal and Downtown Orlando. *Rooms from: $119 ✉ 1850 Hotel Plaza Blvd., Downtown Disney Resort Area, Lake Buena Vista ☎ 407/828–4444 🌐 www.wyndhamlakebuenavista.com 619 rooms, 7 suites No meals ✣ 1:F4.*

UNIVERSAL ORLANDO AREA

Take I–4 Exit 74B or 75A.

Universal Orlando's on-site hotels were built in a little luxury enclave that has everything you need, so you never have to leave Universal property. In minutes, you can walk from any hotel to CityWalk, Universal's dining and entertainment district, or take a ferry that cruises the adjacent artificial river.

The newest Universal lodging, Cabana Bay Beach Resort, with 900 family suites and 900 standard rooms, is so close to Islands of Adventure, you may see the spires of Hogwarts Castle from your room. This more affordable, motor court–style resort is designed to evoke 20th-century driving vacations with a hip, retro look.

A burgeoning hotel district across Kirkman Road and down to Sand Lake Road offers convenient accommodations and some even less expensive rates. Although these off-property hotels don't have the perks of the on-site places, you'll probably be smiling when you see your hotel bill.

$ HOTEL **Comfort Suites Universal Studios Area.** If Universal's roller coasters and Diagon Alley are your destinations, these homey accommodations just outside the park should fit the bill. **Pros:** free breakfast; free Wi-Fi; free parking; free shuttle to Universal and SeaWorld. **Cons:** a bit of a hike to shops, restaurants; long way to Disney parks; no on-site full-service restaurant or room service. *Rooms from: $129 ✉ 5617 Major Blvd., Universal Orlando Area, Orlando ☎ 407/363–1967, 800/951–7829 🌐 www.comfortorlando.com 150 suites Breakfast ✣ 2:D1.*

$ HOTEL **DoubleTree by Hilton at the Entrance to Universal Orlando.** The name is a mouthful, but it's an accurate description for this hotel, which caters to business-trippers and pleasure seekers alike, thanks to a location close to the Universal Orlando entrance and not far from the Convention Center. **Pros:** three on-site restaurants; within walking distance of Universal, shops, and restaurants; free shuttle to Universal; on I-Drive trolley route; free Wi-Fi. **Cons:** fee for parking; on a fast-lane tourist strip; need a car to reach Disney and Downtown Orlando. *Rooms from: $139 ✉ 5780 Major Blvd., Universal Orlando Area, Orlando ☎ 407/351–1000, 800/327–2110 🌐 www.doubltreeorlando.com 742 rooms, 19 suites No meals ✣ 2:D1.*

$ HOTEL Fodor's Choice ★ **Drury Inn & Suites Orlando.** This reasonably priced, centrally located hotel is really shaking up the competition in Orlando with free Wi-Fi, free parking, free hot breakfast, free long-distance and local phone calls, and free hot food and cold beverages in the late afternoon. **Pros:** free everything; central location; reasonable price. **Cons:** if Disney is your destination, this might be a little far afield. *Rooms from: $129 ✉ 7301 W. Sand Lake Rd., at I–4, Universal Orlando Area, Orlando ☎ 407/354–1101 🌐 www.druryhotels.com 238 Some meals ⊕ 2:C3.*

$$$$ HOTEL **Hard Rock Hotel.** Music rules in this California Mission–style building, where guests can pretend they are rock stars as their hotel key card lets them skip the lines at Universal and grants early park admission. **Pros:** shuttle, water taxi, or short walk to Universal Parks and CityWalk; preferential treatment at Universal rides; charge privileges extend to the other on-property Universal hotels. **Cons:** rooms and meals are pricey; resort fee for parking, gym, and in-room Wi-Fi; loud rock music in public areas, even the pool, but that's why you're here, right? *Rooms from: $354 ✉ 5800 Universal Blvd., Universal Orlando Area, Orlando ☎ 407/503–7625, 800/232–7827 🌐 www.hardrockhotelorlando.com 621 rooms, 29 suites No meals ⊕ 2:D1.*

$ HOTEL **Hyatt Place Orlando/Universal.** Hyatt Place supports tech-savvy guests in what Hyatt calls the "24/7" lifestyle, which means that essentially any of the hotel amenities available to guests at 3 in the afternoon are also on tap at 3 in the morning. **Pros:** walking distance to Universal as well as a free shuttle; free breakfast, parking, and high-speed Wi-Fi throughout. **Cons:** no kids' programs or babysitting service; no shuttles to Disney. *Rooms from: $134 ✉ 5895 Caravan Ct., Universal Orlando Area, Orlando ☎ 407/351–0627 🌐 www.orlandouniversal.place.hyatt.com 151 rooms Breakfast ⊕ 2:D1.*

$$$$ HOTEL Fodor's Choice ★ **Loews Portofino Bay Hotel at Universal Orlando.** The charm and romance of Portofino, Italy—destination of Europe's rich and famous—are conjured up at this lovely luxury resort, where part of the fun is exploring the waterfront "village" from end to end and not knowing what you'll find around a corner or down some steps. **Pros:** Italian villa atmosphere; large spa; restaurants on-site; short walk or ferry ride to CityWalk, Universal Studios, and Islands of Adventure; guests skip lines at Universal rides; kids' activities; shuttles to SeaWorld. **Cons:** rooms and meals are pricey; daily fee for in-room high-speed Internet or Wi-Fi as well as for parking. *Rooms from: $378 ✉ 5601 Universal Blvd., Universal Orlando Area, Orlando ☎ 407/503–1000, 800/232–7827 🌐 www.loewshotels.com/Portofino-Bay-Hotel 750 rooms, 49 suites Breakfast ⊕ 2:D1.*

$$$ RESORT Fodor's Choice ★ **Loews Royal Pacific Resort at Universal Orlando.** The entrance—a broad, covered footbridge high above a tropical stream—sets the tone for the Pacific Rim theme of this hotel, which lies amid 53 acres of lush shrubs, soaring bamboo, orchids, and palms. **Pros:** preferential treatment at Universal rides; early admission to Islands of Adventure (Wizarding World of Harry Potter); serene, Zen garden vibe. **Cons:** rooms car feel cramped; steep fees for in-room Internet access, fitness center, parking. *Rooms from: $309 ✉ 6300 Hollywood Way, Un*

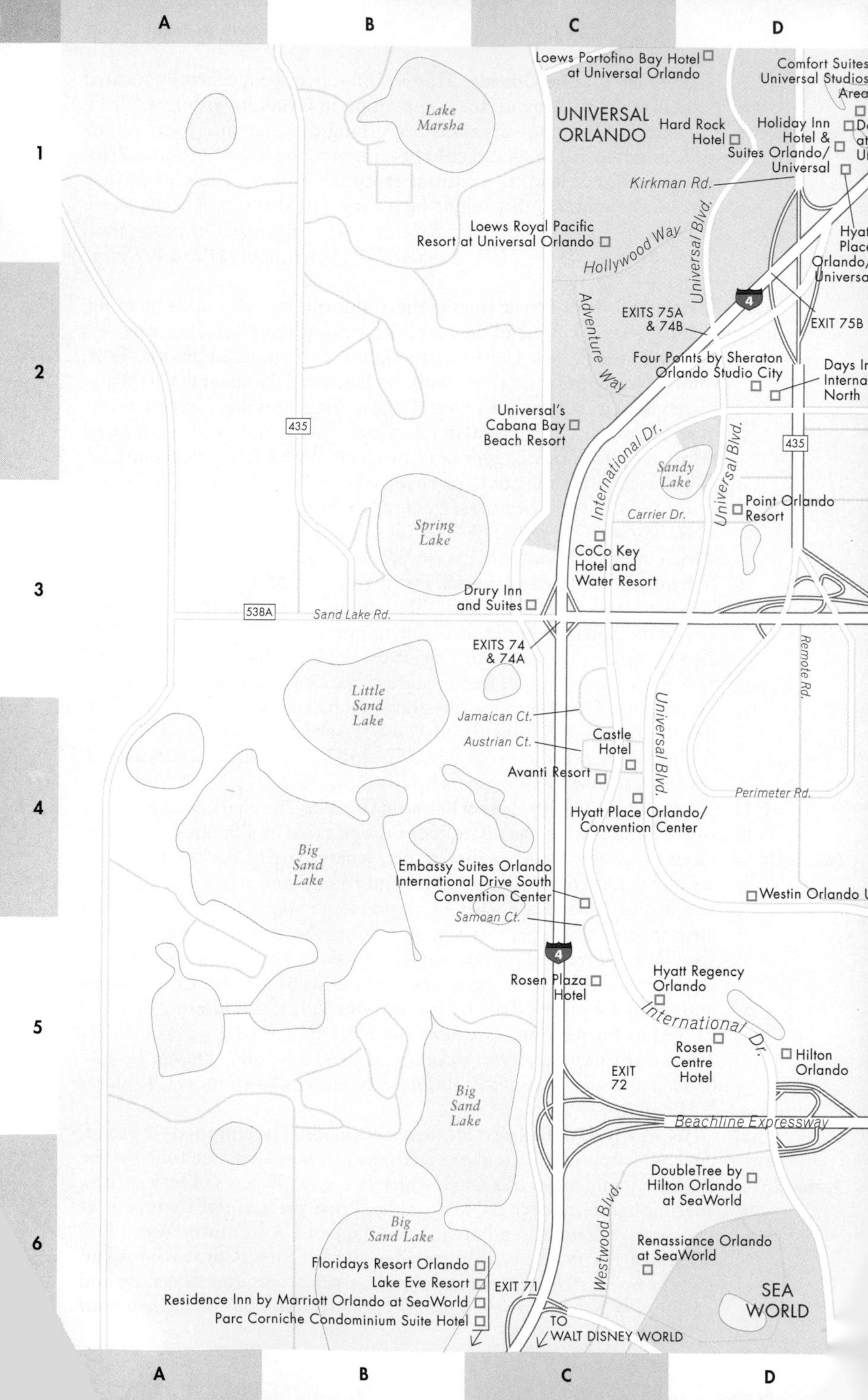

A
B
C
D
1
2
3
4
5
6
Loews Portofino Bay Hotel at Universal Orlando
Comfort Suites Universal Studios Area
UNIVERSAL ORLANDO
Hard Rock Hotel
Holiday Inn Hotel & Suites Orlando/ Universal
Lake Marsha
Kirkman Rd.
Loews Royal Pacific Resort at Universal Orlando
Hollywood Way
Universal Blvd.
Adventure Way
EXITS 75A & 74B
EXIT 75B
4
Four Points by Sheraton Orlando Studio City
Universal's Cabana Bay Beach Resort
435
International Dr.
Sandy Lake
Universal Blvd.
Carrier Dr.
Point Orlando Resort
Spring Lake
CoCo Key Hotel and Water Resort
Drury Inn and Suites
538A
Sand Lake Rd.
EXITS 74 & 74A
Remote Rd.
Little Sand Lake
Jamaican Ct.
Austrian Ct.
Castle Hotel
Avanti Resort
Universal Blvd.
Perimeter Rd.
Hyatt Place Orlando/ Convention Center
Big Sand Lake
Embassy Suites Orlando International Drive South Convention Center
Samoan Ct.
Rosen Plaza Hotel
Hyatt Regency Orlando
International Dr.
Rosen Centre Hotel
Hilton Orlando
EXIT 72
Beachline Expressway
Big Sand Lake
DoubleTree by Hilton Orlando at SeaWorld
Westwood Blvd.
Big Sand Lake
Renassiance Orlando at SeaWorld
Floridays Resort Orlando
Lake Eve Resort
Residence Inn by Marriott Orlando at SeaWorld
Parc Corniche Condominium Suite Hotel
EXIT 71
TO WALT DISNEY WORLD
SEA WORLD

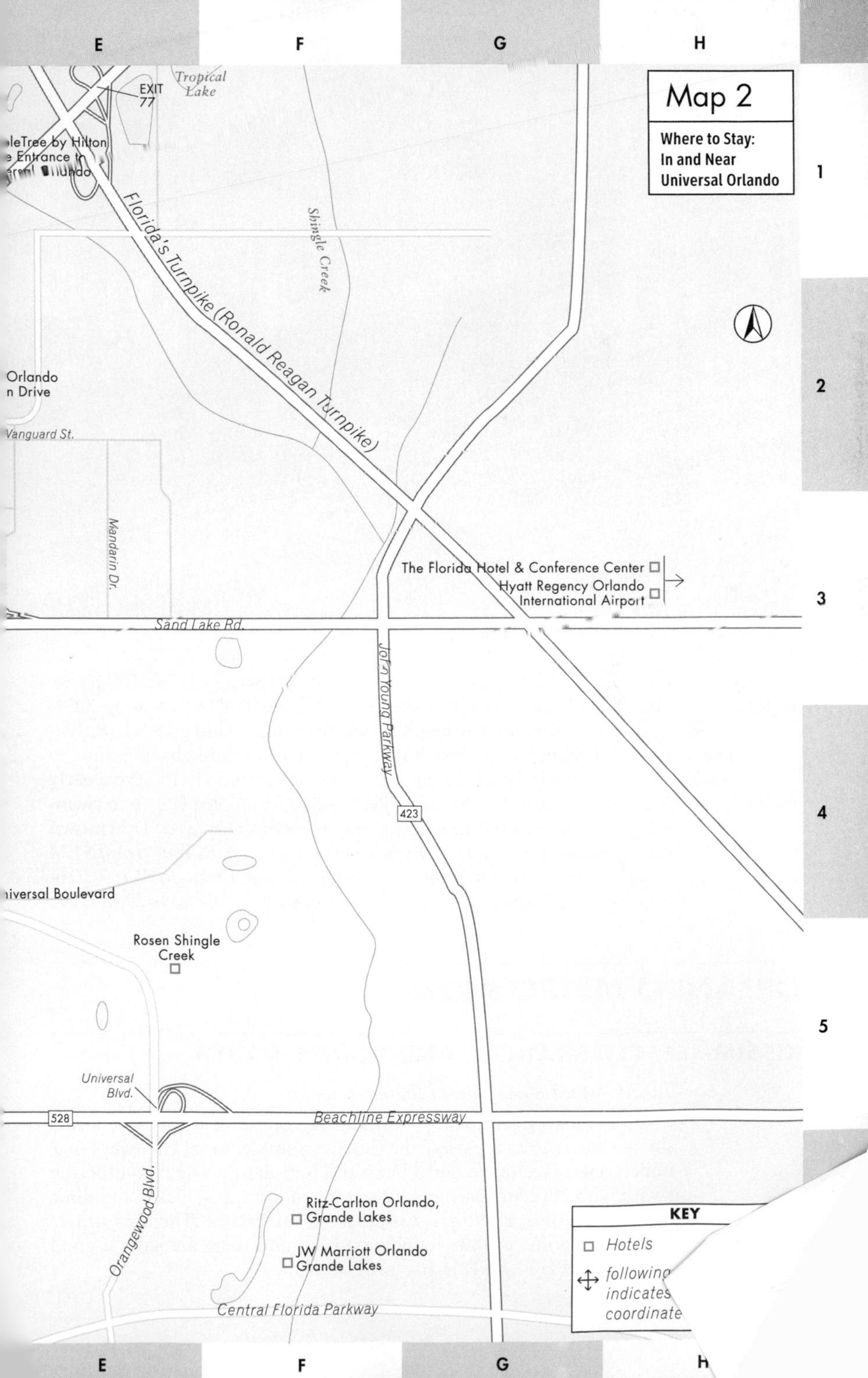

E
F
G
H
Map 2
Where to Stay: In and Near Universal Orlando
1
2
3
4
5
Tropical Lake
EXIT 77
Florida's Turnpike (Ronald Reagan Turnpike)
Shingle Creek
Orlando
n Drive
Vanguard St.
Mandarin Dr.
The Florida Hotel & Conference Center
Hyatt Regency Orlando International Airport
Sand Lake Rd.
John Young Parkway
423
iversal Boulevard
Rosen Shingle Creek
Universal Blvd.
528
Beachline Expressway
Orangewood Blvd.
Ritz-Carlton Orlando, Grande Lakes
JW Marriott Orlando Grande Lakes
Central Florida Parkway
KEY
Hotels
E
F
G

Loews Portofino Bay Hotel at Universal Orlando

Orlando Area, Orlando ☎ *407/503–3000, 800/232–7827* 🌐 *www.universalorlando.com* 🛏 *1,000 rooms, 113 suites* 🍽 *No meals* ✥ *2:C1.*

$ RESORT FAMILY Fodor's Choice ★ **Universal's Cabana Bay Beach Resort.** Arriving at Universal's latest on-site hotel, Cabana Bay Beach Resort, is a bit like going back in time to a 1950s Florida beach town with a modern, ironic twist. **Pros:** early and easy access to Universal parks; food court on property; two swimming pools with sand beaches. **Cons:** access to Disney or Downtown Orlando requires a journey via busy Interstate 4. $ *Rooms from: $174* ✉ *6550 Adventure Way, Universal Orlando Area, Orlando* ☎ *407/503–4000* 🌐 *www.loewshotels.com/Cabana-Bay* 🛏 *1,800 rooms, 900 suites* 🍽 *No meals* ✥ *2:C2.*

ORLANDO METRO AREA

KISSIMMEE, CELEBRATION, AND POINTS SOUTH

Take I–4 Exit 64A, unless otherwise noted.

If you're looking for quaint, charming, or sophisticated, move on. Kissimmee's U.S. 192 strip—aka the Irlo Bronson Memorial Highway—has undergone a face-lift recently, but it still is primarily a neon-and-plastic swath with bargain-basement motels, fast-food spots, nickel-and-dime attractions, overpriced gas stations, and minimarts. The area nearer Disney has some upscale lodging choices, and there are several good options if LEGOLAND is also on your list.

When Disney was in its infancy, U.S. 192 was the best place to find affordable rooms. But now that budget hotels have cropped up all along I-Drive, you can often find better rooms closer to the theme parks. There are exceptions, however—some of the older hotels have maintained decent standards and kept their prices very tempting.

$$ HOTEL **Bohemian Hotel Celebration.** Like everything in the Disney-created town of Celebration, this boutique hotel in the middle of the charming village borrows from the best of the 19th, 20th, and 21st centuries. **Pros:** in the heart of Celebration village; rental bikes and golf carts make touring town a breeze; free shuttle to Celebration Golf and Fitness Center. **Cons:** daily fee for Internet and parking; shuttle to Disney is about $25 per family of four, round-trip; need a car (or lots of cab money) to get anywhere other than Celebration. *Rooms from: $229 700 Bloom St., Celebration 407/566–6000, 888/249–4007 www.celebrationhotel.com 115 rooms No meals 1:D6.*

$$$ RESORT **Gaylord Palms Resort and Convention Center.** Built in the style of a grand turn-of-the-20th-century Florida resort, this huge building is meant to inspire awe: inside its enormous atrium, covered by a 4-acre glass roof, are re-creations of Florida destination icons such as the Everglades, Key West, and old St. Augustine. **Pros:** you could have a great vacation without ever leaving the grounds; free shuttle to Disney. **Cons:** daily resort and parking fee; rooms can be pricey; not much within walking distance (although the hotel is so big that you can take quite a hike inside the building); shuttles to Universal and SeaWorld are available for a fee. *Rooms from: $279 6000 W. Osceola Pkwy., I–4 Exit 65, Kissimmee 407/586–0000 www.gaylordpalms.com 1,406 rooms, 86 suites No meals 1:F6.*

$$ HOTEL Fodor's Choice ★ **Meliá Orlando Suite Hotel at Celebration.** Much like a European boutique hotel in style and service, the Meliá Orlando is very human in scale and crisply minimalist in decor, and is only minutes from Disney. **Pros:** shuttle to Celebration, Disney parks, Universal, and SeaWorld; golf privileges at Celebration Golf; spa privileges at Celebration Day Spa. **Cons:** busy U.S. 192 is close by; daily resort fee; need a car to go anywhere besides Celebration and the parks. *Rooms from: $199 225 Celebration Pl., Celebration 866/404–6662, 407/964–7000 www.solmelia.com 240 suites Breakfast 1:D6.*

$$ RESORT **Omni Orlando Resort at ChampionsGate.** This huge Mediterranean-style complex just six miles south of Disney, and within a 45-minute drive of LEGOLAND, includes a 1,200-acre golf club with two Greg Norman–designed courses and a David Leadbetter academy. **Pros:** Mokara spa; huge, water-park-style pool; five restaurants ranging from a casual café to upscale dining; golf school and two golf courses. **Cons:** remote location; daily resort fee for Internet, shuttles, newspapers, gym; separate daily fee for parking. *Rooms from: $209 I–4 Exit 58, 1500 Masters Blvd., South of Kissimmee, ChampionsGate 407/390–6664, 800/843–6664 www.omniorlandoresort.com 720 rooms, suites, 57 villas Breakfast 1:E6.*

$$ RESORT **Reunion Resort & Club Wyndham Grand Resort.** This 2, built on the rolling hills of a former orange grove, 10 m of Disney and 45 minutes from LEGOLAND, contains

golf courses designed by Tom Watson, Arnold Palmer, and Jack Nicklaus, along with villas and homes designed and decorated to satisfy the most discerning guest. **Pros:** secluded, upscale atmosphere; golf galore; supermarkets and drugstores within a mile; concierge grocery delivery; excellent restaurants on-site; free Internet and parking. **Cons:** daily resort fee; remote; about a 10-mile drive to Disney parks; no theme-park shuttles, so you'll need a car. *Rooms from: $249 ✉ 7593 Gathering Dr., I–4 Exit 58, Reunion ☎ 407/396–3200, 866/880–8563 🌐 www.reunionresort.com 250 villas, 75 homes Breakfast ✥ 1:E6.*

INTERNATIONAL DRIVE

Take I–4 Exit 72, 74A, or 75A.

The sprawl of hotels, time-shares, restaurants, malls, and dozens of small attractions known as International Drive—"I-Drive" to locals—makes a central base for visits to Walt Disney World, Universal, SeaWorld, and other Orlando attractions. Parallel to Interstate 4, this four-lane boulevard stretches from Universal in the north to Kissimmee in the south.

If you're planning a day visiting I-Drive attractions, consider the I-Ride Trolley, which travels the length of I-Drive from Florida's Turnpike to the outlet center on Vineland Avenue, stopping at Wet 'n Wild and SeaWorld. (This trolley does not go to Universal Orlando, even though it's nearby.) I-Ride is a more worthy transportation tool than you might think. Lots of hotels don't offer shuttle service to Disney, even for a fee, but you can take I-Ride to hotels that do offer a fee-based Disney shuttle, which, depending on the size of the family or group, can be cheaper than a cab.

$ RESORT **Avanti Resort.** Smack-dab in the middle of all the activities on International Drive, this once-shuttered resort has been given a total makeover inside and out, offering families a sparkling new home away from home with plenty of amenities at a reasonable price. **Pros:** scheduled shuttles to theme parks; complimentary cribs and high chairs; convenient to I-Drive. **Cons:** daily resort fee, not exorbitant, covers Internet, parking, shuttles. *Rooms from: $99 ✉ 8738 International Dr., I-Drive area ☎ 407/313–0100 🌐 www.avantiresort.com 652 rooms No meals ✥ 2:C4.*

$$ HOTEL **Castle Hotel.** In a bold move from kitsch to classy, this Kessler Signature hotel has been transformed from a kid-focused cartoon castle with pink and purple spires to a sophisticated refuge of white and silver, filled with art. **Pros:** easy walk to I-Drive eateries and attractions; shuttle to Universal, SeaWorld; free parking and Wi-Fi. **Cons:** on a congested stretch of I-Drive; not close to Disney parks. *Rooms from: $179 ✉ 8629 International Dr., I-Drive area, Orlando ☎ 407/345–1511, 800/952–2785 🌐 www.castlehotelorlando.com 214 rooms No meals ✥ 2:C4.*

$ HOTEL **CocoKey Hotel and Water Resort.** If swimming and sliding are among your family's top vacation desires, this resort with an on-property 14-slide, three-pool water park may be for you. **Pros:** on-site water park; free Wi-Fi, parking, and shuttle; kids eat free. **Cons:** substantial daily resort fee; some rooms overlook noisy pools; water park closed some days in winter; on a busy stretch of I-Drive. *Rooms from: $89 7400 International Dr., I-Drive area, Orlando 407/351–2626 www.cocokeyorlando.com 391 rooms Some meals 2:C3.*

$ RESORT **DoubleTree by Hilton Orlando at SeaWorld.** On 28 acres near the Convention Center, this hotel with Bali-inspired decor combines low bungalow-style buildings and a 17-story tower, and offers families and conventioneers a warm welcome and a comforting escape from hectic I-Drive. **Pros:** on-site miniature golf; free theme-parks shuttles, free Wi-Fi; allergy-free rooms available. **Cons:** fee for parking; few shops and restaurants within walking distance. *Rooms from: $169 10100 International Dr., I-Drive area, Orlando 407/352–1100, 800/327–0363 www.doubletreeorlandoseaworld.com 1,094 rooms, 35 suites Breakfast 2:D6.*

$ HOTEL **Embassy Suites Orlando International Drive South Convention Center.** An airy, eight-story atrium with palm trees and fountains lends an air of luxury to this moderately priced all-suites lodging, which offers free shuttles to all theme parks as well as free breakfast, late-afternoon drinks, and parking. **Pros:** easy walk to Convention Center, shopping, and dining; free shuttle to theme parks; free breakfast and afternoon cocktails. **Cons:** on congested stretch of I-Drive; daily Wi-Fi charge in rooms. *Rooms from: $169 8978 International Dr., I-Drive area, Orlando 407/352–1400, 800/433–7275 www.embassysuitesorlando.com 244 suites Breakfast 2:C4.*

$$ RESORT **Floridays Resort Orlando.** This pleasant, two- and three-bedroom condo resort is about halfway between Universal Orlando and Disney World, with six six-story buildings, two pools, a game room, gym, business center, and café with room service. **Pros:** great, self-contained environment for a family vacation; shuttles to all theme parks; on the I-Ride trolley route. **Cons:** a car would be helpful, as it's too far to walk to almost anything meaningful; daily resort fee for Wi-Fi, parking, shuttles. *Rooms from: $245 12562 International Dr., I-Drive area, Lake Buena Vista 407/238–7700 www.floridaysresort.com 432 units No meals 2:C6.*

$ HOTEL **Four Points by Sheraton Orlando Studio City.** With a hard-to-miss giant ball perched on top of its 20-story round tower, this hotel on the north end of International Drive is visible for blocks, and has a contemporary atmosphere, thanks to the clean, airy design of the lobby and guest rooms. **Pros:** convenient to Universal, SeaWorld, and Wet 'n Wild; shuttle to Disney, Universal, and the outlet malls; great night views from upper floors. **Cons:** located on a busy stretch of I-Drive; daily resort fee for Wi-Fi, parking, park shuttles, etc. *Rooms from: $139 5905 International Dr., I-Drive area, Orlando 407/351–2100, 800/327–1366 www.fourpoints.com 301 rooms Breakfast 2:D2.*

$$ HOTEL **Hilton Orlando.** Families visiting this hotel get three pools, a palm-fringed lazy river to relax in, a kids' club, basketball court, tennis court, full-service spa, and a shuttle to SeaWorld; conventioneers, o[illegible] the other hand, appreciate the vast meeting space, direct conn[illegible] the Convention Center, substantial restaurants and ba[illegible] with Herman Miller chairs, and an on-site steakhouse, S[illegible] three pools; shuttle to SeaWorld; direct walkway to Conve[illegible]

3

Cons: about 80% of guests are conventioneers; no free shuttle to Disney World or Universal; daily resort fee; parking fee. *Rooms from: $199* *6001 Destination Pkwy., I-Drive area, Orlando* *407/313–4300* *www.thehiltonorlando.com* *1,417 rooms, 53 suites* *Breakfast* *2:D5.*

$ HOTEL **Hyatt Place Orlando/Convention Center.** Youngish, high-tech-consuming business travelers and vacationing families find value here because of the location and amenities, such as 42-inch flat-panel HDTVs, work areas with computer access panel, and wet bar with mini-refrigerator. **Pros:** free parking, Wi-Fi, and hot breakfast; convenient to Convention Center, shopping, restaurants, and nightlife. **Cons:** no kids' program or babysitting services; no theme-park shuttles. *Rooms from: $139* *8741 International Dr., I-Drive area, Orlando* *407/370–4720, 888/492–8847* *www.orlandoconventioncenter.place.hyatt.com* *149 rooms* *Breakfast* *2:D4.*

$$ RESORT **Hyatt Regency Orlando.** This deluxe, high-rise conference hotel, formerly the Peabody, offers anything a full-service resort customer could want, with richly appointed rooms, two pools with cabanas, a full-service spa and fitness center the size of your local Y, two large restaurants, and a 360-seat glass-walled lounge overlooking the pool. **Pros:** good spa; close to shops and more restaurants. **Cons:** check-in can take a while if a convention is arriving; long walk from end to end; daily resort fee. *Rooms from: $199* *9801 International Dr., I-Drive area, Orlando* *407/284-1234* *www.orlandoregency.hyatt.com* *1,641 rooms, 193 suites, 5 penthouse suites* *No meals* *2:C5.*

$$ RESORT **Lake Eve Resort.** Even though the address is on International Drive, this all-suites resort sits back off the road in 54 acres of semi-rural serenity, with a heated pool, tastefully furnished rooms with full kitchens, and a fitness center and sauna. **Pros:** relatively secluded, especially for I-Drive; free shuttles to all theme parks; free parking and Wi-Fi. **Cons:** too remote to walk anywhere; daily resort fee; few shuttle runs. *Rooms from: $197* *12388 International Dr. S., I-Drive area, Orlando* *407/597–0370* *www.lakeeveresort.com* *176 suites* *No meals* *2:C6.*

$ HOTEL **Parc Corniche Condominium Suite Hotel.** Set back from traffic on the south end of International Drive, this condo hotel offers a good deal for a family who loves golf and theme parks. **Pros:** great for golf lovers; well-equipped kitchens; free theme-parks shuttle; free breakfast; no resort fee. **Cons:** not much within walking distance; daily $4 fee for Wi-Fi. *Rooms from: $97* *6300 Parc Corniche Dr., I-Drive area, Orlando* *407/239–7100, 800/446–2721* *www.parccorniche.com* *210 suites* *Breakfast* *2:C6.*

$ HOTEL **The Point Orlando Resort.** In the center of the entertainment triangle bounded by I–4, Florida's Turnpike, and the Beachline Expressway, this all-suites resort is a quick walk to Wet 'n Wild and central to Universal, outlet shopping malls, I-Drive attractions and the Convention Center, making it a good option for family vacations, romantic getaways, and business travel. **Pros:** central to I-Drive entertainment; Wi-Fi throughout the resort; shuttles to theme parks; breakfast buffet and light fare in cafe. **Cons:** no on-site, full-service restaurant; daily resort fee. *Rooms* *from: $129 ✉ 7389 Universal Blvd., I-Drive area, Orlando ☎ 407/956–2000 🌐 www.thepointorlando.com 244 suites 🍴 Breakfast ✥ 2:D3.*

$$ HOTEL **Renaissance Orlando at SeaWorld.** With a vast and airy 10-story atrium full of ponds, palm trees, and, ironically, a sushi bar, this SeaWorld neighbor underwent a substantial renovation in 2013; rooms feature a king or two queen beds, sectional couches, flat-screen TVs, lush bedding, and ergonomic work areas. **Pros:** across from SeaWorld; free shuttles to Universal, SeaWorld, and Aquatica; on the Lynx bus line to Disney World. **Cons:** can be a long walk to rooms; many conventioneers; fees for Wi-Fi and parking. *$ Rooms from: $249 ✉ 6677 Sea Harbor Dr., I-Drive area, Orlando ☎ 407/351–5555, 800/468–3571 🌐 www.renaissanceseaworld.com 781 rooms, 65 suites 🍴 Some meals ✥ 2:C6.*

$$ HOTEL FAMILY Fodor'sChoice ★ **Residence Inn by Marriott Orlando at SeaWorld.** From the bright, welcoming lobby to the well-appointed suites (including dishwasher, microwave, pots, pans, dishes) and the parklike atmosphere around the pool, this hotel is a great choice for a family if SeaWorld, Aquatica, I-Drive shopping, or the Convention Center are on your to-do list. **Pros:** free shuttles to all theme parks; well-equipped kitchens; free breakfast; free Wi-Fi; no resort fee. **Cons:** not much within walking distance; right next to busy Interstate 4. *$ Rooms from: $179 ✉ 11000 Westwood Blvd., I–4 Exit 72, I-Drive area, Orlando ☎ 407/313–3600, 800/889–9728 🌐 www.residenceinnseaworld.com 350 suites 🍴 Breakfast ✥ 2:C6.*

$$ RESORT **Rosen Centre Hotel.** Directly across from the convention center, this just-renovated 24-story resort pleases both leisure and business customers by offering something for everyone. **Pros:** central location; free Wi-Fi; five on-site restaurants; preferred tee times at sister resort Rosen Shingle Creek Golf Club; free shuttles to Universal, SeaWorld, and Wet 'n Wild. **Cons:** no free shuttle to Disney; need a car to get anywhere off I-Drive. *$ Rooms from: $186 ✉ 9840 International Dr., I-Drive area, Orlando ☎ 407/996–9840 🌐 www.rosencentre.com 1,334 rooms, 80 suites 🍴 No meals ✥ 2:D5.*

$ HOTEL **Rosen Plaza Hotel.** Close to the Convention Center, this 14-story hotel caters to its corporate clientele—BAGS service, for example, lets you check suitcases in the hotel lobby so you can go straight to the gate at Orlando International—but leisure travelers also like the prime location and long list of amenities, including a heated swimming pool, fitness center and babysitting services. **Pros:** within walking distance of Pointe Orlando and other I-Drive restaurants and cinema; priority reservations at 18-hole golf course at nearby Rosen Shingle Creek; free shuttle to Universal; free Wi-Fi. **Cons:** Convention Center traffic can be heavy; parking fee. *$ Rooms from: $153 ✉ 9700 International Dr., I-Drive area, Orlando ☎ 407/996–9700, 800/366–9700 🌐 www.rosenplaza.com 800 rooms, 32 suites 🍴 No meals ✥ 2:C5.*

$$ HOTEL **Westin Orlando Universal Boulevard.** Directly across Universal Boulevard from the mammoth Orange County Convention Center, this 12-story hotel attracts scores of conventioneers, but its location n[illegible] SeaWorld and Universal and only a block from I-Drive mak[illegible] choice for families, too. **Pros:** easy walk to Convention C[illegible] Orlando, I-Drive; kids' programs. **Cons:** 20–25 minutes f[illegible]

Ritz-Carlton Orlando, Grande Lakes

World; steep daily fees for parking and Internet; conventions bring crowds. *Rooms from: $219* ✉ *9501 Universal Blvd., I-Drive area, Orlando* ☎ *407/233–2200* 🌐 *www.westinorlandouniversal.com* *315 rooms, 153 suites* *No meals* ✥ *2:D5.*

SOUTH ORLANDO

$$$$ RESORT **JW Marriott Orlando Grande Lakes.** With more than 70,000 square feet of meeting space, this lush resort caters to a convention clientele, but leisure-seekers and families are certainly not ignored: a European-style spa, a Greg Norman–designed golf course, and a lazy river–style pool complex offer plenty of family fun. **Pros:** pool is great for kids and adults; shares amenities with the Ritz, including huge spa; golf course; free shuttle to SeaWorld and Universal. **Cons:** daily resort fees for parking and in-room Wi-Fi; the resort is huge and spread out; need a car to reach Disney or shopping. *Rooms from: $409* ✉ *4040 Central Florida Pkwy.* ☎ *407/206–2300, 800/576–5750* 🌐 *www.grandelakes.com* *1,000 rooms, 64 suites* *Multiple meal plans* ✥ *2:F6.*

$$$$ RESORT Fodor's Choice ★ **Ritz-Carlton Orlando, Grande Lakes.** Orlando's only Ritz-Carlton is a particularly extravagant link in the luxury chain, with exemplary service that extends from the porte-cochere entrance to the 18-hole golf course, restaurants, children's programs, and 40-room spa. **Pros:** truly luxurious; impeccable service; great spa; golf course; award-winning restaurants; transportation to theme parks. **Cons:** pricey; remote from theme parks, attractions; lots of convention and meeting traffic; resort fee. *Rooms from: $499* ✉ *4012 Central Florida Pkwy.* ☎ *407/206–2400,*

800/576–5760 🌐 *www.ritzcarlton.com* ⇆ *582 rooms, 63 suites* 🍽 *Multiple meal plans* ✥ *2:F6.*

$$ RESORT **Rosen Shingle Creek.** Sitting amid 230 acres of lush landscape, including a cypress-fringed creek and a championship golf course, this luxury resort offers a golf academy, fishing, nature trails, four swimming pools, basketball and volleyball courts, and a huge spa to soothe those aching muscles. **Pros:** golf course; spa; free shuttle to Universal, SeaWorld, Aquatica; free Wi-Fi; BAGS airport check-in service; self-service coin laundry; variety of excellent restaurant options on-site. **Cons:** large grounds mean long walks to on-site amenities; no free shuttle to I-Drive or Disney; daily parking fee. [$] *Rooms from: $211* ✉ *9939 Universal Blvd.* ☎ *407/996–9939, 866/996–6338 reservations* 🌐 *www.rosenshinglecreek.com* ⇆ *1,500 rooms, 109 suites* 🍽 *No meals* ✥ *2:E5.*

LAKE BUENA VISTA

Many people stay in resorts outside Downtown Disney because, though equally grand, they tend to be less expensive than those right on Hotel Plaza Boulevard. If you're willing to take a five-minute drive or shuttle ride, you might save as much as 35% off your room tab.

$ RESORT **Caribe Royale All-Suite Hotel & Convention Center.** This big, pink, all-suites palace, on 53 tropical acres 10 minutes from Disney, melds luxurious decor, family-friendly ingredients, and business-traveler amenities. **Pros:** family-friendly; award-winning restaurant; free shuttle to Disney and outlet mall; fitness center; free parking. **Cons:** too far to walk to shops and restaurants; no shuttle to Universal or SeaWorld; daily Internet fee. [$] *Rooms from: $169* ✉ *8101 World Center Dr., Lake Buena Vista area, Orlando* ☎ *407/238–8000, 800/823–8300* 🌐 *www.thecaribehotelsorlando.com* ⇆ *1,218 suites, 120 villas* 🍽 *Breakfast* ✥ *1:G5.*

$ HOTEL **Fairfield Inn & Suites Lake Buena Vista.** Less than a mile from Downtown Disney and within walking distance of a variety of restaurants, this hotel has in-room amenities and a price that make it a good bet for families on a budget. **Pros:** refrigerators and microwaves in every room; free shuttle to Disney; grocery store nearby; free Wi-Fi and Internet; free parking. **Cons:** no real on-site restaurant; small pool; no room service. [$] *Rooms from: $109* ✉ *12191 S. Apopka Vineland Rd., Lake Buena Vista area, Orlando* ☎ *407/239–1115, 888/236–2427* 🌐 *www.marriott.com/mcofv* ⇆ *170 rooms, 50 suites* 🍽 *Breakfast* ✥ *1:F3.*

$ RESORT **Hawthorn Suites by Wyndham Orlando Lake Buena Vista.** The cool marble lobby welcomes guests to this all-suites lodging less than a mile from Disney's door, and the amenities continue into the suites, each with a fully equipped kitchen, living room, and bedroom with TVs. **Pros:** affordable; full kitchens; walk to shops; free Disney shuttle; free Wi-fi and parking; on public bus route. **Cons:** pool area can be noisy; no restaurant; pay shuttle to Universal or SeaWorld. [$] *Rooms from: $137* ✉ *8303 Palm Pkwy., Lake Buena Vista area, Orlando* ☎ *407/5[illegible] 5000, 866/756–3778* 🌐 *www.hawthornlakebuenavista.c[illegible] suites* 🍽 *Breakfast* ✥ *1:G3.*

$$ RESORT **Hilton Orlando Bonnet Creek.** The Hilton more than lives up to its next-door neighbor the Waldorf Astoria Orlando, with plenty of amenities, including a 3-acre lagoon pool with lazy river, rooms with deluxe bedding, flat screen TVs, family-friendly activities, on-site ticket sales and transportation to Disney parks The hotel is part of the Bonnet Creek resort area, tucked into a corner of Disney World's vast forest lands. **Pros:** serene setting, just moments from Disney; golf course and forest views; next door to Waldorf and its amenities; Disney shuttle. **Cons:** nothing within walking distance, so car is helpful; daily parking fee; very steep daily resort fee. *Rooms from: $209 14100 Bonnet Creek Resort La., Bonnet Creek, Orlando 407/597–3600 www.hiltonbonnetcreek.com 1,000 rooms, 36 suites Some meals 1:E5.*

$$ RESORT Fodor's Choice ★ **Hyatt Regency Grand Cypress Resort.** Sitting amid 1,500 palm-filled acres just outside Disney's back gate, this huge luxury resort hotel has a private lake with watercraft, three golf courses, and miles of trails for strolling, bicycling, jogging, and horseback riding. **Pros:** huge pool; lots of recreation options, for kids and adults, including nearby equestrian center; free Wi-Fi. **Cons:** need a car or taxi to get to Downtown Orlando or Universal; steep resort fee. *Rooms from: $239 1 Grand Cypress Blvd., Lake Buena Vista area, Orlando 407/239–1234, 800/233–1234 www.hyattgrandcypress.com 815 rooms No meals 1:F3.*

$ RESORT FAMILY Fodor's Choice ★ **Nickelodeon Suites Resort.** This 24-acre Nickelodeon-themed resort is so kid-friendly that you can barely take a step without bumping into images of SpongeBob, Dora the Explorer, Jimmy Neutron, or other Nick characters. **Pros:** extremely kid-friendly; Disney, Universal, and SeaWorld shuttles included in resort fee; discounts (up to 50% off standard rates) for active-duty military; mini-golf course. **Cons:** daily resort fee of $30; not within walking distance of Disney or Downtown Disney; way too frenetic for folks without kids. *Rooms from: $149 14500 Continental Gateway, Lake Buena Vista area, Orlando 407/387–5437, 866/462–6425 www.nickhotel.com 777 suites No meals 1:F5.*

$$$ RESORT **Orlando World Center Marriott.** With 2,000 rooms and 110 suites, this luxury resort is one of Orlando's largest, catering to conventions (nearly a half million square feet of meeting space) and families. **Pros:** full-service spa; good on-site steak house; golf course; lobby Starbucks. **Cons:** daily fee for parking and Internet; on-site restaurants have expense-account-size prices; nothing worth seeing within walking distance. *Rooms from: $251 8701 World Center Dr., Lake Buena Vista area, Orlando 407/239–4200, 800/621–0638 www.marriottworldcenter.com 2,000 rooms, 110 suites Breakfast 1:F5.*

$ HOTEL **Sheraton Lake Buena Vista Resort.** This hotel, just outside a Walt Disney World entrance, completed a total upgrade in 2013, transforming into a pool-centered oasis of cool, the perfect place to decompress after a busy day at the parks, with some guest rooms transformed into family suites with separate bedroom and bunk beds. **Pros:** short walk to shops and restaurants; free Disney shuttle; small pets allowed; on-site restaurant. **Cons:** on a busy commercial strip; close to Downtown Disney but a tad too far to walk in the summer heat (about 1 mile); resort fee covers parking, Wi-Fi, shuttles to parks. *Rooms from: $159 12205 Apopka Vineland Rd., Lake Buena Vista area, Orlando 407/239–0444, 800/423–3297 www.starwoodhotels.com 489 rooms, 105 suites No meals 1:F3.*

$ HOTEL **Staybridge Suites Lake Buena Vista.** Just minutes from a Disney entrance, this sparkling all-suites (one- and two-bedroom, two-bath) accommodation offers its own brand of luxury, perfect for a big family on a small budget. **Pros:** free scheduled shuttle service to Disney; free hot breakfast; free Wi-Fi and parking. **Cons:** no restaurant, no shuttles to other parks. *Rooms from: $144 8751 Suiteside Dr., Lake Buena Vista area, Orlando 407/238–0777 www.staybridge.com 150 suites Multiple meal plans 1:F3.*

$$$$ RESORT **Villas of Grand Cypress.** The serene views from the terraces of this 1,500-acre, award-winning golf resort's villas and suites take in the fairways of the Jack Nicklaus–designed North Course, waterways where migrating birds stop to rest, and lush tropical foliage; you'd never know you were right next door to a busy tourist area. **Pros:** upscale, golf resort atmosphere; free transportation to all theme parks; in-room Wi-Fi; on-site golf courses; kids' activities at Hyatt. **Cons:** daily resort fee; pricey. *Rooms from: $405 1 N. Jacaranda St., Lake Buena Vista area, Orlando 407/239–4700, 800/835–7377 www.grandcypress.com 191 units Some meals 1:F2.*

$$$ RESORT Fodor's Choice ★ **Waldorf Astoria Orlando.** Although it doesn't duplicate the famed Waldorf Astoria Hotel in New York, this Waldorf echoes the original with imagination and flair, from the iconic clock in the center of the circular lobby to tiny, black-and-white accent tiles on guest room floors. **Pros:** lavish and luxurious hotel with spa and golf, next to Disney; free transportation to Disney parks. **Cons:** pricey, but you knew that; if you can bear to leave your cabana, you'll need a car to see anything else in the area; steep daily resort fee. *Rooms from: $339 14200 Bonnet Creek Resort La., Bonnet Creek, Orlando 407/597–5500 www.waldorfastoriaorlando.com 328 rooms, 169 suites Breakfast 1:E5.*

$$ RESORT **Wyndham Grand Orlando Resort, Bonnet Creek.** Despite being within Mickey's gates, this family-friendly resort hotel feels remote and serene, as the entrance meanders through pristine Florida forest and bamboo-laden landscaping, creating a sense of remoteness and serenity. **Pros:** practically in Mickey's lap; free shuttles to Disney parks; lots of activities. **Cons:** not convenient to Universal or Downtown Orlando; daily resort fee and parking fee. *Rooms from: $229 14651 Chelonia Pkwy., Bonnet Creek, Orlando 407/390–2300 www.wyndhamgrandorlando.com 398 rooms, 2 suites Breakfast 1:E5.*

3

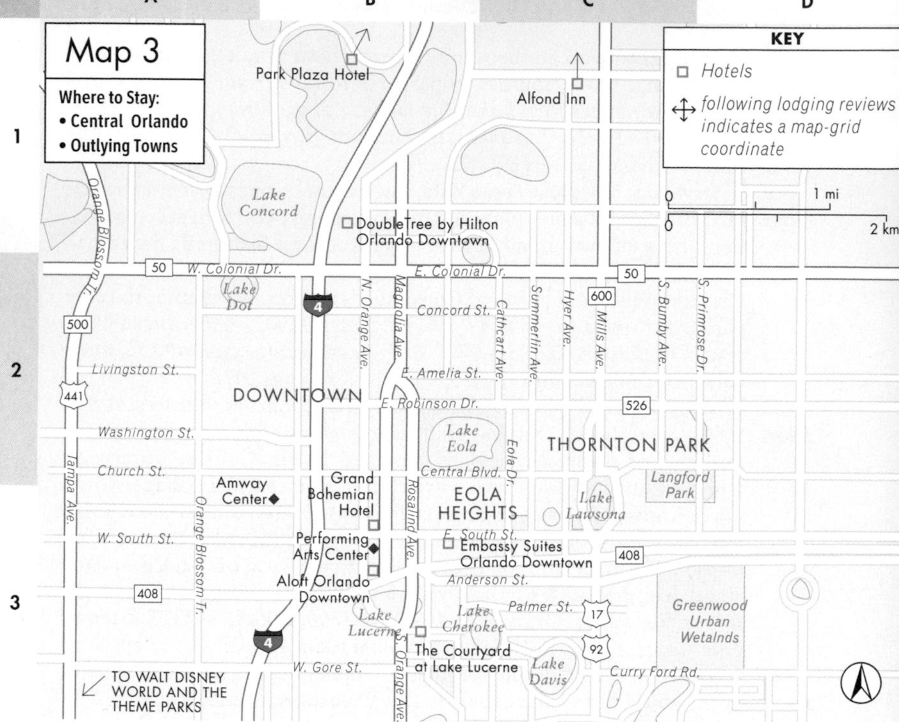

CENTRAL ORLANDO

Take Exit 83B off Interstate 4 westbound, Exit 84 off Interstate 4 eastbound.

Central Orlando, north of Walt Disney World and the I-Drive area, is a thriving business district on weekdays and attracts a club and restaurant crowd on weekend nights.

$ HOTEL **Aloft Orlando Downtown.** Just steps from the Dr. Philips Center for the Performing Arts, the Amway Center, City Hall, and Church Street nightlife, this former utilities building, now an urban hotel in the middle of everything, greets guests with a sparkling lobby, floors of gleaming polished concrete, a busy bar-lounge-meeting place, and innovatively designed rooms. **Pros:** literally steps to downtown nightlife and arts and sporting events; easy access to highways. **Cons:** if Disney is your destination, it's a 45-minute hike down Interstate 4 to get there; only parking choice is valet or street parking. *Rooms from: $169 ✉ 500 S. Orange Ave., Downtown Orlando, Orlando ☎ 407/380–3500 www.aloftorlandodowntown.com 118 rooms, 75 suites No meals 3:B3.*

$ B&B/INN **The Courtyard at Lake Lucerne.** Four beautifully restored Victorian houses surround a palm-lined courtyard within blocks of the Amway Center and the Dr. Philips Center for the Performing Arts. **Pros:** great Victorian architecture; short walk to Downtown restaurants, the

Amway Center and performing arts center; free parking and Wi-Fi. **Cons:** far from theme parks and I-Drive; walking in some parts of downtown at night can be a bit dicey. *Rooms from: $125* ✉ *211 N. Lucerne Circle E, Downtown Orlando, Orlando* ☎ *407/648–5188* *www.orlandohistoricinn.com* *30 rooms, 10 suites* *Breakfast* *3:B3.*

$ HOTEL **DoubleTree by Hilton Orlando Downtown.** Just north of Downtown, this hotel is a gem for business guests, with a clubby, leather-chair-filled lobby, and easy access to the central business district, but it doesn't neglect families, who can occupy themselves at the nearby Orlando Science Center, Museum of Art, and Shakespeare Theater complex. **Pros:** easy access to Downtown and I–4; close to museums and nightlife. **Cons:** no kids' program; distance and traffic between hotel and Disney; parking fee. *Rooms from: $129* ✉ *60 S. Ivanhoe Blvd., Downtown Orlando, Orlando* ☎ *407/425–4455* *www.doubletreeorlandodowntown.com* *341 rooms* *Breakfast* *3:B1.*

$$ HOTEL **Embassy Suites Orlando Downtown.** Although designed primarily for business travelers, this property has nice touches for vacationers, too; many suites have views overlooking nearby Lake Eola and its centerpiece fountain, swan boats, and jogging path, and the hotel is a short walk from a half-dozen cafés and restaurants, the Orange County History Center, the new Dr. Phillips Center for the Performing Arts, and the Amway Center with its NBA basketball games and concerts. **Pros:** near Lake Eola and Downtown; free continental breakfast and beverages; nearby restaurants deliver (front desk has menus). **Cons:** traffic can be heavy; finding on-street parking is hard and there's a fee for on-site parking; daily fee for Wi-Fi; Disney is at least 45 minutes away (an hour or more during rush hours). *Rooms from: $209* ✉ *191 E. Pine St., Downtown Orlando, Orlando* ☎ *407/841–1000, 800/609–3339* *www.embassysuites.com* *167 suites* *Breakfast* *3:B3.*

$$$ HOTEL **Grand Bohemian Hotel.** Decorated in a sophisticated and eclectic "Bohemian" style, this European-style property is Downtown Orlando's only Four Diamond luxury hotel. **Pros:** art gallery; quiet, adult-friendly atmosphere; great restaurant; sophisticated entertainment; short walk to Amway Center, arts center, and Downtown restaurants and clubs. **Cons:** kids may find it boring; meals are pricey; fees for parking, far from Disney and Universal. *Rooms from: $279* ✉ *325 S. Orange Ave., Downtown Orlando, Orlando* ☎ *407/313–9000, 866/663–0024* *www.grandbohemianhotel.com* *212 rooms, 35 suites* *No meals* *3:B3.*

ORLANDO INTERNATIONAL AIRPORT

The area around the airport, especially the neighborhood just north of the Beachline Expressway, has a surfeit of hotels, mostly used by business travelers and airline staff. They're worth checking out if you have an early departure.

$ HOTEL **The Florida Hotel & Conference Center.** Five miles from the airport [illegible] the hotel is midway between Orlando International and I-D[illegible] you like to shop, you're in for a treat. **Pros:** in-room Wi-Fi a[illegible] access; free parking; short drive to airport. **Cons:** neighborhood less than scenic; besides adjoining mall, little to walk to; Disney is 18 miles away; no free shuttles; pricey resort fee. *Rooms from: $166 1500 Sand Lake Rd., at S. Orange Blossom Trail, Orlando International Airport Area 407/859–1500, 800/588–4656 www.thefloridahotelorlando.com 511 rooms, 5 suites Breakfast 2:H3.*

$$ HOTEL **Hyatt Regency Orlando International Airport.** If you have to catch an early-morning flight, this hotel inside the main terminal complex is a convenient option; counting the time you spend waiting for the elevator, your room is a five-minute walk from the nearest ticket counter. **Pros:** despite being at the airport, rooms are quiet; people-watching from terminal-side balconies can be fun; terminal has 24-hour shopping and dining; shuttles to Disney and Universal (fee); free Internet access. **Cons:** nothing around but the airport; Downtown Orlando and theme parks at least 30 minutes away; daily fee for parking. *Rooms from: $209 9300 Jeff Fuqua Blvd., Orlando International Airport Area 407/825–1234, 800/233–1234 www.orlandoairport.hyatt.com 445 rooms; 23 suites No meals 2:H3.*

WINTER PARK

Take I–4 Exit 87 or 88.

Home of Rollins College, Winter Park is a charming small town just north of Orlando. Brick streets overhung by moss-draped oaks lead to flower-bedecked Park Avenue, the main drag. Chic shops and restaurants line its east side, and a beautifully landscaped park graces the west side. It feels a million miles from the tourist trail, but it's just a 25- to 45-minute drive from the major attractions, and a great place for people-watching from the sidewalk cafés.

$$ HOTEL **The Alfond Inn.** This newly built, serenely sophisticated building in the heart of charming Winter Park, just steps from the shops and restaurants of Park Avenue, combines an upscale hotel with an art gallery. **Pros:** five-minute walk to Park Avenue for pleasant strolls; restaurant on property. **Cons:** at least an hour's drive to the theme parks. *Rooms from: $249 300 E. New England Ave., Winter Park 407/998–8090 www.thealfondinn.com 112 rooms No meals 3:C1.*

$$ HOTEL **Park Plaza Hotel.** Small and intimate, this beautifully updated 1922 establishment on Park Avenue offers the charm of fern-bedecked wrought-iron balconies along with free Wi-Fi and free breakfast in bed. **Pros:** free valet parking, romantic ambience; view of Park Avenue shops and restaurants; rail station about a block away. **Cons:** railroad tracks are close, sometimes making for train noise at night; no small children allowed; small rooms; a long way from theme parks. *Rooms from: $178 307 Park Ave. S, Winter Park 407/647–1072, 800/228–7220 www.parkplazahotel.com 27 rooms Breakfast 3:B1.*

4

WHERE TO EAT

Visit Fodors.com for advice, updates, an

EPCOT INTERNATIONAL FOOD & WINE FESTIVAL

For six autumn weeks, Epcot hosts the Epcot International Food & Wine Festival, attracting folks more interested in a fine phyllo than a photo op with Cinderella.

(Above) A family digs in at the Epcot International Food & Wine Festival. (Bottom right) Diners at Epcot's Teppan Edo. (Top right) Marinated strawberries with basil served at the Argentina kiosk.

The festival is essentially a compendium of food- and beverage-related offerings, some free with the price of Epcot admission, others costing anywhere from $3 to a few hundred. You can attend mixology or cheese seminars, have cookbooks signed by authors, and sample tapas-size portions of foods from around the world. And that's just the basics. Throughout the event, Disney and guest chefs host brunches, lunches, and wine-pairing dinners at Epcot and in hotels, some posh, others festive, and yet more T-shirt-and-shorts-friendly. The headliners change annually but might include names like Jacques Torres, Jamie Deen, or Andrew Zimmern. The festival's food and beverage lineup changes every year, too, so for more information and to make reservations (during festival season only, generally midsummer through early November), call ☎ *407/939–3378* or visit 🌐 *www.disneyworld.com/foodandwine*.

MASTER OF THE HOUSE

Visitors with a serious interest in the fruit of the vine should consider enrolling in one of the festival's Wine School classes, some taught by Master Sommeliers. Each two-hour course focuses on a single subject, which may include the regions from which pinot noir is derived or the wines of Argentina.

SHOPPING FOR A SNACK

The heart of the Food & Wine Festival—and the most approachable event for hungry tourists on a budget—takes place around Epcot's World Showcase. Ordinarily a miniature world of 11 pavilions themed around one country apiece, the area takes on new life as 27 "international marketplaces" take up residence.

Most of the 27 marketplaces, from Brazil to South Korea, offer a taste of one country, selling approximately three appetizer-size food items and a few beverages that pair well—nearly all for $3 to $7 apiece. Indisputably popular creations like the garlicky escargots at the France counter and the cheddar soup ladled out endlessly at Canada are keepers; regulars might revolt if those were absent at any time. Still, a majority of the menu can change in a given year. Attendees who stop by every autumn might taste Belgian potato-leek waffles with braised beef (with a Stella Artois beer or Godiva-chocolate iced coffee) or Moroccan harissa chicken roll (with Ksar white wine) one time, an Irish fisherman's pie (with Bunratty Meade honey wine) or a Korean lettuce wrap with roast pork and kimchi slaw (with a soju fruit slushy) another.

At a few marketplaces a certain item is featured instead of a locale. The Desserts and Champagne booth, for instance, pours a bounty of bubbly and special sweets. A cheese marketplace puts out treats like an almond-crusted blue cheese soufflé with fig jam and a trio of artisanal cheeses. And the all-American Hops & Barley Market often specializes in fare U.S. citizens can be proud of, such as Maine lobster rolls and Samuel Adams beers.

Lines tend to get very long, especially on weekends, when locals pour in for their regular fix of foreign fare, so consider timing your tour during the day or on a weekday evening, when most spots have shorter waits.

FESTIVAL OF THE SENSES

Every Saturday evening throughout the festival, food and wine enthusiasts clad in cocktail attire saunter into the gala called Party for the Senses. Billed as a "grand tasting," the bash is a huge all-you-can-eat fancy-food fest. In a dramatically decorated, high-ceilinged room, 10 to 15 chefs from around the country host one food station apiece, serving a hearty appetizer-size portion of one passionately prepared dish. Some are Disney chefs eager to show their talents, and others are known nationally. Big names such as François Payard, Allen Susser, and Walter Staib have been known to participate. Wines and beers are poured freely throughout the night. Live entertainment such as acrobats and vocalists—some years, from Cirque du Soleil's *La Nouba*—gives attendees something to watch while taking a break between bites. The price runs $145 to $285, depending on if, and where, you have reserved seats, with or without perks such as an artisanal-chees station and a pre

Updated by
Rona Gindin

You'll find burger-and-fries combos everywhere in Orlando, yet the ambitious chefs behind Orlando's theme-park and independent restaurants provide loads of better options—much better. Locally sourced foods, creative preparations, and clever international influences are all the rage here. Theme-park complexes have some of the best restaurants in town, although you may opt for a rental car to seek out the local treasures.

The signs of Orlando's dining progress is most evident in the last place one would look: Disney's fast-food outlets. Every eatery on Disney property offers a tempting vegetarian option, and kiddie meals come with healthful sides and drinks unless you specifically request otherwise. Chefs at Disney's table-service restaurants consult face-to-face with guests about food allergies.

Around town, locals flock to the Ravenous Pig, the Rusty Spoon, the Smiling Bison, and other gastropubs where the menu changes regularly; Luma on Park, a suave home of thoughtfully created cutting-edge meals; and any number of dining establishments competing to serve the very finest steak. Orlando's culinary blossoming began in 1995, when Disney's signature California Grill debuted, featuring farm-to-table cuisine and wonderful wines by the glass. Soon after, celebrity chefs started opening up shop. And in 2013, Disney completely revamped California Grill so it's a trendsetter once again.

Orlando's destination restaurants can be found in the theme parks, as well as in the outlying towns. Sand Lake Road is now known as Restaurant Row for its eclectic collection of worthwhile tables. Here you'll find fashionable outlets for sushi and seafood, Italian and chops, Hawaiian fusion and upscale Southwestern. Heading into the residential areas, the neighborhoods of Winter Park (actually its own city), Thornton Park, and College Park are prime locales for chow. Scattered throughout Central Florida, low-key ethnic restaurants specialize in the fare of Turkey, India, Peru, Thailand, Vietnam—you name it. Prices in these family-owned finds are usually delightfully low.

DINING PLANNER

WHERE SHOULD WE EAT?

With thousands of eateries competing for your attention, it may seem like a daunting question. But fret not—our expert writers and editors have done most of the legwork. The selections here represent the best this city has to offer—from hamburger joints to fine dining. Search "Best Bets" for top recommendations by price, cuisine, and experience. Or find a review quickly in the listings, organized alphabetically within theme park or neighborhood. Dive in and enjoy!

4

CONSIDERATIONS FOR DIFFERENT TYPES OF TRAVELERS

FAMILIES WITH YOUNG KIDS

If you're traveling with small children, you really should include a character meal. Walt Disney World offers breakfast, lunch, and dinner with characters at each of its four parks and some of its resorts. Some are buffets; others are family-style or à la carte. Regardless of the format, Mickey, Donald, Goofy, Chip 'n' Dale, Cinderella, and other favorites show up to sign autographs and pose for snapshots.

At Universal, character meals move around. Cafe La Bamba might feature characters from *Hop* and *Despicable Me*. At Christmastime, one Islands of Adventure restaurant hosts a Grinchmas character breakfast featuring the Grinch and friends. Universal's hotels also have character dinners, including the Simpsons, on select nights.

When possible, reserve your spot far in advance.

■ TIP→ If your young children are theme-park newbies, have your character meal near the end of a visit, so they'll be used to seeing the large and sometimes frightening figures.

Except for two, the ultraformal Victoria & Albert's and Christini's, all restaurants in and near the theme parks welcome children. Crayons, games, and kiddie menus are standard.

FAMILIES WITH TWEENS

Tweens are impressed by highly themed concepts. Consider the 50's Prime Time Café in Disney's Hollywood Studios, a kitschy 1950s-themed space where "Mom," the waitress, may make parents finish their vegetables. At the Sci-Fi Dine-In Theater nearby, guests eat in top-down convertible cars that face a big screen airing '50s and '60s sci-fi and monster trailers.

Universal's Islands of Adventure also has themed eateries based on superheroes or other classic characters. The Three Broomsticks replicates a Hogsmeade tavern, a boon for Harry Potter fans.

FAMILIES WITH TEENS

CityWalk is filled with high-energy themed eateries that teens love. In fact, local high schoolers tend to congregate in the CityWalk common areas on weekend evenings. The high-energy Hard Rock Cafe is a consistent favorite.

On the Disney boardwalk, the ESPN Club is a great choice for teen sports fans. Even its bathrooms are equipped with video monitors, so you don't have to miss a second of a great game.

COUPLES

Truly, you'd be hard-pressed to find more romantic restaurants than the ones on Disney property. Jiko, at the Animal Kingdom Lodge, pairs superb African-accented cuisine with an exceptional South African wine list and dramatic decor. If you really want to go all out, there's absolutely nothing like Victoria & Albert's, in the Grand Floridian. Treat yourself to a gourmet, seven-course prix-fixe meal to live harp music.

Outside the theme parks, Norman's, at the Ritz-Carlton, has a sophisticated dining room and impressive New World cuisine.

SINGLES OR GROUPS OF FRIENDS

Singles often dine at the bars of upscale-casual favorites, including Seasons 52, Prato, and Bonefish Grill. Groups enjoy the festive antics of International Drive's Taverna Opa, where visitors often find themselves dancing around the dining room.

LARGE GROUPS

Restaurants in theme-park hotels, in nearby convention hotels, on Sand Lake Road, and on International Drive have private party rooms for large groups more often than not. For an alternative, consider dinner shows. The food is plentiful and the entertainment keeps younger family members engaged. The luaus at Disney and Universal hotels are good for all ages, as is the wonderfully hokey Hoop-Dee-Doo Musical Revue at Disney's Fort Wilderness Resort.

Many off-park venues also offer themed dining with shows. The concepts range from medieval jousting on horseback to pirates to crime and comedy.

MEAL PLANS

Disney Magic Your Way Plus Dining Plan allows you one table-service or buffet meal, one counter-service meal, and one snack per day of your trip at more than 100 theme-park and resort restaurants, provided you stay in a Disney hotel. You'll also receive a refillable drink mug for use at your hotel's fast fooderies. For more money, you can upgrade the plan to include more; to save, you can downgrade to a counter-service-only plan. Used wisely, a Disney dining plan is a steal, but be careful to buy only the number of meals you'll want to eat. Moderate eaters can end up turning away appetizers and desserts to which they're entitled. Plan ahead, and use "extra" meals to your advantage by swapping two table-service meals for a Disney dinner show, say, or an evening at a high-end restaurant like California Grill.

Universal Meal Deal offers one sit-down and one quick-service meal at participating walk-up eateries inside Universal Studios and Islands of Adventure, plus a snack and soft drink. Daily prices are $46 and $18 (both parks) and must be purchased with a resort stay. A quick-service-only arrangement, with one meal a day, is $20 and $13. All-you-can-drink soft drinks are $12 daily for all.

WHAT IT COSTS

	$	$$	$$$	$$$$
AT DINNER	under $14	$15–$21	$22–$30	over $30

Prices are per person for a median main course, at dinner, excluding tip and tax of 6.5%.

RESERVATIONS

Reservations are strongly recommended throughout the theme parks. Indeed, make reservations for Disney restaurants and character meals at both Universal and Disney at least 90 (and up to 180) days out. And be sure to ask about the cancellation policy—at a handful of Disney restaurants, for instance, you may be charged penalties if you don't give 24 to 48 hours' notice.

For restaurant reservations within Walt Disney World, call ☎ *407/939–3463* (*WDW–DINE*) or book online at 🌐 *www.disneyworld.com/dining*. You can also get plenty of information on the website, including the meal periods served, price range, and specialties of all Disney eateries. Menus for all restaurants are posted online and tend to be up to date. For Universal Orlando reservations, call ☎ *407/224–9255* (theme parks and CityWalk) or ☎ *407/503–3463* (hotels). Learn about the complex's 50-plus restaurants at 🌐 *www.universalorlando.com/dining*.

In our reviews, reservations are mentioned only when they're essential or not accepted. Unless otherwise noted, the restaurants listed are open daily for lunch and dinner.

TIPPING AND TAXES

In most restaurants, tip the waiter 15%–20% of the food and beverage charges before tax. Tip at least $1 per drink at the bar, and $2 for valet parking.

WHAT TO WEAR

Because tourism is king around Orlando, casual dress is the rule. Flip-flops and cutoffs are acceptable in just about all fast-food and midprice restaurants. Although it's best to dress up for the ritzier restaurants, don't be shocked to find diners beside you in Levi's and polo shirts. Men need jackets only in the most exclusive establishments; however, such establishments are strict about enforcing dress code. If you plan to at a nicer place, check on dress codes so you aren't caught un and turned away at the door.

ABOUT OUR PRICE CATEGORIES AND MAPS

Prices in the restaurant reviews are the average cost of a main course at dinner or, if dinner is not served, at lunch; taxes and service charges are generally included.

Throughout the chapter, you'll see mapping symbols and coordinates (⊕ 3:F2) at the end of each review. Maps are within the chapter. The first number after the ⊕ symbol indicates the map number. After that is the property's coordinate on the map grid.

WALT DISNEY WORLD AREA

MAGIC KINGDOM

Dining options in the Magic Kingdom are mainly counter service, with a few delightful exceptions, and every land has its share of fast-food places selling burgers, hot dogs, grilled-chicken sandwiches, and salads. Each has a different regular and children's menu. The walkways are peppered with carts dispensing smoked turkey legs, popcorn, ice-cream bars, lemonade, bottled water, and soda. The Magic Kingdom's almost no-liquor policy (wine and beer is offered only during dinner at Be Our Guest) fits the theme park most suited for little kids. The spirits ban does not extend to the rest of Walt Disney World.

$$$ BRASSERIE Fodor's Choice ★ ✕ **Be Our Guest.** Traverse a bridge flanked by gargoyles and gas lamps to reach the Beast's castle, home of this massive new restaurant with a *Beauty and the Beast* theme, French flair, and the Magic Kingdom's first and only wine and beer served at dinner. The 500-seat restaurant has three rooms: a gilded ballroom, whose ceiling sports cherubs with the faces of Imagineers' children; the tattered West Wing, with a slashed painting that changes from prince to beast during faux storms; and the Rose Gallery. Decor comprises French provincial furniture, suits of armor, and heavy drapes. Food, scratch-prepared on-site, includes pan-seared salmon, grilled steak, and maybe a pork rack with red wine au jus. The signature kids' soft drink comes in a light-up castle cup, and desserts, while sweet, are made without refined sugar. Be sure to accept a dollop of "the gray stuff—it's delicious." Lunch is a no-reservations fast-casual affair with the likes of quinoa salad and a braised pork stew with mashed potatoes, ordered on a touch screen and delivered to the table. $ *Average main: $25* ✉ *Fantasyland* ☎ *407/939–3463* 🌐 *www.disneyworld.disney.go.com/dining* ✍ *Reservations essential* ⊕ *1:B1.*

$$$$ AMERICAN ✕ **Cinderella's Royal Table.** Cinderella and other Disney princesses appear at this eatery in the castle's old mead hall; you should book reservations up to 180 days in advance to be sure to see them. The Fairytale Breakfast offers all-you-can-eat options such as lobster-crab crepes, and caramel apple–stuffed French toast. The Fairytale Lunch and Dinner, prix-fixe table-service meals, include entrées like gnocchi with roasted vegetables or roasted bone-in pork with sweet potato hash. When you arrive at the Cinderella Castle, a photographer snaps a shot of your group in the lobby. A package of photographs will be delivered to your table during your meal. $ *Average main: $59* ✉ *Cinderella Castle*

☎ *407/939–3463* 🌐 *www.disneyworld.disney.go.com/dining* ✍ *Reservations essential* ✥ *1:B1.*

$$$$ AMERICAN ✕ **Liberty Tree Tavern.** This "tavern" is dry, but it's a prime spot on the parade route, so you can catch a good meal while you wait. Order Colonial-period comfort food for lunch like hearty pot roast cooked with a Cabernet wine–and-mushroom sauce, or turkey and dressing with mashed potatoes. Dinner is the family-style Patriot's Platter, with turkey, carved beef, sliced pork, and sides. The restaurant is decorated in lovely Williamsburg colors with Early American–style antiques and lots of brightly polished brass. Each of the six dining rooms commemorates a historical U.S. figure, like Betsy Ross or Benjamin Franklin. 💲 *Average main: $32* ✉ *Liberty Sq.* ☎ *407/939–3463* 🌐 *www.disneyworld.disney.go.com/dining* ✥ *1:B1.*

$$$ ITALIAN ✕ **Tony's Town Square Restaurant.** Inspired by the animated classic *Lady and the Tramp,* Tony's offers everything from spaghetti with meatballs to a New York strip steak with red wine butter to garlicky shrimp scampi with sun-dried tomatoes. There's no wine list, but you can get the lemonade punch in a light-up collector's mug. The most tempting desserts are the chocolate cake with chocolate-hazelnut filling and the pistachio crème brûlée. If you can't get a table right away, you can watch *Lady and the Tramp* in the waiting area. 💲 *Average main: $23* ✉ *Main St., U.S.A.* ☎ *407/939–3463* 🌐 *www.disneyworld.disney.go.com/dining* ✥ *1:B1.*

EPCOT

Epcot's World Showcase offers some of the finest dining in Orlando. Every pavilion has at least one and often two or even three eateries. Where there's a choice, it's between a relatively expensive full-service restaurant and a more affordable, ethnic fast-food spot, plus carts and shops selling snacks ranging from French pastries to Japanese ices—whatever's appropriate to the pavilion.

$$$$ SCANDINAVIAN ✕ **Akershus Royal Banquet Hall.** This restaurant has character buffets at all three meals, with an array of Disney princesses, including Ariel, Belle, Jasmine, Snow White, Mulan, Mary Poppins, and even an occasional cameo appearance by Cinderella. The breakfast menu is American, but lunch and dinner find an ever-changing assortment of Norwegian specialties. Appetizers are offered buffet style, and usually include herring, goat-milk cheese, peppered mackerel, and gravlax (cured salmon served with mustard sauce) or *fiskepudding* (a seafood mousse with herb dressing). For your main course, chosen à la carte, you might try traditional ground pork and beef *kjottkake* (dumplings) or roasted rack of lamb. Aquavit, wine, and specialty drinks are offered. All meals are fixed price. 💲 *Average main: $52* ✉ *Norway Pavilion* ☎ *407/939–3463* 🌐 *www.disneyworld.disney.go.com/dining* ✍ *Reservations essential* ✥ *1:D4.*

$$$$ GERMAN ✕ **Biergarten.** Oktoberfest runs 365 days a year here. The cheerful, sometimes raucous, crowds are what you would expect in a place with a[n] oompah band. The menu and level of frivolity are the same at l[unch] and dinner. Mountains of sauerbraten, bratwurst, chicken ...

BEST BETS FOR ORLANDO AND THE PARKS DINING

If it can be fried and put under a heat lamp, you can probably find it in Orlando, but the dining scene both within the parks and the city itself has long transcended prototypical fast food. High-quality restaurants operate within the parks, Downtown Disney, and several Orlando neighborhoods. Here are our top recommendations, organized by price, cuisine, and experience. The restaurants we consider the very best are indicated in the listings with the Fodor's Choice logo.

Fodor's Choice ★

Be Our Guest, $$$, p. 122
Boma—Flavors of Africa, $$$$, p. 136
California Grill, $$$$, p. 133
Christner's Prime Steak & Lobster, $$$$, p. 168
Emeril's Orlando, $$$$, p. 147
Flying Fish, $$$$, p. 135
4 Rivers Smokehouse, $, p. 168
Hawkers, $$, p. 166
Jiko, $$$$, p. 137
K Restaurant & Wine Bar, $$$, p. 166
Luma on Park, $$$, p. 169
Monsieur Paul, $$$$, p. 128
Norman's, $$$$, p. 157
Prato, $$$, p. 169
Primo, $$$$, p. 157
The Ravenous Pig, $$$, p. 170
The Rusty Spoon, $$$, p. 166
The Smiling Bison, $, p. 167
Todd English's bluezoo, $$$$, p. 136
Victoria & Albert's, $$$$, p. 134

By Price

$

Anh Hong, p. 163
Confisco Grille, p. 138
4 Rivers Smokehouse, p. 168
Mel's Drive-In, p. 138
The Smiling Bison, p. 167

$$

Cask & Larder, p. 168
ESPN Club, p. 135
50's Prime Time Café, p. 130
Hawkers, p. 166
Mama Melrose's Ristorante Italiano, p. 130
Mythos, p. 138
Seasons 52, p. 162

$$$

Be Our Guest, p. 122
Bosphorous Turkish Cuisine, p. 159
K Restaurant & Wine Bar, p. 166
Les Chefs de France, p. 128
Luma on Park, p. 169
Prato, p. 169
The Ravenous Pig, p. 170
The Rusty Spoon, p. 166
Sanaa, p. 137

$$$$

Boma—Flavors of Africa, p. 136
California Grill, p. 133
Christner's Prime Steak & Lobster, p. 168
Emeril's Orlando, p. 147
Emeril's Tchoup Chop, p. 150
Flying Fish, p. 135
Jiko, p. 137
Monsieur Paul, p. 128
Norman's, p. 157
Primo, p. 157
Todd English's bluezoo, p. 136
Victoria & Albert's, p. 134

By Cuisine

AFRICAN

Boma—Flavors of Africa, $$$$, p. 136
Jiko, $$$$, p. 137
Sanaa, $$$, p. 137

AMERICAN

California Grill, $$$$, p. 133
Cask & Larder, $$, p. 168
Cinderella's Royal Table, $$$$, p. 122
50's Prime Time Café, $$, p. 130
Luma on Park, $$$, p. 169

The Ravenous Pig, $$$, p. 170

The Rusty Spoon, $$$, p. 166

Seasons 52, $$, p. 162

Victoria & Albert's, $$$$, p. 134

Wolfgang Puck, $$, p. 132

ASIAN

Dragonfly, $$$, p. 160

Hawkers, $$, p. 166

CONTINENTAL

Park Plaza Gardens, $$$, p. 169

The Venetian Room, $$$$, p. 158

ECLECTIC

The Boheme Restaurant, $$$, p. 163

Café Tu Tu Tango, $$$, p. 153

Citricos, $$$$, p. 133

FRENCH

Be Our Guest, $$$, p. 122

Les Chefs de France, $$$, p. 128

Monsieur Paul, $$$$, p. 128

IRISH

Finnegan's Bar & Grill, $$, p. 138

Raglan Road Irish Pub, $$$, p. 132

ITALIAN

Bice Ristorante, $$$$, p. 150

Café d'Antonio, $$, p. 152

Fiorella's Cucina Toscana, $$$, p. 154

La Luce by Donna Scala, $$$, p. 158

Mama Della's Ristorante, $$$, p. 151

Mama Melrose's Ristorante Italiano, $$, p. 130

Peperoncino, $$$, p. 161

Prato, $$$, p. 169

Primo, $$$$, p. 157

Tutto Italia Ristorante, $$$, p. 129

JAPANESE

Kimonos, $$$, p. 135

Shari Sushi Lounge, $$$, p. 167

Tokyo Dining and Teppan Edo, $$$, p. 129

LATIN

Columbia Restaurant, $$$, p. 152

Cuba Libre, $$$, p. 154

PIZZA

Via Napoli, $$$, p. 129

SEAFOOD

Cityfish, $$, p. 163

Flying Fish, $$$$, p. 135

MoonFish, $$$$, p. 161

Ocean Prime, $$$$, p. 161

Oceanaire Seafood Room, $$$$, p. 155

Sunset Sam's, A Key West Grill, $$$$, p. 152

Todd English's bluezoo, $$$$, p. 136

STEAK HOUSE

Christner's Prime Steak & Lobster, $$$$, p. 168

Linda's La Cantina, $$$, p. 166

Morton's The Steakhouse, $$$$, p. 161

The Palm, $$$$, p. 151

Shula's Steak House, $$$$, p. 135

Yachtsman Steakhouse, $$$$, p. 136

By Experience

BEST BUFFET

Biergarten, $$$$, p. 123

Boma—Flavors of Africa, $$$$, p. 136

Chef Mickey's, $$$$, p. 133

Tusker House, $$$$, p. 131

BEST VIEWS

California Grill, $$$$, p. 133

Sanaa, $$$, p. 137

BEST DISNEY RESTAURANT

Be Our Guest, $$$, p. 122

Boma—Flavors of Africa, $$$$, p. 136

California Grill, $$$$, p. 133

Flying Fish, $$$$, p. 135

Jiko, $$$$, p. 137

Monsieur Paul, $$$$, p. 128

Victoria & Albert's, $$$$, p. 134

BEST OFF-SITE RESTAURANT

K Restaurant & Wine Bar, $$$, p. 166

Luma on Park, $$$, p. 169

Norman's, $$$$, p. 157

Prato, $$$, p. 169

Primo, $$$$, p. 157

The Ravenous Pig, $$$, p. 170

SPECIAL OCCASION

Norman's, $$$$, p. 157

Ocean Prime, $$$$, p. 161

Victoria & Albert's, $$$$, p. 134

BEST SUNDAY BRUNCH

The Boheme Restaurant, $$$, p. 163

House of Blues, $$, p. 132

K Restaurant & Wine Bar, $$$, p. 166

MOST ROMANTIC

Christini's Ristorante Italiano, $$$$, p. 160

Norman's, $$$$, p. 157

The Venetian Room, $$$$, p. 158

Victoria & Albert's, $$$$, p. 134

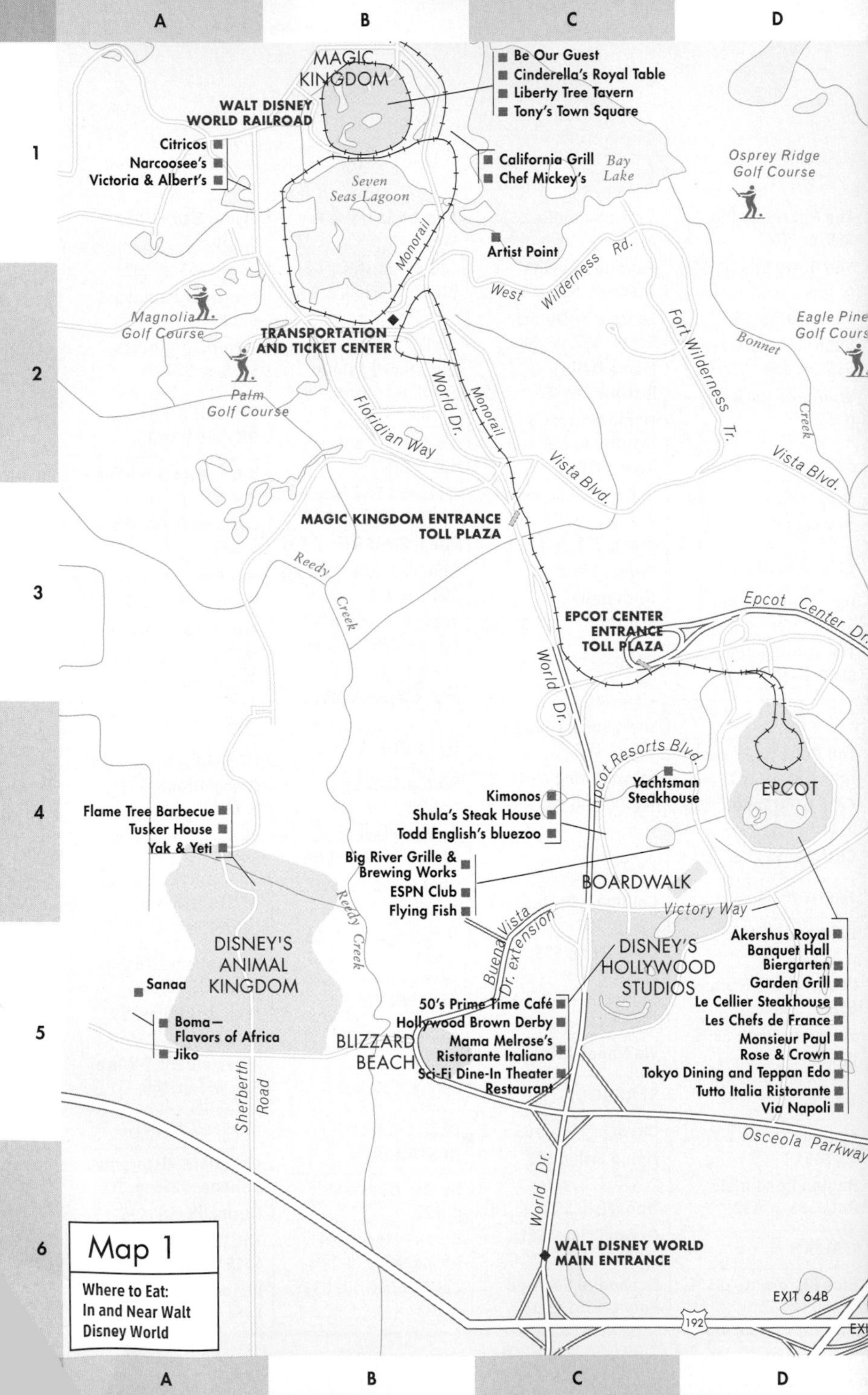
A
B
C
D
1
2
3
4
5
6
MAGIC KINGDOM
WALT DISNEY WORLD RAILROAD
Be Our Guest
Cinderella's Royal Table
Liberty Tree Tavern
Tony's Town Square
Citricos
Narcoosee's
Victoria & Albert's
California Grill
Chef Mickey's
Bay Lake
Seven Seas Lagoon
Osprey Ridge Golf Course
Monorail
Artist Point
West Wilderness Rd.
Magnolia Golf Course
TRANSPORTATION AND TICKET CENTER
Eagle Pine Golf Cours
Bonnet
Fort Wilderness Tr.
Creek
Palm Golf Course
Floridian Way
World Dr.
Monorail
Vista Blvd.
Vista Blvd.
MAGIC KINGDOM ENTRANCE TOLL PLAZA
Reedy Creek
Epcot Center Dr.
EPCOT CENTER ENTRANCE TOLL PLAZA
World Dr.
Epcot Resorts Blvd.
Yachtsman Steakhouse
EPCOT
Kimonos
Shula's Steak House
Todd English's bluezoo
Flame Tree Barbecue
Tusker House
Yak & Yeti
Big River Grille & Brewing Works
ESPN Club
Flying Fish
BOARDWALK
Reedy Creek
Victory Way
Buena Vista Dr. extension
DISNEY'S ANIMAL KINGDOM
DISNEY'S HOLLYWOOD STUDIOS
Akershus Royal Banquet Hall
Biergarten
Garden Grill
Le Cellier Steakhouse
Les Chefs de France
Monsieur Paul
Rose & Crown
Tokyo Dining and Teppan Edo
Tutto Italia Ristorante
Via Napoli
Sanaa
Boma—Flavors of Africa
Jiko
50's Prime Time Café
Hollywood Brown Derby
Mama Melrose's Ristorante Italiano
Sci-Fi Dine-In Theater Restaurant
BLIZZARD BEACH
Sherberth Road
Osceola Parkway
World Dr.
WALT DISNEY WORLD MAIN ENTRANCE
EXIT 64B
192
Map 1
Where to Eat: In and Near Walt Disney World
A
B
C
D

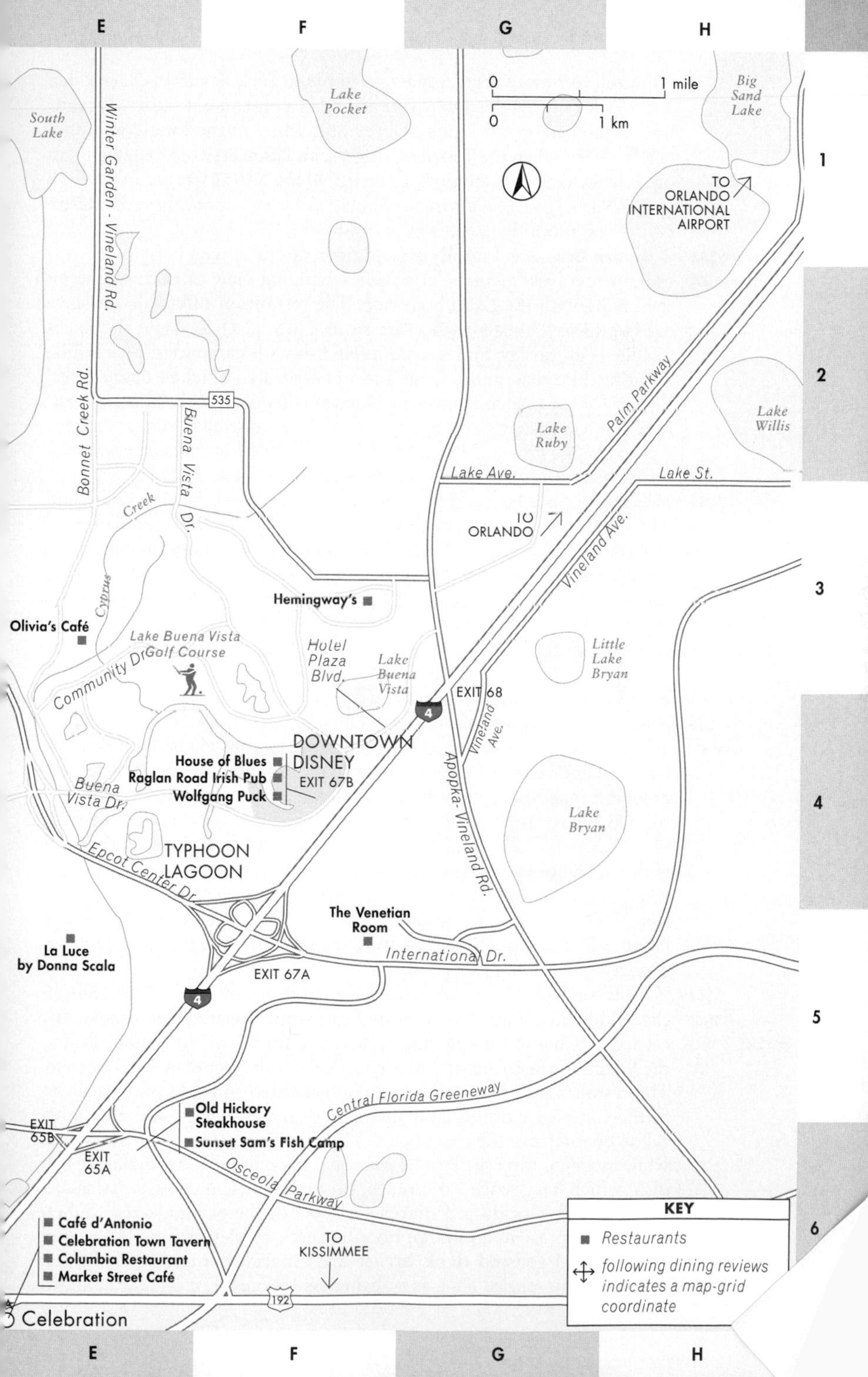

E
F
G
H
1
2
3
4
5
6
0
1 mile
0
1 km
South Lake
Lake Pocket
Big Sand Lake
Winter Garden - Vineland Rd.
TO ORLANDO INTERNATIONAL AIRPORT
Bonnet Creek Rd.
535
Buena Vista Dr.
Palm Parkway
Lake Ruby
Lake Willis
Lake Ave.
Lake St.
Creek
TO ORLANDO
Vineland Ave.
Cyprus
Hemingway's
Olivia's Café
Lake Buena Vista Golf Course
Community Dr.
Hotel Plaza Blvd.
Lake Buena Vista
Little Lake Bryan
EXIT 68
4
Vineland Ave.
DOWNTOWN DISNEY
House of Blues
Raglan Road Irish Pub
Wolfgang Puck
EXIT 67B
Buena Vista Dr.
Apopka- Vineland Rd.
Lake Bryan
TYPHOON LAGOON
Epcot Center Dr.
The Venetian Room
La Luce by Donna Scala
International Dr.
EXIT 67A
4
Central Florida Greeneway
Old Hickory Steakhouse
Sunset Sam's Fish Camp
EXIT 65B
EXIT 65A
Osceola Parkway
KEY
Restaurants
following dining reviews indicates a map-grid coordinate
Café d'Antonio
Celebration Town Tavern
Columbia Restaurant
Market Street Café
TO KISSIMMEE
192
Celebration
E
F
G
H

schnitzel, German sausage, spaetzle, apple strudel, Bavarian cheesecake, and Black Forest cake await you at the all-you-can-eat buffet. Patrons pound pitchers of all kinds of beer and wine on the long communal tables—even when the yodelers, singers, and dancers aren't egging them on. Prices change seasonally. *Average main: $40 ✉ Germany Pavilion ☎ 407/939–3463 www.disneyworld.disney.go.com/dining Reservations essential ⊕ 1:D4.*

$$$$ AMERICAN **Garden Grill.** Solid family-style dinner fare is served here as the restaurant revolves, giving you an ever-changing view of each biome on the Living with the Land boat ride. The restaurant offers all-you-can-eat family-style meals with visits from Chip 'n' Dale. Typical choices include beef, turkey, and a sustainable fish with trimmings, plus kiddie favorites like mac and cheese and oven-roasted chicken drumsticks. Except for the princess meals in Norway, this is the only Epcot restaurant that has Disney character meet-and-greets during meals. *Average main: $39 ✉ The Land Pavilion ☎ 407/939–3463 www.disneyworld.disney.go.com/dining No lunch ⊕ 1:D4.*

$$$$ CANADIAN **Le Cellier Steakhouse.** This charming eatery with stone arches and dark-wood paneling has a good selection of wine and Canadian beer. Options are à la carte and include the signature filet mignon with wild-mushroom risotto and white truffle–butter sauce. Of the many non-beef entrees, consider the rack of venison with a fig and Port wine reduction, and porcini-dusted veal tenderloin. Desserts pay tribute to the land up north with crème brûlée made with maple sugar. *Average main: $42 ✉ Canada Pavilion ☎ 407/939–3463 www.disneyworld.disney.go.com/dining ⊕ 1:D4.*

$$$ FRENCH **Les Chefs de France.** What some consider the best restaurant at Disney was created by three of France's most famous chefs: Paul Bocuse, Gaston Lenôtre, and Roger Vergé. Classic escargots, a good starter, are prepared in a casserole with garlic butter; you might follow up with roasted breast and leg of duck confit, or grilled beef tenderloin with black pepper sauce. Make sure you finish with profiteroles drizzled with chocolate sauce. The three-course prix-fixe menu is a great value when it's available. An Audio-Animatronics Remy, from the movie *Ratatouille*, makes the rounds atop a roving chef's cart. *Average main: $30 ✉ France Pavilion ☎ 407/939–3463 www.disneyworld.disney.go.com/dining ⊕ 1:D4.*

$$$$ FRENCH Fodor's Choice ★ **Monsieur Paul.** A mere staircase away from Epcot's busy World Showcase, Monsieur Paul is a subdued and sophisticated fine dinery. It's owned by Chef Jerome Bocuse and named for his world-famous father, the Culiniary Institute of America's Chef of the Century, Paul Bocuse. The restaurant is expensive and sophisticated—in odd juxtaposition to the rumpled clothing and sneakers of most diners—and a delightful diversion from the theme park's bustle. The menu is overtly French while incorporating the best of America. For example, the signature fish dish, which has "scales" of potato, braised fennel, and rosemary sauce, is made with Florida red snapper instead of the original's red mullet. Escargot is presented in large raviolis and a parsley cream. The seared scallops and roasted duck breast are especially interesting entrées. Although the service isn't as polished as the menu, it is heartening to

hear the waitstaff converse in French. *Average main: $41 France Pavilion 407/939–3463 www.disneyworld.disney.go.com/dining No lunch 1:D4.*

$$$ BRITISH **Rose & Crown.** If you're an Anglophile and you love a beer so thick you could stand a spoon up in your mug, this is the place to soak up both the suds and British street culture. "Wenches" serve up traditional English fare—fish-and-chips, cottage or shepherd's pie (ground beef or lamb with onions, carrots, and peas, topped with mashed potatoes and cheddar cheese), and, at times, the ever-popular bangers and mash (sausage over mashed potatoes). Scotch egg makes a good appetizer. Vegetarians can always find one item adapted for them, such as vegetable pie 'n' mash. For dessert, try the sticky toffee pudding. The terrace has a splendid view of IllumiNations. *Average main: $23 United Kingdom Pavilion 407/939–3463 www.disneyworld.disney.go.com/dining 1:D4.*

4

$$$ JAPANESE **Tokyo Dining and Teppan Edo.** Above the Mitsukoshi department store in Epcot's Japan pavilion are sister restaurants Teppan Edo, a teppanyaki steak house where chefs do performance cooking at 20 grills, and Tokyo Dining, for sushi and preplated meals. Menu standouts at Teppan Edo include the filet mignon and the Tori chicken breast. It also has a small sushi selection and a kids' menu with Teppan-style chicken or shrimp with rice and veggies. The more stylish Tokyo Dining offers up tempura dishes, katsu dinners, and salmon or chicken teriyaki. Both restaurants have something great to watch: Teppan Edo has the performing chefs; Tokyo Dining has a great view of the Japan pavilion. *Average main: $25 Japan Pavilion 407/939–3463 www.disneyworld.disney.go.com/dining 1:D4.*

$$$ ITALIAN **Tutto Italia Ristorante.** Tutto Italia may have an old-world look, but its menu is under the contemporary tutelage of Joachim Splichal, the prestigious Patina Restaurant Group's celebrity chef. Although freshened up significantly in 2012, the restaurant still has a certain formality, even though typical diners are wearing shorts, T-shirts, and flip-flops. Offerings include polenta with braised short ribs and meatballs, pan-roasted salmon baked with green lentils and herb butter, and pasta with braised lamb ragu. Desserts include gelato and cannoli. Expect a wait at peak lunch and dinner times. Outdoor seating is available. An adjacent canvernous wine cellar, Tutto Gusto, has small bites and 200 wine options. *Average main: $27 Italy Pavilion 407/939–3463 www.disneyworld.disney.go.com/dining Reservations essential 1:D4.*

$$$ PIZZA **Via Napoli.** When the Patina Restaurant Group decided to open a second Italian eatery in Epcot (the first was Tutto Italia Ristorante), they opted to specialize in authentic Neapolitan wood-fired pizza, importing the mozzarella from Italy and using only San Marzano tomatoes. The result is crusty, thin pies topped with your choice of pepperoni; portobello and crimini mushrooms; or eggplant, artichokes, cotto ham, and mushrooms. The eggplant parmigiana is an outstanding alternative. *Average main: $24 Italy Pavilion 407/939–3463 www.disneyworld.disney.go.com/dining 1:D4.*

DISNEY'S HOLLYWOOD STUDIOS

The Studios tends to have more highly themed restaurants than the other parks, and some serve good, imaginative food, too. Dinner packages that include the Fantasmic! after-dark show can be booked by phone or online, in person at a Disney hotel, or at the park's Guest Relations (aka Guest Services). With the package, you secure your reservation by credit card for dinner and then receive "designated seating" for the extravaganza. For a less expensive option, pick up a picnic dinner at Min & Bill's Dockside Diner as part of "A Taste of Hollywood to Go!" It's available during the park's busiest seasons only.

$$ AMERICAN FAMILY **50's Prime Time Café.** Who says you can't go home again? If you grew up in middle America in the 1950s, just step inside. While *I Love Lucy* and *The Donna Reed Show* clips play on a television screen, you can feast on meat loaf, pot roast, or fried chicken, all served on a Formica tabletop. At $16, the meat loaf is one of the best inexpensive, filling dinners in any local theme park. Enjoy it with a malted-milk shake or root-beer float (or a bottle of wine). The place offers some fancier dishes, like the olive oil–poached salmon, which is a good choice for lighter eaters. If you're not feeling totally wholesome, go for Dad's Electric Lemonade (rum, vodka, blue curaçao, sweet-and-sour mix, and Sprite), which is worth every bit of the $10.75 price tag. Just like Mother, the menu admonishes, "Keep your elbows off the table." [$] *Average main: $18* ✉ *Echo Lake* ☎ *407/939–3463* 🌐 *www.disneyworld.disney.go.com/dining* ✣ *1:C5.*

$$$ AMERICAN **Hollywood Brown Derby.** At this reproduction of the famous 1940s Hollywood restaurant, the walls are lined with movie-star caricatures, just as in Tinseltown. The specialty is the Cobb salad, which by legend was invented by Brown Derby founder Robert Cobb; the salad consists of finely chopped lettuce enlivened by loads of tomato, bacon, turkey, blue cheese, chopped egg, and avocado, all tossed table-side. Other menu choices include grilled salmon with black beluga lentil stew and lemon-thyme sabayon, and filet of beef with white truffle oil forest mushroom mashed potatoes. Dining with an Imagineer is a special option; you will have lunch or dinner with one of Disney's creative engineers while enjoying a set-price four-course meal including soup, salad, entrée, and dessert. If you request the Fantasmic! dinner package, make a reservation for no later than two hours before the start of the show. [$] *Average main: $30* ✉ *Hollywood Blvd.* ☎ *407/939–3463* 🌐 *www.disneyworld.disney.go.com/dining* ✣ *1:C5.*

$$ ITALIAN **Mama Melrose's Ristorante Italiano.** To replace the energy you've no doubt depleted by miles of theme-park walking, you can load up on carbs at this casual Italian restaurant that looks like an old warehouse. Good main courses include spaghetti with meatballs, and wood-grilled chicken in a four-cheese sauce with pasta and vegetables. Wood-fired flatbreads are available as an entrée choice here (a great bargain at $13 and up) with toppings ranging from grilled chicken with ricotta and onion to wild mushroom. The sangria is popular. Ask for the Fantasmic! dinner package if you want priority seating for the show. [$] *Average main: $22* ✉ *Streets of America* ☎ *407/939–3463* 🌐 *www.disneyworld.disney.go.com/dining* ✣ *1:C5.*

$$ AMERICAN **Sci-Fi Dine-In Theater Restaurant.** If you don't mind zombies leering at you while you eat, then head to this enclosed faux drive-in, where you can sit in a fake candy-color '50s convertible and watch trailers from classics like *Attack of the Fifty-Foot Woman* and *Teenagers from Outer Space*. The menu includes choices like steak and garlic-mashed potatoes, an Angus or veggie burger, shrimp with pasta, and a huge Reuben sandwich with fries or cucumber salad. End with a hot-fudge sundae. *Average main: $22 Commissary La. 407/939–3463 www.disneyworld.disney.go.com/dining 1:C5.*

DISNEY'S ANIMAL KINGDOM

Disney's Animal Kingdom is far from a foodie destination, but Disney's highly themed zoo does offer variety, including an African-theme buffet, a Chinese restaurant with table service, and surprises like a tea stand, a fruit market, and, at times, picnic lunches packaged to go.

$ FAST FOOD **Flame Tree Barbecue.** This counter-service eatery is one of the relatively undiscovered gems of Disney's culinary offerings. There's nothing fancy here, but you can dig into ribs and pulled pork sandwiches. For something with a lower calorie count, try the smoked turkey sandwich served with cranberry mayo or a great barbecued chicken served with baked beans and coleslaw. The outdoor tables, set beneath intricately carved wood pavilions, make great spots for a picnic, and they're not usually crowded. *Average main: $12 Discovery Island www.disneyworld.disney.go.com/dining Reservations not accepted 1:A4.*

$$$$ AFRICAN **Tusker House.** This restaurant offers all-buffet dining three meals a day: a Donald's safari-theme character breakfast and lunch, and a bountiful dinner without Donald and his crew. Tusker House offers healthier fare like curry chicken, *peri-peri* (African hot pepper) marinated salmon, strip loin rubbed with *berbere* (an African spice mix), and saffron-infused root vegetables, along with the standard kids' fare. This restaurant has a large vegetarian selection. *Average main: $36 Africa 407/939–3463 www.disneyworld.disney.go.com/dining Reservations essential 1:A4.*

$$$ ASIAN **Yak & Yeti.** The location of this pan-Asian cuisine, sit-down eatery—the only full-service restaurant inside Disney's Animal Kingdom—certainly makes sense. It's just at the entrance to the Asia section, in a two-story, 250-seat building that is pleasantly faux-Asian, with cracked plaster walls, wood carvings, and tile mosaic tabletops. Standout entrées include seared miso salmon, roasted duck with orange-wasabi glaze, and tempura shrimp with jasmine rice and chili-plum sauce. Also tasty, if not authentically Asian, are the baby back ribs with a hoisin barbecue sauce and sweet chili slaw. *Average main: $22 Asia 407/939–3463 www.disneyworld.disney.go.com/dining 1:A4.*

DOWNTOWN DISNEY

Downtown Disney is a shopping and dining complex broken into three sections: Marketplace, which is known more for its shopping but boasts quite an array of restaurants; Pleasure Island, originally a nightlife center that, at this writing, has plenty of dining, shopping, and entertainment options; and West Side, with its enviable lineup of dining spots plus entertainment venues. By 2016, the area will be doubled in size and renamed Disney Springs. There is no cover charge to enter any part of the enterprise.

$$ AMERICAN **House of Blues.** You're unlikely to like this place unless you enjoy listening to high-decibel music during your meal. But if you do, this is a great spot to chow down from an eclectic menu that offers everything from ribs to shrimp and grits to a tasty chicken Caesar salad. The Juicy Lucy is a bacon cheeseburger with jalapeño and chipotle mayo. A worthy dessert is the bourbon–white-chocolate banana-bread pudding. The Gospel Sunday Brunch offers a Southern cooking buffet and live gospel music. Reservations are available only for Sunday brunch. For a quicker meal, visit the quick-service barbecue counter that debuted in 2014. *Average main: $21 West Side, 1490 E. Buena Vista Dr. 407/934–2583 www.houseofblues.com 1:F4.*

$$$ IRISH **Raglan Road Irish Pub.** An authentic Irish pub in Downtown Disney seems oxymoronic, particularly when that pub seats 600 people. But if Irish grub's your thing, Raglan's is the place to go. The shepherd's pie served here is of higher quality than the usual version, prepared with beef and lamb and jazzed up with house spices. And you don't have to settle for plain fish-and-chips (though you can for $19); there's also baked salmon with smoked salmon and maple glaze; shiitake risotto; and lamb shanks braised with rosemary jus. Massive and ornate bars, imported from Ireland and more than a century old, help anchor the pub. The entertainment alone makes this place worth the visit. The house bands play nightly, and a troupe of Irish dancers performs every evening and during Sunday brunch. Another band plays outside for guests dining alfresco. *Average main: $22 Downtown Disney, 1640 E. Buena Vista Dr. 407/938–0300 www.raglanroadirishpub.com 1:F4.*

$$ AMERICAN **Wolfgang Puck Grand Cafe.** There are lots of choices here, from wood-oven pizza at the informal Puck Express to fine-dining meals in the upstairs formal dining room. There's also a sushi bar and an informal café; the café is quite literally a happy medium, and may be the best bet for families hoping for a bit of elegance without the pressure of a formal dinner. At Express try the butternut squash soup or the Margherita pizza. At the café, midprice entrées like rosemary chicken Alfredo and crispy pork loin with shaved fennel, oranges, and radishes are winners, and you can always have a personal pizza, such as barbecued chicken with smoked mozzarella. The dining room offers creative entrées liked seared chicken with truffled polenta. *Average main: $21 1482 E. Buena Vista Dr., West Side 407/938–9653 www.wolfgangpuckcafeorlando.com 1:F4.*

WALT DISNEY WORLD RESORTS

MAGIC KINGDOM RESORT AREA

$$$$ AMERICAN

Artist Point. If you're not a guest at the Wilderness Lodge, a meal here is worth it just to see the giant totem poles and huge rock fireplace in the lobby of the hotel. The specialty at this restaurant, which focuses on foods of the American Northwest, is cedar-plank salmon, served with seasonal items like rainbow cauliflower, root spinach, lemon-butter sauce, applewood-smoked bacon jam, and short rib strudel (worth its $35 price tag). The buffalo is another signature item, sometimes char-grilled and served with luscious enhancements like Zellwood corn–sausage hash, Yukon gold–potato smear, and blackberry pinot noir reduction. There's a good Northwestern U.S. wine list and a wine-flight-pairing option for an additional cost. *Average main: $39 Wilderness Lodge, 901 Timberline Dr. 407/939–3463 www.disneyworld.disney.go.com/dining Reservations essential No lunch 1:C1.*

$$$$ AMERICAN

Fodor's Choice ★

California Grill. The view from the surrounding Disney parks from this 15th-floor restaurant—the World's signature dining establishment since 1995—is as stunning as the food, especially after dark, when you can watch the nightly Magic Kingdom fireworks. The entire space and menu underwent major transformations in 2013, from new midcentury modern furnishings and chandeliers to kitchen equipment such as a cast-iron flat grill designed specifically for cooking fish. Expect locally sourced foods where possible, made-from-scratch items such as the sausage-in-a-duck sampler appetizer, and many items cooked in the wood-fired oven. Sushi remains a highlight, alongside creative, globally inspired entrées. Specialties include a short-rib fillet cooked at a low temperature for 24 hours sous-vide style and served with red-wine butter, and scallops with homemade gnocchi, smoked pork, and Parmesan foam. A 10- to 14-course *omakase* (tasting menu) is available. *Average main: $41 Contemporary Resort, 4600 N. World Dr. 407/939–3463 www.disneyworld.disney.go.com/dining Reservations essential No lunch 1:B1.*

$$$$ AMERICAN

Chef Mickey's. This is the holy shrine for character meals, with Mickey, Minnie, or Goofy around for breakfast and dinner. Folks come here for entertainment and comfort food, not a quiet spot to read the *Orlando Sentinel.* The breakfast buffet includes "pixie-dusted" challah French toast, mountains of pancakes, and even a breakfast pizza. The dinner buffet doesn't disappoint with Thai-curry-chipotle barbecue chicken, roasted ham, and spice-rubbed beef sirloin. Finish off your meal at the all-you-can-eat dessert bar of sundaes. *Average main: $44 Contemporary Resort, 4600 N. World Dr. 407/939–3463 www.disneyworld.disney.go.com/dining No lunch 1:B1.*

$$$$ ECLECTIC

Citricos. Although the name implies that you'll be eating lots of local citrus specialties, you won't necessarily find them here (unless you count the "Citropolitan" martini, made with limoncello, or the veal shank's toasted citrus gremolata). But you will find an ambitious menu that's fundamentally American with influences of southern Europe's low-fat, high-flavor cuisines, namely Tuscan, Provençal, and

4

Spanish-Mediterranean. Standout entrées include the aforementioned braised veal shank and butter-poached monkfish with Américaine sauce and preserved lemon. The wine list, one of Disney's most extensive, includes vintages from around the world. *Average main: $41* *Grand Floridian Resort & Spa, 4401 Floridian Way* *407/939–3463* *www.disneyworld.disney.go.com/dining* *Reservations essential* *No lunch* *1:A1.*

$$$$ SEAFOOD **Narcoossee's.** The dining room, with Victorian-style columns, high ceilings, and hardwood floors, makes a great place not only to enjoy "coastal cuisine"—especially steaks and seafood—but to gaze out at the nightly fireworks over the Seven Seas Lagoon. The menu changes daily. Typical choices are wild line-caught Alaskan halibut and the surf-and-turf centerpiece: a butter-poached lobster tail and a tender grilled filet mignon. The name of the place, incidentally, was not coined by Disney Imagineers; it's the name of a river and a small Central Florida town, both of which predate Disney. Diners should note that no tank tops or cut-offs are permitted. *Average main: $52* *Grand Floridian, 4401 Floridian Way* *407/939–3463* *www.disneyworld.disney.go.com/dining* *No lunch* *1:A1.*

$$$$ MODERN AMERICAN Fodor's Choice ★ **Victoria & Albert's.** At this ultraposh award-winning Disney restaurant, a well-polished service team will anticipate your every need during a gourmet extravaganza. This is one of the plushest fine-dining experiences in Florida, with an ambience so sophisticated that children under 10 aren't on the guest list. The seven-course, prix-fixe menu changes daily, and you'd do well to supplement the $135 tab with a $65 wine pairing. Appetizer choices may include roast duck with mango vinaigrette, octopus with black-garlic aioli, and masago-crusted shrimp with coconut-curry sauce. Entrées may feature braised oxtail and cherry ravioli or Australian Kobe-style beef with smoked garlic-potato puree. For most of the year, there are two seatings, at 5:45 and 9 pm. In July and August, however, there's generally just one seating at 6:30 pm. For a more luxe experience, reserve a table in the intimate Queen Victoria Room or at the Chef's Table, which have more courses (10 to 12) and a bigger bill ($210, wine pairing $105). *Average main: $173* *Grand Floridian, 4401 Floridian Way* *407/939–3862* *www.victoria-alberts.com* *Reservations essential* *Jacket required* *No lunch* *1:A1.*

EPCOT RESORT AREA

$$ AMERICAN **Big River Grille & Brewing Works.** Strange but good brews, like Rocket Red Ale, Southern Flyer Light Lager, and Gadzooks Pilsner, abound here at Walt Disney World's only microbrewery. You can dine inside among the giant copper brewing tanks or sip your suds outside on the lake-view patio. The menu emphasizes meat and fish, with pork ribs dry-rubbed and topped with Rocket Red barbecue sauce, a flame-grilled meat loaf made with ground beef and Italian sausage, and grilled Atlantic salmon fillet with dill butter. The garlic–mashed potatoes are a perfect accompaniment. *Average main: $19* *BoardWalk Inn, 2101 Epcot Resorts Blvd.* *407/560–0253* *www.bigrivergrille.com* *1:C4.*

$$ AMERICAN **ESPN Club.** Not only can you watch sports on a big-screen TV here (the restaurant has about 100 monitors), but you can also periodically see ESPN programs being taped in the club itself and be part of the audience of sports-radio talk shows. Food ranges from a variety of half-pound burgers, made with Angus chuck (and one topped with lobster salad), to an excellent Reuben with plenty of corned beef, sauerkraut, and cheese. If you want an appetizer, try the Pub Nachos for Two, crispy corn tortilla chips piled high with barbecued pulled pork, spicy chili, shredded cheddar cheese, cheddar cheese sauce, sour cream, pico de gallo, and sliced jalapeños. This place is open quite late by Disney standards—until 1 am daily. Beware, the place can be pretty loud during any broadcast sports event, especially football games. *Average main: $16* *BoardWalk Inn, 2101 Epcot Resorts Blvd.* *407/939–3463* *www.disneyworld.disney.go.com/dining* *1:C4.*

4

$$$$ SEAFOOD Fodor's Choice ★ **Flying Fish.** One of Disney's best restaurants, Flying Fish is whimsically decorated with murals, along the upper portion of the walls, that pay tribute to Atlantic seaboard spots of the early 1900s. This is a place where you put on your "resort casual" duds to "dine," as opposed to putting on your flip-flops and shorts to "chow down." The chefs take the food so seriously that the entire culinary team takes day trips to local farms to learn their foodstuffs' origins. Flying Fish's best dishes include potato-wrapped red snapper, which is so popular it has been on the menu for several years, and oak-grilled salmon. Groups of up to six can sit at the counter that directly faces the exhibition kitchen for a five-course wine tasting menu. The restaurant now hosts Dine with an Imagineer meals. *Average main: $36* *BoardWalk Inn, 2101 Epcot Resorts Blvd.* *407/939–2359* *www.disneyworld.disney.go.com/dining* *No lunch* *1:C4.*

$$$ JAPANESE **Kimonos.** Knife-wielding sushi chefs prepare world-class sushi and sashimi but also other Japanese treats like soups and salads at this sleek hotel sushi bar, where bamboo-style floor tiles and pink and purple furnishings create a cheerful environment. Popular rolls include the Dragon Roll (giant shrimp and tuna), Dancing Eel Roll (faux crab, avocado, and eel), and the Bagel Roll (smoked salmon, cream cheese, and cucumber). Cocktails are a draw here, too, along with entertainment in the form of nightly karaoke. *Average main: $23* *Walt Disney World Swan, 1200 Epcot Resorts Blvd.* *407/934–3000* *www.swandolphinrestaurants.com/kimonos* *Reservations not accepted* *No lunch* *1:C4.*

$$$$ STEAKHOUSE **Shula's Steak House.** The hardwood floors, dark-wood paneling, and pictures of former Miami Dolphins coach Don Shula make this restaurant resemble an annex of the NFL Hall of Fame. Among the best selections are the porterhouse and prime rib. Ambitious diners may be interested in the 48-ounce porterhouse challenge: finish the dish and you get a signed picture of coach Don Shula, plus your name will be displayed on a virtual plaque on the restaurant's website. If you're not a carnivore, go for the daily market fish or the huge (up to 4 pounds) Maine lobster. *Average main: $79* *Walt Disney World Dolphin, 1500 Epcot Resorts Blvd.* *407/934–1362* *www.swandolphinrestaurants.com/shulas* *No lunch* *1:C4.*

$$$$ SEAFOOD Fodor's Choice ★ ✕ **Todd English's bluezoo.** Celebrity chef Todd English oversees this cutting-edge seafood eatery, a sleek, modern restaurant that resembles an underwater dining hall, with blue walls and carpeting, aluminum fish suspended from the ceiling, and bubble-like lighting fixtures. The menu is creative and pricey, with entrées like the two-pound Maine "Cantonese lobster," fried and tossed in a sticky soy glaze, and the daily "dancing fish," cooked on an upright rotisserie with an apple-soy marinade. If you don't care for fish, you can opt for seasonal chicken or steak preparations. The children's menu is especially good. *Average main: $44 ✉ Walt Disney World Dolphin, 1500 Epcot Resorts Blvd. ☎ 407/934–1111 🌐 www.thebluezoo.com ⊙ No lunch ✢ 1:C4.*

$$$$ STEAKHOUSE ✕ **Yachtsman Steakhouse.** Aged beef, the attraction at this casual steak house in the upscale Yacht and Beach Club, can be seen mellowing in the glassed-in butcher shop near the entryway. The chefs are proud of their beef in this woodsy, family-friendly spot, and the quality seems to prove it. Meats are hand-cut on the premises. The 12-ounce New York strip with peppercorn-brandy sauce and white cheddar twice-baked potato is quite tasty, but at $48, it's not soft on the wallet. Other menu options include porterhouse, filet mignon, and a fish, such as ahi tuna with farro-fried rice and hibiscus gel. An artisanal cheese platter and nice selections of dessert wines and scotches round out the menu. *Average main: $50 ✉ Yacht and Beach Club, 1700 Epcot Resorts Blvd. ☎ 407/939–3463 🌐 www.disneyworld.disney.go.com/dining ⊙ No lunch ✢ 1:C4.*

DOWNTOWN DISNEY RESORT AREA

$$ AMERICAN ✕ **Olivia's Café.** This is like a meal at Grandma's—provided she lives in Key West and likes to gussy up her grub with trendy twists. The menu ranges from a shrimp pasta with sundried tomato to grilled pork chops with chipotle barbecue sauce and a side of smoked-cheddar mac 'n' cheese. Desserts are indulgent, such as the banana-bread-pudding sundae with bananas Foster topping and vanilla ice cream. The outdoor seating, which overlooks a waterway, is a nice place to dine any time the midsummer heat is not bearing down. *Average main: $21 ✉ Old Key West Resort, 1510 N. Cove Rd. ☎ 407/939–3463 🌐 www.disneyworld.disney.go.com/dining ✢ 1:E3.*

ANIMAL KINGDOM RESORT AREA

$$$$ AFRICAN Fodor's Choice ★ ✕ **Boma—Flavors of Africa.** Boma takes Western-style ingredients and prepares them with an African twist—then invites guests to walk through an African marketplace–style dining room to help themselves at the extraordinary buffet. The dozen or so serving stations have entrées such as roasted pork, Durban-style chicken, spice-crusted beef, and fish served with tamarind and other robust sauces; intriguing salads; and some of the best hummus this side of the Atlantic. Don't pass up the soups, as the coconut-curry seafood stew is excellent. The zebra dome dessert is chocolate mousse covered with white chocolate and striped with dark chocolate. All meals are prix fixe, and prices change seasonally. The South African wine list is outstanding. *Average main:*

$44 ✉ *Animal Kingdom Lodge, 2901 Osceola Pkwy.* ☎ *407/939–3463* 🌐 *www.disneyworld.disney.go.com/dining* ✍ *Reservations essential* ⏰ *No lunch* ✥ *1:A5.*

$$$$ AFRICAN Fodor'sChoice ★ ✕ **Jiko.** The name of this restaurant means "the cooking place" in Swahili, and it is certainly that. The dining area surrounds two big, wood-burning ovens and a grill area where you can watch cooks in North African–style caps working on your meal. The menu here is more African-inspired than purely African, but it does include authentic flavors in entrées like peri-peri chicken flatbread and Zanzibar fish stew. Menu items often change, but entrées might include maize-crusted fish with tomato-butter sauce orspicy Botswana-style beef short ribs with cassava-potato puree. The restaurant offers dozens of wines by the glass, including a large selection of South African vintages. Ask about the wine-and-dine experiences, the Wanyama vehicle safari-dinner combo (only for hotel guests), and the Wednesday wine tastings. [$] *Average main: $36* ✉ *Animal Kingdom Lodge, 2901 Osceola Pkwy.* ☎ *407/939–3463* 🌐 *www.disneyworld.disney.go.com/dining* ✍ *Reservations essential* ⏰ *No lunch* ✥ *1:A5.*

$$$ AFRICAN ✕ **Sanaa.** Most of the flavors are from India, yet Sanaa is really a celebration of the Spice Islands—locales off the coast of Africa that for centuries hosted traders from the world's corners. Exotic yet approachable lunches and dinners make it a true find on the outer edges of the Disney empire; views of zebras and giraffes right out the picture windows are another draw. Potato-pea samosas and an appetizer sampler are good starters. For the main course, be sure to try the tandoori shrimp or the sampler with two of five protein options. There is a reservations-only Dine with an Animal Specialist program consisting of a four-course meal and fascinating company. [$] *Average main: $23* ✉ *Animal Kingdom Villas—Kidani Village, 3701 W. Osceola Pkwy.* ☎ *407/989–3463* 🌐 *www.disneyworld.disney.go.com/dining* ✥ *1:A5.*

UNIVERSAL ORLANDO AREA

With dozens of restaurants, including the world's largest Hard Rock Cafe, Universal Orlando is a mecca for those seeking a meal, plain or fancy. Islands of Adventure has from one to six eateries—not all of them strictly burger-and-fries affairs—in each of its lands. Universal Studios Florida has yet more places for lunch and dinner. And at CityWalk, a dining, retail, and entertainment complex that you have to pass as you leave the two theme parks, you'll find even more tempting eateries. In fact, CityWalk recently added several new eateries including a highly themed Mexican concept, a sushi-burger duo, and a so-called artisan pizza place.

UNIVERSAL STUDIOS

Behind-the-scenes movie action is the theme at Universal Studios Florida, and dining options are purposely cliché versions of restaurants you might see on the silver screen: an old-fashioned Italian joint, a '50s drive-in, an Irish pub, and a seafood house, for example. Be sure to snack on a sundae at a replica of Schwab's Pharmacy, where many starlets were "discovered."

$$ IRISH **Finnegan's Bar & Grill.** In an Irish pub that would look just right in downtown New York during the Ellis Island era, Finnegan's offers classic Irish comfort food like shepherd's pie, corned beef and cabbage, bangers and mash (sausage and mashed potatoes), and fish-and-chips, plus Guinness on tap. If shepherd's pie isn't your thing, opt instead for a steak, burger, entrée salad, or sandwich. Irish folk music, sometimes live, completes the theme. *Average main: $16 New York 407/363–8757 www.universalorlando.com 2:D1.*

$$ SEAFOOD **Lombard's Seafood Grille.** Fresh fried fish, fried shrimp, and assorted other takes on seafood are the specialty at this restaurant designed to resemble a Fisherman's Wharf warehouse from 19th-century San Francisco. You can also get a Boursin steak sandwich with fried onion strips, hamburgers, chicken sandwiches, and big salads. The New England clam chowder is a standout, especially for the price. *Average main: $16 San Francisco 407/224–6400 www.universalorlando.com 2:D1.*

$ AMERICAN **Mel's Drive-In.** At the corner of Hollywood and Vine is a flashy '50s eatery with a pink-and-white 1956 Ford Crown Victoria parked out in front. For burgers and fries, this is one of the best choices in the park, and it comes complete with a roving doo-wop group during peak seasons. You're on vacation, so go ahead and have that extra-thick shake or the decadent chili-cheese fries. Mel's is also a great place to meet up, in case you decide to go your separate ways in the park. *Average main: $9 Hollywood 407/363–8766 www.universalorlando.com Reservations not accepted 2:D1.*

ISLANDS OF ADVENTURE

Here the food always fits the "island," from green eggs and ham at Seuss Landing (open seasonally) to an otherworldly grotto in the Lost Continent to the British fare on tap in the Wizarding World of Harry Potter's Hogsmeade Village.

$ AMERICAN **Confisco Grille.** You could walk right past this full-service restaurant without noticing it, but if you want a good meal and sit-down service, don't pass by too quickly. This is one of the better eateries inside the theme parks. The menu changes often, but typical entrées include pad Thai, grilled or blackened fresh fish of the day with mashed potatoes and sautéed spinach in a lemon-butter-cilantro sauce, and penne puttanesca—the vodka-cream tomato sauce is enhanced with sausage, kalamata olives, fried pepperoncini, and roasted garlic. Wash it all down with refreshing sangria, available by glass, pitcher, and half pitcher. *Average main: $13 Port of Entry 407/224–4404 www.universalorlando.com No dinner. 2:D2.*

$$ ECLECTIC **Mythos.** The name may be Greek, but the dishes are eclectic. The seasonally changing menu usually includes such mainstays as pad Thai and pan-seared salmon with pineapple sauce. The building itself—which looks like a giant rock formation from the outside and a huge cave

Continued on page 147

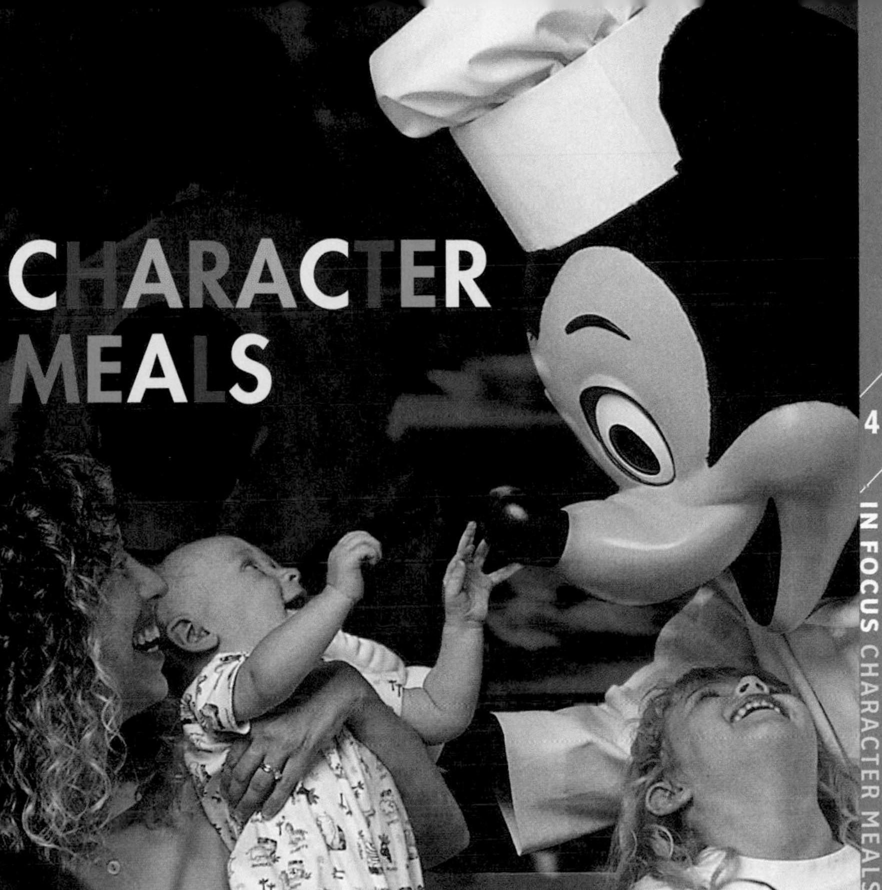

CHARACTER MEALS

Little ones get personal attention from Mickey Mouse at Chef Mickey's.

Character meals are larger-than-life experiences that might be the high point of your child's visit to Walt Disney World or Universal. Mickey, Minnie, and more come alive and welcome your kids as if they were old friends. By Joseph Hayes

These meals, ranging from Alice in Wonderland–themed tea parties to Mickey Mouse–hosted barbecues (and everything in between) are unique, one-on-one opportunities where characters pose for pictures and engage with the little ones. Kids adore hugging or getting an autograph from their favorites; even tots who may be shy at first will usually warm up to their most-loved character. Here we give our picks for the best character breakfast, lunch, and dinner options at both Walt Disney World and Universal, and provide a comprehensive chart, listing all dining experiences for every budget, location, and character preference. Choose the meal that's best for your family, and watch as your youngsters go giddy over meeting Cinderella or Scooby Doo.

Ohana's Best Friend Breakfast at Disney's Polynesian Resort.

BREAKFAST: TOP PICKS

WDW

PRINCESS STORYBOOK DINING at Akershus Royal Banquet Hall, Epcot. Belle, Jasmine, Snow White, the Little Mermaid's Ariel and many more princesses could appear at this medieval castle-styled Norwegian building. Price includes an imaging package. **$43.99 adult; $25.99 child.**

CHEF MICKEY'S FUN TIME BUFFET, Disney's Contemporary Resort. Kids love seeing the monorail pass overhead while greeting the Big Cheese. Chef Mickey's Buffet combines space-age Disney styling with Mickey Mouse, Donald, and the gang, plus the ever-popular Mickey-shaped waffles. **$35.99 adult; $18.99 child.**

'OHANA'S BEST FRIENDS BREAKFAST WITH LILO & STITCH, Disney's Polynesian Resort. The intergalactic Stitch and his human friend, Lilo, join your family in a tropical setting for this very popular breakfast. Every 30 minutes, Mickey and Pluto join in while kids parade around the restaurant with maracas and wide grins. **$24.99 adult; $13.99 child.**

UNIVERSAL

SUPERSTAR CHARACTER BREAKFAST, Universal Studios. SpongeBob Square Pants, Gru from *Despicable Me*, and E.B. from *Hop* are among the superstars who may stop by to say hi at this Universal breakfast, held in Café La Bamba every morning. **$24.99 adult, $10.99 child, plus park admission.**

DRESS UP

If your little ones want to look like a princess when meeting a princess, head to the **Bibbidi Bobbidi Boutique** (407/939–7895) in the World of Disney store at Downtown Disney's Marketplace, where little girls can transform into fairytale princesses or pop divas. There's also a branch right in **Cinderella Castle**. Boys can get their buccaneer on at **The Pirates League** (407/939–2739), next to the Pirates of the Caribbean ride, with costumes, eye patches, and gold teeth. Bibbidi Bobbidi Boutique packages range from **$54.95–$189.95**; Pirates League, **$29.95–$44.95.**

Prices for meals at Disney are prepaid and include tax. Rates increase during peak seasons.

BREAKFAST OPTIONS

CHARACTER MEAL	LOCATION	POSSIBLE CHARACTERS	PRICES; ADULT/CHILD	HOURS
WALT DISNEY WORLD				
Fairytale Dining	Cinderella's Royal Table, Cinderella Castle, Magic Kingdom	Cinderella, the Royal family, Jasmine, Sleeping Beauty, Snow White, Belle	$47.99/$30.99*	Daily
Princess Storybook Dining	Akershus Royal Banquet Hall, Norway Pavilion, Epcot	Ariel, Belle, Jasmine, Snow White, Aurora, Mulan, Alice, and Mary Poppins	$43.99/$25.99*	Daily
Chef Mickey's Fun Time Buffet	Disney's Contemporary Resort	Mickey, Minnie, Goofy, Pluto and Donald	$35.99/$18.99	Daily
Donald's Safari Breakfast	Tusker House Restaurant, Animal Kingdom	Donald, Daisy, Goofy, Mickey	$30.99/$16.99*	Daily
'Ohana's Best Friends Breakfast featuring Lilo & Stitch	Disney's Polynesian Resort	Mickey, Pluto, Lilo, Stitch	$24.99/$13.99	Daily
Supercalifragilistic Breakfast	1900 Park Fare, Disney's Grand Floridian	Mary Poppins, Alice, Mad Hatter	$24.99/$13.99	Daily
Beach Club Breakfast Buffet	Cape May Café, Disney's Yacht and Beach Club Resorts	Goofy, Donald	$28.99/$15.99	Daily
Disney Junior Play 'n Dine	Hollywood & Vine, Disney's Hollywood Studios	Handy Manny, Little Einsteins	$28.99/$15.99	Daily
A Buffet with Character	Crystal Palace, Magic Kingdom	Winnie the Pooh, Tigger, Eeyore, Piglet	$26.99/$14.99*	Daily
Good Morning Character Breakfast	Garden Grove at Walt Disney World Swan Resort	Goofy, Pluto (plus Chip and Dale on Sun.)	$24.99/$15.99	Sat., Sun.
Watercress Café Character Breakfast	Buena Vista Palace Hotel + Spa	Minnie, Pluto, Goofy	$25/$11.95	Sun.
Covington Mill Character Breakfast	Hilton in the Walt Disney World Resort	Mickey, Minnie	Buffet $22.50/$9 Continental $18/$7.25	Sun.
Disney Character Breakfast	Ravello at Four Seasons Resort Orlando	Goofy and Pals		Thurs., Sat.
Disney Character Breakfast	Wyndham Lake Buena Vista Resort	Goofy, Pluto	$24.95/$12.95	Tues., Thurs., Sat.
UNIVERSAL				
Character Breakfast	Jake's American Bar, Lowes Royal Pacific Resort	Gru, Hop, the Minions	$26.99/$14.99	Sun.
Superstar Character Breakfast	Café La Bamba, Universal Islands of Adventure	Gru, SpongeBob, Dora, Hop	$24.99/$10.99*	Daily

*Plus park admission

Leo (from the *Little Einsteins*) pictured here at Disney's Hollywood Studios

LUNCH (OR TEA): TOP PICKS

WDW

DISNEY JUNIOR PLAY 'N DINE, Disney's Hollywood Studios. The Hollywood & Vine Restaurant brings Disney Channel stars to life. Handy Manny and Agent Oso from *Handy Manny*, and June from Disney's *Little Einsteins* march around the room, singing and dancing to the delight of their energetic fans. This is a great choice for toddlers. **$32.99 adult; $17.99 child.**

A BUFFET WITH CHARACTER AT THE CRYSTAL PALACE, Magic Kingdom. A lovely Victorian setting is the perfect place for the old-fashioned and lovable Winnie the Pooh and friends to greet your kids. This is the only meal where you can find characters from the Hundred Acre Wood. Lunch includes upscale goodies for adults, and a separate kids buffet featuring pizza and mac 'n cheese. **$28.99 adult; $15.99 child.**

MY DISNEY GIRL'S PERFECTLY PRINCESS TEA PARTY, Disney's Grand Floridian Resort. Girls ages 3 to 11 enjoy the princess experience with Mom (or Dad). Dressing up is encouraged, and lunch, featuring tea and sandwiches, is served on china plates (apple juice, peanut butter, ham-and-cheese sandwiches, and cake for the little darlings; cheeses and finger sandwiches for adults). Princess Aurora (Sleeping Beauty herself) will make an appearance. Little ones receive a special Disney Girl Princess doll, jewelry, a ribbon tiara and a photo scrapbook page; a nice parting gift considering the hefty price. **$275 for one child and one adult.**

TEA PARTY

Tea and Mad Hatter reigns at the Wonderland Tea Party. A kids-only affair (Moms, take a stroll through the Grand Floridian hotel or book a massage at its spa), "tea" consists of apple juice and cupcakes served by a very silly Hatter (the girls love him) and Alice (girls dress like her). Dress-up is encouraged but not required. Games and stories fill the hour for approximately 25 attendees from ages 4 to 12, and autographed photos are the parting gift. **$49 child.**

Alice at Wonderland Tea Party

Prices for meals at Disney are prepaid and include tax.

WDW LUNCH OPTIONS

CHARACTER MEAL	LOCATION	POSSIBLE CHARACTERS	PRICES; ADULT/CHILD	HOURS
Princess Storybook Dining	Akershus Royal Banquet Hall, Norway Pavilion, Epcot	Ariel, Belle, Jasmine, Snow White, Princess Aurora, Mulan, Alice, Mary Poppins	$46.99/$26.99*	Daily
Fairytale Dining	Conderella's Royal Table, Cinderella Castle, Magic Kingdom	Jasmine, Sleeping Beauty, Snow White, and Belle	$50.99/$32.99*	Daily
Disney Junior Play 'n Dine	Hollywood & Vine, Disney's Hollywood Studios	Handy Manny, *Little Einsteins,* Agent Oso, Jake	$32.99/$17.99*	Daily
A Buffet with Character	Crystal Palace, Magic Kindgom	Winnie the Pooh, Tigger, Eeyore, Piglet	$28.99/$15.99*	Daily
Donald's Dining Safari	Tusker House, Animal Kingdom	Donald Duck	$32.99/$17.99*	Daily
TEA PARTIES				
My Disney Girl's Perfectly Princess Tea Party	Garden Tea Room, Disney's Grand Floridian Hotel	Princess Aurora, Rose Petal	$275 for one child and one adult	Sun, Mon., Weds., Thurs., Fri.
Wonderland Tea Party	1900 Park Fare, Disney's Grand Floridian Hotel	Mad Hatter, Alice	$49	Mon.–Fri.

*Plus park admission

Sleeping Beauty, Ariel and Cinderella's mouse at Akershus Royal Banquet Hall.

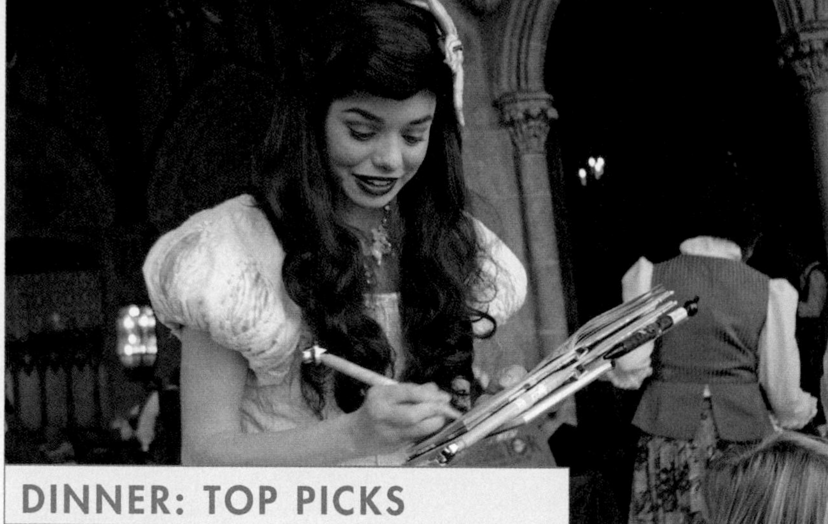

Above, Ariel pictured at Cinderella's Royal Table signing autographs. Below, Cinderella at Cinderella Castle.

DINNER: TOP PICKS

WDW

MICKEY'S BACKYARD BBQ at the Fort Wilderness Resort. This dinner show has everything from dancing and foot-stomping country music, to finger-food goodies like hot dogs and smoked ribs. Cowboy Mickey Mouse is the star of the show. **Tues. and Thurs., Mar.–Dec; $54.99 adult; $31.99 child.**

CINDERELLA'S HAPPILY EVER AFTER DINNER at Disney's Grand Floridian Resort. A dinner buffet of worldly cuisine is complete with Cinderella, Prince Charming, and their family (including the wicked steps) making the rounds. **$39.99 adult; $19.99 child.**

UNIVERSAL

TRATTORIA DEL PORTO, Loews Portofino Bay Hotel. Delectable Italian cuisine will please parents, while Bart Simpson and Scooby Doo may be on hand to distract the kids. Characters appear on Friday nights between 5:30 and 10 pm, coinciding with Pasta Cucina Kitchen, an all-you-can-eat experience where guests create thier own pastas. **Pricing is à la carte.**

THE KITCHEN, Hard Rock Hotel at Universal Orlando. The Simpsons and Scobby-Doo are among those who may appear on Saturdays from 6 to 9 pm. The special child-only Kids' Crib area supplies crayons and cartoon videos, allowing parents to have a break while everyone enjoys their meals. **Pricing is à la carte.**

Prices for meals at Disney are prepaid and include tax. Rates rise in peak seasons.

THE HARDEST TICKET IN TOWN

The magic of fairy tale has never been better realized than at **Cinderella Castle**, where the presence of Princess Charming herself makes this the hottest character meal ticket in Disneytown. With only 130 seats for breakfast, lunch, or dinner, reservations are scarce. Cinderella greets your family in the Castle lobby, pictures (included in the price) are taken, then you are whisked up to your table, where Fairy Godmother and Wicked stepsisters alike stop chairside to chat and sign autographs.

DINNER OPTIONS

CHARACTER MEAL	LOCATION	POSSIBLE CHARACTERS	PRICES; ADULT/CHILD	HOURS
WALT DISNEY WORLD				
Mickey's Backyard BBQ	Fort Wilderness Resort	Mickey, Minnie, and friends	$54.99/$31.99	Tues. and Thurs., Mar.–Dec.
Cinderella's Happily Ever After Dinner	1900 Park Fare, Grand Floridian Resort	Cinderella, Prince Charming, and stepsisters	$39.99/$19.99	Daily
Fairytale Dining	Cinderella's Royal Table, Cinderella Castle, Magic Kingdom	Cinderella, the Royal family, Jasmine, Sleeping Beauty, Snow White, Belle	$58.99/$35.99*	Daily
Chip 'n' Dale's Harvest Feast	Garden Grill, Epcot	Mickey, Chip and Dale	$38.99/$18.99*	Daily
Princess Storybook Dining	Akershus Royal Banquet Hall, Norway Pavilion, Epcot	Ariel, Belle, Jasmine, Snow White, Princess Aurora, Mulan	$51.99/$27.99*	Daily
A Buffet with Character	Crystal Palace, Magic Kingdom	Winnie the Pooh, Tigger, Eeyore, Piglet	a la carte ($35.99/$17.99 for Friday seafood buffet)	Daily
Character Dinner	Garden Grove at Walt Disney World Swan Resort	Goofy, Pluto, Chip and Dale	$29.99 ($35.99 Fri. only) /$13.99	Daily
Chef Mickey's Fun Time Buffet	Chef Mickey's at Disney's Contemporary Resort	Mickey, Donald, Minnie	$43.99/$20.99	Daily
UNIVERSAL				
Universal Orlando Character Dining	Trattoria del Porto at Loews Portofino Bay Hotel	Bart Simpson, Scooby Doo	$25.99/$12	Fri.
Universal Orlando Character Dining	The Kitchen at Hard Rock Hotel	The Simpsons, the Minions	a la carte	Sat.
Universal Orlando Character Dining	Islands Dining Room at Loews Royal Pacific Resort	Scooby Doo, The Simpsons	a la carte	Mon., Wed.

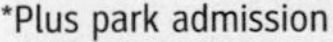

*Plus park admission

Above, Mickey's Backyard BBQ; Left, JoJo at Disney's Hollywood Studios

FAQ

Belle making friends at Cinderella's Royal Table.

■ **How do I make reservations?** Call Disney's Dining Reservation Center at ☎ 407/939–3463 for meals at Disney properties, or check the Disney Dining website at 🌐 www.disneyworld.com/dining. Universal reservations can be made at ☎ 407/224–9255 (theme parks and CityWalk) or ☎ 407/503–3463 (hotels). Resort hotels can be contacted individually; many don't require reservations. Check for last minute cancellations; walking up to the podium and asking for an available table will often bring results.

■ **How far in advance should I book a character meal?** At Disney, reservation dates open 180 days in advance and go very quickly. Disney resort hotel vacationers can book 180 days from the start of their stay rather than the actual desired date, giving them an edge. The most popular meals require a credit card deposit at the time of reservation, which may be charged if cancelled less than 48 hours in advance. Universal character meals, which are relatively easy to get, usually require 30 to 90 days advance booking.

■ **How do I know which characters will be at the meal?** You don't. Cast-members change daily, and all anyone can offer is that you may see a certain list of characters, but usually not all of them. Characters tend to be site-specific and you will see most of the princesses at the castle at any one time. Universal hotels rotate characters regularly.

■ **Are all meals prix-fixe, and what are the different types of meals offered? Buffet, family-style, pre-plated?** Most breakfasts are all-you-can-eat buffets; certain offerings are family-style table service and may be easier for parties if you have multiple children. Lunches and dinner are buffet, family style, or à la carte. Prices for meals at the Disney parks include tax and rise during peak seasons. Some require park admission.

■ **What should I bring to a character meal?** Don't forget your own camera, an autograph book and a large Sharpie (it's hard to handle a tiny pen with big gloves).

(albeit one with plush upholstered seating) from the inside—is enough to grab your attention, but so do sandwiches like crab cake sliders and roast beef paninis with caramelized yellow onions, roasted red peppers, and pepperocinis. Mythos also has a waterfront view of the big lagoon in the center of the theme park. When it's slow in the park, the restaurant is open only for lunch. *Average main: $15 ✉ The Lost Continent ☎ 407/224–4533 🌐 www.universalorlando.com ⊕ 2:D2.*

$ BRITISH **✕ Three Broomsticks.** Now Harry Potter fans can taste pumpkin juice (with hints of honey and vanilla) and butterbeer (sort of like bubbly butterscotch cream soda; some say it tastes like shortbread cookies). They're on the menu along with British foodstuffs at this Hogsmeade restaurant modeled after the fantasy books. Rickety staircases and gaslit chandeliers set the tone for the counter-service restaurant, where families gobble down ample portions of shepherd's pie, fish-and-chips, char-grilled ribs, and smoked chicken. In the adjacent Hog's Head pub, a faux hog's head sneers now and then. *Average main: $12 ✉ Wizarding World of Harry Potter ☎ 407/224–4233 🌐 www.universalorlando.com ⚠ Reservations not accepted ⊕ 2:D2.*

4

CITYWALK

Restaurants, bars, clubs, shops, live entertainment, and movie theaters make Universal CityWalk an attraction on its own. The upbeat expanse serves as the entrance to both Universal Orlando theme parks—you can't reach the parks from the parking lot without walking through—and is an after-dark destination for tourists and locals alike.

$$ MEXICAN **✕ Antojitos Authentic Mexican Food.** The massive Antojitos opened in 2014, bringing the specialties of Mexican cantinas and food carts to CityWalk. The outside looks like it's been spray-painted with shocking pastels. Inside, the grand space is chic yet rustic, sparse but dotted with Mexican folk art. Neon sculptures on the ceiling depict hip versions of Day of the Dead figures. The larger downstairs area has a lower-priced menu filled with tacos, enchiladas, and the like. Start with guacamole, made table-side, and follow up with the duck tacos topped with slaw and green sauce. The quieter upstairs, with a more expensive menu and a lower noise level, serves entrées like the excellent coffee-crusted rib-eye steak with fire-roasted vegetables. End with a coffee crème brûlée with churros or the molten dulce cake. The restaurant stocks 200 tequilas. *Average main: $21 ✉ 6000 Universal Blvd. ☎ 407/224–2807 ⊙ No lunch ⊕ 2:E2.*

$$$$ CAJUN Fodor's Choice ★ **✕ Emeril's Orlando.** The popular eatery is a culinary shrine to Emeril Lagasse, the famous TV chef who occasionally makes an appearance. And although the modern interior of the restaurant with its 30-foot ceilings, blond woods, second-story wine loft, and lots of galvanized steel looks nothing like the French Quarter, the hardwood floors and linen tablecloths create an environment befitting the stellar nature of the cuisine. Entrées, which change frequently, may include andouille-crusted pan-roasted redfish with creole meunière sauce, pork chop with green mole sauce and tamarind glaze, and barbecue-glazed salmon with homemade andouille. Reservations are usually essential, but there's a

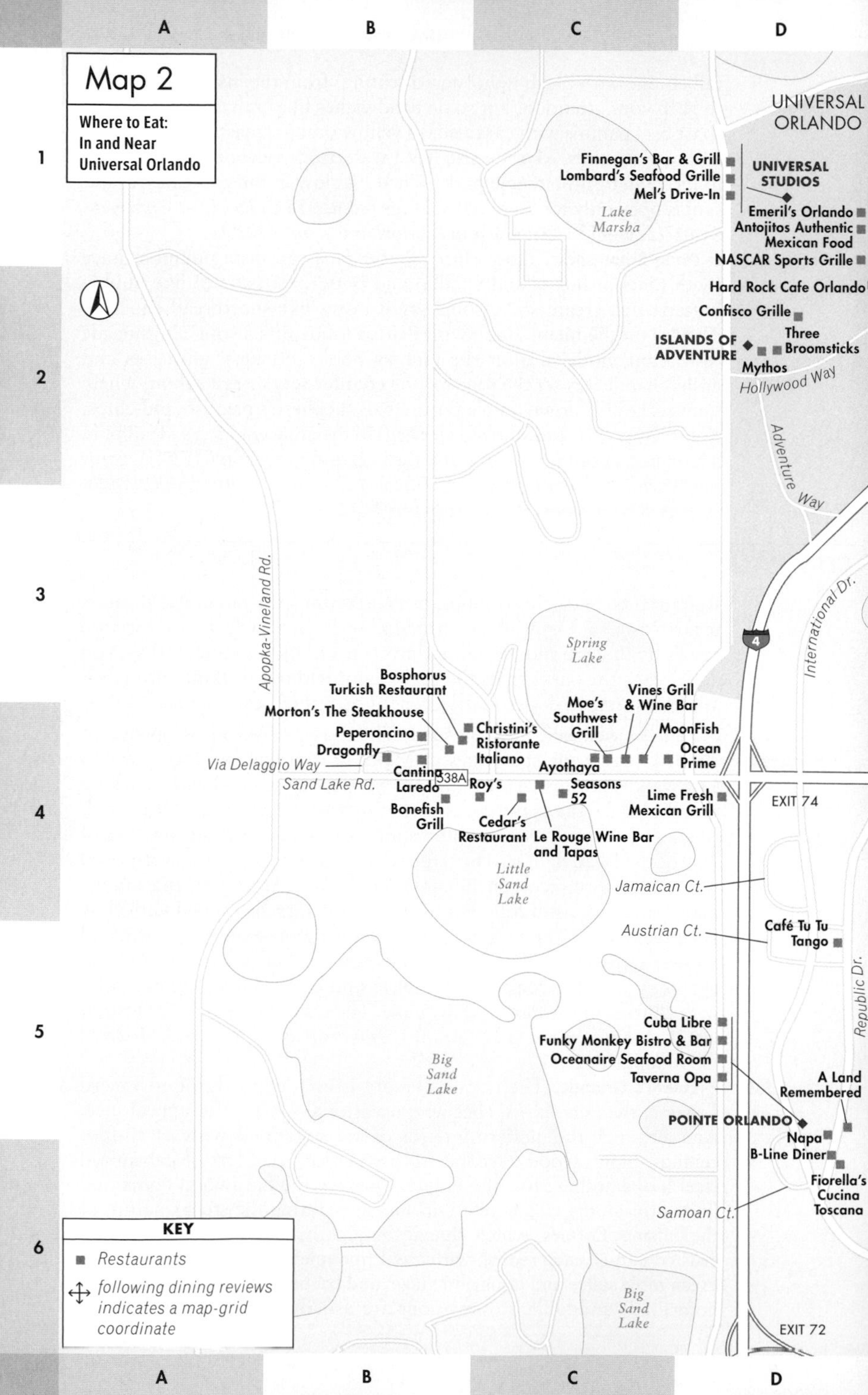

A
B
C
D
Map 2
Where to Eat:
In and Near
Universal Orlando
1
2
3
4
5
6
UNIVERSAL
ORLANDO
Finnegan's Bar & Grill
Lombard's Seafood Grille
Mel's Drive-In
UNIVERSAL
STUDIOS
Lake
Marsha
Emeril's Orlando
Antojitos Authentic
Mexican Food
NASCAR Sports Grille
Hard Rock Cafe Orlando
Confisco Grille
ISLANDS OF
ADVENTURE
Three
Broomsticks
Mythos
Hollywood Way
Adventure
Way
Apopka-Vineland Rd.
International Dr.
4
Spring
Lake
Bosphorus
Turkish Restaurant
Morton's The Steakhouse
Christini's
Ristorante
Italiano
Peperoncino
Dragonfly
Via Delaggio Way
Sand Lake Rd.
Cantina
Laredo
538A
Roy's
Moe's
Southwest
Grill
Vines Grill
& Wine Bar
MoonFish
Ocean
Prime
Ayothaya
Seasons
52
Lime Fresh
Mexican Grill
EXIT 74
Bonefish
Grill
Cedar's
Restaurant
Le Rouge Wine Bar
and Tapas
Little
Sand
Lake
Jamaican Ct.
Austrian Ct.
Café Tu Tu
Tango
Republic Dr.
Cuba Libre
Funky Monkey Bistro & Bar
Oceanaire Seafood Room
Taverna Opa
Big
Sand
Lake
A Land
Remembered
POINTE ORLANDO
Napa
B-Line Diner
Fiorella's
Cucina
Toscana
Samoan Ct.
KEY
Restaurants
following dining reviews
indicates a map-grid
coordinate
Big
Sand
Lake
EXIT 72

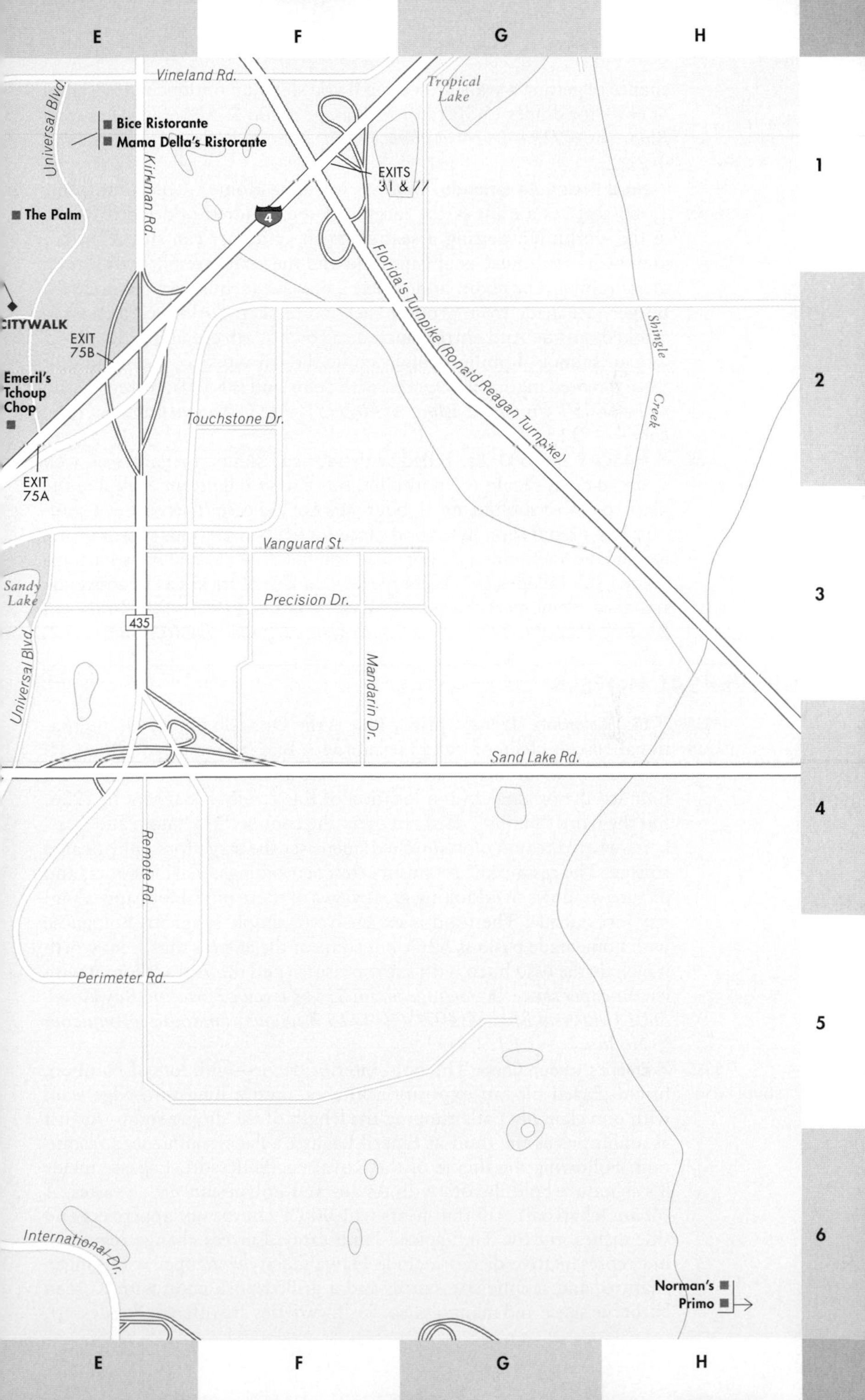

E
F
G
H
1
2
3
4
5
6
Vineland Rd.
Tropical Lake
Universal Blvd.
Bice Ristorante
Mama Della's Ristorante
Kirkman Rd.
EXITS 31 & 77
The Palm
4
Florida's Turnpike (Ronald Reagan Turnpike)
CITYWALK
EXIT 75B
Shingle Creek
Emeril's Tchoup Chop
Touchstone Dr.
EXIT 75A
Vanguard St.
Sandy Lake
Precision Dr.
435
Mandarin Dr.
Universal Blvd.
Sand Lake Rd.
Remote Rd.
Perimeter Rd.
International Dr.
Norman's
Primo

chance of getting a walk-in seating if you show up for lunch (11:30 am) or early for dinner (5:30 pm). *Average main: $39 6000 Universal Blvd. 407/224–2424 www.emerils.com Reservations essential ↔ 2:E2.*

$$ AMERICAN **Hard Rock Cafe Orlando.** Built to resemble Rome's Colosseum, this 1,000-seat restaurant is the largest of the hundred-odd Hard Rocks in the world, but getting a seat at lunch or dinner can still require a long wait. The music is always loud and the walls are filled with rock memorabilia. The chain underwent a massive menu overhaul in 2014. Burgers are made from ground beef and brisket. Barbecued meats are smoked on-site. And entrées include a cowboy rib eye and grilled Norwegian salmon. Imbibers might enjoy the Air Mexico, a sampling of three flavored margaritas served with chips and salsa. *Average main: $21 6050 Universal Blvd. 407/351–7625 www.hardrockcafe.com ↔ 2:D2.*

$$ AMERICAN **NASCAR Sports Grille.** Filled with race-car simulator games as well as arcade and racing memorabilia, this eatery might not look like the place to grab a sublime meal, but that's not the case. This theme restaurant has a reputation as a good place for grub. Selections worth trying include the Southern-style pot roast and the slow-roasted baby back rib platter; the Talladega cheeseburger with a side of fries is a cut above the standard theme-park burger. *Average main: $19 6000 Universal Blvd. 407/224–7223 www.nascarsportsgrilleorlando.com ↔ 2:E2.*

UNIVERSAL HOTELS

$$$$ ITALIAN **Bice Ristorante.** Trendy, pricey Bice is the Orlando unit of an international upscale chain of Italian restaurants. Bice (pronounced "*BEACH*-ay") is an Italian nickname for Beatrice, as in Beatrice Ruggeri, who founded the original Milan location of this family restaurant in 1926. But the word "family" does not carry the connotation "mom and pop" here, where cream-color starched linens set the stage for sophisticated cuisine. The restaurant retains its frescoed ceilings, marble floors, and picture windows overlooking great views of the artificial (but appealing) bay just outside. The food is expensive (a simple spaghetti Bolognese with homemade pasta is $26), but some of the entrées that seem worth it include the osso buco with saffron risotto and the veal scallopini with lemon-caper sauce. *Average main: $35 Loews Portofino Bay Hotel, 5601 Universal Blvd. 407/503–1415 www.orlando.bicegroup.com No lunch ↔ 2:E1.*

$$$$ SOUTH PACIFIC **Emeril's Tchoup Chop.** The bold interior decor—with lots of bamboo, bright glazed tile, an exposition kitchen, and a long zero-edge pool with porcelain lily pads running the length of the dining room—is just as ambitious as the food at Emeril Lagasse's Pacific-influenced restaurant. Following the theme of the Royal Pacific Resort, Lagasse melds his signature bold flavors with Asian- and Polynesian-fusion tastes. A *robata* (charcoal) grill that heats to 1,000°F churns out appetizers and side dishes; try the Thai-spiced lamb satay. Entrées change regularly, but representative dishes include Hawaiian-style snapper with ginger, cilantro, and sesame soy sauce; and a grilled pork chop with Korean barbecue sauce and mango salsa. Sushi varieties are offered. For dessert,

get the Hawaiian-style *malasadas* doughnuts. They're served with three sauces in plastic bottles; you insert the tip into the donuts and squirt in the fillings yourself. *Average main: $32* *Loews Royal Pacific Resort, 6300 Hollywood Way* *407/503–2467* *www.emerils.com* *Reservations essential* *2:E2.*

$$$ ITALIAN **Mama Della's Ristorante.** This playfully themed Italian restaurant happens to have excellent food. The premise is that you're eating at a home-turned-restaurant owned by an Italian woman. That woman, Mama Della, is played by an actress, whose warmth enhances the experience (as does the serenade by an accordianist, guitar player, and vocalist). The menu features Italian classics like chicken parmigiana and lasagna as well as more ambitious dishes like salmon with fennel sofrito and braised lamb with eggplant caponata. Outdoor seating on the patio provides a view of the hotel's nightly *Musica Della Notte* (*Music of the Night*) opera show. *Average main: $29* *Loews Portofino Bay Hotel, 5601 Universal Blvd.* *407/503–3463* *www.loewshotels.com* *No lunch* *2:E1.*

4

$$$$ STEAKHOUSE **The Palm.** With its dark-wood interior and hundreds of framed celebrity caricatures, this restaurant resembles its famed New York City namesake. For most diners the steaks are the star of the show. Aged beef is the predominant house specialty, and the gargantuan lobsters are nearly as popular as the fine steaks. For fish lovers, salmon is a nice choice, as it is broiled and served with mango salsa. Crab cakes, another option, are made of jumbo-lump crabmeat and paired with chipotle tartar sauce. The Italian specialties are top-notch versions of favorites like veal parmigiana. *Average main: $38* *Hard Rock Hotel, 5800 Universal Blvd.* *407/503–7256* *www.thepalm.com* *No lunch* *2:E1.*

ORLANDO METRO AREA

KISSIMMEE

Although Orlando is the focus of most theme-park visitors, Kissimmee is actually closer to Walt Disney World. It offers a huge number of dining choices, many of which are of the "burger barn" variety in accordance with the area's budget lodging options, but there are notable exceptions. While the restaurants featured here are minutes from Walt Disney World's southern tip, allow about 15 to 25 minutes to travel from WDW or about 35 minutes from I-Drive.

$$$$ STEAKHOUSE **Old Hickory Steakhouse.** This upscale steak house is designed to look like rustic cabins in the Everglades. Beyond the playful facade is a polished restaurant with a classic steak-house menu—bone-in rib eye, porterhouse, and filet mignon, supplemented by rack of lamb, veal chop, and Atlantic salmon, all priced for the hotel's convention-goers. The chef gets creative with appetizers like a warm pear-and-goat-cheese tart, but most are standards such as onion soup, shrimp cocktail, and tomato-onion salad. Artisanal cheese plates are on the menu, and desserts are interesting, such as fudge-dipped derby pie. *Average main:*

$50 ✉ *Gaylord Palms Resort, 6000 W. Osceola Pkwy., I–4 Exit 65* ☎ *407/586–1600* 🌐 *www.gaylordpalms.com* ⏲ *No lunch* ✣ *1:E6.*

$$$$ SEAFOOD ✕ **Sunset Sam's, A Key West Grill.** Sunset Sam's looks gimmicky—its bar and dining room encircle two 60-foot masts—yet the food is both excellent and affordable. Starters on the New World Floridian cuisine menu are big enough to be a meal and include crab bisque and conch salsa with kettle chips. Entrées are pricey and might be grilled swordfish with chimichurri or jumbo shrimp with coconut milk cornbread, semolina fondue, and tomato-bacon jam. Entrée salads, priced below $23, are a more wallet-friendly option. For dessert, go for the traditional key lime tart. $ *Average main: $32* ✉ *Gaylord Palms Resort, 6000 W. Osceola Pkwy., I–4 Exit 65* ☎ *407/586–1101* 🌐 *www.gaylordpalms.com* ✣ *1:E6.*

CELEBRATION

If this not-so-small town with early-20th-century-style homes and perfectly manicured lawns reminds you a bit of Main Street, U.S.A, in the Magic Kingdom, it should. The utopian residential community was created by Disney, with all the Disney attention to detail. Every view of every street is warm and pleasant, though the best are out the windows of the town's Market Street–area restaurants, most of which face a pastoral (though man-made) lake. Homes here are on the expensive side, and restaurants reflect the upscale nature of the local customers. To get here, take Interstate 4 to Exit 64 and follow the "Celebration" signs.

$$ ITALIAN ✕ **Café d'Antonio.** The wood-burning oven and grill are worked pretty hard here, and the mountains of hardwood used in the open kitchen flavor the best of the menu—pizza, grilled fish and chicken, steaks and chops, and even the lasagna. A standout is the wood-fired veal chop stuffed with prosciutto, fontina, and spinach. For a less expensive meal, you can pick your own ingredients for a personal, wood-oven pizza. The terrace overlooking the lake is now enclosed and air-conditioned. $ *Average main: $21* ✉ *691 Front St.* ☎ *407/566–2233* 🌐 *www.antoniosonline.com* ✣ *1:E6.*

$$$ SEAFOOD ✕ **Celebration Town Tavern.** This New England–cuisine eatery, operated by a family with Boston roots, has a double personality. The interior is a brass, glass, and dark-wood-paneling kind of place, while the outside patio has table seating plus the Paddy O' Bar. The food ranges from landlubber treats like baby back ribs, prime rib, and half-pound burgers (from $8) to exquisite seafood including Ipswich clams, lobster rolls, Boston scrod, and 2-pound lobsters (all flown in from Boston), plus, on occasion, a salute to the Sunshine State with Florida stone crabs in season. While the place has a polished demeanor, there are plenty of menu choices right out of a working-class Boston bar—meatball hoagies, Philly cheesesteak sandwiches, and Buffalo-style chicken wings. For dessert there's great—what else?—Boston cream pie. $ *Average main: $26* ✉ *721 Front St.* ☎ *407/566–2526* 🌐 *www.thecelebrationtowntavern.com* ✣ *1:E6.*

$$$ LATIN AMERICAN ✕ **Columbia Restaurant.** Celebration's branch of this family-owned high-end chain is generally as good as the original in Tampa, which has been

operating for a century now. Start with the garlic shrimp or the empanadas stuffed with beef, raisins, and olives. For your main course, zero in on the paella—either *à la Valenciana,* with clams, shrimp, scallops, squid, chicken, and pork mixed into tasty yellow rice; or the *paella campesina,* a "farmer's" paella from Spain, with no seafood, but beef, pork, chorizo, and chicken. The best dessert, *brazo gitano cien anos* (sponge cake with strawberries that is soaked in syrup and Spanish sherry and flambéed table-side), was created for the restaurant chain's 100th anniversary in 2005, and is well worth its price just for the show. $ *Average main: $23* ✉ *649 Front St.* ☎ *407/566–1505* 🌐 *www.columbiarestaurant.com* ✣ *1:E6.*

$ AMERICAN

Market Street Café. The menu at this upscale diner ranges from breakfast classics served all day, like French toast and the house-special baked-potato omelet, to comfort classics like beef Stroganoff and homemade chicken potpie. In addition to a hearty version of the quintessential American hamburger (best enjoyed with a creamy milk shake), there are also salmon and portobello burgers for the cholesterol wary. An outdoor seating section in front of the restaurant makes for a pleasant dining destination. $ *Average main: $12* ✉ *701 Front St.* ☎ *407/566–1144* 🌐 *www.market-street-cafe.com* *Reservations not accepted* ✣ *1:E6.*

4

INTERNATIONAL DRIVE

A number of restaurants are scattered among the hotels that line International Drive—the best along the manicured area near the Convention Center, at the very northern tip near the outlet stores, and in upscale convention hotels. Many are branches of chains, from fast-food spots to theme coffee shops and up, but the food here can be quite good. To get to the area, take Interstate 4 Exit 72 or 74A. Count on it taking up to half an hour from the Kissimmee area or from a WDW property.

$$$ AMERICAN

B-Line Diner. As you might expect from its location in the Hyatt Regency, this slick modern diner is not exactly cheap, but the salads, sandwiches, and griddle foods are tops. The classic combo—a thick, juicy burger with fries and a milk shake—is done beautifully. And there are lots of selections you'd never expect to find here, like an appetizer of potato chips with blue cheese sauce and rosemary (on the late-night menu only) and an entrée of miso-broiled Atlantic salmon with eggplant caponata and ponzu-butter sauce. It's open 24 hours, so if you crave a Reuben or Oreo chocolate mousse cake at 3 am, B-Line is the place to go. $ *Average main: $24* ✉ *Hyatt Regency Orlando, 9801 International Dr.* ☎ *407/284–1234* 🌐 *orlando.regency.hyatt.com* ✣ *2:D6.*

$$$ ECLECTIC

Café Tu Tu Tango. The food here is served tapas-style—everything is appetizer size but plentiful, and relatively inexpensive. If you want a compendium of cuisines at one go, try the black-bean soup with cilantro sour cream, guava barbecue-glazed pork ribs, hazelnut-lemongrass fish, and spiced alligator bites. The wine list includes more than 35 wines from several countries, with all but a handful by the bottle and the glass, and 50-plus craft beers. The restaurant is designed to resemble an artist's loft; artists paint at easels while diners take a culinary trip around the world. Belly dancers, flamenco dancers, Bolivian dancers, and African drummers are among the entertainers who perform in the evening. Thanks to a patio, diners can also share their small plates alfresco. *Average main: $23 8625 International Dr. 407/248–2222 www.cafetututango.com Reservations not accepted 2:D5.*

$$$ CUBAN **Cuba Libre.** The dining rooms at this Cuban restaurant feel as if they're movie sets of Old Havana, with dramatic touches upstairs and down. Carved second-level balconies, "weathered" facades, and stained glass replicate the Cuban city. Start your meal with a meat-filled arepa rellena corn cake or a platter of two to four empananadas filled with savory ground beef and olives, chicken, cheese, or pork. For the main course, consider the *churrasco a la Cubana* (grilled skirt steak) with a lemon-onion sauce plus a watercress-mushroom escabeche salad. Go traditional with a pressed Cuban sandwich, which is part of classic platter with black bean soup, salad, and chips, or a good version of the traditional Latin dish *ropa vieja*, shredded beef brisket with tomatoes, bell peppers, and onions in a red wine sauce. *Average main: $26 Pointe Orlando, 9101 International Dr. 407/226–1600 www.cubalibrerestaurant.com No lunch. 2:D6.*

$$$ ITALIAN **Fiorella's Cucina Toscana.** The Tuscan cooking at this quiet little eatery—tucked behind the Orange County Convention Center in the Westin Imagine—is worth the short trip. The decor is vibrant, with dark woods accented by bright, custom-made glass flowers. Worthy dinner selections include lobster ravioli with crabmeat and brown butter, and chicken with prosciutto, sage, mushrooms, and a Marsala wine sauce. Finish your meal with the delectable tiramisu. *Average main: $26 Westin Orlando Universal Blvd., 9501 Universal Blvd. 407/233–2950 www.fiorellasorlando.com 2:D6.*

$$$$ ECLECTIC **Funky Monkey Bistro & Bar.** Funky Monkey brings to the Convention Center area an enticing mix of creative American cuisine, sushi, interesting wines, and occasional entertainment—including Friday- and Saturday-night drag shows. Fried goat cheese, sweet potato-wrapped grouper, and "drunken" salad with rum-soaked pineapple are typical choices. For a respite from touristy watering holes, grab a seat at the low-key bar and sip a glass of chardonnay with a plate of seasoned-rice "monkey balls." There is a second Funky Monkey in Orlando's colorful Mills 50 neighborhood; it has a warmer, more romantic atmosphere. *Average main: $32 Pointe Orlando, 9101 International Dr. 407/418–9463 www.funkymonkeywine.com No lunch Sun. 2:D6.*

$$$$ AMERICAN **Napa.** Within the massive Hyatt Regency Orlando convention hotel, Napa aims to reproduce the concept of a Wine Country restaurant, preparing seasonal farm-to-table foods using ingredients from local producers. The contemporary dining room is a sophisticated space done in gold, brick, and tan, and jazzy tunes play in the background and glass wine racks lining the walls. Begin your meal with a sampling of five seasonal appetizers. Then move on to one of the creative entrées, like the Florida rock shrimp and mussels spaghetini with creamy Maine lobster sauce or whole fried yellowtail snapper with tropical salsa. The menu has a small section specifically for vegans and vegetarians.

$ *Average main: $32* ✉ *Hyatt Regency Orlando, 9801 International Dr.* ☎ *407/284–1234* 🌐 *orlando.regency.hyatt.com* ⊕ *2:D6.*

$$$$ SEAFOOD ✕ **Oceanaire Seafood Room.** Don't let the 1930s-era ocean-liner interior fool you: as theme restaurants go, this place is a good one, packing everything from—depending on the season—Canadian walleye, Costa Rican swordfish, or Ecuadorian mahimahi. The straightforward preparation here—grilled or broiled, brushed with lemon butter—is welcome. The chefs change the menu every day based on what's fresh. Lobster bisque is a standouts, as is the chilled shellfish platter and the day's fish specialties. Make sure to save room for the baked Alaska, which is flamed at the table. $ *Average main: $45* ✉ *Pointe Orlando, 9101 International Dr.* ☎ *407/363–4801* 🌐 *www.theoceanaire.com* ⏲ *No lunch* ⊕ *2:D6.*

4

$$$ GREEK ✕ **Taverna Opa.** This high-energy Greek restaurant bills itself as offering "fun with a capital F." Here the ouzo flows like a mountain stream, the Greek music almost reaches the level of a rock concert, and the roaming belly dancers actively encourage diners to take part in the mass Zorba dancing, which often happens on the tops of dining tables. The only thing missing is the Greek restaurant tradition of throwing dinner plates, made up in part by the throwing of torn-up paper napkins, which sometimes reaches near-blizzard level. The food, by the way, is also excellent. Standouts include traditional staples like spanakopita, *saganaki* (the traditional flaming cheese appetizer), *avgolemono* (lemony chicken-rice soup), and perhaps the most famous Greek entrée, moussaka. Family-style meals for groups of four and up are available at $33 and $44 per person. The best dessert is the baklava. $ *Average main: $27* ✉ *Pointe Orlando, 9101 International Dr.* ☎ *407/351–8660* 🌐 *www.opaorlando.com* ⊕ *2:D6.*

SOUTH ORLANDO

$$$$ STEAKHOUSE ✕ **A Land Remembered.** The name of this award-winning restaurant (from a novel about Florida by Patrick Smith) is somewhat enigmatic, but then so is the location (in the golf clubhouse of the Rosen Shingle Creek resort). But if you're a steak lover, you'll find this place worth seeking out. Notable choices include the 20-ounce chateaubriand-for-two carved tableside and the $54 24-ounce porterhouse with a Vidalia onion gravy, which shouldn't disappoint the most ardent beef connoisseur, sticker price notwithstanding. If you don't like beef, you're still in a good place here, with choices that include cedar plank–broiled fish with onion-and-chive butter, and lamb Tequesta, rubbed with roasted garlic and dry mustard. $ *Average main: $58* ✉ *Rosen Shingle Creek, 9939 Universal Blvd.* ☎ *407/996–9939* 🌐 *www.landrememberedrestaurant.com* ⏲ *No lunch* ⊕ *2:D6.*

$$$$ FRENCH ✕ **Le Coq au Vin.** This traditional French restaurant, owned by Sandy and Reimund Pitz, is hideaway located in a small nondescript house in South Orlando. It seats 100 people in three quaint dining rooms. Knickknacks cover the walls, creating a home-style atmosphere. The namesake dish is always available, and select entrées are available in half portions. For dessert, try the Grand Marnier, chocolate, or raspberry

CLOSE UP

Popular Chain Restaurants

When all you want is a quick bite, consider these chain restaurants. They seem to crop up everywhere, and all have tables where you can sit for a few moments before heading back out to the shops and attractions.

Anthony's Coal-Fired Pizza: Thin-crust pizzas with generous toppings like arugula and pepperoni are baked—charred, really—in a coal-fired oven. The chicken wings are also popular in this bustling space. 🌐 *www.anthonyscoalfiredpizza.com*

Bubbalou's Bodacious Bar-B-Que: A quintet of local smokers serves up mounds of Southern barbecue, from baby back ribs to pulled-pork sandwiches. The restaurant on Kirkman Road and Conroy-Windermere Road is minutes from Universal Orlando. 🌐 *www.bubbalous.com*

Einstein Bros. Bagels: For a light breakfast or lunch, Einstein's satisfies with a menu of bagels, wraps, salads, and sandwiches. 🌐 *www.einsteinbros.com*

First Watch: Breakfast classics like pancakes and waffles make First Watch a popular choice for locals, who line up on weekends for Key West "crepeggs" (a crepe filled with eggs that have been scrambled with turkey, avocado, bacon, tomatoes, and Monterey Jack cheese), and Floridian French toast with bananas, kiwi, and berries. 🌐 *www.firstwatch.com*

Five Guys Burgers and Fries: This burger joint has a nearly cultlike following for its freshly ground beef. Fifteen toppings are available for no charge, and the fries are freshly cut. 🌐 *www.fiveguys.com*

Greens & Grille: Thanks to organic ingredients and house-made soups and dressings, Greens & Grille is a leap beyond typical fast-casual eateries. You can order a signature sandwich or salad (the Fall, with roasted beets, is superb) or customize. Beer and wine are available. Outlets are near the Mall at Millenia and the University of Central Florida. 🌐 *www.greensandgrille.com*

Jimmy John's: Lunchtime lines are out the door at Orlando's 17 Jimmy John's, where the "world's greatest gourmet sandwiches" are essentially subs and clubs. 🌐 *www.jimmyjohns.com*

Johnny Rockets: Burgers, chili dogs, and frothy milk shakes are served in a vibrant, '50s diner–style environment here. There are three branches near the theme parks. 🌐 *www.johnnyrockets.com*

Panera Bread: Fresh-baked pastries and bagels are the mainstays here, although you can grab a hearty and inexpensive meal like smoked-turkey panino on three-cheese bread or a bowl of soup served in a hollowed-out sourdough loaf. 🌐 *www.panerabread.com*

Pei Wei Asian Diner: Bold flavors from all corners of Asia come together at these fast-casual restaurants, where a hearty noodle bowl, orange-peel beef, or sweet-and-sour tofu will come in at less than $10. 🌐 *www.peiwei.com*

TooJay's Gourmet Deli: A New York deli it ain't, but the TooJay's chain offers a welcome pastrami fix for those with a yen for salty meat on crusty seeded rye. 🌐 *www.toojays.com*

soufflé. *Average main: $31* ✉ *4800 S. Orange Ave.* ☎ *407/851–6980* 🌐 *www.lecoqauvinrestaurant.com* ⏲ *No lunch. Closed Mon.* ✣ *3:D6.*

$$$$ ECLECTIC Fodor's Choice ★ **Norman's.** Celebrity-chef Norman Van Aken brings impressive credentials to the restaurant that bears his name, as you might expect from the headline eatery in the Ritz-Carlton Orlando Grande Lakes. Van Aken's culinary roots go back to the Florida Keys, where he's credited with creating "Floribbean" cuisine, a blend that is part Key West and part Caribbean—although he now weaves in flavors from all continents. The Orlando operation is a formal, sleek restaurant with marble floors, starched tablecloths, servers in ties and vests, eight certified sommeliers, and a creative, if expensive, menu. In addition to exceptional ceviches and a signature appetizer called Down Island French toast made with Curacao-marinated foie gras, favorites include a Mongolian-marinated veal chop, pan-cooked Florida snapper with citrus butter, and pork Havana with "21st-century mole sauce." A six-course tasting menu is $95, more with beverage pairings. Covered terrace seating is also available. *Average main: $46* ✉ *Ritz-Carlton Orlando Grande Lakes, 4000 Central Florida Pkwy.* ☎ *407/393–4333* 🌐 *www.normans.com* ⏲ *No lunch* ✣ *2:I16.*

$$$$ ITALIAN Fodor's Choice ★ **Primo.** James Beard Award winner Melissa Kelly cloned her Italian-organic Maine restaurant in an upscale Orlando hotel and brought her farm-to-table sensibilities with her. Here the daily dinner menu pays tribute to Sicily's lighter foods, made with produce grown in the hotel garden. Homemade pasta is served with veal meatballs or braised rabbit; if the butternut-squash ravioli with butter-poached Maine lobster is available, order it. Dry-aged prime New York strip steak is enhanced with crispy potato and horseradish raviolinis. Fish plays prominently, such as a refreshing Florida snapper fillet with Italian couscous and heirloom tomato sauce. Desserts are just as special, with the likes of warm Belgian chocolate *budino* (pudding) cake or hot zeppole tossed in cinnamon and sugar. *Average main: $38* ✉ *JW Marriott Orlando Grande Lakes, 4040 Central Florida Pkwy.* ☎ *407/393–4444* 🌐 *www.primorestaurant.com* ⏲ *No lunch* ✣ *2:H6.*

LAKE BUENA VISTA

Lake Buena Vista, just to the east of Downtown Disney, is essentially a collection of midscale hotels, convention hotels, and chain restaurants catering to off-site visitors to Disney World. The restaurants tend to be well run, well kept, and affordable, with a few destination dining rooms within convention hotels.

$$$$ SEAFOOD **Hemingway's.** Business travelers and vacationers put on their khakis and sundresses to dine in this quiet seafood house loosely themed around Ernest Hemingway's travels. In fact, the Papa Doble cocktail, with rum and grapefruit juice, is reputedly of Papa's own creation. The woodsy dining room provides views of the Hyatt Regency's manicured grounds, a treat in summer when the sun sets late. Choose the Hemingway's "Cayo Hueso" crab cake, served with corn salsa and sweet corn coconut grits. Other options are the Duvall Street shrimp scampi, a tribute to the author's love of shrimp, here served with truffled pasta,

or the paella, a nod to the time he spent in Spain. Because the Keys were another favorite spot, the baked Alaska key lime is a fitting meal ender. *Average main: $32 Hyatt Regency Grand Cypress, 1 Grand Cypress Blvd. 407/239–3854 www.hyattgrandcypress.com No lunch 1:F3.*

$$$ ITALIAN **La Luce by Donna Scala.** Having made a name for herself at California's Bistro Don Giovanni, Donna Scala brought the same Italian cuisine with a Napa Valley farm-fresh flair to this upscale Hilton at the edge of Disney World. The walls are decorated with chalk art, which changes twice a year. Equal effort goes into the menu, where pastas are made fresh. Try the ricotta gnocchi with wild mushrooms and artichokes, the rib eye with fennel, or a simple seared salmon fillet with tomato chive butter sauce. *Average main: $30 Hilton Orlando Bonnett Creek, 14100 Bonnet Creek Resort La., Bonnet Creek 407/597–3600 www.laluceorlando.com No lunch 1:E5.*

$$$$ EUROPEAN **The Venetian Room.** This fine-dining restaurant inside one of Lake Buena Vista's many convention hotels may have been designed as a place for execs on expense accounts to seal deals, but it has also become a haven for nontrendy locals seeking an old-fashioned romantic retreat. The architecture alone—it looks like Renaissance Venice—is enough to lure you. The entry door is topped by a giant copper dome, and the dining room has dark-wood furniture, crystal chandeliers, and carpets that could grace a European palace. Deep booths are surrounded on two sides by etched glass. The waiters wear tuxes. Begin with the signature lobster bisque, an ultrarich soup topped with flaky pastry. Follow that with a good filet mignon, Dover sole, or pan-seared veal chop in porcini cream sauce. Grand Marnier soufflé is the signature dessert. *Average main: $40 Caribe Royale All-Suite Hotel & Convention Center, 8101 World Center Dr. 407/238–8060 www.thevenetianroom.com No lunch. Closed Sun. and Mon. 1:F5.*

SAND LAKE ROAD

This part of Orlando is an anomaly: it's a growing collection of appealing strip centers filled with restaurants—from fast-casual panini and Asian-food restaurants to fine-dining establishments—that's about equidistant from well-to-do residential neighborhoods, Walt Disney World, Universal Orlando, SeaWorld, and International Drive. The result is known as Restaurant Row, and it's the only place in town where locals dine beside convention goers and adventuresome theme-park visitors. From Interstate 4, take the Sand Lake Road exit, 74A.

$$$ THAI **Ayothaya.** Although it is not as fancy or as highly themed as its Sand Lake neighbors, this restaurant has a solid menu. Start with the mandatory (if you are a true Thai fan) chicken satay or the Tulip dumplings with shrimp and chicken stuffing, or go for the Ayothaya sampler, with chicken satay, spring rolls, Tulip dumplings (dumplings stuffed with chicken and crabmeat with sweet-and-sour sauce), crab cakes, fried wonton, and Thai shrimp rolls. There's no sensible need to eat more after that, but forge ahead and try any of the curry or noodle

dishes. $ *Average main: $25* ✉ *The Fountains, 7555 Sand Lake Rd.* ☎ *407/345–0040* 🌐 *www.ayothayathaicuisineoforlando.com* ✣ *2:C4.*

$$ SEAFOOD ✕ **Bonefish Grill.** Divine fish dishes served in an upscale-casual setting distinguish Bonefish Grill from other area chains. Regulars rave about the Bang Bang Shrimp, a spicy appetizer of breaded and fried shrimp tossed in a tangy, spicy, mayonnaise-based sauce. Choose one of the many wood-grilled fresh fish options with your choice of mango salsa, chimichurri, pan-Asian flavorings, or lemon butter. Other selections include a pecan-Parmesan-crusted rainbow trout, chicken marsala, and grilled filet mignon. For the record, there's no bonefish on the menu. It's an inedible game fish, caught for sport (and usually released). The Orlando area has several additional units. $ *Average main: $21* ✉ *Plaza Venezia, 7830 Sand Lake Rd.* ☎ *407/355–7707* 🌐 *www.bonefishgrill.com* ⏲ *No lunch* ✣ *2:B4.*

4

$$$ TURKISH ✕ **Bosphorous Turkish Cuisine.** Exceptional Turkish cuisine served in a relaxing, indoor-outdoor setting is a welcome surprise among the big-budget chains on Sand Lake Road. Servers at this independently owned neighborhood favorite bring to the table piping-hot, oversized *lavas* (hollow bread) to dip in appetizers such as a hummus; *ezme* (a zesty, garlicky, chilled chopped salad); and baba ghanoush. Many twosomes make a meal of the bountiful mixed-appetizer platter with a lavas or two. Following are oversized platters of char-grilled whole or filleted sea bass, kebabs, and any variety of lamb dishes, each prepared expertly. Light eaters enjoy the boat-shaped, spinach-and-cheese, special Turkish pastry. A second unit, also with alfresco tables, is in Winter Park. $ *Average main: $28* ✉ *Marketplace at Dr. Phillips, 7600 Dr. Phillips Blvd., Suite 108* ☎ *407/352–6766* 🌐 *www.bosphorousrestaurant.com* ✣ *2:B4.*

$$ MEXICAN ✕ **Cantina Laredo.** You can tell this is an upscale Mexican eatery, first by the Porsches in the parking lot and then by the aged Mexican tequila that fetches up to $48 a glass. But the prices shouldn't scare off those looking for decent Mexican food in a nice atmosphere. Among the great *especialidades* (special plates) is *camaron poblano asada*—a Mexican steak wrapped around a mild poblano pepper stuffed with shrimp and Jack cheese and topped with chimichurri sauce. If you want representative Mexican dining, go for the Cantina Laredo platter, comprising a cheese chile relleno (breaded, mild pepper, stuffed with cheese, and fried), handmade tamale, chicken enchilada, and fajita beef taco *al carbon.* If you walk in from the front, you may never notice the small covered dining area out back that faces a courtyard with a spectacular fountain—a pleasant setting for a lovely meal. $ *Average main: $18* ✉ *Dellagio, 8000 Via Dellagio Way* ☎ *407/345–0186* 🌐 *www.cantinalaredo.com* ✣ *2:B4.*

$$$ MIDDLE EASTERN ✕ **Cedar's Restaurant.** This family-owned Lebanese eatery, set in a major upscale strip shopping center that's become part of Restaurant Row, serves Middle Eastern standards like shish kebab, baba ghanoush (an ultrasmoky variety that is the very best in town), and hummus as well as tasty daily specials. One of the most notable regular entrées is the *samak harra* (sautéed red snapper fillet topped with onions, tomatoes, and cilantro). More formal than the average Orlando-area Middle Eastern restaurant, and featuring a cocktail menu, Cedar's has tables

with white-linen tablecloths and diners who tend to sport resort-casual attire. A belly dancer performs on Friday and Saturday evenings at 8 pm; hookah pipes are popular on the back patio. $ *Average main: $26* ✉ *Plaza Venezia, 7732 W. Sand Lake Rd.* ☎ *407/351–6000* 🌐 *www.orlandocedars.com* ✥ *2:C4.*

$$$$ ITALIAN ✕ **Christini's Ristorante Italiano.** Locals, visitors, and theme-park execs alike love to spend money at Christini's, one of the city's fanciest places for northern Italian cuisine. The menu is filled with high-end versions of familiar dishes like chicken marsala and veal with lemon-wine sauce. You may be so enchanted by the rose each lady receives and the serenade by a roving accordion player that you forget to check the price of the recommended wine, which will cost you. $ *Average main: $45* ✉ *Marketplace at Dr. Phillips, 7600 Dr. Phillips Blvd.* ☎ *407/345–8770* 🌐 *www.christinis.com* ⏲ *No lunch* ✥ *2:B4.*

$$ MODERN ASIAN ✕ **Dragonfly.** Sleek and stylish, Dragonfly is a bit of everything the young and beautiful people want: a pretty space featuring sushi, colorful martinis, and modern, izakaya-style small plates, both creative and simple. Groups of dressed-up twenty- and thirtysomethings gather indoors and out to share plates of robata-cooked meats and vegetables, along with tempura, rolls, noodle dishes, and salads, all beautifully presented. The daily happy hour is hugely popular with locals. $ *Average main: $14* ✉ *Dellagio, 7972 Via Dellagio Way* ☎ *407/370–3359* 🌐 *www.dragonflyorlando.com* ⏲ *No lunch* ✥ *2:B4.*

$$ WINE BAR ✕ **Le Rouge Wine Bar and Tapas.** Determined to open a sleek tapas lounge reminiscent of the ones he'd visited in Europe, owner Mounir Elidrissi decorated his with red recessed lighting and named it for the French word for the color associated with passion. It looks like a destination for a glass of wine or a first date, but foodies visiting town also find it worth seeking out. The lamb chops with currant–red wine sauce are exceptional, as is the truffle mac and cheese and the mahimahi ceviche. A three-course wine-pairing meal is $35. The wine list is comprehensive, with vintages from California to Lebanon, France to New Zealand. Live music plays Wednesday through Saturday. $ *Average main: $20* ✉ *Plaza Venezia, 7730 W. Sand Lake Rd.* ☎ *407/370–0909* 🌐 *www.lerougewinebar.com* ⏲ *No lunch* ✥ *2:C4.*

$ MEXICAN ✕ **Lime Fresh Mexican Grill.** What was solely a so-hot South Beach quick-service joint is now a rapidly growing mini-chain that serves "fresh-Mex" fare. Orlando's outpost in the Restaurant Row area (there are others in Winter Park and Lake Mary) is a bright corner restaurant that serves up the signature fish tacos, steak fajita quesadillas, and tortilla soup. Six salsas, from mild (*salse verde*) to super hot (habanero), add any needed zest. $ *Average main: $9* ✉ *Phillips Crossing, 8031 Turkey Lake Rd., Suite 100* ☎ *407/370–3810* 🌐 *www.limefreshmexicangrill.com* ✥ *2:D4.*

$ SOUTHWESTERN ✕ **Moe's Southwest Grill.** At this great fast-food alternative, meals cost well south of $10. It is an immensely casual joint but by no means a dive, with a youthful vibrancy (music blares over the sound system) that makes it a great place for a quick meal. The Moe in this equation could almost be the guy who cavorted with Larry and Curly. Dishes are familiar and fresh, such as quesadillas, fajitas, and nachos, and you get to choose what goes into each meal. The franchise has several additional Central Florida restaurants. *Average main: $7 The Fountains, 7541D W. Sand Lake Rd. 407/264–9903 www.moes.com Reservations not accepted 2:C4.*

$$$$ SEAFOOD **MoonFish.** This splashy-looking restaurant caters to the convention crowd, with private rooms, polished service, and high prices—but the food is quite good. At least half a dozen fish varieties are flown in daily and prepared with a fusion of flavors from around the world. The menu is varied, with appetizers like almond-fried lobster tail and sesame duck carpaccio, and entrées like citrus oak-grilled, blackened, or bronzed fish; fish prepared Hong Kong–style with fresh ginger and scallions in a light sherry soy sauce; and Oscar Mignon, a steak with hollandaise and a crabmeat topping. The sushi is consistently fresh, and the wine list is extensive. *Average main: $32 The Fountains, 7525 W. Sand Lake Rd. 407/363–7262 www.talkofthetownrestaurants.com No lunch 2:C4.*

4

$$$$ STEAKHOUSE **Morton's The Steakhouse.** This fine choice among Orlando's many steak houses looks like a sophisticated private club, and youngsters with mouse caps are not common at the nationwide chain's local outpost. Center stage in the kitchen is a huge broiler, kept at 900°F to sear in the flavor of the porterhouses, sirloins, rib eyes, and other cuts of aged beef. For true value, nibble on "bar bites" in the lounge area during happy hour, when they're half price, and you'll enjoy top-quality sliders and such for $6 to $7 a plate. Soufflés are a specialty here and there are four: chocolate, raspberry, lemon, and Grand Marnier (order at the beginning of your meal). The wine list has about 350 vintages from around the world. *Average main: $45 Marketplace at Dr. Phillips, 7600 Dr. Phillips Blvd. 407/248–3485 www.mortons.com No lunch 2:B4.*

$$$$ SEAFOOD **Ocean Prime.** From the Berries & Bubbles martinis (tart cocktails made with citrus and berry flavors and served bubbling and smoking, thanks to dry ice) that start off the meal, to the ultrarich chocolate peanut butter dessert draped in bittersweet chocolate ganache, Ocean Prime wows at every turn. This local outpost of an upscale chain holds its own with consistently good food, if uneven service. The jumbo-lump crab cake with sweet corn cream is a good way to begin, as are the white truffle caviar deviled eggs, ahi tuna tartare, and goat cheese ravioli. Follow with a simple grilled steak, sea scallops with Parmesan risotto and citrus vinaigrette, or the teriyaki salmon. *Average main: $37 Rialto, 7339 W. Sand Lake Rd. 407/781–4880 www.oceanprimeorlando.com No lunch 2:C4.*

$$$ ITALIAN **Peperoncino.** You'll be transported to Milan at this Dr. Phillips Italian, a slim, slightly glitzy newcomer where chef-owner Barbara Alfano puts out a fresh menu of Italian specialties every evening. The finishing kitchen is in the dining room, so diners lucky enough to snag the few indoor seats (the outside patio has extras) can see Alfano and her team composing the dishes. You might feast on fried pecorino drizzled with honey, a lasagna worthy of a return Orlando visit, pear-and-cheese pasta pockets, or the day's fish, whole or filleted, steamed with aromatics in parchment. Some desserts are imported from Italy, others

made in-house. $ *Average main: $25* ✉ *Dellagio, 7988 Via Dellagio Way* ☎ *407/440–2856* 🌐 *www.peperoncinocucina.com* *Reservations essential* ✣ *2:B4.*

$$$ HAWAIIAN ✕ **Roy's.** Chef Roy Yamaguchi has more or less perfected his own cuisine type, using European-style cooking techniques with Asian ingredients, primarily seafood, together with lots of imagination. The menu changes seasonally, but typical dishes include Hawaiian-style butterfish with a sizzling peanut lemon-shoyu vinaigrette, and hibachi-style grilled Atlantic salmon with Japanese citrus ponzu sauce. If your taste buds want to stay on land, go for hearty fare like grilled filet mignon with shiso Bernaise or Hawaii Kai–style braised short ribs. The crunchy golden lobster pot stickers are a Roy's classic. The three-course prix-fixe menu ($37) is a relative bargain if you happen to like that day's dishes. A vegetarian and gluten-free menu is available upon request. $ *Average main: $28* ✉ *Plaza Venezia, 7760 W. Sand Lake Rd.* ☎ *407/352–4844* 🌐 *www.roysrestaurant.com* ⏲ *No lunch* ✣ *2:C4.*

$$ AMERICAN ✕ **Seasons 52.** Parts of the menu change every week at this innovative restaurant that serves different foods at different times of year, depending on what's in season. Meals here tend to be healthful (butter is banned) yet hearty and very flavorful. The beef and black bean chili starter is to die for. For an entrée, you might have wood-roasted pork tenderloin with polenta, portobello mushrooms, caramelized cipollini, and roasted onion jus, or caramelized grilled sea scallops with sundried tomato–mushroom pearl pasta. An impressive wine list with dozens of selections by the glass complements the menu. For dessert, have mini-indulgence classics like pecan pie, rocky road, carrot cake, and key lime pie served in petite portions. Although the cuisine is haute, the prices are modest—not bad for a snazzy, urbane bistro and wine bar. It has live music nightly to boot. Another Seasons is in Altamonte Springs. $ *Average main: $20* ✉ *Plaza Venezia, 7700 Sand Lake Rd., I–4 Exit 75A* ☎ *407/354–5212* 🌐 *www.seasons52.com* ✣ *2:C4.*

$$$$ STEAKHOUSE ✕ **Vines Grille & Wine Bar.** Live jazz and blues music fills the night at the bar section of this dramatically designed restaurant, but the food and drink in the snazzy main dining room are headliners in their own right. The kitchen bills itself as a steak house, but it really is far more than that. Entrées range from a porterhouse (alas, no longer dry-aged) to pan-seared Chilean sea bass with lobster risotto and basil *beurre blanc,* from a one-pound Wagyu burger with truffle fries to pork osso bucco with brown butter Boursin grits. Be sure to start with the grilled octopus, which is simply prepared with red onions, capers, and roasted fennel. The wine list here is extensive, and the cocktails are serious business, too. The crowd tends to dress up, but jackets and ties are not required. $ *Average main: $48* ✉ *The Fountains, 7533 W. Sand Lake Rd.* ☎ *407/351–1227* 🌐 *www.vinesgrille.com* ⏲ *No lunch* ✣ *2:C4.*

CENTRAL ORLANDO

The center of Orlando shows what the town as a whole was like before it became a big theme park. Quiet streets are lined with huge oaks covered with Spanish moss. Museums and galleries are along main thoroughfares, as are dozens of tiny lakes, where herons, egrets, and, yes, alligators, peacefully coexist with human city dwellers. This is quintessential urban Florida. The restaurants in this area, a good half hour from the Disney tourism area via Interstate 4, tend to have more of their own sense of character and style than the eateries going full tilt for your dollars in Kissimmee and Lake Buena Vista or on International Drive.

$$$ JAPANESE **Amura.** Amura, Japanese for "village of love," is a local chain of high-end Japanese restaurants; two of the three also have teppanyaki dining. The Downtown location is lively and hip, while the two suburban outposts are quieter and nearly luxurious—and priced accordingly. The sushi menu has about 40 choices, from clams to yellowtail cheek. The Mexican roll—with avocado, tempura shrimp, and jalapeño peppers—makes for an unusual appetizer. Other entrées include Tokyo orange chicken, spicy pork, and yakisoba noodles. *Average main: $23* *54 W. Church St., Downtown Orlando* *407/316–8500* *www.amura.com* *No lunch weekends* *3:D6.*

$ VIETNAMESE **Anh Hong.** It's nothing fancy, yet this Vietnamese restaurant is among the most popular in an Orlando neighborhood filled with competitors. Asian-Americans fuel up on steaming bowls of soups, chopsticks in one hand, a spoon in the other, stopping periodically to tear fresh herbs off branches and stir them into the broth. The menu is massive and has excellent grilled meats with rice. Adventurous eaters might start with the Vietnamese carpaccio and the cabbage-and-duck salad. "Self prepare and roll your self" is essentially a make-your-own summer roll dish: you moisten a rice-paper pancake, then fill it with proteins, noodles, and herbs. The noodle soups are flavorful, and the chicken with lemongrass and hot chili and the caramel chicken with ginger are can't-miss stir-fries. *Average main: $11* *1124 E. Colonial Dr., Downtown Orlando* *407/999–2656* *www.anhhongorlando.com* *Reservations not accepted* *3:E5.*

$$$ ECLECTIC **The Boheme Restaurant.** The Grand Bohemian, a boutique, luxury hotel, is the setting for a sleek city-center restaurant. As a prelude to your main, try the calamari served with tomatoes, olives, Asiago, and curry-cumin aïoli. For a main course, consider sea bass with beet reduction and asparagus or an aged Black Angus steak. The Sunday brunch here is a worthwhile experience: you can get carved New York strip steak and snow crab as well as omelets. *Average main: $27* *Grand Bohemian Hotel Orlando, 325 S. Orange Ave., Downtown Orlando* *407/313–9000* *www.grandbohemianhotel.com* *3:D6.*

$$ SEAFOOD **Cityfish.** In Downtown Orlando's trendy Thornton Park district, this casual dining spot aims to be urbane. It caters to locals, but it's loud enough and casual enough to welcome kids wearing mouse ears. With the general ambience of a city sports bar—including flat-screen TVs on all the walls (but renovations planned)—Cityfish dispenses basic, well-prepared, fresh fish, most of it simply grilled, blackened, Parmesan-crusted or fried (your choice). Once guests select the fish and preparation, they also choose to have it served in a sandwich, on a Southwestern salad, or plated with smoked-bacon succotash, red bliss potatoes, and jalapeno hushpuppies. The appetizers reveal creative twists introduced or improved by Orlando's homegrown celeb-chef Greg Richie, who took over the kitchen in late 2013. Examples are flash-fried crispy

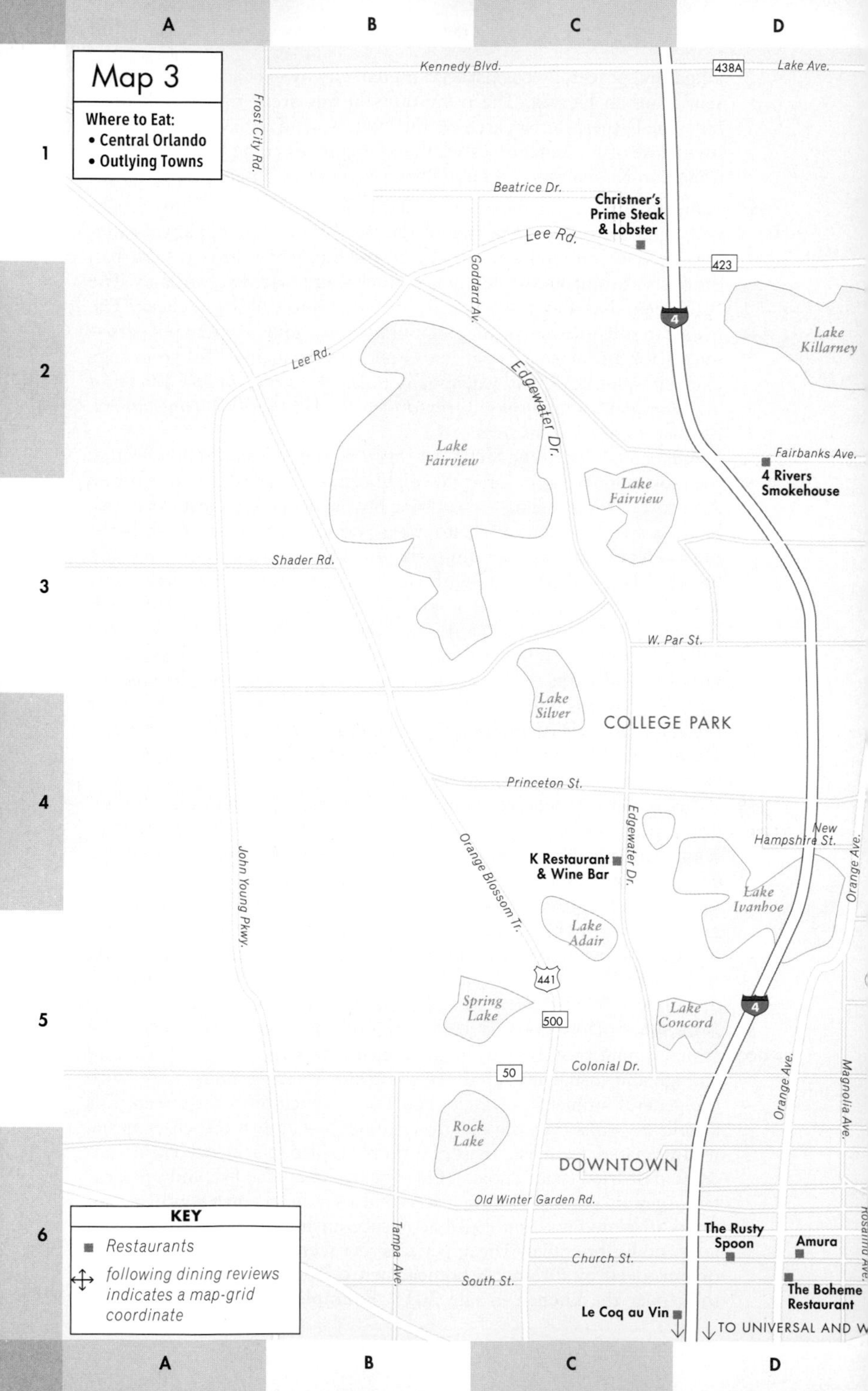

A
B
C
D
Map 3
Where to Eat:
• Central Orlando
• Outlying Towns
1
2
3
4
5
6
Kennedy Blvd.
438A
Lake Ave.
Frost City Rd.
Beatrice Dr.
Christner's Prime Steak & Lobster
Lee Rd.
423
Goddard Av.
4
Lake Killarney
Lee Rd.
Edgewater Dr.
Lake Fairview
Fairbanks Ave.
4 Rivers Smokehouse
Lake Fairview
Shader Rd.
W. Par St.
Lake Silver
COLLEGE PARK
Princeton St.
Edgewater Dr.
New Hampshire St.
Orange Ave.
John Young Pkwy.
Orange Blossom Tr.
K Restaurant & Wine Bar
Lake Ivanhoe
Lake Adair
441
Spring Lake
500
Lake Concord
4
50
Colonial Dr.
Orange Ave.
Magnolia Ave.
Rock Lake
DOWNTOWN
Old Winter Garden Rd.
KEY
Restaurants
following dining reviews indicates a map-grid coordinate
Tampa Ave.
The Rusty Spoon
Amura
Church St.
South St.
The Boheme Restaurant
Le Coq au Vin
TO UNIVERSAL AND W
A
B
C
D

E
F
G
H
0
1 mi
0
2 km
MAITLAND
1
Orlando Ave.
Webster Ave.
Park Ave.
Brio Tuscan Grille
Canton Ave.
Aloma Ave.
Prato
N. Denning Dr.
N. Pennsylvania Ave.
Dexter's
Luma on Park
Osceola Ave.
2
600
New England Ave.
Park Plaza Gardens
ROLLINS COLLEGE
Cask & Larder
Lake Mizell
Lakeview Ave.
17 92
Orange Ave.
WINTER PARK
Minnesota Ave.
The Ravenous Pig
Lake Virginia
3
MEAD BOTANICAL GARDENS
Lake Winyah
Lake Sue
Lake Estelle
Winter Park Blvd.
Glenridge Way
Loch Haven Park
ORLANDO MUSEUM OF ART
4
Lake Rowena
Lake Formosa
HARRY LEU BOTANICAL GARDENS
Corrine Dr.
Bennett Rd.
Lake Susannah
Virginia Dr.
Hawkers
Highland Lake
Weber St.
Hampton Dr.
Bumby Ave.
Humphries Ave.
Marks St.
Mills Ave.
5
Linda's La Cantina
Summerlin Ave.
E. Colonial Dr.
50
Maguire Blvd.
The Smiling Bison
Anh Hong
Amelia St.
Primrose Dr.
Orlando Executive Airport
Livingston St.
Robinson St.
Cityfish
Washington St.
THORNTON PARK
Shari Sushi Lounge
Central Blvd.
6
Lake Lawsome
East-West Expwy.
South St.
408
T DISNEY WORLD
E
F
G
H

pickle slices with smoky Bloody Mary aioli, and buffalo shrimp. The big patio filled with tables shaded by large umbrellas is a great place to spend a few unhurried hours in cool weather. *Average main: $20* ✉ *617 E. Central Blvd., Thornton Park* ☎ *407/849–9779* 🌐 *www.cityfishorlando.com* ✥ *3:E6.*

$$ ASIAN Fodor's Choice ★ ✕ **Hawkers.** Hipsters, families, and business groups dine side by side at this popular restaurant, a laid-back spot that specializes in serving Asian street food. Travel the continent with $3 to $7.50 appetizer-size portions of scratch-made specialties from Malaysia, Singapore, Thailand, and Vietnam. Musts for adventurous diners include roti canai, a flaky bread with a chicken-curry dip; curry laksa, a noodle soup with exotic flavors; and stir-fried udon noodles. More timid eaters adore the marinated beef skewers with Malaysian satay sauce, peanuty chilled sesame noodles, duck tacos, and any of the Americanized (but flavorful) lettuce wraps. *Average main: $15* ✉ *1103 Mills Ave., Mills 50 District* ☎ *407/237–0606* 🌐 *www.facebook.com/hawkersstreetfare* ✥ *3:E5.*

$$$ AMERICAN Fodor's Choice ★ ✕ **K Restaurant & Wine Bar.** A vibrant restaurant down the road from College Park's restaurant hub, K is a hot spot for locals, serving upscale, eclectic, American and Italian cuisine in an intimate setting. Besides lunch and dinner, K hosts flip-flop-friendly wine tastings in the garden or on the patio, a monthly brunch, and popular wine dinners—generally four courses for $50. Menus change daily and feature appetizers such as fried green tomatoes with roasted corn, crab salad, and grain mustard sauce, and country-fried chicken livers with caramelized onion marmalade. For entrées, check out the mushroom-dusted filet mignon with red wine sauce, or the mac and cheese gussied up with lobster, homemade sausage, or another treat. *Average main: $27* ✉ *1710 Edgewater Dr., College Park* ☎ *407/872–2332* 🌐 *www.kwinebar.com* ⏲ *Closed Sun., except for brunch 2nd Sun. each month.* ✥ *3:C4.*

$$$ STEAKHOUSE ✕ **Linda's La Cantina.** A favorite among locals since the Eisenhower administration, this down-home steak house serves good cuts of meat, cooked expertly and served at a reasonable price. The menu is short and to the point, including about a dozen steaks (most of them different sizes of top sirloin strip, filet mignon, or T-bone) and just enough ancillary items to fill a single page. Among the fish selections is the 12-ounce blackened red snapper. The chicken, veal, or eggplant parmigiana topped with marinara sauce and mozzarella is good for nonsteak lovers. With every entrée you receive a salad plus a heaping order of spaghetti (which isn't particularly noteworthy), baked potato, steak fries, green beans, or broccoli. *Average main: $26* ✉ *4721 E. Colonial Dr., near Orlando Executive Airport, Downtown Orlando* ☎ *407/894–4491* 🌐 *www.lindaslacantina.com* ⏲ *No lunch. Closed Sun. and Mon.* ✥ *3:G5.*

$$$ SOUTHERN Fodor's Choice ★ ✕ **The Rusty Spoon.** Lovingly raised animals and locally grown produce are the menu foundation at this Downtown gastropub, an ideal spot for a business lunch or a pre–basketball game, -theater, or -concert dinner. The wood-and-brick dining room is a comfortable backdrop to hearty American meals with a Southern bent. Creatively stuffed eggs and buttermilk-soaked Vidalia onion rings are top starters. The salads—with ultrafresh greens—are always sensational. All pastas are

made from scratch, whether a butternut squash lasagna or a winter pappardelle with wilted escarole, parsnips, toasted walnuts, and fried sage. The Dirty South seafood stew is a Dixie take on bouillabaisse. End with a very grown-up take on s'mores. One Sunday a month, there's brunch. *Average main: $22 55 W. Church St., Downtown Orlando 407/401–8811 www.therustyspoon.com No lunch weekends 3:D6.*

$$$ JAPANESE **Shari Sushi Lounge.** Resplendent with metallic leather and chic white seats, this trendy eatery has more the atmosphere of a fast-lane singles bar than of an Asian oasis, but the dishes from the kitchen—fresh sushi and cooked Asian entrées—distinguish the place as a legit dining establishment. If you're here for the sushi, the place will not disappoint. There are 25 different varieties of signature rolls alone, plus traditional sushi including sea urchin and baby octopus and a dozen interesting sashimi creations. The ceviche roll is especially tasty; a tribute to the Latin American fish dish, the sushi mixes the flavors of micro cilantro, a lime-chipotle sauce plus siracha. Start with the *tako* salad, a delicious arrangement of octopus, cucumber, enoki mushrooms, mandarin oranges, and spicy kimchi sauce, or Wagyu steak that you cook yourself on a hot stone. Then move on to one of the mini-courses, like buffalo lobster tempura, or an entrée such as sake salmon: an 8-ounce fillet steamed with sake, garlic, soy sauce, lime juice, and grated ginger. Or sit at the bar and let the sushi chef pamper you with the day's multicourse omakase. *Average main: $24 621 E. Central Blvd., Thornton Park 407/420–9420 www.sharisushilounge.com No lunch 3:E6.*

$ AMERICAN **The Smiling Bison.** A shabby shack located near a standard mall, The Smiling Bison is an ambitious gastropub popular with Orlando's locavores. The owners got their start selling homemade sausages from a food cart, and you can still find smoked kielbasa, curry wurst, or other creations in sandwich form. The menu changes weekly, but soft caraway-coated pretzels with a spicy beer-mustard-cheese dip and a bison burger are always on offer. Dinner might be a chicken potpie, fried grouper cheeks over jalapeno grits, or carrot-and-ricotta agnolotti—all under $20. The beer menu caters to a craft-brew-centric crowd, and wines are interesting and reasonably priced. Musicians entertain several nights a week, with no cover charge. *Average main: $14 745 Bennett Rd., Downtown Orlando 407/898–8580 www.thesmilingbison.com No lunch 3:G5.*

WINTER PARK

Winter Park is a charming suburb on the northern end of Orlando, 35 minutes from Disney. It's affluent, understated, and sophisticated—and can be pleasurable when you need a break from the theme parks. It has four restaurant hubs: Park Avenue, Orange Avenue, Hannibal Square, and Winter Park Village. To get into the area, follow Interstate 4 to Exit 87.

$$ ITALIAN **Brio Tuscan Grille.** Head to this trendy restaurant for wood-grilled meats and fish, Italian classics like chicken Milanese, and plenty of pasta. Try the strip steak topped with Gorgonzola, or the mushroom

ravioli with champagne brown butter sauce. A good appetizer choice is the bruschetta, a wood-baked flatbread covered with toppings like sliced steak or roasted red peppers with mozzarella. The dining room's Italian archways are elegant, its frescoed walls schmaltzy in a grand trattoria sort of way, and the sidewalk tables a good option on cool days. There is another location at Orlando's Mall at Millenia and a similar, sister concept, Bravo!, on Restaurant Row. *Average main: $21* ✉ *480 N. Orlando Ave., Winter Park Village* ☎ *407/622–5611* *www.brioitalian.com* *Reservations not accepted* ✣ *3:E2.*

$$ SOUTHERN
Cask & Larder. Firmly established as local celebs, thanks to their success at the neighboring Ravenous Pig, chef-owners Julie and James Petrakis went the Southern brewpub route for restaurant number two. It's a bustling, casual space for a wallet-friendly home-style meal made with regional ingredients, along with several varieties of house-brewed and other craft beers plus hand-crafted cocktails made with American spirits. Staples include a three-ham tasting platter with pepper jelly "ham jam," pimiento cheese fries, and raw oysters. After that, it's an always-changing array of small entrées, featuring familiar items like chicken and scallops and not-so-common ones like grouper cheeks, rabbit, and bone marrow. Plan ahead for a three-course whole-animal dinner (eight-person minimum), especially a smoked suckling pig. *Average main: $20* ✉ *565 W. Fairbanks Ave.* ☎ *321/280–4200* *www.caskandlarder.com* ✣ *3:F2.*

$$$$ STEAKHOUSE Fodor's Choice ★
Christner's Prime Steak & Lobster. Locals like this quiet, uncomplicated, family-run steak house, which delivers carefully prepared food and attentive service in a traditional setting of red leather and dark wood. When your steak arrives—still sizzling on a hot plate—the waiter asks you to cut into it and check that it was cooked as you ordered. The menu is simple: rib eyes, porterhouses, filet mignon. Seafood such as lobster, shrimp, and salmon fill out the "surf" side of the menu. End your meal with a big slice of mandarin orange cake. *Average main: $39* ✉ *729 Lee Rd., Orlando* ☎ *407/645–4443* *www.christnersprimesteakandlobster.com* *No lunch. Closed Sun.* ✣ *3:C1.*

$$ ECLECTIC
Dexter's. A trio of Central Florida restaurants with a fourth in the works, Dexter's is a low-key concept with a wildly creative menu, surprisingly low prices, a good wine list, and a faithful following among locals. Two of the best-selling entrées are the chicken tortilla pie—a stack of puffy, fried tortillas layered with chicken and cheese—and the Bourbon Street jambalaya, with andouille sausage and salmon. The rotating fish of the day features whatever's freshest in season. In addition to a core menu shared by the restaurants, each has its own café menu with specialties designed by that unit's on-site chef. There's always live music on Thursday night. The other restaurants are in Lake Mary and Orlando's Thornton Park neighborhood. Next up: Dr. Phillips. *Average main: $20* ✉ *558 W. New England Ave., Hannibal Sq.* ☎ *407/629–1150* *www.dexwine.com* *Reservations not accepted* ✣ *3:E2.*

$ BARBECUE Fodor's Choice ★
4 Rivers Smokehouse. Obsessed with Texas-style barbecue brisket, John Rivers decided to turn his passion into a business upon retiring from the corporate world. The result is the uber-popular 4 Rivers, which turns out barbecue standards like pulled pork and cornbread, plus more

unusual items like the addicting bacon-wrapped smoked jalapeño peppers, the Six Shooter with cheese grits, and a sausage-filled pastry called *kolache*. Old-time soft drinks such as Frostie Root Beer and Cheerwine are for sale, along with desserts like the kiddie favorite Chocolate Awesomeness, an indulgent layering of chocolate cake, chocolate pudding, Heath Bar, whipped cream, and chocolate and caramel sauces. Some units have a Sweet Shop that sells whole oversized cakes. Additional 4 Rivers are scattered throughout Central Florida. *Average main: $14 1600 W. Fairbanks Ave. 407/474–8377 www.4rsmokehouse.com Reservations not accepted Closed Sun. 3:D2.*

$$$ MODERN AMERICAN Fodor's Choice ★ **Luma on Park.** Indisputably one of the Orlando area's best restaurants, Luma on Park is a popular spot for progressive American cuisine served in a fashionable setting. Every ingredient is carefully sourced from local producers when possible, and scratch preparation—from pastas to sausages to pickled rhubarb—is the mantra among its dedicated clique of chefs. The menu changes daily. You might discover chestnut agnolotti with Maine lobster or a cauliflower-onion tart as starters, followed by tilefish with tangerine-fennel broth or a duck breast with kale, toasted pine nuts, parsnip purée, and pickled white asparagus. The wine cellar is a high point, holding 7,000 bottles—80 varieties, all available by the half glass, glass, and bottle. The restaurant offers a three-course, prix-fixe dinner Sunday through Tuesday for $35 per person, $45 with wine pairings. *Average main: $26 290 S. Park Ave. 407/599–4111 www.lumaonpark.com Reservations essential No lunch Mon.–Thurs. 3:F2.*

$$$ EUROPEAN **Park Plaza Gardens.** Sitting at the sidewalk café and bar is like sitting on the main street of the quintessential American bustling town. Here you can enjoy casual pub fare like burgers and spinach-artichoke dip, but for a more ambitious menu, head inside to an atrium dining room with live ficus trees, a brick floor, and brick walls that give the place a Vieux Carré feel. A new management team and chef revamped the menu recently, introducing Southern coastal cuisine that is heavy on seafood, from sunflower-crusted tuna to jumbo lump crab ravioli with goat cheese crumbles. *Average main: $29 319 Park Ave. S 407/645–2475 www.parkplazagardens.com 3:F2.*

$$$ ITALIAN Fodor's Choice ★ **Prato.** Progressive Italian cuisine in a casual, bustling wood-and-brick setting immediately made Prato a local favorite. Every item from the pancetta to the amaretti is crafted from scratch. Most are prepared in one of two imported Italian wood-burning ovens, dubbed Johnny Cash and June Cash because "they make music," the chefs say. The menu changes regularly, but standouts include the chicken-liver crostini and pastas such as shrimp ravioli and rigatoni cacciatore made with shredded rabbit and orange zest. The hand-tossed pizzas are also popular, as are the tiramisu and the *budino,* an olive oil–based pudding. *Average main: $22 124 N. Park Ave. 407/262–0050 www.prato-wp.com Reservations essential No lunch Mon. and Tues. 3:F2.*

$$$
MODERN AMERICAN
Fodor's Choice ★

The Ravenous Pig. A trendy, vibrant gastropub in one of Orlando's most affluent enclaves, the Pig is arguably Orlando's most popular foodie destination. Run by husband-and-wife chefs James and Julie Petrakis, the restaurant dispenses delicacies such as pork porterhouse with German potato salad and apple cider gastrique, and five-spice Florida cobia with bacon brussels sprout hash, poached apple, and apple whiskey broth. The menu changes daily and always includes less expensive pub fare like lobster tacos and homemade pretzels with a taleggio-porter fondue. All charcuterie is made in house, from spiced orange salami to game-bird terrine. The signature dessert is the Pig Tails, essentially a basket full of piping hot, pig tail–shaped doughnuts with a chocolate-espresso dipping sauce. *Average main: $25* *1234 N. Orange Ave.* *407/628–2333* *www.theravenouspig.com* *Reservations essential* *Closed Sun. and Mon.* *3:E3.*

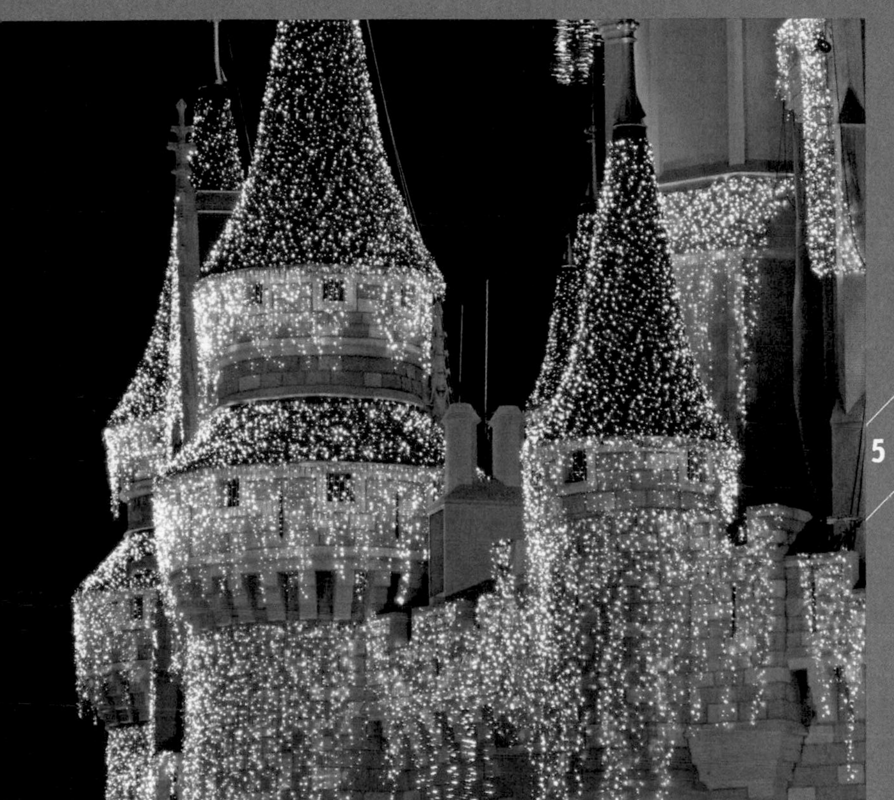

5

WALT DISNEY WORLD

WELCOME TO WALT DISNEY WORLD

TOP REASONS TO GO

★ **Nostalgia:** Face it—Mickey and Company are old friends. And you probably have childhood pictures of yourself in front of Cinderella Castle. Even if you don't, nobody does yesteryear better: head to Main Street, U.S.A, or Hollywood Boulevard and see.

★ **Memories in the Making:** Who doesn't want to snap photos of Sis on the Dumbo ride or of Junior after his Splash Mountain experience? The urge to pass that Disney nostalgia on to the next generation is strong.

★ **The Thrills:** For some this means roller coasting to an Aerosmith soundtrack or simulating space flight; for others it's about cascading down a waterslide or going on safari.

★ **The Chills:** If the Pirates of the Caribbean cave doesn't give you goose bumps, try the Haunted Mansion or Twilight Zone Tower of Terror.

★ **The Spectacle:** The list is long—fireworks, laser-light displays, arcade games, parades . . .

1 Magic Kingdom. Disney's emblematic park is home to Space Mountain, Pirates of the Caribbean, and an expanded Fantasyland full of new experiences.

2 Epcot. Future World's focus is science, technology, and hands-on experiences. In the World Showcase, you can tour 11 countries without getting jet-lagged.

3 Disney's Hollywood Studios. Attractions at this re-creation of old-time Hollywood include Rock 'n' Roller Coaster Starring Aerosmith and Twilight Zone Tower of Terror.

4 Disney's Animal Kingdom. Amid a 403-acre wildlife preserve are an Asian-themed water ride, an African safari ride, a runaway-train coaster, and shows.

5 Blizzard Beach. Water thrills range from steep flume rides to tubing expeditions in the midst of a park that you'd swear is a slowly melting ski resort. There's plenty for little ones, too.

6 Typhoon Lagoon. Sandy beaches, oceanlike waves, and a themed water coaster invite castaways to enjoy a day of fun and relaxation. Take the kids on Bay Slides and don snorkels to explore Shark Reef.

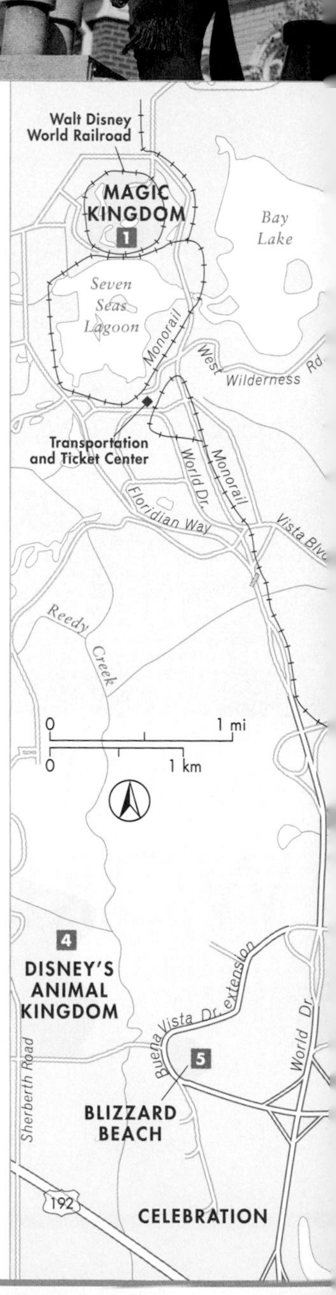

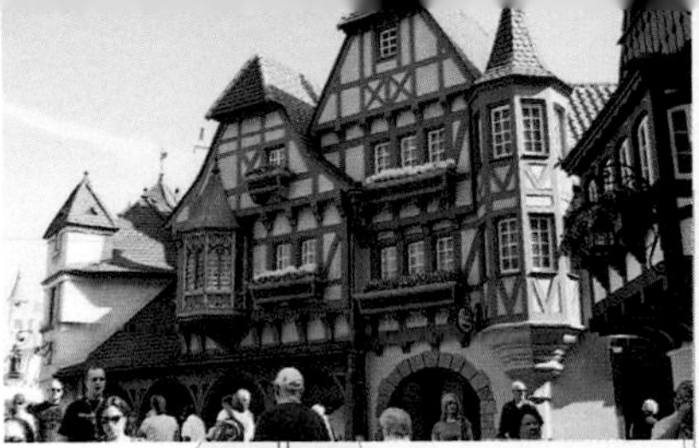

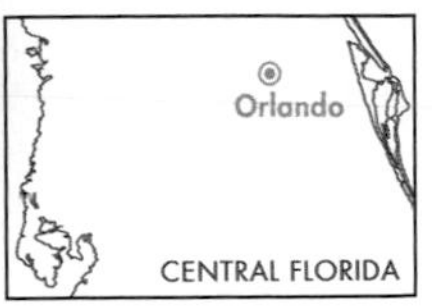

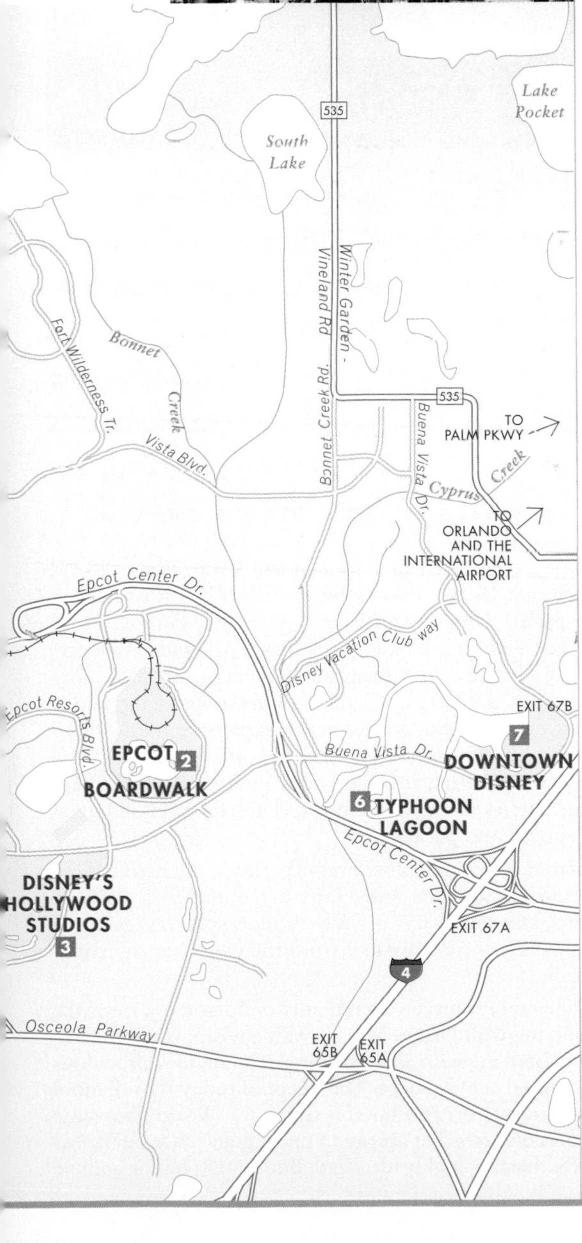

Orlando
CENTRAL FLORIDA

Lake Pocket
535
South Lake
Winter Garden - Vineland Rd
Bonnet Creek Rd.
Fort Wilderness Tr.
Bonnet Creek
Vista Blvd.
535
Buena Vista Dr.
TO PALM PKWY
Cypress Creek
TO ORLANDO AND THE INTERNATIONAL AIRPORT
Epcot Center Dr.
Disney Vacation Club way
Epcot Resorts Blvd.
EXIT 67B
7
DOWNTOWN DISNEY
EPCOT 2
BOARDWALK
Buena Vista Dr.
6 TYPHOON LAGOON
Epcot Center Dr.
DISNEY'S HOLLYWOOD STUDIOS
3
EXIT 67A
4
Osceola Parkway
EXIT 65B
EXIT 65A

7 Disney's Other Worlds. Downtown Disney is the place to go for shopping, dining, and great entertainment from morning through late night. Disney's BoardWalk is a nostalgia trip, with bicycles built for two, surreys with a fringe on top, pizza, bars, and a dance hall.

GETTING ORIENTED

Walt Disney World straddles Orange and Osceola counties to the west of Interstate 4. Four exits will get you to the parks and resort areas: 64B, 65, 67, and 68. To reach hotels along I-Drive, use Exit 72, 74A, or 75A.

Mickey Mouse. Tinker Bell. Cinderella. What would childhood be like without the magic of Disney? When kids and adults want to go to *the* theme park, they're heading to Disney. Here you're walking amid people from around the world and meeting characters like Snow White and Donald Duck while rides whirl nonstop and the irrepressible "it's a small world" tune and lyrics run through your head. You can't help but believe dreams really do come true here.

The **Magic Kingdom** is the heart and soul of the Walt Disney World empire. It was the first Disney outpost in Florida when it opened in 1971, and it's the park that launched Disney's presence in France, Japan, and Hong Kong. For a landmark that wields such worldwide influence, the 142-acre Magic Kingdom may seem small—indeed, Epcot is more than double the size of the Magic Kingdom, and Animal Kingdom is almost triple the size when including the park's expansive animal habitats. But looks can be deceiving. Packed into six different "lands" are nearly 50 major crowd-pleasers, and that's not counting all the ancillary attractions: shops, eateries, live entertainment, character meet-and-greet spots, fireworks shows, and parades.

Nowhere but at **Epcot** can you explore and experience the native food, entertainment, culture, and arts and crafts of countries in Europe, Asia, North Africa, and the Americas. What's more, employees at the World Showcase pavilions actually hail from the countries the pavilions represent.

Epcot, or "Experimental Prototype Community of Tomorrow," was the original inspiration for Walt Disney World. Walt envisioned a future in which nations coexisted in peace and harmony, reaping the miraculous harvest of technological achievement. The Epcot of today is both more and less than his original dream. Less, because the World Showcase presents views of its countries that are, as an Epcot guide once put it, "as Americans perceive them"—highly idealized. But this is a minor quibble in the face of the major achievement: Epcot is that rare paradox—a successful educational theme park that excels at entertainment, too.

Disney's Hollywood Studios were designed to be a trip back to Tinseltown's golden age, when Hedda Hopper, not tabloids, spread celebrity gossip and when the girl off the bus from Ohio could be the next Judy Garland.

The result is a theme park that blends movie-production capabilities and high-tech wonders with breathtaking rides and nostalgia. The park's old-time Hollywood atmosphere begins with a rosy-hued view of the moviemaking business presented in a dreamy stage set from the 1930s and '40s, amid sleek art-moderne buildings in pastel colors, funky diners, kitschy decorations, and sculptured gardens populated by roving actors playing, well, roving actors. There are also casting directors, gossip columnists, and other colorful characters.

Thanks to a rich library of film scores, the park is permeated with music, all familiar, all evoking the magic of the movies, and all constantly streaming from the camouflaged loudspeakers at a volume just right for humming along. The park icon, a 122-foot-high Sorcerer Mickey Hat that serves as a gift shop and Disney pin-trading station, towers over Hollywood Boulevard.

Disney's Animal Kingdom explores the stories of all animals—real, imaginary, and extinct. Enter through the Oasis, where you hear exotic background music and find yourself surrounded by gentle waterfalls and gardens alive with exotic birds, reptiles, and mammals.

At 403 acres and several times the size of the Magic Kingdom, Animal Kingdom is the largest in area of all Disney theme parks. Animal habitats take up much of that acreage. Creatures here thrive in careful re-creations of landscapes from Asia and Africa. Throughout the park, you'll also learn about conservation in a low-key way.

Amid all the nature are thrill rides, a 3-D show (housed in the "root system" of the iconic Tree of Life), two first-rate musicals, and character meet and greets. Cast members are as likely to hail from Kenya or South Africa as they are from Kentucky or South Carolina. It's all part of the charm. New park areas based on the movie *Avatar* are expected to open in 2017, a fitting addition, since the film's theme of living in harmony with nature reflects the park's eco-philosophy.

Typhoon Lagoon and **Blizzard Beach** are two of the world's best water parks. What sets them apart? It's the same thing that differentiates all Disney parks—the detailed themes. Whether you're cast away on a balmy island at Typhoon Lagoon or washed up on a ski-resort-turned-seaside-playground at Blizzard Beach, the landscaping and clever architecture will add to the fun of flume and raft rides, wave pools, and splash areas. Another plus: the vegetation has matured enough to create shade. The Disney water parks give you that lost-in-paradise feeling on top of all those high-speed, wedgie-inducing waterslides. They're so popular that crowds often reach overflow capacity in summer. If you're going to Disney for five days or more between April and October, add the Water Park Fun & More option to your Magic Your Way ticket.

PLANNING

ADMISSION

At the gate, the per-person, per-day price for Magic Kingdom guests is $99 for adults (ages 10 and older) and $93 for children (ages 3–9). At Disney's other three parks, Epcot, Hollywood Studios and Animal Kingdom, the per-person, per-day price is $94 for adults (ages 10 and older) and $88 for children (ages 3–9). You can buy tickets at the Ticket and Transportation Center (TTC) in the Magic Kingdom, from booths at other park entrances, in all on-site resorts if you're a guest, at the Disney store in the airport, and at various other sites around Orlando. You can also buy them in advance online—the best way to save time and money.

If you opt for a multiday ticket, you'll be issued a nontransferable pass that uses your fingerprint for ID. Hold your pass up to the reader, just like people with single-day tickets, and also slip your finger into the V-shaped reader. A new option, the MagicBand wristband, serves as park ticket, attraction FastPass+ ticket, and even hotel room key.

OPERATING HOURS

Walt Disney World operates 365 days a year. Opening and closing times vary by park and by season, with the longest hours during prime summer months and year-end holidays. The parking lots open at least an hour before the parks do.

In general, openings hover around 9 am, though certain attractions might not start up till 10 or 11. Closings range between 5 and 8 pm in the off-season and between 8 and 10, 11, or even midnight in high season. Downtown Disney and BoardWalk shops stay open as late as 11 pm.

EXTRA MAGIC HOURS

The Extra Magic Hours program gives Disney resort guests free early and late-night admission to certain parks on specified days—check ahead (🌐 *www.disneyworld.disney.go.com/calendars*) for information about each park's "magic hours" days to plan your early- and late-visit strategies.

PARKING AND IN-PARK TRANSPORT

Parking at Disney parks is free to resort guests; all others pay $17 for cars and $18 for RVs and campers. Parking is free for everyone at Typhoon Lagoon, Blizzard Beach, Downtown Disney, and the BoardWalk. Trams take you between the theme-park lots (*note your parking location!*) and turnstiles. Disney's buses, boats, and monorails whisk you from resort to park and park to park. If you're staying on Disney property, you can use this system exclusively. Either take a Disney bus or drive to Typhoon Lagoon and Blizzard Beach. Once inside the water parks, you can walk, swim, slide, or chill out. Allow up to an hour for travel between parks and hotels on Disney transportation.

FASTPASS+

FastPass+ helps you avoid lines, and it's included in regular park admission. Using the new My Disney Experience app or FastPass+ kiosks in each park, you can select up to three attractions at one time; each appointment will give you a one-hour window within which you can experience each attraction. The FastPass+ appointments are loaded directly to your plastic theme-park ticket or your new MagicBand. It's best to make appointments only for the most popular attractions and to stick with the standby queue for attractions that aren't in such demand. Strategy is everything.

Guests can get FastPass+ reservations for some designated character greetings, parades, and shows. These "experience" FastPass+ reservations count just the same as those for the rides. You get three to start with (in a single park) and can add as many more as you have time for (and these can be in a different park if you have the Park Hopper option). Best FastPass+ practices are explained by the program. It will direct you to the attractions where FastPass+ is most helpful. If these attractions don't meet your family's specific needs—your kids are too young to ride coasters, for example—the program will also help you customize your FastPass+ selections.

DISNEY STRATEGIES

Keep in mind these essential strategies, tried and tested by generations of Disney fans.

■ **Buy tickets before leaving home.** It saves money and gives you time to look into all the ticket options. It also offers an opportunity for you to consider vacation packages and meal plans and to register with the My Disney Experience program and mobile app for vacation planning.

■ **Make dining reservations before leaving home.** If you don't, you might find yourself eating fast food (again) or leaving Disney for dinner. On-site restaurants, especially those featuring character appearances, book up months ahead.

■ **Arrive at least 30 minutes before the parks open.** We know, it's your vacation and you want to sleep in. But you probably want to make the most of your time and money, too. Plan to be up by 7:30 am each day to get the most out of your park visits. After transit time, it'll take you 15–20 minutes to park, get to the gates, and pick up your park guide maps and *Times Guide*.

■ **See top attractions in the morning.** And we mean *first thing*. Decide in advance on your can't-miss attractions, find their locations, and hotfoot it to them before 10 am.

■ **Use FastPass+.** The system is free, easy, more streamlined than ever with the new FastPass+ online prebooking system, and it's your ticket to the top attractions with little or no waiting in line. Even if you wait to book once you're in the park, you can now schedule up to three Fastpasses at one time; paper tickets and Fastpasses are obsolete. Instead, your attraction appointments are loaded onto your MagicBand or plastic ticket, whichever you choose to use.

- **Use Baby Swap.** Disney has a theme-park "rider switch" policy that works like this: one parent waits with the baby or toddler while the other parent rides the attraction. When the ride ends, they switch places with minimal wait.
- **Build in rest time.** Start early and then leave the parks around 3 or 4 pm, thus avoiding the hottest and often most crowded period. After a couple of hours' rest at your hotel, head back for a nighttime spectacle or to ride a big-ticket ride (lines often are shorter around closing time).
- **Create an itinerary, but leave room for spontaneity.** Don't try to plot your trip hour by hour. If you're staying at a Disney resort, find out which parks have Extra Magic Hours on which days.
- **Eat at off hours.** To avoid the mealtime rush hours, have a quick, light breakfast at 7 or 8 am, lunch at 11, and dinner at 5 or 6.

OTHER DISNEY SERVICES

If you can shell out $315–$380 an hour (with a six-hour minimum), you can take a customized **VIP Tour** with guides who help you park hop and get good seats at parades and shows. These tours don't help you skip lines, but they make navigating easy. Groups can have up to 10 people; book up to three months ahead.

WDW Tours. Reserve with WDW Tours up to 180 days in advance for behind-the-scenes tours. Participant age requirements vary, so be sure to check before you book. ☎ *407/939–8687*.

Character meals. Mickey, Belle, or other characters sign autographs and pose for photos. Book through Disney's dining reservations line up to 180 days out; these hugging-and-feeding frenzies are wildly popular.

DISNEY CONTACTS

Cruise Line: ☎ *800/370–0097* 🌐 *www.disneycruise.com*

Dining Reservations: ☎ *407/939–3463*

Extra Magic Hours: 🌐 *www.disneyworld.disney.go.com/calendars*

Fairy-Tale Weddings: ☎ *321/939–4610* 🌐 *www.disneyweddings.disney.go.com*

Golf Reservations: ☎ *407/939–4653*

Guest Info: ☎ *407/824–4321*

VIP Tours: ☎ *407/560–4033*

WDW Travel Company: ☎ *407/828–8101*

Web: 🌐 *www.disneyworld.disney.go.com*

THE MAGIC KINGDOM

5

Whether you arrive at the Magic Kingdom via monorail, boat, or bus, it's hard to escape that surge of excitement or suppress that smile upon sighting the towers of Cinderella Castle or the spires of Space Mountain. So what if it's a cliché by now? There's magic beyond the turnstiles, and you aren't going to miss one memorable moment.

Most visitors have some idea of what they'd like to see and do during their day in the Magic Kingdom. Popular attractions like Space Mountain and Splash Mountain are on the lists of any thrill seeker, and the recently expanded Fantasyland is Destination One for parents of small children. Visitors who steer away from wilder rides are first in line at the Jungle Cruise or Pirates of the Caribbean in Adventureland.

It's great to have a strategy for seeing the park's attractions, grabbing a bite to eat, or scouring the shops for souvenir gold. But don't forget that Disney Imagineers—the creative pros behind every themed land and attraction—are famous for their attention to detail. Your experience will be richer if you take time to notice the extra touches—from the architecture to the music to the costumes. The same genius is evident even in the landscape, from the tropical setting of Adventureland to the red-stone slopes of Frontierland's Big Thunder Mountain Railroad.

Wherever you go, watch for hidden Mickeys—silhouettes and abstract images of Mickey Mouse—tucked by Imagineers into every corner of the Kingdom. For instance, at the Haunted Mansion, look for him in the place settings in the banquet scene.

Much of the Magic Kingdom's pixie dust is spread by the people who work here, the costumed cast members who do their part to create fond memories for each guest who crosses their path. Maybe the grim ghoul who greets you solemnly at the Haunted Mansion will cause you to break down and giggle. Or the sunny shop assistant will help your daughter find the perfect sparkly shoes to match her princess dress.

TOP ATTRACTIONS

FOR AGES 7 AND UP

Big Thunder Mountain Railroad. An Old West–theme, classic coaster that's not too scary; it's just a really good, bumpy, swervy thrill.

Buzz Lightyear's Space Ranger Spin. A shoot-'em-up ride where space-ranger wannabes compete for the highest score.

Haunted Mansion. With its razzle-dazzle special effects, this classic is always a frightful hoot.

Pirates of the Caribbean. Don't miss this family cruise through pirate territory, especially if you're a fan of the movies.

Seven Dwarfs Mine Train. It's the newest coaster on the block, with train cars that swing to and fro during the rollicking, musical ride through a mine full of glittery gems.

Space Mountain. The Magic Kingdom's scariest ride zips you along the tracks in near-total darkness except for the stars.

FOR AGES 6 AND UNDER

Dumbo the Flying Elephant. The elephant ears get them every time, and the renovated ride offers double the number of pachyderm vehicles.

Enchanted Tales with Belle. Young girls and boys, and some parents, too, clamor to play characters from "Beauty and the Beast" in this well-done interactive story adventure.

The Magic Carpets of Aladdin. On this must-do for preschoolers, you can make your carpet go up and down to avoid occasional water spurts as mischievous camels spit at you.

The Many Adventures of Winnie the Pooh. Hang on to your honey pot as you get whisked along on a windy-day adventure with Pooh, Tigger, Eeyore, and friends.

Under the Sea: Journey of the Little Mermaid. Wander past waterfalls and tide pools into the cave beneath Prince Eric's Castle for some interactive fun and a clamshell ride through Ariel's story.

You get the feeling that everyone's in on the fun; in fact, you wonder if they ever go home!

ORIENTATION AND PLANNING

GETTING ORIENTED

The park is laid out on a north–south axis, with Cinderella Castle at the center and the various lands surrounding it in a broad circle.

As you pass underneath the railroad tracks, symbolically leaving behind the world of reality and entering a world of fantasy, you'll immediately notice the adorable buildings lining Town Square and Main Street, U.S.A, which runs due north and ends at the Hub (also called Central Plaza), in front of Cinderella Castle. If you're lost or have questions, cast members are available at almost every turn to help you.

MAGIC KINGDOM PLANNER

PARK AMENITIES

Baby Care: The quiet baby-care center is next to the Crystal Palace between Main Street and Adventureland. Rocking chairs and low lighting make nursing comfortable, though it can get crowded. Toddler-size toilets are a hit with tots. There are also changing tables, formula, baby food, pacifiers, diapers, and children's pain relievers. Most park restrooms also have changing tables.

Cameras: The camera center at Town Square Theater (formerly Exposition Hall), opposite City Hall, sells film, batteries, and digital memory cards. If a Disney photographer took your picture in the park, you can buy the photos here or pick up your PhotoPass to view and order them online. A 5-inch-by-7-inch photo costs $12.95 for the first print; the more prints you buy, the less each additional print costs. An 8-inch-by-10-inch costs $16.95 and less for each extra print. Or you can go completely digital with the $199 Memory Maker option to view and download all PhotoPass images. This area is a Mickey Mouse meet-and-greet spot and features the first-ever Fastpass ticket to meet Mickey.

5

First Aid: The first-aid center, staffed by registered nurses, is beside the Crystal Palace. More than a dozen automated external defibrillators are across the park.

Guest Relations. To the left in Town Square as you face Main Street, **City Hall** houses Guest Relations (aka Guest Services), the Magic Kingdom's principal information center (☎ *407/824–4521*). Here you can search for misplaced belongings or companions, ask questions of staffers, and pick up a guide map and a *Times Guide* with schedules of events and character-greeting information. ■ **TIP→ If you're trying for a last-minute lunch or dinner reservation, you may be able to book it at City Hall.**

Lockers: Lockers ($7 or $9 plus $5 deposit) are in an arcade under the Main Street railroad station. If you're park hopping, use your locker receipt to get a free locker at the next park.

Lost People and Things: Instruct your kids to talk to anyone with a Disney name tag if they lose you. **City Hall** also has a lost and found and a computerized message center, where you can leave notes for your companions in the Magic Kingdom and other parks.

Main Lost and Found. After a day, found items are taken to the Lost and Found at the Ticket and Transportation Center. ✉ *Ticket and Transportation Center [TTC]* ☎ *407/824–4245.*

Package Pick-Up: Have large purchases sent to Package Pick-Up at the Chamber of Commerce next to City Hall, so you won't have to carry them around. Allow three hours for the delivery. You also can have packages delivered to your Disney hotel.

Services for People with Disabilities: The Magic Kingdom gets decent marks from visitors with disabilities. Level entrances and ramps provide wheelchair access. Frontierland is the only area of the park, aside from Main Street, that has sidewalk curbs; there are ramps in several locations.

Pick up a *Guide for Guests with Disabilities* at Guest Relations. It gives mobility details and notes where you can use handheld-captioning, assisted-listening, video-captioning, and other devices (which are available for free but require a deposit). The guide also indicates which attractions have sign-language interpretation and when, which attractions don't permit service animals, and locations of designated "break" areas for animals.

At the hub by the Tip Board across from Casey's Corner, there's a large Braille map of the park. You can rent wheelchairs only at the park's entrance before passing under the train station for $12 daily, $10 a day for multiday rental. Electronic convenience vehicles (ECV) are $50 per day plus a refundable $20 security deposit. **■ TIP→ Neither wheelchairs nor ECVs can be booked ahead, so arrive early to rent them—ECV availability is limited.**

Stroller Rentals: The Stroller Shop is near the entrance on the east side of Main Street. Single strollers are $15 daily, $13 for multiday rental; doubles are $31 daily, $27 for multiday rental.

Wait-time updates: At the end of Main Street, on the left as you face Cinderella Castle, just before the Hub, is the **Tip Board**, a large board with constantly updated information about attractions' wait times.

PARK TOURS

Book any park tours ahead of your visit by calling ☎ *407/939–8687*.

Family Magic Tour. It's a two-hour "surprise" scavenger hunt in which your guide encourages you to find things that have disappeared. Disney officials don't want to reveal the tour's components—after all, it's the Family "Magic" Tour—but they will say that a special character-greeting session awaits you at the end of the adventure. Tours leave City Hall daily ($34 for adults and children 3 and up). ✉ *Main Street, U.S.A.* ☎ *407/939–8687* 🎫 *$34* ⏲ *Daily.*

Keys to the Kingdom Tour. The five-hour tour gives you a feel for the Magic Kingdom's layout and what goes on behind the scenes. The walking tour, which costs $79, includes lunch. Park admission must be purchased separately. No one younger than 16 is allowed. Tours leave from City Hall several times daily. Included are visits to "backstage" zones: the parade staging area, the wardrobe area, and other locations in the web of tunnels beneath the Magic Kingdom. ✉ *Main Street, U.S.A.* ☎ *407/939–8687* 🎫 *$79* ⏲ *Daily.*

Magic Behind Our Steam Trains. This tour, which gives you an inside look at the daily operation of the WDW railroad, became so popular that it was lengthened from two to three hours and is offered on six days. Tours begin at the front-entrance turnstile at 7:30 am Monday through Saturday. Visitors 10 years old and up may participate. The cost is $54 per person, plus park admission. ✉ *Magic Kingdom* ☎ *407/939–8687* 🎫 *$54* ⏲ *Mon.–Sat.*

Magic Kingdom guided tours. Several Disney-run Magic Kingdom guided tours are available. Ask about discounts when booking, and arrive 15 minutes ahead of time to check in. Park admission is required in addition to the tour fee unless otherwise noted. ✉ *Magic Kingdom* ☎ *407/939–8687.*

Walt Disney: Marceline to Magic Kingdom Tour. Walt Disney spent much of his early childhood in Marceline, Missouri, and this insider's walking tour offers insight into the boy who became the man behind the Disney kingdom. Open to ages 12 and up, tours ($30) leave from the Main Street Chamber of Commerce, next to City Hall, on Monday, Wednesday, Friday and Saturday at 8 am. ✉ *Main Street, U.S.A.* ☎ *407/939–8687* *$30* *Mon., Weds., Fri., and Sat.*

VISITING TIPS

■ Try to come toward the end of the week, because most families hit the Magic Kingdom early in a visit.

■ Ride a star attraction during a parade; lines ease considerably. (But be careful not to get stuck on the wrong side of the parade route when it starts, or you may never get across.)

■ At City Hall, near the park's Town Square entrance, pick up a map and a *Times Guide,* which lists showtimes, character-greeting times, and hours for attractions and restaurants.

■ Book character meals early. Main Street, U.S.A's The Crystal Palace, A Buffet with Character has breakfast, lunch, and dinner with Winnie the Pooh, Tigger, and friends. All three meals at the Fairy Tale Dining experience in Cinderella Castle are extremely popular—so much so that you should reserve your spot six months out. The same advice goes for booking the full service dinner at the new Be Our Guest Restaurant in the Beast's Castle in Fantasyland.

5

EXPLORING THE MAGIC KINGDOM

MAIN STREET, U.S.A

With its pastel Victorian-style buildings, antique automobiles ahoohga-oohga-ing, sparkling sidewalks, and an atmosphere of what one writer has called "almost hysterical joy," Main Street is more than a mere conduit to the other enchantments of the Magic Kingdom. It's where the spell is first cast.

You emerge from beneath the Walt Disney World Railroad Station into a realization of one of the most tenacious American dreams. The perfect street in the perfect small town in a perfect moment of time is burnished to jewel-like quality, thanks to a four-fifths-scale reduction, nightly cleanings with high-pressure hoses, and constant repainting. And it's a very sunny world, thanks to an outpouring of welcoming entertainment: live bands, barbershop quartets, and background music from Disney films and American musicals played over loudspeakers. Horse-drawn trolleys and omnibuses with their horns tooting chug along the street. Vendors in Victorian costumes sell balloons and popcorn. And Cinderella's famous castle floats whimsically in the distance where Main Street disappears.

Although attractions with a capital A are minimal on Main Street, there are plenty of inducements—namely, shops and eateries—to while away your time and part you from your money. The largest of these, the Emporium, is often the last stop for souvenir hunters at day's end. At the Main Street Bakery, you can find your favorite Starbucks latte and a sandwich or baked treats like cupcakes and brownies. If you can't resist an interactive challenge while making your way through the park, head first to the Firehouse, next to City Hall, to join the legendary wizard Merlin in the Sorcerers of the Magic Kingdom role-playing game. For no extra charge, you can take ownership of special cards with "magic spells" that help you search for symbols and bring down Disney villains like Yzma and Kronk from the Disney film *The Emperor's New Groove*. Don't worry—you'll have time between fireball battles and cyclone spells to ride Space Mountain.

The Harmony Barber Shop lets you step back in time for a haircut ($15 for children 12 and under, $19 for anyone older). Babies or tots get free Mickey Ears, a souvenir lock of hair, and a certificate if it's their first haircut ever, but you pay $19 for the experience. Tweens like to get colored hair gel or "pixie dust" applications (about $8 a pop). At the Town Square Theater (formerly Exposition Hall), presented by Kodak, Mickey Mouse meets you for photos and autographs. And, for the first time in Disney history, you can pick up a FastPass+ appointment for such meet and greets. While you're here, stock up on batteries and memory cards or disposable cameras.

Walt Disney World Railroad. If you click through the turnstile just before 9 am with young children in tow, wait at the entrance before crossing beneath the station. In a few moments, you'll see the day's first steam-driven train arrive laden with the park's most popular residents: Mickey Mouse, Donald Duck, Goofy, Pluto, and characters from every corner of the World. Once they disembark and you've collected the stars' autographs and photos, step right up to the elevated platform above the Magic Kingdom's entrance for a ride into living history. All the locomotives date from 1928, the same year Mickey Mouse was created.

Disney scouts tracked down these vintage carriers in Mexico (where they transported sugarcane in the Yucatán), brought them back, and overhauled them. They're splendid, with striped awnings, brightly painted benches, authoritative "choo-choo" sounds, and hissing plumes of steam.

The 1½-mile track runs along the perimeter of the Magic Kingdom, with much of the trip through the woods and stops in Frontierland and the newly expanded Fantasyland. The four trains run at five-to-seven-minute intervals. **For people with disabilities:** You can remain in a standard wheelchair or transfer to one if you're in an ECV. Equipped for handheld-captioning. **■ TIP→ The ride is a good introduction to the layout of the park; it's also great as relief for tired feet.** You can't load bulky strollers—like those Disney rents. Go midafternoon, when there's no line, or early, before 9 am, to greet Disney characters. ✉ *Magic Kingdom* ☞ *Duration: 21 mins or less depending where you disembark. Crowds: Moderate. Audience: All Ages.*

ADVENTURELAND

From the scrubbed brick, manicured lawns, and meticulously pruned trees of the Central Plaza, an artfully dilapidated wooden bridge leads to the jungles of Adventureland. Here, South African cape honeysuckle droops, Brazilian bougainvillea drapes, Mexican flame vines cling,

Adventureland Adventure Number 1: Being shipwrecked with the Swiss Family Robinson and exploring their tree house.

spider plants clone, and three varieties of palm trees sway. The bright, all-American sing-along tunes that fill the air along Main Street and Central Plaza are replaced by the recorded repetitions of trumpeting elephants, pounding drums, and squawking parrots. The architecture is a mishmash of the best of Thailand, the Middle East, the Caribbean, Africa, and Polynesia, arranged in an inspired disorder that recalls comic-book fantasies of far-off places.

Once contained within the Pirates of the Caribbean attraction, Captain Jack Sparrow and the crew of the Black Pearl are brazenly recruiting new hearties at the Pirates League, adjacent to the ride entrance. You can get pirate and mermaid makeovers (for lots of doubloons) here. On a nearby stage furnished with pirate booty, the captain instructs scurvy dog recruits on brandishing a sword at Captain Jack Sparrow's Pirate Tutorial (several shows a day). And that's not all! The new "A Pirate's Adventure: Treasures of the Seven Seas" sends park guests on an interactive quest with a pirate map and talisman to complete "raids" through Adventureland as they fight off pirate enemies along the way. Shiver me timbers—it's a pirate's life for ye!

Enchanted Tiki Room. The latest version of Disney's first Audio-Animatronics attraction brings back the original show, *Tropical Serenade*. Winged hosts Jose, Fritz, Pierre, Michael, and the boys take you on a tour of the attraction while cracking lots of jokes. The original ditty "In the Tiki, Tiki, Tiki, Tiki, Tiki Room" is second only to "it's a small world" as the Disney song you most love to hate. Speaking of which, many people do hate this attraction, finding the talking birds obnoxious and the music too loud and peppy. But you can also hear

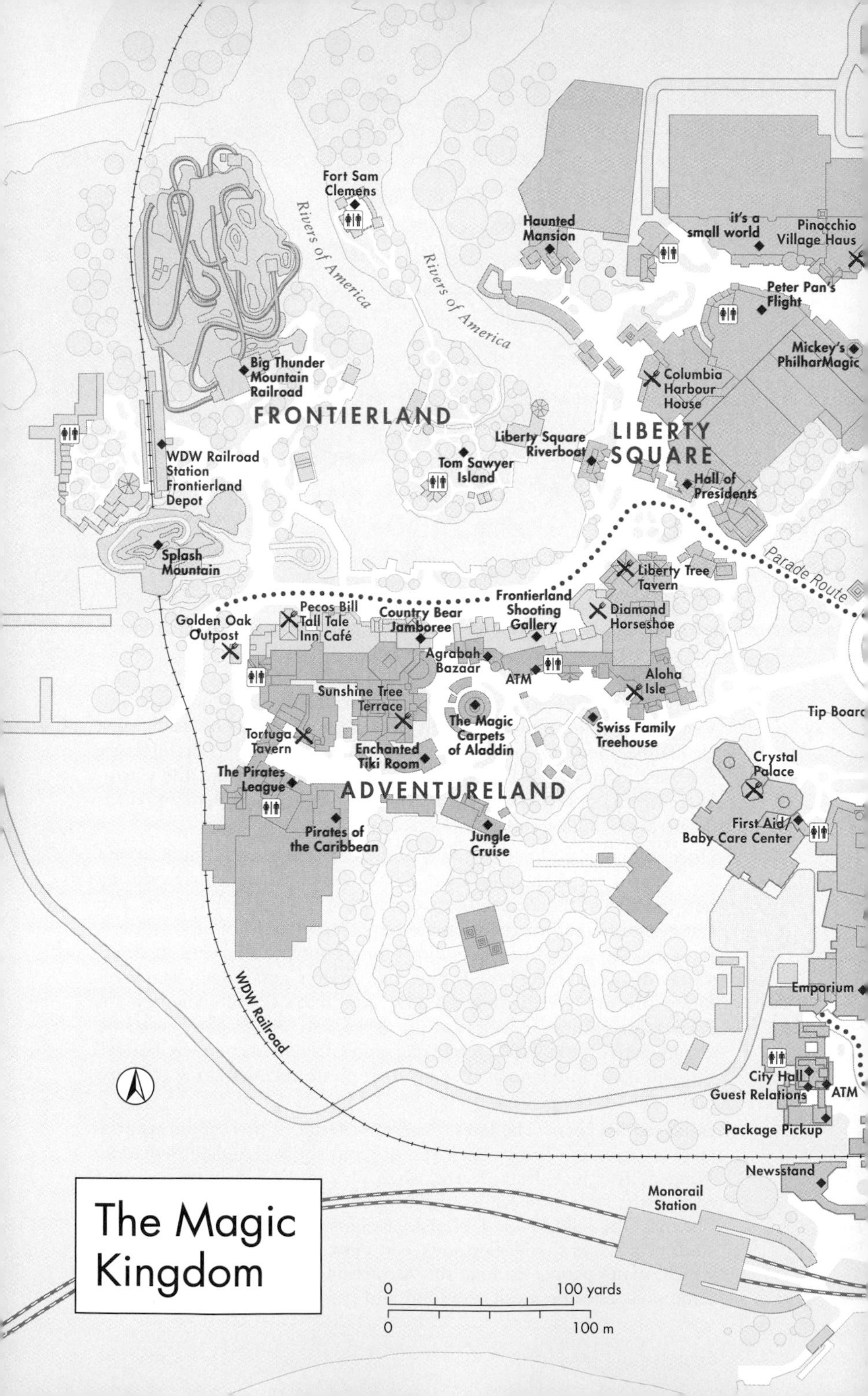

The Magic Kingdom
Fort Sam Clemens
Rivers of America
Rivers of America
Haunted Mansion
it's a small world
Pinocchio Village Haus
Peter Pan's Flight
Mickey's PhilharMagic
Big Thunder Mountain Railroad
Columbia Harbour House
FRONTIERLAND
LIBERTY SQUARE
Liberty Square Riverboat
Tom Sawyer Island
Hall of Presidents
WDW Railroad Station Frontierland Depot
Splash Mountain
Parade Route
Liberty Tree Tavern
Frontierland Shooting Gallery
Diamond Horseshoe
Pecos Bill Tall Tale Inn Café
Country Bear Jamboree
Golden Oak Outpost
Agrabah Bazaar
ATM
Aloha Isle
Sunshine Tree Terrace
The Magic Carpets of Aladdin
Swiss Family Treehouse
Tip Board
Tortuga Tavern
Enchanted Tiki Room
Crystal Palace
The Pirates League
ADVENTURELAND
Pirates of the Caribbean
Jungle Cruise
First Aid/ Baby Care Center
Emporium
WDW Railroad
City Hall
Guest Relations
ATM
Package Pickup
Newsstand
Monorail Station
0
100 yards
0
100 m

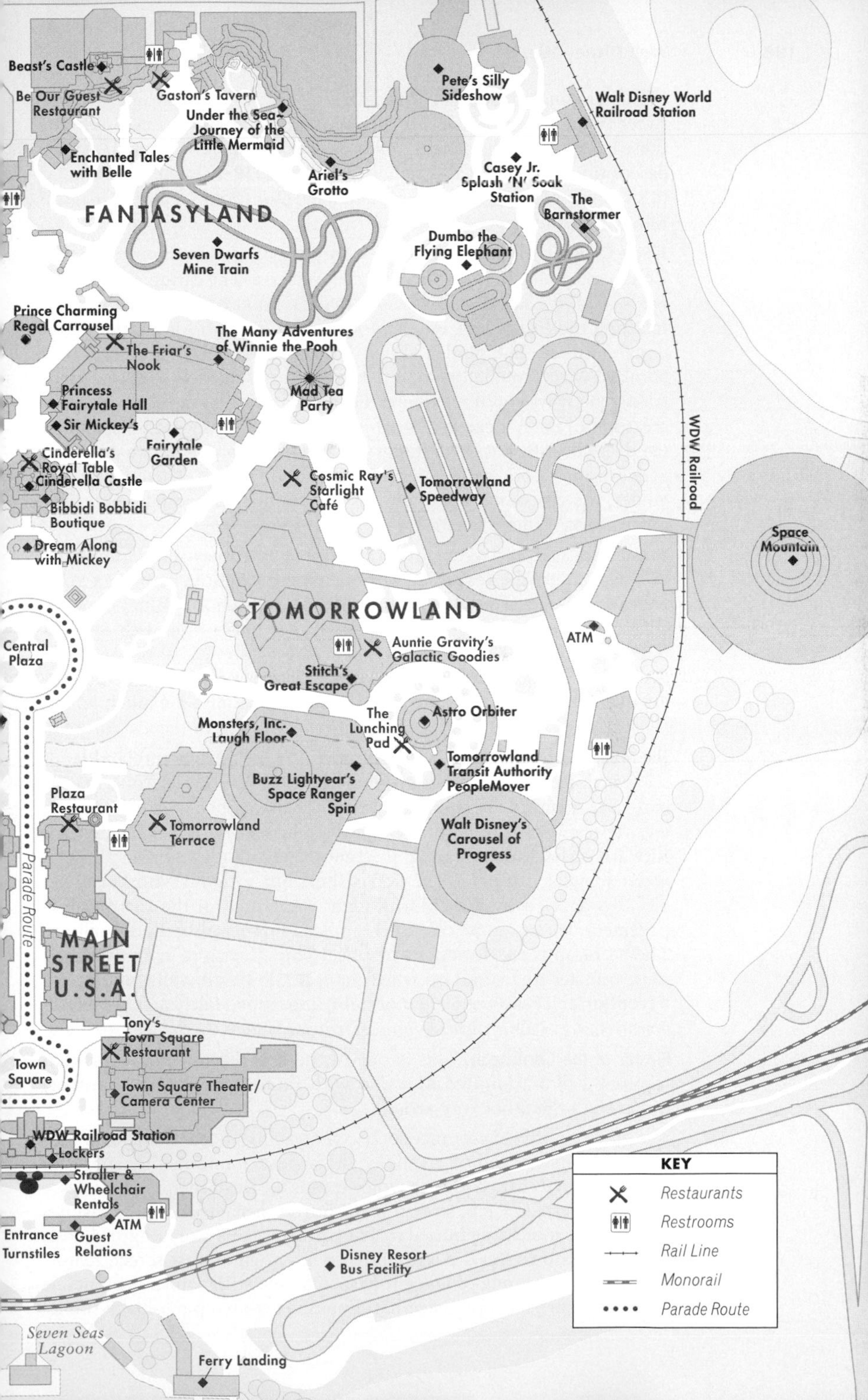

Beast's Castle
Be Our Guest Restaurant
Gaston's Tavern
Under the Sea~ Journey of the Little Mermaid
Enchanted Tales with Belle
Pete's Silly Sideshow
Walt Disney World Railroad Station
Ariel's Grotto
Casey Jr. Splash 'N' Soak Station
The Barnstormer
FANTASYLAND
Seven Dwarfs Mine Train
Dumbo the Flying Elephant
Prince Charming Regal Carrousel
The Many Adventures of Winnie the Pooh
The Friar's Nook
Mad Tea Party
Princess Fairytale Hall
Sir Mickey's
Fairytale Garden
Cinderella's Royal Table
Cinderella Castle
Bibbidi Bobbidi Boutique
Dream Along with Mickey
Cosmic Ray's Starlight Café
Tomorrowland Speedway
WDW Railroad
Space Mountain
TOMORROWLAND
Central Plaza
ATM
Auntie Gravity's Galactic Goodies
Stitch's Great Escape
Astro Orbiter
The Lunching Pad
Monsters, Inc. Laugh Floor
Tomorrowland Transit Authority PeopleMover
Buzz Lightyear's Space Ranger Spin
Plaza Restaurant
Tomorrowland Terrace
Walt Disney's Carousel of Progress
Parade Route
MAIN STREET U.S.A.
Tony's Town Square Restaurant
Town Square
Town Square Theater/ Camera Center
WDW Railroad Station
Lockers
Stroller & Wheelchair Rentals
ATM
Entrance Turnstiles
Guest Relations
Disney Resort Bus Facility
Seven Seas Lagoon
Ferry Landing
KEY
Restaurants
Restrooms
Rail Line
Monorail
Parade Route

old-timers singing along to "Let's All Sing Like the Birdies Sing," tweet, tweet tweet, tweet, tweet. **For people with disabilities:** Accessible for those in standard wheelchairs; equipped for handheld-captioning, audio description, and assisted-listening devices. **■TIP→ Go when you need to sit down with a/c.** ✉ *Adventureland* ☞ *Duration: 12 mins. Crowds: Moderate. Audience: All Ages.*

Jungle Cruise. Cruise through three continents and along four rivers: the Congo, the Nile, the Mekong, and the Amazon. The canopied launches are loaded, the safari-suited guides make a point of checking their pistols, and the *Irrawady Irma* or *Mongala Millie* is off for another "perilous" journey. The guide's shtick is surprisingly funny in a wry and cornball way, provided he or she has mastered the art of enunciation. Along the way, you'll encounter Disney's famed Audio-Animatronics creatures of the African veld: bathing elephants, slinky pythons, an irritated rhinoceros, a tribe of hungry headhunters, and a bunch of hyperactive hippos (good thing the guide's got a pop pistol). Then there's Old Smiley, the crocodile, who's always waiting for a handout—or, as the guide quips, "a foot out."

The animals are early-generation and crude by Disney standards—anyone who's seen the real thing at the Animal Kingdom or even a good zoo won't be impressed. Unless you're an old-school Disney fan, the Jungle Cruise isn't really worth a FastPass+. **For people with disabilities:** Several boats have lifts that allow wheelchair access; equipped for assisted-listening. Sign language is provided some days. **■TIP→ Go during the afternoon parade, but not after dark—you miss too much.** ✉ *Adventureland* ☞ *Duration: 10 mins. Crowds: Heavy. Audience: All Ages.*

The Magic Carpets of Aladdin. Brightening the lush Adventureland landscape is this jewel-toned ride around a giant genie's bottle. You can control your own four-passenger, state-of-the-art carpet with a front-seat lever that moves it up and down and a rear-seat button that pitches it forward or backward. Part of the fun is dodging the right-on aim of a water-spewing "camel." The ride is short but a big hit with kids, who are also dazzled by the colorful gems implanted in the surrounding pavement. Parents must ride with toddlers. **For people with disabilities:** There's ramp access for guests in wheelchairs. If you're in an ECV, you must transfer to a standard wheelchair. **■TIP→ Visit while waiting for a Frontierland FastPass+ appointment; lines move fairly quickly.** ✉ *Adventureland* ☞ *Duration: 3 mins. Crowds: Heavy. Audience: All Ages.*

Pirates of the Caribbean. This is one of the few rides in the world that inspired a film (*Haunted Mansion* with Eddie Murphy was another) rather than the other way around.

The gracious arched entrance soon gives way to a dusty dungeon, redolent of dampness and of a spooky, scary past. Lanterns flicker as you board the boats and a ghostly voice intones, "Dead men tell no tales." Next, a deserted beach, strewn with shovels, a skeleton, and a disintegrating map indicating buried treasure prefaces this story of greed, lust, and destruction. You'll pass right through a water-mist screen featuring the maniacal mug of Davy Jones, complete with squirming tentacle beard and barnacle-encrusted hat. Emerging from a pitch-black tunnel

Adventureland Adventure Number 2: Gliding through the muggy, steamy Caribbean world of pirates. Yo ho ho!

after a mild, tummy-tickling drop, you're caught between a pirate ship cannon-blasting a stone fortress. Look for Captain Barbossa, evil nemesis of Captain Jack Sparrow. Audio-Animatronics pirates hoist the Jolly Roger while brave soldiers scurry to defend the fort—to no avail.

Politically correct nerves may twinge as the women of the town are rounded up and auctioned, but the wenches rule in another scene, where they chase roguish rapscallions with glee. The wild antics of the pirates—Captain Jack Sparrow pops up in several situations—result in a conflagration; the town goes up in flames, and all go to their just reward amid a catchy chorus of "A Pirate's Life For Me." **For people with disabilities:** Boarding requires transferring from a standard wheelchair to the ride vehicle; the very small flume drop may make the attraction inappropriate for those with limited upper-body strength or those wearing neck or back braces. Equipped for audio-description and handheld-captioning devices. **■TIP→ This is a great destination in the heat of the afternoon, and lines move steadily.** ✉ *Adventureland* ☞ *Duration: 12 mins. Crowds: Moderate. Audience: All Ages.*

Swiss Family Treehouse. Inspired by the classic novel by Johann Wyss about the adventures of the Robinson family, who were shipwrecked en route to America, the tree house shows what you can do with a big faux tree and a lot of imagination. Disney detail abounds: the kitchen sink is a giant clamshell; the boys' room, strewn with clothing, has two hammocks instead of beds; and an ingenious system of rain barrels and bamboo pipes provides running water in every room.

As you clamber around the narrow wooden steps and rope bridges that connect the rooms in this split-level dwelling, take a look at the Spanish moss. It's real, but the tree itself—some 90 feet in diameter, with more than 1,000 branches—was constructed by the props department. The 300,000 leaves are vinyl. Toddlers unsteady on their feet may have trouble with the stairs. **For people with disabilities:** With its 100 steps and lack of narration, this attraction gets low ratings among those with mobility and visual impairments. ■ **TIP→ If you're with children 4 to 12 who like to explore, visit while waiting for a parade or FastPass+ appointment.** ✉ *Adventureland* ☞ *Duration: Up to You. Crowds: Light–moderate. Audience: All Ages.*

NEED A BREAK?

If you're looking for real refreshment and an energy boost, stop by Aloha Isle, where you'll find some of the tastiest and most healthful goodies. Try the fresh pineapple spears, or sip a smoothie or just some fruit juice, while you relax on one of the benches scattered around Adventureland.

FRONTIERLAND

Frontierland evokes the American frontier and is planted with mesquite, twisted Peruvian pepper trees, slash pines, and cacti. The period seems to be the latter half of the 19th century, and the West is being won by Disney cast members dressed in checked shirts, leather vests, cowboy hats, and brightly colored neckerchiefs. Banjo and fiddle music twangs from tree to tree, and snackers walk around munching turkey drumsticks so large that you could best an outlaw single-handedly with one. (Beware of hovering seagulls that migrate to the parks during cooler months—they've been known to snatch snacks.)

The screams that drown out the string music aren't the result of a cowboy surprising an Indian. They come from two of the Magic Kingdom's more thrilling rides: Splash Mountain, an elaborate flume ride, and Big Thunder Mountain Railroad, a roller coaster. The Walt Disney World Railroad tunnels past a colorful scene in Splash Mountain and drops you off between it and Thunder Mountain.

Fodor's Choice ★ **Big Thunder Mountain Railroad.** Set in gold-rush days, this thrilling roller coaster simulates a runaway train. It's a bumpy ride with several good drops (pregnant women and guests wearing back, neck, or leg braces should avoid this one). There are moments when you feel like you're going to fly right off the tracks. Overall it's more fun than scary, and you'll see kids as young as 7 lining up to ride. The train rushes and rattles past 20 Audio-Animatronics figures—mostly critters—as well as $300,000 worth of genuine antique mining equipment, tumbleweeds, a derelict mining town, hot springs, and a flash flood.

The 197-foot mountain landscape is based on the windswept scenery of Arizona's Monument Valley, and thanks to 650 tons of steel, 4,675 tons of concrete, and 16,000 gallons of paint, it replicates the area's gorges, tunnels, caverns, and dry river beds. **For people with disabilities:** You must be able to step into the ride vehicle and walk short distances. Service animals aren't permitted. ■ **TIP→ Use FastPass+ unless the wait is less than 15 minutes. The ride is most exciting at night, when you can't anticipate the curves and the track's rattling really sounds as if something's about to give.** ✉ *Frontierland* ☞ *Duration: 4 mins. Crowds: Absolutely. Audience: Not Young Kids.*

Country Bear Jamboree. Wisecracking, cornpone, lovelorn Audio-Animatronics bears joke, sing, and play country music and 1950s rock and roll in this stage show. Even timid youngsters love them. The emcee, the massive but debonair Henry, leads the stellar cast of Grizzly Hall, which includes the robust Trixie, who laments love lost while perching on a swing suspended from the ceiling; Bubbles, Bunny, and Beulah, harmonizing on "All the Guys That Turn Me On Turn Me Down"; and Big Al, the off-key cult figure who has inspired his own shopping kiosk. **For people with disabilities:** Wheelchair accessible; reflective captioning provided; equipped for assisted-listening devices. If you lip-read, ask to sit up front. **■ TIP→ Visit before 11 am, during the afternoon parade, or late in the day. Stand to the far left in the anteroom for the front rows and to the far right for the last row, where small kids can perch atop seats to see better.** ✉ *Frontierland* ☞ *Duration: 17 mins. Crowds: Heavy. Audience: All Ages.*

Fodor's Choice ★ **Splash Mountain.** The second-most-popular thrill ride after Space Mountain, this log-flume water ride was based on animated sequences in Disney's 1946 film *Song of the South.* Here the Audio-Animatronics creations of Brer Rabbit, Brer Bear, Brer Fox, and a menagerie of other Brer beasts frolic in bright, cartoonlike settings. Settle into the eight-person hollowed-out logs, and the fun begins.

As the boat carries you up the mountain, Brer Rabbit's silhouette hops merrily ahead to the tune of the ride's theme song, "Time to Be Moving Along." Every time some critter makes a grab for the bunny, your log boat drops out of reach. But Brer Fox has been studying his book *How to Catch a Rabbit,* and our lop-eared friend looks as if he's destined for the pot. Things don't look so good for the flumers, either. You get one heart-stopping pause at the top of the mountain—just long enough to grab the safety bar—and then the boat plummets about five stories at a 45-degree angle into a large, wet briar patch. It's enough to reach speeds of 40 mph—and makes you feel weightless. Clench your teeth and smile: as you begin to drop, a flashbulb pops. Another photographic memento for sale as you "Zip-a-Dee-Doo-Dah" your way to the next ride.

You may get wet, so plan accordingly. If you need to use Baby Swap you can take the young ones to a play area in a cave under the attraction; riders must be at least 40 inches tall. Do not ride if you're pregnant or have heart, back, or neck problems. **For people with disabilities:** You must be able to step into the ride vehicle and walk short distances. Service animals aren't permitted. **■ TIP→ Plan to use FastPass+ or ride when the park opens, during meal or parade times.** ✉ *Frontierland* ☞ *Duration: 11 mins. Crowds: Yes! Audience: Not Young Kids.*

Tom Sawyer Island. Tom Sawyer Island is a playground of hills, trees, rocks, and shrubs. Most attractions are on the main island, where your raft docks. The Mystery Mine is like a secret passageway to exploration. Children love Injun Joe's Cave, where there are lots of columns and crevices from which to jump out and startle siblings. As you explore the shoreline on the dirt paths, watch out for the barrel bridge—the whole contraption bounces at every step.

Coasting down Splash Mountain in Frontierland will put some zip in your doo-dah and some water on your clothes.

On the other island is Fort Langhorn, a log fortress from which you can fire air guns with great booms and cracks at the passing *Liberty Belle* riverboat. **For people with disabilities:** With its stairs, bridges, inclines, and narrow caves, this attraction isn't negotiable by those using a wheelchair. **■ TIP→ Try it as a refreshing afternoon getaway. Just mind your toddlers, as it's easy to lose track of them here.** ✉ *Frontierland* ☞ *Duration: Up to You. Crowds: Light. Audience: Kids and Tweens.*

LIBERTY SQUARE

The rough-and-tumble Western frontier gently folds into Colonial America as Liberty Square picks up where Frontierland leaves off. The weathered siding gives way to solid brick and neat clapboard. The mesquite and cactus are replaced by stately oaks and masses of azaleas. The theme is Colonial history, which Northerners will be happy to learn is portrayed here as solid Yankee. The buildings, topped with weather vanes and exuding prosperity, are pure New England.

A replica of the Liberty Bell, crack and all, seems an appropriate prop to separate Liberty Square from Frontierland. There's even a Liberty Tree, a more than 150-year-old live oak, transported here from elsewhere on Disney property. Just as the Sons of Liberty hung lanterns on trees as a signal of solidarity after the Boston Tea Party, the Liberty Tree's branches are decorated with 13 lanterns representing the 13 original colonies. Around the square are tree-shaded tables for an alfresco lunch and plenty of carts and fast-food eateries to supply the goods.

NEED A BREAK?

Sleepy Hollow offers quick pick-me-ups in the form of funnel cakes, soft-serve ice cream, espresso drinks, and waffle sandwiches.

Hall of Presidents: A Celebration of Liberty's Leaders. With the latest in Disney Audio-Animatronics (this attraction introduced the technology in 1971) this show tells a moving story of the bond between the presidents and "We, the People." Producers re-shot the accompanying film in high-definition video and added more than 130 images culled from the National Archives, Library of Congress, and other collections. A digital soundtrack, LED lighting, and narration by Morgan Freeman further enhance the experience. The film covers 220 years of U.S. history and emphasizes anecdotes about presidents who've reached out to people in times of strife. Both George Washington and Abraham Lincoln grab a bit of the spotlight, the latter by delivering his famous Gettysburg Address.

DID YOU KNOW?

It's hard to keep the Haunted Mansion's 200-odd trunks, chairs, harps, dress forms, statues, rugs, and knickknacks appropriately dusty. Disney buys its dust in 5-pound bags and scatters it with a gadget resembling a fertilizer spreader. Word is, enough dust has been dumped since the park's 1971 opening to completely bury the mansion. Where does it all go? Perhaps the voice is right in saying that something will follow you home.

5

The best part of the show is a roll call of all 43 U.S. presidents. (Fun fact: Obama is officially the 44th president because Grover Cleveland is counted twice due to his having served nonconsecutive terms.) Each chief executive responds with a nod, and those who are seated rise (except for wheelchair-bound Franklin Delano Roosevelt, of course). The robots nod and whisper to each other as the roll call proceeds. During Obama's turn, he takes the presidential Oath of Office (recorded in the White House by Imagineers) and delivers a speech about the American Dream. Anyone interested in presidential artifacts will enjoy the wait in the lobby area, where First Ladies' dresses, presidential portraits, and even George Washington's dental instruments are on display. **For people with disabilities:** Wheelchair accessible; enter through a door on the right. Reflective captioning available; equipped for assisted-listening devices. ■**TIP→ Visit anytime.** ✉ *Liberty Sq.* ☞ *Duration: 22 mins. Crowds: Moderate–Heavy. Audience: Not Young Kids.*

Fodor's Choice ★ **Haunted Mansion.** The special effects here are a howl. You're greeted at the creaking iron gates of this Gothic mansion by a lugubrious attendant, who has one of the few jobs at Disney for which smiling is frowned upon, and ushered into a spooky picture gallery. A disembodied voice echoes from the walls: "Welcome, foolish mortals, to the Haunted Mansion. I am your ghost host." An audio system with 30-plus surround-sound speakers ups the ghost-host fright factor. A scream shivers down, the room begins to "stretch," and you're off into one of Disney's classic attractions. ■**TIP→ Don't rush out of this room when other visitors depart; linger for some ghoulish bonus whispers.**

Consisting mainly of a slow-moving ride in a cocoonlike "doom buggy," the Haunted Mansion is only really scary for younger children, and that's mostly because of the darkness. Everyone else will laugh while they gawk at the special effects. Watch the ghostly ballroom dancers;

Liberty Square's Haunted Mansion in lights—pretty scary or just pretty? You decide.

Madame Leota's talking head in the crystal ball; and ghostly footprints that move along a staircase. In the "bride in the attic" scene, keep an eye on the portraits. Just when you think the Imagineers have exhausted their bag of ectoplasmic tricks, you discover that your doom buggy has gained an extra passenger. This is a high-capacity, fast-loading ride, and lines usually move steadily. **For people with disabilities:** Those in wheelchairs must transfer to the "doom buggies" and take one or more steps; however, if you can walk up to 200 feet, you'll enjoy the preshow as well as the ride's sensations and eerie sounds. Equipped for handheld-captioning and audio-description devices. **■ TIP→ When you reach a fork in the queue before entering the mansion, go left through the cemetery for interactive graveyard fun. Nighttime adds an extra fright factor.** ✉ *Liberty Sq.* ☞ *Duration: 8 mins. Crowds: Heavy. Audience: Not Young Kids.*

Liberty Square Riverboat. An old-fashioned steamboat, the *Liberty Belle* is authentic, from its calliope whistle and the gingerbread trim on its three decks to the boilers that produce the steam that drives the big rear paddle wheel. In fact, the boat misses authenticity on only one count: there's no mustachioed captain to guide it during the ride around the Rivers of America. That task is performed by an underwater rail. The 1½-mile cruise is slow and not exactly thrilling, but there are lovely views of Tom Sawyer Island and surrounding attractions. Children like exploring the boat. Lines move quickly. **For people with disabilities:** Wheelchair accessible; enter through exit on right or left. **■ TIP→ Come when you need a break from the crowds. Check Times Guide—the riverboat is**

open seasonally. ✉ *Liberty Sq.* ☞ *Duration: 15 mins. Crowds: Light–Moderate. Audience: All Ages.*

FANTASYLAND

Walt Disney called this "a timeless land of enchantment," and Fantasyland does conjure pixie dust. Perhaps that's because the fanciful gingerbread houses, gleaming gold turrets, and, of course, the rides are based on Disney-animated movies.

Many of these rides, which could ostensibly be classified as rides for children, are packed with enough delightful detail to engage the adults who accompany them. Fantasyland has always been the most heavily trafficked area in the park, and its rides and shows are almost always crowded.

The good news is that Fantasyland has undergone the largest expansion in the park's history to add several new attractions and experiences. Dumbo the Flying Elephant now is double the size, flying above circus-themed grounds that also include the Great Goofini coaster, starring Goofy as stuntman. There's also a Walt Disney World Railroad station in Fantasyland. And a circus-themed Casey Jr. Splash 'N' Soak Station provides water-play respite for kids. Ariel of *The Little Mermaid* invites you to her own state-of-the-art attraction, Under the Sea: Journey of the Little Mermaid. Disney princesses welcome you for a photo op in the glittering Princess Fairytale Hall. You can be part of the show when you join Belle, Lumiere, and Madame Wardrobe of *Beauty and the Beast* at the Enchanted Tales with Belle attraction for a story performance. Meanwhile, Beast may be brooding in his castle, where the Be Our Guest dining room beckons to lunch and dinner guests. And the musical Seven Dwarfs Mine Train family coaster just opened in 2014 to complete the expansion.

You can enter Fantasyland on foot from Liberty Square, Tomorrowland, or via the Walt Disney World Railroad, but the classic introduction is through Cinderella Castle. As you exit the castle's archway, look left to discover a charming and often overlooked touch: Cinderella Fountain, a lovely brass casting of the castle's namesake, who's dressed in her peasant togs and surrounded by her beloved mice and bird friends.

From the southern end of Liberty Square, head toward the park hub and stop at the Disney PhotoPass picture spot for one of the park's best, unobstructed ground-level views of Cinderella Castle. It's a great spot for that family photo.

Ariel's Grotto. Every mermaid princess should have a giant seashell throne, and that's where Ariel fans can meet the fashionably finned, red-headed beauty. Built into the rockwork of Prince Eric's castle, the grotto provides shade for those waiting in the queue and a more secluded experience for families who want to photograph or videotape the royal meet-up. ■ **TIP→ Families with young children should head here after exiting Under the Sea: Journey of the Little Mermaid.** ✉ *Fantasyland* ☞ *Duration: About 2 mins. Crowds: Yes. Audience: Young kids.*

The Barnstormer. This coaster, which used to feature Goofy at his Wiseacre Farm, now stars The Great Goofini, stuntmaster—a perfect fit

Continued on page 202

A MAN, A MOUSE, A LEGACY

By Jennie Hess

Walt Disney once said, "I only hope that we never lose sight of one thing—that it was all started by a mouse." His legendary mouse, Mickey, took the world by storm in 1928 in the theatrical debut of the animated short film *Steamboat Willie*. Today, Walt is Mickey, Mickey is Walt, and their legacy is legendary.

Above: Walt Disney; below: Mickey from *Fantasia*, 1940; right: *Pinocchio*, 1940

There's a tale still told (and disputed) that Walt imagined Mickey while on a train from New York to California, after a disastrous meeting where he lost the rights to a character called Oswald the Lucky Rabbit. Walt's friend and colleague, gifted Dutch cartoonist Ub Iwerks, first drew Mickey, but it was Walt who gave him a voice and personality.

He planned to name the mouse Mortimer, but his wife, Lilian, insisted the name didn't fit the cheerful little rodent.

The man behind the mouse, Walter Elias Disney, was born December 5, 1901, in Chicago. His early Midwestern years were spent nurturing his love of drawing. After driving an ambulance for the Red Cross in France during World War I, Walt returned to the States and worked for an ad company, where he met Ub.

Though Mickey appeared in the silent short *Plane Crazy* in May of 1928, the amiable mouse didn't really take a bow until the November debut of *Steamboat Willie*. Walt's use of synchronized sound made all the difference. By 1937, Walt and company had released their first animated feature-length film, *Snow White and the Seven Dwarfs*.

The many films that followed formed the creative and financial bedrock for a legacy of one theme park after another. But perhaps the greatest legacy of Walt and his mouse is that they both make memories for generation upon generation.

Hollywood studio opens

Steamboat Willie released

1930

Snow White wins special Oscar

Shirley Temple presents Disney with one big and seven dwarf-size Oscars for *Snow White*, 1939; right: *Snow White; Steamboat Willie* poster, 1928

1920s–30s A Mouse Is Born

Walt and his brother, Roy, establish a Hollywood studio in 1923. Animated shorts *Plane Crazy* and *Steamboat Willie*, starring both Mickey and Minnie, are released in 1928. Thereafter, Walt and his artists create dozens of Mickey shorts like 1930's *The Chain Gang*, when an orange pup named Pluto first appears.

Two years later, good-natured Goofy debuts as an audience extra in *Mickey's Revue*. His spasmodic laugh earns him a series of his own animated short films. Hot-tempered Donald Duck and his loyal girlfriend, Daisy, follow.

In 1937, America's first full-length animated feature, *Snow White and the Seven Dwarfs*, becomes the highest-grossing feature of its time. *Gone with the Wind* doesn't blow by that record until 1939, the same year that Disney's groundbreaking feature earns a special Academy Award: one full-size Oscar and seven dwarf Oscars presented by Shirley Temple.

■ **Visit:** Walt Disney: One Man's Dream; The Magic of Disney Animation

Goofy

1940s–50s Characters Come to Life

Fans of all ages flock to see successive hits, from *Pinocchio* and *Fantasia* (both 1940) to *Dumbo* (1941) and *Bambi* (1942). Though *Fantasia* is panned by some, it earns Academy Awards kudos for innovating in the area of visualized music—specifically, animation set to music by composers such as Bach, Tchaikovsky, and Beethoven and recorded under the direction of conductor Leopold Stokowski.

During World War II, the Disney studio springs to patriotic action with a series of military training and propaganda films. After the war, the animation wizards cast a spell over the

First Disney theme park opens in California

1950 | 1960 | 1970

Left: *Dumbo* and *Lady and the Tramp;* right: entrance to Sleeping Beauty's Enchanted Castle, Disneyland, late 1960s

country with *Cinderella* (1950), *Alice in Wonderland* (1951), *Peter Pan* (1953), *Lady and the Tramp* (1955), *Sleeping Beauty* (1959), and others.

Walt's love for nature leads him to produce 13 True-Life Adventure films, eight of which win Oscars. Walt also brings his first live-action adventure film, *Treasure Island,* to the screen. He and his brother, Roy, begin dreaming up a new adventure altogether—Disneyland.

The first Disney theme park opens on July 17, 1955, in Anaheim, California. Many attractions and rides have Disney film themes. Drawing on his lifelong train infatuation, Walt encircles the park with the Disneyland Railroad.

- **Visit:** Cinderella Castle
- **Ride:** Prince Charming Regal Carrousel, Peter Pan's Flight, Dumbo the Flying Elephant, and Walt Disney World Railroad
- **See:** Mickey's PhilharMagic

Cinderella Castle today

1960s–70s

A Magical New Frontier

In the early 1960s, Walt purchases 27,500 Orlando acres—an area twice the size of Manhattan. Sadly, he dies (December 1966) before Walt Disney World opens.

On October 1, 1971, the Magic Kingdom gates swing open, and a sleek monorail glides to the Contemporary and the Polynesian resort hotels. In November, a 640-acre western-style camping resort, Fort Wilderness, opens.

- **Visit:** Magic Kingdom
- **Ride:** The Monorail

Tokyo Disneyland opens

Disneyland Paris opens

1990

2000

Above: Disney Paris; Mickey hat; right: EPCOT's iconic Spaceship Earth

1980s–90s

A Worldlier Walt

Prior to his death, Walt begins work on what he hopes will be an ideal city. He names the project Experimental Prototype Community of Tomorrow. After the Magic Kingdom opens, Disney executives use some of Walt's ideas to create EPCOT Center. What opens in 1982 is the second Florida theme park—celebrating the world's cultures, the past, and the future—rather than an experimental community.

The 1980s are banner years for Disney Parks and Resorts. In 1983, the company's first international park—Tokyo Disneyland—opens. In 1989, Florida's third park, Disney-MGM Studios (later Disney's Hollywood Studios) premiers with celebrity fanfare. Not far from it, a new nightlife district, Pleasure Island, pumps up the volume, and Typhoon Lagoon crashes onto the scene with 6-foot waves and thrill-slide appeal.

The decade that follows is no less ambitious. In 1992 Euro Disney Resort (now Disneyland Paris) becomes the Mouse's second international destination; the first Disney cruise ships are launched from Port Canaveral, Florida; and the fourth Florida park, Disney's Animal Kingdom, earns raves for its authentic habitats. The icing on the Magic Kingdom's 20th anniversary cake? The animation studio is once again making big-screen hits with *Beauty and the Beast* (1991), *Aladdin* (1992), and *The Lion King* (1994)

■ **Visit:** Spaceship Earth at EPCOT; Beauty and the Beast—Live on Stage at the Studios; Kilimanjaro Safaris at Animal Kingdom; Typhoon Lagoon

Aladdin

Hong Kong Disneyland opens

Disney Dream cruise ship makes its maiden voyage

2010

2020

Finding Nemo's, Dory and Nemo

New Millennium

To Infinity and Beyond!

The new millennium sends the Mouse into overdrive. Hong Kong Disneyland opens (2005), as do several World attractions, among them one with a *Toy Story* theme, and two with a *Nemo* theme. Disney World also adds to its accommodations, bringing the total to 30,000 rooms, 3,200 Disney Vacation Club villas, and 800 campsites. New eateries like Spice Road Table at the Morocco pavilion in Epcot open, as do luxurious on-Disney property resorts including Waldorf Astoria and Four Seasons Resort Orlando.

Looking ahead, it seems as if pixie dust will permeate the World for years to come. The Magic Kingdom's new Fantasyland is complete with a 2014 final-phase opening of the Seven Dwarfs Mine Train family coaster. Disney Cruise Line now sails with four ships including the newer *Disney Fantasy* and *Disney Dream.* The multimillion-dollar makeover of Downtown Disney—to be renamed Disney Springs—will bring in new shops, restaurants, and entertainment, plus two much-needed parking garages by 2016.

Toy Story's Buzz Lightyear

FINDING MICKEY

A Hidden Mickey at Epcot

Hidden Mickeys began as an inside joke among Disney Imagineers, the creative folks behind the theme parks. When finishing an attraction, they'd slip a Mickey into the motif to see who might notice. You can get a list of Hidden Mickeys at any Guest Relations location, at www.allears.net, or at www.hiddenmickeys.org. Here are just a few to get you started, though:

Big Thunder Mountain Railroad (Magic Kingdom). As your train nears the station, look to your right for three rusty gears on the ground.

DINOSAUR (Animal Kingdom). Stare at the bark of the painted tree in the far left background of the wall mural at the entrance.

Haunted Mansion (Magic Kingdom). As you move through the ballroom, notice the Mouse-eared place setting on the table.

Spaceship Earth (Epcot). Mickey smiles down from a constellation behind the loading area.

Twilight Zone Tower of Terror (Hollywood Studios). In the boiler room, look for a water stain on the wall after the queue splits.

for Fantasyland's new Storybook Circus area. The twisting, turning roller coaster "flight" takes you high above the circus fun. It's perfect for young children's first thrill ride. Circus props and themed posters tell Goofini's tale with references to some of the short films of Goofy's heyday. **For people with disabilities:** You must be able to walk a few steps from your wheelchair to board the ride. Service animals are not permitted. **■TIP→ First thing in the morning, take the Walt Disney World Railroad to Fantasyland and hop in line before the crowds arrive.** ✉ *Fantasyland* ☞ *Duration: 1 min. Crowds: Heavy. Audience: All but Youngest Kids. Height minimum: 35 inches.*

Casey Jr. Splash 'N' Soak Station. The Casey Jr. circus train has just pulled into town, and train cars full of faux circus animals are taking a break in this circus-themed play area across from Dumbo the Flying Elephant. The critters may not be real, but they sure do put out a lot of water as children run hooting and squealing past spitting camels, spraying elephants, and other water hazards. **■TIP→ While the kids cool off and burn energy, parents can take a break and grab a hot dog or soft pretzel from nearby carts.** ✉ *Fantasyland* ☞ *Duration: As long as you like. Crowds: Not Bad. Audience: Young Kids.*

Cinderella Castle. Although often confused with Disneyland's Sleeping Beauty Castle, at 180-plus feet this castle is more than 100 feet taller; and with its elongated towers and lacy fretwork, it's more graceful. Don't miss the elaborate mosaic murals on the walls of the archway as you rush toward Fantasyland from the Hub. The five panels, measuring some 15 feet high and 10 feet wide were created from a million bits of multicolor Italian glass, silver, and 14-karat gold by mosaicist Hanns-Joachim Scharff. The mosaics tell the story of the little cinder girl as she goes from pumpkin to prince to happily ever after.

The fantasy castle has feet, if not of clay, then of solid steel beams, fiberglass, and 500 gallons of paint. Instead of dungeons, there are service tunnels for the Magic Kingdom's less-than-magical quotidian operations, such as Makeup and Costuming. These are the same tunnels that honeycomb the ground under much of the park.

Within the castle's archway is the **Bibbidi Bobbidi Boutique**, where the "royal treatment" transforms little girls age 3 and older into princesses or divas. Hair and makeup are by a "Fairy Godmother-in-training." The Knight Package offers a heroic alternative makeover that includes hair-style, sword, and shield. If you have reservations to dine at **Cinderella's Royal Table,** you enter the castle by way of an ascending spiral staircase. You are attended by costumed waiters and joined by Cinderella and other princesses in one of Disney's most popular character-dining experiences. **For people with disabilities:** For those with limited mobility, elevator access to the dining experience is provided. **■TIP→ Call 180 days ahead, or as soon as you can, to reserve the character breakfast, lunch, or dinner known as Fairytale Dining.** ✉ *Fantasyland.*

Dumbo the Flying Elephant. Based on the movie about the gigantic-eared baby elephant who learns he can fly, the ride consists of flying pachyderms, each packing a couple of kids and a parent. A joystick controls your Dumbo's up-and-down movement. A popular new feature

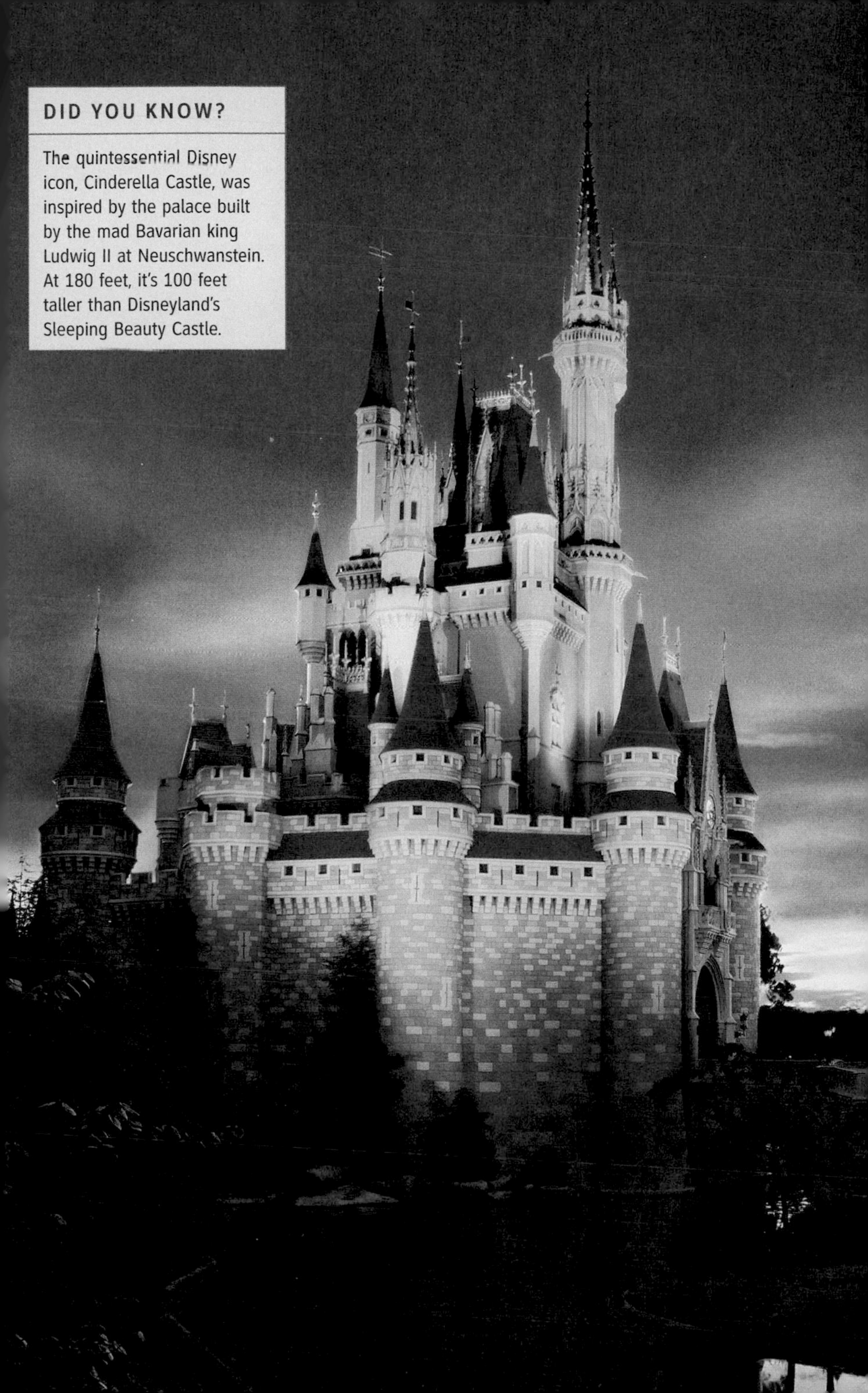

DID YOU KNOW?

The quintessential Disney icon, Cinderella Castle, was inspired by the palace built by the mad Bavarian king Ludwig II at Neuschwanstein. At 180 feet, it's 100 feet taller than Disneyland's Sleeping Beauty Castle.

See Lumiere chat with Belle at Enchanted Tales with Belle in Fantasyland.

for parents and children: the Big Top "play while you wait" indoor area chock full of climbing equipment for kids of most ages. As you enter the colorful circus tent, a Disney "ringmaster" hands you a pager that buzzes when it's your turn to ride. Parents can supervise tots in a small circus ring of play equipment while older kids burn up energy on multilevel climbers like the "Thrilling Tower of Flames." Adults enjoy the bench seating. **For people with disabilities:** If using a wheelchair, prepare to transfer to a ride vehicle. ■ **TIP→ Hop the train from Main Street to Fantasyland and ride early.** ✉ *Fantasyland* ☞ *Duration: 2 mins. Crowds: Heavy. Audience: Young Kids.*

Fodor's Choice ★ **Enchanted Tales with Belle.** Stroll the path through an artfully planted woodland and meadow to a rustic French cabin complete with waterwheel, where Belle's father, Maurice, tinkers with his inventions. The small homestead oozes Belle's provincial life, with a giant pot hanging in the fireplace and books stacked on a simple wooden chair. Inside her father's workshop, amid blueprints and tools, a giant gold-framed mirror hangs. A costumed cast member welcomes your group to the workshop (*Bonjour!*) and implores everyone to chant, "Take me back to the day Belle and Beast fell in love!" *Voila!* The mirror becomes an animated screen straight from the Disney film *Beauty and the Beast* before transforming into a portal that leads to an elegant room of Beast's Castle. Inside, an Animatronic Madame Armoire encourages guests to grab props and play character roles from the "tale as old as time." Then, it's on to the library, where a spot-on Animatronic Lumiere holds court from the mantle. Families grab a cushy bench as a coiffed actress playing Belle joins guests to act out a scene from the enchanted tale. You'll dance around the room to "Be Our Guest," and you may shed a tear as the interactive story unfolds. This live performance gets to the heart of Disney storytelling, and every participant poses for photos with Belle before a very happy ending. **For people with disabilities:** Wheelchair accessible; equipped for handheld captioning and assisted listening. **■ TIP→ Don't miss this enchanting experience while waiting for your Under the Sea: Journey of the Little Mermaid or other Fantasyland FastPass+ appointments.** ✉ *Fantasyland* ☞ *Duration: 15 mins. Crowds: Yes. Audience: All Ages; Perfect for Families.*

it's a small world. Visiting Walt Disney World and not stopping for this tribute to terminal cuteness—why, the idea is practically un-American. The attraction is essentially a boat ride through several candy color lands, each representing a continent and each crammed with musical moppets, all madly singing. Disney raided the remains of the 1964–65 New York World's Fair for sets, and then appropriated the theme song of international brotherhood and friendship for its own. Some claim that it's the "revenge of the Audio-Animatrons," as 450 simplistic dolls differentiated mostly by their national dress—Dutch babies in clogs, Spanish flamenco dancers, sari-wrapped Indians waving temple bells, Swiss yodelers, Japanese kite fliers, Middle East snake charmers, and young French cancan dancers, to name just a few—parade past, smiling away and wagging their heads in time to the song. Now all together: "It's a world of laughter, a world of tears. It's a world of hope and a world of fears." Take enchanted tots through again if the line is short.

5

For people with disabilities: You can board with your standard wheelchair through the designated entrance; if you use a scooter, transfer to one of the attraction's standard chairs available at the ride entrance. Equipped for handheld-captioning and audio-description devices. **■ TIP→ Come back later if there's a long line, because crowds truly do ebb and flow here.** ✉ *Fantasyland* ☞ *Duration: 11 mins. Crowds: Heavy. Audience: All Ages.*

Mad Tea Party. This carnival staple is for the vertigo addict looking for a fix. The Disney version is based on its own 1951 film *Alice in Wonderland*, in which the Mad Hatter hosts a tea party for his un-birthday. You hop into oversize, pastel-color teacups and whirl around a giant platter. Add your own spin to the teacup's orbit with the help of the steering wheel in the center. Check out the soused mouse that pops out of the teapot centerpiece. **For people with disabilities:** If using a wheelchair, enter through the exit on right, then transfer to a ride vehicle. **■ TIP→ Lines move slowly; skip this ride if the wait is longer than 30 minutes and if spinning could ruin your day.** ✉ *Fantasyland* ☞ *Duration: 2 mins. Crowds: Moderate. Audience: Young Kids.*

Fodor's Choice ★ **The Many Adventures of Winnie the Pooh.** The famous honey lover and his exploits in the Hundred Acre Wood are the theme for this ride. You can read posted passages from A.A. Milne's stories as you wait in line. Once you board your honey pot, Pooh and his friends wish you a "happy windsday." Pooh flies through the air, held aloft by his balloon, in his perennial search for "hunny," and you bounce along with Tigger, ride with the Heffalumps and Woozles, and experience a cloudburst. This ride replaced Mr. Toad's Wild Ride; look for the painting of Mr. Toad handing the deed to Owl. **For people with disabilities:** If using a wheelchair, obtain a FastPass+ or enter through standard queue. Equipped for handheld-captioning and audio-description devices. **■TIP→ Use a FastPass+ if crowds are heavy.** ✉ *Fantasyland* ☞ *Duration: 3 mins. Crowds: Heavy. Audience: Young Kids.*

Mickey's PhilharMagic. Mickey Mouse may be the headliner here, but it's Donald Duck's misadventures—reminiscent of Mickey's as the sorcerer's apprentice in *Fantasia*—that set the comic pace in this gorgeous, 3-D animated film. As you settle into your seat, the on-screen action takes you behind the curtains at a grand concert hall where Donald and Mickey are preparing for a musical performance. But when Donald misuses Mickey's sorcerer's hat, he finds himself on a whirlwind journey that includes a magic carpet ride and an electrifying dip under the sea. And you go along for the ride. On the way you meet Ariel, Simba, Aladdin, Jasmine, Peter Pan, Tinker Bell, and others.

The film startles with its special-effects technology—you'll smell a fresh-baked apple pie, feel the rush of air as champagne corks pop, and get lost in the action on the 150-foot-wide screen. The 3-D film marks the first time that classic Disney characters appear in a computer-generated animation attraction. Some of the effects can startle small children, and some of the darker scenes are a bit muddy through the recycled 3-D glasses. **For people with disabilities:** There's a special viewing area for guests in wheelchairs. Reflective captioning is provided; equipped for assisted-listening and audio-description devices. **■TIP→ It's a big theater, so waits aren't long.** ✉ *Fantasyland* ☞ *Duration: 12 mins. Crowds: Heavy. Audience: All Ages.*

Peter Pan's Flight. This sweet indoor ride was inspired by Sir James M. Barrie's 1904 novel about the boy who wouldn't grow up, which Disney animated in 1953. Aboard two-person magic sailing ships with brightly striped sails, you soar into the skies above London en route to Neverland. Along the way you can see Wendy, Michael, and John get sprinkled with pixie dust while Nana barks below, wave to Princess Tiger Lily, spot the evil Captain Hook, and cheer for the tick-tocking, clock-swallowing crocodile who breakfasted on Hook's hand.

Children—especially preschoolers—love this ride. Adults enjoy the dreamy views of London by moonlight. The downsides are the ride's brevity and its low-tech look. **For people with disabilities:** You must transfer from your wheelchair to the ride vehicle. Service animals aren't permitted. Equipped for handheld-captioning and audio-description devices. **■TIP→ Use FastPass+ here or ride early, late, or during the parade.** ✉ *Fantasyland* ☞ *Duration: 2.5 mins. Crowds: Heavy. Audience: Young Kids.*

Pete's Silly Sideshow. No other Disney character meet-and-greet location is quite as much fun as Pete's Silly Sideshow, named after the Mickey Mouse archnemesis created in 1925. But you won't meet Pete under this big top; instead, you'll grip and grin with Disney Fab Five characters Goofy, Minnie, and Donald, as well as Donald's sweetheart, Daisy. Each character poses for photos and signs autographs against a sideshow backdrop: the Great Goofini, "Broken Bone Record Holder," in his stunt garb; the Astounding Donaldo dressed as a snake charmer; Minnie Magnifique, pretty in pink feathers, and her "pirouetting Parisian poodles," and Madame Daisy Fortuna with crystal ball as "seer of all fate and destinies." Two queues move guests along fairly quickly, and elaborate, themed backdrops offer extra fun photo ops. Strongman Pete does make a poster appearance. ■ **TIP→ Grab your Under the Sea: Journey of the Little Mermaid FastPass+, then head back to the Storybook Circus area to meet these characters and ride Dumbo the Flying Elephant.** ⊠ *Fantasyland* ☞ *Duration: About 1–2 mins per character meet and greet. Crowds: Yes, but double queue makes wait shorter. Audience: Young Kids.*

Prince Charming Regal Carrousel. This ride is great for families and for romantics, young and old. Seventy-two of the 90 dashing wooden steeds date from the original carousel built in 1917 by the Philadelphia Toboggan Company; additional mounts were made of fiberglass. All are meticulously painted, and each one is completely different. One wears a collar of bright yellow roses; another, a quiver of Native American arrows. Eighteen panels beneath the wooden canopy depict scenes from Disney's 1950 film *Cinderella*. As the ride spins, the mirrors sparkle, the fairy lights glitter, and the band organ plays favorite Disney movie tunes. **For people with disabilities:** If using a wheelchair, or if you have a service animal, check with a host for boarding information. ■ **TIP→ Lines move quickly. Come while waiting for your Peter Pan's Flight FastPass+ reservation.** ⊠ *Fantasyland* ☞ *Duration: 2 mins. Crowds: Moderate–Heavy. Audience: Families.*

5

Fodor's Choice ★ **Seven Dwarfs Mine Train.** Quick! Can you name all Seven Dwarfs in seven seconds? Sleepy, Doc, Grumpy, Bashful, Sneezy, Happy, and Dopey. Snow White's hard-working pals debut impressive Audio-Animatronics flair as they mine a steep mountain-full of glittering gems and "Heigh-ho" their way into theme-park fans' hearts at the new Seven Dwarfs Mine Train. Set amid a steep Enchanted Forest landscaped with red poppies, cedars and birch trees, the long-awaited attraction is a visual feast of LED-illuminated gems, playful woodland creatures and beloved characters from Walt Disney's 1937 animated film classic, "Snow White and the Seven Dwarfs." A rough-hewn entrance to the mine leads to a covered queue designed to keep riders occupied as they wend their way toward the train load area. Fun interactive diversions include animated "floating" gems that you can catch and match in a touch-screen jewel-washing trough. The musical family coaster serves up thrills, but no stomach-churning plunges, with cars that twist, climb, drop rapidly and rock gently when slowing down for riders to enjoy the artfully crafted scene of the dwarfs at work in the mine. As the train rounds its final curve, you'll see Snow White dancing with her diminutive pals in the storybook cottage as the Wicked Queen, disguised as an old hag, lurks outside. The ride is not appropriate if you're pregnant or have heart, back, or neck problems. Expect this to be the highest-demand attraction in Disney World's four-park playbook for some time. **For people with disabilities:** You must transfer from wheelchair to ride vehicle.

MAGIC KINGDOM

NAME	Height Req.	Type of Entertainment	Duration	Crowds	Audience	Tips
Adventureland						
Enchanted Tiki Room	n/a	Show	12 mins.	Light	All Ages	Visit when you need a refresher in a/c.
Jungle Cruise	n/a	Cruise	10 mins.	Heavy	All Ages	Use FastPass+ or come during the parade.
The Magic Carpets of Aladdin	n/a	Thrill Ride for Kids	3 mins.	Heavy	All Ages	Visit while waiting for a FastPass+ appointment.
Pirates of the Caribbean	n/a	Cruise	10 mins.	Moderate	All Ages	A good destination in the heat of the afternoon.
Swiss Family Treehouse	n/a	Walk-through	Up to you	Moderate	All Ages	Visit while waiting for a FastPass+.
Fantasyland						
The Barnstormer	35″	Thrill Ride for Kids	1 min.	Heavy	All but Young Kids	Ride early after hopping train to Fantasyland.
★ Dumbo the Flying Elephant	n/a	Thrill Ride for Kids	2 mins.	Heavy	Young Kids	New circus tent queue offers air-conditioned play area.
★ Enchanted Tales with Belle	n/a	Show	15 mins.	Heavy	All Ages	Go while waiting for Mermaid FastPass+ appointment.
it's a small world	n/a	Cruise	11 mins.	Moderate	All Ages	Tots may beg for a repeat ride; it's worth it.
Mad Tea Party	n/a	Thrill Ride for Kids	2 mins.	Moderate	Young Kids	Skip it if wait is 30 mins.
★ The Many Adventures of Winnie the Pooh	n/a	Thrill Ride for Kids	3½ mins.	Heavy	All Ages	Use FastPass+. Come early, late in the afternoon, or after dark.
Mickey's PhilharMagic	n/a	3-D Film	12 mins.	Heavy	All but Young Kids	Use FastPass+ or arrive early or during a parade.
Peter Pan's Flight	n/a	Thrill Ride for Kids	2½ mins.	Heavy	All Ages	Try evening or early morning. Use FastPass+ first.
Prince Charming Regal Carrousel	n/a	Thrill Ride for Kids	2 mins.	Moderate to Heavy	Families	Come while waiting for Peter Pan's Flight FastPass+, during afternoon parade, or after dark.
★ Seven Dwarves Mine Train	At least 38″	Thrill Ride	2½ mins.	Heavy	All but Young Kids	This ride just opened use a FastPass+.
Under the Sea: Journey of the Little Mermaid	n/a	Ride-Through	7 mins.	Absolutely!	All Ages	You can get a FastPass+, but you'll miss the interactive queue.

Frontierland						
★ Big Thunder Mountain Railroad	At least 40"	Thrill Ride	4 mins.	Absolutely!	All but Young Kids	Use FastPass+. Most exciting at night when you can't anticipate the curves.
Country Bear Jamboree	n/a	Show	17 mins.	Heavy	All Ages	Visit before 11 am. Stand to the far left lining up for the front rows.
★ Splash Mountain	At least 40"	Thrill Ride with Water	11 mins.	Yes!	All but Young Kids	Use FastPass+. Get in line early, or ride during meal or parade time. You may get wet.
Liberty Square						
Hall of Presidents	n/a	Show/Film	22mins.	Moderate	All but Young Kids	Visit anytime.
★ Haunted Mansion	n/a	Thrill Ride	8 mins.	Moderate	All Ages	Nighttime adds extra fear factor.
Liberty Square Riverboat	n/a	Cruise	15 mins.	Moderate	All Ages	Good for a break from the crowds.
Main Street U.S.A.						
Walt Disney World Railroad	n/a	Railroad	21 mins.	Moderate to Heavy	All Ages	Board with young children for an early start in Frontierland or Fantasyland or hop on midafternoon.
Tomorrowland						
Astro-Orbiter	n/a	Thrill Ride for Kids	2 mins.	Moderate to Heavy	All Ages	Skip unless there's a short line.
★ Buzz Lightyear's Space Ranger Spin	n/a	Interactive Ride	5 mins.	Heavy	All Ages	Come in the early morning and use FastPass+. Kids will want more than one ride.
Monster's Inc. Laugh Floor	n/a	Film with special effects	15 mins.	Moderate to Heavy	All Ages	Come when you're waiting for your Buzz Lightyear or Space Mountain FastPass+.
★ Space Mountain	At least 44"	Thrill Ride	2½ mins.	You Bet!	All but Young Kids	Use FastPass+, or come at the beginning or the end of day or during a parade.
Stitch's Great Escape	At least 40"	Simulator Exp.	15 mins.	Moderate to Heavy	All but Young Kids	Visit early after Space Mountain.
Tomorrowland Speedway	54" to drive	Thrill Ride for Kids	5 mins.	Moderate	All but Young Kids	Come in the evening or during a parade; skip on a first-time visit; 32" height requirement to ride shotgun.
Tomorrowland PeopleMover	n/a	Railroad	10 mins.	Light	All Ages	Come with young kids if you need a restful ride.
Walt Disney's Carousel of Progress	n/a	Show	20 mins.	Light to Moderate	All Ages	Skip on a first-time visit unless you're heavily into nostalgia.

★ Fodor's Choice

■ **TIP→ Book your FastPass+ at the closest park kiosk if you didn't reserve it at the MyDisney Experience.com website or mobile app. If circumstances deposit you in the stand-by queue, enjoy the clever hands-on activities along the way.** ✉ *Fantasyland* ☞ *Duration: 2.5 mins. Crowds: Heavy. Audience: All but children under the 38 in. height minimum.*

Under the Sea: Journey of the Little Mermaid. The shipwreck theming, craggy grotto rockwork, waterfalls, lagoons, and magical landscape of this attraction draw you into Ariel's world long before you board a giant clamshell for a journey under the sea. As you wend your way throught the long queue, you'll see starfish embedded in rocks, a sandy beach, palm trees, sea-grape plants, and other authentic seaside touches. Once inside the cavern beneath Prince Eric's Castle, you can join in an interactive game that plays out around every corner starring Scuttle the seagull and his animated crab pals. Through a cave portal, you'll enter the castle's stone hallways where you hop aboard a clamshell ride vehicle and, thanks to cold air and light effects, feel the sensation of descending under the sea. You'll float past animated and Audio-Animatronic scenes from *The Little Mermaid* film, including a Broadway-style "Under the Sea" number with Sebasian conducting the undersea orchestra. There are fish conga lines and ominous scenes starring villainess Ursula but, of course, a fairy-tale ending is in store featuring Menken-Ashman showstopper "Kiss the Girl." Most children love this ride, but some tots are afraid in the dark Ursula scene. ■ **TIP→ You can get a FastPass+, but you'll miss the fun of the interactive stand-by queue.** ✉ *Fantasyland* ☞ *Duration: 7 mins. Crowds: Absolutely! Audience: All Ages.*

TOMORROWLAND

The "future that never was" spins boldly into view as you enter Tomorrowland, where Disney Imagineers paint the landscape with whirling spaceships, flashy neon lights, and gleaming robots. This is the future as envisioned by sci-fi writers and moviemakers in the 1920s and '30s, when space flight, laser beams, and home computers were fiction, not fact. Retro Jetsonesque styling lends the area lasting chic.

Gamers who want a break from the crowds can find their favorite video challenges in the arcade attached to Space Mountain. SEGA race car, NASCAR, and Fast and Furious Super Bikes games draw tweens and teens; Lil' Hoops give young kids a manageable basketball challenge. Though Tomorrowland Transit Authority (TTA) PeopleMover isn't a big-ticket ride, it's a great way to check out the landscape from above as it zooms in and out of Space Mountain and curves around the entire land.

Astro Orbiter. This gleaming superstructure of revolving planets has come to symbolize Tomorrowland as much as Dumbo represents Fantasyland. Passenger vehicles, on arms projecting from a central column, sail past whirling planets; you control your car's altitude but not the velocity. The line is directly across from the entrance to the TTA PeopleMover. **For people with disabilities:** You must be able to walk several steps and transfer to the vehicle. ■ **TIP→ The line moves slowly; come while waiting for a Space Mountain FastPass+ appointment or if there's a**

In Tomorrowland, interplanetary travel is within your reach on the Astro Orbiter.

short line. Skip on your first visit if time is limited. ✉ *Tomorrowland* ☞ *Duration: 2 mins. Crowds: Moderate–Heavy. Audience: All Ages.*

Fodor's Choice ★ **Buzz Lightyear's Space Ranger Spin.** Based on the wildly popular *Toy Story*, this ride gives you a toy's perspective as it pits you and Buzz Lightyear against the evil Emperor Zurg. You're seated in a fast-moving two-passenger Star Cruiser vehicle with an infrared laser gun and a centrally located lever for spinning your ship to get a good vantage point. Throughout the ride you shoot at targets to help Disney's macho space toy, Buzz, defeat the emperor and save the universe. You have to hit the targets marked with a "Z" to score, and the rider with the most points wins. To infinity and beyond! **For people with disabilities:** To board you must transfer to a standard wheelchair. Equipped for audio-description and handheld-captioning devices. **■ TIP→ Come first thing in the morning and get a FastPass+ (if available). If you're with kids, time the wait and—if it's only 15 or 20 minutes—ride twice so they can have a practice run.** ✉ *Tomorrowland* ☞ *Duration: 5 mins. Crowds: Heavy. Audience: All Ages–Truly.*

Monsters, Inc. Laugh Floor. The joke's on everyone at this interactive attraction starring Mike Wazowski, the one-eyed hero from Disney-Pixar's hit film *Monsters, Inc.* In the 400-seat theater, you can interact with an animated Mike and his sidekicks in the real-time, unscripted way that the character Crush from *Finding Nemo* performs at Epcot in Turtle Talk with Crush at The Seas with Nemo & Friends. Here the premise is that Mike realizes laughter can be harnessed as a power source, and Mike's new comedy club is expected to generate power for the future. The more the audience yuks it up, the greater the power produced. You can text-message jokes from cell phones to the show's producer; they might even be used in the show. **For people with disabilities:** Wheelchair accessible. Sign language is available some days. Equipped for assisted-listening and video-captioning devices. ■**TIP→ Come when you're waiting for your Buzz Lightyear or Space Mountain FastPass+ appointment.** ✉ *Tomorrowland* ☞ *Duration: 15 mins. Crowds: Heavy. Audience: All Ages.*

Fodor's Choice ★ **Space Mountain.** The needlelike spires and gleaming, white, concrete cone of this 180-foot-high attraction are almost as much of a Magic Kingdom landmark as Cinderella Castle. Inside is what is arguably the world's most imaginative roller coaster. Although there are no loop-the-loops or high-speed curves, the thrills are many as you take a trip into the depths of outer space—in the dark.

You can pass the wait time playing big-screen interactive space games in the long, dark queue area. As you walk to the loading area, you'll pass whirling planets and hear the screams and shrieks of the riders, pumping you up for your own launch. Once you blast off, the ride lasts only two minutes and 38 seconds, with a top speed of 28 mph, but the devious twists and invisible drops in the dark make it seem twice as long. You can hear the screams from other cars, but you don't know where they are, adding an additional fright factor. Stow personal belongings securely. Not appropriate for pregnant women or guests wearing back, neck, or leg braces. **For people with disabilities:** You must be able to step into the ride vehicle and walk short distances. Guests in wheelchairs should obtain a FastPass+ or see a cast member for boarding options. Service animals aren't permitted. ■**TIP→ The wait can be long. Get a FastPass+, or come early, late, or during a parade.** ✉ *Tomorrowland* ☞ *Duration: 2.5 mins. Crowds: You Bet! Audience: Not Young Kids. Height minimum: 44 inches.*

Stitch's Great Escape. Once again, Disney seizes upon a hit film to create a crowd-pleasing attraction. The film is *Lilo & Stitch,* and the attraction is built around a back-story to the film about the mischievous alien, Stitch, before he meets Lilo in Hawaii. You're invited, as a new security recruit for the Galactic Federation, to enter the high-security teleportation chamber, where the ill-mannered Stitch is being processed for prison. In the form of a 3½-foot-tall Audio-Animatronics figure, Stitch escapes his captors and wreaks havoc on the room during close encounters with the audience in near-darkness. Sensory effects are part of the package. Beware the chili-dog "belch" odor and other tactile surprises.

Young children may be frightened by shoulder restraints, periods of darkness, and loud, startling noises. **For people with disabilities:** Guests in motorized scooters must transfer to an on-site standard wheelchair. Equipped for assisted listening, handheld-captioning, and video-captioning devices. Guests with service animals should check with a host before entering. ■**TIP→ Come during a parade or whenever lines dwindle.** ✉ *Tomorrowland* ☞ *Duration: 15 mins. Crowds: Moderate–Heavy. Audience: Not Young Kids. Height minimum: 40 inches.*

Tomorrowland Speedway. This is one of those rides that incite instant addiction in children and immediate regret in their parents. The reasons

MAGIC KINGDOM KIDS TOUR

The Magic Kingdom is alive with thrilling distractions for young children, so let them take the lead now and then. Toddlers may want to jump from their strollers and dance along to the barbershop quartet on Main Street. Children who love to explore will have a ball scrambling around Frontierland and hopping a raft to Tom Sawyer's playground.

STOP AND SMELL THE ROSES

Head down Main Street, U.S.A, and, if you're lucky, the park's **Dapper Dan's barbershop quartet** will be harmonizing sweet tunes and tossing out one-liners from a small alcove along the street (check the park's *Times Guide* for performances). Young children are jazzed by the music and colorful costumes of these talented singers.

As you continue on, veer right toward the rose garden for a scenic picture spot where you can snap one of the prettiest shots in the park: the kids by the garden amid Mickey and Minnie topiaries, with Cinderella Castle in the background.

Fantasyland is dead ahead, and after you've soared on **Dumbo the Flying Elephant** and nabbed a FastPass+ for Under the Sea: Journey of the Little Mermaid or the new Seven Dwarfs Mine Train family coaster, head straight to Enchanted Tales with Belle where the kids get to participate. Then, try and catch a character performance in front of **Cinderella Castle** or during one of the daily parades or street parties.

PUT THE ZIP IN YOUR DOO-DAH

With little ones in tow, when it's time for food, fast is best. **Cosmic Ray's Starlight Café** is a high-energy quick stop with multiple choices for the entire family. Kids can head straight to the dance floor where an Audio-Animatronics entertainer keeps the tunes coming. After refueling, board the **Walt Disney World Railroad** at Main Street, U.S.A, Fantasyland, or Frontierland. While in Frontierland, too-short-to-ride kids can burn energy in the cave-like play area beneath **Splash Mountain** while parents take turns riding. And the short raft trip to **Tom Sawyer Island** is worth it for kids who like exploring. Not far from the Country Bear Jamboree, sure shots can take aim at Western-style targets in the often-missed **Frontierland Shootin' Arcade**—at about $1 per 35 shots, it's a blast for any aspiring sheriff.

BECOME THE CHARACTER

Get the makeover of a lifetime ($55–$190) at **Bibbidi Bobbidi Boutique,** in Cinderella Castle. Hair, nails, makeup—even a sprinkling of pixie dust—it's all here. At the **Pirates League,** in Adventureland by Pirates of the Caribbean, a scurvy sea-dog makeover ($29.95–$45) lets the inner buccaneer emerge. Don't want to be a pirate? Try the mermaid makeover ($75).

But the best-buy makeover (and fastest, too) is in Town Square, where the **Harmony Barber Shop** transforms your hair with colored gel at about $8 a pop. After, be sure to catch a character meet and greet (see *Times Guide* for schedule) so the little rascals get all the hugs, autographs, photos, and magical memories they deserve.

If Pooh can, you can—enjoy a Main Street parade, that is.

for the former are evident: the brightly colored Mark VII model cars that swerve around the four 2,260-foot tracks with much *vroom-vroom-vrooming*. Like real sports cars, the vehicles are equipped with rack-and-pinion steering and disc brakes; unlike the real thing, these run on a track. However, the track is so twisty that it's hard to keep the car on a straight course. Expect to spend a lot of time waiting your turn on the track and returning your vehicle after your lap. All this for a ride that achieves a top speed of 7 mph.

For people with disabilities: To drive the cars, you must be able to steer, press the gas pedal, and transfer into the low car seat. ■ **TIP→ Skip on a first-time visit unless you'll break your child's heart.** ✉ *Tomorrowland* ☞ *Duration: 5 mins. Crowds: Moderate. Audience: Young kids and Tweens. Height requirements: With an adult must be at least 32 inches; those who wish to drive must reach 54 inches.*

Tomorrowland Transit Authority PeopleMover. A reincarnation of what Disney old-timers may remember as the WEDway PeopleMover, the TTA PeopleMover gives you a nice, leisurely ride with great views of Tomorrowland, circling the Astro-Orbiter and gliding through the middle of Space Mountain. Disney's version of future mass transit is smooth and noiseless, thanks to an electromagnetic linear induction motor that has no moving parts, uses little power, and emits no pollutants. **For people with disabilities:** You must be able to walk several steps and step on and off of a moving ramp to transfer to a ride vehicle. Equipped for handheld-captioning and audio-description devices. ■ **TIP→ Come to view Tomorrowland, to preview Space Mountain, if you have young children,**

or if you need a relaxing ride. ✉ *Tomorrowland* ☞ *Duration: 10 mins. Crowds: Light. Audience: All Ages.*

Walt Disney's Carousel of Progress. Originally seen at New York's 1964–65 World's Fair, this revolving theater traces the impact of technological progress on the daily lives of Americans from the turn of the 20th century into the near future. Representing each decade, an Audio-Animatronics family sings the praises of modern-day gadgets that technology has wrought. **For people with disabilities:** Wheelchair accessible; equipped for assisted-listening, handheld-captioning, audio-description, and video-captioning devices. **■TIP→ Skip on a first-time visit unless you adore nostalgia. May close early or entirely in low season.** ✉ *Tomorrowland* ☞ *Duration: 20 mins. Crowds: Moderate. Audience: All Ages.*

MAGIC KINGDOM SPECTACLES

5

Celebrate the Magic!. Before the popular Wishes fireworks show each evening, and some nights twice, Cinderella Castle lights up to tell a story to park guests with the help of cutting-edge projector technology that wraps colorful images around the castle in sequences enhanced by music. For 10 minutes, the castle is a magical canvas that transforms into Alice's rabbit hole, Simba's savanna, and Dumbo's big top. Playful sequences feature popular Disney and Pixar characters, and even Walt Disney himself. Watch for seasonal updates like the villains' appearance around Halloween. **For people with disabilities:** Ask any cast member along Main Street for the best wheelchair viewing location; several areas are set aside. **■TIP→ Try for a better view and some breathing room away from the crowds by migrating to one of the walkways that lead from the castle hub to Tomorrowland or Adventureland.** ✉ *Magic Kingdom* ☞ *Duration: 10 mins. Crowds: Heavy. Audience: All Ages.*

Fodor's Choice ★ **Disney Festival of Fantasy Parade.** Who'd want to miss a parade that delivers in 12 entertainment-packed minutes a lineup of Disney characters and royalty, a Steampunk-inspired, fire-breathing dragon, elaborate towering floats, and handsome pairs of dancers twirling to some of Disney's best tunes? This newest daily 3 pm parade celebrates Walt's legacy with vignettes featuring the glamour, drama, and fun of classic films like *Sleeping Beauty* and *Peter Pan* while also catering to fans of contemporary box-office hits like *Brave* and *Frozen*. The colorful pageant of nine floats out-performs its predecessors with über-creative costuming, inventive float technology, a cast of nearly 100 gung-ho performers, and a new musical score that invites singing along with familiar medleys. From the 50-foot-long topiary garden float of Disney royal couples led by dancers in swan-neck-collared ball gowns with iridescent feathers to the 32-foot-tall Airship float finale with Mickey and Minnie, the parade energizes spectators as it rolls past. A Lost Boy from *Peter Pan* may grab your hand and kiss it. A stilt-walker might lean into your camera for a snapshot. You'll hear viewers gasp or shout when the towering 53-foot-long, green-eyed Maleficent Dragon, created with help from Tony-award-winning designer Michael Curry, rears its head and spews flames. **For people with disabilities:** There are viewing areas for guests in wheelchairs along the route; ask any cast member for guidance. A sign-language schedule is available at Guest Relations. ■ **TIP→ The parade runs from Frontierland to Town Square. Check your guidemap for the complete route. Disney now distributes a limited number of FastPass+ reservations, but book as far ahead as possible. Otherwise, find shade beneath a Frontierland porch at least an hour before showtime. If you've seen the parade, this is a good time to head for popular rides while crowds gather along the route.** ✉ *Magic Kingdom* ☞ *Duration: 12 mins. Crowds: Heavy. Audience: All Ages.*

Dream Along with Mickey. The Cinderella Castle forecourt provides the perfect location for several daily performances of this Disney character spectacle starring Donald Duck, Mickey Mouse, Minnie Mouse, Goofy, and others. As the show begins, Donald is a "dreams-come-true" skeptic, but he has joined his optimistic pals anyway at a party where Disney princes and princesses dance in a romantic, dreamy number. There's adventure, too, when Peter Pan, pirates, and wenches take the stage. When pesky Disney villains crash the party, Donald decides to challenge evil and fight for the dreams of all his character friends and family. If you want to sit (and don't mind an obstructed view), arrive 30 to 40 minutes before showtime to get a seat on a bench. ■ **TIP→ If you have children, plan to stand or sit on the pavement near the stage for an unobstructed view.** ✉ *Magic Kingdom* ☞ *Duration: 20 mins. Crowds: Heavy. Audience: All Ages.*

Fodor's Choice ★ **Main Street Electrical Parade.** The Main Street parade, with 23 illuminated floats, 80 performers, and a half-million lights in all, first debuted at Disneyland in California in 1972. It lights up Magic Kingdom nights with plenty of power and its distinctive synthesizer-infused "Baroque Hoedown" musical theme. The lead float features Tinker Bell showering guests with 25,000 pixie-dusted points of light, and a finale float with a patriotic tribute that includes a majestic bald eagle shining with golden lights. Check *Times Guide;* the parade sometimes runs twice in one night and occasionally not at all. ■ **TIP→ Take your place on the curb at least 40 minutes before the parade begins.** ✉ *Magic Kingdom* ☞ *Duration: 20 mins. Crowds: Heavy. Audience: All Ages.*

Fodor's Choice ★ **Wishes.** When the lights dim on Main Street and orchestral music fills the air, you know this fireworks extravaganza is about to begin. In Wishes, Jiminy Cricket's voice comes to life and tries to convince you that your wishes really can come true. He gets plenty of support from the Disney stars of classic films such as *Pinocchio, Fantasia, Cinderella,* and *The Little Mermaid.* Portions of famous film songs play over loudspeakers, and you hear the voices of film characters like Peter Pan and Aladdin as more than 680 individual fireworks paint the night sky. Oh, and don't worry that Tinker Bell may have been sealed in her jar for the night—she comes back to fly above the crowd in grand pixie-dust style. Check the *Times Guide* for performance time, which varies seasonally. ■ **TIP→ Best views are in the Castle forecourt or on surrounding bridges; or find a place near the front of the park for a quick postshow exit.** ✉ *Magic Kingdom* ☞ *Duration: 12 mins. Crowds: Heavy. Audience: All Ages.*

SHOPPING

The Main Street buildings, with forced-perspective architecture and elaborately decorated facades, beckon, but don't waste precious touring time shopping in the morning. Come back later for Disney watches, hand-blown crystal, cookware, princess dresses, mouse ears, and, of course, fairy-tale-themed snow globes. For sweet souvenirs, don't miss the Main Street Confectionery, the most popular destination for consumables anywhere on Walt Disney World property. Chocolate-covered pineapple spears, anyone? Sip and nosh at the Main Street Bakery, which recently underwent some sprucing up and now serves Starbucks signature beverages and treats, along with artisanal sandwiches and Disney favorites like cookies and seasonal cupcakes.

MAIN STREET, U.S.A

The Chapeau. Classic monogrammed mouse ears are always in style, and there's a large selection here including fancy ear hats and bride-and-groom ears. You can have your name stitched on the ears while you wait. Mouse ear headbands with hero and villain themes are all the rage, or you can buy a Disney baseball cap to block the sun. ✉ *Main Street, U.S.A.*

5

Crystal Arts. This shop dazzles with Arribas Brothers engraved crystal pieces like a sparkling Cinderella coach or an iconic glass slipper in one of many sizes (though none will fit your foot!). ■ **TIP→ Be sure to visit the glass studio and its 2,100°F furnaces in the back, where a glassblower explains the process while creating wineglasses and bowls. Fascinating!** ✉ *Main Street, U.S.A.*

The Emporium. At 17,000 square feet, it's one of the largest souvenir shops in any of the parks. You'll find thousands of Disney character products, from sunglasses to plush toys. Princess items rock for little girls; the costume jewelry is an inexpensive souvenir. This is the place to buy Mickey sweatshirts or T's. Inquire about deals or marked-down merchandise. ✉ *Main Street, U.S.A.*

Uptown Jewelers. It's a treasure chest of jewelry, figurines, and accessories by Vera Bradley, Dooney and Bourke, and other leading designers. If dressing up is your thing, Uptown has your bling. ✉ *Main Street, U.S.A.*

ADVENTURELAND

Agrabah Bazaar. In addition to the expected Aladdin-wear and Jasmine costumes, you'll also find maracas and other inexpensive percussion instruments, gold- and silver-plated bangles, collectible pins, sunglasses, and snappy safari hats. ✉ *Adventureland.*

Pirate's Bazaar. Just outside the Pirates of the Caribbean, you can stock up on pirate hats, swords, flintlocks, and hooks-for-hands. The ultimate scalawag topper is a Captain Jack Sparrow hat complete with braids if it's not sold out when you visit. ✉ *Adventureland.*

FRONTIERLAND

Big Al's. This merchandise cart across the walkway from the Country Bear Jamboree has Davy Crockett coonskin caps, cowboy hats like Woody wears in *Toy Story*, and other gear that draws oohs and ahs from cowboy and -girl wannabes. ✉ *Frontierland.*

LIBERTY SQUARE

Ye Olde Christmas Shoppe. Shoppers who arrive after Christmas may discover some markdowns on ornaments. Mickey, princess, and other character-themed stockings are hot items. Character ornaments, Mickey wedding top hats, and Minnie bridal veils are always in stock. ✉ *Liberty Sq.*

FANTASYLAND

Castle Couture. Sparkly, shimmering dresses, hats, dolls, jewelry, and princess nightgowns and slippers are all the rage here. ✉ *Fantasyland.*

SPAS

MAGIC KINGDOM RESORT AREA

Senses—A Disney Spa at Disney's Grand Floridian Resort. All the senses—sound, sight, smell, touch, and taste—are engaged when you enter this new, Disney-designed and -owned, 15-room spa near the Wedding Pavilion at the Grand Floridian Resort. Soothing fruit-based elixirs start the journey toward serenity, while soft lighting, gentle music, and the aroma of lavender encourage you to shed your stress along with your clothes. Lounge chairs in separate and secluded men's and women's relaxation areas offer you a spot to further unwind as you wait. Pure silk sheets on the heated massage tables surround you in heavenly luxury. Tiny green-glass tiles form a floral mosaic on the walls and on heated lounge chairs in the restful wet room (spend some time looking for the hidden Mickey on the wall). Swimsuits are required in all wet relaxation areas. Treatments include facials, scrubs, warm-stone, Swedish, and aromatherapy massages. A whimsical Mad Hatter chair offers little princesses a special place for a pedicure. Massage from $135. Packages from $375. 20% gratuity added. ✉ *Grand Floridian Resort, 4401 Floridian Way* ☎ *407/824–3000* 🌐 *www.disneyworld.disney.go.com* ☞ *Parking: complimentary self-parking.*

DOWNTOWN DISNEY RESORT AREA

Blue Harmony. Infused with the colors of ocean and sky, this spa lives up to its name from the moment you enter. Its signature treatment combines exfoliation with marine salt and oil, polishing with marine salt and lavender, and a massage based in Thai techniques. Body treatments use oil-infused seawater gels to add natural minerals to the skin, and end with a cozy wrap and massage. Two of the eight treatment rooms are outdoors near the relaxation spa garden and hot tub, taking advantage of the blue Florida sky. The serene relaxation lounge offers beverages and tea as you wait for your treatment. Bring the family, as the spa offers treatments for teens and men. Massage from $120. Packages from $140. ✉ *14651 Chelonia Pkwy.* ☎ *407/390–2442.*

Kay Casperson Lifestyle Spa and Boutique. At the Buena Vista Palace's 10,000-square-foot haven for the frazzled fun-seeker, you can settle back in one of 14 treatment rooms for an invigorating facial using botanicals, minerals, and ingredients from the sea, or enjoy a relaxing deep-tissue massage. The Kay Casperson philosophy balances inner health and outer beauty, so after a treatment, guests are offered a free makeup application of Casperson's hypoallergenic products. Those ages

12 and under who choose the Princess Package receive a tiara along with a mani-pedi and makeup session. The spa has a full-service salon, private steam showers, a large dry sauna, separate whirlpools, and an adults only lap pool for serene swimming. Massage from $120. Packages from $305. There is a 20% service charge. ✉ *Buena Vista Palace Hotel & Spa, 1900 E. Buena Vista Dr.* ☎ *407/827–3200* 🌐 *www.buenavistapalace.com.*

Senses Spa at Disney's Saratoga Springs Resort. The spa may share its name with the Grand Floridian's, and the senses are just as successfully nourished, but the ambience is quite different at this two-story stone-and-wood spa, inspired by the legendary lodges at the mineral springs of the Adirondacks. Fruit-infused elixirs and the scent of frankincense sooth you as you enter either the separate men's or women's waiting room. Signature treatments include the Hydrotherapy package that combines water and stone to exfoliate, soak, wrap, and relax that stressed-out body, and the Bamboo Fusion massage that combines warm stones and an ancient technique using heated bamboo segments. The pure silk sheets surround you with dreamlike luxury. Don't miss the spa's two wet relaxation rooms, with steam bath, pool, and heated, glass-tile-covered lounge chairs. You can even bring the family—there's a couples' treatment room and a manicure and pedicure for kids ages 4–12. Swimsuits are required in wet rooms. Massages from $145. Spa packages from $375. ✉ *Disney's Saratoga Springs Resort, 1960 Broadway* ☎ *407/939–7727.*

EPCOT

Walt Disney said that Epcot would "take its cue from the new ideas and new technologies that are now emerging from the creative centers of American industry." He wrote that Epcot—never completed, always improving—"will never cease to be a living blueprint of the future, a showcase to the world for the ingenuity of American free enterprise."

But the permanent settlement that Disney envisioned wasn't to be. Epcot opened in 1982—16 years after his death—as a showcase, ostensibly, for the concepts that would be incorporated into the real-life Epcots of the future. (Disney's vision *has* taken an altered shape in the self-contained city of Celebration, an urban-planner's dream opened in 1996 on Disney property near Kissimmee.)

Epcot, the theme park, has two key areas: Future World, where most pavilions are collaborations between Walt Disney Imagineering and U.S. corporations and are designed to demonstrate technological advances through innovative shows and attractions; and the World Showcase, where shops, restaurants, attractions, and live entertainment create microcosms of 11 countries from four continents.

For years, Epcot was considered the more staid park, a place geared toward adults. But after its 10th anniversary, Epcot began to evolve into a livelier, more child-friendly park, with interactive fun at Innoventions and such "wow" attractions as Future World's Test Track, Mission: SPACE, and Soarin'.

There's something for everyone here. The World Showcase appeals to younger children with the Kidcot Fun Stop craft stations and the Norway pavilion's Princess Storybook Dining. Soarin', in the Land Pavilion, is a family favorite. And the Seas with Nemo & Friends—with one of the world's largest saltwater aquariums and a Nemo-themed ride—is a must-see for all. The hottest new ticket? The greatly improved Test

TOP ATTRACTIONS

The American Adventure. Many adults and older children love this patriotic look at American history; who can resist the Audio-Animatronics hosts, Ben Franklin and Mark Twain?

IllumiNations. This amazing musical laser-fountains-and-fireworks show is Disney nighttime entertainment at its best.

Mission: SPACE. Blast off on a simulated ride to Mars, if you can handle the turbulence.

Soarin'. Everyone's hands-down favorite: feel the sweet breeze as you "hang glide" over California landscapes.

Test Track. Design your concept car, then rev up to 60 mph on a hairpin turn in this wild ride on a Chevrolet proving ground.

MIND GAMES

Although several attractions provide high-octane kicks, Epcot's thrills are mostly for the mind. The park is best for school-age children and adults, but there's interactive entertainment for everyone at **Innoventions** and with the **Disney Phineas and Ferb: Agent P's World Showcase Adventure,** with starting points in several locations. Most attractions provide some diversions for preschool children. At the 11 **Kidcot Fun Stops,** younger children can try their hands at crafts projects—like designing a mask and adding special touches at each pavilion along the way.

5

Track presented by Chevrolet, where you can design your own custom concept car, then put it through its high-speed paces.

Wear comfortable shoes—there's *a lot* of territory to cover here. Arrive early, and try to stay all day, squeezing in extras like high-tech games at Innoventions and a relaxing meal. If you enter through International Gateway before 11 am, cast members will direct you to Future World, which usually opens two hours before World Showcase.

ORIENTATION AND PLANNING

GETTING ORIENTED

Epcot is composed of two areas: Future World and the World Showcase. The inner core of Future World's pavilions has the Spaceship Earth geosphere and a plaza anchored by the computer-animated Fountain of Nations. Also at the core is Innoventions, popular for its hands-on, high-tech exhibits, and immersion entertainment.

Six pavilions compose Future World's outer ring. Each of the three east pavilions has a ride and the occasional postride showcase; a visit rarely takes more than 30 minutes. The blockbuster exhibits on the west side contain rides and interactive displays; each exhibit can take up to 90 minutes for the complete experience.

World Showcase pavilions are on the promenade that circles the World Showcase Lagoon. Each houses shops, restaurants, and friendly international staffers; some have films or displays. Mexico and Norway offer tame rides. Live entertainment is scheduled at every pavilion except Norway.

Disney's monorail and buses drop you off at the main entrance in front of Future World. But if you're staying at one of the Epcot resorts (the BoardWalk, Yacht Club, Beach Club, Dolphin, or Swan), you can use the International Gateway entrance between World Showcase's France and U.K. pavilions.

EPCOT PLANNER

PARK AMENITIES

Baby Care: The baby-care center at Odyssey Center in Future World has rocking chairs and low lighting. The center sells formula, baby food, pacifiers, and disposable diapers. Changing tables are available here, as well as in all women's and some men's restrooms.

Cameras: Disposable cameras and memory cards are widely available, and you can use the Disney PhotoPass Service to gather memories throughout the park. Other photo services are available at the Imagination! pavilion.

First Aid: Staffed by registered nurses, first aid is in the Odyssey Center. More than a dozen automated external defibrillators are located across the park.

Guest Relations: To the right of the ticket windows at the park entrance and to the left of Spaceship Earth inside the park, this is the place to pick up schedules and maps. You also can get maps at the park's International Gateway entrance and most shops. Guest Relations will also assist with dining reservations, ticket upgrades, and services for guests with disabilities.

Lockers: Lockers ($7 and $9, with $5 refundable deposit) are at the International Gateway and to the west of Spaceship Earth. Coin-operated lockers also are at the bus information center by the bus parking lot.

Lost People and Things: Instruct children to speak to someone with a Disney name tag if you become separated. Guest Relations has a computerized message center for contacting companions in any of the parks.

Epcot Lost and Found. Located in the Guest Relations lobby east of Spaceship Earth. ✉ *Future World, Epcot* ☎ *407/560–7500.*

Main Lost and Found office. After one day, all articles are sent here. ✉ *Ticket and Transportation Center [TTC], Magic Kingdom* ☎ *407/824–4245.*

Package Pick-Up: Ask shop clerks to forward large purchases to Package Pick-Up at the Gift Stop in the Entrance Plaza and at the World Traveler at International Gateway. Allow three hours for delivery. You also can have packages sent to your Disney hotel.

Services for People with Disabilities: Accessibility standards are high. Many attractions and most restaurants and shops are fully wheelchair accessible. There are large Braille park maps at Guest Relations in Future World and International Gateway as well as to the left of the walkway from Future World to the World Showcase Plaza.

At Guest Relations there's a schedule for sign-language presentations at some of the park attractions; you also can pick up special devices for hearing- and sight-impaired visitors.

At World Showcase most people stroll around the promenade, but there are also Friendship boats, which require visitors using oversize wheelchairs or scooters to transfer to Disney chairs.

You can rent wheelchairs at the gift stop outside the main entrance, at the Stroller & Wheelchair Rental Shop to the left of Spaceship Earth, or at the International Gateway. A limited number of electronic convenience vehicles (ECV) are available only at the Stroller & Wheelchair Rental.

Wheelchairs are $12 daily, $10 for multiday rental. ECVs are $50 per day plus a refundable $20 security deposit. Arrive early, because neither conveyance can be reserved.

Stroller Rentals: You can rent strollers on the east side of the Entrance Plaza and at the International Gateway. Singles are $15 daily, $13 for multiday rental; doubles cost $31 daily, $27 for multiple days. Even preschoolers will be glad for a stroller in this large park.

PARK TOURS

Dolphins in Depth. At 9:45 am Dolphins in Depth ($199, neither park admission nor diving certification required) guides escort you from Epcot Guest Relations outside the main park entrance. Tours run Tuesday through Saturday and last about three hours. Participants must be 13 or older; a parent or legal guardian must accompany anyone under 18. ✉ *Epcot* ☎ *407/939–8687* 🎟 *$199* ⏲ *Tues.–Sat.*

Epcot Divequest. On the three-hour Epcot Divequest ($175, park admission not required or included) at the Seas with Nemo & Friends pavilion, you spend 40 minutes in the mammoth aquarium under the supervision of a master diver. The tours take place Tuesday through Saturday in the afternoon. Guests 10 and up must have open-water adult scuba certification; children under 17 must dive with a parent or legal guardian. ✉ *Epcot* ☎ *407/939–8687* 🎟 *$175* ⏲ *Tues.–Sat.*

Epcot Seas Aqua Tour. For this tour ($140, no park admission required or included) you wear a flotation device and diving gear, but you remain on the water's surface. Anyone age 8 and older can join the tour (those ages 8–12 must be with a parent or legal guardian). Tours are limited to 12 guests, meet Tuesday through Saturday, and run about 2½ hours, with 30 minutes in the water. ✉ *Epcot.*

UnDISCOVERed Future World. This tour ($64, plus park admission) leaves at 9 am Monday through Friday from Guest Relations at the main entrance. The four-hour behind-the-scenes walk for guests 16 and older covers all Future World pavilions and some VIP lounges and backstage areas including the Epcot marina where IllumiNations fireworks floats are docked. ✉ *Epcot* ☎ *407/939–8687* 🎟 *$64* ⏲ *Weekdays.*

VISITING TIPS

■ Epcot is so vast and varied that you really need two days to explore. With just one day, you'll have to be highly selective.

■ Go early in the week, when others are at Magic Kingdom.

EPCOT BY BOAT

Epcot is a big place at 305 acres; a local joke suggests that the acronym actually stands for "Every Person Comes Out Tired." But still, the most efficient way to get around is to walk.

To vary things, you can cruise across the lagoon in an air-conditioned, 65-foot water taxi. Also called Friendship Boats, they depart every 12 minutes from two World Showcase Plaza docks at the border of Future World.

The boat closer to Mexico zips to a dock by the Germany pavilion; the one closer to Canada heads to Morocco. You may have to stand in line to board, however.

- If you like a good festival, visit during the International Flower & Garden Festival (early to mid-March through May) or the International Food & Wine Festival (late September through mid-November).
- Once through the turnstiles at either the main Future World entrance or the back World Showcase entrance, make a beeline for the popular Mission: SPACE and Test Track (for fast-paced thrills) or the Seas with Nemo & Friends and Soarin' (for family fun). Or get a FastPass+ and return later.

EXPLORING EPCOT

FUTURE WORLD

Future World's inner core is composed of the iconic Spaceship Earth geosphere and, beyond it, a plaza anchored by the awe-inspiring computer-animated Fountain of Nations, which shoots water 150 feet skyward. Don't miss interactive fun at Innoventions.

Six pavilions compose Future World's outer ring. On the east side, they are the Ellen's Energy Adventure, Mission: SPACE, and Test Track. Each pavilion presents a single, self-contained ride and an occasional postride showcase; a visit rarely takes more than 30 minutes, but it depends on how long you spend in the postride area. On the west side are the Seas with Nemo & Friends, The Land, and Imagination! These blockbuster exhibits contain both rides and interactive displays; you could spend at least 1½ hours at each of these pavilions, but there aren't enough hours in the day, so prioritize.

■ TIP→ Before setting out, look into the Disney PhotoPass at the Camera Center in the Entrance Plaza. It tracks photos of your group shot by Disney photographers, which you can view and purchase later at the center or online.

SPACESHIP EARTH

Balanced like a giant golf ball waiting for some celestial being to tee off, the multifaceted silver geosphere of Spaceship Earth is to Epcot what Cinderella Castle is to the Magic Kingdom. As much a landmark as an icon, it can be seen on a clear day from an airplane flying down either coast of Florida.

Spaceship Earth ride. Inside the giant geosphere you are transported past a series of tableaux that explore human progress and the continuing search for better forms of communication. Oscar-winner Dame Judi Dench narrates the journey that begins in the darkest tunnels of time, proceeds through history, and ends poised on the edge of the future. Ten-time Emmy winner Bruce Broughton composed the musical score.

Audio-Animatronics figures present Cro-Magnon man daubing mystic paintings on cave walls, Egyptian scribes scratching hieroglyphics on papyrus, Roman centurions building roads, Islamic scholars mapping the heavens, and 11th- and 12th-century Benedictine monks hand-copying manuscripts. As you move into the Renaissance, there's Michelangelo and Gutenberg and, in rapid succession, the telegraph, radio, television, and computer come into being. A family views the moon landing on TV, and soon the personal computer is born.

5

As your ride vehicle swings backward and descends slowly, touch screens ask how you envision your own future, then play back an animated, *Jetsons*-esque scenario based on the answers. Siemens, which presents the higher-tech attraction, created a fun-packed postshow with high-demand interactive games. As you enter the post-show, watch the giant digital map screen to see your photo taken during the ride and posted in your hometown location.

For people with disabilities: You must be able to transfer to a standard wheelchair, then walk four steps to the ride vehicle. Guests with service animals should check with an attraction host for boarding information. The ride is equipped for handheld captioning and audio-description devices available at Guest Relations. **■ TIP→ Ride while waiting for a Mission: SPACE or Soarin' FastPass+ appointment. Lines are longest in the morning and shortest just before closing.** ✉ *Future World, Spaceship Earth* ☞ *Duration: 15 mins. Crowds: Moderate–Heavy. Audience: All Ages.*

INNOVENTIONS

This walk-through attraction contains interactive exhibits that entertain kids (some are especially designed for preschoolers) and adults as they investigate the innovations now improving the world around us.

Innoventions. Innoventions is loaded with activities designed to entertain and inspire kids and adults, and it's a great place for families to play together. Take Sum of All Thrills, by technology company Raytheon, for instance. This is not your typical "design a coaster" ride. Here, you get your own multi-touch-screen table with math- and engineering-based tools (and simple instructions) to design and customize your bobsled, jet, or roller-coaster ride with corkscrews, inversions, and steep hills. Along the way, you'll apply math and engineering principles to measure the energy you need to make it over a hill. Then you and a partner get to climb aboard a robotic simulator for the high-def immersion ride that's as mild or as wild as you design it. At Habit Heroes presented by Florida Blue and Anthem Blue Cross and Blue Shield, you and your team tackle three interactive experiences designed to help you create

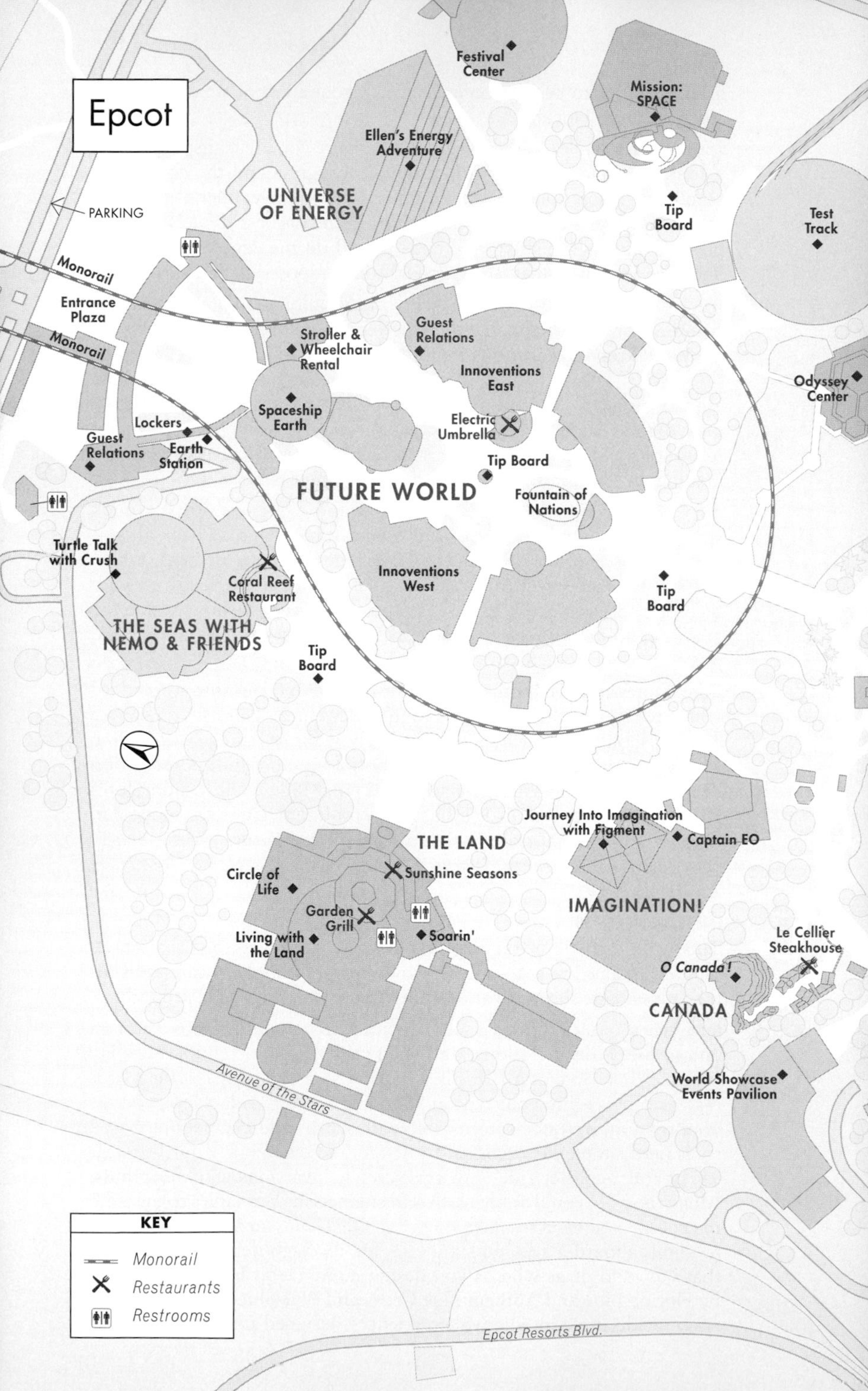
Epcot
Festival Center
Mission: SPACE
Ellen's Energy Adventure
UNIVERSE OF ENERGY
PARKING
Tip Board
Test Track
Monorail
Entrance Plaza
Monorail
Guest Relations
Stroller & Wheelchair Rental
Innoventions East
Odyssey Center
Spaceship Earth
Lockers
Guest Relations
Earth Station
Electric Umbrella
Tip Board
FUTURE WORLD
Fountain of Nations
Turtle Talk with Crush
Coral Reef Restaurant
Innoventions West
Tip Board
THE SEAS WITH NEMO & FRIENDS
Tip Board
Journey Into Imagination with Figment
Captain EO
THE LAND
Sunshine Seasons
Circle of Life
Garden Grill
IMAGINATION!
Living with the Land
Soarin'
Le Cellier Steakhouse
O Canada!
CANADA
World Showcase Events Pavilion
Avenue of the Stars
KEY
Monorail
Restaurants
Restrooms
Epcot Resorts Blvd.

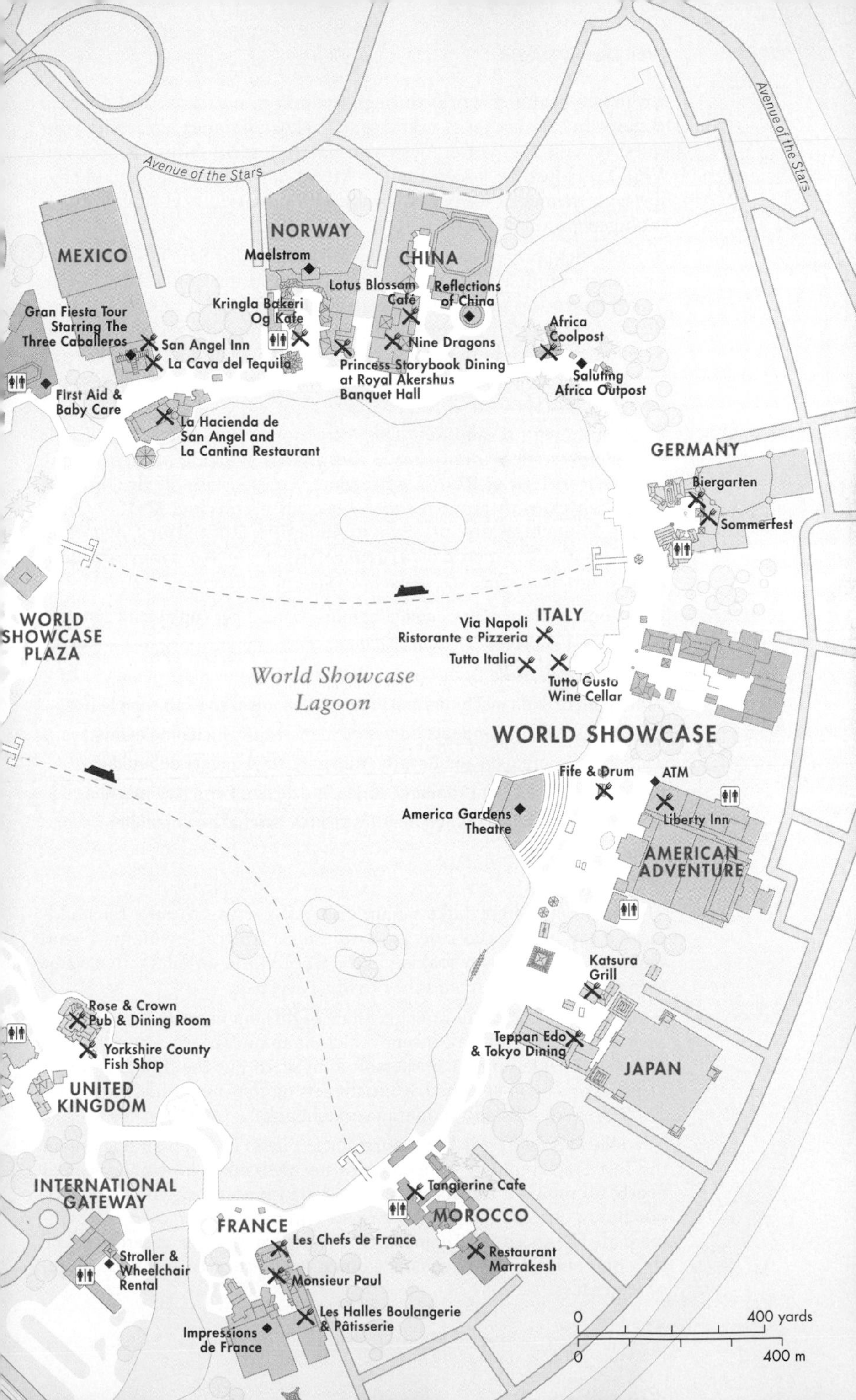

Avenue of the Stars
Avenue of the Stars
MEXICO
NORWAY
CHINA
Maelstrom
Lotus Blossom Café
Reflections of China
Kringla Bakeri Og Kafe
Gran Fiesta Tour Starring The Three Caballeros
San Angel Inn
La Cava del Tequila
Nine Dragons
Princess Storybook Dining at Royal Akershus Banquet Hall
Africa Coolpost
Saluting Africa Outpost
First Aid & Baby Care
La Hacienda de San Angel and La Cantina Restaurant
GERMANY
Biergarten
Sommerfest
WORLD SHOWCASE PLAZA
ITALY
Via Napoli Ristorante e Pizzeria
Tutto Italia
Tutto Gusto Wine Cellar
World Showcase Lagoon
WORLD SHOWCASE
Fife & Drum
ATM
Liberty Inn
America Gardens Theatre
AMERICAN ADVENTURE
Katsura Grill
Rose & Crown Pub & Dining Room
Yorkshire County Fish Shop
Teppan Edo & Tokyo Dining
JAPAN
UNITED KINGDOM
INTERNATIONAL GATEWAY
Tangierine Cafe
MOROCCO
FRANCE
Les Chefs de France
Restaurant Marrakesh
Stroller & Wheelchair Rental
Monsieur Paul
Les Halles Boulangerie & Pâtisserie
Impressions de France
0
400 yards
0
400 m

a happier, healthier world through hydration, nutrition, and physical activity. In each scenario, you'll get to battle villainous hazards in your quest to save the world. Wish you had a "green" home? Check out VISION House by Green Builder Media, a model of sustainable living with themes of energy efficiency, indoor-environment quality, and multigenerational design.

StormStruck, presented by the Federal Alliance for Safe Homes, serves up severe weather that'll make you jump and duck in a 4-D theater. You have your own electronic buttons for voting on how you'd protect your property from future storms before the "big reveal" tells you whether you're right or wrong. New experiences and adventures were in the planning stage as this edition went to press; some are expected to open in 2015.

For people with disabilities: This attraction is completely wheelchair accessible—some exhibits inside this always-evolving attraction may require transferring from a wheelchair. Guests with service animals should check with an attractions host when entering. ■**TIP→ Come before 11 am or after 2 pm. Sum of All Thrills, StormStruck, and Habit Heroes have drawn crowds.** ✉ *Future World, Innoventions* ☞ *Duration: Up to You. Crowds: Moderate–Heavy. Audience: All Ages.*

NEED A BREAK?

Club Cool. With soft drinks going for more than $2 per cup at park concessions, Club Cool is the place to visit when you're thirsty and in the mood to be adventurous. Here Coca-Cola's bold red-and-white colors guide you to a room full of soda machines and logo merchandise. You can sample (for free) the cola king's products from around the world, including mainstays Vegitabeta from Japan and Beverly from Italy. New flavors debuted in late 2013 that hail from Thailand, Africa, Brazil, and Peru. It's entertaining to watch kids' faces when their taste buds react to an unfamiliar flavor. ✉ ***Future World.***

TEST TRACK

This pavilion is shaped like a giant disk. As you wait to enter the building for the high-speed ride, cars on the return track whiz past you. Outside, kids can get a soaking in the Cool Wash, an interactive water area that lets them pretend they're in a car wash.

Fodor's Choice ★ **Test Track ride.** The white-knuckle finale of this fan favorite is as thrilling as ever. Create a custom concept vehicle at an interactive design station, and then buckle up in a six-person SimCar to put the design through its paces in a neon-splashed, futuristic setting that surrounds the attraction's original hills and mountain switchbacks.

The High-Speed Test is last: your vehicle bursts through an opening in the Test Track building to negotiate a steeply banked loop at a speed of nearly 60 mph. At the special effects–laden post-show, you can check out how your custom car performed and create your own car commercial. The speeds and some jarring effects may prove unsettling. The ride isn't suitable for pregnant women or guests wearing back, neck, or leg braces.

For people with disabilities: Visitors in wheelchairs are provided a special area in which to practice transferring into the ride vehicle before actually boarding. One TV monitor in the preshow area is closed-captioned. Service animals aren't permitted on board. ■ **TIP→ If you use a FastPass+ ticket, you won't get to customize your vehicle—it will be a predesigned version. A Single Rider queue lets you skip a long wait. The ride won't function on wet tracks, so don't head here after a downpour.** ✉ *Future World, Test Track* ☞ *Duration: 5 mins. Crowds: Heavy. Audience: Not Young Kids. Minimum height: 40 inches.*

MISSION: SPACE

The exterior of this pavilion has a sleek, futuristic look with a planetary theme. When the weather is warm enough, kids like to hop around in the fountain out front.

Fodor's Choice ★ **Mission: SPACE ride.** It took five years for Disney Imagineers, with the help of 25 experts from NASA, to design Mission: SPACE, the first ride ever to take people "straight up" in a simulated rocket launch. The story transports you and co-riders to the year 2036 and the International Space Training Center, where you are about to embark on your first launch. Before you board the four-person rocket capsule, you're assigned to a position: commander, navigator, pilot, or engineer. And at this point you're warned several times about the intensity of the ride and the risks for people with health concerns. Pregnant women and anyone with heart, back, neck, balance, blood-pressure, or motion-sickness problems shouldn't ride.

■ **TIP→ Many people exit this ride feeling nauseated and disoriented from the high-speed spinning, which is what makes you feel as if you're rocketing into space. These effects are often cumulative, so stick with one go round.**

For those who can handle the intense spinning, the sensation of liftoff is a turbulent, heart-pounding experience that flattens you against your seat. Once you break into outer space, you'll even feel weightless. After landing, you exit your capsule into the Advanced Training Lab, where you can play some very entertaining space-related games.

For people with disabilities: This ride requires a transfer from wheelchair to seat. Service animals aren't permitted to board. Video-captioning devices can be used on the ride; assisted-listening devices can be used in the post-show Training Lab. ■ **TIP→ Arrive before 10 am or use FastPass+ during peak season. Don't ride on a full stomach.** ✉ *Future World, Mission: SPACE* ☞ *Duration: 4 mins. Crowds: You Bet! Audience: Not Young Kids. Minimum height: 44 inches.*

UNIVERSE OF ENERGY

The first of the pavilions on the left, or east, side of Future World, the Universe of Energy occupies a large, lopsided pyramid sheathed in thousands of mirrors—solar collectors that power the attraction inside.

Ellen's Energy Adventure. Comedian Ellen DeGeneres plays the lead role in this attraction that has fun with pop culture at the same time it gives a crash course in Energy 101. As Ellen naps and dreams, you'll meet Alex Trebek of *Jeopardy!* and Bill Nye, the Science Guy. Actress Jamie Lee Curtis, as Ellen's irritating former college roommate, and Albert

Einstein play Ellen's game show challengers.

Your Energy 101 primer reveals the history of the universe—in one minute—on three 70-millimeter screens, 157 feet wide by 32 feet tall. Next the theater separates into six 96-passenger vehicles that lurch into a primeval forest. Through this swampy, damp, (and chilly) landscape, apatosauruses wander, a tyrannosaurus fights it out with a triceratops, and pterodactyls swoop through the air. A terrified Ellen is even cornered by a menacing elasmosaurus.

The ride concludes with another film in which Ellen learns about the world's present-day energy needs, resources, and concerns. It's shown on three screens, each 30 feet tall, 74 feet wide, and curved to create a 200-degree range of vision. Does Ellen win in her *Jeopardy!* dream? You'll have to travel back in time for the answer.

MISSION: SPACE CAUTION

Parents should exercise caution when deciding whether to let children ride Mission: SPACE. Even if your child meets the height requirement, she may not be old enough to enjoy the ride. In the capsule, you're instructed to keep your head back against the seat and to look straight ahead for the duration of the ride. (Closing your eyes or not looking straight ahead can bring on motion sickness.) Your role as a "crew member" also means you're supposed to hold on to a joystick and push buttons at certain times. All these instructions can confuse younger kids and get in the way of their enjoyment of the ride.

For people with disabilities: This attraction is accessible to guests using standard wheelchairs and those who can transfer to them. Equipped for assisted-listening, handheld-captioning, and audio-description devices. ■ **TIP→ To experience the primeval landscape unspoiled by rows of modern heads, sit in the seats to the far left and front of the theater; to get these, position yourself similarly in the preshow area.** ✉ *Future World, Universe of Energy* ☞ *Duration: 45 mins. Crowds: Moderate. Audience: All ages, though a bit lengthy and possibly frightening for young children.*

THE SEAS WITH NEMO & FRIENDS

This pavilion has always been a draw with its 5.7-million-gallon aquarium filled with 65 species of sea life, including sharks, but it was reworked to capitalize on the popularity of the Disney-Pixar film *Finding Nemo*.

The Seas with Nemo & Friends experience. Hop into a "clamobile" and take a ride under the sea to look for Nemo, who has wandered off from Mr. Ray's class field trip. This ride adds fresh zip to an aging, but relevant, attraction—an astonishing animation-projection effect makes it appear as if Nemo and his pals are swimming among the marine life of the actual Seas aquarium. As your ride progresses, Dory, Nemo's spacey sidekick, helps Bruce, Squirt, and other pals find him. After the ride, walk around the tank to Bruce's Shark World for some fun photo ops and shark facts with graphics, plus displays about the endangered Florida manatee and dolphins.

DID YOU KNOW?

Disney's original conception for the Epcot Center—as sort of a futuristic master-planned community—didn't quite pan out in the park but instead took form in the town of Celebration, near Kissimmee.

EPCOT

NAME	Height Req.	Type of Entertainment	Duration	Crowds	Audience	Tips
Future World						
Captain EO (Imagination!)	n/a	3-D Film	17 mins.	Moderate to Heavy	All but Young Kids	Come in the early morning or just before closing. Take off the 3-D glasses if little kids get scared.
Journey into Imagination with Figment (Imagination!)	n/a	Ride-Through	8 mins.	Light	Young Kids	Ride after Captain EO. Warn toddlers about darkness at the end of the ride.
Ellen's Energy Adventure (Universe of Energy)	n/a	Ride-Through	45 mins.	Moderate	All but very Young Kids	Best seats are to the far left and front of the theater.
Innoventions	n/a	Walk-Through	Up to you	Moderate to Heavy	All Ages	Come anytime.
The Circle of Life (The Land)	n/a	Film	20 mins.	Moderate to Heavy	All Ages	Come early or for your toddler's afternoon nap.
Living with the Land (The Land)	n/a	Cruise	14 mins.	Moderate	Small Kids	The line moves quickly, so come anytime.
★ Soarin' (The Land)	At least 40"	Simulator Ride	5 mins.	Heavy	All but very Young Kids	Use FastPass+, or come early, or just before closing.
The Seas with Nemo & Friends	n/a	Ride- and Walk-Through	Up to you	Moderate to Heavy	All Ages	Get Nemo fans here early in the morning.
Turtle Talk with Crush	n/a	Animated Show	20 mins.	Moderate to Heavy	Young Kids and Families	Line up after "clamobile" ride.

★	Mission: SPACE	At least 44"	Thrill Ride	4 mins.	You Bet!	All but Young Kids	Come before 10 am or use FastPass+. Don't ride on a full stomach.
	Spaceship Earth	n/a	Ride-Through	15 mins.	Moderate to Heavy	All Ages	Ride while waiting for Mission: SPACE or Soarin' FastPass+ appointment or just before closing.
★	Test Track	At least 40"	Thrill Ride	5 mins.	Heavy	All but Young Kids	Come early or use FastPass+. The ride can't function on wet tracks, so don't come after a downpour.
	World Showcase						
★	The American Adventure Show	n/a	Show/Film	20 mins.	Heavy	All Ages	Arrive 10 mins. before the Voices of Liberty or the Spirit of America Fife & Drum Corps are slated to perform.
	America Gardens Theatre	n/a	Live Show	Varies	Varies	Varies	Arrive more than an hour or so ahead of time for holiday and celebrity performances.
	Gran Fiesta Tour Starring the Three Caballeros	n/a	Cruise	9 mins.	Light to Moderate	All Ages	Especially good if you have young children.
	Impressions de France	n/a	Film	20 mins.	Moderate	All Ages	Come anytime.
	Maelstrom	n/a	Thrill Ride for Kids with Water	10 mins.	Moderate to Heavy	All Ages	Use FastPass+ for after lunch or dinner.
	O Canada!	n/a	Film	14 mins.	Moderate to Heavy	All Ages	Stop in any time. Be prepared to stand for the film. No strollers permitted.
	Reflections of China	n/a	Film	14 mins.	Moderate	All Ages	Come anytime. Be prepared to stand during the film. No strollers permitted.

★ Fodor's Choice

EPCOT FAMILY TOUR

A trip to Italy is on hold, but Mom knows she can find a taste of Venice in the World Showcase. Dad, the *Popular Mechanics* devotee, can't wait to check out Test Track and Innoventions. Each can have a great day—in his or her own way.

STRATEGIZE

Devise a plan before pushing through the Epcot turnstiles. Everyone will probably want to take off at Soarin' in The Land for the one-ride-fits-all thrill of simulated hang gliding (there are even special safety restraints for little ones). If your kids are too small for the height restrictions at Test Track, let Dad shift into overdrive while the rest of you play Innoventions games. Meet up with Dad at the Imagination! pavilion to see Michael Jackson circa 1980s dance his way through Captain EO, or head back to the Land for a Sunshine Seasons treat. Don't miss an under-the-sea ride at the Seas with Nemo & Friends before meeting the coolest dude of all at Turtle Talk with Crush.

GET YOUR WORLD SHOWCASE PASSPORTS

On the way into the World Showcase, let the kids get their own passports, complete with stickers, at any merchandise location. As you visit each country, they can get their passports stamped—not only fun, but a great keepsake. But before you cross the Future World border, stop and let young kids play in the dancing fountains—it'll be one of their happiest memories. Bring a towel and a change of clothing, and you'll be happy, too.

FOR THE LITTLE ONES (AND MOM)

Younger children can be creative at Kidcot Fun Stops, where a Disney cast member gets them started on a craft activity, such as coloring a Carnivale-style mask on a stick. At each of 11 Fun Stops, the kids can add something to the mask, such as a Viking ship at Norway. Children love Mexico because they can ride the boats at Gran Fiesta Tour starring the Three Caballeros. The Norway ride, Maelstrom, is next door, and offers an adventure involving Viking ships and menacing trolls. Now it's your turn, Mom. Italy is right around the corner, and the kids can watch a juggler or comedy troupe in the courtyard while you taste some wine at Enoteca Castello or go shopping.

LIVE MUSIC

The Beatles, the Rolling Stones, Elton John, and more: hear top hits by iconic British musicians when the tribute band British Revolution amps up the fun outside the United Kingdom showcase five days each week. Grab a bench or dance to favorite tunes. Young children are thrilled to explore hedge mazes that surround the gazebo stage.

Live entertainment is one of Epcot's strong suits—best shows for younger kids are the Jeweled Dragon Acrobats at China, Mariachi Cobre musicians at Mexico, Sergio the clown and juggler at Italy, and the JAMMitors percussion group at Future World East and West (check the daily *Times Guide*).

For people with disabilities: Guests in standard wheelchairs can wheel onto an accessible "clamshell" vehicle; those in ECVs must transfer to a standard wheelchair or the ride vehicle. Equipped for audio-description and handheld captioning devices. ■ **TIP→ Come early; the wait will only get longer.** ✉ *Future World, The Seas with Nemo & Friends* ☞ *Duration: Up to You. Crowds: Moderate–Heavy. Audience: All Ages.*

Turtle Talk with Crush. Head for the Sea Base area to line up for this real-time animated show starring Crush, the ancient sea turtle from *Finding Nemo*. Crush chats and jokes with kids so convincingly that young children, eyes wide as sand dollars, have walked up and touched the screen where Crush "swims." It's in a small theater and there's often a wait, but it's a hit with young children as well as their parents. **For people with disabilities:** The theater is wheelchair accessible, assisted-listening devices can be used, and sign-language presentations are offered twice a week. ■ **TIP→ Come early and prepare to be amazed.** ✉ *Future World, The Seas with Nemo & Friends* ☞ *Duration: 20 mins. Crowds: Moderate–Heavy. Audience: Young Kids, but Great for All Ages.*

5

THE LAND

Shaped like an intergalactic greenhouse, the enormous, skylighted Land pavilion dedicates 6 acres and a host of attractions to everyone's favorite topic: food. You can easily spend two hours exploring here, more if you take one of the guided greenhouse tours available throughout the day.

NEED A BREAK?

Talk about a self-contained ecosystem: The Land Pavilion grows its own produce, including tomatoes and cucumbers, some of which show up on the menu at the healthful Sunshine Seasons food court. Much of the fare is cooked on a 48-inch Mongolian grill. The eatery's Asian shop offers chicken noodle bowls and spicy stir-fries. A sandwich shop delivers oak-grilled veggie sandwiches on fresh breads, and a yummy turkey on ciabatta with chipotle mayonnaise. The salad shop wows with roasted beets, goat cheese, and seared tuna—among other options—over mixed greens. Wood-fired grills and rotisseries sizzle with chicken, pork, and salmon, and the bakery's pastries are sure bets. To avoid crowds, eat at nonpeak times—after 2 for lunch and before 5 or after 7 for dinner.

The Circle of Life. Featuring three stars of *The Lion King*—Simba the lion, Timon the meerkat, and Pumbaa the waddling warthog—this film delivers a powerful message about protecting the world's environment for all living things. Part animation, part *National Geographic*–like film using spectacular 70-millimeter live-action footage, Circle of Life tells a fable about a "Hakuna Matata Lakeside Village" that Timon and Pumbaa are developing by clearing the African savanna. Simba cautions about mistreating the land by telling a story of a creature who occasionally forgets that everything is connected in the great Circle of Life. "That creature," he says, "is man." The lilting accompaniment is Tim Rice and Elton John's popular song, and James Earl Jones is the narrator.

For people with disabilities: Wheelchair accessible. Has reflective captioning and is equipped for assisted-listening and audio-description devices. ■ **TIP→ It's enlightening for children and adults; a nap**

opportunity for toddlers. Squeeze in other attractions and see this before leaving. ✉ *Future World, The Land* ☞ *Duration: 20 mins. Crowds: Moderate–Heavy. Audience: All Ages.*

Living with the Land. A canopied boat cruises through three artificial biomes—rain forest, desert, and prairie ecological communities—and into an experimental live greenhouse that demonstrates how food sources may be grown in the future, not only on the planet but also in outer space. Shrimp, tilapia, eels, catfish, and alligators are raised in controlled aquacells, and tomatoes, peppers, squash, and other fruits and vegetables thrive in the Desert Farm area via drip irrigation that delivers just the right amount of water and nutrients to their roots. Gardeners are usually interested in the section on integrated pest management, which relies on "good" insects like ladybugs to control more harmful predators.

See Mickey Mouse–shaped fruits and vegetables (there may be pumpkins, cucumbers, or watermelons) nurtured with the help of molds created by the Land's science team; scientists also have grown a "tomato tree"—the first of its kind in the United States—that yields thousands of tomatoes from a single vine. Many of the growing areas are actual experiments-in-progress, in which Disney and the U.S. Department of Agriculture have joined forces to produce, say, a sweeter pineapple or a faster-growing pepper. The plants (including the tomato tree's golf-ball-size tomatoes) and fish that grow in the greenhouse are regularly harvested for use in The Land's restaurants. **For people with disabilities:** Those using an oversize wheelchair or ECV must transfer to a standard wheelchair. Equipped for handheld-captioning and audio-description devices. ■ **TIP→ The line moves fairly quickly, so come anytime. In case of a crowd, use FastPass+.** ✉ *Future World, The Land* ☞ *Duration: 14 mins. Crowds: Moderate. Audience: All.*

Fodor's Choice ★ **Soarin'.** If you've ever wondered what it's like to fly, or at least hang glide, this attraction is your chance to enjoy the sensation without actually taking the plunge. It uses motion-based technology to literally lift you in your seat 40 feet into the air within a giant projection-screen dome.

As you soar above the Golden Gate Bridge, Napa Valley, Yosemite, and other California wonders, you feel the wind and smell pine forests and orange blossoms. Navy buffs get a kick out of swooping over a massive aircraft carrier. The accompanying score created by Jerry Goldsmith (*Mulan, Star Trek*) builds on the thrill, and the crispness and definition of the film, projected at twice the rate of a typical motion picture, adds realism.

The flight is so mild (and the view so thrilling) that even very shy children love it. **For people with disabilities:** Those with mobility impairments must transfer from their wheelchairs to the ride system. Equipped for video-captioning devices. Service animals aren't permitted on the ride. ■ **TIP→ Ride early or late or grab a FastPass+.** ✉ *Future World, The Land* ☞ *Duration: 5 mins. Crowds: Heavy. Audience: All who can be strapped into a seat. Height minimum: 40 inches.*

IMAGINATION!

The focus is on the fun that can be had when you turn your imagination loose. The fanciful leaping fountains outside the pavilion make the point, as do the 3-D film *Captain EO,* the Journey into Imagination with Figment ride, and Image Works, a sort of interactive fun house devoted to music and art.

Captain EO. Directed by Francis Ford Coppola and produced by George Lucas, the 17-minute 3-D film stars pop legend Michael Jackson as Captain EO and Oscar-winner Anjelica Huston as the Supreme Leader of a colorless planet of droids from the dark side. After an opener that mimics space-fantasy action scenes from Lucas's epic *Star Wars* series, EO's motley crew of furry space creatures lands on the planet and magically transforms into an electronic band, prepared to shed light on the Supreme Leader and her robotic forces of darkness.

Music and light save the day as evil robot guards transform into dancers with hair and costumes straight from the '80s. Young children may be frightened by the dark nature of the film and its special effects.

For people with disabilities: The attraction is wheelchair accessible, although you must transfer to a theater seat to experience some special effects. Equipped with reflective captioning and for assisted-listening, video-captioning, or audio-description devices. The preshow area has closed-captioned TV monitors for the show intro featuring a behind-the-scenes look at how Lucas and Coppola made the film. Guests with service animals should check with a show host before entering. **■ TIP→ Come early or late, or get a FastPass+.** ⊠ *Future World, Imagination!* ☞ *Duration: 18 mins. Crowds: Moderate. Audience: Not Young Kids.*

Journey into Imagination with Figment. Figment, a fun-loving dragon, takes you on a sensory adventure designed to engage your imagination through sound, illusion, gravity, dimension, and color. After the ride—which could use some updating—you can check out Image Works, where several interactive displays allow you to further stretch your imagination. Although this ride is geared to smaller kids, be sure to prepare yours for a brief period of darkness.

For people with disabilities: Ride and Image Works are wheelchair accessible. Equipped for handheld-captioning and audio-description devices. **■ TIP→ Ride only if lines are short and you'll have plenty of time for preferred attractions on your list.** ⊠ *Future World, Imagination!* ☞ *Duration: 8 mins. Crowds: Light. Audience: Young Kids.*

WORLD SHOWCASE

Nowhere but at Epcot can you explore a little corner of nearly a dozen countries in one day. As you stroll the 1 miles around the 40-acre World Showcase Lagoon, you circumnavigate the globe-according-to-Disney by experiencing native food, entertainment, culture, and arts and crafts at pavilions representing countries in Europe, Asia, North Africa, and the Americas. Pavilion employees are from the countries they represent—Disney hires them as part of its international college program.

Instead of rides, you have solid film attractions at the Canada, China, and France pavilions; several art exhibitions; and the chance to try

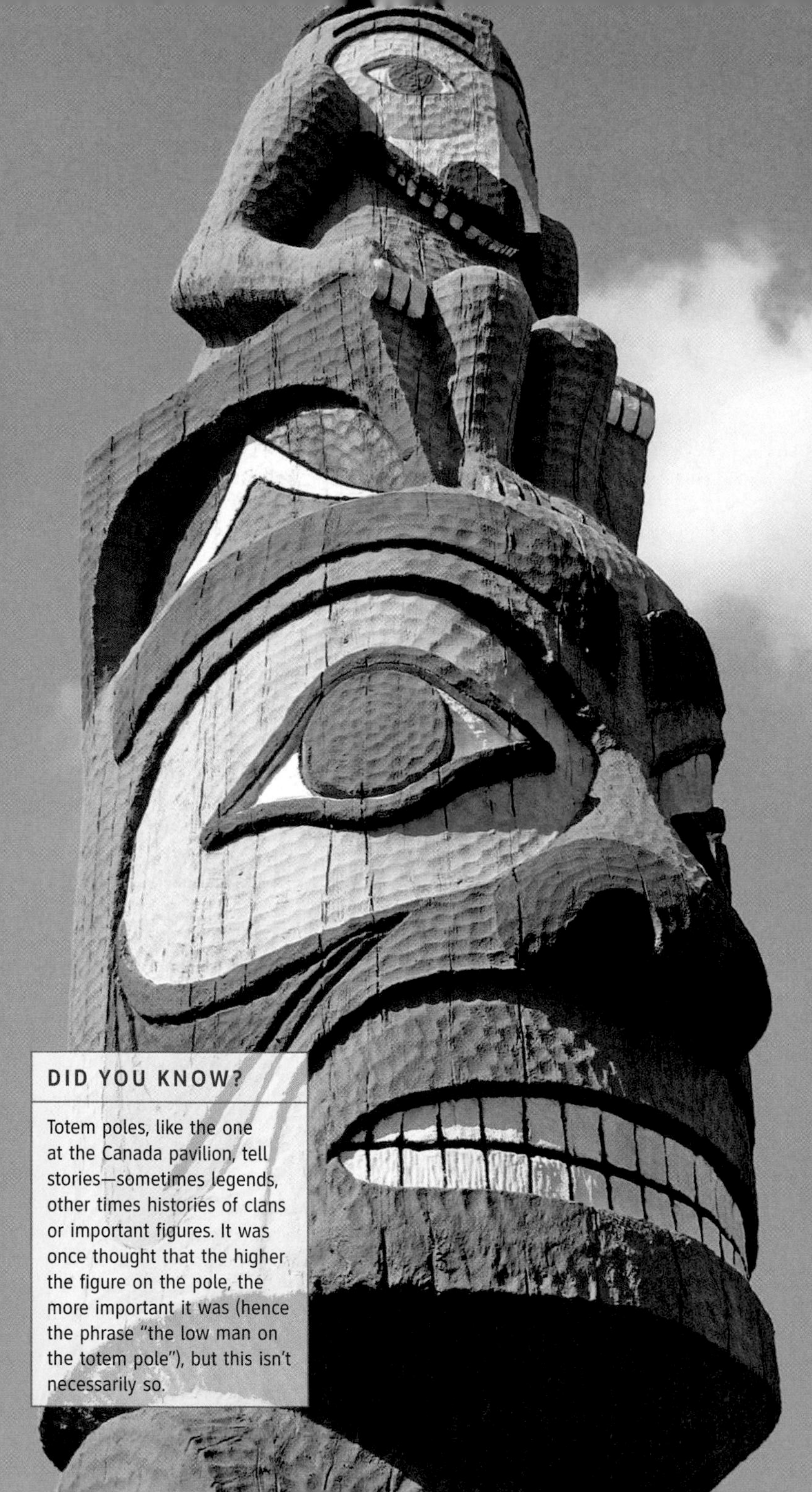

DID YOU KNOW?

Totem poles, like the one at the Canada pavilion, tell stories—sometimes legends, other times histories of clans or important figures. It was once thought that the higher the figure on the pole, the more important it was (hence the phrase "the low man on the totem pole"), but this isn't necessarily so.

your foreign language skills with the staff. Each pavilion also has a designated Kidcot Fun Stop, open daily from 11 or noon until about 8 or 9, where youngsters can try a cultural crafts project. Live entertainment is an integral part of the experience, and you'll enjoy watching the incredibly talented Jeweled Dragon Acrobats in China, singing along with terrific British rock band impersonators in the United Kingdom and the Off Kilter band in Canada, or laughing along with some improv fun in the Italy courtyard.

WATER PLAY

Preschoolers love to play in the interactive fountains in front of Mission: SPACE and in the walkways between Future World and the World Showcase. Bring swimsuits and a towel!

Dining is another favorite pastime at Epcot, and the World Showcase offers tempting tastes of the authentic cuisines of the countries here.

For People with Disabilities. Attractions at Mexico, American Adventure, France, China, and Canada are all wheelchair accessible, as are the plaza areas where shows are presented. Norway's Maelstrom boat ride requires transferring to the ride vehicle; personal-translator units amplify sound tracks. Most of the live entertainment around the World Showcase features strong aural as well as visual elements.

EN ROUTE

A World Showcase Passport ($9.95) is a wonderful way to keep a kid interested in this more adult area of Epcot. The passports, available at vendor carts, come with stickers and a badge, and children can have them stamped at each pavilion. The World Showcase is also a great place to look for unusual gifts—you might pick up a Oaxacan wood carving in Mexico, a tea set in China, or a kimonoed doll in Japan.

CANADA

"Oh, it's just our Canadian outdoors," said a typically modest native guide upon being asked about the model for the striking rocky chasm and tumbling waterfall that represent just one of the pavilion's high points. The beautiful formal gardens do have an antecedent: Butchart Gardens, in Victoria, British Columbia. And so does the Hôtel du Canada, a French Gothic mansion with spires, turrets, and a mansard roof; anyone who's ever stayed at Québec's Château Frontenac or Ottawa's Château Laurier will recognize the imposing style favored by architects of Canadian railroad hotels.

Like the size of the Rocky Mountains, the scale of the structures seems immense; unlike the real thing, it's managed with a trick called forced perspective, which exaggerates the smallness of the distant parts to make the entire thing look gigantic.

You can browse shops that sell maple syrup; Canadian sports jerseys; and plush huggable bears, beavers, and huskies. Le Cellier Steakhouse is a great place for a relaxing lunch or dinner; due to its increasing popularity, book reservations far ahead.

O Canada!. That's just what you'll say after seeing this CircleVision film's stunning opening shot—footage of the Royal Canadian Mounted Police surrounding you as they circle the screen. From there, you whoosh over waterfalls, venture through Montréal and Toronto, sneak up on bears and bison, mush behind a husky-pulled dogsled, and land pluck in the middle of a hockey game. The only downsides: this is a standing-only theater, strollers aren't permitted, and toddlers and small children can't see unless they're held aloft. ■ **TIP→ Stop in on your stroll around World Showcase Promenade.** ✉ *World Showcase, Canada* ☞ *Duration: 14 mins. Crowds: Moderate–Heavy. Audience: All Ages.*

UNITED KINGDOM

The United Kingdom rambles between the elegant mansions lining a London square to the bustling, half-timber shops of a village High Street to thatch-roof cottages from the countryside. (The thatch is made of plastic broom bristles due to local fire regulations.) And, of course, there's a pair of iconic red phone booths.

The pavilion has no single major attraction. Instead, you wander through shops selling tea, Welsh handicrafts, and English lavender fragrance by Taylor of London. There's a store with Beatles T-shirts, CDs, and memorabilia. Next door is the Historic Research Center, where you can research your family name and purchase printed, hand-painted, or embroidered versions of your family coat of arms.

Outside, the strolling World Showcase Players coax audience members to participate in lowbrow versions of Shakespeare. There's also a lovely garden and park with benches in the back that's easy to miss—relax and kick back to the tunes of the British Revolution, a band known for its on-target Beatles and other Brit-band performances. Kids love to run through the hedge maze as their parents travel back in time to "Yesterday." Check the *Times Guide* and arrive 30 minutes early for a bench or 15 minutes early for a curb. Restrooms are near the red phone booths.

NEED A BREAK?

Revive yourself with a pint of the best at the Rose & Crown, a pub where you'll jostle for space any evening the Hat Lady performs her piano magic. The dining room serves hearty fare for lunch and dinner (reservations often required). The outdoor terrace is one of the best spots for watching IllumiNations. Arrive at least an hour or so in advance for a seat. If you're in a hurry, grab fish-and-chips to go from Yorkshire County Fish Shop then nab a lagoon-side table.

FRANCE

You don't need the scaled-down model of the Eiffel Tower to tell you that you've arrived in France, specifically Paris. There's the poignant accordion music wafting out of concealed speakers, the trim sycamores pruned in the French style to develop signature knots at the end of each branch, and the delicious aromas surrounding Les Halles Boulangerie & Pâtisserie bakeshop. This is the Paris of dreams, a Paris of the years just before World War I, when solid mansard-roof mansions were crowned with iron filigree, when the least brick was drenched in romanticism.

Here's a replica of the conservatory-like Les Halles—the iron-and-glass barrel-roof market that no longer exists in the City of Light; there's an arching footbridge; and all around, of course, there are shops. You can inspect Parisian impressionist artwork at Galerie des Halles; sample perfume at the Guerlain shop; and acquire a Julia Child cookbook or bottle of Pouilly-Fuisse at Les Vins de France. If you plan to dine at Les Chefs de France, make a reservation for a late lunch or dinner; the second-floor Monsieur Paul (dinner only) is a gourmet treat.

NEED A BREAK?

The lines at Les Halles Boulangerie Pâtisserie, a large Parisian-style counter-service café, are worth the wait. Have wine with a cheese plate, quiche, or sandwich on crusty French bread. Or go for a creamy café au lait and a napoleon. The new L'Artisan des Glaces ice cream–and-sorbet shop is praiseworthy for its ultracreamy treats that include an ice cream "martini" with Grand Marnier and flavor-customized ice-cream sandwiches made with brioche or French *macaron*.

Impressions de France. The intimate Palais du Cinema, inspired by the royal theater at Fontainebleau, screens this homage to the glories of the country. Shown on five screens spanning 200 degrees, in an air-conditioned, sit-down theater, the film takes you to vineyards at harvest time, Paris on Bastille Day, the Alps, Versailles, Normandy's Mont-St-Michel, and the stunning châteaux of the Loire Valley. The music sweeps you away with familiar segments from Offenbach, Debussy, and Saint-Saëns, all woven together by longtime Disney musician Buddy Baker. **■ TIP→ Visit anytime during your stroll around the World Showcase; theatre seats are comfy and a great way to rest weary legs.** ✉ *World Showcase, France* ☞ *Duration: 20 mins. Crowds: Moderate. Audience: All Ages.*

5

MOROCCO

Walk through the pointed arches of the Bab Boujouloud gate and you're transported to this mysterious North African country. The arches are ornamented with wood carvings and encrusted with mosaics made of 9 tons of handmade, hand-cut tiles; 19 native artisans were sent to Epcot to install them and to create the dusty stucco walls that seem to have withstood centuries of sandstorms. Look closely and you'll see that every tile has a small crack or other imperfection, and no tile depicts a living creature—in deference to the Islamic belief that only Allah creates perfection and life.

Koutoubia Minaret, a replica of the prayer tower in Marrakesh, acts as Morocco's landmark. Winding alleyways—each corner bursting with carpets, brasses, leatherwork, and other wares—lead to a tiled fountain and lush gardens. A highlight is Restaurant Marrakesh. Enjoy couscous and roast lamb while a lithesome belly dancer makes for a pleasant diversion. One of the hottest fast-food spots in Epcot is Tangierine Café, with tasty Mediterranean specialties like pita-pocket lamb and chicken sliders, killer baklava, and share-worthy vegetable platters with hummus, tabbouleh, falafel, lentils, and couscous. Just opened in 2014, Spice Road Table is the ideal lagoon-side spot for tapas and the best sangria in Orlando. All eateries are open for lunch and dinner. Restrooms on the France side of the pavilion offer quick access.

JAPAN

A brilliant vermilion torii gate, based on Hiroshima Bay's much-photographed Itsukushima Shrine, frames the World Showcase Lagoon and stands as an emblem of Disney's serene version of Japan.

Disney horticulturists deserve a hand for authenticity: 90% of the plants they used are native to Japan. Rocks, pebbled streams, pools, and pruned trees and shrubs complete the meticulous picture. At sunset, or during a rainy dusk, the twisted branches of the corkscrew willows frame a perfect Japanese view of the five-story winged pagoda that is the heart of the pavilion. Based on the 8th-century Horyuji Temple in Nara, the brilliant blue pagoda has five levels, symbolizing the five elements of Buddhist belief—earth, water, fire, wind, and sky.

PHOTO TIP

You'll get a great shot of Spaceship Earth across the lagoon by framing it in the torii gate.

The peace is occasionally interrupted by performances on drums and gongs. Mitsukoshi, an immense retail firm known as Japan's Sears Roebuck, carries everything from T-shirts to kimonos and rows of Japanese dolls. For lunch and dinner, you'll be entertained by the culinary feats of chefs at Teppan Edo (which carries on the chop-toss-applaud antics of the original Teppanyaki Dining Room). Tokyo Dining focuses on presentation of traditional ingredients and cuisine from Japan, including sushi. At the pavilion's rear is a sake tasting bar that you'll miss if you don't look for it.

AMERICAN ADVENTURE

In a Disney version of Philadelphia's Independence Hall, the Imagineers prove that their kind of fantasy can beat reality hands down. The 110,000 bricks, made by hand from soft, pink, Georgia clay, sheathe the familiar structure, which acts as a beacon for those across Epcot's lagoon. The pavilion includes an all-American fast-food restaurant, a shop, lovely rose gardens, and an outdoor theater. Restrooms are tucked away along the far left side of the restaurant, and a roomier, more modern restroom accommodation opened recently by the gift shop.

NEED A BREAK?

What else would you order at the counter-service **Liberty Inn** but burgers, apple pie, and other all-American fare? On a summer evening this is the place to get an ice-cream sundae before IllumiNations starts. On a chilly winter day, the hot cocoa is a hit. At the **Fife & Drum** along the promenade, you can pair a beer with a turkey leg for a satisfying snack.

Fodor's Choice ★ **The American Adventure.** The pavilion's key attraction is this 100-yard dash through history, and you'll be primed for the lesson after watching a courtyard performance of the Spirit of America Fife & Drum Corps or reaching the main entry hall and hearing the stirring a cappella Voices of Liberty. Inside the theater, the main event begins to the accompaniment of "The Golden Dream," performed by the Philadelphia Orchestra. This show combines evocative sets, a rear-projection screen (72 feet wide), enormous movable stages, and 35 Audio-Animatronics players.

Beginning with the arrival of the Pilgrims at Plymouth Rock and their grueling first winter, Benjamin Franklin and a wry, pipe-smoking Mark Twain narrate the episodes, both praiseworthy and shameful, that have shaped the American spirit. Each speech and scene seems polished like

Morocco's open-air market is like something out of an Indiana Jones movie. It's a maze of shops selling straw bags, colorful carpets, leather goods, and, of course, ceramics.

a little jewel. You feel the cold at Valley Forge. You're moved by Nez Percé Chief Joseph's forced abdication of Native American ancestral lands and by women's rights campaigner Susan B. Anthony's speech. You laugh with Will Rogers's aphorisms and learn about the pain of the Great Depression through an affecting radio broadcast by Franklin Delano Roosevelt. **■TIP→ Arrive 10 minutes before the Spirit of America Fife & Drum Corps or Voices of Liberty are slated to perform. See the drum corps outside, then head inside to enjoy the a cappella tunes.** ✉ *World Showcase, American Adventure* ☞ *Duration: 30 mins. Crowds: Heavy. Audience: All Ages.*

America Gardens Theatre. On the edge of the lagoon, directly opposite Disney's magnificent bit of colonial fakery, is this open-air, partially tree-shaded venue for concerts and shows. Some are of the "Yankee Doodle Dandy" variety. Others are hot tickets with themes tied to Epcot events, such as Flower Power concerts with '60s pop legends during the March through May Epcot International Flower & Garden Festival and Eat to the Beat! concerts during the late-September through mid-November Epcot International Food & Wine Festival. This is also the setting for the annual yuletide Candlelight Processional—a not-to-be-missed event if you're at WDW during the holidays. The Candlelight Dinner Package (available through Disney's dining reservations hotline) includes lunch or dinner in a select World Showcase restaurant and preferred seating for the moving performance. Roomy new restrooms are now open behind the Kidcot Fun Stop. **■TIP→ Arrive more than an hour ahead of time for holiday and celebrity performances.** ✉ *World Showcase,*

American Adventure ☞ Duration: Performances vary. Crowds: Vary. Audience: Varies.

ITALY

Architectural reproductions of Venice's Piazza San Marco and Doge's Palace are accurate right down to the gold leaf on the ringlets of the angel perched 100 feet atop the Campanile; the seawall stained with age, with barbershop-stripe poles to which two gondolas are tethered; and the Romanesque columns, Byzantine mosaics, Gothic arches, and stone walls that have all been carefully antiqued. Mediterranean plants such as grapevines, kumquat, and olive trees add verisimilitude. Shops sell Venetian beads and glasswork, leather purses, perfumes, olive oils, pastas, and Perugina cookies and chocolate kisses.

At Tutto Italia Ristorante, the cuisine—wines, handmade mozzarella, and fresh bread—is from several regions of Italy. Limited outdoor dining beneath umbrellas is lovely. The hot ticket is on the edge of the piazza: Via Napoli is a casual 300-seat pizzeria with wood-burning ovens and an airy, noisy dining room. Chefs use Caputo flour, San Marzano tomatoes, and fresh, handmade mozzarella to craft some of the best margherita pizza outside of Naples! The Tutto Gusto Wine Cellar is a cool escape for a glass of prosecco and a small plate.

The Ziti Sisters comedy troupe and a clown–juggler bring crowds to the piazza several times each day. This is a great spot for viewing IllumiNations if you're in the vicinity.

GERMANY

Germany, a make-believe village that distills the best folk architecture from all over that country, is so jovial that you practically expect the Seven Dwarfs to come "heigh-ho"-ing out to meet you. If you time it right, you will spot Snow White as she poses for photos and signs autographs. The fairy tale continues as a specially designed glockenspiel on the clock tower chimes on the hour. You'll also hear musical toots and tweets from cuckoo clocks, folk tunes from the spinning dolls sold at Der Teddybär, and the satisfied grunts of hungry visitors chowing down on hearty German cooking.

The Biergarten's wonderful buffet serves several sausage varieties, as well as sauerkraut, spaetzle, and roasted potatoes, rotisserie chicken, and German breads, all accompanied by yodelers, dancers, and other lederhosen-clad musicians who perform a year-round Oktoberfest show. There are shops aplenty, including Die Weihnachts Ecke (the Christmas Corner), which sells nutcrackers and other Christmas ornaments. It's hard to resist watching the miniature trains that choo-choo along a garden track dotted with tiny villages. Restrooms are just steps away.

NEED A BREAK?

Sommerfest. Bratwurst and cold beer from the Sommerfest snack counter at the entrance of the Biergarten restaurant make a perfect quick and hearty lunch, while the soft pretzels and strudel are ever-popular snacks. There's not much seating, so you may have to eat on the run. ✉ *World Showcase, Germany.*

Saluting Africa–Outpost. The Saluting Africa–Outpost, between Germany and China, isn't one of the 11 World Showcase pavilions, but kids love to test their drumming skills on bongos and other drums that invite players to improvise their own African folklore performances. Village Traders sells African handicrafts and—you guessed it—souvenirs relating to *The Lion King*. Buy an ice cream or frozen yogurt at the Africa Coolpost, and enjoy the break at a table by the lagoon. A cool mist is set up to offer respite on hot days. ✉ *World Showcase*.

CHINA

A shimmering red-and-gold, three-tier replica of Beijing's Temple of Heaven towers over a serene Chinese garden, an art gallery displaying treasures from the People's Republic, a spacious emporium devoted to Chinese goods, and two restaurants. The gardens—planted with a native Chinese tallow tree, water lilies, bamboo, and a 100-year-old weeping mulberry tree—are tranquil.

5

Piped-in traditional Chinese music flows gently over the peaceful hush of the gardens, which come alive with applause and cheers when the remarkable Jeweled Dragon Acrobats tumble into a roped-off area for their breathtaking act. At China's popular Nine Dragons Restaurant try the shrimp summer rolls or the salt-and-pepper shrimp with spinach noodles; there are also several chicken and stir-fry favorites.

NEED A BREAK?

Lotus Blossom Café. The open-air Lotus Blossom Café offers some authentic Chinese fare: pot stickers, soups, and egg rolls. Entrées include orange chicken with steamed rice, vegetable curry, and a beef noodle soup bowl. The Joy of Tea cart along the promenade serves hot and cold tea, plus trendy green-tea frozen drinks and plum wine. ✉ *World Showcase, China*.

Reflections of China. Think of the Temple of Heaven as an especially fitting theater for a movie in which sensational panoramas of the land and people are dramatically portrayed on a 360-degree CircleVision screen. Highlights include striking footage of Hong Kong, Shanghai, and Macao. This may be the best of the World Showcase films—the only drawbacks are that strollers aren't permitted and the theater has no chairs; lean rails are provided. **■TIP→ Come anytime and, before the show, visit the Tomb Warriors gallery, where you can see replicas of the terra-cotta soldiers unearthed by farmers in Xi'an, China, in 1974.** ✉ *World Showcase, China* ☞ *Duration: 14 mins. Crowds: Moderate. Audience: All Ages.*

NORWAY

Among the rough-hewn timbers and sharply pitched roofs here—softened and brightened by bloom-stuffed window boxes and figured shutters—are lots of smiling young Norwegians, all eager to speak English and show off their country. The pavilion complex contains a 14th-century, fortresslike castle that mimics Oslo's Akershus, cobbled streets, rocky waterfalls, and a stave church modeled after one built in 1250, with wood dragons glaring from the eaves. The church houses an exhibit called "To the Ends of the Earth," which uses vintage artifacts

The Temple of Quetzalcoatl (ket-zel-co-WAH-tal) at Teotihuacán (tay-o-tee-wah-CON), just outside Mexico City, is the model for the pyramid at the Mexico pavilion.

to tell the story of two early-20th-century polar expeditions. It all puts you in the mood for the pavilion's shops, which sell spears, shields, and other Viking necessities perfect for next Halloween.

At Akershus Royal Banquet Hall, Princess Storybook Dining is a big deal. Visit the Norwegian *koldtbord* (buffet) for smoked salmon, fruit, and pastries, followed by a family-style hot breakfast of eggs, meats, and other treats served at the table. For lunch and dinner, you'll find traditional treats like chilled shrimp, salads, meats, and cheeses. Hot entrées served à la carte might include oven-roasted chicken breast, short ribs, or the traditional Scandinavian meatball dish called *kjottkaker*. Family-style dessert is a treat with three of the chef's sweet specialties.

■ TIP→ The restaurant is the only one in the park where you can dine with Disney princesses, who may include Aurora, Belle, or Snow White. You can reserve up to 180 days in advance, and we recommend booking as early as possible. However, you can always check at Guest Relations for seats left by cancellations.

NEED A BREAK?

Kringla Bakeri Og Kafe. You can order smoked salmon and other open-face sandwiches, pastries, or Norwegian Ringnes beer at Kringla Bakeri Og Kafe. **■ TIP→ Go early or late for speediest service and room to sit in the outdoor seating area.** ✉ ***World Showcase, Norway.***

Maelstrom. In Norway's dandy boat ride you pile into a 16-passenger, dragon-headed longboat for a voyage through time that, despite its scary name and encounters with evil trolls, is actually more interesting than frightful. The journey begins in a 10th-century village, where a boat, much like the ones used by Eric the Red, is being readied for a Viking voyage. You glide steeply up through a mythical forest populated by trolls, who cause the boat to plunge backward down a mild waterfall, then cruise amid the grandeur of the Geiranger Fjord. Then you experience a storm in the North Sea and, as the presence of oil rigs signals the 20th century, end up in a peaceful coastal village. Disembarking, you proceed into a theater for a quick film about Norway's scenic wonders, culture, and people.

For people with disabilities: You must step down into and up out of a boat to ride. Equipped with reflective captioning and for assisted-listening, audio-description, or handheld-captioning devices. ■**TIP→ Grab a FastPass+ appointment if the queue is long so you can return after lunch or dinner.** ✉ *World Showcase, Norway* ☞ *Duration: 10 mins. Crowds: Moderate–Heavy. Audience: All Ages.*

MEXICO

5

Housed in a spectacular Mayan pyramid surrounded by dense tropical plantings and brilliant blossoms, Mexico welcomes you onto a "moonlit" plaza that contains the Gran Fiesta Tour boat ride; an exhibit of pre-Columbian art; a very popular restaurant; and, of course, shopping kiosks where you can unload many, many pesos.

Modeled on the market in the town of Taxco, Plaza de los Amigos is well named: there are lots of friendly people—the women dressed in peasant blouses and bright skirts, the men in white shirts and dashing sashes—all eager to sell you trinkets from a cluster of canopied carts. The perimeter is rimmed with stores with tile roofs, wrought-iron balconies, and flower-filled window boxes. What to buy? Sombreros, baskets, pottery, jewelry, and maracas.

One of the pavilion's key attractions is the San Angel Inn, featuring traditional Mexican cuisine and wine and beer, and overlooking the faux-moonlit waterway traversed by Gran Fiesta Tour boats. The pavilion's Cava del Tequila bar serves up tequila flights, tapas like blue-crab tostados, and exotic blended margaritas. The casual, outdoor La Cantina de San Angel is a 150-seat quick-service eatery adjacent to La Hacienda de San Angel, a 250-seat table-service restaurant with waterside view. You won't want to miss trying Mexican treats like *chiles toreados y chorizitos* (roasted sweet peppers with lime and sea salt, served with mini chorizo) or La Hacienda mixed grill served with beans and fresh salsa.

FAMILY **Gran Fiesta Tour Starring the Three Caballeros.** In this attraction—which shines with the polish of enhanced facades, sound system, and boat-ride props—Donald teams with old pals José Carioca (the parrot) and Panchito (the Mexican charro rooster) from the 1944 Disney film *The Three Caballeros*. The Gran Fiesta Tour film sweeps you along for an animated jaunt as the caballeros are reunited for a grand performance in Mexico City. Donald manages to disappear for his own tour of the country, leaving José and Panchito to search for their missing comrade. **For people with disabilities:** The boat is accessible to guests using wheelchairs, but those using ECVs or oversize chairs must transfer to a Disney model. Equipped for handheld-captioning and audio-description devices. ■**TIP→ It's worth a visit if lines aren't long, especially if**

you have small children, who usually enjoy the novelty of a boat ride. ✉ *World Showcase, Mexico* ☞ *Duration: 9 mins. Crowds: Moderate. Audience: All Ages.*

EPCOT SPECTACLE

Fodor's Choice ★ **IllumiNations: Reflections of Earth.** This marvelous nighttime spectacular takes place over the World Showcase Lagoon every night before closing. Be sure to stick around for the lasers, lights, flames, fireworks, fountains, and music that fill the air over the water. The show's Earth Globe—a gigantic, spherical, video-display system rotating on a 350-ton floating island—is three stories tall with 180,000 light-emitting diodes. It houses six computer processors and 258 strobe lights and projects images celebrating the diversity and unified spirit of humankind. The globe opens like a lotus flower in the grand finale, revealing a huge torch that rises 40 feet into the air as additional flames spread light across the lagoon. Nearly 2,800 fireworks shells paint colorful displays across the night sky.

Although there's generally good viewing from all around the lagoon, some of the best spots are in front of the Italy pavilion, on the bridge between France and the United Kingdom, on the promenade in front of Canada, at the World Showcase Plaza, and at La Hacienda de San Angel and La Cantina de San Angel in Mexico. **For people with disabilities:** During the show, certain areas along the lagoon's edge at Showcase Plaza, Canada, and Germany are reserved for guests using wheelchairs. **■ TIP→ For best views (and if you have young children), find your place 45 minutes in advance and send someone in your group for ice cream or other treats.** ✉ *World Showcase* ☞ *Duration: 13 mins. Crowds: Heavy. Audience: All Ages.*

SHOPPING

Fine goods and trinkets from all over the world, some handcrafted, are sold at the pavilions representing individual countries here. Check out the Japanese and Chinese kimonos, Moroccan fezzes, French wines, Norwegian sweaters, and Mexican wood carvings. A United Kingdom shop even helps you research your family coat of arms, which you can buy as a paper printout or dressed up with paint or embroidery.

FUTURE WORLD

Mouse Gear. The usual Disney suspects—plush toys, Mickey cookware, Disney pins, Epcot-themed sweatshirts and T-shirts—are all at this Future World emporium. A few gems include designer mouse ears and character-themed iPad cases. ✉ *Future World.*

WORLD SHOWCASE

Enoteca Castello. This Italy pavilion shop sells some of the country's popular wines, olive oils, pastas, and sweets. ✉ *World Showcase.*

Historic Research Center. The focus at this United Kingdom outpost in The Crown & Crest is tracking down your family name and coat of arms. Take home a printout of both for $65. Drop the bigger bucks for a framed, embroidered, or hand-painted version. ✉ *World Showcase.*

House of Good Fortune. China's sprawling bazaar has a huge selection of tea sets ranging in style from traditional to contemporary ($45 and up) and fragranced candles that are sure to align your chi. Butterfly hair combs and brocade pajamas are beautiful, but the hottest items are little Buddha statues, available for $6 and up. ✉ *World Showcase.*

Il Bel Cristallo. For chic Italian totes, accessories, and collectibles, stop at this Italy pavilion. You'll also find fragrances by Fendi, Prada, and Bulgari. ✉ *World Showcase.*

La Signature. In the France pavilion, follow your nose for a sniff and a spritz of high-end French perfumes. Guerlain fragrances, cosmetics, and skin-care products like the Orchidée Impériale eye cream (most recently selling for a whopping $200 apiece) draw fans from around the globe. ✉ *World Showcase.*

Les Vins de France. Enjoy tasting some wine and shopping for a bottle or two of your favorite. A fun, practical souvenir is the sparkly Mickey wine stopper. ✉ *World Showcase.*

The Market. Morocco's open-air market is like something out of an Indiana Jones movie. It's a maze of shops selling straw bags and colorful carpets. It's also a great place to pick up something really different, like a Moroccan fez or belly-dancing gear, including a bright scarf, finger cymbals, and a CD with all the music you need to wow your audience. ✉ *World Showcase.*

Mexican Folk Art Gallery. As you enter the Mexico pavilion and descend the staircase, stop here to browse the hand-painted wood carvings crafted by Zapotec Indians of Oaxaca in southern Mexico. Artisans use brilliant colors to complete the detail of these intricate wood animal figures, which range in price from $16 to $700. ✉ *World Showcase.*

Mitsukoshi. Hello Kitty, one of Japan's most popular toys, is on hand here. Another toy favorite is a four-inch collectible Bebichhichi doll with pacifier. Dress up with a washable poly kimono or a more luxurious silk version ($40–$400), or check out the shimmering pearl jewelry. You'll be tempted to take home some sweets after watching a Japanese Candy Art demonstration just outside the store (see *Times Guide* for demo schedule). ✉ *World Showcase.*

Plaza de los Amigos. Descend a ramp at this Mexico shop to find sombreros ($17 to $54), baskets, pottery, and leather goods. You'll also find brightly colored ponchos, jewelry, and pinatas. ✉ *World Showcase.*

Puffin's Roost. In Norway, Viking wannabes go crazy for the soft toy spears and shields ($11–$15). The plush seals are sweet for tots, and you can find Norwegian pewter, leather goods, and colorful sweaters. ✉ *World Showcase.*

Weinkeller. In Germany, you can buy a wine-flight passport ($20) here for two 2-ounce samples of German wine—Rieslings and ice wines are popular—as well as two samples each of Italian and French wines at the Italy and France pavilions (or you can pick up the same passport when visiting those other two countries). ✉ *World Showcase.*

NIGHTLIFE

BARS

Cava del Tequila. Set inside the Mexico pavilion, this intimate bar serves tasty tapas, tequila flights, and some of the best margaritas anywhere, including the Cava Organic Skinny Lime Margarita. ✉ *World Showcase, Mexico.*

Rose & Crown Pub. Great piano sets by the Hat Lady and, on busy nights, four-to-six-deep at the bar guarantees good times at this United Kingdom watering hole. The fish-and-chips are first rate, and the Trio of United Kingdom Cheeses includes aged Irish cheddar and Stilton. Grab a beer or a cordial and let the fun begin! ✉ *World Showcase, United Kingdom.*

Tutto Gusto. This cool, cozy wine cellar adjoining Tutto Italia is the ideal place to kick back at a table or on a sofa and sip a bubbly Prosecco or a glass of Italian wine while noshing on antipasto or tapas-sized pastas. For quicker service, head straight for the bar. ✉ *World Showcase Italy pavilion.*

SHOWS

Illuminations. Epcot's 13-minute show, which takes place over the reflective World Showcase lagoon, usually begins at 9 pm and features lasers, fireworks, fountains, and a floating sphere that displays video scenes.

DISNEY'S HOLLYWOOD STUDIOS

The first thing you notice when you pass through the Hollywood Studios turnstiles is the laid-back California attitude. Palm-lined Hollywood Boulevard oozes glamour—but in a casual way that makes you feel as if you belong, even without your slinky Michael Kors jersey and Jimmy Choos.

When the park opened in May 1989 its name was Disney-MGM Studios. Disney changed the name in 2008 to broaden its appeal. Unlike the first movie theme park—Universal Studios in California—Hollywood Studios combined Disney detail with MGM's motion-picture legacy and Walt Disney's own animated classics. Imagineers built the park with real film and television production in mind, and during its first decade, the Studios welcomed films like *Ernest Saves Christmas* and TV shows like *Wheel of Fortune* to its soundstages.

The Animation Studios, too, were busy. Stories such as *Aladdin* and *Lilo & Stitch* came to life on the easels and computers of Disney's Florida animators. Though production has mostly halted at the park, you can enjoy plenty of attractions that showcase how filmmakers practice their craft. Want to see how special effects are created? Visit the Studio Backlot Tour. If you're wowed by action-film stunts, you can learn the tricks of the trade at the Indiana Jones Epic Stunt Spectacular! or the Lights, Motors, Action! Extreme Stunt Show. No trip to the Studios would be complete without a tour of the Magic of Disney Animation, where you can sit down and draw a character like Mickey or Donald.

In a savvy effort to grab a big piece of the pop-culture pie, in late 2008 Disney opened its own *American Idol* attraction, where performers earn audience votes to compete in an end-of-day contest for a spot in the TV show's regional audition process. Imagineers continue to "bring it," with big-hit attractions such as Toy Story Midway Mania! and new twists on old favorites like the 3-D Star Wars–themed simulator ride, Star Tours—The Adventures Continue.

TOP ATTRACTIONS

AGES 8 AND UP

The American Idol Experience. If you don't get chosen to test your pipes, you can vote for your favorite Idol wannabe.

Indiana Jones Epic Stunt Spectacular! The show's cast reenacts *Raiders of the Lost Ark* scenes with panache.

The Magic of Disney Animation. It's always fun to immerse yourself in Disney's world of animation.

Rock 'n' Roller Coaster Starring Aerosmith. Blast off to rockin' tunes on a high-speed, hard-core coaster.

Star Tours—The Adventures Continue. Prepare for a high-speed chase on this updated simulator thrill ride through multiple scenarios in the *Star Wars* galaxy.

Toy Story Midway Mania! 3-D glasses? Check. Spring-action shooter? Check. Ride and shoot your way through the midway with Buzz, Woody, and others.

Twilight Zone Tower of Terror. The TV classic theming of this free-fall "elevator" screamer is meticulous.

AGES 7 AND UNDER

Beauty and the Beast—Live on Stage. Memorable music, talented performers, dancing kitchen objects, and a fairy-tale ending make this a must-see show.

Disney Junior—Live on Stage! The preschool crowd can't get enough of the characters here from Disney Channel shows like *Jake and the Never Land Pirates, Mickey Mouse Clubhouse*, Doc McStuffins, and Sofia the First.

Honey, I Shrunk the Kids Movie Set Adventure. Youngsters love to romp among the giant blades of grass and bugs.

Muppet*Vision 3-D. Children (and most adults) shriek with laughter during this 3-D movie.

ORIENTATION AND PLANNING

GETTING ORIENTED

The park is divided into sightseeing clusters. **Hollywood Boulevard** is the main artery to the heart of the park, and is where you find the glistening replica of Graumann's Chinese Theater.

Encircling it are **Sunset Boulevard,** the **Animation Courtyard, Mickey Avenue, Pixar Place, Commissary Lane, the Streets of America area,** and **Echo Lake**.

The entire park is 135 acres, and has just 20 major attractions (compared with Magic Kingdom's 40-plus). It's small enough to cover in a day and even repeat a favorite ride or two.

If you're staying at one of the Epcot resorts (BoardWalk, Yacht or Beach Club, Swan, or Dolphin), getting to the Entrance Plaza on a motor launch is part of the fun. Disney resort buses also drop you at the entrance.

If you're staying off-property and driving, your parking ticket will remain valid for parking at another Disney park later in the day—provided, of course, you have the stamina.

DISNEY'S HOLLYWOOD STUDIOS PLANNER

PARK AMENITIES

Baby Care: The small baby-care center next to Guest Relations has nursing and changing facilities. Formula, baby food, pacifiers, and disposable diapers are for sale next door at Movieland and at Oscar's Super Service. There are also diaper-changing areas in all women's rooms and some men's rooms.

Cameras: At the Darkroom (or next door at Cover Story) on Hollywood Boulevard, you can buy memory cards and disposable cameras. And if a Disney photographer takes your picture in the park, you can pick up a Disney PhotoPass from him or her that lets you see the pictures online. PhotoPass CD packages are $169.95 and $199.95, and you can pur chase prints ($16.95 for an 8- by10-inch photo; other sizes available).

First Aid: The station is in the Entrance Plaza adjoining Guest Relations.

Guest Relations: You'll find it just inside the turnstiles on the left side of the Entrance Plaza. The **Studios Tip Board**, with updated information on events and attraction wait times, is at the corner of Hollywood and Sunset boulevards.

Lockers: You can rent lockers at the Crossroads of the World kiosk in the center of the Entrance Plaza. The cost is $7 or $9 with a $5 refundable key deposit. The lockers themselves are at Oscar's Super Service.

Lost People and Things: Instruct your kids to go to a Disney staffer with a name tag if they can't find you. If you lose them, ask any cast member for assistance; logbooks of lost children's names are kept at Guest Relations, which also has a computerized message center where you can leave notes for companions.

Disney's Hollywood Studios Lost and Found. Report lost or found articles at Guest Relations. ✉ *Hollywood Blvd.* ☎ *407/560–4666.*

Main Lost and Found. Seek out articles lost for more than one day here. ✉ *Ticket and Transportation Center [TTC], Magic Kingdom* ☎ *407/824–4245.*

Package Pick-Up: You can ask shop clerks to forward purchases to your hotel if you're staying on Disney property or to Package Pick-Up next to Oscar's Super Service in the Entrance Plaza, so you won't have to carry them around. Allow three hours for delivery.

Services for People with Disabilities: The Studios' restaurants, shops, theaters, and attractions are wheelchair accessible, although there are boarding restrictions on some rides. Parade routes have special sections for guests with disabilities.

Some theater-type attractions, including Muppet*Vision 3-D, have reflective captioning, and most other attractions are equipped for assisted-listening and video- or handheld-captioning devices. There are large Braille park maps near the Guest Relations lobby and near the Tip Board at Hollywood and Sunset. Note that restaurants don't have Braille menus.

You can pick up Braille guides ($25 same-day refundable deposit) and assisting devices (also $25 deposit) and check on sign-language interpretation schedules at Guest Relations. Although interpreters appear only two days each week, you can request them (at least 14 days in advance) on other days by calling ☎ *407/824–4321* or TTY *407/827–5141*.

Oscar's Super Service, to the right in the Entrance Plaza, rents wheelchairs ($12 daily, $10 multiday) and electronic convenience vehicles (ECVs; $50 per day plus a refundable $20 security deposit). Reservations aren't an option, so arrive early, especially to snag an ECV.

Stroller Rentals: Oscar's Super Service rents strollers. Single strollers are $15 daily, $13 for more than one day; doubles are $31 daily, $27 multiday.

DINNER AND A SHOW

***Fantasmic!* Dinner Package.** Call or check ahead to visit on a day when you can see the after-dark *Fantasmic!* show, with its 25 powerful minutes of Disney characters, special effects, fireworks, flames, fountains, and even animation sequences projected onto water screens. If you're not crazy about the idea of arriving at the huge Hollywood Hills Amphitheater more than an hour ahead of showtime for a good seat, it's worth booking a *Fantasmic!* dinner package.

You get a prix-fixe meal at buffet-style Hollywood & Vine or a full table-service dinner at Hollywood Brown Derby or Mama Melrose's, along with a preferred-entry pass to sidestep the main line at the *Fantasmic!* show. Each dinner includes appetizer, entrée, dessert (the Brown Derby's grapefruit cake is a sweet-tart wonder), and a nonalcoholic beverage. A seasonal option is the quick-service package at Min & Bill's Dockside Diner.

There's a small catch (well, actually, there are three):

You'll have to book an early dinner so you have plenty of time between your dining time and your arrival for showtime. (Disney recommends that you show up at the theater 30 or more minutes ahead of time to choose your seat).

The dinner package is offered only for the first show on peak nights when *Fantasmic!* is performed twice.

If it rains, *Fantasmic!* might be canceled. You still get dinner, but you lose out on seeing the show with preferred seating.

It's best to reserve the package several months in advance. You'll have to provide a credit-card number and, if you cancel 48 hours or less before the show, your card will be charged $10 per person. ✉ *Sunset Blvd.* ☎ *407/939–3463 reservations* 🎫 *$38–$60 adults, $13–$22 children 3–9 (prices vary by restaurant and exclude tax and gratuity; quick-service option priced under $20 for adults)* ⏲ *Fantasmic! usually performed once nightly during off-peak seasons; twice nightly during holidays and other peak visiting times.*

VISITING TIPS

■ Visit early in the week, when most people are at Magic Kingdom and Animal Kingdom.

■ Check the Tip Board periodically for attractions with short wait times to visit between FastPass+ appointments.

■ Be at the Fantasmic! amphitheater at least an hour before showtime if you didn't book the dinner package.

■ Need a burst of energy? On-the-run hunger pangs? Grab a slice at **Pizza Planet** at Streets of America. Alternatively, **Hollywood Scoops ice cream** on Sunset is the place to be on a hot day.

EXPLORING DISNEY'S HOLLYWOOD STUDIOS

HOLLYWOOD BOULEVARD

With its palm trees, pastel buildings, and flashy neon, Hollywood Boulevard paints a rosy picture of 1930s Tinseltown. There's a sense of having walked right onto a movie set of old, with art-deco storefronts and roving starlets and nefarious agents—actually costumed actors known as the Citizens of Hollywood. Throughout the park, characters from Disney movies new and old—from *Mickey Mouse* to *Toy Story* friends—pose for photos and sign autographs.

5

Great Movie Ride. At the end of Hollywood Boulevard, just behind the Sorcerer Mickey Hat, are the fire-engine-red pagodas of a replica of Graumann's Chinese Theater, where you enter this attraction. The preshow queue snakes through a screening room with continuously running clips from *Mary Poppins, Raiders of the Lost Ark, Singin' in the Rain, Fantasia,* and, of course, *Casablanca.* Once you board the ride,

Disney cast members dressed as 1920s newsboys (and girls) steer past a Hollywood Hills backdrop as you begin this tour of cinematic climaxes—with a little help from Audio-Animatronics, scrim, smoke, and Disney magic. Along the way you'll see Gene Kelly "Singin' in the Rain" as he clutches that immortal lamppost and Mary Poppins with her umbrella as her sooty admirers reprise "Chim-Chim-Cher-ee." A gangland shoot-out with James Cagney in *Public Enemy* is just around the corner. Gangsters or Western gunslingers (it depends on which tram you board) hijack your tram and whisk you off to a showdown. You'll meet some slimy characters from *Alien*—look up for truly scary stuff—before rolling onto the snake-ridden set of *Indiana Jones and the Temple of Doom,* where your hijacker attempts to steal an idol. We won't give away the scene stealer here.

Keep an eye out as Tarzan swings into action and Bogey bids Bergman goodbye with a "Here's looking at you, kid" by the plane to Lisbon. You'll know you're not in Kansas anymore with the Yellow Brick Road finale and the cackling imprecations by the Wicked Witch of the West. Remember to check out Dorothy's tornado-tossed house—you might spot the ruby slippers. **For people with disabilities:** You may remain in your wheelchair or ECV. Handheld captioning and audio description available. The sounds and effects on this ride might scare service animals. **■TIP→ Come while waiting out a FastPass+ appointment for another attraction.** ✉ *Hollywood Blvd.* ☞ *Duration: 22 mins. Crowds: Moderate. Audience: All but Very Young Kids.*

SUNSET BOULEVARD

This avenue honors Hollywood with facades derived from the Cathay Circle, the Beverly Wilshire Theatre, and other City of Angels landmarks.

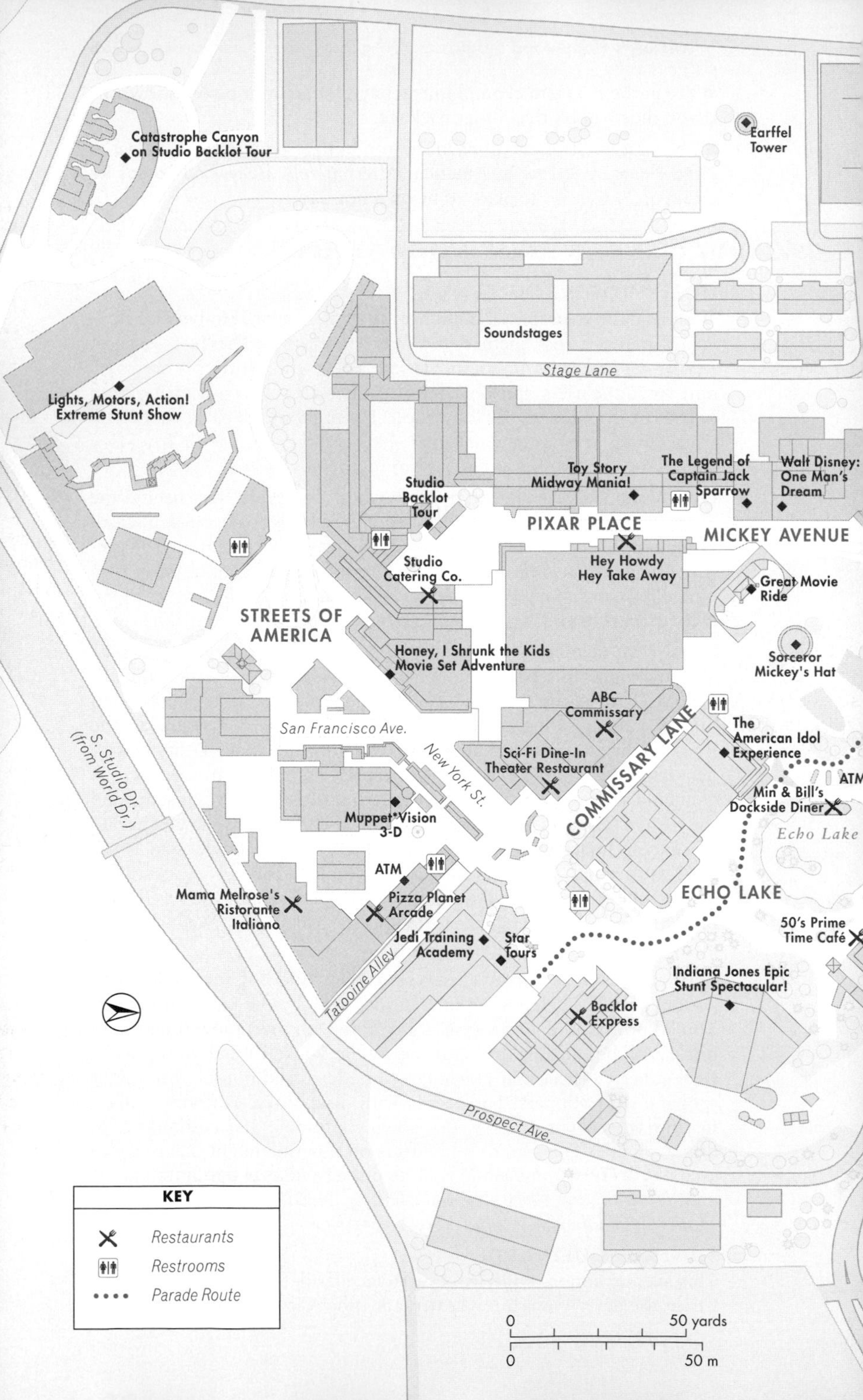

Catastrophe Canyon on Studio Backlot Tour
Earffel Tower
Soundstages
Stage Lane
Lights, Motors, Action! Extreme Stunt Show
Toy Story Midway Mania!
The Legend of Captain Jack Sparrow
Walt Disney: One Man's Dream
Studio Backlot Tour
PIXAR PLACE
MICKEY AVENUE
Hey Howdy Hey Take Away
Studio Catering Co.
Great Movie Ride
STREETS OF AMERICA
Sorceror Mickey's Hat
Honey, I Shrunk the Kids Movie Set Adventure
ABC Commissary
The American Idol Experience
San Francisco Ave.
New York St.
Sci-Fi Dine-In Theater Restaurant
COMMISSARY LANE
ATM
Min & Bill's Dockside Diner
S. Studio Dr. (from World Dr.)
Muppet*Vision 3-D
Echo Lake
ATM
ECHO LAKE
Mama Melrose's Ristorante Italiano
Pizza Planet Arcade
50's Prime Time Café
Jedi Training Academy
Star Tours
Indiana Jones Epic Stunt Spectacular!
Tatooine Alley
Backlot Express
Prospect Ave.
KEY
Restaurants
Restrooms
Parade Route
0
50 yards
0
50 m

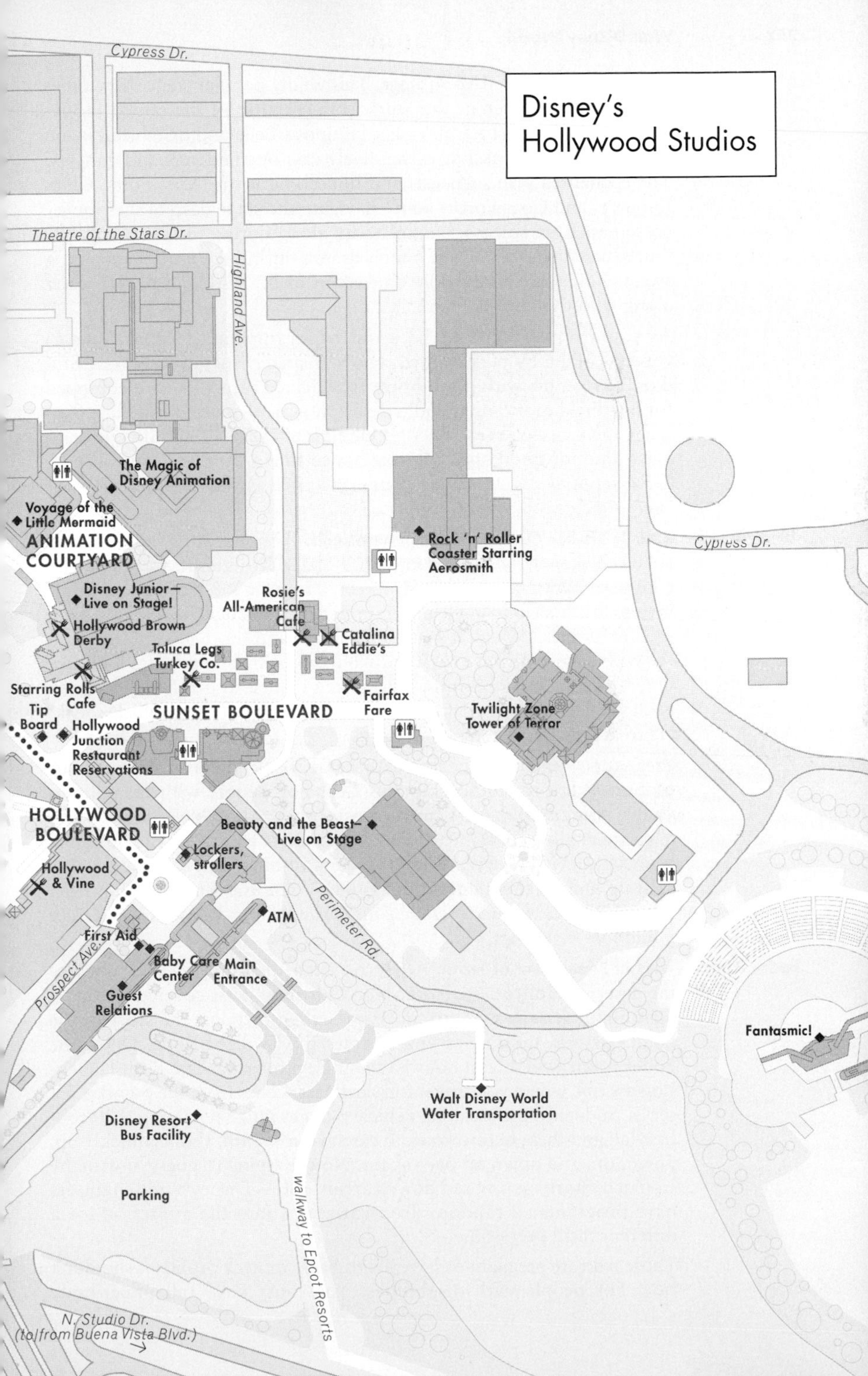

Disney's Hollywood Studios
Cypress Dr.
Theatre of the Stars Dr.
Highland Ave.
The Magic of Disney Animation
Voyage of the Little Mermaid
ANIMATION COURTYARD
Disney Junior—Live on Stage!
Hollywood Brown Derby
Rosie's All-American Cafe
Catalina Eddie's
Toluca Legs Turkey Co.
Rock 'n' Roller Coaster Starring Aerosmith
Cypress Dr.
Starring Rolls Cafe
Fairfax Fare
SUNSET BOULEVARD
Tip Board
Hollywood Junction Restaurant Reservations
Twilight Zone Tower of Terror
HOLLYWOOD BOULEVARD
Beauty and the Beast–Live on Stage
Lockers, strollers
Hollywood & Vine
Perimeter Rd.
ATM
First Aid
Prospect Ave.
Baby Care Center
Main Entrance
Guest Relations
Fantasmic!
Walt Disney World Water Transportation
Disney Resort Bus Facility
Parking
walkway to Epcot Resorts
N. Studio Dr. (to/from Buena Vista Blvd.)

Beauty and the Beast—Live on Stage. This wildly popular stage show takes place at the Theater of the Stars, a re-creation of the famed Hollywood Bowl. The actors playing a luminous Belle and delightfully vain Gaston sing with passion with a lively cast of characters and dancers. The enchanted prince (Beast) and household items (Mrs. Potts, Chip, Lumiere, and Cogsworth) deftly navigate the stage despite their bulky costumes. Even some set pieces sway along during the charming "Be Our Guest" number. There's high drama during the mob scene and a sweet ending when ballroom dancers in frothy pink and purple waltz along with the fairy-tale couple.

As you arrive or depart, check out handprints and footprints set in concrete of the TV personalities who've visited Disney's Hollywood Studios. **For people with disabilities:** Wheelchair accessible and equipped for handheld captioning, audio description, and assisted listening. Sign language twice a week. **■ TIP→ Line up at least 30 minutes prior to showtime for good seats. Performance times vary, so check ahead.** ✉ *Sunset Blvd.* ☞ *Duration: 30 mins. Crowds: Moderate–Heavy. Audience: All Ages.*

Fodor's Choice ★ **Rock 'n' Roller Coaster Starring Aerosmith.** Although this is an indoor roller coaster like Magic Kingdom's Space Mountain, the similarity ends there. With its high-speed launch (0 to 60 in 2.8 seconds), multiple inversions, and loud rock music, it generates delighted screams from coaster junkies, though it's smooth enough and short enough that even the coaster-phobic have been known to enjoy it. The vehicles look like limos, and the track resembles the neck of an electric guitar that's been twisted. Hard-driving rock tunes by Aerosmith blast from vehicle speakers to accentuate the flips and turns.

Pregnant women and guests with heart, back, or neck problems or motion sickness should skip this one. **For people with disabilities:** Guests using wheelchairs must transfer to a ride vehicle. Service animals aren't allowed. **■ TIP→ Ride early, and get a FastPass+ to go again, especially if visiting with tweens or teens. Another way to avoid a wait—split up and try the Single Rider Queue.** ✉ *Sunset Blvd.* ☞ *Duration: 1 min., 22 secs. Crowds: Huge. Audience: All but Young Kids. Height minimum: 48 inches.*

Fodor's Choice ★ **Twilight Zone Tower of Terror.** After you enter the dimly lighted lobby of the deserted Hollywood Tower Hotel, then the dust-covered library, a lightning bolt zaps a TV to life. Rod Serling recounts the story of the hotel's demise and invites you to enter the Twilight Zone. On to the boiler room, where you board a giant elevator ride. The Fifth Dimension awaits, where you travel forward past scenes from the popular TV series. Suddenly, the creaking vehicle plunges into a terrifying, 130-foot free-fall and then, before you can catch your breath, shoots quickly up, down, up, and down all over again. No use trying to guess how many stomach-churning ups and downs are in store—Disney's ride engineers have programmed random drop variations into the attraction for a different thrill every time.

Those who are pregnant or have heart, back, or neck problems shouldn't ride. **For people with disabilities:** You must have full upper-body strength and be able to transfer to a ride seat. Equipped for video captioning. Service animals can't ride. ■**TIP→ Get a FastPass+ reserved-time ticket. Otherwise, come early or wait until evening, when crowds thin.** ✉ *Sunset Blvd.* ☞ *Duration: 10 mins. Crowds: You Bet! Audience: All but Young Kids. Height minimum: 40 inches.*

ANIMATION COURTYARD

As you exit Sunset Boulevard, veer right through the high-arched gateway to the Animation Courtyard. Straight ahead are *Disney Junior—Live on Stage!*, the Magic of Disney Animation, and *Voyage of the Little Mermaid.*

Disney Junior—Live on Stage!. This is one of Walt Disney World's best shows for tots and preschoolers. A cast of Disney Channel characters joins the show's perky host, Casey, on a larger-than-life storybook stage. Puppets of Mickey Mouse, Goofy, and friends team up on the Mickey Mouse Clubhouse set to prep for Minnie's surprise birthday bash. In another skit, characters from Jake and the Never Land Pirates devise a clever way to thwart Captain Hook and defend their treasure chest. The newest show segment features princess-in-training Sofia the First and Doc McStuffins. Sofia enlists sorcerer Mr. Cedric to cast a spell and make her father's royal ball a success. Meanwhile, Lambie's dance moves cause a bad case of "the rippies," cured only after Stuffy the Dragon and friends gather in Doc's office for some bubbly cheering-up fun.

5

Throughout the 24-minute show, preschoolers sing and dance along as the characters cha-cha-cha their way through the fun. Surprise special effects are icing on Minnie's birthday cake. **For people with disabilities:** Wheelchair accessible, equipped with preshow-area TV monitors with closed captioning, and equipped for assisted-listening, audio description, and video- and handheld-captioning devices. ■**TIP→ Come early, when your child is most alert and lines are shorter. Be prepared to sit on the carpet. Don't miss character meet-and-greets before or after the show.** ✉ *Animation Courtyard* ☞ *Duration: 24 mins. Crowds: Moderate– Heavy. Audience: Young Kids.*

The Magic of Disney Animation. More than any other backstage peek, this tour truly takes you inside the magic as you follow the many steps of 2-D animation, an art expected to be totally replaced in years to come by computer-generated films such as the Disney/Pixar blockbuster *Toy Story.* You begin in a small theater with a performance of *Drawn to Animation,* in which an actor plays the role of an animator interacting with Mushu, the wisecracking character from *Mulan.* Depending on when you visit, new characters from upcoming Disney films may be introduced near the end of this show.

Then you enter a creative zone to play with computer touch screens. You can voice your favorite character and discover which one is most like you. Watch for popular costumed Disney toon stars to appear in this area for autographs and photos.

The final stop is the Animation Academy. Children and adults can participate as an artist explains how to draw the Disney character du jour—your sketch is your souvenir. As you exit, don't miss the collection of drawings and cels of characters from *Snow White, Fantasia,* and other classics. Here, too, are the actual Academy Awards that Disney has won for its animated films. The entire experience can take 15 to 30 minutes or more if you play at interactive exhibits or take part in the Animation Academy. **For people with disabilities:** Wheelchair accessible, has reflective captioning and equipped for audio-description devices. **■ TIP→ Come early or late. To test your talents at Animation Academy, go there first or get in line quickly after the Drawn to Animation show. Toddlers may get bored.** ✉ *Animation Courtyard* ☞ *Duration: 15+ mins. Crowds: Moderate. Audience: All Ages.*

Voyage of the Little Mermaid. You join Ariel, Sebastian, and the underwater gang in this stage show, which condenses the movie into a marathon presentation of the greatest hits. In an admirable effort at verisimilitude, a fine mist sprays the stage; if you're sitting in the front rows, expect to get spritzed. Although this show is suitable for all ages, smaller children might be frightened by the dark theater and the evil, larger-than-life Ursula. **For people with disabilities:** Wheelchair accessible, has reflective captioning and preshow-area TVs with closed-captioning, and equipped for audio description and assisted-listening devices. **■ TIP→ If you're not riding Rock 'n' Roller Coaster or Tower of Terror, come first thing and put FastPass+ (if available) to good use. Or wait until the stroller brigade's exodus after 5.** ✉ *Animation Courtyard* ☞ *Duration: 15 mins. Crowds: Heavy. Audience: All Ages.*

MICKEY AVENUE

The Legend of Captain Jack Sparrow. This walk-through attraction combines elaborate set pieces and special effects to re-create a dark and forbidding high-seas adventure with Captain Jack Sparrow. Bits of scenes from all four *Pirates of the Caribbean* films come to life through impressive animation, audio, and projection technology. The narrator, a large disembodied skull floating above the scene, interacts with guests as lightning flashes, waves crash, mermaids entice, a Kraken threatens, and undead skeletons jump to life. You are recruited to join Sparrow's crew and, ultimately, you meet the very convincing (and soused) Sparrow himself, played by Johnny Depp. The climax features a high-seas battle with Davy Jones and the *Flying Dutchman* ship. **For people with disabilities:** Wheelchair accessible and equipped for handheld captioning, audio-description and assisted-listening listening devices. **■ TIP→ Young children may be frightened and tired park-hoppers may be irritated by the lack of seating. Skip if the wait is longer than 15 minutes.** ✉ *Mickey Avenue* ☞ *Duration: 12 mins. Crowds: Moderate. Audience: Not young kids.*

Walt Disney: One Man's Dream. One Man's Dream is a photo, film, and audio tour through Walt's life. For baby boomers, it's a real nostalgia trip to see Walt resurrected on film as his Wonderful World of Color intro splashes across the screen. There's also plenty of Walt memorabilia to view. Imagineers have added displays that include a towering Audio-Animatronics figure of Abraham Lincoln. Featured by Disney at the 1964–65 New York World's Fair in a "Great Moments with Mr. Lincoln" exhibit, the robotic president offers a transparent view of the mechanical innards that provide his movements. The film at the end of your self-guided tour is 15 minutes long. **For people with disabilities:** Wheelchair accessible; has reflective captioning; and equipped for assisted-listening, handheld-captioning, and audio-description devices. ■ **TIP→ Come while waiting for a FastPass+ appointment at a high-demand ride like Rock 'n' Roller Coaster.** ✉ *Mickey Ave.* ☞ *Duration: 15+ mins. Crowds: Light–Moderate. Audience: Not Young Kids.*

PIXAR PLACE

Pixar Place has a fresh look tied to one of the park's biggest attractions, Toy Story Midway Mania! Where TV- and film-production soundstages once stood, warm brick facades welcome you to the land of Woody and Buzz. Open-air kiosks invite you to browse for themed toys and souvenirs. The brick building featuring Toy Story Friends is the place to mix and mingle with characters from the blockbuster movie *Toy Story*. Check schedules on your *Times Guide*.

Fodor's Choice ★ **Toy Story Midway Mania!.** Great toys like Mr. Potato Head, Woody, and Buzz Lightyear from Disney's hit film *Toy Story* never lose their relevance. The action here involves these beloved characters and takes place inside the toy box of Andy, the boy whose toys come to life when he's gone. Step right up and grab a pair of 3-D glasses before boarding your jazzed-up carnival tram. Soon, you're whirling onto the midway where you can use your spring-action shooter to launch darts at balloons, toss rings at aliens, and splatter eggs at barnyard targets.

You'll rack up points for targets hit and see your tally at ride's end. Try to hone a rat-a-tat shooting system to increase your score. Don't let Rex's fear of failure slow you down—shoot for the stars and you'll deserve a salute from the Green Army Men. **For people with disabilities:** Guests using ECVs must transfer to a standard wheelchair. Equipped for video-captioning and audio-description devices. Check with a host about boarding with a service animal. ■ **TIP→ It's so addictive, you might want to come first thing, ride, and get a FastPass+ for another go.** ✉ *Pixar Pl.* ☞ *Duration: 7 mins. Crowds: Heavy. Audience: All Ages.*

STREETS OF AMERICA

It's fun to tour the New York and San Francisco sets here on foot so that you can check out the windows of shops and apartments, the taxicabs, and other details. If you're lucky (or smart enough to check the *Times Guide* show schedule), you'll join the street party for a performance by Mulch, Sweat & Shears—Live in Concert, as they play a 30-minute set of rock classics or rockin' seasonal tunes during holidays. The band also performs later in the day by the Sorcerer Hat on Hollywood Boulevard.

Honey, I Shrunk the Kids Movie Set Adventure. In this playground based on the movie, youngsters can slide down a gigantic blade of grass, crawl through caves, climb a mushroom mountain, and dodge sprinklers set in resilient flooring made of ground-up tires. All the requisite playground equipment is present: net climbs, ball crawls, caves, and slides. Because the area is enclosed, there's often a line to get in—but attraction hosts don't fudge on capacity limits, which maintains a comfort zone for those inside. **For people with disabilities:** Barrier-free, but uneven surfaces make maneuvering a wheelchair difficult. ■ **TIP→ Come when you've visited several attractions and your kids need to cut loose. Keep**

a close eye on toddlers—it's easy to lose track of them in the caves and on slides. ✉ *Streets of America* ☞ *Duration: Up to You. Crowds: Moderate. Audience: Young Kids.*

Lights, Motors, Action! Extreme Stunt Show. Here Disney show producers reveal the secrets behind Hollywood's greatest stunts, including heart-pounding car chases and explosions. The scene is a 177,000-square-foot Mediterranean village movie set inside a 5,000-seat, open-air theater. The premise? Filmmakers are producing a spy thriller, and the director is organizing out-of-sequence stunts. Heroes and villains perform high-speed spinouts, two-wheel driving, jumps, and high falls using various vehicles, including watercraft. Amid the action, you learn how filmmakers combine shots of various stunts to create a completed scene.

The show is pretty long, the benches are hard, some children become frightened by all the loud noises. Consider sitting toward the back in case you or your kids want to leave early. **For people with disabilities:** Wheelchair accessible and equipped for assisted-listening devices. **■ TIP→ For the best seats, line up for this while others are lining up for the parade.** ✉ *Streets of America* ☞ *Duration: 38 mins. Crowds: Moderate–Heavy. Audience: Not Young Kids.*

Muppet*Vision 3-D. You don't have to be a Miss Piggyphile to get a kick out of this combination 3-D movie and musical revue. All the Muppet characters make appearances, including Miss Piggy in roles that include the Statue of Liberty. In the waiting area, movie posters advertise the world's most glamorous porker in *Star Chores* and *To Have and Have More,* and Kermit the Frog in an Arnold Schwarzenegger parody, *Kürmit the Amphibian,* who's "so mean, he's green." Special effects are built into the walls and ceilings of the theater; the 3-D effects are coordinated with other sensory stimulation. **For people with disabilities:** Wheelchair accessible; has reflective captioning and preshow-area TVs with closed-captioning; and equipped for assisted-listening, video-captioning, and audio-description devices. **■ TIP→ Arrive 10 minutes early. And don't worry—there are no bad seats.** ✉ *Streets of America* ☞ *Duration: 25 mins. Crowds: Moderate–Heavy. Audience: All Ages.*

Studio Backlot Tour. The first stop on this tour, which you enter at the far end of Pixar Place where it meets Streets of America, is an outdoor special-effects water tank, where some of you are recruited for an unforgettable (and very wet) video moment. The line for the tram ride passes through a huge prop warehouse, which stores everything from traffic lights to British phone booths.

Board the tram for a tour of different departments—set design, costumes, props, lighting—as well as the movie set for *Catastrophe Canyon.* A simulated earthquake sets off multiple reactions—beware disaster! As the tram pulls out, you see the backstage workings of the catastrophe: the canyon is actually a mammoth steel slide wrapped in copper-colored concrete, and 70,000 gallons of "floodwater"—enough to fill 10 Olympic-size swimming pools—are recycled every 3½ minutes.

You also ride past the Streets of America back lot, where you can glimpse the New York Street with its brownstone facades. Pose for a photo by the Empire State and Chrysler buildings. You'll have to

DID YOU KNOW?

Pixar Place's Toy Story Midway Mania! combines the fun of a video game with 3-D technology *and* interaction with favorite *Toy Story* characters, like Mr. Potato Head. Man your spring-action shooter and take aim at playful targets along the colorful ride route. Scores are tallied at the end—will yours make you master of the midway?

walk the Streets set after exiting the tram to see the San Francisco and Chicago side streets. Film buffs will want to browse the American Film Institute Showcase with revolving exhibits about motion picture special effects. **For people with disabilities:** Wheelchair accessible and equipped for handheld- and video-captioning devices. **■TIP→ Come early (it closes at dusk) and remember that people sitting on the left side of the tram get a bit wet.** ⊠ *Streets of America* ☞ *Duration: 35 mins. Crowds: Moderate. Audience: Not Young Kids.*

ECHO LAKE

In the center of an idealized slice of Southern California is a cool, blue lake—an oasis fringed with trees, benches, and things like pink-and-aqua, chrome-trimmed restaurants with sassy waitresses and black-and-white TVs at the tables; the shipshape Min & Bill's Dockside Diner; and Gertie, an emotive dinosaur that dispenses ice cream (seasonally) as well as Disney souvenirs and the occasional puff of smoke. (Look for Gertie's giant footprints in the sidewalk.) The hot ticket here is the American Idol Experience, where you can act out your own *American Idol* ambitions. You'll also find two of the park's longest-running attractions, the Indiana Jones Epic Stunt Spectacular! and Star Tours—The Adventures Continue, where a 3-D attraction transformation jazzes up the galaxy.

The American Idol Experience. So you want to be a rock star? How about an American Idol? If you're 14 or older and can sing on key, head to auditions as soon as you enter the park in the morning. You may be chosen by a Disney casting director to belt out a tune during shows at The American Idol Experience stage. At day's end, the top singers are invited back for a grand finale, and the winning performer earns The American Idol Experience "Dream Ticket"—a sort of FastPass+ to the front of the line at a future regional audition for the *American Idol* TV show.

Not an *Idol* fan? No problem. This show, performed on a high-tech Hollywood-style stage complete with neon flash and high-energy show hosts, is a blast for all who enjoy live entertainment. Idol wannabes can choose their tunes from many music genres, so performers and songs vary with every show. The best part? You and every other audience member vote for the show's top singer.

When it's time to vote, your armrest keypad lights up for 10 seconds. While votes are tallied, you're treated to a big-screen music video starring 2007 *American Idol* champion Jordin Sparks. Other *Idol* stars make video appearances.

Preliminary shows last 25 minutes; finale shows are 45 minutes. Dying to see who wins the Dream Ticket but can't get into the theater for the evening finale? Take heart. A stadium-size LED screen outside the theater offers a live simulcast. To learn about auditions ahead of time, visit 🌐 *www.disneyworld.com/idol*. **For people with disabilities:** Wheelchair accessible. Twice weekly sign-language interpretations. Equipped for assisted-listening and video-captioning devices. **■TIP→ To get a seat inside the theater, arrive at least 30 minutes before showtime.** This attraction is scheduled to close in January 2015. ⊠ *Echo Lake* ☞ *Duration: 25 or 45 mins. Crowds: Yes! Audience: All but Young Kids.*

Fodor's Choice ★ **Indiana Jones Epic Stunt Spectacular!.** The rousing theme music from the Indiana Jones movies heralds action delivered by veteran stunt coordinator Glenn Randall, whose credits include *Raiders of the Lost Ark, E.T.,* and *Jewel of the Nile.* Presented in a 2,200-seat amphitheater, the show starts with a series of near-death encounters in an ancient Mayan temple. Indy slides down a rope from the ceiling, dodges spears, avoids getting chopped by booby-trapped idols, and snags a forbidden gemstone, setting off a gigantic boulder that threatens to flatten him.

Next comes the Cairo street scene, circa 1940, where lucky audience members are chosen to perform as extras. When the nasty Ninja-Nazi stuntmen come out, you start to think that it's probably better to be in the audience.

Eventually Indy returns with his redoubtable girlfriend, Marian Ravenwood, portrayed by a Karen Allen look-alike. She's kidnapped and tossed into a truck while Indy fights his way free with bullwhip and gun, and bad guys tumble from every corner and cornice.

5

The actors do a commendable job of explaining their stunts, and you'll learn how cameras are camouflaged for trick shots. Only one stunt remains a secret: how do Indy and Marian escape the grand finale explosion? That's what keeps 'em coming back. **For people with disabilities:** Wheelchair accessible. Equipped for assisted-listening, audio-description, and handheld-captioning devices. There's sign language interpretation twice weekly. ■ **TIP→ Don't waste a FastPass+ here; there's plenty of room. Come at night to see the idols' eyes glow.** ✉ *Echo Lake* ☞ *Duration: 30 mins. Crowds: Moderate–Heavy. Audience: All but Very Young Kids.*

Fodor's Choice ★ **Star Tours: The Adventures Continue.** *Star Wars* fans, wield those light sabers! This fan favorite multiplies the thrills with more than 50 ride scenarios powered up by Dolby 3-D video combined with motion-simulator technology. Here's the basic storyline: C-3PO and R2-D2, at the helm of a misappropriated spaceship, must navigate the galaxy with a rebel spy on board (it could be you!) while Imperial forces try to thwart the journey.

Each ride is different: you'll encounter multiple thrills from the *Star Wars* universe including the lush Wookiee planet Kashyyyk and the underwater world of Naboo. One flight propels you through a dangerous asteroid field before skimming the second Death Star construction zone. You may come face-to-menacing-mask with Darth Vader, or meet favorite sage Yoda. Other characters sprinkled throughout the different films included Admiral Ackbar, Chewbacca, and Boba Fett. Your 40-passenger Starspeeder 1000 rockets through space with enough high-speed twists, turns, and nosedives to guarantee that the Force is, indeed, with you.

Those who are pregnant or have heart, back, neck, or motion-sickness issues shouldn't ride. Children less than 40 inches tall may not ride. **For people with disabilities:** Guests using wheelchairs must transfer to a ride seat. Equipped for handheld-captioning and video-captioning devices. Service animals aren't allowed. ■ **TIP→ Lines swell when the Indiana Jones show lets out. Come early or late or use FastPass+. For**

DISNEY'S HOLLYWOOD STUDIOS

NAME	Height Req.	Type of Entertainment	Duration	Crowds	Audience	Tips
Animation Courtyard						
Disney Junior—Live on Stage!	n/a	Show	24 mins.	Moderate to Heavy	Young Kids	Come first thing in the morning, when your child is most alert and lines are shorter.
The Magic of Disney Animation	n/a	Tour	15+ mins.	Moderate	All Ages	Come in the morning or late afternoon. Toddlers may get bored.
Voyage of the Little Mermaid	n/a	Show	15 mins.	Heavy	All Ages	Come first thing in the morning. Otherwise, wait until after 5.
Echo Lake						
The American Idol Experience	n/a	Show	25 mins./ 45 mins.	Yes!	All but Young Kids	Check *Times Guide*, for showtimes. Arrive at least 30 minutes early for seats inside the theater.
Indiana Jones Epic Stunt Spectacular!	n/a	Show	30 mins.	Moderate to Heavy	All but Young Kids	Come at night, when the idol's eyes glow. Sit up front to feel the heat of a truck on fire.
★ Star Tours 3-D—The Adventure Continues	At least 40"	Simulator Exp.	6 mins.	Heavy	All but Young Kids	Get a FastPass+. Sit in rear for wildest ride.
Hollywood Boulevard						
Great Movie Ride	n/a	Ride/Tour	22 mins.	Moderate	All but Young Kids	Come while waiting for FastPass+ appointment. Lines out the door mean 25-min. wait—or longer.
Mickey Avenue						
Walt Disney: One Man's Dream	n/a	Walk-Through/ Film	15+ mins.	Light to Moderate	All but Young Kids	See this attraction while waiting for a FastPass+ appointment.

The Legend of Captain Jack Sparrow	n/a	Show/Film	12 mins.	Moderate	All but Young Kids	Standing room only; children may be restless.
Pixar Place						
Toy Story Midway Mania!	n/a	Interactive Ride	7 mins.	Heavy	All Ages	Come early; use FastPass+.
Streets of America						
Honey, I Shrunk the Kids Movie Set Adventure	n/a	Playground	Up to you	Moderate	Young Kids	Come after you've done several shows and your kids need to cut loose. Keep an eye on toddlers who can quickly get lost in the caves and slides.
Lights, Motors, Action! Extreme Stunt Show	n/a	Show	38 mins.	Heavy	All but Young Kids	For the best seats, line up for the show while others are lining up for the parade.
Muppet*Vision 3-D	n/a	3-D Film	25 mins.	Moderate	All Ages	Arrive 10 mins. early. And don't worry—there are no bad seats.
Studio Backlot Tour	n/a	Tour	35 mins.	Moderate	All but very Young Kids	People sitting on the left can get wet. Come early; it closes at dusk.
Sunset Boulevard						
Beauty and the Beast—Live on Stage!	n/a	Show	30 mins.	Moderate to Heavy	All Ages	Come 30 mins. before showtime for good seats. Performance times vary, so check ahead.
★ Rock 'n' Roller Coaster Starring Aerosmith	At least 48"	Thrill Ride	1 min., 22 secs.	Huge	All but Young Kids	Ride early, then use FastPass+ for another go later.
★ Twilight Zone Tower of Terror	At least 40"	Thrill Ride	10 mins.	You Bet!	All but Young Kids	Use FastPass+. Come early or late evening.

★ Fodor's Choice

HOLLYWOOD STUDIOS KIDS TOUR

Young children always get a kick out of Hollywood Boulevard's wacky street performers and the park's lively street parades and energetic stage shows.

The minute you enter, head straight to Toy Story Midway Mania! and get in line (unless you made a FastPass+ reservation). Everyone loves this busy ride—even young children who have to learn how to operate their spring-action shooters to rack up midway points. If you can ride *and* come back for your FastPass+ reservation, you'll be your kids' hero.

Now take a deep breath and lead the little ones to hands-on activities inside the Magic of Disney Animation (where they'll first enjoy a short film) and Honey, I Shrunk the Kids Movie Set Adventure, where they can whoop their way through a larger-than-life playground.

Combine lunch with more playtime at the Play 'N Dine at Hollywood & Vine family buffet, where characters from Disney Junior: Live on Stage! mix and mingle with the children. Don't forget your camera and the kids' autograph books!

SEE THE CHARACTERS COME TO LIFE

Shows and attractions based on Disney films and TV series really grab young children. Check your *Times Guide* for performances of Beauty and the Beast: Live on Stage and Disney Junior: Live on Stage! After tots and preschoolers have danced along at the Disney Junior show, they can meet the characters in the Animation Courtyard, then catch a Beauty and the Beast performance or watch Ariel "under the sea" in *Voyage of the Little Mermaid.*

Check other character greeting locations and times—the Green Army Men from *Toy Story* put the kids through their marching paces on Pixar Place; Mickey Mouse, Lotso from *Toy Story 3,* or the Incredibles might turn up at the Magic of Disney Animation. Make time to meet Phineas and Ferb near Mama Melrose's Ristorante Italiano. Then watch Kermit display his wry wit and Miss Piggy steal the show at Muppet*Vision 3-D. It's not easy being green. . . .

GRAB THE SPOTLIGHT

Jedi wannabes can suit up to clash with the Dark Force at Jedi Training Academy, which is scheduled throughout the day. Just outside Star Tours, children ages 4–12 can grab a light saber and let the Force be with them. During each 20-minute show, crowds gather and cheer the kids as they learn to "cut to the left shoulder, step back, and duck!" when clashing with a costumed Darth Vader. Needless to say, the Dark Force can't compete.

the wildest ride, sit in the back. ✉ *Echo Lake* ☞ *Duration: 6 mins. Crowds: Heavy. Audience: All but Young Kids.*

NEED A BREAK?

If you have a sweet tooth, save room for some soft-serve Ice Cream of Extinction at Gertie's ice-cream bar and snack shop, open seasonally inside the big green dinosaur on the shore of Echo Lake. Nearby, Min & Bill's Dockside Diner is the spot for a quick sandwich and a shake. You can even buy a beer here. Step right up to the counter.

HOLLYWOOD STUDIOS GROWN-UP TOUR

At the Studios, movie classics like *The Wizard of Oz* and *Casablanca* come to life on the Great Movie Ride, and the best of Disney animation—from *Toy Story* to *Beauty and the Beast*—is reborn as park attractions. The old small-screen favorite *The Twilight Zone* is taken to new heights, and the modern TV phenomenon *American Idol* goes live.

FIND YOUR ADRENALINE RUSH

Two words—thrills and chills—define the top two attractions for older kids and adults. Head straight to Sunset Boulevard and grab the thrills at Rock 'n' Roller Coaster Starring Aerosmith, where multiple inversions, twists, and turns rock to the tune of "Dude (Looks Like a Lady)." Feel the chills at the Twilight Zone Tower of Terror, when something goes terribly wrong with your elevator car, and it veers off its ghostly course.

A quick walk to Echo Lake lands you in Wookiee territory, where you can climb aboard the Star Tours flight simulator for a wild flight to the Moon of Endor; 3-D upgrades and more than 50 different ride scenarios increase the thrill factor.

DISCOVER YOUR TALENT

Are you an actor, an artist, a singer, or a midway-game fanatic? If the Citizens of Hollywood Talent Agent doesn't get your number, you can try out your act at one of several park attractions. At the Indiana Jones Epic Stunt Spectacular! 10 guests are chosen to perform as show extras (arrive early and get noticed). At the American Idol Experience, you can test your pipes in an audition—and maybe even make it onto the show. All those years filling notebooks with doodles might just have been training for the Magic of Disney Animation Academy experience. At Toy Story Midway Mania! join Woody and Buzz for a manic midway ride past moving targets that test your spring-action-shooter mettle.

LEARN TRICKS OF THE TRADE

Refuel at one of the park's many quick-service stands, let "Mom" serve you meat loaf and a peanut butter-and-jelly shake at the '50s Prime Time Café, or boost your image with a plush booth and a Cobb salad at the Hollywood Brown Derby.

Then head for the Studio Backlot Tour and a look at how filmmakers create special effects. Stroll the Streets of America before queuing up for a seat at the Lights, Motors, Action! Extreme Stunt Show and a peek at how high-speed vehicle action is shot.

Back at Echo Lake, the Tune-In Lounge is a great place to grab a mojito or margarita before heading to the nighttime extravaganza Fantasmic! That's a wrap.

5

HOLLYWOOD STUDIOS SPECTACLE

Fantasmic!. The Studios' after-dark show wows huge audiences with its special effects and Disney characters. The omnipresent Mickey, in his Sorcerer's Apprentice costume, plays the embodiment of Good in the struggle against forces of Evil, personified by Disney villains such as Cruella DeVil, Scar, and Maleficent. Animated clips of these famous bad guys (and gals), alternating with clips of Disney nice guys (and dolls), are projected onto screens made of water—high-tech fountains surging high in the air. The epic battle plays out amid water effects and flames, explosions, and fireworks worthy of a Hollywood shoot-'em-up. All this, plus the villainous action, is why small kids may find this show frightening.

Arrive early at the Hollywood Hills Amphitheater opposite the Twilight Zone Tower of Terror. Check ahead for information on show days and times. This show runs two or three times nightly during peak season; fewer times during nonpeak periods. **For people with disabilities:** Wheelchair accessible. Equipped with reflective captioning and for assisted-listening devices. **■TIP→ Arrive at least an hour early and sit toward the rear, near the entrance/exit. Or consider the dinner package, which includes a special block of seating for the show. If you sit in front rows you will get wet.** ✉ *Sunset Blvd.* ☞ *Duration: 30 mins. Crowds: Heavy. Audience: Not Young Kids.*

SHOPPING

HOLLYWOOD BOULEVARD

You can upgrade your look at Keystone Clothiers or make the kiddies happy with a splurge at L.A. Prop Cinema Storage across the boulevard. Mickey's of Hollywood has something for everyone in the family.

Keystone Clothiers. This shop pops with stylish clothing and accessories for adults. Handbags and totes sport classic Mickey Mouse artwork. Colorful scarves with hidden Mickeys and other designs are popular buys. Character-theme clothing for men, including ties, hats, and even Hawaiian shirts, elicit smiles. ✉ *Hollywood Blvd.*.

L.A. Prop Cinema Storage. Pink and red Minnie Mouse togs get noticed even in Tinseltown. Little girls gravitate toward the Tinker Bell Fashion Set of tiny dolls and costumes. Boys want to check out the Buzz Lightyear Star Command Blasters. ✉ *Hollywood Blvd.*.

Mickey's of Hollywood. The largest store in Hollywood Studios is a mini-version of the Magic Kingdom's Emporium with toys, T-shirts, and doodads. Blue velvety Sorcerer's Apprentice hats have Mouse ears, plus a moon and stars that light up. You'll also find plush Minnie Mouse and Donald Duck character key chains and lots of Disney-character-embossed tech accessories. ✉ *Hollywood Blvd.*.

ECHO LAKE

Indiana Jones Adventure Outpost. Almost as popular as the pirate hats in the Magic Kingdom are the Indiana Jones felt fedoras sold at this outpost near the stunt amphitheater. Young kids can get a complete Indy play set with fedora, machete, pistol, and gems for about $20. ✉ *Echo Lake.*

Tatooine Traders. This spot outside of the Star Tours ride is jammed with kids clamoring to build their own single or double light sabers complete with crystals, hilts, and blades. Collectible pins and Vinylmation characters are popular here. ✉ *Echo Lake.*

STREETS OF AMERICA

The Writer's Stop. A cup of coffee or a spot of tea pairs well with some browsing here. If you happen to hit it right, you might get a book signed by a celebrity author. ✉ *Streets of America.*

ANIMATION COURTYARD

Animation Gallery. If you appreciate the art of animation, this is the place. It's loaded with interesting art pieces, some valuable, some not. You can watch artists sketch characters and hand paint animation cels; you can also buy limited-edition hand-painted cels that include "Goofy Moments," and "Off to Neverland" ($125–$290). You'll also find statuettes, posters, and animation books. ✉ *Animation Courtyard.*

In Character. Little girls love this open-air shop next to the Voyage of the Little Mermaid for the dolls, plush princess toys, and dress-up costumes. You can drop a small bundle on glass (plastic) slippers and a magical light-up wand or spring for the coveted Ariel mermaid costume gown. ✉ *Animation Courtyard.*

SUNSET BOULEVARD

Sunset Club Couture. It's the one shop you don't want to miss on Sunset Boulevard. Vintage-style T-shirts of Mickey, Pluto, Donald, and Grumpy are classy alternatives to standard-issue Ts, and a white sequined Mickey hat adds flair to any outfit. Women's fashion T's ($30) and costume bling ($12–$30) draw lots of shoppers. Customized watches like those sold at the Magic Kingdom's Uptown Jewelers are sold here, too. ✉ *Sunset Blvd.*

NIGHTLIFE

SHOWS

***Fantasmic!*.** This Hollywood Studios 25-minute special-effects blockbuster is held after dark in an often-packed 6,500-seat amphitheater. Mickey Mouse in the guise of the Sorcerer's Apprentice emcees this special effect–packed revue. Performances run two or three times nightly during high season, less frequently in slow periods. ✉ *Disney's Hollywood Studios.*

ANIMAL KINGDOM

If you're thinking, "Oh, it's just another zoo, let's skip it," think again. Walt Disney World's fourth theme park, opened in 1998, takes its inspiration from humankind's enduring love for animals and pulls out all the stops. Your day will be packed with unusual animal encounters, enchanting entertainment, and themed rides that'll leave you breathless.

A large chunk of the park is devoted to animal habitats, especially the forest and savanna of Africa's Kilimanjaro Safaris. Towering acacia trees and tall grasses sweep across the land where antelopes, giraffes, and wildebeests roam. A lion kopje, warthog burrows, a zebra habitat, and an elephant watering hole provide ample space for inhabitants.

About 94 acres contain foliage like hibiscus and mulberry, perfect for antelope and many other species. The largest groups of Nile hippos and African elephants in North America live along the winding waterway that leads to the savanna. The generously landscaped Pangani Forest Exploration Trail provides roaming grounds for troops of gorillas and authentic habitats for meerkats, birds, fish, and other creatures.

Beyond the park's Africa territory, similar large spaces are set aside for the homes of Asian animals like tigers and giant fruit bats, as well as for creatures such as Galápagos tortoises and a giant anteater.

Disney Imagineers didn't forget to include their trademark thrills, from the Kali River Rapids ride in Asia to the fast-paced DINOSAUR journey in DinoLand U.S.A. Expedition Everest, the park's biggest thrill attraction, is a "runaway" train ride on a faux rugged mountain complete with icy ledges, dark caves, and a yeti legend. Next up: Imagineers are designing a new land in the former Camp Minnie-Mickey location based on the blockbuster film *Avatar* and expected sequels.

The only downside to the Animal Kingdom layout is that walking paths and spaces can get very crowded and hot in the warmest months. Your

TOP ATTRACTIONS

AFRICA

Festival of the Lion King. Singers and dancers dressed in fantastic costumes representing many wild animals perform uplifting dance and acrobatics numbers and interact with children in the audience.

Kilimanjaro Safaris. You're guaranteed to see dozens of wild animals, including giraffes, gazelles, hippos, rhinos, zebras, and elephants, living in authentic, re-created African habitats. If you're lucky, the lions and cheetahs will be stirring, too.

ASIA

Expedition Everest. This roller coaster is a spine-tingling trip into the snowy Himalayas to find the abominable snowman. It's best reserved for brave riders 7 and up.

DINOLAND U.S.A

DINOSAUR. Extremely lifelike giant dinosaurs jump out as your vehicle swoops and dips. We recommend it for fearless kids 8 and up.

Finding Nemo: The Musical. Don't miss a performance of this outstanding musical starring the most charming, colorful characters ever to swim their way into your heart.

DISCOVERY ISLAND

Tree of Life: *It's Tough to Be a Bug!* This clever and very funny 3-D movie starring Flik from the Disney film *A Bug's Life* is full of surprises, including "shocking" special effects. Some young children are scared of the loud noises.

TOUR

Wild Africa Trek. The price tag is hefty, but this behind-the-scenes wild-animal adventure is a memory maker.

best bet is to arrive very early and see the animals first before the heat makes them (and you) woozy.

Just before the park opens, Minnie Mouse, Pluto, and Goofy arrive at the iconic Tree of Life in a safari vehicle to welcome the first guests into the heart of the park. Let the adventure begin!

ORIENTATION AND PLANNING

GETTING ORIENTED

Animal Kingdom's hub is the Tree of Life, in the middle of Discovery Island. The park's lands, each with a distinct personality, radiate from Discovery Island. To the southwest, home of the former Camp Minnie-Mickey, Disney Imagineers are creating the new land of Pandora based on the *Avatar* film and upcoming sequels. The new area is expected to open in 2017. North of the hub is Africa, where Kilimanjaro Safaris travel across extensive savanna. In the northeast corner is Rafiki's Planet Watch with conservation activities.

Asia, with thrills like Expedition Everest and Kali River Rapids, is east of the hub, and DinoLand U.S.A brings *T. rex* and other prehistoric creatures to life in the park's southeast corner.

If you're staying on-site, you can take a Disney bus to the Entrance Plaza. If you drive, the $15 parking fee allows you to park at other Disney lots throughout the day.

Although this is technically Disney's largest theme park, most of the land is reserved for the animals. Pedestrian areas are actually quite compact, with relatively narrow passageways. The only way to get around is on foot or in a wheelchair or electronic convenience vehicle (ECV).

ANIMAL KINGDOM PLANNER

PARK AMENITIES

Baby Care: At Discovery Island you can stop in to nurse babies in the quiet baby-care center, which is equipped with rocking chairs and low lighting. There are changing tables, which are also available in restrooms (including some men's restrooms), and you can buy disposable diapers, formula, baby food, and pacifiers.

Cameras: You can buy film and digital memory cards at several shops throughout the park. If a Disney photographer takes your picture, sign up for a Disney PhotoPass—later, you can view and purchase the pictures online ($199 for full digital Memory Maker access) or at the park's photo center in the Oasis.

First Aid: The first-aid center, staffed by registered nurses, is in Discovery Island, and at least a dozen automated external defibrillators are in key park areas.

Guest Relations: This office will help with tickets at a window to the left just before you pass through the turnstile. Once you've entered, Guest Relations staffers in the Oasis can provide park maps, schedules, and answers to questions. They can also assist with dining reservations, ticket upgrades, and services for guests with disabilities.

Lockers: Lockers are in Guest Relations in the Oasis. Rental fees are $7 to $9 (depending on size) for a day plus a $5 key deposit.

Lost People and Things: Instruct your kids to speak to someone with a Disney name tag if you become separated. Lost children are taken to the baby-care center, where they can watch Disney movies, or to Guest Relations, whichever is closer. If you do lose your child, contact any cast member immediately and Disney security personnel will be notified.

Animal Kingdom Lost and Found. To retrieve lost articles on the same day, visit or call Lost and Found, which is at Guest Relations. ✉ *Oasis* ☎ *407/938–2785.*

Main Lost and Found. If more than a day has passed since you've lost something, contact the Main Lost and Found office at the Magic Kingdom Ticket and Transportation Center. ☎ *407/824–4245.*

Package Pick-Up: You can have shop clerks forward purchases to Package Pick-Up near the Main Entrance in the Oasis, so that you won't have to carry them around all day. Allow three hours for the journey. If you're staying at a Disney hotel, you also can have packages delivered there.

SERVICES FOR PEOPLE WITH DISABILITIES

Guests using wheelchairs will have ready access to restaurants, shops, and most attractions—including the Finding Nemo: The Musical theater in DinoLand U.S.A, and the Tree of Life theater showing *It's Tough to Be a Bug!* (Theaters also are accessible to ECVs.) Some monitor-equipped attractions have reflective-captioning boxes.

Scripts and story lines for all attractions are available, and you can book sign-language interpreters with notice of two or more weeks. Large Braille park maps are by Guest Relations and near the Tip Board at the entrance to Discovery Island. Guest Relations is also where you can borrow assisted-listening, handheld-captioning, and video-captioning devices with a refundable deposit. Service animals are allowed in most, but not all, areas of the park.

You can rent wheelchairs ($12 daily, $10 for multiple days) and ECVs ($50 per day plus a refundable $20 security deposit) at Garden Gate Gifts in the Oasis. You can't, however, reserve these items, so arrive early to get one—particularly if you want an ECV.

Stroller Rentals: Garden Gate Gifts in the Oasis rents strollers. Singles are $15 daily, $13 multiday; doubles run $31 daily, $27 multiday.

TOURS

Animal Kingdom Guided Tours. For a closer look at the park's animals or design features, call WDW Tours to reserve a behind-the-scenes tour. ☎ *407/939–8687.*

Backstage Safari. This tour ($72) takes an in-depth look at animal conservation, stopping at the state-of-the-art veterinary hospital and other behind-the-scenes areas. It's a great way to learn about animal behaviors and how handlers manage a diverse population of critters in captivity. The tour includes the park's Kilimanjaro Safaris ride, so you will see plenty of exotic creatures in their habitats. Participants must be at least 16 years old. ☎ *407/939–8687* *$72* *Mon., Wed.–Fri.*

Fodor's Choice ★ **Wild Africa Trek.** You and 11 other guests will cover exciting new ground on this three-hour, walking-riding adventure into unexplored areas of the park. For a close-up view of the hippos, you'll wear a special vest with a harness that's tethered to a rail at the edge of a bluff. You'll cross a rope bridge above a pool of Nile crocodiles. Your exclusive open-air safari vehicle makes multiple stops for leisurely viewing of giraffes, wildebeests, cheetahs, and other creatures of the savanna. Burning all those calories pays off when breakfast or lunch treats are served (think prosciutto, Brie, fresh fruit) at the open-air Boma Landing on the edge of the savanna. The tour is good for anyone age 8 and older who's fit. Included in the admission price is a CD-photo souvenir of your trek. A portion of the tour price is donated to the Disney Worldwide Conservation Fund. ☎ *407/939–8687* *$189* *Up to 8 times daily, beginning at 8 am.*

Wild By Design. This tour offers insights into the art, architecture, history, and landscape of Animal Kingdom. You'll learn how stories of exotic lands like Harambe in Africa are told and about Discovery Island's architectural touches, including exotic folk art from Bali and masterful animal carvings that grace the iconic Tree of Life. You'll also get a glimpse of behind-the-scenes buildings where animals receive care. The tour is for ages 14 and older. ☎ *407/939–8687* *$60* *Mon., Wed.–Fri.*

VISITING TIPS

- Try to visit during the week. Pedestrian areas are compact, and the park can feel uncomfortably packed on weekends.
- Plan on a full day here. That way, while exploring Africa's Pangani Forest Exploration Trail, say, you can spend 10 minutes (rather than just two) watching vigilant meerkats stand sentry or tracking a mama gorilla as she cares for her youngster.
- Arrive a half hour before the park opens as much to see the wild animals at their friskiest (morning is a good time to do the safari ride) as to get a jump on the crowds.
- For updates on line lengths, check the Tip Board, just after crossing the bridge into Discovery Island.
- Good places to rendezvous include the outdoor seating area of Tusker House restaurant in Africa, in front of DinoLand U.S.A's Boneyard, or on one of the benches outside Expedition Everest in Asia.

EXPLORING ANIMAL KINGDOM

THE OASIS

This entrance makes you feel as if you've been plunked down in the middle of a rain forest. Cool mist, the aroma of flowers, playful animals, and colorful birds enliven a miniature landscape of streams and grottoes, waterfalls, and glades fringed with banana leaves and jacaranda. It's also where you can take care of essentials before entering. Here you'll find guide maps, stroller and wheelchair rentals, Guest Relations, and an ATM.

DISCOVERY ISLAND

The park hub and site of the Tree of Life, this island is encircled by Discovery River, which isn't an actual attraction but makes for attractive views from the bridge to Harambe and another between Asia and DinoLand U.S.A. The island's whimsical architecture, with wood carvings from Bali, lends charm and a touch of fantasy. The Discovery Island Trails that lead to the Tree of Life provide habitats for African crested porcupines, lemurs, Galápagos tortoises, and other creatures you won't want to miss.

You'll discover some great shops and good counter-service eateries here, and the island is also the site of the daily Mickey's Jammin' Jungle Parade. Visitor services that aren't in the Oasis are here, on the border with Harambe, including the baby-care center and the first-aid center.

Fodor's Choice ★ **Tree of Life—*It's Tough to Be a Bug!*.** A monument to all Earth's creatures, the park's centerpiece is an imposing 14 stories high and 50 feet wide at its base. Its 100,000-plus leaves are several shades of green fabric, each carefully placed for a realistic effect. Carved into its thick trunk, gnarled roots, and soaring branches—some of which are supported by joints that allow them to sway in a strong wind—are nearly 350 intricate animal forms that include a baboon, a whale, a horse, the mighty lion, and even an ankylosaurus. Outside, paths tunnel underneath the roots as the fauna-encrusted trunk towers overhead.

The path leads you inside the tree trunk, where you get a bug's-eye view of life. The witty 3-D film adventure *It's Tough to Be a Bug!* is modeled on the animated film *A Bug's Life* from Disney-Pixar. Special effects spray you with "poison," zap you with a swatter, and even poke you with a stinger—all in good fun.

Although the show has something for all ages, it's very loud. Some effects frighten young children. **For people with disabilities:** Wheelchair accessible, but, to fully experience all the special effects, guests using wheelchairs should transfer to a seat. Equipped with reflective captioning and for audio-description and assisted-listening devices. If you have a service animal, check with a host before entering the theater. **■ TIP→ Enter across from the Disney Outfitters store via the Discovery Island Trails.** ✉ *Discovery Island* ☞ *Duration: 20 mins. Crowds: Moderate–Heavy. Audience: All but Young Kids.*

5

DINOLAND U.S.A

Just as it sounds, this is the place to come in contact with re-created prehistoric creatures, including the fear-inspiring carnotaurus and the gentle iguanodon. The landscaping includes live plants that have evolved over the last 65 million years. In collaboration with Chicago's Field Museum, Disney displays a complete, full-scale skeleton cast of Dino-Sue—also known as "Sue"—the 65-million-year-old *Tyrannosaurus rex* discovered near the Black Hills of South Dakota.

After admiring Sue, you can go on the thrilling DINOSAUR ride, play in the Boneyard, or take in the Finding Nemo: The Musical show at the Theater in the Wild. Kids will want to try the TriceraTop Spin and the Primeval Whirl family coaster, which has spinning "time machines." There's no need to dig for souvenirs at Chester and Hester's Dinosaur Treasures gift shop—all you need is your wallet.

NEED A BREAK?

Famished, but not much time for lunch? Make tracks for a counter-service burger and fries or a hearty salad at Restaurantosaurus and you'll be ready to take on *T. rex*.

Boneyard. Youngsters can slide, dig, bounce, slither, and stomp around this archaeological dig site–cum–playground, the finest play area in any of the four Disney parks. In addition to a huge sand pit where children can dig for mammoth bones, there are twisting short and long slides, climbing nets, caves, and a jeep to climb on. Stomp on the dino footprints to make 'em roar. **For people with disabilities:** This fossil play maze is wheelchair accessible. **■ TIP→ Let the kids burn off energy here while waiting for a DINOSAUR FastPass+ appointment. Or head over late in the day when kids need to run free.** ✉ *DinoLand U.S.A* ☞ *Duration: Up to You. Crowds: Moderate–Heavy. Audience: Young Kids.*

DINOSAUR. This wild adventure through time puts you face-to-face with huge dinosaurs that move and breathe with uncanny realism. When a carload of guests rouses a cantankerous carnotaurus from his Cretaceous slumber, it's showtime. You travel back 65 million years on a fast-paced, twisting adventure and try to save the last living iguanodon as a massive asteroid hurtles toward Earth. Exciting Audio-Animatronics and special effects bring to life dinosaurs like the raptor, pterodactyl,

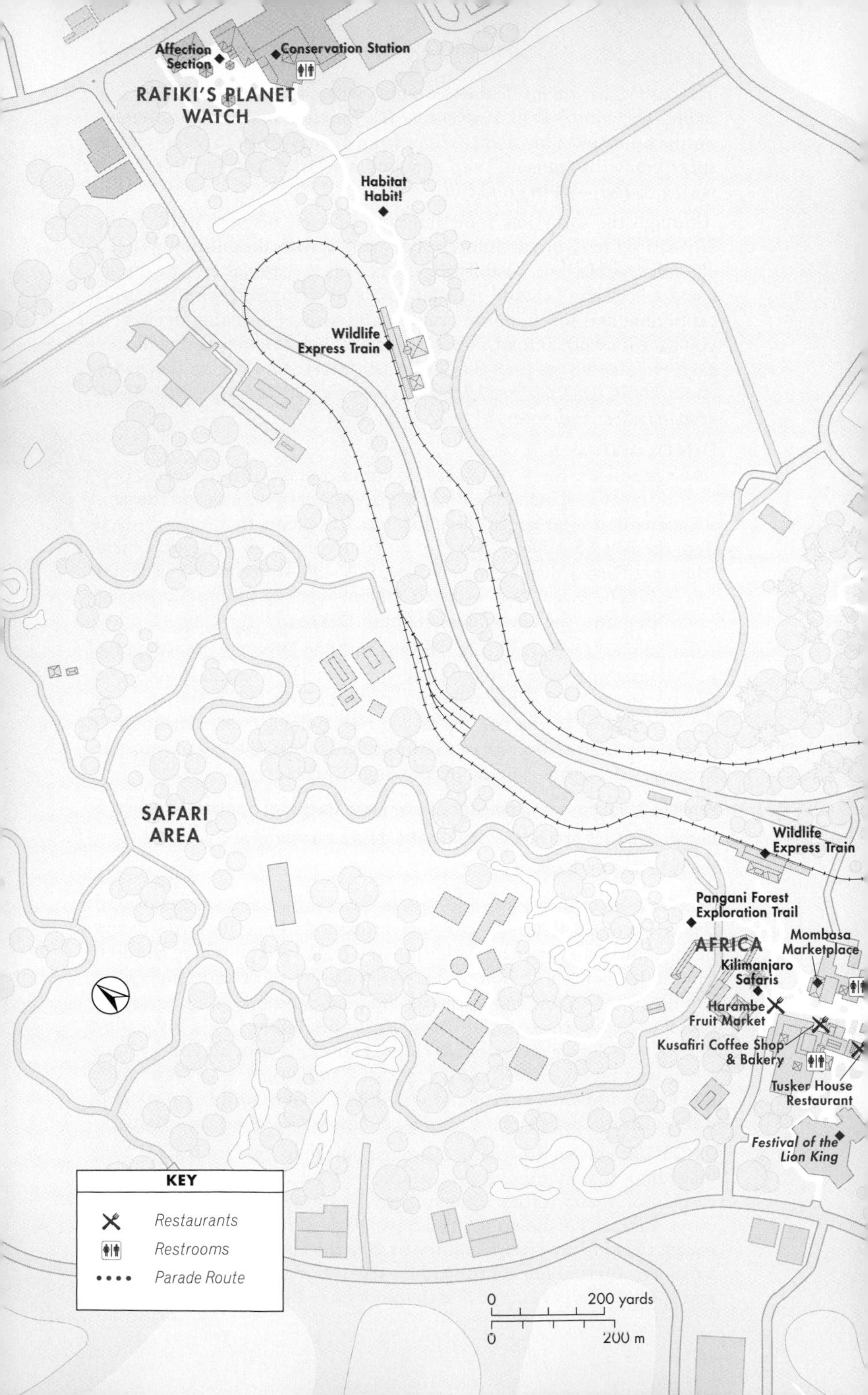

Affection Section
Conservation Station
RAFIKI'S PLANET WATCH
Habitat Habit!
Wildlife Express Train
SAFARI AREA
Wildlife Express Train
Pangani Forest Exploration Trail
AFRICA
Mombasa Marketplace
Kilimanjaro Safaris
Harambe Fruit Market
Kusafiri Coffee Shop & Bakery
Tusker House Restaurant
Festival of the Lion King
KEY
Restaurants
Restrooms
Parade Route
0
200 yards
0
200 m

Disney's Animal Kingdom

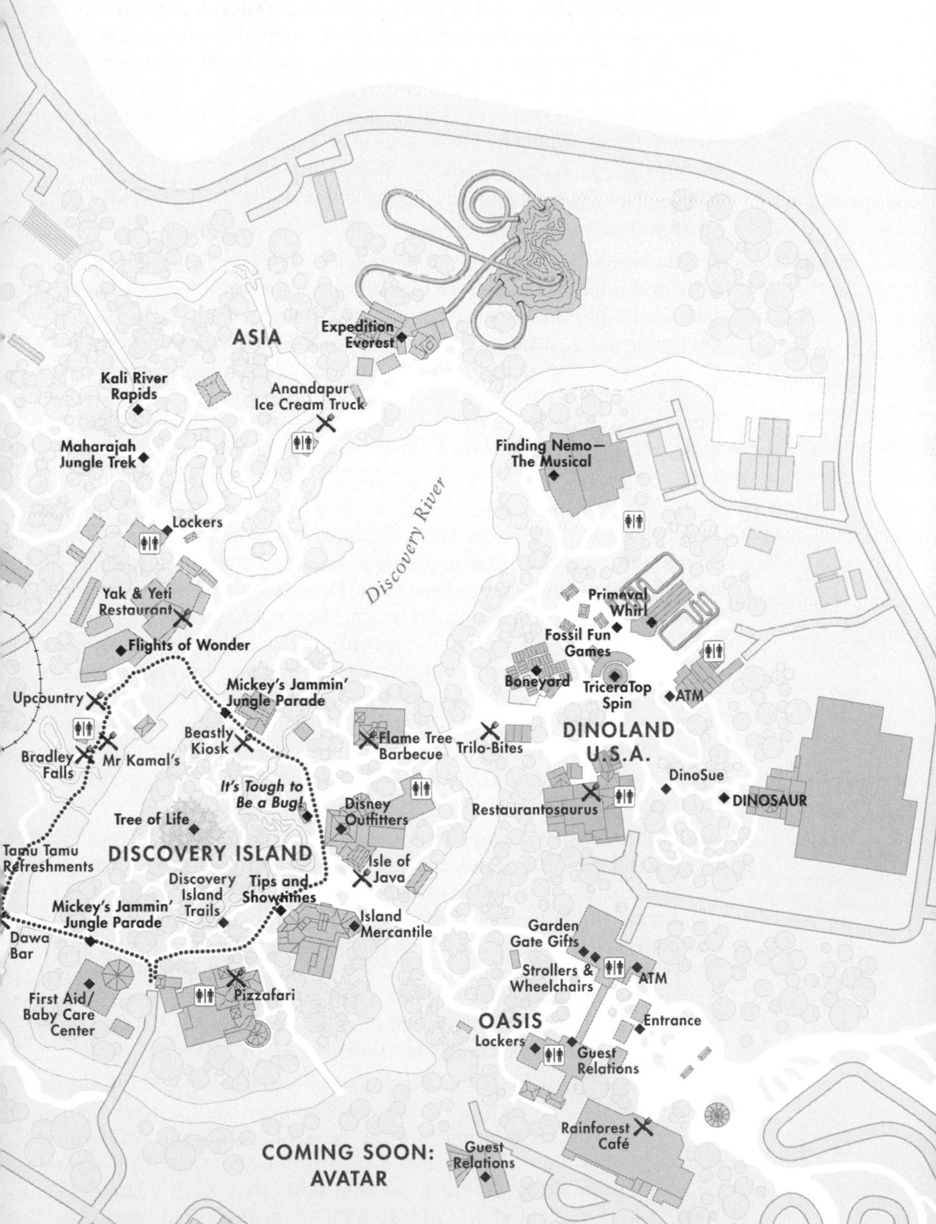
ASIA
Expedition Everest
Kali River Rapids
Anandapur Ice Cream Truck
Maharajah Jungle Trek
Lockers
Discovery River
Finding Nemo—The Musical
Yak & Yeti Restaurant
Flights of Wonder
Primeval Whirl
Fossil Fun Games
Boneyard
TriceraTop Spin
ATM
Upcountry
Mickey's Jammin' Jungle Parade
Beastly Kiosk
Bradley Falls
Mr Kamal's
Flame Tree Barbecue
Trilo-Bites
DINOLAND U.S.A.
DinoSue
DINOSAUR
It's Tough to Be a Bug!
Disney Outfitters
Restaurantosaurus
Tree of Life
Tamu Tamu Refreshments
DISCOVERY ISLAND
Isle of Java
Discovery Island Trails
Tips and Showtimes
Mickey's Jammin' Jungle Parade
Island Mercantile
Dawa Bar
Garden Gate Gifts
Strollers & Wheelchairs
ATM
First Aid/ Baby Care Center
Pizzafari
OASIS
Entrance
Lockers
Guest Relations
Rainforest Café
COMING SOON: AVATAR
Guest Relations

styracosaurus, alioramus, and compsognather. Be prepared for a short but steep drop toward the end of the ride.

Guests who are pregnant or have back, neck, or heart problems should avoid this very bumpy ride. The jostling and realistic carnivores may frighten young children. **For people with disabilities:** You must transfer from your wheelchair to board this ride. Equipped for video-captioning and assisted-listening devices. No service animals. **■ TIP→ Come first thing in the morning or at the end of the day, or use FastPass+.** ✉ *DinoLand U.S.. ☞ Duration: Under 4 mins. Crowds: Heavy. Audience: All but Young Kids. Height minimum: 40 inches.*

Timing Tip: Because of the proximity of the two attractions, Finding Nemo: The Musical is a good place to take younger kids while older siblings do Expedition Everest.

Fodor's Choice ★ **Finding Nemo–The Musical.** The performance of this fish tale is so creative and fun that many have likened it to a first-rate Broadway show. Indeed, Disney Imagineers collaborated with several Broadway talents to produce it. Original songs by Tony Award–winning *Avenue Q* co-composer-creator Robert Lopez and a-cappella musical *Along the Way* co-creator Kristen Anderson-Lopez add depth and energy. Michael Curry, who co-designed the character puppets of Broadway's *The Lion King,* also created this show's eye-popping puppetry.

Multigenerational humor; special effects; and larger-than-life puppets acted by gifted performers, dancers, and acrobats all bring you into Nemo's world. The sweet story remains the same as in the movie—Nemo and his father Marlin go on separate journeys that teach them how to understand each other. Zany Dory, with her memory lapses, Crush the sea-turtle dude, tap-dancing sharks, and others give memorable supporting-role turns. **For people with disabilities:** Wheelchair accessible. Equipped with reflective captioning and for audio description and assisted-listening devices. Check with Guest Relations for sign-language schedule. **■ TIP→ Arrive 30 to 40 minutes before showtime. Bring little kids here while older tweens and teens ride Expedition Everest.** ✉ *DinoLand U.S.A ☞ Duration: 40 mins. Crowds: Heavy. Audience: All Ages.*

Fossil Fun Games. A carnival-style midway in the middle of DinoLand U.S.A., this fun fair draws crowds with games like Whack a Packycephalosaur and the mallet-strength challenge, Dino-Whamma. The prehistoric fun comes at a price, however, and stone currency is not accepted. Prizes are mostly of the plush-character variety—you might win your sweetheart a stuffed Nala. **For people with disabilities:** Wheelchair accessible. **■ TIP→ It costs $4 a game, or $10 for 3 games. Bring a pocketful of change and a stash of ones.** ✉ *DinoLand U.S.A ☞ Duration: Up to You. Crowds: Light. Audience: All but Young Kids.*

Primeval Whirl. In a free-spinning, four-passenger vehicle, you head on a brief journey back in time on this outdoor open-air coaster, twisting, turning, and even venturing into the jaws of a dinosaur "skeleton." Crazy cartoon dinosaurs in shades of turquoise, orange, yellow, and purple pop up along the track bearing signs that warn "The End is Near." More signs alert you to incoming "Meteors!" and suggest that

On Asia's Expedition Everest, you'll chug, twist, turn, and plunge up, through, and down Mt. Everest on nearly a mile of track. Oh, yeah, and beware of the yeti!

you "Head for the Hills!"—coaster hills, that is. Halfway through the ride, your car seems to spin out of control and you take the next drop backward. The more weight in the vehicle, the more you spin.

Pregnant women or guests with back, neck, or heart problems should skip this one. **For people with disabilities:** Guests using wheelchairs must transfer to the ride vehicle. No service animals. **■ TIP→ Kids might want to ride twice. Take your first spin early; get a FastPass+ to return later if the wait is over 20 minutes.** ✉ *DinoLand U.S.A* ☞ *Duration: 2½ mins. Crowds: Heavy. Audience: All but Young Kids. Height minimum: 48 inches.*

TriceraTop Spin. TriceraTop Spin is designed for playful little dinophiles who ought to get a kick out of whirling around this ride's giant spinning toy top and dodging incoming comets in their dino-mobiles. "Pop!" goes the top and out comes a grinning dinosaur as four passengers in each vehicle fly in a circle and maneuver up and down. **For people with disabilities:** Wheelchair accessible, but guests using ECVs must transfer to standard wheelchairs. **■ TIP→ Ride early or take little ones while older kids are riding DINOSAUR.** ✉ *DinoLand U.S.A* ☞ *Duration: 2 mins. Crowds: Heavy. Audience: Young Kids.*

ASIA

Meant to resemble an Asian village, this land is full of remarkable rainforest scenery and ruins. Groupings of trees grow from a crumbling tiger shrine, and massive towers—representing Thailand and Nepal—are the habitat for gibbons, whose hooting fills the air.

Fodor's Choice ★ **Expedition Everest—Legend of the Forbidden Mountain.** A fierce yeti guards the route to Mt. Everest. Of course, you're willing to risk running across the big guy in your roller-coaster quest to reach the summit. So, you board an "aging," seemingly innocuous, 34-passenger, steam-engine train into the mountains. You roll past bamboo forests, waterfalls, and glacier fields as you climb higher through snowcapped peaks. Suddenly the train becomes a runaway, barreling forward then backward around icy ledges and through dark snowy caverns.

Nearly a mile of twists and turns cut through the dark mountain, and at one point your train plunges a harrowing 80 feet. Will you find the yeti? Buildings along the queue look like Himalayan mountain dwellings and teem with things like prayer flags, totems, and other artifacts from Tibet, Nepal, and the entire region.

The coaster is supposed to be less intense than, say, Space Mountain, so brave children who meet the 44-inch minimum-height requirement can ride. Pregnant women or guests with back, neck, or heart problems shouldn't ride. **For people with disabilities:** You must transfer from your wheelchair to a ride vehicle. No service animals. ■**TIP→ Unless you prefer to see the animals first, rush here as soon as the park opens and the wait isn't too long. Otherwise, grab a FastPass+ or choose the Single Rider Queue.** ✉ *Asia* ☞ *Duration: 2½ mins. Crowds: Huge. Audience: Anyone 44 inches or taller.*

Flights of Wonder. This outdoor show area near the border with Africa has spectacular demonstrations of skill by falcons, hawks, and other rare birds, which swoop down over the audience. Twenty species of birds are part of the show, including the bald eagle. **For people with disabilities:** Wheelchair accessible. Sign-language interpretation sometimes offered. Equipped for assisted-listening devices. ■**TIP→** Check the Times Guide for showtimes and **arrive 15 minutes ahead to find a shaded seat beneath one of the awnings—the sun can be brutal in summer.** ✉ *Asia* ☞ *Duration: 25 mins. Crowds: Light. Audience: All Ages.*

Kali River Rapids. Asia's thrilling water adventure ride mixes the fun of a rafting experience with a solemn message to save pristine lands and animal habitats that are threatened by development. Aboard a round raft that seats 12, you run the Chakranadi River. After passing through a huge bamboo tunnel filled with jasmine-scented mist, your raft climbs 40 feet upriver, lurches and spins through sharp twists and turns, and then approaches an immense waterfall, which curtains a giant carved tiger face. Past rain forests and temple ruins, you find yourself face-to-face with the denuded slope of a logged-out woodland burning out of control. There are many more thrills, but why spill the beans?

You will get wet and you may get soaked. Unless you want to wring out your clothing in the nearest restroom afterward, bring a poncho. Better yet, bring a change of clothing in a plastic bag. The ride-height minimum is 38 inches. If you are pregnant or have heart, back, neck, or motion-sickness problems, sit this one out. **For people with disabilities:** Guests using wheelchairs must transfer to a ride raft. No service animals. ■**TIP→ Use FastPass+, or come during the parade.** ✉ *Asia* ☞ *Duration: 7 mins. Crowds: Heavy. Audience: All but Young Kids.*

Maharajah Jungle Trek. Get an up-close view of some unusual animals along this trail: a Komodo dragon perched on a rock; giant fruit bats

A silverback gorilla from Kilimanjaro Safaris

that hang to munch fruit from wires and fly very close to the open and glass-protected viewing areas; and Bengal tigers in front of a maharajah's palace ruins. The tigers have their own view (with no accessibility, of course) of Asian deer and black buck, an antelope species. At the end of the trek, you walk through an aviary with a lotus pool. Disney interpreters, many from Asian countries, are on hand to answer questions. **For people with disabilities:** Wheelchair accessible; equipped for audio-description devices. Guests with service animals should check with a host before entering the aviary. **■ TIP→ Come anytime. Crowds stay fairly light, as people are constantly on the move.** ✉ *Asia* ☞ *Duration: Up to You. Crowds: Light. Audience: All Ages.*

AFRICA

The largest of the lands is an area of forests and grasslands, predominantly an enclave for wildlife from the continent. Harambe, on the northern bank of Discovery River, is Africa's starting point. Inspired by several East African villages, this Disney town has so much detail that it's mind-boggling to try to soak it all up. Signs on the apparently peeling stucco walls are faded, as if bleached by the sun, and everything has a hot, dusty look. For souvenirs with Disney and African themes, browse through the Mombasa Marketplace and Ziwani Traders.

NEED A BREAK?

The tantalizing aroma of fresh-baked cinnamon buns leads to the Kusafiri Coffee Shop & Bakery, where, after just one look, you may give in to the urge. These buns are worth the banknotes, and they pair well with a cappuccino or espresso. Kids may opt for a giant cookie and milk.

The Tree of Life is the iconic centerpiece of Disney's Animal Kingdom.

Fodor's Choice ★ ***Festival of the Lion King.*** If you think you've seen enough *Lion King* to last a lifetime, you're wrong, unless you've seen this show. Disney presents a delightful tribal celebration of song, dance, and acrobatics that uses huge moving stages and floats. The show's singers are first-rate; lithe dancers wearing exotic animal-theme costumes portray creatures in the wild. Timon, Pumba, and other *Lion King* stars have key roles. Once a mainstay in the park's Camp Minnie-Mickey land, the show has moved to the park's Africa area; at press time, the show's exact location had not been announced. **For people with disabilities:** Information was not available at press time regarding the new show venue and accessibility, though it's certain to accommodate wheelchairs. Sign-language interpretation is sometimes offered. Expected to be equipped for assisted-listening and handheld-captioning devices. **■ TIP→ Arrive 30–40 minutes before showtime. If you have a child who might want to go on stage, try to sit up front to increase his or her chance of getting chosen.** ✉ *Africa* ☞ *Duration: 30 mins. Crowds: Moderate. Audience: All Ages.*

Fodor's Choice ★ **Kilimanjaro Safaris.** A giant Imagineered baobab tree is the starting point for this adventure into the upcountry. Although re-creating an African safari in the United States isn't a new idea, this safari takes great pains to create an authentic environment, allowing you to observe rhinos, hippos, antelopes, wildebeests, giraffes, cheetahs, elephants, lions, and the like. There are illustrated game-spotting guides above the seats in the open-air safari vehicles, and as you lurch and bump over some 100 acres of savanna, forest, rivers, and rocky hills, you'll see most of these animals—sometimes so close you feel that you could reach out and touch them. It's easy to suspend disbelief here because the landscape is so effectively modeled and replenished by Disney horticulturists.

Recent savanna additions include a zebra habitat and a watering hole for many species. Keep an eye out for animal babies; the park's breeding programs have been extremely successful, with new additions including elephants, white and black rhinos, okapi, giraffes, and several gorillas.

Parents should hang on tightly to their small tykes. The ride is very bumpy and should be avoided by expectant guests or those with heart, back, or neck problems. **For people with disabilities:** Wheelchair accessible, but ECV users must transfer to standard wheelchairs. Equipped for assisted-listening and video-captioning devices. Guests with service animals should check with a host for boarding information. **■ TIP➔ During the hottest months, come first thing in the morning, using FastPass+ if necessary. Otherwise come at day's end when it cools down a bit.** ⊠ *Africa* ☞ *Duration: 22 mins. Crowds: Moderate– Heavy. Audience: All Ages.*

5

Pangani Forest Exploration Trail. Calling this a nature walk doesn't really do it justice. A path winds through dense foliage, alongside streams, and past waterfalls. En route there are viewing points where you can watch a beautiful rare okapi (a member of the giraffe family) munching the vegetation, a family and a separate bachelor group of lowland gorillas, hippos (which you usually can see underwater), comical meerkats (a kind of mongoose), exotic birds, and a bizarre colony of hairless mole rats. Native African interpreters are at many viewing points to answer questions. **For people with disabilities:** Wheelchair accessible. Guests with service animals should check with a host before entering. **■ TIP➔ Come while awaiting a safari FastPass+ appointment; avoid coming at the hottest time of day, when the gorillas like to nap.** ⊠ *Africa* ☞ *Duration: Up to You. Crowds: Moderate–Heavy. Audience: All Ages.*

RAFIKI'S PLANET WATCH

While in the Harambe, Africa, section, board the 250-passenger rustic Wildlife Express steam train for a ride to a unique center of eco-awareness named for the wise baboon from *The Lion King*. Young children especially enjoy the chance to explore these three animal-friendly areas.

Affection Section. In this petting zoo, children and adults can pet and even borrow brushes to groom goats, sheep, donkeys, and other domesticated creatures from around the world. **For people with disabilities:** Guests must transfer from ECVs to standard wheelchairs. No service animals are allowed in this area. **■ TIP➔ If you visit at the right time, you might see pigs demonstrate how they've learned to paint with their snouts.** ⊠ *Rafiki's Planet Watch* ☞ *Duration: Up to You. Crowds: Light–Moderate. Audience: All Ages; Mostly Children.*

Conservation Station. This is a great place to meet some of the park's animal handlers and to gather round for a critter encounter. You'll learn about the park's veterinary care, ongoing research, and food preparation for hundreds of animal inhabitants. Interactive exhibits are simple fun for younger children and have messages about worldwide efforts to protect endangered species and their habitats. Here, you also can find out how to connect with conservation efforts in your own community.

ANIMAL KINGDOM

	NAME	Height Req.	Type of Entertainment	Duration	Crowds	Audience	Tips
	Africa						
★	Festival of the Lion King	n/a	Show	30 mins.	Moderate	All Ages	Arrive 30–40 mins. before showtime. Sit in one of the front rows to increase your kid's chance of being chosen to participate in a show number.
★	Kilimanjaro Safaris	n/a	Riding Tour	22 mins.	Moderate to Heavy	All Ages	Do this first thing in the morning or use FastPass+. If you arrive at the park late morning, save it for day's end, when it's not so hot.
	Pangani Forest Exploration Trail	n/a	Zoo/Aviary	Up to you	Light to Moderate	All Ages	Come while waiting for your safari FastPass+; try to avoid coming at the hottest time of day, when the gorillas like to nap.
	Asia						
★	Expedition Everest	At least 44"	Thrill Ride	2½ mins.	Huge	All but Young Kids	Arrive early or use FastPass+. This is the park's biggest thrill ride.
	Flights of Wonder	n/a	Show	25 mins.	Light	All Ages	Arrive 15 mins. before showtime, and find a shaded seat beneath one of the awnings—the sun can be brutal.
	Kali River Rapids	At least 38"	Thrill Ride	7 mins.	Heavy	All but Young Kids	Use your FastPass+ or come during the parade. You'll get wet.
	Maharajah Jungle Trek	n/a	Zoo/Aviary	Up to you	Light to Moderate	All Ages	Come anytime.
	DinoLand U.S.A.						
	Boneyard	n/a	Playground	Up to you	Moderate to Heavy	Young Kids	Play here while waiting for DINOSAUR FastPass+, or come late in the day.

	DINOSAUR	At least 40″	Thrill Ride	4 mins.	Heavy	All but Young Kids	Come first thing in the morning or at the end of the day, or use FastPass+.
★	Finding Nemo–The Musical	n/a	Show	40 mins.	Heavy	All Ages	Arrive 40 mins. before showtime. Take young kids here while older kids wait for Expedition Everest.
	Fossil Fun Games	n/a	Arcade/Fair	Up to you	Light	All Ages	Bring a stash of ones to buy play tickets.
	Primeval Whirl	At least 48″	Thrill Ride	2½ mins.	Heavy	All but Young Kids	Kids may want to ride twice. Take your first spin early, then use FastPass+ if the wait is more than 20 mins.
	TriceraTop Spin	n/a	Thrill Ride for Young Kids	2 mins.	Heavy	Young Kids	Ride early while everyone else heads for the safari or while waiting for your FastPass+ appointment for DINOSAUR.
	Discovery Island						
★	Tree of Life—It's Tough to Be a Bug!	n/a	3-D film	20 mins.	Moderate to Heavy	All but Young Kids	Do this after Kilimanjaro Safaris or Expedition Everest. Small children may be frightened.
	Rafiki's Planet Watch						
	Affection Section	n/a	Petting Yard	Up to you	Light	All Ages	Pet exotic goats and other rare domesticated animals.
	Conservation Station	n/a	Walk-Through	Up to you	Light to Moderate	All Ages	Wait for the critter encounter and learn how to protect endangered species.
	Habitat Habit!	n/a	Trail Walk	Up to you	Light	All Ages	Watch cotton-top tamarins along this discovery trail.
	Wildlife Express Train	n/a	Train Ride	5 mins.	Moderate	All Ages	Head straight to Affection Section with little kids to come face-to-face with domesticated critters.

★ Fodor's Choice

ANIMAL KINGDOM GROWN-UP TOUR

When the park first opened, Disney went to great marketing lengths to be sure visitors would know that this is "Nahtazu" (as in "not-a-zoo"). Adults and older children needed assurance that there was plenty to do besides see animals. And there is. Several thrill rides, a hilarious 3-D-and-special-effects-laden film, and two Broadway-style shows with animal and conservation themes can fill a memorable day.

ADVENTURE SEEKERS WANTED

If a trip to the Himalayas is on your wish list, but your budget says, "Dream on," make a beeline for Asia and **Expedition Everest.** If there's a wait for the attraction's high-speed train ride, the queue snakes through authentic rammed-earth and stacked-stone buildings of a Himalayan village, where museum-quality artifacts from Nepal and Tibet are worth browsing. While in Asia, pile into a **Kali River Rapids** raft for a white-water ride on the park's Chakranadi River.

Time-travel back to **DinoLand U.S.A** for a DINOSAUR journey through a primeval forest and white-knuckle encounters with carnivorous creatures like the razor-toothed carnotaurus, a swooping pterodactyl, and other menacing creatures of prehistoric doom.

If it's a cool day, the park's animals should be active, so head to Africa. Your **Kilimanjaro Safaris** open-air journey is a bumpy 20-minute quest for exotic-animal sightings, and you won't be disappointed. Adventurous guests with dollars to spare should sign up for the park's Wild Africa Trek. It's one of Disney's most thrilling guided tours.

EAT, SHOP, LAUGH

Dining can be an adventure, too, at **Tusker House Restaurant** in Africa, where a colorful buffet of vegetables and carved meats is enhanced with African-inspired chutneys, hummus, spiced tandoori tofu, and couscous salad. You can even sip on an African margarita or a sugar-cane mojito as you savor the exotic flavors.

Burn the calories during a shopping excursion to **Mombasa Marketplace,** where you can buy a bottle of South African wine or pick up hand-painted dishes from Zimbabwe. Onward to Discovery Island for a stroll along Discovery Island Trails into the Tree of Life show *It's Tough to Be a Bug!* Expect to laugh a lot.

DISCOVER ANIMAL ATTRACTION

Along the **Pangani Forest Exploration Trail,** you can view gorillas both through a glassed-in area and from a bridge as these magnificent primates move among the rocks and lush greenery.

Even though you feel safe from Bengal tigers on the **Maharajah Jungle Trek,** several raised viewing spots offer clear views with no glass or fence to mar your photos. Habitat backdrops like the Maharajah palace ruins create scenic props.

Before your day comes to a close, catch a **Flights of Wonder** performance to see hawks, eagles, and other imposing birds. If you can squeeze in only one live show, choose to take in the beautiful dance moves of "animal" performers at ***Festival of the Lion King.***

For people with disabilities: Guest may remain in wheelchairs or ECVs. ■ **TIP→ This is a great place to begin a family conservation project.** ✉ *Rafiki's Planet Watch* ☞ *Duration: Up to You. Crowds: Light–Moderate. Audience: All Ages.*

Habitat Habit!. On this educational wildlife trail that focuses heavily on animal conservation efforts, you get a close-up look at cotton-top tamarins (small white-headed monkeys) and their entertaining antics while you learn how to live with all the earth's animals. The South American primates are named for their flowing white mane of hair. **For people with disabilities:** Wheelchair accessible. ■ **TIP→ Ask questions; the animal-care cast members enjoy telling you about these cute critters.** ✉ *Rafiki's Planet Watch* ☞ *Duration: Up to You. Crowds: Light–Moderate. Audience: All Ages.*

SHOPPING

DISCOVERY ISLAND

Creature Comforts. This spot close to the border at Africa specializes in toys, toys, and more toys—including plenty of princess and fairy merchandise. Plush baby Simba, Tigger, and Pooh toys are adorable. Popular inexpensive souvenirs are rubber snakes and spiders and zebra-print Mickey-head pencils. By early 2015, the store may be made over into a Starbucks shop, a park insider said.

Disney Outfitters. The Outfitters, near the Tip Board, features unusual keepsakes like hand-painted ostrich eggs ($85–$185). There's a broad selection of upscale men's and women's apparel as well as jewelry and pottery handcrafted by African artisans.

Island Mercantile. To the left as you enter Discovery Island from the Oasis, the Animal Kingdom's largest shop stocks clothing, cookware, photo frames, and souvenirs. Safari hats, caps, and straw hats range from $20 to $30, and you can buy a backpack or messenger bag. Load it with towels for when you emerge soaked from Kali River Rapids.

DINOLAND U.S.A

Chester & Hester's Dinosaur Treasures. Dinophiles can't resist the finds here. It has a big display of quite large and scary-looking, yet soft and huggable, T-rex, velociraptor, and other dinosaur figures ($13–$23). Beyond the prehistoric, the shop has an attractive bin of rocks for collectors.

ASIA

Bhaktapur Market. At this gem of a shop you'll find bejeweled sandals and thongs and gorgeous, colorful print scarves of silk, satin, or India chiffon. There's also a good chance you'll find something on the clearance shelves—anything from a calligraphy kit to a Buddha figurine.

AFRICA

Mombasa Marketplace and Ziwani Traders. In Harambe Village, this is a great stop for unusual items like hand-painted dishes from Zimbabwe and South African wines such as a Chakalaka red varietal by Spice Route Winery. Young kids like to play with the small, inexpensive figurines of giraffes, elephants, rhinos, and other critters they just saw on their Kilimanjaro Safaris ride.

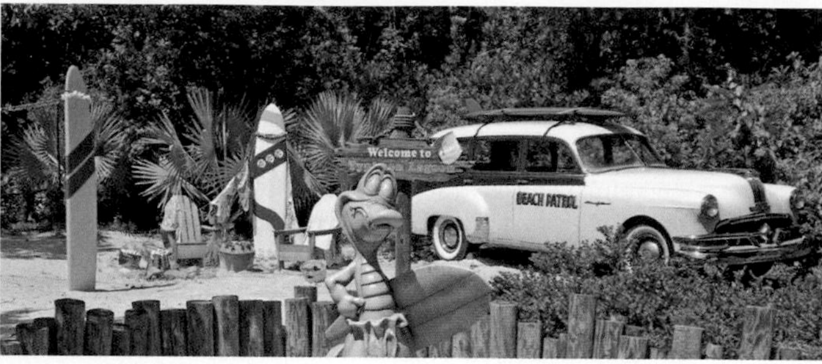

TYPHOON LAGOON

The beauty of Disney's water parks is that you can make either experience fit your mood. Like crowds? Head for the lounge chairs along the Surf Pool at Typhoon Lagoon or Melt-Away Bay at Blizzard Beach. Prefer peace? Walk past lush foliage along each park's circular path until you spot a secluded lean-to or tree-shaded patch of sand.

According to Disney legend, Typhoon Lagoon was created when the lush Placid Palms Resort was struck by a cataclysmic storm. It left a different world in its wake: surfboard-sundered trees, once-upright palms imitated the Leaning Tower of Pisa, and part of the original lagoon was cut off, trapping thousands of tropical fish—and a few sharks. Nothing, however, topped the fate of *Miss Tilly,* a shrimp boat from "Safen Sound, Florida," which was hurled high in the air and became impaled on Mt. Mayday, a magical volcano that periodically tries to dislodge *Miss Tilly* with huge geysers.

Ordinary folks, the legend continues, would have been crushed by such devastation. But the resourceful residents of Placid Palms were made of hardier stuff—and from the wreckage they created 56-acre Typhoon Lagoon, the self-proclaimed "world's ultimate water park."

ORIENTATION AND PLANNING

GETTING ORIENTED

The layout is so simple. The wave and swimming lagoon is at the park's center. Note that the waves are born in the Mt. Mayday side and break on the beaches closest to the entrance. Any attraction requiring a gravitational plunge starts around the summit of Mt. Mayday. Shark Reef and Ketchakiddee Creek flank the head of the lagoon, to Mt. Mayday's right and left, respectively, as you enter. The Crush 'n' Gusher water coaster is due right of Singapore Sal's.

You can take WDW bus transportation or drive to Typhoon Lagoon. There's no parking charge. Once inside, your options are to walk, swim, or slide.

WDW Information. Call WDW Information or check www.disneyworld.com's park calendars for days of operation. ✉ *Blizzard Beach* ☎ *407/824–4321.*

TYPHOON LAGOON PLANNER

WHAT TO EXPECT

You can speed down waterslides with names like Crush 'n' Gusher and Humunga Kowabunga or bump through rapids and falls at Mt. Mayday. You can also bob along in 5-foot waves in a surf pool the size of two football fields or, for a mellow break, float in inner tubes along the 2,100-foot Castaway Creek. Go snorkeling in Shark Reef, rubberneck as fellow human cannonballs are ejected from the Storm Slides, or hunker down in a hammock or lounge chair and read a book. Ketchakiddee Creek, for young children, replicates adult rides on a smaller scale. It's Disney's version of a day at the beach—complete with friendly Disney lifeguards. Most people agree that kids under 7 and older adults prefer Typhoon Lagoon. Bigger kids and teens like Blizzard Beach.

During the off-season between October and April, Typhoon Lagoon closes for several weeks for routine maintenance and refurbishment.

PARKS AMENITIES

Dining: Picnicking is permitted, but coolers too large for one person to carry, glass containers, and alcoholic beverages not bought in the park are forbidden. There are tables at Getaway Glen, Typhoon Tilly's (near Shark Reef), and at pavilions across the park. You can always fork out $40 a day for a reserved spot at Getaway Glen, with chairs, an umbrella and small table, and four beach towels. Arrive early, though, and you can stake out a great spot for free. Park eateries and food stands have salads, burgers, pizza, and other treats. One popular snack is a carton of hot mini-doughnuts with warm chocolate, vanilla, or strawberry dipping sauce from the Donut Hut.

Dressing Rooms and Lockers: There are thatched-roof dressing rooms and lockers to the right on your way into the park. It costs $8 a day to rent a small locker and $10 for a large one; there's also a $5 deposit. There are restrooms in every nook and cranny. Most have showers and are much less crowded than the dressing rooms. If you forgot your towel, rent ($2) or buy one at Singapore Sal's.

First Aid: The small first-aid stand, run by a registered nurse, is on your left as you enter the park.

Guest Services: The staff at Typhoon Lagoon's Guest Services window outside the entrance turnstiles, to your left, can answer many questions. ■ **TIP→ A chalkboard inside gives water temperature and surfing information.**

Lost People and Things: Ask about your misplaced people and things at the Guest Services window near the entrance turnstiles. Lost children are taken to an area by the Tip Board near the front of the park, where Disney cast members entertain them with games.

Private Patios: The park has a dozen premium, roped-off Beachcomber Shacks (patios, really) that groups of as many as six can rent. They generally offer shade and sun as well as plush loungers and other chairs, a table with an umbrella, and an ice chest with two bottles of water per guest (up to six). Each guest also gets two beach towels and a refillable soft-drink mug. The whole group gets a locker to share and an attendant to take and deliver food orders (cost of meals not included). The patios cost $345 during peak season (usually March through late August), $240 in September, and $160 the rest of the year. Reserve (☏ *407/939–8687*) well in advance or arrive very early to book one at High 'N Dry. In summer, any patio that isn't prebooked sells out within a half hour of the park opening.

Services for People with Disabilities: The paths connecting the different areas are wheelchair accessible, but most of the waterslides are not. There is, however, an elevator that takes you to the loading zone of the Crush 'n' Gusher water coaster. If you transfer from your chair to a raft or inner tube, you can float in Typhoon Lagoon Surf Pool or Castaway Creek.

Wheelchairs are available at the entrance turnstile area and are free with ID. You can trade a land-based wheelchair for chairs that go into the water by asking a lifeguard.

Supplies: You can get inner tubes at Castaway Creek and inner tubes, rafts, or slide mats at the rides. Borrow snorkel gear at **Shark Reef** (your own isn't allowed) and life vests at **High 'N Dry**. Near the main entrance is **Singapore Sal's,** where you can pick up free life jackets, buy sundries, and rent (or buy) towels and lockers.

VISITING TIPS

■ In summer, come first thing in the morning (early birds can ride several times before the lines get long), late in the afternoon when park hours run later, or when the weather clears after a thundershower (rainstorms drive away crowds). Afternoons are also good in cooler weather, as the water is a bit warmer. To make a whole day of it, avoid weekends, when locals and visitors pack in.

■ Women and girls should wear one-piece swimsuits unless they want to find their tops somewhere around their ears at the bottom of the waterslide.

■ Invest in sunscreen and water shoes. Plan to slather sunscreen on several times throughout the day. An inexpensive pair of water shoes will save tootsies from hot sand and walkways and from restroom floors.

■ Arrive 30 minutes before opening so you can park, buy tickets, rent towels, and snag inner tubes before the crowds descend and, trust us, it gets very crowded.

EXPLORING TYPHOON LAGOON

Bay Slides. Kids scramble up several steps tucked between faux-rock formations, where a lifeguard sits to supervise their slide into Blustery Bay. The incline is small, but the thrill is great for young kids, who whoosh into the bay (sometimes into the arms of waiting parents).

These scaled-down versions of the Storm Slides are geared to kids shorter than 60 inches. ■ **TIP→ Kids really burn up energy going up the steps and down the slides repeatedly. Parents should be prepared for their wanting to ride over and over again..** ✉ *Typhoon Lagoon* ☞ *Duration: Up to You. Crowds: Light–Moderate. Audience: Young Kids.*

Castaway Creek. This circular, 15-foot-wide, 3-foot-deep waterway is chill. Snag an inner tube, and float along a creek that winds through the park and around the Surf Pool and beaches. You pass through a rain forest that showers you with spray, you slide through caves and grottoes, you float by overhanging trees and flowering bushes, and you get dumped on at the Water Works with "broken" pipes. The current flows a gentle 2½ feet per second. Along the way there are five landing areas where you can hop in and out. **For people with disabilities:** Guests using wheelchairs must transfer to an inner tube. ■ **TIP→ A full circuit takes about 20 minutes, longer if you stop at one of the five lifeguard-manned launches.** ✉ *Typhoon Lagoon* ☞ *Duration: Up to 20 mins. Crowds: Vary by Season. Audience: All Ages.*

5

Fodor's Choice ★ **Crush 'n' Gusher.** If flume rides, storm slides, and tube races aren't wild enough for your inner thrill-seeker, get ready to defy gravity on Disney's first water coaster. Designed to propel you uphill and down along a series of flumes, caverns, and spillways, this ride should satisfy the most enthusiastic daredevil. Keeping with park lore, Crush 'n' Gusher flows through what appears to be a rusted-out tropical fruit factory, weaving in and out of the wreckage and debris that once transported fruit through the plant's wash facilities. Three fruit spillways are aptly named Banana Blaster, Coconut Crusher, and Pineapple Plunger. Guests shouldn't ride if they are pregnant or have heart, back, or neck problems. **For people with disabilities:** An elevator takes guests using wheelchairs to the loading area; there's a short distance between this area and the ride. ■ **TIP→ Ride first thing in the morning, before lines get too long. And don't forget to say cheese for the cameras!** ✉ *Typhoon Lagoon* ☞ *Duration: 1 min. Crowds: Moderate–Heavy. Audience: Anyone 48 inches or taller.*

Gangplank Falls. Families who climb Mt. Mayday for this ride are in for an adventure—more of an adventure than they might expect. Upon takeoff, a 6½-foot-long inflated raft plunges down the slide with impressive speed. It even gets bumpy at times along the 300-foot river. Not too scary for the tykes, and yet not a bore for parents, Gangplank Falls is great family fun! Those who are pregnant or have heart, back, or neck problems should sit this one out. ■ **TIP→ The inner tubes are heavy, so be sure to have at least two willing carriers. Also, be prepared to ride with two to four riders (five if some are kids).** ✉ *Typhoon Lagoon* ☞ *Duration: 1 min. Crowds: Vary by Season. Audience: Not Young Kids.*

Humunga Kowabunga. There's little time to scream, but you'll hear just such vociferous reactions as the survivors emerge from the catch pool opposite Shark Reef. The basic questions are: want to get scared out of your wits in four seconds flat—and did you like it enough to go back for more? The three side-by-side Humunga Kowabunga speed

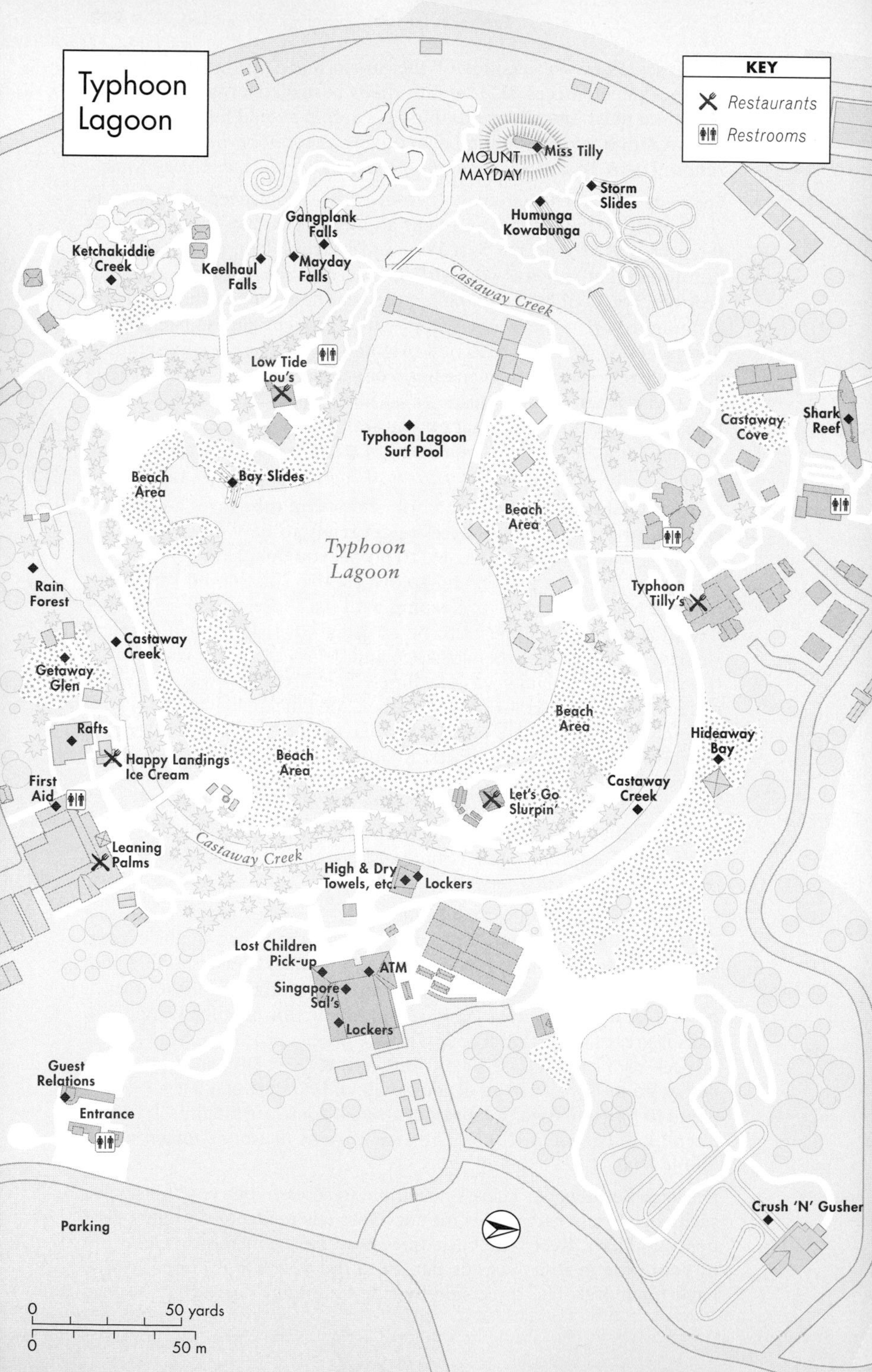

Typhoon Lagoon
KEY
Restaurants
Restrooms
MOUNT MAYDAY
Miss Tilly
Storm Slides
Humunga Kowabunga
Gangplank Falls
Mayday Falls
Keelhaul Falls
Ketchakiddie Creek
Castaway Creek
Low Tide Lou's
Typhoon Lagoon Surf Pool
Castaway Cove
Shark Reef
Beach Area
Bay Slides
Beach Area
Typhoon Lagoon
Rain Forest
Typhoon Tilly's
Castaway Creek
Getaway Glen
Beach Area
Rafts
Hideaway Bay
Happy Landings Ice Cream
Beach Area
First Aid
Castaway Creek
Let's Go Slurpin'
Leaning Palms
Castaway Creek
High & Dry Towels, etc.
Lockers
Lost Children Pick-up
ATM
Singapore Sal's
Lockers
Guest Relations
Entrance
Crush 'N' Gusher
Parking
0
50 yards
0
50 m

slides deserve acclaim among thrill lovers, as they drop more than 50 feet in a distance barely four times that amount. For nonmathematicians, that's very steep. Oh yes, and then you go through a cave. In the dark. The average speed is 30 mph; however, you can really fly if you lie flat on your back, cross your ankles, wrap your arms around your chest, and arch your back. One caveat: the ride only lasts a few seconds—too short for us—and lines are often too long to requeue for another plunge. This ride isn't appropriate for guests who are pregnant or who have heart, back, or neck problems. ■ **TIP→ Race against your friends or family; there are three slides at the top.** ⊠ *Typhoon Lagoon* ☞ *Duration: 4 secs. Crowds: Heavy. Audience: Daring souls 48 inches or taller.*

PARK VIEWS

Mt. Mayday. What goes down can also go up—and up and up. Climbing Mt. Mayday "[is] like climbing Mt. Everest," wailed one teenager about a climb that seems a lot steeper than an 85-foot peak should be. However, it's Mt. Everest with hibiscus flowers, a rope bridge, and stepping-stones set in plunging waters. The view encompasses the entire park. Lovers of white-water rafting should head to Mayday Falls, Keelhaul Falls, and Gangplank Falls at Mt. Mayday. These rides in oversize inner tubes plunge down the mountain's left side. They have caves, waterfalls, and intricate rockwork. ⊠ *Typhoon Lagoon.*

Keelhaul Falls. Do you need to chill out after the Mach 5 speeds of Humunga Cowabunga? Then venture up to Keelhaul Falls, a laid-back trip down the left side of Mt. Mayday. Just kick back and relax as your blue tube cruises down the 400-foot slide and splashes into the pool below. Keelhaul feels a little slow if you ride it right after Mayday Falls, so thrill-seekers may be disappointed. Yet its winding path and scenic descent make for a satisfying ride. This ride isn't appropriate for guests who are pregnant or who have heart, back, or neck problems. ■ **TIP→ Ride before or after Mayday Falls.** ⊠ *Typhoon Lagoon* ☞ *Duration: 1 min. Crowds: Vary by Season. Audience: Not Young Kids.*

Ketchakiddee Creek. Typhoon Lagoon's play area for young children has slides, mini-rapids, faux sand castles, squirting whales and seals, bouncing barrels, waterfalls, sprinklers, and all the other ingredients of a splash fiesta. The bubbling sand ponds, where youngsters can sit in what seems like an enormous whirlpool bath, are special favorites. Little ones also love the tiny-scale tube ride. Small water cannons let kids engage in water-spray wars. Families can camp beneath lots of shady lean-tos when not in the water. **For people with disabilities:** Accessible for people using water-appropriate wheelchairs. ■ **TIP→ Parents can take turns watching the kiddies here and riding the thrill slides.** ⊠ *Typhoon Lagoon* ☞ *Duration: Up to You. Crowds: Light. Audience: Young Kids. Height requirements: Adults must be accompanied by a child under 48 inches and vice versa.*

Mayday Falls. This 460-foot slide in bright yellow inner tubes is the longest and bumpiest of the three falls. It's a long trek up to Mayday Falls—even higher than Keelhaul—but the increased speed and longer descent are well worth the climb. It's a relatively straight slide over the

From the wreckage—like that shown here—in the wake of a storm, Placid Palms Resort residents created 56-acre Typhoon Lagoon. Or so the story goes. . . .

falls into a catchment, but it's not as thrilling as the up-and-down water jets on the Crush 'n' Gusher. This ride isn't appropriate for guests who are pregnant or who have heart, back, or neck problems. ■ **TIP→ While you're in the neighborhood, ride Keelhaul Falls, too.** ⊠ *Typhoon Lagoon* ☞ *Duration: 1 min. Crowds: Vary by Season. Audience: Not Young Kids.*

Shark Reef. If you felt like jumping into the tank at Epcot's The Seas with Nemo & Friends, make tracks for this 362,000-gallon snorkeling tank. The coral reef is artificial, but the 4,000 tropical fish—including rainbow parrotfish, sting rays, trigger fish, yellowtail damselfish, and amiable leopard and bonnet-head sharks (only 2 to 3 feet long)—are quite real. A sunken ship divides the reef; its portholes give landlubbers access to the underwater scene, though the windows are filmy and viewing is a bit blurry. During the warmest months (late March through September), adults and children ages 5 and older can don personal supplied-air snorkeling equipment at no charge. Life vests are provided for weak swimmers. To prevent algae growth, Shark Reef is kept at a brisk 72°F, which is about 15° cooler than the rest of Typhoon Lagoon. For those who prefer a long, leisurely snorkel, this experience will be too brief. **For people with disabilities:** The sunken-ship viewing area is wheelchair accessible. ■ **TIP→ This is popular, but even in the busy summer months, the wait is often under 20 minutes.** ⊠ *Typhoon Lagoon* ☞ *Duration: Up to You. Crowds: Moderate– Heavy depending on season. Audience: Most ages; children under 10 must be accompanied by an adult.*

Fodor's Choice ★ **Storm Slides.** Each of these three body slides is about 300 feet long and snakes in and out of rock formations, through caves and tunnels, and under waterfalls, but each has a slightly different view and offers a twist. The one in the middle has the longest tunnel; the others feature secrets you'll have to discover for yourself. Brace for splashdown on all three slides! Maximum speed is about 20 mph, and the trip takes about 30 seconds. These slides are not appropriate for guests who are pregnant or who have heart, back, or neck problems. ■ **TIP→ Try each of the three slides for different twists.** ✉ *Typhoon Lagoon* ☞ *Duration: 15–20 secs. Crowds: Moderate–Heavy. Audience: Not Young Kids.*

Fodor's Choice ★ **Typhoon Lagoon Surf Pool.** This is the heart of the park, a swimming area that spreads out over 2½ acres and contains almost 3 million gallons of clear, chlorinated water. It's scalloped by coves, bays, and inlets, all edged with white-sand beaches—spread over a base of white concrete, as bodysurfers soon discover when they try to slide into shore. Ouch! The waves are the draw. Twelve huge water-collection chambers hidden in Mt. Mayday dump their load into trapdoors with a resounding whoosh to create waves large enough for Typhoon Lagoon to host amateur and professional surfing championships.

A piercing double hoot from *Miss Tilly* (the boat that purportedly landed at Mt. Mayday at the park's highest level) signals the start and finish of wave action: every 2 hours, for 1½ hours, 5-foot waves issue forth every 90 seconds; the last half hour is devoted to moderate bobbing waves. Even during the big-wave periods, however, the waters in Blustery Bay and Whitecap Cove are protected. Surfers who don't want to risk a fickle ocean can surf here on certain days before the park opens. Instruction and soft-sided surfboard are included in the $165 cost, and the surfing experience (ages 8 and older) lasts for 2½ hours. Reserve your waves by calling ☎ *407/939–7529*. **For people with disabilities:** Accessible for people using water-appropriate wheelchairs. ■ **TIP→ Waves come every 90 seconds if you want to time your bodysurfing.** ✉ *Typhoon Lagoon* ☞ *Duration: Up to You. Crowds: Heavy. Audience: All Ages.*

NEED A BREAK?

Leaning Palms, to your left as you enter the park, has burgers, pizzas, turkey sandwiches, Asian salads, beer, and, of course, ice cream and frozen yogurt. **Let's Go Slurpin'** is a beach shack on the edge of Typhoon Lagoon that dispenses frozen margaritas as well as wine and beer. **Typhoon Tilly's,** on the right just south of Shark Reef, serves sandwiches, salads, and snacks of all kinds and pours mostly sugary, nonalcoholic grog—though you can grab a Davy Jones "lager."

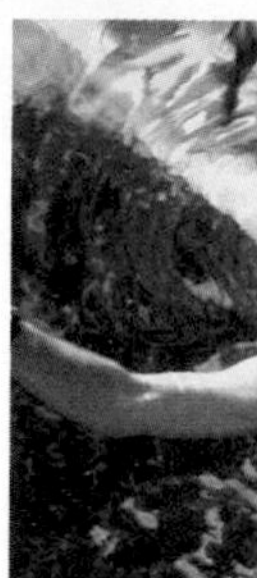

BLIZZARD BEACH

With its oxymoronic name, Blizzard Beach promises the seemingly impossible—a seaside playground with an alpine theme. As with its older cousin, Typhoon Lagoon, Disney Imagineers have created a legend to explain the park's origin.

The story goes that after a freak winter storm dropped snow over the western side of Walt Disney World, entrepreneurs created Florida's first downhill ski resort. Sauna-like temperatures soon returned. But as the 66-acre resort's operators were ready to close up shop, they spotted a playful alligator sliding down the 120-foot-tall "liquid ice" slopes. The realization that the melting snow had created the world's tallest, fastest, and most exhilarating water-filled ski and toboggan runs gave birth to the ski resort–water park.

From its imposing ski-jump tower to its 1,200-foot series of rushing waterfalls, Blizzard Beach delivers cool fun even in the hot summertime. Where else can you wear your swimsuit on the slopes?

ORIENTATION AND PLANNING

GETTING ORIENTED

The park layout makes it fairly simple to navigate. Once you enter and rent a locker, you'll cross a small bridge over Cross Country Creek before choosing a spot to park your towels and cooler. To the left is the Melt-Away Bay wave pool. Dead ahead you can see Mt. Gushmore, a chairlift to the top, and the park's many slopes and slides.

If thrills are your game, come early and line up for Summit Plummet, Slush Gusher, and Downhill Double Dipper before wait times go from light to moderate (or heavy). Anytime is a good time for a dip in Melt-Away Bay or a tube trip around Cross Country Creek. Parents with young children should claim their spot early at Tike's Peak, to the park's right even before you cross the bridge.

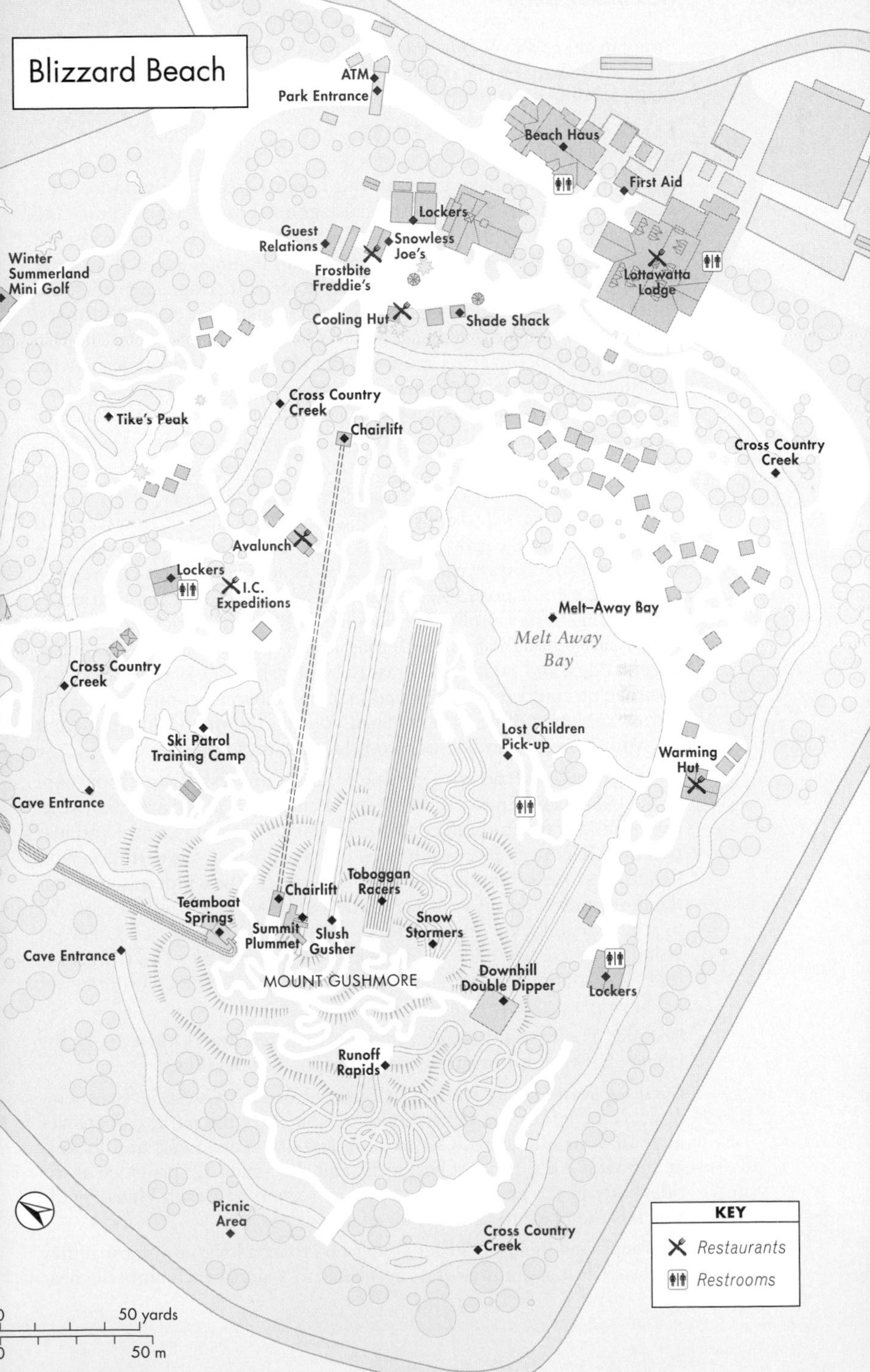

Blizzard Beach
ATM
Park Entrance
Beach Haus
First Aid
Lockers
Guest Relations
Snowless Joe's
Frostbite Freddie's
Lottawatta Lodge
Winter Summerland Mini Golf
Cooling Hut
Shade Shack
Cross Country Creek
Tike's Peak
Chairlift
Cross Country Creek
Avalunch
Lockers
I.C. Expeditions
Melt-Away Bay
Melt Away Bay
Cross Country Creek
Ski Patrol Training Camp
Lost Children Pick-up
Warming Hut
Cave Entrance
Toboggan Racers
Chairlift
Teamboat Springs
Snow Stormers
Summit Plummet
Slush Gusher
Cave Entrance
Downhill Double Dipper
Lockers
MOUNT GUSHMORE
Runoff Rapids
Picnic Area
Cross Country Creek
KEY
Restaurants
Restrooms
0
50 yards
0
50 m

You can take WDW bus transportation or drive to Blizzard Beach. There's no charge for parking. Once inside, your options are to walk, swim, or slide.

BLIZZARD BEACH PLANNER

WHAT TO EXPECT

Disney Imagineers have gone all out here to create the paradox of a ski resort in the midst of a tropical lagoon. Lots of verbal puns and sight gags play with the snow-in-Florida motif. The centerpiece is Mt. Gushmore, with its 120-foot-high Summit Plummet. Attractions have names like Teamboat Springs, a white-water raft ride. Themed speed slides include Toboggan Racers, Slush Gusher, and Snow Stormers. Between Mt. Gushmore's base and its summit, swim-skiers can also ride a chairlift converted from ski-resort to beach-resort use—with multihued umbrellas and snow skis on their undersides. Older kids and devoted waterslide enthusiasts generally prefer Blizzard Beach to other water parks.

PARKS AMENITIES

Dining: You can't bring oversize coolers, glass containers, or your own alcoholic beverages into the park. Picnicking is welcome, however, and there are several pleasant pavilions and other spots, most notably the terrace outside Lottawatta Lodge. This is also where you can reserve your own picnic spot ($40 for a day), which includes chairs (two of them loungers), an umbrella and small table, and four beach towels. Arrive early enough, and you'll snag a spot for free. You can get burgers, hot dogs, and salads at Lottawatta Lodge or other eateries and food stands. You could go for the usual snacks—snowballs or ice cream. But a truly sublime nibble is the melt-in-your-mouth mini-doughnut from the Mini Donuts stand across from Lottawatta Lodge.

Dressing Rooms and Lockers: Dressing rooms, showers, and restrooms are in the village area, just inside the main entrance. There are other restrooms in Lottawatta Lodge, at the Ski Patrol Training Camp, and just past the Melt-Away Bay beach area. Lockers are near the entrance, next to Snowless Joe's Rentals, and near Tike's Peak (the children's area and the most convenient if you have little swim-skiers in tow). It costs $8 to rent a small locker and $10 for a large one, and there's a $5 deposit. Note that there are only small lockers at Tike's Peak. The towels for rent ($2) at Snowless Joe's are tiny. If you forgot yours, you're better off buying a proper one at the Beach Haus.

First Aid: The first-aid stand, overseen by a registered nurse, is in the village, between Lottawatta Lodge and the Beach Haus.

Guest Services: Disney staffers at Blizzard Beach's Guest Services window, to the left of the ticket booth as you enter the park, can answer most of your questions. Get free life vests or rent towels and lockers at **Snowless Joe's**. Inner tubes, rafts, and slide mats are provided at the rides. Buy beach gear or rent towels or lockers at **Beach Haus. Shade Shack** is the place for a new pair of sunglasses.

Lost People and Things: Instruct youngsters to let a lifeguard know if they get lost. The lost-children station is beneath a large beach umbrella near the front of the park. And don't worry about the kids—a Disney cast member will keep them busy with activities.

Private Patios: The park has 14 Polar Patios to rent to groups of as many as six people. For $345 a day in peak season (usually March through late August), $240 in September, and $160 off-peak, you get plush loungers, chairs, a table with umbrella, refillable beverage mugs, an ice chest with two water bottles per person, a group locker, and an attendant who will take your orders for and deliver lunch and snacks (food costs extra). It's best to book a patio far ahead of time (☎ *407/939–8687*). If you arrive early enough, there might be an open patio; check at the Shade Shack.

SERVICES FOR PEOPLE WITH DISABILITIES

Most of Blizzard Beach's paths are flat and level. If you can transfer from your chair a short distance, you can also access all the waterslides except Summit Plummet. Or settle into a large inner tube and float in Cross Country Creek.

5

A limited number of wheelchairs—some suitable for the water—are available near the park entrance and are free if you leave an ID.

EXPLORING BLIZZARD BEACH

Chairlift. No subtropical skiing paradise would be complete without a chairlift, and this one is an attractive alternative to trekking to the top of Mt. Gushmore over and over again. The two-minute chairlift ascent is a great opportunity to scout out other slides and to enjoy the "ski beach" scenery. **For people with disabilities:** Guests using wheelchairs must transfer to a ride seat and subsequent attractions. A companion will have to meet you with the wheelchair at the base of Mt. Gushmore. **■TIP→ If the wait is too long or you have children under 32 inches tall, hiking up is good exercise.** ☞ *Duration: 2 mins. Crowds: Light–Moderate. Audience: Not Young Kids. Height requirements: At least 32 inches tall to ride.*

Cross Country Creek. Just grab an inner tube, hop on, and circle the entire park during a leisurely 25-minute float on this creek. Along the way, you'll get doused with frigid water in an ice cave—wonderful on a steamy Florida day. Tubes are provided at six launch sites, but they're not required. In fact, kids soon discover that the fastest and most enjoyable way to get around the park is to glide with the current and hop off at whichever exit they wish. **For people with disabilities:** Guests using wheelchairs must transfer to inner tubes. **■TIP→ There are exits near most thrill rides, and moving through the park this way is oodles more fun than walking.** ☞ *Duration: 25 mins. Crowds: Vary by Season. Audience: All Ages.*

Fodor's Choice ★ **Downhill Double Dipper.** If you're on your way to Snow Stormers or Toboggan Racers on the purple slopes, you may notice a cool-looking slide on the left. This is the Downhill Double Dipper, and it's well worth the stop. The best thing about this slide is that you are timed from blastoff to finish line! Competition may get heated as kids (48 inches or taller) vie for the glory of fastest speed slider, but even the least competitive will enjoy tearing down Mt. Gushmore in their racing tubes. Expectant mothers shouldn't ride, nor should guests with heart conditions or neck or back problems. **For people with disabilities:** Guests using wheelchairs must transfer to the tube-launch site. ■ **TIP→ Ride early; this popular purple-slope attraction gets crowded after lunch. (And, oh yeah—our fastest time was 5.89 seconds—can you beat that?)** ☞ *Duration: Under 10 secs. Crowds: Heavy. Audience: Thrill seekers 48 inches and taller.*

Melt-Away Bay. The park's main pool is a 1-acre oasis that's constantly fed by "melting snow" waterfalls. The man-made waves are positively oceanlike. If you're not a strong swimmer, stay away from the far end of the pool, where the waves originate. You can get temporarily stuck in a pocket even if your head is still above water. If you prefer to stay beached, there are plenty of recliner chairs spread out around the bay. This is where moms and dads often relax and watch their kids swim in the lifeguard-protected waters. **For people with disabilities:** Guests using water-appropriate wheelchairs can enjoy shallow waters here. ■ **TIP→ Get an inner tube if you plan to venture to deeper waters, and arrive early if you want to find a shady spot (there are limited giant umbrellas).** ☞ *Duration: Up to You. Crowds: Vary by Season. Audience: All Ages.*

Runoff Rapids. It's easy to overlook this three-track flume ride hidden on the far red slope of Mt. Gushmore. Yet if you have the courage to carry your tube all the way up to the top, you'll eventually come upon three twisting, turning flumes—even one that's in the dark (keep in mind the tunnel slide is for single riders only, while the open slides are for one- or two-passenger tubes). Once you're in, it's way more fun than scary. Still, guests who are pregnant or who have heart, neck, or back problems should skip it. **For people with disabilities:** Guests using wheelchairs must transfer to inner tubes. ■ **TIP→ It's worth riding both an open slide and the tunnel slide, but remember that the tunnel slide is only for single riders.** ☞ *Duration: 35 secs. Crowds: Light–Moderate. Audience: Not Young Kids.*

Ski Patrol Training Camp. Preteens might want to spend most of their time on the T-bar drop, Cool Runners slides, and Snow Falls downhill body slide. In addition, there's a chance to take on the Thin Ice Training Course, a wide-open area where kids can jump from one slippery mogul to the next. The moguls really look more like bobbing baby icebergs, and kids don't mind when they miss a berg and plop into the pool. **For people with disabilities:** Guests using water-appropriate wheelchairs can enjoy wading areas here. ■ **TIP→ The optimum time to come is early in the day or after a thunderstorm, when crowds thin out. That said, lines are often short at the zip-line drop and the iceberg obstacle course.** ☞ *Duration: Up to You. Crowds: Light–Moderate. Audience: Tweens.*

Fodor's Choice ★ **Slush Gusher.** This speed slide, which drops through a snow-banked mountain gully next door to Summit Plummet on the green slopes, isn't quite as intimidating, but it's a real thriller nonetheless. Instead of one scream-inducing steep drop, the Slush Gusher features a fast, hilly descent to the base of Mt. Gushmore. While the Slush Gusher will not disappoint thrill-seekers, it is perfect for those who want some adventure but tremble at the sight of Summit Plummet. For guests who are pregnant or who have heart, back, or neck problems, this ride is less than perfect. **For people with disabilities:** Guests using wheelchairs must transfer to the ride. ■ **TIP→ The earlier you ride, the better. On crowded days waits last up to 90 minutes.** ☞ *Duration: 15 secs. Crowds: You Bet! Audience: Not Young Kids; must be 48 inches or taller to ride.*

NEED A BREAK?

Lottawatta Lodge—a North American ski lodge with a Caribbean accent—is the park's main emporium of fast food. Lines are long at peak feeding times. The Warming Hut, which is open seasonally, offers smoked turkey legs, salads, sandwiches, and ice cream. Specialty hot dogs, turkey legs, and salads are on the menu at Avalunch. Frostbite Freddie's and Polar Pub, on the main beach, both sell frozen drinks and spirits.

5

Snow Stormers. No water park would be complete without a meandering waterslide, and Blizzard Beach has one. Here three flumes, each 350 feet long, descend from the top of Mt. Gushmore along a switchback course of ski-type slalom gates on the purple slopes. Snow Stormers offers an exciting change of pace from the straight-down slides of the green slopes, and riders are in for a grand total of eight hairpin turns before finally splashing into the pool at the bottom. This ride isn't appropriate for guests who are pregnant or who have heart, neck, or back problems. **For people with disabilities:** Guests using wheelchairs must transfer to a toboggan-style slide mat with handles. ■ **TIP→ This is a belly-down ride. Hold on tight!** ☞ *Duration: 20 secs. Crowds: Moderate–Heavy. Audience: All Ages.*

Fodor's Choice ★ **Summit Plummet.** This is Mt. Gushmore's big gun, which Disney bills as "the world's tallest, fastest free-fall speed slide." From Summit Plummet's "ski jump" tower at the very top of the green slopes, it's a wild 55-mph, 12-story plunge straight down to a splash landing at the base of the mountain. It looks almost like a straight vertical drop, and you can't help but feel like a movie stunt double as you take the plunge. If you're watching from the beach below, you can't hear the yells of the participants, but you can bet many of them are screaming their heads off. The ride is not for guests who are pregnant or who have heart, back, or neck problems. ■ **TIP→ Make this one of your first stops. The line will only get longer as the day goes on. (Summer-afternoon waits can be up to two hours.)** ☞ *Duration: 10 crazy secs. Crowds: Absolutely. Audience: Not Young Kids; must be 48 inches or taller to ride.*

Teamboat Springs. Six-passenger rafts zip along green slopes in one of the world's longest family white-water raft rides. Since its original construction, it has doubled its speed of departure onto its twisting, 1,200-foot channel of rushing water, which ends with a refreshing waterfall dousing. This ride is a good place for kids too big for Tike's Peak to test more grown-up waters. Those who are pregnant or have heart, neck, or back problems should avoid this one. **For people with disabilities:** Guests using wheelchairs must transfer to the ride. ■ **TIP→ This is an excellent ride for the whole family: there are no age or height requirements (other than "no infants"), tubes seat four to six people, and lines**

generally move quickly. ☞ *Duration: 1½ mins. Crowds: Moderate. Audience: Families.*

Fodor's Choice ★ **Tike's Peak.** Disney never leaves the little ones out of the fun, and this junior-size version of Blizzard Beach, set slightly apart from the rest of the park, has scaled-down elements of Mt. Gushmore, with sand, slides (including one with tubes), faux snow drifts, and igloo-like tunnels. Parents can find sun or shade beneath lean-tos while watching over the little ones. Several lifeguards are on hand, but parents should still watch their youngsters at all times. **For people with disabilities:** Guests using water-appropriate wheelchairs can enjoy the wading areas. **■ TIP→ Stake out lounge chairs early, especially for a shady spot. If your tykes don't swim well, get them fitted with a free life vest, and pull your chair up to the water's edge.** ☞ *Duration: Up to You. Crowds: Vary by Season. Audience: Young Kids. Height requirement: Children shorter than 48 inches must be accompanied by adults.*

Toboggan Racers. Grab your mat, wait for the signal, and go. You and eight other racers whiz simultaneously down the watery trail on the purple slopes toward the finish line at the base of the mountain. The racing aspect makes the ride fun, but it lacks the speed of single-rider green-slope rides like Slush Gusher. For a ride combining speed and friendly competition, check out the Downhill Double Dipper. Expectant mothers shouldn't ride, nor should guests with heart, neck, or back problems. **For people with disabilities:** Guests using wheelchairs must transfer to slide mats. **■ TIP→ It's more fun when you race family members or friends—up to eight people can ride at the same time.** ☞ *Duration: 10 secs. Crowds: Moderate–Heavy. Audience: Not Young Kids.*

DOWNTOWN DISNEY

EXPLORING

5

East of Epcot and close to Interstate 4 along a large lake, this shopping, dining, and entertainment complex currently has three areas: the Marketplace, West Side, and the connecting district, Pleasure Island. Major changes are in store by 2016 after a massive makeover featuring new shops, restaurants, and promenades is complete and the area is renamed Disney Springs. A huge parking garage will open in early 2015. You can rent lockers, strollers, or wheelchairs, and there are two Guest Relations centers.

DisneyQuest. In a five-story virtual-reality mini-theme park in Downtown Disney's West Side, DisneyQuest lets you pay a hefty cover to participate in high-tech virtual adventures and play video games. To be fair, you can play all day, and there are cutting-edge games and interactive adventures that make the admission worthwhile. It's also a great place for teens and older tweens (children under 10 must be accompanied by an adult). Newest game with play consoles on every floor: Fix-It Felix, Jr. from the popular Disney movie "Wreck-It Ralph."

In **Explore Zone,** fly through the streets of Agrabah with the help of a virtual-reality helmet on Aladdin's Magic Carpet Ride. Take a Virtual Jungle Cruise down the roiling rapids of a prehistoric world, and paddle (yes, *really* paddle) to adventure amid volcanoes, dinosaurs, and other cretaceous threats. At Pirates of the Caribbean: Battle for Buccaneer Gold, you and the gang must brave the high seas and sink pirate ships to acquire treasure.

In the **Score Zone,** battle super villains while flying, headset firmly intact, through a 3-D comic world in Ride the Comix. Escape evil aliens and rescue colonists during Invasion! An ExtraTERRORestrial Alien Encounter. Or hip-check your friends in a life-size Mighty Ducks Pinball Slam game.

In the **Create Zone** learn the secrets of Disney animation at the Animation Academy. Create your own twisted masterpiece at Sid's Create-A-Toy, based on the popular animated film *Toy Story.* Or, at Living Easels, make a *living* painting on a giant electronic screen. Thrills await at Cyberspace Mountain, where you can design your own roller coaster

Downtown Disney

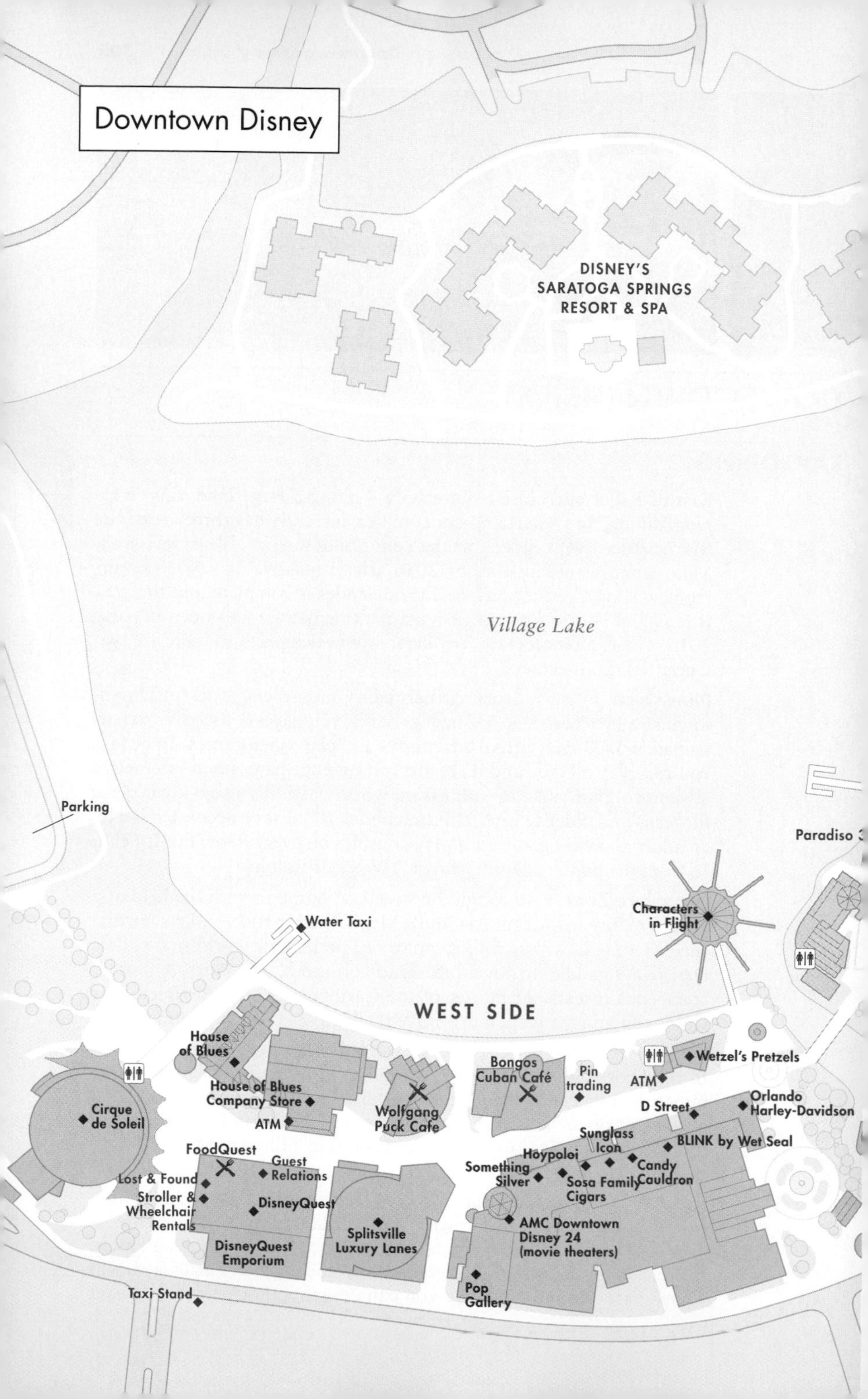

DISNEY'S SARATOGA SPRINGS RESORT & SPA

Village Lake

Parking

Paradiso 3

Water Taxi

Characters in Flight

WEST SIDE

House of Blues

Bongos Cuban Café

Pin trading

ATM

Wetzel's Pretzels

House of Blues Company Store

ATM

Wolfgang Puck Cafe

D Street

Orlando Harley-Davidson

Cirque de Soleil

Sunglass Icon

BLINK by Wet Seal

FoodQuest

Guest Relations

Hoypoloi

Something Silver

Candy Cauldron

Sosa Family Cigars

Lost & Found

Stroller & Wheelchair Rentals

DisneyQuest

Splitsville Luxury Lanes

AMC Downtown Disney 24 (movie theaters)

DisneyQuest Emporium

Taxi Stand

Pop Gallery

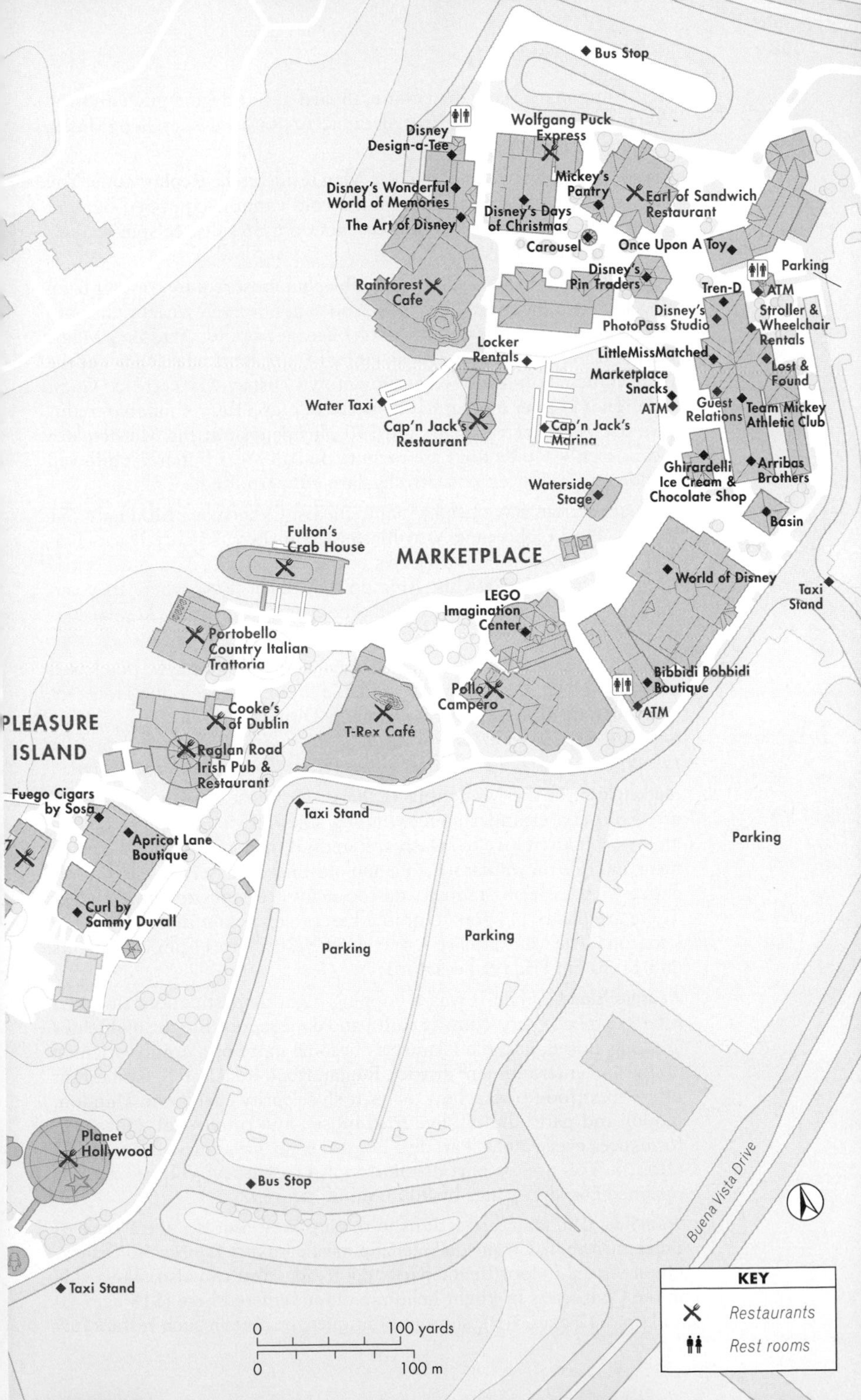
Bus Stop
Wolfgang Puck Express
Disney Design-a-Tee
Disney's Wonderful World of Memories
The Art of Disney
Mickey's Pantry
Earl of Sandwich Restaurant
Disney's Days of Christmas
Carousel
Once Upon A Toy
Parking
Rainforest Cafe
Disney's Pin Traders
Tren-D
ATM
Disney's PhotoPass Studio
Stroller & Wheelchair Rentals
Locker Rentals
LittleMissMatched
Lost & Found
Marketplace Snacks
ATM
Water Taxi
Guest Relations
Team Mickey Athletic Club
Cap'n Jack's Restaurant
Cap'n Jack's Marina
Ghirardelli Ice Cream & Chocolate Shop
Arribas Brothers
Waterside Stage
Basin
Fulton's Crab House
MARKETPLACE
World of Disney
Taxi Stand
LEGO Imagination Center
Portobello Country Italian Trattoria
Bibbidi Bobbidi Boutique
Pollo Campero
ATM
Cooke's of Dublin
T-Rex Café
PLEASURE ISLAND
Raglan Road Irish Pub & Restaurant
Fuego Cigars by Sosa
Taxi Stand
Apricot Lane Boutique
Parking
Curl by Sammy Duvall
Parking
Parking
Planet Hollywood
Bus Stop
Buena Vista Drive
KEY
Restaurants
Rest rooms
Taxi Stand
0
100 yards
0
100 m

on a computer screen, then climb aboard a 360-degree pitch-and-roll simulator for the ride of your dreams. At Radio Disney SongMaker, produce your own hit.

Classic free-play machines like Pac Man reside in the **Replay Zone.** You can also sit with a partner in an asteroid cannon–equipped bumper car and blast others to make their cars do a 360-degree spin in Buzz Lightyear's AstroBlaster.

All attractions are wheelchair accessible, but most require transfer from wheelchair to the attraction itself. You can, however, wheel right onto Pirates of the Caribbean: Battle for Buccaneer Gold, Aladdin's Magic Carpet Ride, and Mighty Ducks Pinball Slam. Rent wheelchairs at the DisneyQuest Emporium or at Downtown Disney Marketplace Guest Relations ($12 per day for hand operated, plus $100 refundable credit-card deposit); electric chairs are $50 plus deposit at the Marketplace location only. Guide dogs are permitted in all areas but aren't allowed to ride several attractions. Strollers are *not* permitted.

Four attractions have height requirements: Cyberspace Mountain (51 inches), Buzz Lightyear's AstroBlaster (51 inches), Mighty Ducks Pinball Slam (48 inches), and Pirates of the Caribbean (35 inches). Little ones 2–7 can enjoy a Kids' Area on the fourth floor, where they can play smaller versions of video and other games like air hockey, basketball, and bowling.

Lost and Found is at the Guest Relations window, film can be purchased at the Emporium, and cash is available at ATMs inside the House of Blues merchandise shop not far from the DisneyQuest entrance. ✉ *West Side* ☎ *407/828–4600* 🎫 *$45 adults, $39 children 3–9, excluding sales tax* ⏲ *Sun.–Thurs. 11:30 am–10 pm, Fri. and Sat. 11:30 am–11 pm.*

Marketplace. In the Marketplace, the easternmost Downtown Disney area, you can meander along winding sidewalks and explore hidden alcoves. Children love to splash in fountains that spring from the pavement and ride the miniature train and old-time carousel ($2). Toy stores entice with creation-stations and too many treasures to comprehend. There are plenty of spots to grab a bite or sip a cappuccino along the lakefront. The Marketplace is open from 9:30 am to 11 pm weeknights and 11:30 pm Friday and Saturday.

Pleasure Island. When it was a hopping nightlife destination, this area offered a mix of bars, comedy clubs, and dance spots. But the nightclubs are long closed, and the Island has become more of a family-oriented dining and entertainment district. Raglan Road Irish Pub & Restaurant offers great food by Raglan Road's Irish celebrity chef Kevin Dundon, indoor and patio dining, live Irish music, and traditional dance performances every night. Paradiso 37 also welcomes diners indoors and alfresco. This area is part of the Downtown Disney renovation to be renamed Disney Springs by 2016, if not before.

West Side. The main attractions in the hip West Side are the House of Blues music hall, Cirque du Soleil, Splitsville Luxury Lanes, and DisneyQuest virtual indoor theme park and arcade. You can also take a ride in the Characters in Flight helium balloon tethered here ($18 ages 10 and up, $12 ages 3–9), shop in boutiques, or dine in such restaurants as the Wolfgang Puck Café and Planet Hollywood. Shops open at 9:30 or 10:30 am, and closing time is between 11 pm and 2 am. The Splitsville entertainment center offers plenty of fresh fun with 30 bowling lanes on two floors, weekend DJs, and upscale eats like filet sliders and sushi at indoor and outdoor tables. Starbucks plans to move in as part of the mega-makeover that will transform the area to Disney Springs.

SHOPPING

Why spend valuable touring time shopping in the theme parks when you can come here (for no entry fee) on your first or last day? The perfect place for one-stop souvenir shopping, Downtown Disney has dozens of stores, including the vast, hard-to-top World of Disney; the super-kid-friendly LEGO Imagination Center; and the überhip Tren-D clothing and accessory shop.

5

MARKETPLACE

Disney's Design-a-Tee. Tucked next to the long-standing Art of Disney gallery, this shop wows creative types with eight touch-screen computer stations where you can select your Hanes shirt (color, size, style), then choose from among hundreds of Disney images (contemporary and vintage) to complete your design ($22.95 children's size; $26.95 adult size). These are perfect for a family-reunion keepsake. ✉ *Marketplace.*

LEGO Imagination Center. An impressive backdrop of large, elaborate LEGO sculptures and piles of colorful LEGO bricks welcomes children and their parents who want to build toy castles, cars, and pirate ships. The center, including its covered outdoor play area, has been expanded by 3,500 square feet to accommodate more brick-building stations and merchandise. ■ **TIP→ Ask a clerk to point out the discounted merchandise shelf.** ✉ *Marketplace.*

LittleMissMatched. Girls and their moms are goofy for the candy-colored T-shirts, jammies, duffels, and miss-matched socks (a pack of three pairs of knee-high socks for $13) at this Marketplace shop. ■ **TIP→ Seasonal sales run periodically, and there's a good chance you can dress up with quirky flair for a bargain.** ✉ *Marketplace.*

Mickey's Pantry. If you're dying to get the recipe for a Disney dish you love, explore the cookbooks at Mickey's Pantry. It's hard to resist Mickey's own brand of kitchen items, and kids clamor for a bag of Mickey-shaped pasta. Look for savory spices, gourmet teas, and seasonings from the Spice & Tea Exchange. ✉ *Marketplace.*

Once Upon A Toy. Toy rooms are themed to boys with kinetic train displays and Star Wars sets and to girls with princess and fairy items. There are lots of classic games redesigned with Disney themes, like the Haunted Mansion Game of Life. You can test-drive many of the toys, and, at the Mr. Potato Head Creation Station, you can fill a box with assorted lips, noses, and even Mickey ears ($20). ✉ *Marketplace.*

Pin Traders. It's nice to know that you can visit the biggest and best location for pin collectors without paying park admission. There are so many pins lining the walls, including many hard-to-find limited-edition pins, that you could go cross-eyed. Certain days you may find

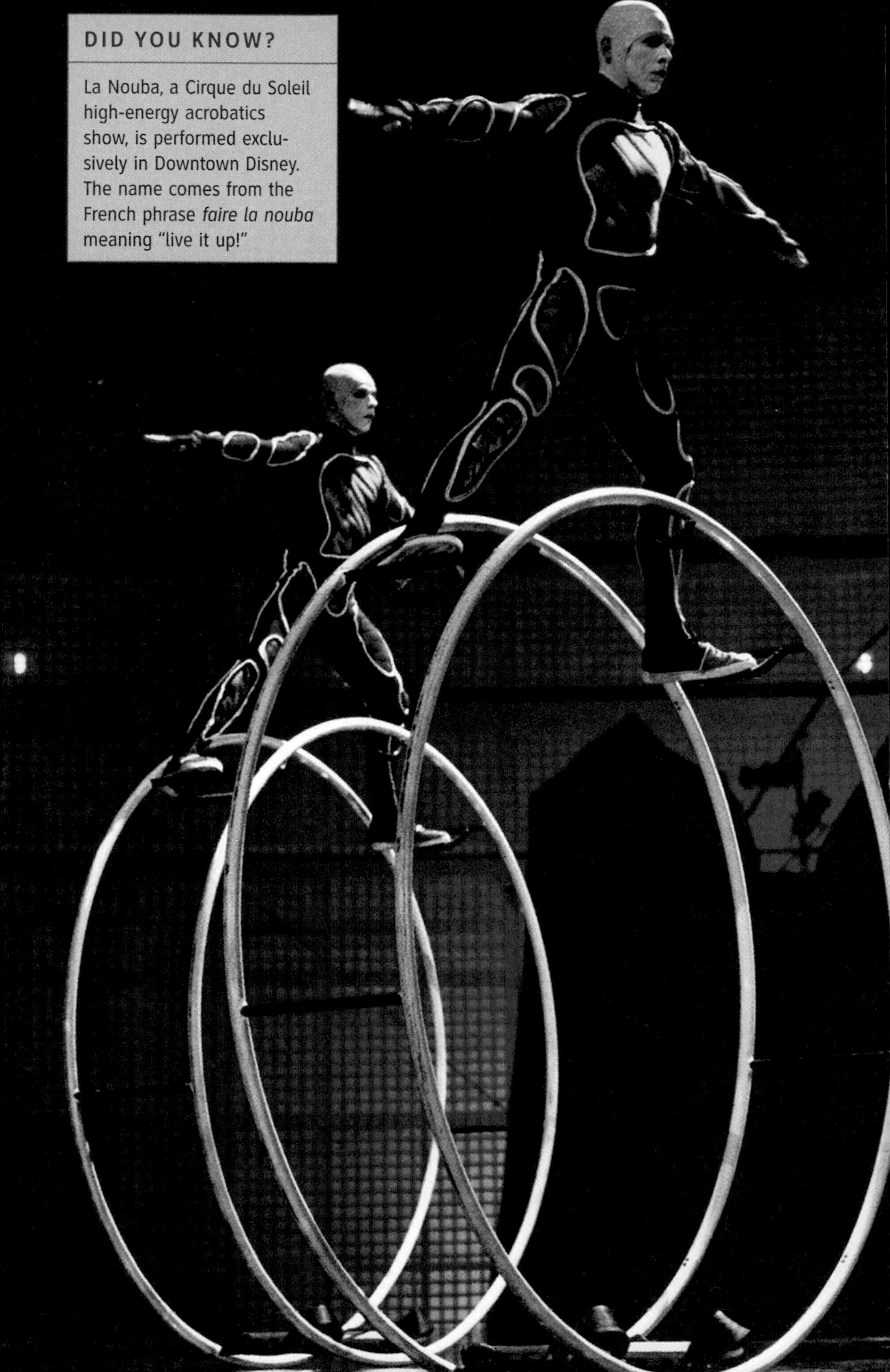

DID YOU KNOW?

La Nouba, a Cirque du Soleil high-energy acrobatics show, is performed exclusively in Downtown Disney. The name comes from the French phrase *faire la nouba* meaning "live it up!"

a pin-trading station staffed by a Disney cast member who'll help you search for that Snow White or teacup pin. ✉ *Marketplace.*

Tren-D. This Marketplace boutique has "hip" and "eclectic" written all over it. Chic sundresses with subtle Mickey-ear designs are perfect for an evening at Cirque du Soleil or dinner at House of Blues. Designer items are from Billabong, Dooney & Bourke, Harveys (The Original Seatbealtbags), and Roxy. ✉ *Marketplace.*

World of Disney. At *the* Disney superstore—with 50,000 square feet and nearly half a million Disney items—beware of sensory overload. Themed shopping areas like the princess room ($65 for that Cinderella dress or Ariel costume) help steer you to just the right toys, clothing, housewares, and more. The Bibbidi Bobbidi Boutique, similar to one at the Magic Kingdom, does princess makeovers ($55–$200). Disney media, from software to CDs, is everywhere, and there's candy for every sweet tooth. ✉ *Marketplace.*

WEST SIDE

Blink. Wet Seal owns this new denim boutique that carries a juniors line (sizes 0–13) of sundresses, distressed denim, fashion tops, and skinny jeans ($20–$40 most items). You can accessorize with jewelry starting at $5.50. ✉ *West Side.*

Hoypoloi. It's easy to lose track of time in this little oasis of fine art, handcrafted jewelry, and Zen paraphernalia. Big sellers include solid bronze frogs by Frogman; signed, digitized paintings by Alan Foxx; Josh Simpson glass-planet art pieces; and handsome menorahs and mezuzahs. ✉ *West Side.*

Orlando Harley-Davidson. Climb aboard an iconic hog for a photo op. Harley riders of all ages can buy biker vests, patches, and other popular gear. ✉ *West Side.*

NIGHTLIFE

Bongos Cuban Café. Latin rhythms provide the beat at this restaurant and bar with a pre-Castro theme owned by pop singer Gloria Estefan. Four bars are especially busy on weekends, when a Latin band kicks it up a notch with *muy caliente* music. Samba, tango, salsa, and merengue rhythms roll throughout the week. ✉ *West Side* ☎ *407/828–0999* ⏲ *Sun.–Thurs. 11–10:30, Fri. and Sat. 11 am–2 am.*

House of Blues. The restaurant serves up live blues performances and rib-sticking Mississippi Delta cooking all week long. The attached concert hall has showcased such artists as Aretha Franklin, David Byrne, Steve Miller, Willie Nelson, and Journey. Many swear by the "World Famous Gospel Brunch" each Sunday. ✉ *West Side* ☎ *407/934–2583* 🎫 *Covers vary* ⏲ *Restaurant open 11:30–11 Sun.–Thurs; 11:30–1 am Fri. and Sat. Concert times vary.*

EPCOT RESORT AREA

In the good ol' days, Americans escaped their city routines for breezy seaside boardwalks. Disney's BoardWalk is within walking distance of Epcot, across Crescent Lake from Disney's Yacht and Beach Club Resorts, and fronting a hotel of the same name. You may be drawn to its good restaurants, bars, shops, surreys, and performers. After sunset, the mood is festive. ■ **TIP→ If you're here when Epcot is ready to close, you can watch the park fireworks from the bridge that connects BoardWalk to the Yacht and Beach Club Resorts.**

NIGHTLIFE

Atlantic Dance Hall. This high-energy Top 40 dance club has a huge screen showing videos requested by the crowd. The parquet dance floor is set off by furnishings of deep blue, maroon, and gold, and the ceiling glows with gold stars and twinkling lights. Signature cocktails are in demand, and you can sip a cognac or choose from a selection of popular beers to inspire your dance floor moves. ✉ *BoardWalk* ☎ *407/939–2444* *No cover* ⏲ *Tues.–Sat. 9 pm–1:45 am.*

Big River Grille & Brewing Works. Disney World's only brewpub has intimate tables where brew masters tend to their potions. You can order an $8 sampler with five-to-seven 3-ounce pours of whatever's on tap that day, usually including Red Rocket, Southern Flyer Light Lager, Gadzooks Pilsner, and Steamboat Pale Ale. Upscale pub grub and sandwiches pair well. There's also a sidewalk café. ✉ *BoardWalk* ☎ *407/560–0253* *No cover* ⏲ *Daily 11–11.*

ESPN Club. The sports motif here is carried into every nook and cranny—the main dining area looks like a sports arena, with a basketball-court hardwood floor and a giant scoreboard that projects the day's big game. While you watch, munch on wings, nachos, and linebacker-sized burgers. There are more than 100 TVs throughout (even in the restrooms). The place is packed for big games; call ahead to see if special seating rules are in effect. ✉ *BoardWalk* ☎ *407/939–1177* *No cover* ⏲ *Daily 11:30 am–1 am.*

Jellyrolls. In this rockin', boisterous piano bar, comedians act as emcees and play dueling grand pianos nonstop. The steady stream of conventions at Disney makes this the place to catch CEOs doing the conga to Barry Manilow's "Copacabana"—if that's your idea of a good time. ✉ *BoardWalk* ☎ *407/560–8770* *$12 cover* ⏲ *Daily 7 pm–1:45 am.*

CELEBRATION

Celebration. This community, where every blade of grass in every lawn seems perfect, is as picturesque as a movie set—although, to some critics, it would be one used in *The Stepford Wives*. But Celebration is a model of American architecture and urban planning as well as a delightful place to spend a morning or afternoon.

Things appear nearly as faux as on Main Street, U.S.A, but as they unfold, you see signs of reality—and a pleasant one it is. Celebration is a real town, with its own hospital and school system. Houses and apartments spread out from the compact downtown area, which wraps around the edge of a lake. Sidewalks are built for strolling, restaurants have outdoor seating with lake views, and inviting shops beckon. After a walk around the lake, take youngsters over to the huge interactive fountain and have fun getting soaked.

The town has a year-round roster of special events and a noteworthy Sunday Farmers' Market. Starting the last Saturday in November and continuing through New Year's Eve, honest-to-goodness snow sprinkles softly down over Main Street every night on the hour from 6 to 9. ✉ *Celebration* ✣ *6 miles south of Epcot; take I–4 to Exit 64A and follow "Celebration" signs* ☎ *407/566–1200* 🌐 *www.celebrationfl.com.*

6

UNIVERSAL ORLANDO

WELCOME TO UNIVERSAL ORLANDO

TOP REASONS TO GO

★ **The Variety:** Universal Orlando is much more than just a single Hollywood-themed amusement park. It's also the fantasy-driven Islands of Adventure (IOA) theme park; the clubs and restaurants of the CityWalk entertainment complex; and the upscale, on-site Hard Rock Hotel, Portofino Bay, and Royal Pacific resorts. Nearby Wet 'n Wild water park is also affiliated with Universal.

★ **Theme-Park Powerhouse:** Neither SeaWorld nor any of Disney's four theme parks can match the collective energy at Universal Studios and Islands of Adventure. Wild rides, clever shows, constantly updated attractions, and an edgy attitude all push the envelope here.

★ **Party Central:** Throughout the year, Universal hosts festive park-wide events such as Mardi Gras, Halloween Horror Nights, Grinchmas, the Summer Concert Series, and the Rock the Universe Christian-music celebration.

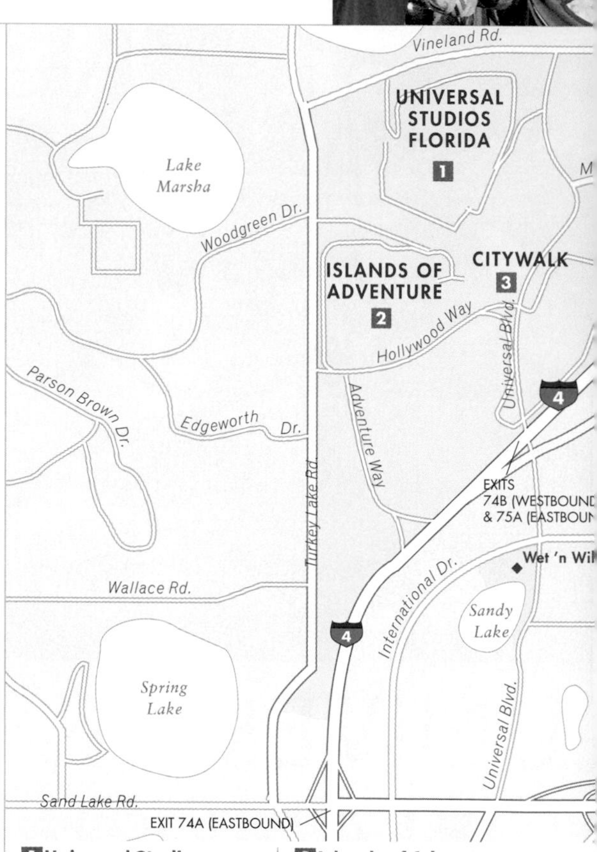

1 Universal Studios Florida. The centerpiece of Universal Orlando is a creative and quirky tribute to Hollywood past, present, and future. Overall, the collection of wild rides, quiet retreats, live shows, street characters, and clever movies (both 3-D and 4-D) are as entertaining as the motion pictures they celebrate (and they're always adding something new).

2 Islands of Adventure. Certainly the most significant addition to any Orlando theme park came when IOA introduced an entire land dedicated to Harry Potter, which, in turn, sparked a substantial surge in attendance. Also at IOA are Spider-Man, the Hulk, velociraptors, the Cat in the Hat, and dozens of other characters that give guests every reason to head to the islands.

Orlando
CENTRAL FLORIDA

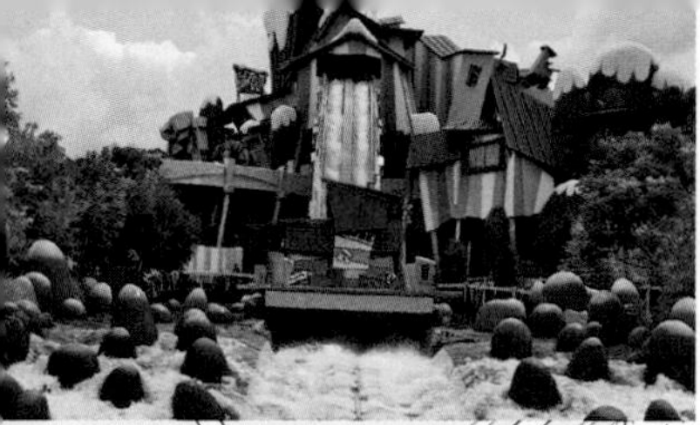

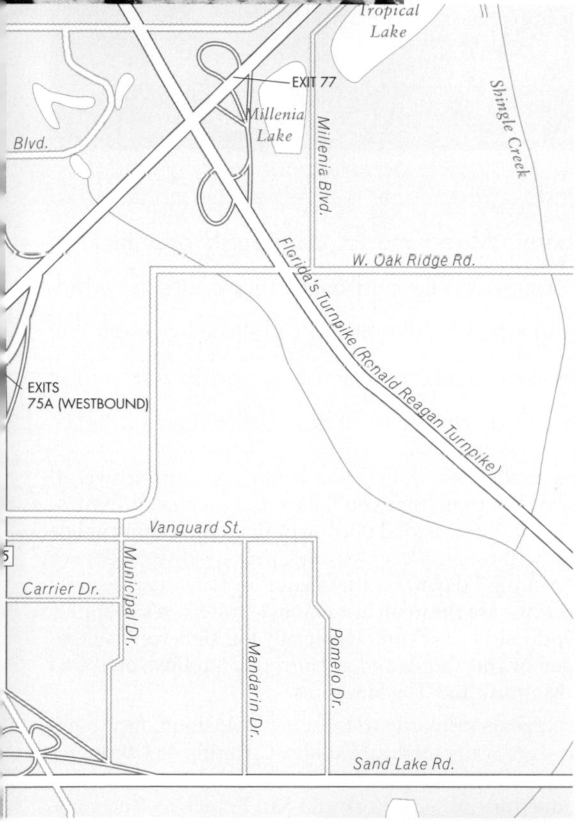

Tropical Lake
EXIT 77
Millenia Lake
Blvd.
Millenia Blvd.
Shingle Creek
W. Oak Ridge Rd.
Florida's Turnpike (Ronald Reagan Turnpike)
EXITS 75A (WESTBOUND)
Vanguard St.
Carrier Dr.
Municipal Dr.
Mandarin Dr.
Pomelo Dr.
Sand Lake Rd.

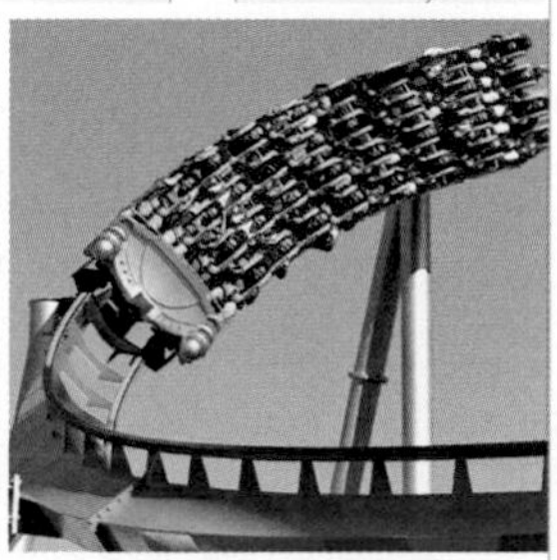

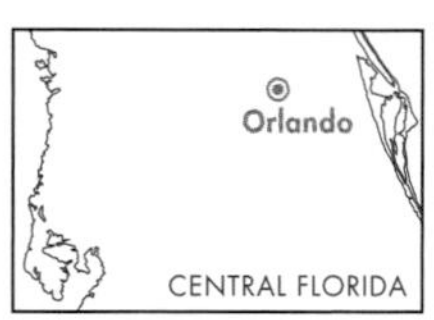

GETTING ORIENTED

Universal Orlando is tucked into a corner created by the intersection of Interstate 4 and Kirkman Road (Highway 435), midway between Downtown Orlando and the Walt Disney World Resort. Here you'll be about 15 minutes from each and just 10 minutes from SeaWorld.

3 CityWalk. Even when the parks are closed (especially when the parks are closed), locals and visitors come to this sprawling entertainment and retail complex to watch movies; dine at theme restaurants; shop for everything from cigars to surf wear; and stay up late at nightclubs celebrating the French Quarter, Jamaica, and the coolest clubs of NYC.

Universal Orlando's personality is revealed the moment you arrive on property. Mood music, cartoonish architecture, abundant eye candy, subtle and overt sound effects, whirling and whizzing rides plus a throng of fellow travelers will follow you to nearly every corner of the park. For peace and quiet, seek out a sanctuary at one of the resort hotels.

At a breathless pace, there's a chance you could visit both Universal parks in a single day, but to do that you'll have to invest in an Express Pass. Without it, you'll spend a good portion of that day waiting in line at the premium attractions. So allow two days, perhaps three; a day for each park and a "pick-up" day to return to your favorites at a leisurely pace. Which attractions are the main attractions? At IOA, it's definitely The Wizarding World of Harry Potter (especially the high-volume/low-capacity Ollivanders wand shop), and at Universal Studios you'll find long lines at The Mummy and The Simpsons.

Universal Studios appeals primarily to those who like loud, fast, high-energy attractions—generally teens and adults. Covering 444 acres, it's a rambling montage of sets, shops, and soundstages housing themed attractions, reproductions of New York and San Francisco, and some genuine moviemaking paraphernalia.

When Islands of Adventure (IOA) first opened in 1999, it took attractions to a new level. Most—from Marvel Super Hero Island and Toon Lagoon to Seuss Landing and the Lost Continent—are impressive; some even out-Disney Disney. In 2010, IOA received well-deserved worldwide attention when it opened the 20-acre Wizarding World of Harry Potter. And it's destined to receive even more coverage with the arrival of two new Potter-related areas—one atop the old Amity area at Universal Studios, and another tacked onto the Wizarding World by the Lost Continent.

PLANNING

GETTING HERE AND AROUND

East on Interstate 4 (from WDW and Tampa), exit at Universal Boulevard (75A); take a left into Universal Orlando, and follow the signs. Heading west on Interstate 4 (from Downtown or Daytona), exit at Universal Boulevard (74B), turn right, and follow Hollywood Way.

Both Universal Studios and IOA require a lot of walking—a whole lot of walking. Start off by using the parking area's moving walkways as much as possible. Arrive early at either park, and you may be able to complete a single lap that will get you to the main attractions.

OPERATING HOURS

Universal Studios and IOA are open 365 days a year, from 9 am to 7 pm, with hours as late as 10 pm in summer and at holidays. Wet 'n Wild is also open 365 days a year, weather permitting, but with widely varying hours. Usually it's open from 9 to 6—sometimes earlier, often much later, with summer hours from 9:30 am until 9 pm. Call for exact hours during holiday periods.

PARKING

Universal's two garages total 3.4 million square feet, so *note your parking space*. The cost is $16 for cars and motorcycles ($5 after 6 pm and free after 10), $22 for RVs and preferred parking. Although moving walkways get you partway, you could walk up to a half mile to reach the gates. Valet parking ($15 for up to two hours, $30 for more than two hours) is much closer.

ADMISSION

The at-the-gate, per-person, per-day rate for either Universal Studios Florida or IOA is $92 (ages 10 and up) and $86 for children (ages 3–9). Far less expensive are multiday passes.

EXPRESS PASSES

The Express Pass ranges in price from about $20 off-season to $80 in peak season. This pass gets you to the front of most lines and saves a tremendous amount of time. If you're a guest at a Universal hotel, this perk is free; your room key serves as the pass.

UNIVERSAL DINING PLAN

If you prefer to pay in advance, Quick Service meals include, for adults, one meal, two snacks, and a nonalcoholic beverage ($19). The kids' version covers a kids meal, one snack, and a nonalcoholic beverage ($13). Universal Studios locations include Mel's Drive-In, Louie's Italian, Beverly Hills Boulangerie, and the Classic Monsters Café. At Islands of

Adventure, your choices are the Comic Strip Café, Croissant Moon, the Burger Digs, and Café 4.

UNIVERSAL TIPS AND ADVICE

Arrive early. Come as early as 8 am if the parks open at 9. Seriously. Better to share them with hundreds of people than with thousands.

Visit on a weekday. Crowds are lighter, especially fall through spring, when kids are in school.

Don't forget anything in your car. Universal's parking areas are at least a half mile from park entrances, and a round-trip hike will eat up valuable time. Consider valet parking. It costs $30 for longer than two hours before 6 pm (almost twice as much as regular parking), but it puts you much closer to Universal's park entrances and just steps from CityWalk.

Know the restrictions. A few things aren't allowed in the parks: alcohol and glass containers; hard-sided coolers; soft-sided coolers larger than 8½ inches wide by 6 inches high by 6 inches deep; and coolers, suitcases, and other bags with wheels. But if your flight's leaving later, you can check your luggage at the parks (unless you just leave them in your car).

Look into the Express Pass. Jumping to the front of the line with this pass really is worth the extra cost on busy days—unless you stay at a resort hotel, in which case front-of-line access is one of the perks.

Ride solo. At Universal some rides have a Single Rider line that moves much faster than regular lines.

Get expert advice. The folks at Guest Services (aka Guest Relations) have great insight. The reps can even create a custom itinerary free of charge.

Check out Child Swap. At certain Universal attractions, one parent can enter the attraction, take a spin, and then return to take care of the baby while the other parent rides without having to wait in line again.

FOR PEOPLE WITH DISABILITIES

The *Studio Guide for Guests with Disabilities* (aka *Rider's Guide*) details attractions with special entrances and viewing areas, interpreters, Braille scripts, and assistance devices. In general, if you can transfer from your wheelchair unassisted or with the help of a friend, you can ride many attractions. Some rides have carts that accommodate manual wheelchairs, though not motorized wheelchairs or electronic convenience vehicles (ECVs).

CONTACTS

Universal ☎ *407/363–8000* 🌐 *www.universalorlando.com*

Universal Dining and Tickets ☎ *407/224–7840*

Universal (Loews Resorts) Room Reservations ☎ *877/819–7884*

Universal Vacation Packages ☎ *800/407–4275*

Wet 'n Wild ☎ *407/351–1800 or 800/992–9453* 🌐 *www.wetnwild.com*

UNIVERSAL STUDIOS

By Gary McKechnie

Inspired by the California original and opened in Orlando in 1990 (when the city assumed it would become "Hollywood East"), Universal Studios celebrates the movies. The park is a jumble of areas and attractions. But the same is true of back-lot sets at a film studio. Suspend any disbelief you might have, and just enjoy the motion-picture magic.

At Production Central large soundstages house attractions based on TV programs and films like *Shrek, Despicable Me,* and *Twister*. Because it's right near the entrance it may be the park's most crowded area.

Here you see firsthand that not every film or program based in New York is actually shot in New York. Cleverly constructed sets mean that nearly every studio can own its own Big Apple. Universal is no exception. As you explore Production Central, a collection of sparkling public buildings, well-worn neighborhoods, and back alleys are the next-best thing to Manhattan itself.

As you enter the area known as San Francisco, you're roughly one-third of the way through the park. The crowds spread out, and the pace seems to slow. You can stop to see a show starring Beetlejuice or dine at the waterfront Lombard's Seafood Grille.

There's not much shaking between San Francisco and World Expo and its two large attractions—MEN IN BLACK: Alien Attack and the Simpsons Ride. The scarcity of rides here is, however, offset by the colorful spectacle surrounding the Simpson's hometown of Springfield and the abundant attractions at Woody Woodpecker's KidZone. It matches the energy of toddlers and the under-10 crowd with diversions that include a junior-size roller coaster, a mini water park, and a chance to meet E.T. and Barney the dinosaur. In Hollywood, quiet parks and flashy Rodeo Drive really do make you think you've stepped into vintage Tinseltown.

All in all, Universal Studios fulfills its promise: to put you in the movies.

TOP ATTRACTIONS

AGES 7 AND UP

Hollywood Rip Ride Rockit. On this superwild coaster, you select the soundtrack.

MEN IN BLACK: Alien Attack. The "world's first ride-through video game" gives you a chance to compete for points by plugging away at an endless swarm of aliens.

Revenge of the Mummy. It's a jarring, rocketing indoor coaster that takes you past scary mummies and billowing balls of fire (really).

Shrek 4-D. The 3-D film with sensory effects picks up where the original film left off—and adds some creepy extras in the process.

The Simpsons Ride. It puts you in the heart of Springfield on a wild-and-crazy virtual-reality experience.

Transformers: The Ride - 3-D. Universal Studios' version of IOA's fantastic Spider-Man experience, but this one features a rough-and-tumble encounter with the mechanical stars of the film franchise.

Twister . . . Ride It Out. Okay, it's just a special-effects show—but what special effects! You experience a tornado without having to head to the root cellar.

Universal Orlando's Horror Make-Up Show. This sometimes gross, often raunchy, but always entertaining demonstration merges the best of stand-up comedy with creepy effects.

AGES 6 AND UNDER

Animal Actors on Location! It's a perfect family show starring a menagerie of animals whose unusually high IQs are surpassed only by their cuteness and cuddle-ability.

Curious George Goes to Town. The celebrated simian visits the Man with the Yellow Hat in a small-scale water park.

A Day in the Park with Barney. Young children love the big purple dinosaur and the chance to sing along.

ORIENTATION AND PLANNING

GETTING ORIENTED

On a map, the park appears neatly divided into six areas positioned around a huge lagoon. There's Production Central, which covers the entire left side of the Plaza of the Stars; New York, with street performances at 70 Delancey; San Francisco; futuristic World Expo; Woody Woodpecker's KidZone; and Hollywood.

What's tricky is that—because it's designed like a series of movie sets—there's no straightforward way to tackle the park. You'll probably make some detours and do some backtracking. To save time and shoe leather, ask theme-park hosts for itinerary suggestions and time-saving tips. Here are a few of our own suggestions.

TOURING TIPS

We highly recommend you purchase your tickets online because it gives you plenty of time to consider your many options and includes a discount. Entering Universal Studios can be overwhelming as you and thousands of others flood through the turnstiles at once. Pick up a map in the entryway to CityWalk or by the park turnstiles and spend a few minutes reviewing it. Map out a route, find show schedules, and select restaurants. If a host is nearby, ask for insider advice on what to see first.

The "right" way. Upon entering, avoid the temptation to go left toward the towering soundstages, looping the park clockwise. Instead, head right—bypassing shops, restaurants, and some crowds to primary attractions like the Simpsons Ride and MEN IN BLACK: Alien Attack.

Photo ops. Universal Studios posts signs that indicate photo spots and show how best to frame your shot.

Rendezvous. Good meeting spots include Lucy: A Tribute, near the entrance; Mel's Drive-In, midway through the park on the right; and Beetlejuice's Graveyard Revue midway through the park on the left.

UNIVERSAL STUDIOS PLANNER

PARK AMENITIES

Baby Care: There are diaper-changing stations in many of the men's and women's restrooms, and a nursing station offers comfort and privacy at the park's first-aid station near the entrance. Baby supplies (diapers, food, wipes, and so on) are available at larger stores; ask for them at the counter, though, as they're not displayed on shelves.

6

Cameras: Just inside the main entrance, On Location is a shop with nearly everything you need for a picture-perfect vacation, including batteries, chargers, disposable cameras, and digital memory cards. This is also the pickup location for the souvenir photos taken in the park by Universal's squad of photographers.

First Aid: There are two first-aid centers: one just inside the turnstiles, to the right near the Studio Audience Center, and another directly across from the entrance to Beetlejuice's Graveyard Revue.

Guest Services: Get strategy advice *before* visiting by calling Guest Services at ☎ *407/224–4233*.

Lockers: Daily rates for lockers near the park entrance are $8 for a small unit and $10 for a larger one. There are free lockers near the entrances of some high-speed attractions (such as MEN IN BLACK: Alien Attack and Revenge of the Mummy), where you can stash your stuff before your ride; they're available to you for up to 90 minutes total.

Lost People and Things: If you plan to split up, be sure everyone knows where and when to reconnect. Staffers take lost children to Guest Services near the main entrance. This is also where you might find lost personal items.

Services for People with Disabilities: Universal has made it as easy as possible for guests with disabilities to enjoy the park. It starts when you arrive in the parking garage, where you can rent wheelchairs or ECVs before making the long trek to the park entrance (though there's also chair rental at the entrance), and extends to guidebooks with icons indicating which shows feature sign-language interpreters.

Guest Services (near the entrance just outside and inside the park) is the place to pick up assisted-listening and other devices, such as clickers that trigger closed-captioning. Other services include special viewing areas for people in wheelchairs, automatic doors, well-equipped restrooms, and walking areas for service animals. Be sure to pick up the *Studio Guide for Guests with Disabilities* (aka *Rider's Guide*), which is full of details on equipment and other services.

Accessibility information is posted at each attraction. Note that although ride lines can accommodate standard wheelchairs, often you'll be ushered into a waiting area while the rest of your party goes through the line. Many shows have seating to accommodate manual wheelchairs, but, in general, you'll have to transfer from your chair to ride vehicles.

Assisted-listening devices are available for Despicable Me, *Shrek,* Disaster!, *Twister,* MEN IN BLACK, Transformers: The Ride 3-D, Terminator, Beetlejuice, Animal Actors, and A Day in the Park with Barney.

Stroller Rentals: Just inside the main entrance, there are strollers for $15 (single) and $25 (double) a day. You can also rent small kiddie cars ($18) or large ones ($28) by the day.

Wheelchair Rentals: You can rent manual wheelchairs ($12 per day) at the parking garages and inside the main entrance. Because there are limited quantities of electronic convenience vehicles (ECVs, available in the park for $50), reserve one in advance. A photo ID and a $50 deposit on a credit card are required for wheelchairs.

Where to Snack: The three restaurants on the Universal Dining Plan are **Mel's Drive-In**, a Happy Days–era soda shop–burger joint; **Louie's Italian Restaurant** (pizza, spaghetti, salads); and the **Classic Monsters Café** (pizzas, pasta, salads, rotisserie chicken). Also on the plan is **Beverly Hills Boulangerie** for breakfast croissants and pastries. Full-service restaurants include **Finnegan's Bar and Grill** (Irish pub) and **Lombard's Seafood Grille** (seafood).

Among the self-serve restaurants are **Richter's Burger Co.** (burgers, salads); **Schwab's Pharmacy** for ice cream; and the **Kid Zone Pizza Company** for pizza, chicken tenders, and other kid-geared dishes. Near the Simpson's Ride, a strip called Fast Food Boulevard includes several Springfield-inspired eateries including **Krusty Burger** (hamburgers, hot dogs), **Cletus' Chicken Shack** (chicken sandwiches, platters), the **Frying Dutchman** (fried seafood), **Luigi's Pizza, Lard Lad Donuts** (pastries, sweets), **Bumblebee Man's Taco Truck** (Mexican), and **Lisa's Teahouse of Terror** (salads, wraps, sandwiches). Want a cold one? Drop by **Moe's Tavern** for a Duff's beer or a Flaming Moe.

TOURS

VIP Tours. Universal has several VIP tours that are worthwhile if you're in a hurry, if crowds are heavy, if you're with a large group—and if you have the money to burn. The tours include extras like front-of-the-line access (that is, the right to jump the head of the line). You can also arrange for extras like priority restaurant seating, bilingual guides, gift bags, refreshments at check-in, wheelchairs and strollers, and valet parking. Prices cited here do not include sales tax or park admission, and may edge up in peak seasons (or may not be available in peak season—so call ahead).

Nonexclusive one-day tours (i.e., you'll tour with other park guests) cost $169.99 per person for one park (five hours) and $189.99 for two parks (seven hours). Then there are exclusive tours for your group only. If you're traveling with up to 10 people, consider splitting the cost of an eight-hour tour customized to your interests, which includes a sit-down lunch at the park of your choice. The eight-hour one-park exclusive price is $2,399; two parks in eight hours will cost you $2,750. What does $4,250 get you? How about a two-day tour of both parks with backstage access and discussions on park history, decorating, and landscaping? And lunch. ✉ *Universal Orlando* ☎ *407/363–8295* 🌐 *www.universalorlando.com.*

EXPLORING UNIVERSAL STUDIOS

PRODUCTION CENTRAL

Expect plenty of loud, flashy, rollicking rides that appeal to tweens, teens, and adults. Clear the turnstiles and go straight. You can use Express Pass at all attractions.

Despicable Me: Minion Mayhem. Even if you've never seen the hit animated film, it doesn't take long to fall for Gru, the Scourge of Humanity, in this wild virtual-reality chase through the movie. Two extremely funny (and cute) preshow rooms—Gru's living room and laboratory—set the stage for the 3-D ride. With help from his adopted daughters Margo, Edith, and Agnes (and ever-so-anxious minions), Gru reviews everyone to make sure they're ready to become minions. Sporting your "minion goggles," you are transformed into minions for the ride itself, which is filled with close calls and colorful characters as you pursue the ever-elusive prize: the girls' gift for their dad on the one-year anniversary of their adoption. To celebrate, the ride exits into a minion disco. Of course. The experience, with preshows, lasts about 20 minutes (about five minutes on the ride itself). Not recommended for expectant mothers or anyone with motion sickness or back, neck, or heart problems. **For people with disabilities:** Closed-captioned devices are available; wheelchair guests may remain in their chairs; all guests must be more than 40 inches tall. ■ **TIP→ Arrive early, late, or use an Express Pass. Go for the stationary seats if you think you'll suffer from motion sickness.** ✉ *Production Central* 🌐 *www.universalorlando.com* ☞ *Duration: 5 mins. Crowds: Heavy. Audience: All Ages. Height minimum: 40 inches.*

Fodor's Choice ★ **Hollywood Rip Ride Rockit.** Looking like an endless strand of spaghetti, this half-mile-plus coaster loops, twists, dives, and winds above and through Production Central. After you're locked into your seat, you'll select your personal soundtrack (choose from heavy metal, techno, country, rap, and pop) to accompany the video (starring you) that's shot as you scream your way along. And you will scream! It all starts as you're hauled nearly *17 stories straight up* before you drop nearly *17 stories straight down* before being lifted again into a towering loop and released into what seems like a never-ending series of twists, curves, sideways slings, and snap rolls at speeds up to 65 mph. By the time you return to the station, you might be woozy and a little spent—but you might spend a little more: the video with the soundtrack you selected is available for purchase. Off-season, the line never seems too bad. In season, consider using a Universal Express pass. The ride isn't suitable

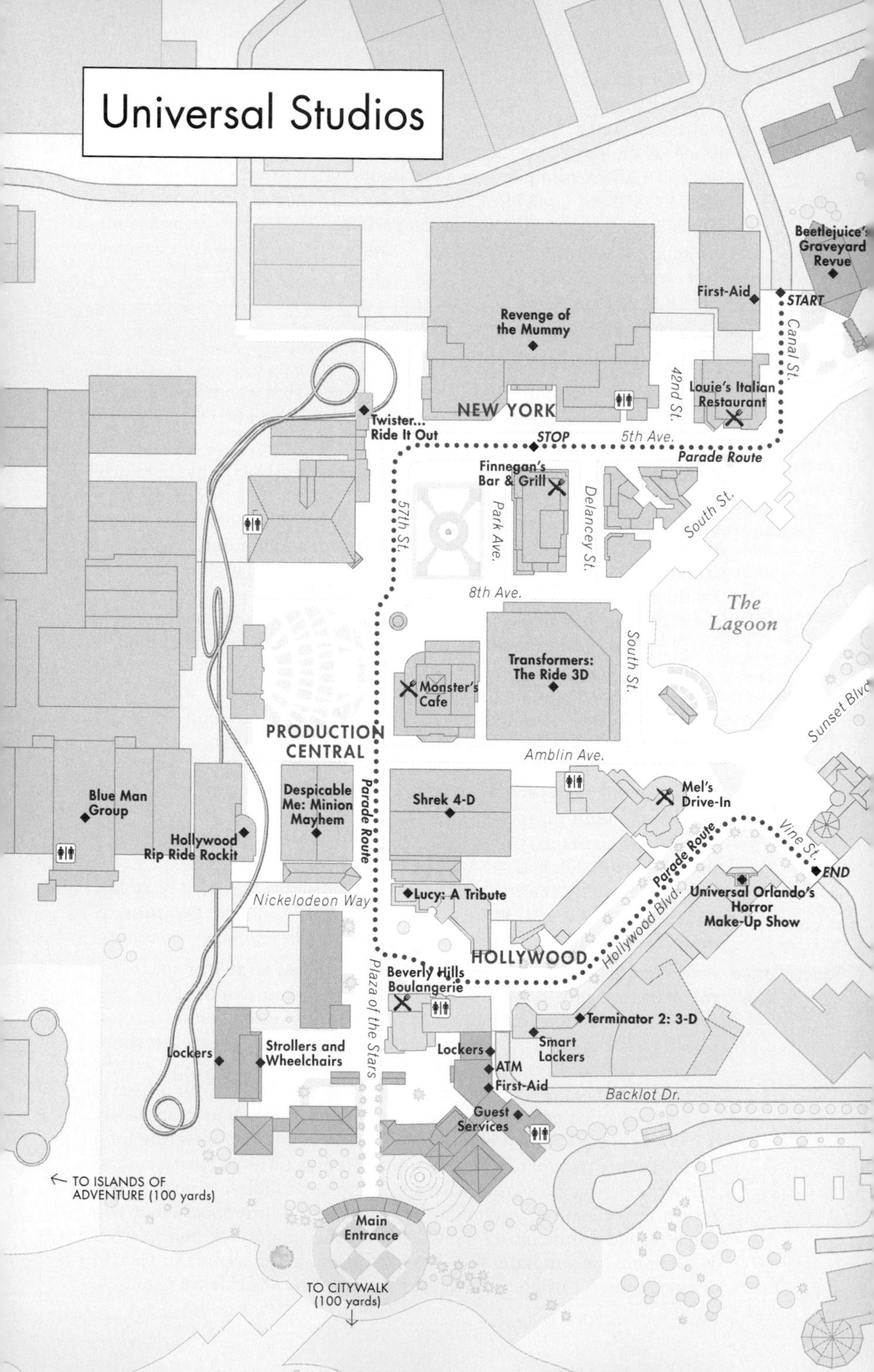

Universal Studios
Beetlejuice's Graveyard Revue
First-Aid
START
Canal St.
Revenge of the Mummy
42nd St.
Louie's Italian Restaurant
NEW YORK
Twister... Ride It Out
STOP
5th Ave.
Parade Route
Finnegan's Bar & Grill
57th St.
Park Ave.
Delancey St.
South St.
8th Ave.
The Lagoon
Transformers: The Ride 3D
South St.
Monster's Cafe
Sunset Blvd
PRODUCTION CENTRAL
Amblin Ave.
Blue Man Group
Despicable Me: Minion Mayhem
Parade Route
Shrek 4-D
Mel's Drive-In
Hollywood Rip Ride Rockit
Parade Route
Vine St.
END
Lucy: A Tribute
Universal Orlando's Horror Make-Up Show
Nickelodeon Way
Hollywood Blvd.
HOLLYWOOD
Plaza of the Stars
Beverly Hills Boulangerie
Terminator 2: 3-D
Lockers
Smart Lockers
Lockers
Strollers and Wheelchairs
ATM
First-Aid
Backlot Dr.
Guest Services
TO ISLANDS OF ADVENTURE (100 yards)
Main Entrance
TO CITYWALK (100 yards)

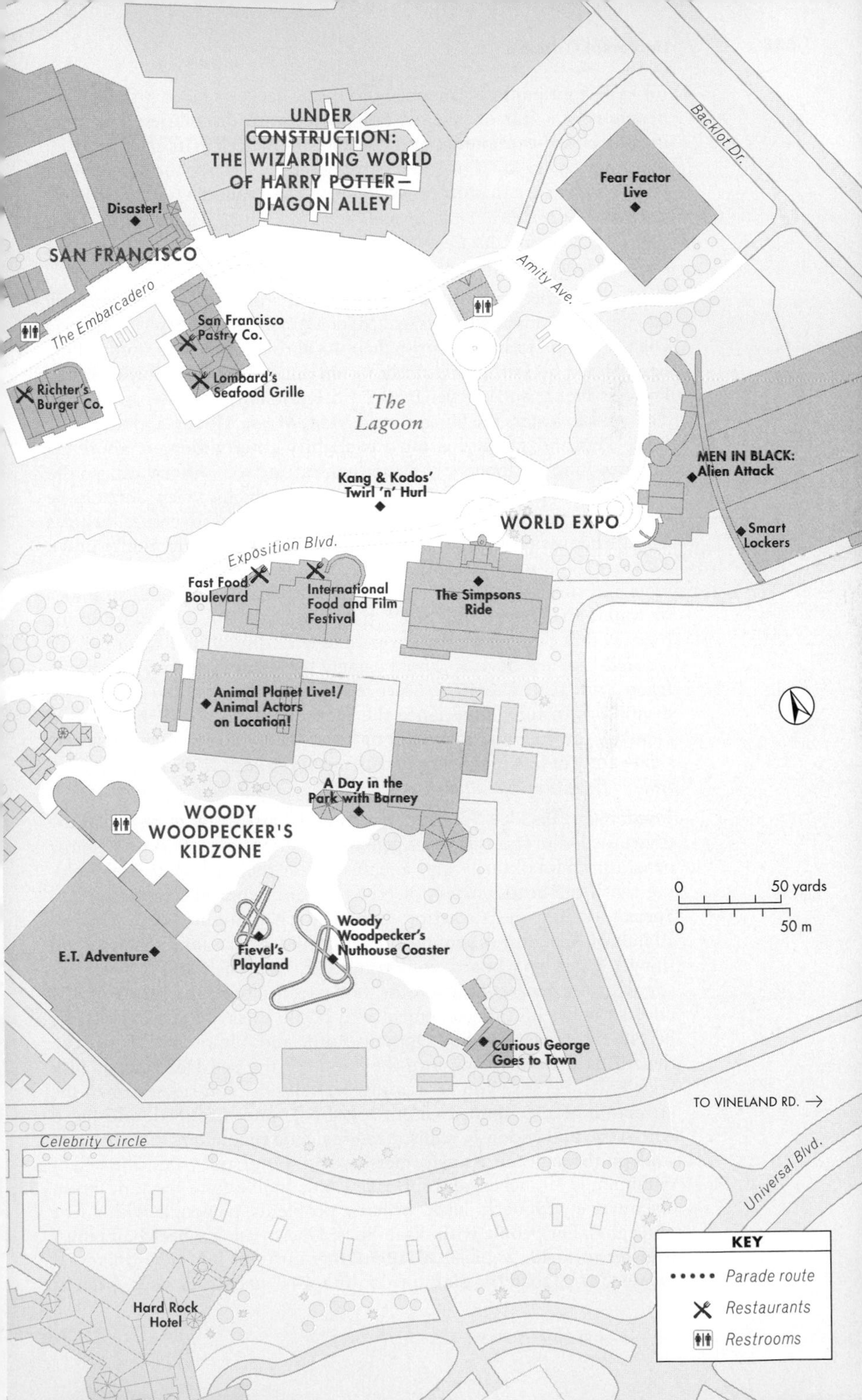

UNDER CONSTRUCTION: THE WIZARDING WORLD OF HARRY POTTER— DIAGON ALLEY
Backlot Dr.
Fear Factor Live
Disaster!
SAN FRANCISCO
Amity Ave.
The Embarcadero
San Francisco Pastry Co.
Lombard's Seafood Grille
Richter's Burger Co.
The Lagoon
MEN IN BLACK: Alien Attack
Kang & Kodos' Twirl 'n' Hurl
WORLD EXPO
Smart Lockers
Exposition Blvd.
Fast Food Boulevard
International Food and Film Festival
The Simpsons Ride
Animal Planet Live!/ Animal Actors on Location!
A Day in the Park with Barney
WOODY WOODPECKER'S KIDZONE
0
50 yards
0
50 m
E.T. Adventure
Fievel's Playland
Woody Woodpecker's Nuthouse Coaster
Curious George Goes to Town
TO VINELAND RD. →
Celebrity Circle
Universal Blvd.
Hard Rock Hotel
KEY
Parade route
Restaurants
Restrooms

for expectant mothers; anyone with neck, back, or heart problems; or people with a fear of heights. **For people with disabilities:** This does include closed-captioning, and guests using wheelchairs must transfer to a ride vehicle. **■ TIP→ Come early or late or choose the single-rider line—and be sure to stow loose items in the available lockers.** ✉ *Production Central* 🌐 *www.universalorlando.com* ☞ *Duration: 2 mins. Crowds: You Bet! Audience: Not Young Kids. Height minimum: 51 inches. Height maximum: 79 inches.*

Shrek 4-D. It's been years since the hit film premiered, but *Shrek* fans still line up at this animated 3-D saga. Mike Myers, Eddie Murphy, Cameron Diaz, and John Lithgow reprise their vocal roles as the swamp-dwelling ogre, Shrek; his faithful chatterbox companion, Donkey; Shrek's bride, Princess Fiona; and the vengeful Lord Farquaad (or rather his ghost). The pre-show stars the Gingerbread Man, Magic Mirror, and the Three Little Pigs and while this intro is slightly entertaining, at about 15 minutes long it's longer than the main attraction. Afterward, you're given OgreVision (aka 3-D) glasses through which to view Shrek as he attempts to rescue Fiona from Lord Farquaad. The adventure includes a battle between fire-breathing dragons and a pretty scary plunge down a virtual 1,000-foot waterfall—all made more intense by special theater seats and surprising sensory effects (mainly blasts of air and sprinkles of water) that create the "4-D" part. The ride can be unsettling for those with motion sickness. **For people with disabilities:** Equipped for assisted-listening devices. Those using wheelchairs don't need to transfer to a ride seat. There are, however, eight seats that allow guests with disabilities to fully experience the sensory effects. **■ TIP→ Despite a capacity for 300, you may wait up to an hour to reach the preshow. Come early or late in the day. Accepts Express Pass.** ✉ *Production Central* ☞ *Duration: 12 mins. Crowds: Heavy. Audience: All Ages.*

Transformers: The Ride 3-D. The new-in-2013 attraction is based on the toy-turned–film franchise that generated billions of dollars and is now generating a lot of thrills and screams. Inside the stark industrial building that's the headquarters of NEST (Nonbiological Extraterrestrial Species Treaty), the attraction is the Universal Studios' equivalent of Islands of Adventure's ground-breaking Spider-Man (and that's a good thing.) When you board your transport, in a flash you're in a illusory world where 60-foot screens, fast-paced action, and plenty of 3-D effects ratchet up the excitement in a battle to save the planet as the heroic Autobots (including Optimus Prime and Bumblebee) try to keep the Allspark from falling into the hands of the evil Decepticons (ask your kids). Because you're wearing 3-D glasses, you ride through the attraction getting spun, twirled, splashed, spun, dropped, and faced with some tremendously realistic intergalactic encounters that rock and roll you through the Transformers' world. Loud and wild. The height minimum is 40 inches, and this ride isn't suitable for expectant mothers; anyone with neck, back, or heart problems; or people with a fear of heights. **For people with disabilities:** Guests using wheelchairs must transfer to a ride vehicle. **■ TIP→ Come early or late, use Universal Express, or choose the single-rider line.** ✉ *Universal Studios* 🌐 *www.*

DID YOU KNOW?

On Production Central's Hollywood Rip Ride Rockit, you choose the soundtrack for your roller-coaster ride from songs within several genres of music. After the whole experience, you can buy a video of your ride with the music you selected.

universalorlando.com ☞ Duration: 5 mins. Crowds: You Bet! Audience: Not Young Kids.

NEED A BREAK?

In the heart of Production Central, the self-serve Classic Monsters Cafe resembles a mad scientist's lab. It offers wood-fired-oven pizzas, pastas, chef salads, four-cheese ravioli, and rotisserie chicken. Frankenstein's monster and other characters from vintage Universal horror films may make the rounds as you eat.

WHAT'S NEW

Whether it's a Wizarding World in 2010, Despicable Me in 2012, or a real-life version of the Simpson's Springfield in 2013, Universal rarely takes a break from creating new lands and attractions. In 2013 the resort opened Transformers: The Ride 3-D, and in early 2014 was well on its way with a new hotel, Cabana Bay. Also, Harry Potter's fantasy world was such a success that two new areas were developed—one atop the old Amity section at Universal Studios and the other next to the Lost Continent at Islands of Adventure. You might feel like you're seeing a whole new park!

NEW YORK

Universal has gone all out to re-create New York's skyscrapers, commercial districts, ethnic neighborhoods, and back alleys—right down to the cracked concrete. Hidden within these structures are restaurants, arcades, gift shops, and key attractions. And, although they're from Chicago, the Blues Brothers drive from the Second City to New York City in their Bluesmobile for free performances at 70 Delancey. Here you can use Express Pass at Revenge of the Mummy and Twister.

Revenge of the Mummy. Action, adventure, and horror are in abundance in this $40 million spine-tingling thrill ride that combines roller-coaster technology, pyrotechnics, and some super-scary skeletal warriors. The entrance is set up like the tomb of a pharaoh. You walk by Egyptian artifacts and through winding catacombs before boarding a multi-passenger coaster car and zipping into the heart of a haunted labyrinth. "Dead" ahead, you're given the chance to sell your soul for safety and riches. Regardless of your decision, a guardian mummy sends you hurtling through underground passageways and Egyptian burial chambers where highlights include escaping a beetle-infested burial chamber, zipping backwards through fog, and then racing full-tilt into the mummified mouth of Imhotep. Take note: you feel the 1.5 g-forces when flying uphill, and much of the ride takes place in the dark—so it's pretty intense. Not good for expectant mothers or anyone with neck, back, or heart problems. **For people with disabilities:** Guests using wheelchairs must transfer to a ride vehicle. **■TIP→ Cut down on wait times: head for the single-rider line. Otherwise, use Express Pass or come early or late. Free lockers are available for loose items. Use them.** ✉ *New York* 🌐 *www.universalorlando.com ☞ Duration: 3 mins. Crowds: Heavy. Audience: Not Young Kids. Height minimum: 48 inches.*

Twister. Ride It Out. After you proceed through a slow-moving line and hear a so-so discussion about the destructive force of tornadoes, you arrive in a standing-room theater—*and this is where the magic happens.*

As you face a pastoral town setting, a make-believe windstorm builds in the distance and soon becomes an ominous five-story-high funnel cloud that weaves in from the background until it commands center stage. Amid the cacophony created by 110 decibels of wind noise, crackling electrical lines, and shattered windows, a truck, signs, car, and a cow earn frequent-flyer points by sailing across the stage. Then when the roof starts to blow off, your instinct is to head for the root cellar. Don't. Stay to marvel at the work of the special-effects masters who put this together, only to have it torn apart every few minutes. **For people with disabilities:** The theater is wheelchair accessible. Strong sound effects and assisted-listening devices make it possible for people with vision impairments to enjoy the show. ■ **TIP→ Use a Universal Express Pass or come first thing in the morning or at closing.** ✉ *New York* 🌐 *www.universalorlando.com* ☞ *Duration: 3 mins. Crowds: Heavy. Audience: Not Young Kids.*

SAN FRANCISCO

This area celebrates the West Coast with the wharves and warehouses of San Francisco's Embarcadero and Fisherman's Wharf districts. *Use your Express Pass at both attractions.*

6

Beetlejuice's Graveyard Revue. Whew! This is *some* show. A Transylvanian castle is the backdrop for Beetlejuice, your ghost host who warms you up with snappy lines, rude remarks, and a heapin' helpin' of sarcasm—a theme that lasts throughout the performance. He then introduces the stars: Frankenstein's monster, his bride, the Wolfman, and Dracula. The creatures doff their traditional garb for glitzy, hip threads to sing hits by such diverse artists as Gloria Gaynor, AC/DC, Van Halen, and Springsteen, albeit with a few changes (e.g., "Jesse's Girl" would become "Frankie's Girl"). Ghoul Girl cheerleaders, Hip and Hop, up the weirdness factor and add sex appeal. This is the only place you'll see Frankenstein's monster pretending to play an electric guitar and shouting "Are you ready to rock, Orlando?" *We are not kidding.* Wayne Brady and Backstreet Boy Joey Fatone were once part of the cast. *We are still not kidding.* **For people with disabilities:** The theater is wheelchair accessible and equipped for assisted-listening devices. Some shows feature a sign language interpreter. ■ **TIP→ You can use Express Pass, but the amphitheater's high capacity means little chance of waiting.** ✉ *San Francisco* 🌐 *www.universalorlando.com* ☞ *Duration: 25 mins. Crowds: Moderate–Heavy. Audience: Not Young Kids.*

NEED A BREAK?

Richter's Burger Co. (across from Beetlejuice) lets you drop in and dress up your own burger or grilled-chicken sandwich. It's pretty quick, pretty convenient, and there are seats inside and out.

Disaster!. Packed with clever comedy, manic energy, tongue-in-cheek comedy, and some clever effects, here's how this two-part story unfolds: Since all of the movie's stars are in rehab, a harried production assistant must cast park guests for various roles in another blockbuster disaster film—*Mutha Earth*. After this guest-star cast is selected, everyone moves to the special-effects set where disaster-movie producer Frank Kincaid (Christopher Walken) magically appears and interacts with the production assistant to explain his vision of a blockbuster film. From here, selected "guest stars" (park guests) are put through some stunt-filled paces before everyone boards San Francisco–style trams for a short ride through a tunnel. When the trams park at a subway station, a two-minute, 8.3–Richter-scale tremor begins; there are collapsing ceilings, blackouts, explosions, fire, and a massive flood that comes at you from every angle—*and you'd swear it was real!* At the end of the experience you get to see the hilarious "finished" film on the tram's monitors: the *Mutha Earth* trailer starring Dwayne "The Rock" Johnson as a heroic park ranger and your fellow guests as his co-stars. This ride isn't suitable for pregnant women or guests with heart, back, neck, or motion-sickness problems. **For people with disabilities:** If you use a standard-size wheelchair or can transfer to a ride vehicle, you can board this attraction. Service animals should not ride, sign language interpreters are available at some shows. **■TIP→ Use Express Pass; otherwise, come early or late.** ✉ *San Francisco* 🌐 *www.universalorlando.com* ☞ *Duration: 20 mins. Crowds: Heavy. Audience: Not Young Kids. Height minimum: 40 inches to ride without an adult.*

WORLD EXPO

At the far end of the park is a futuristic set of buildings containing a few of Universal Studios' most popular attractions, MEN IN BLACK: Alien Attack, the Simpsons Ride, and the new Kang & Kodos' Twirl 'n' Hurl, which offer fast admission with Express Pass.

Kang & Kodos' Twirl 'n' Hurl. Inspired by the intergalactic creatures that make an occasional appearance in Springfield, here's a new spin on an old favorite. About a dozen flying saucers encircle a towering statue of Kang (or Kodos), the one-eyed, fang-toothed, octopus-tentacled alien. Once you've climbed into your saucer the ride begins when, as at Seuss Landing's One Fish, Two Fish, Red Fish, Blue Fish, the spinning ride takes flight and whirls you and your co-pilot around Kang (or Kodos). Kids who love the opportunity to take the controls raise and lower the craft in hopes of avoiding the jets of water shot from surrounding poles. A pleasing, fun, low-thrill attraction that kids enjoy. ✉ *Universal Studios* 🌐 *www.universalorlando.com* ☞ *Duration: 3 mins. Crowds: Light–Medium. Audience: Young Kids and Up.*

MEN IN BLACK: Alien Attack. The preshow of "the world's first ride-through video game" provides the storyline: To earn membership in MIB you must round up aliens that escaped when their shuttle crashed on Earth. On board your vehicle with a few others, you enter the backstreets of a city where aliens pop out from windows, trash cans, and doorways. Fire at them with that laser gun mounted to your futuristic car, and since there's no limit to the number of shots you can take, blast away. Even though the gun's red laser dot is just a pinpoint, an onboard scoreboard helps you keep track of what you've hit. Aliens fire back at you, and if they score a hit it'll cause your car to spin out of control. Depending on the collective score, your ride will wrap up with one of 35 endings, ranging from a hero's welcome to a loser's farewell. All in all, it's pretty exciting. The spinning nature of the cars may cause dizziness, so use caution if you're prone to motion sickness. Don't ride if you have heart, back, or neck problems. **For people**

UNIVERSAL OPENS DIAGON ALLEY

Impressed by the success of the Wizarding World of Harry Potter's Hogsmeade Village at Islands of Adventure, Universal Studios saw an opportunity. Razing the midway and tired JAWS attraction in the Amity Section, it's created an entire land called Diagon Alley.

Scheduled to premiere in June 2014, like its IOA counterpart this area will feature a variety of shops and experiences centered around a single major attraction, Harry Potter and the Escape from Gringotts. The goblin-managed bank is the focal point of this land, and when you enter its hallowed halls, the ride itself is similar to the sensory overload you feel at attractions like Harry's Forbidden Journey and the Amazing Adventures of Spider-Man, as you spin, twist, and twirl through a blend of fast-moving virtual effects (and encounter Harry, Ron, and Hermione along the way).

Throughout the district are shops familiar to anyone who knows of Harry's adventures. There is Universal Studios' version of Ollivanders wand shop as well as Weasleys' Wizard Wheezes (magical jokes and novelty items), the Magical Menagerie (all creatures furry, feathered, or scaly), Madam Malkin's Robes for All Occasions (wizard wear), as well as Wiseacre's Wizarding Equipment and Quality Quidditch Supplies. For practitioners of the Dark Arts, venture down Knockturn Alley and step inside Borgin and Burkes.

J. K. Rowling's vivid descriptions helped paint a picture for designers and they've created spot-on re-creations from the pages of the Potter series. You'll see this at the Leaky Cauldron, the land's signature restaurant, and at Florean Fortescue's Ice-Cream Parlour. And when you're ready to head to Hogwarts, make sure you have a park-to-park pass before stepping aboard the new Hogwarts Express—now departing to Islands of Adventure from Platform 9¾.

6

with disabilities: Equipped for assisted-listening devices. Guests using wheelchairs must transfer to a ride vehicle. ■ **TIP→ In summer, waits are up to an hour. Come first thing or save time by splitting up and using the shorter single-riders line or by using Express Pass.** ✉ *World Expo* 🌐 *www.universalorlando.com* ☞ *Duration: 4½ mins. Crowds: Heavy. Audience: Not Young Kids. Height minimum: 42 inches to ride without an adult.*

Fodor's Choice ★ **The Simpsons Ride.** As you enter this ride through Krusty the Clown's gaping mouth, and then receive a video greeting by citizens of Springfield, police chief Clancy Wiggum reminds you that if you must get sick, do it in your hat—and thus the tone is set for your arrival in one of television's most popular animated communities. The preshow explains that Krusty has expanded his empire to include a theme park, which his disgruntled former sidekick, Sideshow Bob, plans to sabotage. After a fairly tame start, your virtual soars through virtual Springfield, plunging toward familiar businesses and buildings, and narrowly escaping disaster as Sideshow Bob tears up the tracks and sends you racing through wild scenes in a variety of locations such as Disney, SeaWorld—and hell. Several times you're saved by the split-second timing of an unexpected hero. If you have even a scintilla of motion sickness, this one will throw you for a colorful, cartoonish loop. Guests who are pregnant or who have heart, back, or neck problems shouldn't ride. **For people with disabilities:** Guests in wheelchairs must transfer to a ride vehicle. ■ **TIP→ Use Express Pass.** ✉ *World Expo* 🌐 *www.universalorlando.com* ☞ *Duration: 6 mins. Crowds: Heavy. Audience: Not Young Kids. Must be at least 40 inches to ride; adults must accompany kids between 40 and 48 inches.*

WOODY WOODPECKER'S KIDZONE

With its colorful compilation of rides, shows, and play areas, this entire section caters to preschoolers. It's a pint-size Promised Land, where kids can try out a roller coaster and get sprayed, splashed, and soaked in a water-park area. It's also a great place for parents, since it gives them a needed break after nearly circling the park. All shows and attractions except Curious George and Fievel accept Universal Express Pass.

Animal Actors on Location!. Animal shows are usually fun—and this one is better than most thanks to an arkful of animal stars. The tricks (or *behaviors*) they perform are mostly audience-participation segments, which makes it entertaining for young and old alike. You'll see birds, roosters, pigs, parrots, otters, ducks, dogs, and a skunk—and that's in just the first *two minutes*. Dogs demonstrate a range of thespian actions you've seen performed in movies and on television; the parrot from *Evan Almighty* (and *Ace Ventura, Pet Detective*) has a knack for plucking cash from the outstretched hand of an audience member; and an orangutan seems the simian equivalent of Jerry Lewis as it plays opposite a straight-man trainer. The lineup of animals may vary, but the variety of scenes makes it like seeing several shows in one. Best of all, these are some of the cutest actors ever to hit the stage. **For people with disabilities:** The theater is equipped for assisted-listening devices and is wheelchair accessible. Some shows include a sign language interpreter. ■ **TIP→ Come early for a good seat.** ✉ *Woody Woodpecker's KidZone* 🌐 *www.universalorlando.com* ☞ *Duration: 20 mins. Crowds: Moderate–Heavy. Audience: All Ages.*

Curious George Goes to Town. The celebrated simian visits the Man with the Yellow Hat in a no-line, no-waiting, small-scale water park. The main town square has brightly colored building facades, and the plaza is an interactive aqua playground that adults avoid but kids are drawn to like fish to water. Yes, there's water, water everywhere, especially atop the clock tower, which periodically dumps a mighty 500 gallons down a roof and straight onto a screaming herd of preschoolers. Kids love the levers, valves, pumps, and hoses that gush at the rate of 200 gallons per minute, letting them get sprayed, spritzed, splashed, and splattered. At the head of the square, footprints lead to a dry play area, with a rope climb and a ball cage where youngsters can frolic among thousands of foam balls. You can get into the act, sit it out on nearby benches, or take a few minutes to buy souvenir towels to dry off your waterlogged kids. **For people with disabilities:** Most of this attraction is barrier-free. ■ **TIP→ Crowds are heavy midmorning: come in late afternoon or early evening. Kids will get drenched; stash a bathing suit or**

Save the planet from interstellar invaders in World Expo's interactive MEN IN BLACK: Alien Attack. Zap aliens in city streets and compete with other guests to score points.

change of clothing in a nearby locker. ✉ *Woody Woodpecker's KidZone* 🌐 *www.universalorlando.com* ☞ *Duration: Up to You. Crowds: Moderate–Heavy. Audience: Young Kids.*

A Day in the Park with Barney. If your kids can't get enough of the big purple dinosaur, here he is again! A fairly long preshow features a goofy, kid-friendly emcee before you and your preschoolers enter a pleasant theater-in-the-round filled with brilliantly colored trees, clouds, and stars. Within minutes, the kids will cheer like baby boomers at a McCartney concert as their beloved TV playmate and Baby Bop dance and sing though clap-along, sing-along monster classics including "Mr. Knickerbocker," "If You're Happy and You Know It," and (of course) "I Love You." Following the very pleasing and thoughtful show and a chance to meet Barney up close, you exit to an elaborate play area with hands-on activities—a water harp, wood-pipe xylophone, and musical rocks—that propel the already excited kids to even greater heights. **For people with disabilities:** The theater is equipped for assisted-listening devices and is wheelchair accessible. ■ **TIP→ Arrive 10–15 minutes early for a good seat—up close and in the center.** ✉ *Woody Woodpecker's KidZone* 🌐 *www.universalorlando.com* ☞ *Duration: 20 mins. Crowds: Light. Audience: Young Kids.*

E.T. Adventure. This well-meaning, circa 1990, ride is looking (and even smelling) a little tired, although you may still get a kick out of the take on Steven Spielberg's *E.T.* Once Spielberg himself advises you that it's your mission to help E.T. return to his planet, you board a bicycle mounted on a movable platform and fly 3 million light years from Earth, past a squadron of policemen and FBI agents to reach E.T.'s home.

UNIVERSAL STUDIOS GROWN-UP TOUR

A stroll through Universal Studios will make you feel as if you've covered 3,000 miles in just a few hours. Hollywood is just a short walk from New York City; San Francisco a stone's throw from the fictional Middle America of Springfield. The genius here is in the details, so take your time and notice the secondhand items in the windows of New York shops, for instance, or the cable-car tracks running through San Francisco.

SOUTH SIDE

Upon entering, don't head straight to Production Central; instead, turn right—onto Rodeo Drive. In a few steps you're in the heart of **Hollywood.** Although you'll probably drop into attractions such as Terminator 2: 3-D and Universal Orlando's Horror Make-Up Show, you can also have a soda at Schwab's or a hot dog at Mel's. Not even folks in the real Hollywood can do this. Notice the lovely Garden of Allah bungalows that look as if they were actually moved from Tinseltown.

Next stop: Springfield. Although **The Simpsons Ride** is a thrill, so is the amazing pop art that sets the stage for it. The facade is decorated like a carnival, with games of chance bordering the towering face of Krusty the Clown. Watch for the kiosk that sells Squishees ("America's favorite icy goo") and take your time along Fast Food Boulevard where you'll have plenty of food ops—and photo ops—including Lard Lad (of donut fame), Moe's Tavern, and Bumblebee Man's taco truck. Really.

NORTH SIDE

San Francisco comes into view with cobblestone streets, redbrick buildings, and a waterfront inspired by Fisherman's Wharf.

New York captures nearly every borough. There are narrow alleys, fire escapes, a Chinese laundry, pawnshops, and secondhand stores. Round a corner and you'll see the Guggenheim Museum, newspaper offices, Italian restaurants, and Irish pubs. It's an amazing assemblage of styles, with clever signage, props, and effects.

Production Central takes you into the world of soundstages, movies, and TV shows. Look for the posters for the movies and albums being released by the stars of *Shrek* and other witty details.

At Universal Studios, the fun isn't just about the rides.

Here colorful characters climb on vines, play xylophones, and swing on branches in what looks like an alien Burning Man festival. Listen very closely for the payoff: Having given your name to a host at the start of the ride, E.T. is supposed to bid you a personalized good-bye. This ride isn't suitable for guests with heart, back, neck, or motion-sickness problems. **For people with disabilities:** Guests with mobility issues must be in a standard-size wheelchair or transfer to a ride vehicle. Service animals aren't permitted. There's some sudden tilting and accelerating, but those for whom these movements are a concern can ride in E.T.'s orbs (spaceships) instead of the flying bicycles. **■ TIP→ Use Universal Express Pass or come early.** ✉ *Woody Woodpecker's KidZone* 🌐 *www.*

universalorlando.com ☞ Duration: 5 mins. Crowds: Moderate–Heavy. Audience: All Ages. Minimum height: 34 inches.

Fievel's Playland. Based on the Spielberg animated film *An American Tail,* this playground features larger-than-life props and sets designed to make everyone feel mouse-size. An ingenious collection of massive boots, cans, and other ordinary objects disguise tunnel slides, water play areas, ball crawls, and a gigantic net-climb equipped with tubes, ladders, and rope bridges. A harmonica slide plays music when you slide along the openings, and a 200-foot waterslide gives kids (and a parent if so desired) a chance to swoop down in Fievel's signature sardine can. It should keep the kids entertained for hours. The downside? You might have to build one of these for your backyard when you get home. **For people with disabilities:** Unfortunately, this ride isn't fully accessible to people using wheelchairs, although an elevator can transport wheelchairs to the top of the waterslide. ■ **TIP→ On hot days, come after supper to avoid waits for the waterslide. Kids will get drenched; stash a bathing suit or change of clothing in a nearby locker.** ✉ *Woody Woodpecker's KidZone* 🌐 *www.universalorlando.com ☞ Duration: Up to You. Crowds: Light–Moderate. Audience: Young Kids.*

Woody Woodpecker's Nuthouse Coaster. Unlike the maniacal coasters that put you through zero-g rolls and inversions, this is a low-speed, mild-thrill version (top speed 22 mph) that makes it a safe bet for younger kids (who must be at least 36 inches tall) and action-phobic adults. It races (a relative term) through a structure that looks like a gadget-filled factory; the cars are shipping crates—some labeled "mixed nuts," others "salted nuts," and some tagged "certifiably nuts." Children generally love this low-level introduction to thrill rides (which is duplicated at Flight of the Hippogriff at The Wizarding World of Harry Potter). **For people with disabilities:** Guests using wheelchairs must transfer to a ride vehicle. ■ **TIP→ Use Express Pass and/or come at park closing, when most little ones have gone home.** ✉ *Woody Woodpecker's KidZone* 🌐 *www.universalorlando.com ☞ Duration: 1½ mins. Crowds: Moderate–Heavy. Audience: Young Kids.*

HOLLYWOOD

The quintessential tribute to the golden age of the silver screen, this area to the right of the park entrance celebrates icons like the Brown Derby, Schwab's Pharmacy, and art deco Hollywood. There are only a few attractions here, and all except Lucy accept Universal Express Pass.

Lucy: A Tribute. If you can't help smiling when you recall Lucy Ricardo stomping grapes, practicing ballet, gobbling chocolates, or wailing when Ricky won't let her be in the show, then a visit to this mini-museum and major gift shop will be a pleasant, nostalgic visit. The low-key attraction pays tribute to Lucille Ball through scripts, props, costumes, awards, and clips from the comedian's estate, and a challenging trivia quiz game on computer monitors has you trying to get Lucy, Ricky, Fred, and Ethel across the country to Hollywood. It's a fun place to take a break and spend time with one of the wackiest women of television, and the adjacent gift shop has Lucy souvenirs galore. **For people with disabilities:** This attraction is wheelchair accessible; the

UNIVERSAL STUDIOS

NAME	Height Req.	Type of Entertainment	Duration	Crowds	Audience	Tips
Hollywood						
Lucy: A Tribute	n/a	Walk-Through	15 mins.	Light	Adults	Save this for a hot afternoon or for on your way out.
Terminator 2 3-D	n/a	3-D Film/ Simulator Exp.	21 mins.	Heavy	All but Young Kids	Come first thing in the morning or use Express Pass.
★ Universal Orlando's Horror Make-Up Show	n/a	Show	25 mins.	Moderate	All but Young Kids	Come in the afternoon or evening. Young children may be frightened; older children eat up the blood-and-guts comedy.
Production Central						
★ Hollywood Rip Ride Rockit!	At least 51"	Thrill Ride	2 mins.	You Bet!	All but Young Kids	Come early, late, or use a Express Pass. Be patient.
Shrek 4-D	n/a	3-D Film	12 mins.	Heavy	All Ages	Come early or late, or use Express Pass.
New York						
Revenge of the Mummy	At least 48"	Thrill Ride	3 mins.	Heavy	All but Young Kids	Use Express Pass, or come first thing in the morning.
Twister . . . Ride It Out	n/a	Show/ Simulator Exp.	3 mins.	Heavy	All but Young Kids	Come first thing in morning or at closing. This "ride" involves standing and watching the action unfold.
San Francisco/Amity						
Beetlejuice's Graveyard Revue	n/a	Show	25 mins.	Light to Moderate	All but Young Kids	You can use Express Pass here, but there's really no need as there's little chance of a wait.

Disaster!	n/a	Thrill Ride	20 mins.	Heavy	All but Young Kids	Come early, before closing, or use Universal Express Pass. This is loud.
TRANSFORMERS	40″	3-D Thrill Ride	5 mins.	Heavy	All but Young Kids	No Express Pass. Come early.
Woody Woodpecker's KidZone						
A Day in the Park with Barney	n/a	Show	20 mins.	Light	Young Kids	Arrive 10–15 mins. early on crowded days for a good seat—up close and in the center. Can use Express Pass.
Animal Actors on Location!	n/a	Show	20 mins.	Moderate to Heavy	All Ages	Stadium seating, but come early for a good seat. Express Pass accepted.
Curious George Goes to Town	n/a	Playground with Water	Up to you	Moderate	Young Kids	Come in late afternoon or early evening. Bring a towel.
E.T. Adventure	At least 34″	Thrill Ride for Kids	5 mins.	Moderate to Heavy	All Ages	Come early morning or use Express Pass.
Fievel's Playland	n/a	Playground with Water	Up to you	Light to Moderate	Young Kids	Generally light crowds, but there are waits for the waterslide. On hot days come late.
Woody Woodpecker's Nuthouse Coaster	At least 36″	Thrill Ride for Kids	1½ mins.	Moderate to Heavy	Young Kids	Come at park closing, when most little ones have gone home. Try Express Pass.
World Expo						
MEN IN BLACK: Alien Attack	At least 42″	Thrill Ride	4½ mins.	Heavy	All but Young Kids	Solo riders can take a faster line, so split up. This ride spins. Use Express Pass.
★ The Simpsons Ride	40″	Thrill Ride/ Simulator Exp.	6 mins.	Heavy	All but Young Kids	Use Express Pass.

★ Fodor's Choice

TV-show excerpts shown on overhead screens aren't closed-captioned. ■ **TIP→ Save this for your way out or a hot afternoon.** ✉ *Hollywood* 🌐 *www.universalorlando.com* ☞ *Duration: 15 mins. Crowds: Light. Audience: Adults.*

Terminator 2: 3-D. Entering the headquarters of the futuristic consortium Cyberdyne, a "community relations and media control" hostess greets your group and introduces the latest line of law-enforcing robots, but a slight snafu foreshadows what's ahead. After the preshow you enter a theater to watch a James Cameron–directed 12-minute 3-D movie. The cyber-patrol goes haywire, and the excitement escalates courtesy of Schwarzenegger, icy fog, live actors, gunfights, and a chilling finale. Overall, it's loud and fast-paced. Though some kids may be scared enough to require parental counseling, other visitors may feel that the franchise is a bit dated and the 3-D effects are few and far between. See for yourself and decide where you'd place it on the thrill-o-meter. **For people with disabilities:** The theater is wheelchair accessible and offers closed-captioning as well as specialized sound through assisted-listening devices. ■ **TIP→ If it's your first visit, skip this. Express Pass accepted.** ✉ *Hollywood* 🌐 *www.universalorlando.com* ☞ *Duration: 21 mins. Crowds: Heavy. Audience: Not Young Kids.*

NEED A BREAK?

In the heart of Hollywood, Schwab's Pharmacy is a re-creation of the legendary drugstore where—studio publicists claim—Lana Turner was discovered. What you'll discover is a quick stop where you can order soda-fountain treats as well as hand-carved turkey and ham sandwiches.

Fodor's Choice ★

Universal Orlando's Horror Make-Up Show. This funny, highly entertaining show begins in an intriguingly creepy preshow area where masks, props, and rubber skeletons from classic and contemporary horror films and tributes to great make-up artists like Lon Chaney, Rick Baker, and Jack Pierce make a great backdrop for a horrifying family photo. Once inside the theater, your host brings out a special-effects expert who describes and shares some secrets about what goes into (and oozes out of) creepy movie effects (e.g., corn syrup and food coloring make for a dandy blood substitute). Despite the potentially frightening topic, most of the audience gets a kick out of the whole show, because the subject is handled with an extraordinary amount of dead-on humor. Older children, in particular, eat up the blood-and-guts stories. One-liners delivered with comedy-club timing, audience participation, knives, guns, loose limbs—all this goes into creating a flat-out fantastic show that entertains everyone. **For people with disabilities:** The theater is wheelchair accessible. Good scripts and good schtik mean that those with visual impairments can enjoy the show. ■ **TIP→ If busy, use Express Pass or come in the afternoon or evening. Arrive about 15 minutes before showtime (doors close immediately after show starts).** ✉ *Hollywood* 🌐 *www.universalorlando.com* ☞ *Duration: 25 mins. Crowds: Light. Audience: Not Young Kids.*

SHOPPING

At Universal Studios the merchandise is geared toward the attractions themselves; nearly every themed ride channels you from the exit into a gift shop with related merchandise.

The largest collection of stores is near the park gates around **Production Central** and **Hollywood.** Here the inventory ranges from silver-screen collectibles to the usual souvenirs and kitsch. The Universal Studios Store offers one-stop shopping with items from different areas in the studio—and even adds some merchandise from Islands of Adventure's most popular attractions.

Brown Derby. Felt fedoras, bush hats that seem straight from wardrobe for *Jurassic Park,* Cat in the Hat red-and-white stovepipes, and Duff beer mug hats are among the many novelty chapeaus for sale at this Hollywood store. ✉ *Hollywood* 🌐 *www.universalorlando.com.*

Kwik-E-Mart. This re-creation of the animated original from the Simpsons is one of the park's most popular shopping stops. You'll find Kwik-E-Mart (Apu Nahasapeemapetilon, proprietor) caps and smocks, Duff Beer mugs, Lard Lad donuts, Marge-style blue bouffant wigs, and Homer T-shirts packaged in Duff Beer cans. In 2013, an assortment of Springfield-inspired locales appeared, making the shop and its surroundings one of the park's best photo ops. ✉ *World Expo, Universal Studios Orlando.*

6

Silver Screen Collectibles. The Queen of Comedy, Lucille Ball, still makes people smile—and makes a wonderful subject for souvenirs from cookie jars to aprons. Celebrity photos, books on TV and film, and the world's largest selection of Betty Boop souvenirs also feature prominently in this shop perfectly located near the entrance/exit. ✉ *Hollywood* 🌐 *www.universalorlando.com.*

SpongeBob StorePants. There seems to be no end to the desire to own items featuring SpongeBob and friends. When you see this shop with its cartoonish nautical theme—pink jellyfish overhead, a pineapple home in the middle of the store, and SpongeBob merchandise from mugs to shorts to swimwear all around—there's scarcely a chance you can pass it by. ✉ *Woody Woodpecker's KidZone* 🌐 *www.universalorlando.com.*

Super Silly Stuff. Talk about truth in advertising. This colorful gift shop tied to Despicable Me: Minion Mayhem is filled with what seems to be millions of cute minions (both one-eyed and two-eyed) on T-shirts, mugs, and stuffed dolls. Gru fans can also sport a black-and-gray scarf like the one worn by the super villain—sold separately or silk-screened onto a T-shirt. ✉ *Production Central* 🌐 *www.universalorlando.com.*

Universal Studios Store. This sizable store doesn't have all the merchandise that's sold in individual park gift shops, but as the park's central shopping destination, it does have most of it—and some of the best, including T-shirts, stuffed animals, and limited-edition Universal trading pins. A big plus is that you'll also find popular merchandise sold primarily at Islands of Adventure. ✉ *Production Central* 🌐 *www.universalorlando.com.*

ISLANDS OF ADVENTURE

More so than just about any other theme park, Islands of Adventure has gone all out to create settings and attractions that transport you from reality into the surreal. What's more, no one island here has much in common with any other, so in a way, a visit here is almost like a visit to half a dozen different parks.

IOA's unique nature is first revealed when you arrive at the Port of Entry and are greeted by a kaleidoscope of sights and a cacophony of sounds. It's all designed to put you in the frame of mind for adventure.

When you reach the central lagoon, your clockwise journey commences with Marvel Super Hero Island and its tightly packed concentration of roller coasters and thrill rides. Of special note is the amazingly high-tech and dazzling Amazing Adventures of Spider-Man. In just minutes you'll have experienced a day's worth of sensations—and you've only just begun.

Stepping into Toon Lagoon is like stepping into the pages of a comic book, just as entering the upcoming island, Jurassic Park, is like entering a research center where reconstituted dinosaur DNA is being used to create a new breed of *brontosaurus*.

You move from the world of science into the world of magic when you segue into the Wizarding World of Harry Potter. For the first time anywhere, you—and not just a few fortunate actors—can wander through the magnificently fictional, yet now very realistic, realm of the young wizard and his Hogwarts classmates and tutors. Beyond belief.

But that's not the end of it. In the Lost Continent the mood is that of a Renaissance fair, where crafters work inside colorful tents. It's as pronounced an atmosphere as that of the final island, Seuss Landing, which presents the incredible, topsy-turvy world of Dr. Seuss. It's a riot of colors and shapes and fantastic wildlife that pay tribute to the good doctor's vivid imagination.

TOP ATTRACTIONS

AGES 7 AND UP

Amazing Adventures of Spider-Man. Get ready to fight bad guys and marvel at the engineering and technological wizardry on this dazzling attraction.

Dudley Do-Right's Ripsaw Falls. Even if its namesake is a mystery to anyone born after the 1960s, everyone loves the super splash-down at the end of this log-flume ride dedicated to the exploits of the animated Canadian Mountie.

Harry Potter and the Forbidden Journey. This ride brings J. K. Rowling's books to life on a wild, virtual-reality adventure through Hogwarts and beyond with Harry, Hermione, and Ron.

Incredible Hulk Coaster. This superscary coaster blasts you skyward before sending you on seven inversions. It's hard to walk straight after this one.

AGES 6 AND UNDER

The Cat in the Hat. It's like entering a Dr. Seuss book: all you have to do is sit on a moving couch and see what it's like when the Cat in the Hat drops by to babysit.

Flight of the Hippogriff. Some of the younger Hogwarts "students" will enjoy this low-key coaster in Harry Potter's world.

Popeye & Bluto's Bilge-Rat Barges. This tumultuous (but safe) raft ride lets younger kids experience a big-deal ride that's not too scary—just wild and wet.

ORIENTATION AND PLANNING

GETTING ORIENTED

Getting your bearings at IOA is far easier than at its sister park, Universal Studios. Brochures in a multitude of languages are in a rack a few steps beyond the turnstiles. The brochures include a foldout map that will acquaint you with the park's simple layout (it's a circle). And, ahead by the lagoon, boards are posted with up-to-the-minute ride and show information—including the length of lines at the major attractions.

You pass through the turnstiles and into the Port of Entry plaza, a bazaar that brings together bits and pieces of architecture, landscaping, music, and wares from many lands—Dutch windmills, Indonesian pedicabs, African masks, restrooms marked "Loo's Landing," and Egyptian figurines that adorn a massive archway inscribed with the notice "The Adventure Begins." From here, themed islands—arranged around a large lagoon—are connected by walkways that make navigation easy. When you've done the full circuit, you'll recall the fantastic range of sights, sounds, and experiences and realize there can be truth in advertising. This park really *is* an adventure.

TOURING TIPS

Hosts. Just about any employee is a host, whether they're at a kiosk or attraction or turnstile. Ask them about their favorite experiences—and for suggestions for saving time.

Photo Ops. Islands of Adventure posts signs that indicate picture spots and show how best to frame your shot.

Retreat. Explore little-used sidewalks and quiet alcoves to counter IOA's manic energy.

Split the difference. If the park's open late, split the day in half. See part of it in the morning, head off-site to a restaurant for lunch (your parking ticket is good all day) then head to your hotel for a swim or a nap (or both). Return in the cooler, less crowded evening.

ISLANDS OF ADVENTURES PLANNER

PARK AMENITIES

Baby Care: There are diaper-changing stations in many of the men's and women's restrooms at IOA, as well as a nursing station for comfort and privacy at the first-aid station near the entrance. Baby supplies (diapers, food, wipes, and so on) are available at larger stores; ask for those items at the counter, though, as they aren't out on the shelves.

Cameras: Just inside the park, on your right after the turnstiles, is DeFoto's camera shop. It has nearly everything you need to make your vacation picture-perfect, including batteries, chargers, disposable cameras, cleverly themed photo frames, and digital memory cards. This is also IOA's pickup location for the souvenir photos taken by the active contingent of park photographers.

First Aid: There are two health-services/first-aid centers: one at the front entrance inside Guest Services, and another near Sindbad's Village in the Lost Continent. Just look for the Red Cross symbol on the building across from Oasis Coolers (or ask a park host).

Guest Services. Guest Services is right near the turnstiles, both before and after you enter Islands of Adventure (IOA). ☎ *407/224–6350* 🌐 *www.universalorlando.com.*

Lockers: There are $8-a-day lockers across from Guest Services at the entrance; for $10 a day you can rent a family-size model. You have unlimited access to both types throughout the day—although it's a hike back to retrieve things. Scattered strategically throughout the park—notably at the Incredible Hulk Coaster, Jurassic Park River Adventure, and Forbidden Journey—are so-called Smart Lockers. These are free for the first 45 to 75 minutes, $2 per hour afterward, and max out at $14 per day. Stash backpacks and cameras here while you're being drenched on a watery ride or going through the spin cycle on a twisty one.

Lost People and Things: If you've misplaced something, head to Guest Services in the Port of Entry. This is also where park staffers take lost children.

Services for People with Disabilities: Islands of Adventure has made an all-out effort to make the premises accessible for people with disabilities. Most attractions and all restaurants are wheelchair accessible, and all employees attend workshops on how to meet the needs of guests with disabilities. You may occasionally spot staffers using wheelchairs; many employees have had basic sign-language training. There's also a counter in Guest Services where you can pick up assisted-listening and other devices.

You can rent manual wheelchairs ($12 per day) and electronic convenience vehicles (ECVs; $50 per day) at the Port of Entry to the left after you enter the turnstiles. A photo ID and a $50 deposit on a credit card are required. Because it's a long way between the parking garages and the park entrance, you may want to rent a push wheelchair at the garages and then upgrade to an ECV when you reach the park entrance. Quantities of the latter are limited, so reserve in advance.

Even when the crowds are heavy, the park's avenues are wide enough to maneuver a wheelchair. Hosts and hostesses will direct you to a special attraction entrance or a special show seating area. Icons on the guide maps indicate which of the shows include an interpreter.

Assisted-listening devices are available for Cat in the Hat, Sindbad, Spider-Man, Incredible Hulk, Doctor Doom, Jurassic Park, and Poseidon's Fury.

Stroller Rentals: You can rent strollers ($15 per day for singles, $25 for doubles) at the Port of Entry to your left after the turnstiles. You can also rent kiddie cars—small ones for $18, and large ones for $28.

Where to Snack: If you prefer to pay in advance, Quick Service meals includes, for adults, one meal, two snacks, and a nonalcoholic beverage ($19). The kids' version ($13) includes one kids meal, one snack, and a nonalcoholic beverage. At Islands of Adventure, your choices are the Comic Strip Café (Asian, Italian, American, and fish), the Burger Digs (hamburgers, chicken sandwiches, chicken fingers, milk shakes), Café 4 (pizzas, subs, and salads), and Croissant Moon (deli sandwiches, paninis, and pastries).

Other popular options include **Circus McGurkus Cafe Stoo-pendous** (chicken, pasta, pizza, burgers, salads) in Seuss Landing and, in Toon Lagoon, **Blondie's** (jumbo deli sandwiches). **Pizza Predattoria** and **Thunder Falls Terrace** (rotisserie chicken and ribs) are in Jurassic Park, and near the Port of Entry is the comparably more upscale **Confisco Grille,** with its steaks, salads, sandwiches, soups, pasta, and neat little pub. At IOA, the ultimate dining experience is the Lost Continent's **Mythos Restaurant.** Although its Continental dishes change seasonally, the warm, gooey, chocolate-banana cake is a constant.

EXPLORING ISLANDS OF ADVENTURE

MARVEL SUPER HERO ISLAND

The facades on Stanley Boulevard (named for Marvel's famed editor and co-creator Stan Lee) put you smack in the middle of an alternatively pleasant and apocalyptic comic-book world—complete with heroes, villains, and cartoony colors and flourishes. Although the spiky, horrific towers of Doctor Doom's Fearfall and the vivid green of the Hulk's coaster are focal points, the Amazing Adventures of Spider-Man is the must-see attraction. At various times Doctor Doom, Spider-Man, and the Incredible Hulk are available for photos, and sidewalk artists are on hand to paint your face like your favorite hero (or villain). All rides here accept Universal Express Pass.

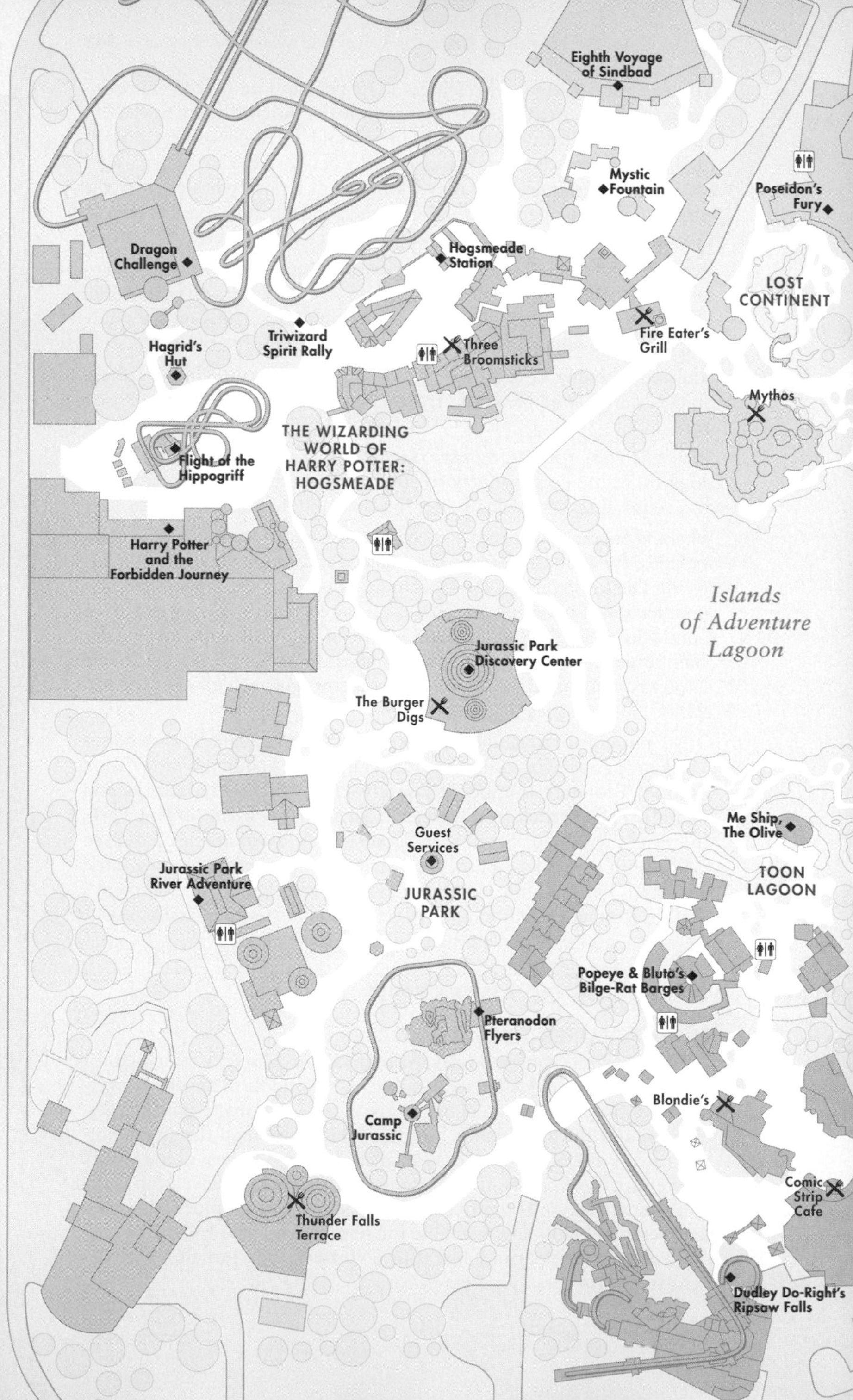
Eighth Voyage of Sindbad
Mystic Fountain
Poseidon's Fury
Dragon Challenge
Hogsmeade Station
LOST CONTINENT
Triwizard Spirit Rally
Hagrid's Hut
Three Broomsticks
Fire Eater's Grill
Mythos
THE WIZARDING WORLD OF HARRY POTTER: HOGSMEADE
Flight of the Hippogriff
Harry Potter and the Forbidden Journey
Islands of Adventure Lagoon
Jurassic Park Discovery Center
The Burger Digs
Guest Services
Me Ship, The Olive
TOON LAGOON
Jurassic Park River Adventure
JURASSIC PARK
Popeye & Bluto's Bilge-Rat Barges
Pteranodon Flyers
Blondie's
Camp Jurassic
Comic Strip Cafe
Thunder Falls Terrace
Dudley Do-Right's Ripsaw Falls

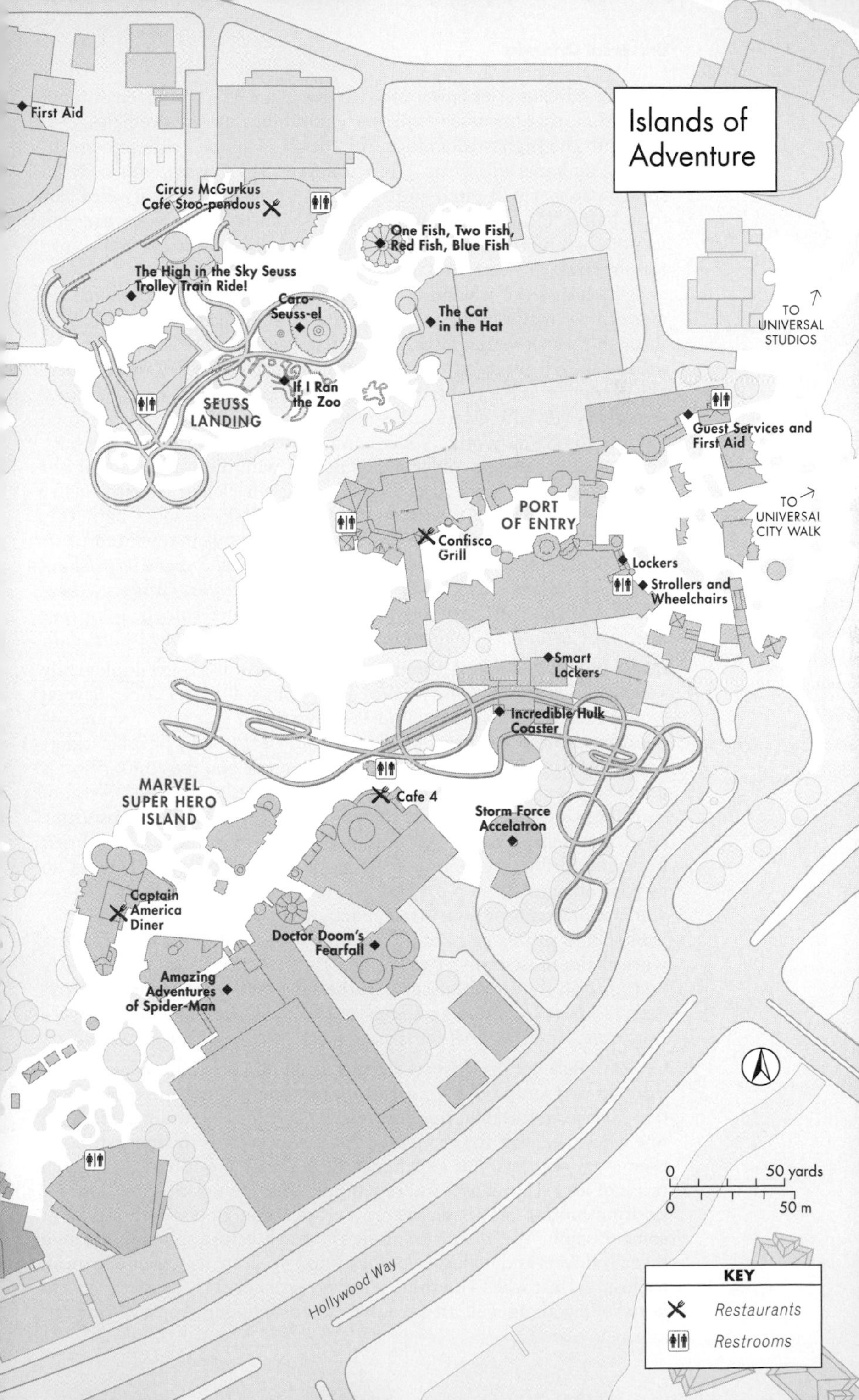

Islands of Adventure
First Aid
Circus McGurkus Cafe Stoo-pendous
One Fish, Two Fish, Red Fish, Blue Fish
The High in the Sky Seuss Trolley Train Ride!
Caro-Seuss-el
The Cat in the Hat
TO UNIVERSAL STUDIOS
If I Ran the Zoo
SEUSS LANDING
Guest Services and First Aid
PORT OF ENTRY
TO UNIVERSAL CITY WALK
Confisco Grill
Lockers
Strollers and Wheelchairs
Smart Lockers
Incredible Hulk Coaster
MARVEL SUPER HERO ISLAND
Cafe 4
Storm Force Accelatron
Captain America Diner
Doctor Doom's Fearfall
Amazing Adventures of Spider-Man
0
50 yards
0
50 m
Hollywood Way
KEY
Restaurants
Restrooms

Amazing Adventures of Spider-Man. Redone in 2012 with even sharper animation, this must-see experience combines moving vehicles, 3-D film with the highest-definition resolution available, simulator technology, and special effects. After donning 3-D glasses, you board a special car that will pitch and roll as you get swept into a weird cartoon battle. How weird? When Spider-Man lands on your car, you feel the bump; when Electro runs overhead, you hear his steps. You feel the sizzle of electricity, the frigid spray of water from Hydro Man, and the heat from a flaming pumpkin tossed by the Hobgoblin. No matter how many times you visit, you cringe when Doc Ock breaks through a brick wall, raises your car to the top of a skyscraper, and then releases it for a 400-foot freefall. The bizarre angles and perspectives really do make you feel as if you're swinging from a web. *Do not miss this one.* Youngsters accustomed to action TV shows should be fine, but timid kids won't. Not recommended if you're pregnant or have heart, back, or neck problems. **For people with disabilities:** Equipped for assisted-listening devices. Guests using wheelchairs must transfer to a ride vehicle. **■TIP→ Come early or at dusk—or most definitely head to the single rider line. Be sure to check out the wanted posters of Spider-Man villains on the walls.** ✉ *Marvel Super Hero Island* 🌐 *www.universalorlando.com* ☞ *Duration: 4½ mins. Crowds: Absolutely. Audience: All but Young Kids. Height requirements: 40 inches minimum; between 40 and 48 inches must be accompanied by an adult.*

Doctor Doom's Fearfall. Although the 200-foot-tall towers look really scary, the ride itself is just kind of scary (but still pretty cool). Several sets of four chairs wrap around the tower, and you and three fellow guests are seated and strapped in just out of the sight of other riders before the disembodied voice of Dr. Doom tells you the contraption is designed to extract fear he'll collect to use and rule the world. Without warning, all the chairs are rocketed to the peak, which jumpstarts a surge of adrenalin as it rises, falls, rises and falls again in a very brief, but quite thrilling, experience. It's easy enough to have a second go as you can actually step off and get right back into line again. Guests who are pregnant or have heart, back, neck, or motion-sickness problems should sit this one out. **For people with disabilities:** Guests using wheelchairs must transfer to a ride vehicle. **■TIP→ Line moves fairly fast, though it's crowded early in the day; come late or use Express Pass.** ✉ *Marvel Super Hero Island* ☞ *Duration: 1 min. Crowds: Light–Moderate. Audience: All but Young Kids. Minimum height: 52 inches.*

Incredible Hulk Coaster. Just seeing this attraction from the sidewalk is a thrill: its cars shoot out from a 150-foot catapult that propels them from 0 to 40 mph in less than *two seconds*. If this piques your interest, get in line where the wait for the prized front-row seats is the longest; however, every seat lets you experience flesh-pressing g-forces that match those of an F-16 fighter. You're whipped into an upside-down, zero-g position more than 10 stories up before being zipped into a dive at some 60 mph. You then race along the track before spinning through seven rollovers and making a plunge into two deep, foggy subterranean enclosures. Just when you think it's over—it's not. This coaster seems to keep rolling along well after you've exhausted your supply of screams and shrieks. Powerful. Pregnant women and people with neck, back, or heart problems and/or motion-sickness issues shouldn't ride. **For people with disabilities:** Guests using wheelchairs must transfer to a ride vehicle. **■ TIP→ Come here first (effects are best in the morning and up front). Use Express Pass. Loose articles are not permitted, so stow things in a convenient locker.** ⊠ *Marvel Super Hero Island* ☞ *Duration: 2¼ mins. Crowds: Yes! Audience: All but Young Kids. Minimum height: 54 inches.*

Storm Force Accelatron. On this whirling ride X-Men character Storm harnesses the weather to battle Magneto by having people like you board Power Orbs. Yes, the story line is that the containers convert human energy into electrical forces through the power of "cyclospin." Strip away the veneer, however, and what you've got seems like a faster version of Disney World's twirling teacups. Still, it's a high-adrenaline ride that's not for anyone who suffers from motion sickness. It's also not suitable for guests who are pregnant or who have heart, back, or neck problems. **For people with disabilities:** Guests using wheelchairs must transfer to a ride vehicle. **■ TIP→ Ride whenever—except right after eating. Use Express Pass when needed.** ⊠ *Marvel Super Hero Island* ☞ *Duration: 2 mins. Crowds: Light. Audience: All but Young Kids.*

6

TOON LAGOON

The main street, Comic Strip Lane, makes use of cartoon characters that are recognizable to anyone—anyone born before 1940, that is. Pert little Betty Boop, gangly Olive Oyl, muscle-bound Popeye, Krazy Kat, Mark Trail, Flash Gordon, Pogo, and Alley Oop are all here, as are the relatively more contemporary Dudley Do-Right, Rocky, Bullwinkle, Beetle Bailey, Cathy, and Hagar the Horrible. With its colorful backdrops, chirpy music, hidden alcoves, squirting fountains, and highly animated scenery, Toon Town is a natural for younger kids (even if they don't know who these characters are). All attractions here accept Universal Express Pass except Me Ship, The Olive.

Dudley Do-Right's Ripsaw Falls. In the 1960s, Dudley Do-Right was recognized as the well-intentioned—but considerably dim—Canadian Mountie who somehow managed to always save the damsel and "get his man" (that is, foil the villain). But you don't need to be familiar with this character to enjoy this "waterlogged" attraction. The twisting, up-and-down flume ride through the Canadian Rockies begins with your mission to help Dudley rescue Nell, his belle, from the evil, conniving Snidely Whiplash. Tucked inside a hollow log, you'll drift gently down the stream before dropping through the rooftop of a ramshackle dynamite shack. After an explosive dive into a 400,000-gallon lagoon, you're not just damp—you're soaked. If the weather is cold or you absolutely must stay dry, pick up a poncho at Gasoline Alley, opposite the ride entrance—and store other items in a locker. This isn't suitable for guests who are pregnant; experience motion sickness; or have heart, back, or neck problems. **For people with disabilities:** Guests using wheelchairs must transfer to a ride vehicle. **■ TIP→ Use Express Pass, and come in late afternoon, when you're hot as can be, or at day's end, when you're ready to head back to your car. Expect to get wet.** ⊠ *Toon Lagoon* ☞ *Duration: 5½ mins. Crowds: Heavy in Summer. Audience: All but*

Young Kids. Height requirements: 44 inches minimum; under 48 inches must ride with an adult.

NEED A BREAK?

Blondie's is home of the Dagwood—the jumbo club sandwich that's sold in sections (much too large for any one person to tackle). The eatery also sells cookies and Nathan's hot dogs (Chicago, chili, Reuben, slaw) as well as turkey, roast beef, and tuna sandwiches.

Me Ship, The Olive. At heart, this is a fantastic playground disguised as a teetering-tottering ship. From bow to stern, there are dozens of participatory activities to keep kids busy as they climb around this jungle-gym shaped like a boat moored on the edge of Toon Lagoon. Toddlers enjoy crawling in Swee' Pea's Playpen, and with high-powered squirt guns, older children and their parents can take aim at unsuspecting riders twisting through the rapids over at Popeye & Bluto's Bilge-Rat Barges ride. Primarily, though, this is designed for small kids, with whistles, bells, tunnels, and ladders. Check out the view of the park from the top of the ship. **For people with disabilities:** The playground area is wheelchair accessible. **■ TIP→ Come in the morning or around dinnertime.** ✉ *Toon Lagoon* ☞ *Duration: Up to You. Crowds: Heavy. Audience: Young Kids.*

Popeye & Bluto's Bilge-Rat Barges. As with every ride at IOA, there's a story line here, but the real attraction is boarding the wide circular raft with 11 other passengers and then getting soaked, splashed, sprayed, or deluged as the watercraft bounces and bobs down and around the twisting stream. The degree of wetness varies, since the direction your raft spins may or may not place you beneath torrents of water flooding from a shoreline water tower or streaming from water guns fired with enthusiasm by guests at an adjacent play area. Pregnant women and guests with heart, back, neck, or motion-sickness problems should skip this one. **For people with disabilities:** Guests using wheelchairs must transfer to a ride vehicle. **■ TIP→ Come first thing in the morning or an hour before closing. Use Express Pass, and stow your items in a locker if needed.** ✉ *Toon Lagoon* ☞ *Duration: 5 mins. Crowds: Heavy. Audience: All but Young Kids. Height requirements: 42 inches minimum; 42 to 48 inches must be accompanied by an adult.*

JURASSIC PARK

Pass through the towering gates of Jurassic Park and the music becomes slightly ominous, the vegetation tropical and junglelike. All of this, plus the high-tension wires and warning signs, does a great job of re-creating the Jurassic Park of Steven Spielberg's blockbuster movie (and its insipid sequels). The half-fun, half-frightening Jurassic Park River Adventure (the only attraction here that uses Universal Express Pass) is the standout, bringing to life key segments of the movie's climax.

Camp Jurassic. Remember when you were content with just a swing set and monkey bars? Well, such toys have been replaced by themed play areas like this. Though the camp is primarily for kids, some adults join in, racing along footpaths through the forests, slithering down slides, clambering over swinging bridges and across streams, scrambling up net climbs and rock formations, and exploring mysterious caves full of faux lava. Watch for the dinosaur footprints; when you jump on them, a dinosaur roars somewhere (different footprints are associated with different roars). Also, look out for the watery crossfire nearby—or join in the shooting yourself. **For people with disabilities:** Much of this attraction is wheelchair accessible (its upper levels probably aren't). ■ **TIP→ Great anytime.** ✉ *Jurassic Park, Universal Studios Orlando* ☞ *Duration: Up to You. Crowds: Light–Moderate. Audience: All Ages.*

Jurassic Park Discovery Center. If there's a scintilla of information your kids don't know about dinosaurs, they can learn it here. There are demonstration areas where a realistic raptor is being hatched, and where you can see what you'd look like (or sound like) if you were a dino. In the Beasaur area ("Be-a-Saur"), you get a dinosaur's view of the world. There are numerous hands-on exhibits and a dinosaur trivia game, although the museum-like feel seems a little off-kilter at an amusement park. Burger Digs, the casual restaurant upstairs, is a nice place to take an air-conditioned break, and tables on the balcony overlook the lagoon. Step outside and a wide promenade affords a lovely perspective of the entire park. **For people with disabilities:** The attraction is fully wheelchair accessible. ✉ *Jurassic Park* 🌐 *www.universalorlando.com* ☞ *Duration: Up to You. Crowds: Light. Audience: All but Young Kids.*

6

Jurassic Park River Adventure. Your excursion begins as a peaceful raft cruise on a mysterious river past friendly, vegetarian dinosaurs. Naturally, something has to go awry, and a wrong turn is all that it takes. When you enter one of the research departments, you'll see that it's been overrun by spitting dinosaurs and razor-clawed raptors. This is when things get plenty scary: straight ahead a towering, roaring T. rex with sharp claws and teeth the size of hams guards the getaway route. Just when you think you're about to become a Cretaceous period entrée, your raft slips down a tremendously steep 85-foot plunge that will start you screaming. Smile! This is when the souvenir photos are shot. Thanks to high-capacity rafts, the line moves fairly quickly.

Not suitable for guests who are pregnant or who have heart, back, or neck problems. **For people with disabilities:** Guests using wheelchairs must transfer to a ride vehicle, and assisted-listening devices are available. ■ **TIP→ Come early in the morning and/or use Express Pass.** ✉ *Jurassic Park* ☞ *Duration: 6 mins. Crowds: Heavy. Audience: All but Young Kids. Minimum height: 42 inches.*

NEED A BREAK?

Thunder Falls Terrace is open for lunch and dinner. Beneath towering ceilings in a spacious setting, one side is entirely glass, which makes it a great place to view the plunge at the adjacent Jurassic Park River Adventure. On a nice day, consider sitting outdoors next to the thundering waterfall and dine on barbecue ribs, wraps, chicken, turkey legs, soup, and salads. If Thunder Falls is too crowded, a short distance away are Burger Digs and Pizza Predattoria.

Pteranodon Flyers. These prehistoric bird-style gondolas are eye-catching and may tempt you to stand in line for a lift. The problem? This is a very slow, very low-capacity ride that will eat up a lot of your park time. Do it only if (1) your child asks, (2) you want a prehistoric-bird's-eye view

ISLANDS OF ADVENTURE

NAME	Height Req.	Type of Entertainment	Duration	Crowds	Audience	Tips
Jurassic Park						
Camp Jurassic	n/a	Playground	Up to you	Light to Moderate	All Ages	Come anytime.
Jurassic Park Discovery Center	n/a	Walk-Through	Up to you	Light	Young Kids to Teens	Come anytime.
Jurassic Park River Adventure	At least 42″	Thrill Ride with Water	6 mins.	Heavy	All but Young Kids	Use Express Pass. Come early or late.
Pteranodon Flyers	36″ to 56″	Thrill Ride for Kids	2 mins.	Heavy	All Ages	Skip this on your first visit. 36″ to 48″ can ride but must do so with an adult.
Lost Continent						
Eighth Voyage of Sindbad	n/a	Show	25 mins.	Heavy	All but Young Kids	Stadium seating for everyone, but arrive at least 15 mins. early. Don't sit too far up front. Use Express Pass.
Poseidon's Fury	n/a	Walk-through Simulator Exp.	20 mins.	Heavy	All but Young Kids	Come at the end of the day. Stay to the left for best spot. Get in first row each time. Express Pass accepted.
Marvel Super Hero Island						
★ The Amazing Adventures of Spider-Man	At least 40″	Simulator Exp.	4½ mins.	Absolutely	All but Young Kids	Use Express Pass, or come early or late in day. Don't miss the bad guys in the wanted posters. Try it twice if you can.
Doctor Doom's Fearfall	At least 52″	Thrill Ride	1 min.	Light to Moderate	All but Young Kids	Use Express Pass, or come later in the day. Regardless, come with an empty stomach.
Incredible Hulk Coaster	At least 54″	Thrill Ride	2¼ mins.	Yes!	All but Young Kids	Come here first. Effects are best in the morning. The front row is best.
Storm Force Accelatron	n/a	Thrill Ride	2 mins.	Light	All but Young Kids	Come whenever—except right after eating.
Seuss Landing						

Caro-Seuss-el	n/a	Thrill Ride for Kids	2 mins.	Moderate	All Ages	Use Express Pass, or end your day here.
The Cat in the Hat	n/a	Thrill Ride for Kids	4½ mins.	Heavy	All Ages	Use Express Pass here, or come early or at the end of the day.
High in the Sky Seuss Trolley Train Ride!	At least 34"	Railroad	3 mins.	Heavy	All Ages	Kids love trains, so plan to get in line! 34" to 48" can ride but must do so with an adult. Express Pass accepted.
If I Ran the Zoo	n/a	Playground with Water	Up to you	Heavy	Young Kids	Come toward the end of your visit.
One Fish, Two Fish, Red Fish, Blue Fish	n/a	Thrill Ride for Kids	2+ mins.	Heavy	Young Kids	Use Express Pass, or come early or late in day. Skip it on your first visit
Toon Lagoon						
Dudley Do-Right's Ripsaw Falls	At least 44"	Thrill Ride with Water	5½ mins.	Heavy	All but Young Kids	Ride the flume in late afternoon to cool down, or at day's end. There's no seat where you can stay dry. Express Pass accepted.
Me Ship, The Olive	n/a	Playground	Up to you	Heavy	Young Kids	Come in the morning or at dinnertime.
Popeye and Bluto's Bilge-Rat Barges	At least 42 "	Thrill Ride with Water	5 mins.	Heavy	All but Young Kids	Come early in the morning or before closing. You will get wet. Express Pass accepted.
The Wizarding World of Harry Potter						
Dragon Challenge	At least 54"	Thrill Ride	3 mins.	Heavy	All but Young Kids	Use Express Pass. Avoid if you're prone to motion sickness.
Flight of the Hippogriff	At least 36"	Thrill Ride for Kids	1 min.	Moderate	Young Kids	Keep an eye on the line, and come when there's an opening. Express Pass accepted.
★ Harry Potter and the Forbidden Journey	At least 48"	Walk-Through/ Ride-Through/ Thrill Ride	50 mins.	Yes!	All but Young Kids	Come early and use Express Pass. Steer clear if you have a queasy stomach.

★ Fodor's Choice

In the Jurassic Park Discovery Center, your kids might just learn something about dinosaurs that they didn't already know.

of the Jurassic Park compound, or (3) you've been to the park a dozen times and this is the last ride to conquer. **For people with disabilities:** Guests using wheelchairs must transfer to a ride vehicle. **■ TIP→ Crowds are usually perpetual, and because the ride loads slowly, waits can take quite a while. Skip this on your first visit.** ✉ *Jurassic Park* 🌐 *www.universalorlando.com* ☞ *Duration: 2 mins. Crowds: Heavy. Audience: All Ages. Height requirements: Between 36 and 56 inches tall; taller adults must be accompanied by a child who meets these height requirements.*

THE WIZARDING WORLD OF HARRY POTTER

In mid-2010, Islands of Adventure fulfilled the fantasy of Harry Potter devotees when it unveiled the biggest theme-park addition since the arrival of Disney's Animal Kingdom in 1998. At the highly publicized premiere, even the actors from the Potter film franchise were amazed. Having performed their roles largely before a green screen, they had never seen anything like this. Neither have you. It's fantastic and unbelievable. The movie-magic-perfect re-creations of mythical locales such as Hogwarts, Hogsmeade Village, and Diagon Alley are all here, while playing supporting roles are a handful of candy shops, souvenir stores, and restaurants expertly and exquisitely themed to make you believe you've actually boarded the *Hogwarts Express* and arrived in the incredible fantasy world of J. K. Rowling. Wands, candy, novelties, and more are unique to this magical land. Expect to be impressed—and to wait in line. Even if you owned a wand and were a real wizard, the only attractions in this land that accept the Universal Express Pass are Flight of the Hippogriff and Dragon Challenge. In fact, the land is so popular that in peak season it sometimes reaches capacity, and you have to wait for others to leave before you can enter.

Dragon Challenge. On this tandem roller coaster the Chinese Fireball and Hungarian Horntail rocket you in a half-mile, screaming snap-crackle-pop ride along the rails. In the line watch for iconic elements from the Tri-Wizard Tournament, but when you get hung up in your seat (you're suspended beneath the track) get ready to be launched on one of the park's great rides. Each coaster is on a separate track, and when they rocket out of the station at the same time, it means they'll soon be rocketing *toward* each other at a combined speed of *120 mph*. Making it even more exciting, the coasters are programmed by computer to bring them just feet apart as they blaze through the track. This isn't appropriate for anyone with neck, back, or heart problems or for anyone who is pregnant or suffers from motion sickness. **For people with disabilities:** Guests using wheelchairs must transfer to a ride vehicle. **■TIP→ Make use of Express Pass. It's perfect for teens and adventurous tweens.** ⊠ *The Wizarding World of Harry Potter* 🌐 *www.universalorlando.com* ☞ *Duration: 3 mins. Crowds: Heavy. Audience: All but Young Kids. Minimum height: 54 inches.*

6

Flight of the Hippogriff. This kid-friendly coaster is a simple way to introduce your children to the pleasures of g-force and vertigo. The queue takes you past Hagrid's hut and then onboard for a "training flight" above the grounds of Hogwarts Castle. On the brief journey, there are some nice little twists and dips that'll give them a pint-size dose of adrenaline. This is an easy alternative to the Dragon Challenge, and one that should please parents and their kids. That said, this ride isn't appropriate for people with heart, back, or neck problems or who are prone to motion sickness. **For people with disabilities:** Guests using wheelchairs must transfer to a ride vehicle. **■TIP→ Bring smaller kids here while the older kids ride Dragon Challenge. Use Express Pass.** ⊠ *The Wizarding World of Harry Potter* 🌐 *www.universalorlando.com* ☞ *Duration: 1 min. Crowds: Moderate. Audience: Young Kids. Minimum height: 36 inches.*

Fodor's Choice ★

Harry Potter and the Forbidden Journey. Of all of Universal's rides, this is the one that really puts you in the movies. The queue leads you through the hallowed halls of Hogwarts, introducing you to the founders of the school and the story of the journey. You'll enter the academy and see the sights you know from the books and films: Headmaster Dumbledore's office, Defence Against the Dark Arts classroom, Gryffindor common room, Room of Requirement, and the greenhouse. You'll also encounter the Sorting Hat, the One-Eyed Witch statue, and several talking portraits. Before you reach the actual ride, heroes Harry, Ron, and Hermione appear to persuade you to skip a lecture and follow them on a soaring journey. Thanks to a combination of live-action, robotic technology and innovative film making, you come face-to-face with a flying dragon and the Whomping Willow before being propelled into the heart of a Quidditch match. You also zip through a dozen scenes and encounter supporting characters Albus Dumbledore, Rubeus Hagrid, Draco Malfoy, and members of the Weasley family. All in all, a fantastic attraction – especially for fans of the series. Not suitable for those with

CLOSE UP

Hogsmeade Village

In Hogsmeade, the village that's the home of Hogwarts, you'll find the signature restaurant, Three Broomsticks, which serves traditional British fare (as well as an assortment of kids' meals), and the Hog's Head Pub, where you can down a pint of Butterbeer (tastes like cream soda, butterscotch, and shortbread cookies) or pumpkin juice (pumpkin, apple cider, and spices). The village is also a fantastic place to run errands and pick up sundries and pretend you're really in Harry Potter's world. Send a postcard or letter stamped with a novelty (and very real cancellation mark) at Owl Post before selecting (or being selected by) a magic wand at Ollivanders. If you can't get into Ollivanders (there's always a long line), kiosks and small shops sell an impressive 25 different styles of wands at a profit-making price (about $30). Pick up some practical jokes (shrunken heads, extendable ears, screaming yo-yos) at Zonko's, and sample strange sweets at Honeydukes. But the best place to shop for Potterabilia is Dervish and Banges, where there are Hogwarts school uniforms, robes, scarves, T-shirts, and broomsticks—including the legendary Nimbus 2000.

neck, back, or heart problems. If you're pregnant or suffer from motion sickness, take a pass. **For people with disabilities:** Guests using wheelchairs must transfer to a ride vehicle. **■TIP→ Be patient; Express Pass isn't an option here, so relax and enjoy your tour of the school before boarding the ride.** ✉ *The Wizarding World of Harry Potter, Universal Studios Orlando* 🌐 *www.universalorlando.com* ☞ *Duration: 50–60 mins. Crowds: Yes! Audience: All but Young Kids. Height requirements: 48 inches minimum, 6 feet 3 inches maximum Weight requirement: less than 250 pounds.*

LOST CONTINENT

Just beyond a wooden bridge, huge mythical birds guard the entrance to a land where trees are hung with weathered metal lanterns, and booming thunder mixes with chimes and vaguely Celtic melodies. Farther along the path, the scene looks similar to a Renaissance fair. Seers and fortune-tellers practice their trade in tents, and, in a huge theater, Sindbad leaps and bounces all over Arabia. This stunt show and Poseidon let you bypass lines using Universal Express Pass.

Eighth Voyage of Sindbad. The story line of this live stunt show is simple: Sindbad and his sidekick Kabob arrive in search of treasure, get distracted by the beautiful Princess Amoura, and are threatened by the evil sorceress Miseria. That's all you really need to know, and it's enough to get the good guy kicking off 25 nonstop minutes of punching, climbing, diving, leaping, and Douglas Fairbanks–ing his way through the performance. Kids are pleased with the action, and women are pleased with Sindbad. The downside is that it's sometimes hard to understand the stuntmen who (1) aren't exactly actors and (2) lip-sync to a script that's not always as funny as the writers intended. Still, you'll probably be satisfied by the water explosions, flames, and pyrotechnics that end

DID YOU KNOW?

The Wizarding World of Harry Potter has been the most popular attraction at Universal Orlando's Islands of Adventure since it debuted in 2010.

with a daring, flaming high dive. Also, the 1,700-seat theater is a nice place to sit a spell and replenish your energy. **For people with disabilities:** The theater is wheelchair accessible and is equipped for assisted-listening devices. Some shows have sign language interpreters. ■ **TIP→ Find seats about 15 minutes before showtime. Don't sit too far up front—the experience is better a few rows back.** ✉ *Lost Continent* 🌐 *www.universalorlando.com* ☞ *Duration: 25 mins. Crowds: Light. Audience: All but Young Kids.*

WORD OF MOUTH

"The wait at Harry Potter's Forbidden Journey around 1 pm was just over an hour (can't use Express Pass for this one). Butterbeer is delicious, although pricey at $11 if you keep the plastic mug. It's available frozen or regular, and we decided the frozen was better. Harry Potter and Spider-Man were our favorite attractions except for our grandson who found some attractions including Harry Potter a bit too intense." –Jeff49

Poseidon's Fury. After a long walk through cool ruins guarded by the Colossus of Rhodes, a young archeologist arrives to take you on a trek to find Poseidon's trident. Each chamber you enter looks interesting, and there's a story told in each one, but actually very little happens in most of them. Most of the time your group is simply walking through the ruins until the attraction attempts to bring the entertainment quotient up for the final scene. That comes after you've walked through a water vortex and enter the final hall where, on a 180-degree movie screen, actors playing Poseidon and his archenemy appear. As they shout at each other, a memorable fire- and waterworks extravaganza erupts all around you as massive waves crash and scorching fireballs fly. This finale is loud, powerful, and hyperactive. Is it worth the investment of time? Meh. Give it a whirl if you've done everything else.

For people with disabilities: The theater is equipped for assisted-listening devices and is wheelchair accessible. ■ **TIP→ Stay left against the wall as you enter, and position yourself opposite the central podium. In each succeeding section of the presentation, get into the very first row, particularly if you aren't tall.** ✉ *Lost Continent* ☞ *Duration: 20 mins. Crowds: Heavy. Audience: All but Young Kids.*

SEUSS LANDING

This 10-acre tribute to Dr. Seuss puts you in the midst of his classic children's books. This means spending quality time with the Cat, Things 1 and 2, Horton, the Lorax, and the Grinch. From topiary sculptures to lurching lampposts to curvy fences (there was never a straight line in any of the books) to buildings that glow in lavenders, pinks, peaches, and oranges, everything seems surreal. It's a wonderful place to wrap up a day. Even the Cat would approve. All rides here except If I Ran the Zoo accept Express Pass.

Caro-Seuss-el. Ordinary horse-centric merry-go-rounds seem so passé compared with the menagerie on this one: the cowfish from *McElligot's Pool*, the elephant birds from *Horton Hatches the Egg*, and the Birthday Katroo from *Happy Birthday to You!* It's an entire ark of imaginary and interactive animals—indeed, the animals' eyes blink, and their tails wag. It may be a cliché, but there's a good chance you'll feel like a kid again when you hop aboard one of these fantastic creatures. You'll love it. **For people with disabilities:** Modified mounts let guests using wheelchairs ride without having to transfer to a ride vehicle. **■TIP→ Use Express Pass, and/or make this a special end to your day. Lines move pretty well, so don't be intimidated.** ✉ *Seuss Landing* 🌐 *www.visitorlando.com* ☞ *Duration: 2 mins. Crowds: Moderate. Audience: All Ages. Height requirement: children under 48 inches must be accompanied by an adult.*

The Cat in the Hat. Enter the pages of this classic book and you'll encounter a crazy cat ready to wreak havoc while your mom is out. As you sit on a couch that spins, whirls, and rocks its way through the house, you'll roll past 18 scenes, 30 characters, and 130 effects. You're never alone. The mischievous cat appears balanced on a ball; hoists china on his umbrella; introduces Thing 1 and his wild sibling, Thing 2; and flies kites in the house while the voice of reason, the fish in the teapot, sounds the warning about the impending return of the family matriarch. As the tension builds, so does the fun—and kids love pointing out scenes from the book. **For people with disabilities:** The ride accommodates guests using wheelchairs and is equipped for assisted-listening devices. This isn't the right ride for anyone who's pregnant; prone to motion sickness; or suffers from heart, neck, or back problems. **■TIP→ Use Express Pass and/or come early or late.** ✉ *Seuss Landing* 🌐 *www.universalorlando.com* ☞ *Duration: 4½ mins. Crowds: Heavy. Audience: All Ages. Height requirement: Under 48 inches must be accompanied by an adult.*

The High in the Sky Seuss Trolley Train Ride!. Colorful and quirky miniature Seussian trains on separate tracks embark on a slow and pleasing tour that provides an aerial view of the area, with Seuss-like narration along the way. You'll roll right through the Circus McGurkus Cafe Stoo-pendous and along the shores of the lagoon, where you can see the Sneetches as they enjoy the beaches. Fun for kids—and grown-ups, too. **For people with disabilities:** Guests using wheelchairs must transfer to a ride vehicle. **■TIP→ Kids love trains, so plan to get in line—especially if you have young ones. Express Pass is available here.** ✉ *Seuss Landing* 🌐 *www.universalorlando.com* ☞ *Duration: 3 mins. Crowds: Heavy. Audience: Young Kids. Height requirement: 34 to 48 inches must be accompanied by an adult.*

If I Ran the Zoo. In this interactive Seussian maze, kids can ditch the adults and have fun at their level. Here they encounter the trademarked fantasy creatures as they climb, jump, crawl, and push buttons to animate strange and wonderful animals. Park designers have learned that kids' basic needs include eating, sleeping, and getting splashed, so they've thoughtfully added some interactive fountains as well. **For people with disabilities:** The area is wheelchair accessible. **■TIP→ If you can talk your kids into waiting, come at the end of your visit.** ✉ *Seuss Landing* 🌐 *www.universalorlando.com* ☞ *Duration: Up to You. Crowds: Heavy. Audience: Young Kids.*

The Cat and his Hat, McGurkus and the Circus, and fish both red and blue are among the attractions geared to the under-7 set at Seuss Landing.

One Fish, Two Fish, Red Fish, Blue Fish. Dr. Seuss put elephants in trees and green eggs and ham on trains, so it doesn't seem far-fetched that fish can circle "squirting posts" to a Jamaican beat. After a rather lengthy wait for what will seem like a very short experience, you climb into your fish and as it spins around a center pole, you (or your child) control its up-and-down motion. The key is to follow the lyrics of the special song—if you go down when the song tells you to go up, you may be drenched courtesy of the aforementioned squirting post. Then again, if the guests ahead of you miss their cue, the water's still spraying—and will likely splash you, too. Mighty silly, mighty fun.

For people with disabilities: Modified mounts let guests using wheelchairs ride without having to transfer to a ride vehicle. **■ TIP→ Use Express Pass and/or come early or late. Consider skipping it on your first visit.** ✉ *Seuss Landing* 🌐 *www.universalorlando.com* ☞ *Duration: 2+ mins. Crowds: Heavy. Audience: Young Kids. Height requirement: Under 48 inches must be accompanied by an adult.*

SHOPPING

At Islands of Adventure the merchandise varies in each section of the park. If you simply must have a Spider-Man T-shirt or Incredible Hulk coffee mug, for example, head to Marvel Superhero Island.

The largest concentration of stores is near the gates at the **Port of Entry.** And, as at Universal Studios, a central emporium—the Trading Company—carries nearly every coveted collectible from nearly every park shop. Keep in mind that **Hogsmeade Village** in the Wizarding World

ISLANDS OF ADVENTURE FAMILY TOUR

As you go through IOA, try to pretend that you are not so much a park guest as you are a fledgling explorer and amateur sociologist (sometimes just watching people having fun *is* the fun). Imagine that you're taking in an entirely new world, rather than merely visiting a theme park.

In **Marvel Super Hero Island**, most guests race into the Hulk roller coaster and Spider-Man attractions. Instead, spend some time on the bridge or along the waterfront. Watch the frequent launching of the Hulk coaster, and perhaps study the visitors who've gathered for photos and autographs of Marvel superheroes.

In **Jurassic Park's** Camp Jurassic, a series of paths loop through a prehistoric playground. Why not get lost for a while? Take time to explore Hogwarts and Diagon Alley over at the **Wizarding World of Harry Potter.** The **Lost Continent**, with its tents and crafters and colorful bangles, is yet another place to stop and take things in.

Toon Lagoon, the G-rated alternative to Super Hero Island, provides plenty of places to explore, including a marked path that lets you follow the trail of Billy (of *Family Circus* comic fame), who's wandered off on his own. At **Seuss Landing** find a quiet place to sit and spend some time just watching children (and adults). The closest thing here to a fountain of youth is spinning on a carousel, riding on a Seussian trolley, and meeting the fabled Cat in the Hat.

of Harry Potter is the place for Potter-related memorabilia and wizard supplies, although some of the most popular Potter products are also carried at stores such as IOA's Trading Company and the Universal Studios Store at Universal Studios.

TOP SOUVENIRS

Several stores carry superhero and film-themed souvenirs—from Spider-Man gear and Incredible Hulk fists at IOA to Egyptian hats and clothing from The Mummy at Universal Studios.

At Seuss Landing, Thing 1 and Thing 2 T-shirts are always a hit with couples and siblings. Or how about a couple of red-and-white-stripe *Cat in the Hat* mugs?

Visit IOA's Wizarding World of Harry Potter and you may find yourself heading home with a wand, omnioculars, a quaffle ball, Hogwarts robe, or Nimbus 2000 broomstick.

TOP SHOPS

Dervish and Banges. Count on cracking open your wallet in the main repository of Potterabilia. There are Hogwarts school uniforms; hundreds of wands; broomsticks, including the top-of-the-line Nimbus 2000 and Firebolt; magical items such as sneakoscopes, spectrespecs, and omnioculars; and "all your Quidditch needs," including the elusive Golden Snitch. ✉ *Wizarding World of Harry Potter* 🌐 *www.universalorlando.com.*

Dinostore. Above a juvenile chorus of "I want this!" are adults counseling their kids on what they actually *need.* That can be a monumental task in this large store, which is packed with dino hats, shorts, necklaces, cards, mugs, squirt guns, figurines, and the clever T-Rex T-shirt emblazoned with the helpful suggestion "Bite Me." Rest assured there are educational dino toys, too. ✉ *Jurassic Park* 🌐 *www.universalorlando.com.*

Trading Company. The rambling emporium inside the entrance/exit of IOA is the largest store in the park; filled with a little something of everything from everywhere, even items from the attractions of Universal Studios. Here you'll find Shrek, SpongeBob, Spider-Man, the Simpsons, superheroes, and *puh-lenty* of Potter products plastered on sandals, frames, mugs, cups, caps, and clothing. ✉ *Islands of Adventure* 🌐 *www.universalorlando.com.*

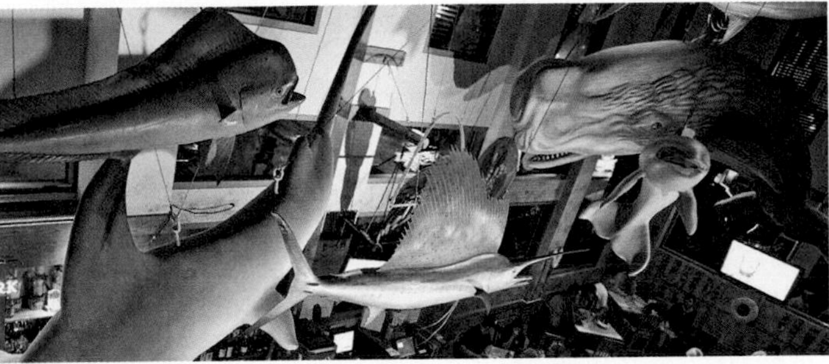

CITYWALK

With an attitude that's distinctly non-Disney, Universal has created nightlife for adults who want to party. The epicenter here is CityWalk, a 30-acre entertainment and retail complex at the hub of promenades that lead to both Universal parks.

When it comes to retail, much of the merchandise includes things you can find elsewhere—and most likely for less. But when you're swept up in the energy of CityWalk and dazzled by the degree of window-shopping (not to mention the fact that you're on vacation and you're more inclined to spend), chances are you'll want to drop into stores selling everything from surf wear and cigars to tattoos and timepieces.

In addition to stores, the open and airy gathering place includes an over-the-top discotheque, a theater for the fabulous and extremely popular Blue Man Group, and a huge hall where karaoke's king. There's a New Orleans bar, a Jamaican reggae lounge, a casual Key West hangout and, as of 2012, Hollywood Drive-In Golf, a pair of fun-filled 1950s sci-fi movie–themed miniature golf courses. On weeknights you find families and conventioneers; weekends a decidedly younger crowd parties until the wee hours.

Clubs have individual cover charges, but it's far more economical to pay for the whole kit and much of the caboodle. Choose a Party Pass (a one-price-all-clubs admission) for $11.99, or upgrade to a Party Pass-and-a-Movie for $15.98 (tax included); a Party Pass-and-a-Meal for $21; a Movie-and-a-Meal for $21.95; or a Meal and a Mini-Golf Deal for $23.95

At AMC Universal Cineplex, with its 20 screens (including IMAX), there's certain to be something you like—including nightly midnight movies. Meals (tax and gratuity included) are served at Jimmy Buffett's Margaritaville, the Hard Rock Cafe, NASCAR Sports Grille, and others. And as if these deals weren't sweet enough, after 6 the $15 parking fee drops to $5. Nevertheless, it's a long haul from the garage to CityWalk—if you prefer, simply call a cab. They run at all hours. ☎ *407/354–3374, 407/363–8000 Universal main line* 🌐 *www.citywalkorlando.com.*

NIGHTLIFE

With the wide range of nightlife you'll find at Universal, you may get the feeling that you're vacationing not in Orlando, but in New York City. CityWalk's stores open by midmorning, and its restaurants come to life between lunchtime and late afternoon. Eateries that double as nightclubs (such as Pat O'Brien's, Bob Marley's, and the Red Coconut Club) start charging a cover before dusk and apply age restrictions (usually 21) around 9. For details on a particular establishment, check with Guest Services.

BARS AND CLUBS

Bob Marley—A Tribute to Freedom. Modeled after the King of Reggae's home in Kingston, Jamaica (even down to the a/c window units), in a way this nightclub is also part museum, with more than 100 photographs and paintings showing pivotal moments in Marley's life. Though the place does serve meals, most patrons are at the cozy bar or by the patio, where they can be jammin' to a (loud) live band that plays nightly. For a nice souvenir, pose by the wonderful Marley statue outside the club. Legendary Thursdays feature drink specials for everyone, and Sunday is ladies' night from 9 pm until closing. ■ **TIP→ Often on Monday and Tuesday, CityWalk's pace is slow enough where some clubs will offer free admission. Ask before you pay.** ✉ *CityWalk* ☎ *407/224–2692* 🌐 *www.universalorlando.com* 🎟 *$7 after 9 pm* ⏲ *Daily 4 pm–2 am.*

CityWalk's Rising Star. Here you and other hopeful (and hopeless) singers can really let loose. Instead of singing to recorded music, you're accompanied by a band complete with backup singers—in front of a live audience. Backup singers are on hand every night, while the live band plugs in Tuesday through Saturday, and a full bar is always on tap. ✉ *6000 Universal Blvd., #717, CityWalk* ☎ *407/224–2961* 🌐 *www.universalorlando.com* 🎟 *$7, no charge to sing* ⏲ *Nightly 8 pm–2 am.*

the groove. In this cavernous hall images flicker rapidly on several screens, and the lights, music, and mayhem appeal to a mostly under-30 crowd. Prepare for lots of fog, swirling lights, and sweaty bodies. The '70s-style Green Room is filled with beanbag chairs and everything you threw out when Duran Duran hit the charts. The Blue Room is sci-fi Jetson-y, and the Red Room is hot and romantic in a bordello sort of way. The music is equally diverse: Top 40, hip-hop, R&B, techno and the occasional live band. ✉ *6000 Universal Blvd., CityWalk* ☎ *407/224–2692* 🌐 *www.universalorlando.com* 🎟 *$7* ⏲ *Daily 9 pm–2 am.*

Jimmy Buffett's Margaritaville. Buffett tunes fill the air at the restaurant here and at the Volcano, Land Shark, and 12 Volt bars. Inside there's a miniature Pan Am Clipper suspended from the ceiling, music videos projected onto sails, limbo and hula-hoop contests, a huge margarita blender that erupts "when the volcano blows," and live music nightly—everything that Parrotheads need to roost. Across the promenade, another full-size seaplane (emblazoned with 'Jimmy Buffett, Captain') is the setting for the Lone Palm Airport, a pleasing and surprisingly popular outdoor waterfront bar. ✉ *6000 Universal Studios Plaza, #704, CityWalk* ☎ *407/224–2692* 🌐 *www.margaritavilleorlando.com* 🎫 *$7 after 10 pm* ⏲ *Daily 11:30 am–2 am.*

Pat O'Brien's. An exact reproduction of the legendary New Orleans original, this comes complete with flaming fountain and dueling pianists who are playing for highly entertained regulars and visitors—even on weekday afternoons. Outside, the cozy and welcoming Patio Bar has a wealth of tables and chairs, allowing you to do nothing but enjoy the outdoors and your potent, rum-based Hurricanes in Orlando's version of the Big Easy. ✉ *6000 Universal Blvd., CityWalk* ☎ *407/224–2692* 🌐 *www.patobriens.com* 🎫 *$7 after 9 pm* ⏲ *Patio Bar daily 4 pm–2 am; piano bar daily 5 pm–2 am, 21 and up after 9 pm.*

Red Coconut Club. Paying tribute to kitsch design of the 1950s, the interior here is part Vegas lounge, part Cuban club, and part Polynesian tiki bar. It's "where tropical meets trendy." There are three full bars on two levels, signature martinis, an extensive wine list, and VIP bottle service. Hang out in the lounge, on the balcony, or at the bar. On a budget? Take advantage of the daily happy hours and gourmet appetizer menu. A DJ (Sunday–Wednesday) or live music (Thursday–Saturday) pushes the energy with tunes ranging from Sinatra to rock. Thursday is ladies' night. ✉ *6000 Universal Blvd., CityWalk* ☎ *407/224–2425* 🌐 *www.universalorlando.com* 🎫 *$7 after 9 pm* ⏲ *Sun.–Wed., 8 pm–2 am, Thurs.–Sat., 6 pm–2 am.*

6

SHOWS

Blue Man Group. At their own venue, the Sharp-Aquos Theatre, the ever-innovative Blue Men continue to pound out new music, sketches, and audience interaction that is nothing like you've ever seen. Attempting to understand the apps on a GiPad (a gigantic iPad), they may appear clueless and perplexed about cutting-edge technology (which for them can be as basic as a can of paint), but they're always excited when they can drum out rhythms on lengths of PVC pipes and throw a rave party finale for all in attendance. The show is a surreal comic masterpiece, so if you have the time and a little extra in your vacation budget, this is a must. Three levels of admission (Poncho, Tier 1, and Tier 2) hint at how messy things can get when the Blue Men cut loose. ✉ *CityWalk* ☎ *407/258–3626* 🌐 *www.universalorlando.com* 🎫 *Adults $69 advance purchase, $84 at box office; children 9 and under from $29* ⏲ *Daily showtimes vary; call for schedule.*

Hard Rock Cafe. The Hard Rock Cafe here is the largest on earth, which means you can see plenty of memorabilia, including such Beatles rarities as John Lennon's famous New York City T-shirt, Paul's original lyrics for "Let It Be," and the doors from London's Abbey Road studios plus hundreds of other fascinating collectibles. And the food's great, too. For savvy locals and many surprised guests, the main attraction is found next door in the Hard Rock Live concert hall ("The Coliseum of Rock.") Frequent performances featuring comedians, solo acts, and internationally recognized bands make it a popular venue and one of

Continued on page 372

UNIVERSAL

PARTY ON

By Gary McKechnie

On any given day at Universal, you can travel from New York to Hollywood, step into the pages of a comic book, or step back to the age of dinosaurs. You may also find yourself at annual celebrations that put you among the Whos in Whoville, in a festive parade through the French Quarter, or at a seriously scary Halloween bash.

Universal's roster of regular and seasonal shows, events, and festivities makes it easy to transform your theme-park vacation into a theme-park party-on vacation. And most—though not all—celebrations are included with regular park admission.

(above) Citywalk's Rising Star; (left) summer concert series performers—rapper LL Cool J, R&B artist Jordin Sparks, British pop star Natasha Bedingfield

Mardi Gras, Universal style

YEAR-ROUND ACTIVITIES

HARD ROCK LIVE

Good For: Large groups; couples; singles

When: Almost nightly, usually at 8

Where: CityWalk

Extra Fee: Ticket prices vary

More Info: www.hardrock.com

In a 3,000-seat concert hall adjacent to the world's largest Hard Rock Café, Hard Rock Live, one of only five in the U.S., gives you the chance to see top-name entertainers. In recent years musical and comedic talents have included Elvis Costello, Ringo Starr, BB King, Alice Cooper, Peter Frampton, and Craig Ferguson. Although Hard Rock Live shows cost extra, it costs nothing to take in the music-industry memorabilia at the café. Highlights include Buddy Holly's glasses, the doors from the Abbey Road studios, a Beatles poster from their days in Hamburg, and a suit worn by Elvis in *Viva Las Vegas*.

BLUE MAN GROUP

Good For: Families with teens; large groups; couples; singles

When: Nightly (usually at 6 and 9 if there are two shows; at 7 or 8 if there's one show)

Where: Sharp-Aquos Theatre, CityWalk

Extra Fee: From $29 (children) or $69 (adults)

More Info: www.blueman.com

Every evening, the Blue Man Group pounds out rhythms on PVC pipes, splatters paint on drums, feasts on marshmallows, unrolls a few miles of paper, and engages in something that can only be described as "spin 'n' spit" art.

Audience participation is part of the show. Afterward, you can mingle with the Blue Men in the lobby. It's a great photo op.

WANTILAN LUAU

Good For: Families; large groups

When: Saturday year-round; also Tuesday in peak season; seating begins at 6

Where: Royal Pacific Resort

Extra Fee: $70 adults, $40 children (including tip)

More Info: www.loewshotels.com

You sit at a table with other guests, taking in the show, and feasting on food from a buffet that includes pit-roasted suckling pig, guava barbecue short ribs, Hawaiian chicken teriyaki, catch of the day, tropical fruits, dessert, and free beer and wine. Performers conduct fire dances and hula navel maneuvers. Luau? No. Lu-wow!

MUSICA DELLA NOTTE

Good For: Large groups; couples

When: Nightly around sunset

Where: Portofino Bay Hotel

Extra Fee: None

More Info: www.loewshotels.com

Each evening, from balconies overlooking the Harbor Piazza, three tenors serenade the audience below with Italian opera classics, Broadway showtunes, and standards made famous by such performers as Andrea Bocelli and Frank Sinatra. If you missed the original Three Tenors (Plácido Domingo, José Carreras, and Luciano Pavarotti) here's your chance to enjoy the "Music of the Night."

VELVET SESSIONS

Good For: Couples; singles

When: Last Thursday of the month, January through October; doors open at 6:30, music begins at 8

Where: Hard Rock Hotel

Extra Fee: $29 online, $35 at door, $50 VIP. All covers include specialty drinks, finger food, and warm-up tunes.

More Info: www.velvetsessions.com

Most music buffs fantasize about seeing their favorite group perform in a small venue. To help fulfill those fantasies, the Hard Rock Hotel presents Velvet Sessions. They're cleverly billed as a "rock n' roll cocktail party" and are presented in the swanky, sexy Velvet Lounge, just off the hotel's lobby. Die-hard fans have a chance to see groups that could once (and, in some instances, could still) fill large concert halls. Performers have included Orleans, Eddie Money, Joan Jett, the Fixx, ABC, and the Romantics. Some of these acts will take some of you back to your high school days. Rock on!

RISING STAR

Good For: Large groups; couples; singles

When: Nightly; with a live band Tuesday through Saturday. Starts at 8; band plays as late as 2 am

Where: CityWalk

Extra Fee: Free with CityWalk pass, or $7 cover (singing is free)

More Info: www.citywalk.com

At this 440-seat venue, you can grab a microphone, select a song, and belt it out. But here, instead of having to wail above computerized backing tracks, you get to sing with a live band (and backup singers) whose members seem to know every possible song that every possible guest could ever possibly want to sing. Will it just be a fun evening out, or will it lead to success and a contract? Who knows? Just look at Susan Boyle.

UNIVERSAL ACCESS

It's not very well promoted, but Universal does offer **backstage tours** (☎ 407/363–8295).

Although they can't begin to compete with the backstage tours of Disney, these may appeal to fans of studio backlots.

Universal also offers five-hour **VIP tours** that usher you around the park (or parks) of your choice and get you front-of-the-line access to major attractions.

A one-day/one park VIP tour costs $169 per person and a one-day/two parks option is $189; this is in addition to park admission.

More exclusive are the one-day/one park tours for groups of up to 12. The price starts at $2,399, with a second park bumping it up to $2,750. Add a second day, and the price hits $4,250.

SEASONAL CELEBRATIONS

SUMMER CONCERT SERIES

Universal's free nighttime summer concert series (🌐 www.universalorlando.com) takes place in the open-air Music Plaza during June and July at, more or less, 8. Some of the pop, hip-hop, and R&B performers featured have topped the charts, earned gold and platinum albums, and been nominated for—or won—Grammy awards.

Member of the O'Jays

The setting is great, too. It's patterned after the famed Hollywood Bowl, so as performers take to the 2,400 square foot stage, you relax under the stars on a 15,000-square-foot lawn. It's not a bad way to spend a summer evening.

ROCK THE UNIVERSE

Rock the Universe (🌐 www.rocktheuniverse.com), a two-day, early-September celebration of Christian rock, has a passionate fan base, thanks to performances by some of the biggest names in the industry, including Pillar, Third Day, Casting Crowns, and tobyMac.

The gates open at 4 pm, and music keeps playing till 1 am. For those who can deal with high decibels and a touch of sleep deprivation, Rock the Universe is truly divine.

Rock the Universe: Group 1 Crew

Entry costs between \$50 and \$85, depending on the number of days you attend and whether or not you pay in advance.

MARDI GRAS

When Orlando's other theme parks are ratcheting down after the busy year-end holiday season, Universal Studios looks forward to February and its take on the New Orleans Mardi Gras (🌐 www.universalorlando.com). Among the festivities (all of them free) are parades and performances that last from February until the arrival of summer. Yes, Mardi Gras rolls on and on with a full slate of concerts by artists such as Daughtry, Nelly, Barenaked Ladies, Foreigner, and Lynyrd Skynyrd. More traditional tunes include Louisiana jazz, blues, zydeco, and Cajun bands played in the French Quarter Courtyard.

Also rolling in are festive floats, costumed marchers, stilt walkers, street performers, and dancers that lead a parade through Universal Studios from Hollywood Boulevard, past the Universal Studios Stores, and across the continent in New York—tossing beads and doubloons. As an onlooker, you'll swear that, for a moment, you're in the heart of N'awlins.

HALLOWEEN HORROR NIGHTS

Universal Studios pulls out all the stops with Halloween Horror Nights (www.halloweenhorrornights.com), which brings the most frightening characters in cinema history to life. Since 1991, Universal has enlisted the talents of maniacal killer clowns, criminally insane morticians, vengeful spinsters, and psychotic psychiatrists (or actors playing them) to scare you silly from late September through Halloween.

Jason is back at Horror Night!

Don't expect a super-sized version of your local Rotary Club's haunted house. The planning for Halloween Horror Nights takes months and utilizes Universal soundstages, movie-ready backlots, skilled makeup artists, existing attractions, eager actors, and horror-flick freaks to create eight haunted houses, six scare zones, and two live shows. It's the most fun you can have with your eyes closed. Prices range between $40 and $60, depending on how close it is to Halloween.

GRINCHMAS

If you owned a theme park that included a place called Seuss Landing, you'd be silly not to stage a holiday celebration starring the legendary Grinch. Each December at Islands of Adventure, Seuss Landing becomes the stage for Grinchmas (www.universalorlando.com), during which an array of Seussian characters come to life. Actors spend hours in makeup to appear as Whoville's Whos—all adorned in their finest holiday apparel.

There's also a free stage show adapted from the classic *How The Grinch Stole Christmas.* Enjoying the season is simply a cinch... when you spend holidays with a warm-hearted Grinch.

MACY'S HOLIDAY PARADE

If you can't travel to New York on Thanksgiving Day, you can still catch the Macy's parade (www.universalorlando.com) live. Granted, Universal's version won't be as much of a spectacle as the one in the Big Apple but, then again, New York doesn't have its own Simpsons Ride, either.

Starting in early December, this free nightly holiday event features marching bands, a Christmas tree lighting, and helium-filled balloons paraded through the heart of Universal Studios—down Hollywood Boulevard, through Production Central, and into New York.

In addition, the open-air Music Plaza hosts the Holiday Concert Series, with performers such as Mannheim Steamroller, Chris Isaak, and Natalie Cole.

How much does Universal charge for the concerts? Nothing. It's their gift to you.

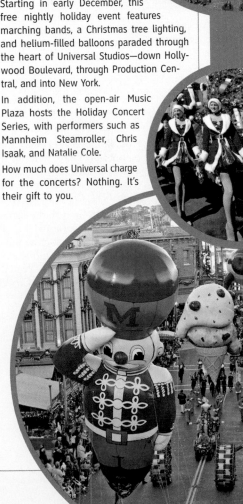

the most active places at Universal. A few drawbacks: The seats are hard and two-thirds don't face the stage; if you arrive at the door carrying a large purse or bags, it won't be time to rock, it'll be time to walk—about a quarter-mile back to the parking garage to stow your stuff. For showtimes, call 407/351–5483. ✉ *CityWalk* 🌐 *www.hardrocklive.com* 💳 *Cover prices vary* ⏲ *Daily from 11 am, with varying closing times, generally around midnight.*

SHOPPING

This 30-acre entertainment and retail complex is at the hub of promenades that lead to Universal Studios and Islands of Adventure. Shops here sell fine jewelry, cool beachwear, fashionable clothing, and stylish accessories. The best stores are near the entrance/exit of the complex.

Cigarz. For years, this perfectly themed cigar sanctuary has lured cigar aficionados with an impressive range of cigars preserved in a well-stocked humidor, as well as a good selection of pipes, lighters, and accessories. A cozy bar has become a popular gathering spot for in-the-know locals and soon-to-be friends. FYI: Smoking's permitted. ✉ *600 Universal Blvd., Suite 740, CityWalk* ☎ *407/370–2999* 🌐 *cigarzcitywalk.com.*

Fresh Produce. Featuring fashions that look right at home in sunny Florida, this boutique showcases comfortable and colorful swimwear, blouses, Capri slacks, dresses, footwear, beach gear, and accessories designed for coastal comfort. ✉ *CityWalk.*

P!Q. Although it's a small shop, there's enough room to hold hundreds of fun and mind-bending toys and books and games for kids (and adults) to teach them about math and physics and sometimes just plain fun stuff—like beer steins. Always interesting. ✉ *6000 Universal Blvd., Suite 745J, CityWalk* 🌐 *www.p!qproducts.com.*

Quiet Flight. Granted the closest beach is about 60 miles east, you can still get outfitted like a surfer at this shop, which sports an inventory featuring brand names such as Billabong, Quicksilver, Hurley, and Oakley. In addition to shorts and shirts, Quiet Flight also sells sandals, watches, sunglasses (Ray-Ban, Prada, and D&G among the featured names), and . . . surfboards! ✉ *CityWalk.*

7

WET 'N WILD

WELCOME TO WET 'N WILD

TOP REASONS TO GO

★ **Year-round fun.** Pools are heated in cooler weather, so Wet 'n Wild is one of the few water parks in the country to stay open year-round.

★ **Dancing waters.** Where else can you spin through a watery 1970s disco but at Wet 'n Wild's Disco H20?

★ **Sheer excitement.** Wet 'n Wild provides high-energy thrills with attractions that spin, drop, slosh, and twirl you through some amazingly creative watery experiences.

★ **Sheer relaxation.** However, when you tire of climbing, walking, and swimming, Wet 'n Wild offers a sandy beach where you can laze the time away in a lounge chair and take a load off.

1 Surf Lagoon. The park's center area, Surf Lagoon and surrounding beach is the park's buffer zone and focal point.

2 West of Surf Lagoon. From the main entrance, the majority of high-speed slides and tube rides are on the left side of the park (along with the kid-friendly Blastaway Beach).

3 East of Surf Lagoon. On the right side of the park there are even more high-adrenaline rides, but they are offset by placid experiences such as the Lazy River and sanctuaries including the Riverside BBQ and tropical cabanas.

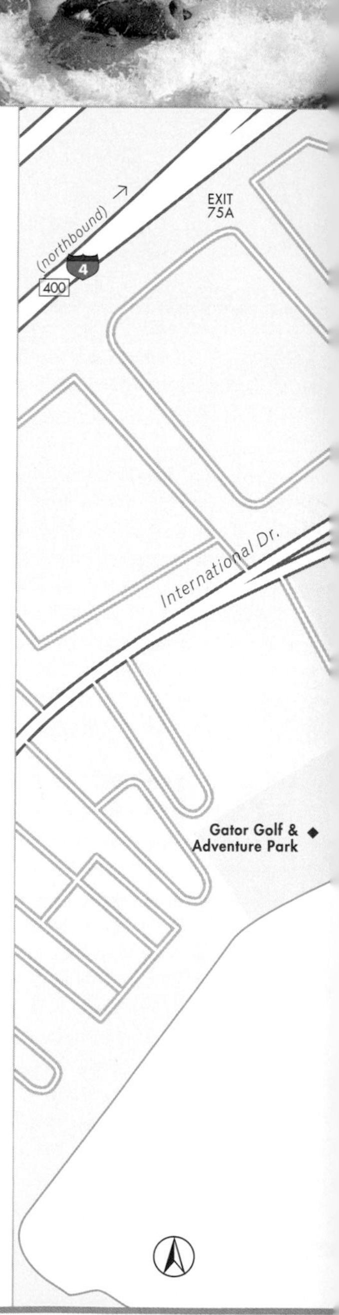

TO
ROUTE 435
(S. Kirkman Rd) →
International Dr.
WET 'N WILD
1
2
3
Universal Blvd.
Sandy Lake
0 1/8 mi
0 1/8 km

GETTING ORIENTED

If you arrive early, when crowds are light to moderate, you should have plenty of time to do each ride once, and possibly twice or more. From the Surf Lagoon straight ahead, head counterclockwise to the most thrilling experiences (Bomb Bay, Der Stuka, The Storm) first. By the time you've circled the park and are worn out, your kids should still have plenty of energy to deplete at Blastaway Beach.

Updated by Gary McKechnie

When you were a kid, chances are all you needed for unlimited summer fun was a simple inflatable pool and a garden hose or sprinkler. Well, about the same time that you were growing up, so were water parks. They started with a few simple slides and are now the aquatic equivalents of megamalls.

It all began in 1977 with Wet 'n Wild, created by George Millay, who was also one of the founders of SeaWorld. Although it's now far from alone, Wet 'n Wild remains extremely popular, thanks to its quality, service, and ability to create more heart-stopping waterslides, rides, and tubing adventures than its competitors. Indeed, new rides seem to be added like clockwork, old ones improved, and settings developed for the comfort of guests. There's a complete water playground for kids, numerous high-energy slides for adults, a lazy-river ride, and some quiet, sandy beaches on which you can stretch out and get a tan.

Speaking of high energy, this is a park that requires a lot of it. A day here is often a marathon of climbing steps, sliding, swimming, and splashing, though you may not notice just how much your stamina is being drained as you scamper from slide to slide. Plan to take breaks: laze in a beach chair and eat high-protein meals and snacks to maintain your strength. You can bring in a cooler for a picnic or eat at a restaurant in one of several food courts.

If you're not a strong swimmer, don't worry. There are plenty of low-key attractions, and all of the ride entrances are marked with warnings to let you know which ones are safe for you. Plus, during peak season, there are as many as 200 lifeguards on duty daily. Also note that all the pools (if not the rides) are ADA-compliant and are heated in cooler weather. This, combined with Orlando's temperate climate, means that Wet 'n Wild is one of the few water parks in the country to stay open year-round.

Surf's up!

TOP ATTRACTIONS

Bomb Bay: You drop through the floor of a cylinder and plummet down a nearly vertical slide—as they say, the first step is a doozy.

Brain Wash: Lighting effects and surreal sounds accompany your five-story drop and spin around a 65-foot domed funnel.

Disco H2O: Why spin through a watery disco to a 1970s soundtrack? For the aquatic dance-hall sensation that makes this ride so popular.

Lazy River: This calming stream is a good antidote to all the adrenaline.

The Storm: Nestled in an inner tube, you slip into a surreal spin around a massive basin that slowly but surely washes you—down the drain.

Surf Lagoon: If the beach is out of reach, take advantage of the sand and surf here.

PLANNING

PARK AMENITIES

Baby Care: There's no specific area for baby care at Wet 'n Wild, nor does the park rent strollers. There are changing stations in both men's and women's restrooms.

First Aid: The First-Aid Stand is between Surf Grill and Manny's Pizza.

Food. The **Wild Tiki Lounge,** a Polynesian restaurant-bar overlooking the lake, has a full menu, table service, and flat-screen TVs. If you're worn out from the attractions, chill out here. It's like being at a South Pacific resort. There's also **Manny's Pizza** (pizza, pasta, and subs), the **Surf Grill** (burgers, hot dogs, and more healthful choices like vegetarian burgers, baked potatoes, and salads), and the all-you-can-eat, seasonal **Riverside BBQ** ($17 adults, $12 children), where you can dine on chicken and pulled pork. Smaller kiosks sell cotton candy, ice cream, funnel cakes, and other carnival-style snacks.

Guest Services: Get maps and other information at Guest Services (aka Guest Relations), to the left as you enter.

Lockers: There are dressing rooms with lockers in three different sizes (personal $6/$3 deposit, standard $9/$3 deposit, family $11/$3 deposit) as well as showers and restrooms to the left of the entrance gates. Additional restrooms are on the island inside the lazy river and near the First-Aid Stand and the Surge.

Lost People and Things: The Lost and Found is at Guest Services, to the left just after you enter the park. This is also where lifeguards and other staffers take lost children.

Picnicking: You're welcome to bring coolers with food into the park, which has many picnic areas—both open and sheltered. Glass containers and alcoholic beverages are not permitted.

Wheelchair Rentals: Near the entrance, you can rent modified wheelchairs (they have large tires that can handle the sand) for $5 per day with a $25

Brain Wash is one of Wet 'n Wild's most thrilling slides.

refundable deposit. Note that although many of the paths are flat and accessible, none of the rides accommodates people using wheelchairs.

ESSENTIALS

Admission: Basic admission is about $55 for adults (ages 10 and up) and $50 for children (but look for discount coupons in flyers and magazines displayed in stores and restaurants throughout the I-Drive area). Full price covers admission for any or all of the next 14 consecutive days, even when you buy in advance online (and by doing so, you'll save an additional $10 per ticket). Other money-saving options include the FlexTicket, which bundles Wet 'n Wild with parks and attractions at Universal Orlando, SeaWorld, and Busch Gardens.

Parking: Costing $12 for cars, vans, and motorcycles and $16 for RVs and cars with trailers, parking is in a large lot along Universal Boulevard.

Wet 'n Wild. For general information, call Wet 'n Wild or visit online. ✉ *Wet 'n Wild* ☎ *407/351–3200 recorded information, 407/351–1800 park operations* 🌐 *www.wetnwildorlando.com.*

TOURING TIPS

- Want to save a bundle? Admission drops to half price during the afternoon; exactly when depends on closing time, but can be as late as 5 pm in the summer. Call ahead for the magic hour. Even better, if you pay for a full-price ticket, you can return for free for 14 consecutive days. It's a great deal for families in town for an extended stay. You can see the big three (Disney, Universal, SeaWorld) during the day and return here in the evening.

- When you arrive, it's a good idea to pick up a map, scan the park layout, and stake out a spot on the beach before heading on or in. To claim a prime beach spot, arrive 30 minutes before the park opens, or visit on a cloudy day. If it looks like rain all day, though, head elsewhere.
- Men should wear a true bathing suit, and women should opt for a one-piece rather than a bikini. Cutoff shorts and garments with rivets, metal buttons, buckles, or zippers aren't allowed.
- Wading slippers are a good idea—hot sidewalks and sandpaper-like pool bottoms can do a number on your feet—but put them in a locker or carry them when taking a plunge, since they can catch on slides.
- Items too large to carry should be stashed in a locker. Some picnic tables have lockable containers (secured to the umbrella stand) that are just large enough to hold smaller items such as keys, glasses, and cell phones.
- For extra privacy, a quiet oasis in the middle of the lazy river features cabanas with a fan, chaise lounges, and a fridge stocked with a dozen bottles of water. It's a nice base for stowing your things, but the privilege costs an extra $150. Don't want to get up? Servers will bring food to you.
- Be patient with the lines here. Just when you think you've arrived, you discover there's another level or two to go.
- To bypass lines at the popular rides, get an Express Pass (available seasonally), accepted at most rides. Prices change based on park attendance and time of day, so call Park Operations at ☎ *407/351–1800* for details. A limited number of passes are sold each day—all the more reason to get here early.
- Okay. So you remembered your swimsuit and towel. But what about sunscreen? You can buy it and other necessities or souvenirs at the **Breakers Beach Shop**, near the park entrance. And if you did forget a towel, renting one here costs $4 with a $3 deposit. Rent a three-pack, though, and you save $2.

7

EXPLORING WET 'N WILD

The Black Hole: The Next Generation. Beneath a massive tower that looks like a UFO, you enter a darkened area that's sealed off from views of the outside world. From here, you're hurtled through the cosmos in a two-person "hydra-capsule" (aka an inner tube). All the while there's a dynamic display of lights flashing around you which ratchets up the drama. Chances are you'll scream your head off as you zip through space and experience the gravitational effects of wormholes and black holes before splashdown. **■ TIP→ Try it very early (or late), or invest in an Express Pass.** ✉ *Wet 'n Wild* ☞ *Duration: 1 min. Crowds: Heavy. Audience: Not Small Kids. Height minimum: 48 inches.*

The Blast. What's the story here? A pipe has ruptured, and the resulting deluge is enough to create this twisting and turning ride. Aboard a two-passenger inner tube, you and a friend will bump down a series of slides and drops and corners through explosive pipe bursts and drenching waterspouts that lead up to a final waterfall plunge. **■ TIP→ Keep**

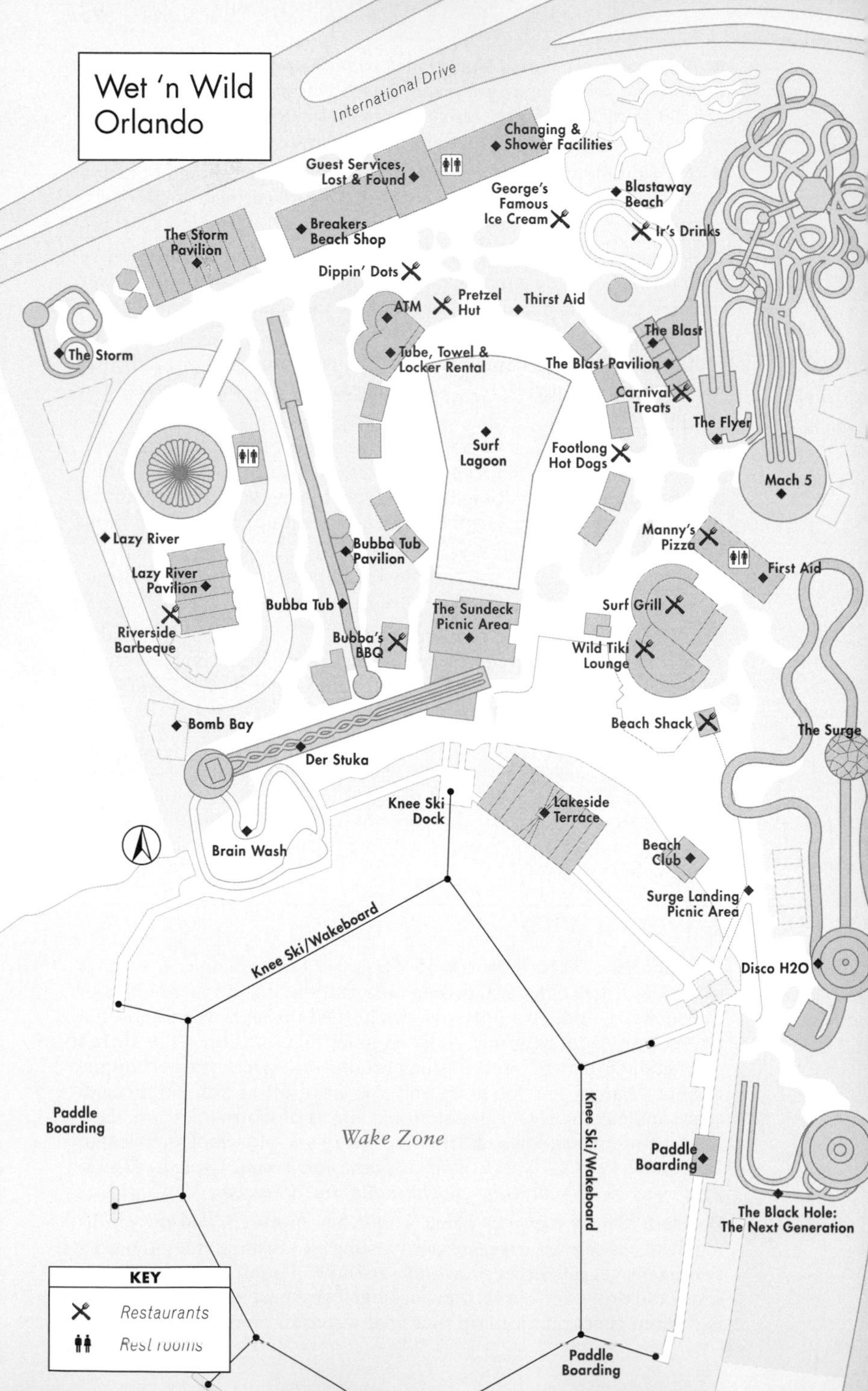
Wet 'n Wild Orlando
International Drive
Changing & Shower Facilities
Guest Services, Lost & Found
George's Famous Ice Cream
Blastaway Beach
Ir's Drinks
The Storm Pavilion
Breakers Beach Shop
Dippin' Dots
Pretzel Hut
Thirst Aid
ATM
The Storm
Tube, Towel & Locker Rental
The Blast
The Blast Pavilion
Carnival Treats
The Flyer
Surf Lagoon
Footlong Hot Dogs
Mach 5
Lazy River
Bubba Tub Pavilion
Manny's Pizza
First Aid
Lazy River Pavilion
Bubba Tub
The Sundeck Picnic Area
Surf Grill
Riverside Barbeque
Bubba's BBQ
Wild Tiki Lounge
Bomb Bay
Beach Shack
The Surge
Der Stuka
Knee Ski Dock
Lakeside Terrace
Brain Wash
Beach Club
Surge Landing Picnic Area
Knee Ski/Wakeboard
Disco H2O
Paddle Boarding
Wake Zone
Knee Ski/Wakeboard
Paddle Boarding
The Black Hole: The Next Generation
KEY
Restaurants
Rest rooms
Paddle Boarding

an eye on the line, and hop on as soon as it gets short. Or you can use your Express Pass. ✉ *Wet 'n Wild* ☞ *Duration: Under 1 min. Crowds: Heavy. Audience: Families. Height minimum: 48 inches; 36 inches with an adult.*

Blastaway Beach. If your kids get a thrill out of a simple waterslide, this may be the highlight of their vacation. It's an amazingly creative 15,000-square-foot section of the park dominated by a towering six-story sand castle that surpasses nearly everything a kid could expect. Adorned with flags and banners and surrounded by two pools that create an 85,000-gallon "moat," the castle is equipped with 15 slides and more than 160 soakers, water jets, waterfalls, water cannons, and huge buckets that fill and dump their contents on the guests below. All of this makes Blastaway Beach the best-equipped—not to mention largest—water playground in Florida. Even better, adults are welcome to join their kids in this splashtacular setting, but if you can't handle this much fun, rest easy: there's plenty of seating amidst lush, tropical landscaping. ■ **TIP→ Come when you need a break but the kids still have energy.** ✉ *Wet 'n Wild* ☞ *Duration: Up to You. Crowds: Moderate–Heavy. Audience: Families.*

Fodor's Choice ★ **Bomb Bay.** Lines move quickly here. Why? Because once they reach the top, a lot of people chicken out and head back down the stairs. Here's why: You step inside a large enclosed capsule. The attendant looks through the glass door to make sure your arms and legs are crossed (thereby preventing wedgies) and punches a button to release the trapdoor. Then, like a bomb dropping out of a plane, you free-fall almost straight down for 76 feet before skimming down the long, steep slide. The force of the water on your feet, legs, and back rivals the emotional toll it took to take the plunge in the first place, but, oh, what a trip! ■ **TIP→ Express Pass accepted here, but although the line might look long, it moves quickly so get on it anytime—if you dare to ride the ride, that is.** ✉ *Wet 'n Wild* ☞ *Duration: Under 1 min. Crowds: Heavy. Audience: Not Small Kids. Height minimum: 48 inches.*

Fodor's Choice ★ **Brain Wash.** At one of Wet 'n Wild's wildest thrill slides, you start by climbing into an inner tube designed for two or four passengers. With lights, video, and surreal sounds washing around you, you and your tube commit to a 53-foot vertical drop—but that's only half of it. Once you've survived the drop, you'll find yourself at the rim of a 65-foot domed funnel and swirl around its massive bowl before finally dropping through into water below. ■ **TIP→ Try it very early (or very late), or invest in an Express Pass.** ✉ *Wet 'n Wild* ☞ *Duration: 1 min. Crowds: Heavy. Audience: Families. Height requirements: 48 inches; 36 inches if riding with an adult.*

Bubba Tub. After scaling the platform, your group (up to four people can ride together) boards a huge inner tube, which floats over the edge of a six-story slide. Your aquatic quartet then launches into an up-and-down triple-dip before finally splashing into the pool. Much of the fun comes from the side-to-side swishing and sloshing of the tube as it travels maniacally down the stream. ■ **TIP→ Try it very early (or very late), or invest in an Express Pass.** ✉ *Wet 'n Wild* ☞ *Duration: Under*

7

1 min. Crowds: Moderate. Audience: Families. Height minimum: 48 inches; 36 inches with an adult.

Der Stuka. It's a steep slide with thrills similar to those of the adjacent Bomb Bay, but without the trapdoor drop. Despite that difference, *Der Stuka* ("Steep Hill" in German) is hard to beat for sheer exhilaration. After climbing the winding six-story platform, you sit down on a horizontal slide, nudge yourself forward a few inches, and then let gravity take over. Before you know it, you're hurtling down a 250-foot-long speed slide that will tax your back and test the security of your bathing suit. This one's a real scream. ■ **TIP→ Express Pass it, or try it very early (or very late).** ✉ *Wet 'n Wild* ☞ *Duration: 1 min. Crowds: Moderate. Audience: Not Small Kids. Height minimum: 48 inches.*

Fodor's Choice ★ **Disco H20.** Here's something even the folks at Studio 54 never dreamed of: a four-person raft that floats into a swirling aquatic nightclub. Once you drift inside the 70-foot-tall building, your raft goes into a spin cycle as disco balls twirl, the lights flash, and the sounds of the '70s greatest hits reverberate. Incredibly, even with the numbing techno music, this is one of the park's most popular attractions. ■ **TIP→ Try it very early (or very late), or invest in an Express Pass.** ✉ *Wet 'n Wild* ☞ *Duration: 1 min. Crowds: Heavy. Audience: Families. Height minimum: 48 inches; 36 inches with an adult.*

The Flyer. If you've ever visited a ski resort during the summer, you've probably seen a toboggan run that you can take in a retrofitted sled. Well, that's kind of the same principle here, but with one difference: there's water, water everywhere. After getting onto your four-person toboggan, you'll slosh around and race into switchback curves and down suddenly steep drops. The turns are similar to those on a real toboggan run—just much warmer and more refreshing. ■ **TIP→ Watch the line, and head over when the timing's right or invest in an Express Pass.** ✉ *Wet 'n Wild* ☞ *Duration: 1 min. Crowds: Heavy. Audience: Families. Height minimum: 48 inches; 36 inches with an adult.*

Lazy River. Just settle into an inner tube for a peaceful trip down a gently moving stream, guided along by the slow current. As you bask in the sun, you drift past waterfalls, colorful flowers, and tropical greenery that grows so incredibly high. Along the way, you'll pass scenes of Old Florida (think rustic boat docks and retro billboards). This is a great place to take a break when your body just can't handle any more climbing or free-falling. ■ **TIP→ Come and go as you wish!** ✉ *Wet 'n Wild* ☞ *Duration: Up to You. Crowds: Moderate. Audience: All Ages. Height minimum: Under 48 inches must wear a life vest (available for free).*

Mach 5. After grabbing a soft foam mat, you scale a few steps and arrive at one of three speedy waterslides. Conventional wisdom says that Lane B is the best, but it's possible all three are the same. Riding on your belly, you zip through some great twists, feel the sensation of hitting the high banks, and then splash down in a flood of water. ■ **TIP→ Try it very early (or very late), or use an Express Pass.** ✉ *Wet 'n Wild* ☞ *Duration: 1 min. Crowds: Moderate. Audience: Not Small Kids. Height minimum: Under 48 inches must wear a life vest.*

DID YOU KNOW?

Lane B of the Mach 5 water-slide is rumored to be the best. You decide by sliding down all three lanes—on your belly using a soft foam board.

The Storm. From the top of the tower you'll see that two flumes are flowing with a torrent of water. No inner tubes or mats here! Just climb in, shove off, and, in the midst of a tidal wave, let the slow, curving arc take you around and around until you reach a 30-foot-diameter bowl. At this point, you spin around again like a human-size soap sud whirling around a sink drain. After angular momentum has had its fun, you drop through a hole in the bottom of the bowl and into a small pool. Once you get your bearings, you may be tempted to climb up and do it again. **■ TIP→ Now's the time for Express Pass, or try this early in the day or later in the evening.** ☒ *Wet 'n Wild* ☞ *Duration: 1 min. Crowds: Moderate. Audience: Not Small Kids. Height minimum: 48 inches.*

Surf Lagoon. Just past the turnstiles, this 17,000-square-foot lagoon is as close to a beach as you'll find in the park. With a zero-depth entry and a maximum depth of 6 feet, plus a wide beach, lounge chairs, and umbrellas surrounding it, it's generally packed. Every so often the lagoon is buffeted by 4-foot-high waves (which is why it's also known as the wave pool), eliciting screams of delight from kids. Adults are thrilled that the money they spent on floats, surfboards, and inner tubes was worth it. **■ TIP→ Anytime is fine.** ☒ *Wet 'n Wild* ☞ *Duration: Up to You. Crowds: Moderate–Heavy. Audience: All Ages. Height minimum: Under 48 inches must wear an approved flotation device in the wave pool.*

The Surge. If you or your kids are too nervous for rides like Bomb Bay or the Black Hole, then this ride, which *borders* on exhilarating, may be a good alternative. You and up to three other passengers get into a giant raft. After going over the lip of the first drop, the raft zips down five stories while twisting and turning through steeply banked curves and zooming beneath waterfalls. It's a new definition of family fun. **■ TIP→ Try it very early (or very late), or invest in an Express Pass.** ☒ *Wet 'n Wild* ☞ *Duration: Under 1 min. Crowds: Moderate. Audience: Families. Height minimum: 48 inches; 36 inches with an adult.*

Wake Zone. A molasses-slow line marks the entrance to this seasonal attraction (open May through September), which requires an extra $12 for an all-day pass. A moving cable with ski ropes attached encircles a large lake. After donning protective headgear and a life vest, you kneel on a knee skate or try to balance on a wakeboard, grab a ski rope, and are given the chance to circumnavigate the lake. The ½-mile ride includes five turns: roughly 75% of riders wipe out after the first one, and 90% are gone by the second. If you need help, ask the assistants for support; they want to see you go the distance and will suggest ways to help you make it around the lagoon (keep your arms in and lean forward). Riders who can stay afloat enjoy three laps per turn, but you can go back again and again. This is also where you can perfect your skills on a stand-up paddle board (no height requirement). **■ TIP→ The extra fee means that the lines may be shorter (but not necessarily faster). The pass is good all day, so return when there's not a wait.** ☒ *Wet 'n Wild* ☞ *Duration: 5 min. Crowds: Moderate–Heavy in Season. Audience: Teens and Adults. Height minimum: 56 inches.*

8

SEAWORLD, DISCOVERY COVE, AND AQUATICA

WELCOME TO SEAWORLD, DISCOVERY COVE, AND AQUATICA

TOP REASONS TO GO

★ **Animal Magnetism:** If you love animals—slick, shiny, feathery, or furry—SeaWorld, Discovery Cove, and Aquatica are where you want to be. No robotic wildlife here; just well-cared-for and talented dolphins, whales, seals, otters, penguins, cats, dogs. . . .

★ **A Slower Pace:** The shows and natural settings of SeaWorld and Discovery Cove let you enjoy a theme-park vacation without racing from one attraction to the next. Living in the moment is the lesson here.

★ **Getting Smarter:** No one leaves these parks without learning a little something about nature through shows, backstage tours, instructional signage, and well-versed educators and naturalists who are always ready to answer questions.

★ **Memories in the Making:** Chances are SeaWorld and Discovery Cove will afford you the chance to pet a penguin, feed a dolphin, or watch a 5-ton whale leap out of the water. You can't forget things like that.

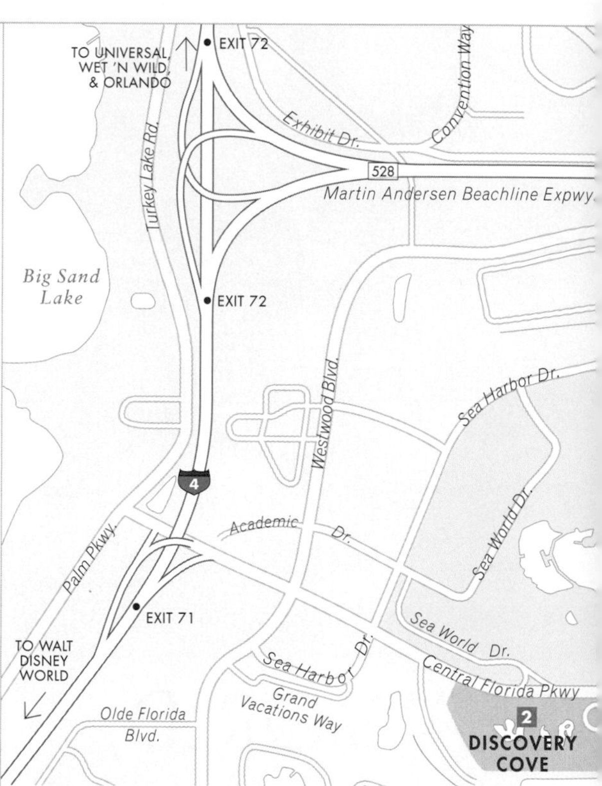

1 SeaWorld. With the exception of a handful of thrill rides, the original park (which opened in 1973 to reroute visitors heading to the then recently opened Walt Disney World) maintains a slow and easy pace. Here it's all about clever shows, shaded sidewalks, and plenty of opportunities to enjoy the natural grace and intriguing personalities of marine life and other animals.

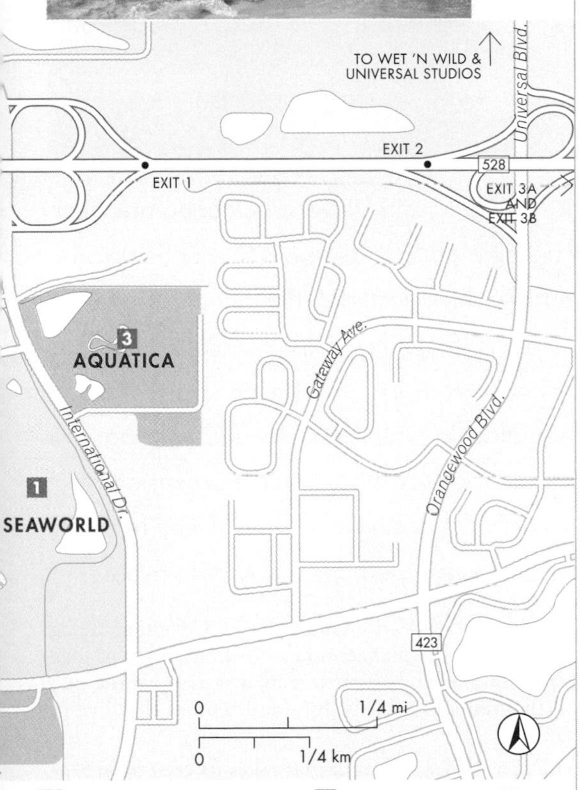

GETTING ORIENTED

SeaWorld is just off the intersection of Interstate 4 and the Beachline Expressway, equidistant from Universal Orlando and the Walt Disney World Resort, which are only about five minutes away. SeaWorld is also a mere 10 minutes from Downtown Orlando and 15 minutes from the airport. Discovery Cove is its own oasis across the street from SeaWorld. Aquatica, a little ways down the road from both, is the first of the three that you'll see after exiting the expressway.

2 Discovery Cove. SeaWorld spun off this park to give you the chance to enjoy a lot more time (and to spend a little more cash) with the animals. A trip to this aquatic oasis feels like a trip to the islands; a daylong, all-inclusive experience that includes breakfast and lunch, drinks, a private beach, snorkeling equipment, and—for approximately an extra $100—the chance to swim with dolphins. Paradise.

3 Aquatica. SeaWorld's water park offers the chance to slip and slide at adrenaline-rush speeds, relax in the current of two wave pools, laze on a wide beach, and take the wee ones to pint-size play areas of their very own. All in all, there's something for everyone, showcased in a tropical, tiki-themed setting.

Just as Walt Disney World and Universal Orlando are much more than just a single park, the same is true of SeaWorld. The original park—which includes the Shamu shows as well as presentations featuring dolphins and seals—has expanded to include Discovery Cove (an immersive tropical retreat), and Aquatica (a water park loaded with aquatic excitement). So, as you plan your vacation, consider that SeaWorld can easily fill a single day or, if you're really eager to take to the waters, perhaps a day or two more.

There's a whole lot more to SeaWorld and Discovery Cove than being splashed by Shamu. You can see manatees face-to-snout, learn to love a shark, swim with dolphins, and be spat at by a walrus. These two parks celebrate all the mammals, birds, fish, and reptiles that live in and near the ocean.

Then there's Aquatica, a wild water park that takes its cues from SeaWorld and Discovery Cove in design and mood—marine-life motifs are everywhere. It also gives competitor water parks a run for their money with thrilling slides, broad beaches, calming rivers, and an area for small kids.

The park also takes some tips from the tropics. Right after you clear the parking lot, you see a tropical pastiche of buildings. Yup. That's definitely an island vibe you're detecting. Upon entering Aquatica, you feel as if you've left Central Florida for the Caribbean or Polynesia, even.

You might be drawn to the series of superfast waterslides (some of which conclude by sending you into serene streams), or you might feel the pull of the white-sand beaches beside the twin wave pools, where you can laze in the sun, venturing out every so often to try a ride or climb into an inner tube and float down a river. Whether you're spending the day at SeaWorld, Discovery Cove, or Aquatica, just go with it. Get into a groove, relax, and enjoy yourself at some of the most pleasant theme parks in Orlando.

PLANNING

GETTING HERE AND AROUND

Heading west on Interstate 4 (toward Disney) take Exit 72; heading east, take Exit 71. After that you'll be going east on the Beachline Expressway (aka Route 528), and the first right-hand exit leads you to International Drive. Turn left, and you'll soon see the entrance to Aquatica on your left. Sea Harbor Drive—leading to SeaWorld's entrance—will be on your right. To reach Discovery Cove, follow International Drive past Aquatica ½ mile to the Central Florida Parkway and turn right. The park's entrance will be on your left.

OPERATING HOURS

SeaWorld opens daily at 9 am and usually closes at 7 pm, with extended hours during the summer and holidays. Hours at Discovery Cove also vary seasonally, although it's generally open daily from 8 to 5:30, with check-in beginning 30 minutes earlier—which is not a bad idea considering Discovery Cove serves a complimentary breakfast until 10 am. Aquatica is open at 9 am, with closing times varying between 5 and 9 pm, depending on the season. Allow a full day to see each attraction.

ADMISSION

SeaWorld, Discovery Cove, Aquatica, and Busch Gardens Tampa Bay fall under the SeaWorld Parks & Entertainment umbrella, and you can save by buying combo tickets. Regular one-day tickets to **SeaWorld** cost $92 (adults) and $87 (children ages 3–9), excluding tax, but if you order in advance over the phone or online, you'll save $10 per ticket—which just may be the best money-saving option you'll find. Combo-park admission prices, which include 14 days at each park, are as follows:

SeaWorld/Aquatica *$129 adults/$124 children*

SeaWorld/Busch Gardens Tampa *$129/$121*

SeaWorld/Aquatica/Busch Gardens Tampa *$159/$154*

Flex Ticket (14 days at SeaWorld/Aquatica/Busch Gardens Tampa) *$345/$325*

Aquatica at-the-gate admission is $56 (adults) and $51 (children 3–9), but if you order online you'll save around $10 per ticket. Add a Banana Beach all-you-can-eat option, and the online price is $55 adults, $50 children.

Reserve **Discovery Cove** visits well in advance—attendance is limited to about 1,000 a day. Tickets (with a dolphin swim) start at about $229 (off-season, in January and February) but are generally around $289. Forgo the dolphin swim and save approximately $100. This park has what's called dynamic pricing (meaning prices change by season, and also at other times without notice). Admission is less expensive the earlier you book (so call well in advance) and includes access to all beach and snorkeling areas and the free-flight aviary; meals and snacks; use of a mask, snorkel, swim vest, towel, locker, and sunscreen; parking; and a pass for 14 days of unlimited admission to SeaWorld Orlando and Aquatica. Upgrade to an "ultimate" pass (about $20), which includes admission (and free transportation) to Busch Gardens Tampa.

Quick Queue Passes. SeaWorld's Quick Queue passes (*$19–$35 per person, depending on season*) get you to the front of the line at major attractions and shows for one admission each. The higher price unlimited pass is good for unlimited admissions. Neither Discovery Cove nor Aquatica has such a pass.

All-Day Dining Deal. Available at select SeaWorld restaurants (Voyager's Smokehouse, Seaport Pizza, Terrace Garden Buffet, The Spice Mill, Seafire Inn, and Mango Joe's), adults will pay from $32.99 and kids from $17.99 to chow down on an entrée, side dish, drink, and dessert for each meal Skip it if you plan on having just one meal in the park.

PARKS TIPS

SMART SEAWORLD

Avoid weekend and school-holiday visits. These are the busiest times, so plan around them if you can.

Wear sneakers or water shoes—no heels or slip-on sandals. It may not seem like it, but there'll be a whole lot of walking as you roam from one end of the park to the other, stand in line, and walk through attractions.

Pack dry clothes. You can get wet just by being toward the front at the Shamu show or riding Journey to Atlantis. Alternatively, carry a rain poncho.

Budget for food for the animals. Participating in animal feedings is a major part of the SeaWorld experience, although it comes at a price: a small carton of fish costs $5.

Pick up a map-and-show schedule inside the entrance. SeaWorld has its show schedule down to a science. If you start by catching the show closest to the entrance, shortly after that one's over, guests are moving farther into the park to grab a seat at the next performance so you'll end up moving with the crowd. Instead, start off at a show further inside the park so you are ahead of the crowds. So spend a few minutes planning so you can casually stroll from show to show and have time for learning, testing out thrill rides, *and* enjoying a leisurely meal.

Be open to learning. SeaWorld's trainers and educators are always at the ready to share information about the park's wildlife.

DISCOVERY DONE RIGHT

Make reservations well in advance. Prized June dates, for instance, can sell out in March. If there aren't openings when you call, though, don't despair. Call back often to inquire about cancellations.

Think about your eyewear. Park masks don't accommodate glasses, but there are a limited number of near- and far-sighted prescription masks (first-come, first-served) available. Just step into a booth and you'll be able to try on a few different pairs with different magnifications. If you don't mind risking lost contacts, just wear those beneath a non-prescription mask.

Don't bring your own wet suit or fins. Every guest must wear a Discovery Cove–issued wet suit or vest—not a bad idea, as the water can be cold.

Leave belongings in your locker. The plastic passes you're given are all you need to pick up your meals, soft drinks, and—if you're over 21—alcoholic drinks.

Be flexible when it comes to weather. If the weather on your reserved day looks like it'll be an all-day downpour, attempts will be made to reschedule your visit while you're in town. If that's not possible, you'll have to settle for a refund.

Have a dolphin relay a message. The Special Occasion Package enlists the help of a bottlenose dolphin to deliver love notes, wedding proposals, birthday or anniversary greetings, and the like.

AQUATICA ADVICE

- **Buy tickets in advance.** Tickets bought ahead of time online or at another SeaWorld park allow early entry (and discounts) to Aquatica, which, in turn, increases your chances of hitting all the big-deal flume and tube rides—possibly more than once.
- **Be open to animal encounters.** The Commerson's dolphins of Dolphin Plunge have scheduled feeding times, and you can see macaws perched on tree limbs and small mammals on display in Conservation Cabanas—usually attended to by knowledgeable educators.
- **Pack beach supplies.** You'll save a few bucks by having your own towels, lotion, water shoes, and snacks.
- **Take care of yourself.** Fight fatigue by eating a good breakfast, drinking plenty of water, and nibbling on high-energy snacks. Avoid sunburn by reapplying sunscreen often—even the waterproof stuff washes off.
- **Save your soles.** Water shoes protect your feet from hot sand and sidewalks and the rough surfaces in some pools.

8

CONTACTS

Aquatica ☎ *888/800–5447* 🌐 *www.aquaticabyseaworld.com*

Busch Gardens Tampa ☎ *888/800–5447* 🌐 *www.buschgardens.com/bgt*

Discovery Cove ☎ *877/557–7404* 🌐 *www.discoverycove.com*

SeaWorld ☎ *888/800–5447* 🌐 *www.seaworld.com*

Parking. Parking is $15 for a car or motorcycle, $20 for an RV or camper. For $25 you can pull into one of the six Preferred Parking rows closest to the front gate and for $30 a valet will take the wheel. At Aquatica, cars and motorcycles are charged $12, RVs $16—although if you already have your parking slip from that day at SeaWorld, it's free. Parking is free at Discovery Cove.

SEAWORLD

By Gary McKechnie

Just as you wouldn't expect to arrive at Disney and see nothing but Mickey Mouse, don't expect to arrive at SeaWorld and see only Shamu. Only a few steps into the park you'll find baby dolphins and their mothers, a pool filled with stingrays, colorful flamingos, rescued sea turtles, rescued pelicans, and even rescued manatees. SeaWorld's objective is to educate as well as entertain.

You'll see how lumbering manatees live and what they look like up close; watch otters and seals perform slapstick routines based on their natural behaviors; learn about the lives of giant tortoises and sea turtles; and be absolutely amazed at the scope of marine life celebrated throughout the park.

Then there are the attractions, each and every one designed not only to showcase the marine world but also to demonstrate ways in which humans can protect the earth's waters and wildlife. And, because there are more exhibits and shows than rides, the difference between SeaWorld and other theme parks is that you can go at your own pace, without that hurry-up-and-wait feeling. It's also worth noting that because shows, attractions, and exhibits are based primarily on nature and animals, designers have created a natural layout as well, with winding lanes and plenty of places to relax by the waterfront or beside bouquets of flowers. There's never a nagging urge to race through anything; indeed, the entire park encourages you to slow down and move at a casual pace.

TOP SEAWORLD ATTRACTIONS

Antarctica: Empire of the Penguin. SeaWorld's latest attraction (and entire land, to boot), centers around a virtual-reality ride that follows a lone penguin through blizzards and past sea lions and into an ice cave where a colony of several hundred real-life penguins await your arrival.

Clyde and Seamore Take Pirate Island. Head for Sea Lion & Otter Stadium to watch this slapstick comedy routine starring an adorable team of water mammals and their trainers.

Kraken. Another fast and furious coaster takes you on a high-speed chase with a dragon. But the storyline doesn't matter as much as the fact this one rockets you through some incredible loops.

Manta. SeaWorld likes to claim that this is two attractions in one: while waiting in line, you walk past 10 supercool aquariums filled with rays and fish. But the big thrill is the amazingly fast coaster you reach at the front of the line.

One Ocean. Replacing Believe, this modified show (no trainers are in the water) can still impress with its killer-whale antics and message to care for the planet and its creatures.

Pets Ahoy. Anyone who has ever loved a pet (or just wanted one) simply has to see the talented cats, dogs, birds, and pig in this cute and clever show.

ORIENTATION AND PLANNING

8

GETTING ORIENTED

SeaWorld's performance venues, attractions, and activities surround a 17-acre lagoon, and the artful landscaping, curving paths, and concealing greenery sometimes lead to wrong turns. But armed with a map that lists showtimes, it's easy to plan an approach that lets you move fluidly from one show and attraction to the next and still have time for rest stops and meal breaks.

TOURING TIPS

Before investing in front-of-the-line Quick Queue passes (*$19–$35*), remember that there are only a handful of big-deal rides, and space is seldom a problem at shows.

If you bring your own food, remove all straws and lids before you arrive—they can harm fish and birds.

Arrive at least 30 minutes early for the Shamu show, which generally fills to capacity. Prepare to get wet in the "splash zone" down front.

In Discovery Cove make the aviary one of your first stops, since the 250-plus birds within will be more active in the morning. Check-in starts at around 7:30 am.

SEAWORLD PLANNER

PARKS AMENITIES

Baby Care: Diaper-changing tables are in or near most women's restrooms and in the men's restroom at the front entrance. Diaper-vending machines are in all changing areas and at Shamu's Emporium. Areas for nursing are alongside the women's restroom at Friends of the Wild gift shop and beside Shamu's Happy Harbor. Baby food is sold at most restaurants and at Sand Castle Toys and Treats. Rent strollers (*$15 for a single, $24 for a double per day*) at the information center.

First Aid: Staffed by registered nurses, first-aid centers are behind Stingray Lagoon and near Shamu's Happy Harbor. Discovery Cove's first-aid station is near the Photo Area entrance.

Guest Services: Ticket booths have become the new Guest Services (aka Guest Relations) center. If you ordered your tickets online, have questions about dining or attractions, or just need tickets to begin with, you can find it here.

Information and Reservation Center: Right inside the entrance you can pick up the park map (which also has info on showtimes, services, and amenities); make dinner reservations; and buy tickets for Discovery Cove, Aquatica, and park tours.

Lockers: One-time-use, coin-op lockers ($1) are near flip-over coasters like Kraken and Manta, Journey to Atlantis, and Shamu's Happy Harbor as well as inside SeaWorld's main entrance. Also near the entrance, next to Shamu's Emporium, are day lockers ($8 small, $10 large per day). At Discovery Cove free lockers await you near the cabanas.

Lost People and Things: SeaWorld's Main Information Center operates as the park's Lost and Found. Lost children are brought here, and it's the place to report lost children. A park-wide paging system also helps reunite parents with kids. At Discovery Cove lost kids and items eventually find their way to the check-in lobby.

Package Pick-Up: If you buy something, you can have it sent to SeaWorld's Package Pick-Up, in Shamu's Emporium, or to the check-in lobby at Discovery Cove. Allow two hours for delivery.

Pet Care Center: SeaWorld's Pet Care Center, near the main entrance, accommodates dogs, cats, hamsters, and whatever other creatures guests are traveling with. Arrive with a copy of your pet's shot record, updated rabies tag, water bowl, food, and a toy or blanket to remind your pet of home. (Note that dogs must be walked at least once a day.) You can drop off your pet 30 minutes before the park opens and must pick it up 30 minutes before closing.

Services for People with Disabilities: Get info on services and rent standard wheelchairs ($12 daily) and electric wheelchairs ($50 daily) at SeaWorld's Main Information Center. Discovery Cove has some free wheelchairs equipped with huge balloon-like tires to cross the sand. Reserve one in advance. At both parks, aquariums, wading areas, theaters, and restaurants are wheelchair accessible. (Note that drinking straws aren't provided, out of concern for the safety of the animals.) Shops are level, but many are so packed with stuff that maneuvering in a wheelchair is a challenge.

DID YOU KNOW?

Performers ski atop the backs of two dolphins, divers leap from towers, and an acrobat does an aerial ballet during the Blue Horizons show. It's a show that blends everything SeaWorld does best above and below the water.

SeaWorld Orlando
TO AQUATICA
Kraken
Pacific Point Preserve
Shark Encounter
Shark's Underwater Grill
Clyde and Seamore Take Pirate Island (Sea Lion & Otter Theater)
Spice Mill Café
Lockers
Antarctica: Empire of the Penguins
Lockers
Journey to Atlantis
ATM
Pearl Dive
Voyager Smokehouse
Antarctic Market
Seaport Pizza
Guest Services, Information
Reservations and Show Schedules
Seaport Theater/ Pets Ahoy
THE WATERFRONT
Blue Horizons (Dolphin Theater)
Manta
Turtle Trek
Lockers
Seafire Inn
Dolphin Nursery
Pelican Preserve
Dolphin Cove
ATM
KEY WEST
ATM
Lockers
Cypress Bakery
Stingray Lagoon
First Aid
Captain Pete's Island Eats
Key West at SeaWorld
Information and Reservations
SeaWorld Rescue
Parking

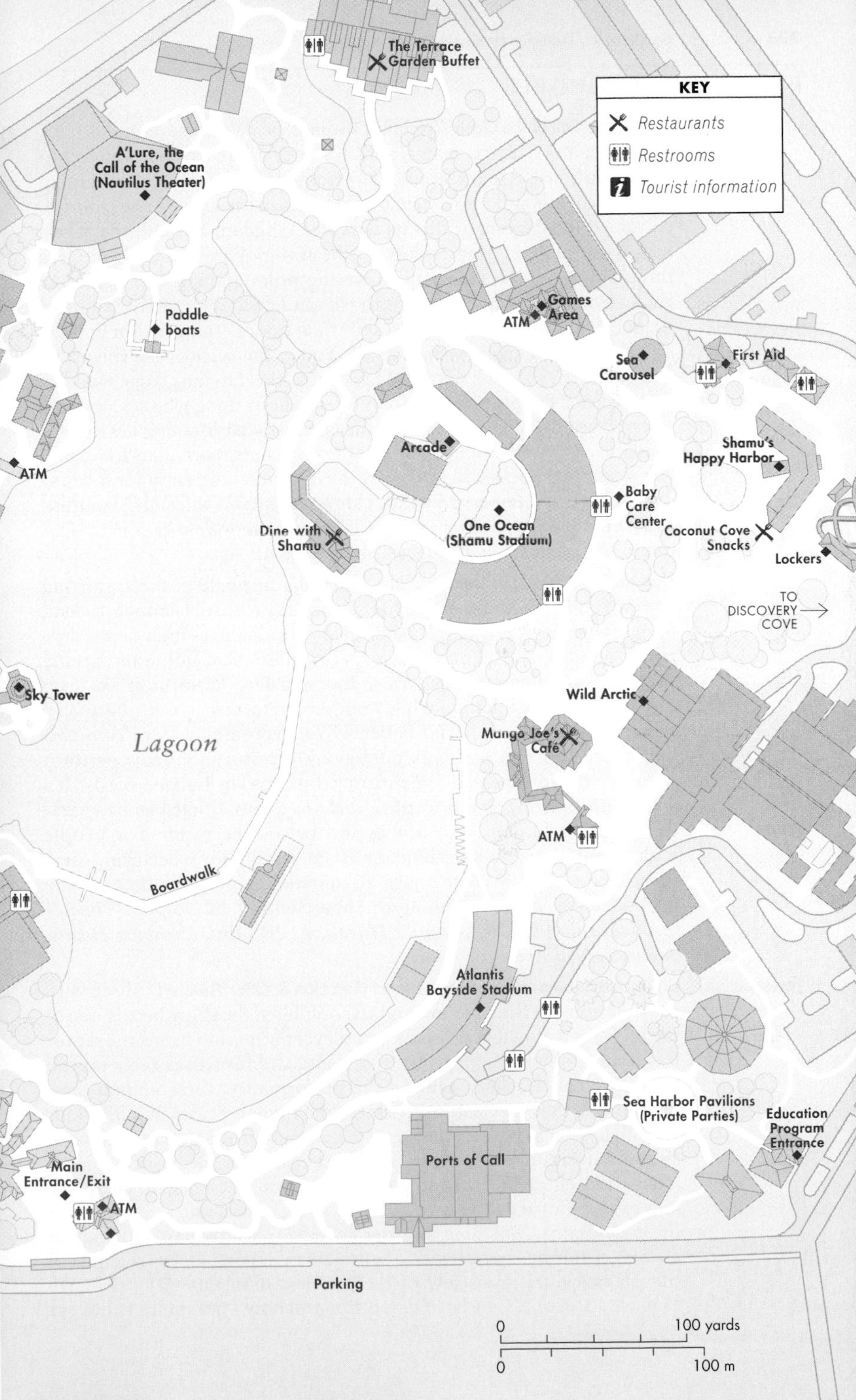
KEY
Restaurants
Restrooms
Tourist information
The Terrace Garden Buffet
A'Lure, the Call of the Ocean (Nautilus Theater)
Paddle boats
Games Area
ATM
Sea Carousel
First Aid
ATM
Arcade
Shamu's Happy Harbor
Baby Care Center
One Ocean (Shamu Stadium)
Dine with Shamu
Coconut Cove Snacks
Lockers
TO DISCOVERY COVE
Sky Tower
Wild Arctic
Lagoon
Mungo Joe's Café
ATM
Boardwalk
Atlantis Bayside Stadium
Sea Harbor Pavilions (Private Parties)
Education Program Entrance
Ports of Call
Main Entrance/Exit
ATM
Parking
0
100 yards
0
100 m

EXPLORING SEAWORLD

A'Lure, the Call of the Ocean (Nautilus Theater). SeaWorld never holds back when it comes to stage shows, and this one, similar in style and feel to Cirque du Soleil, is no exception. It is framed by the story of a fisherman who falls overboard into a new world beneath the waves. The colorful, costumed inhabitants of this underwater kingdom astound the fisherman with their amazing talents on the trampoline, rocket themselves through hoops, and leap onto towering poles and stick to them like chameleons. Acrobats march into the audience with festive Chinese dragons, find wonderful new uses for hula hoops, and perform impressive feats with hanging strips of silk. You might want to see this show twice—there's so much taking place you're likely to miss some wonderful moments. **For people with disabilities:** Guests using wheelchairs have reserved seating at the rear of the theater. Assisted-listening devices are available. ■**TIP→ Although the auditorium seats more than 1,000 and you won't feel packed in, arrive at least 15 minutes early for a wider choice of seats. Reserved seats can be arranged through Signature Show Seating.** ✉ *Nautilus Theater* 🌐 *www.seaworldparks.com* ☞ *Duration: 20 mins. Crowds: Heavy. Audience: All Ages.*

Blue Horizons (Dolphin Theater). The story is a fairytale of sorts, starting with a young girl's fantasy of life in the sea, which is enough to lead off a high-energy, crowd-pleasing show that features high dives, dazzling dolphins, and astounding feats of aquabatics. Dolphins execute perfectly coordinated leaps, arcs, and splashes. Performers ski atop the backs of two dolphins while another performer in a feathery bird costume performs an aerial ballet. Divers repeatedly leap from two high towers as two acrobats portraying the story's villains perform impressive and repeated synchronized jumps on bungee cords. It's active, it's exciting, it's beautiful, and it's a show that blends everything SeaWorld does best above and below the water. **For people with disabilities:** Ask an attendant about seating for wheelchair users toward the front. ■**TIP→ Arrive 20 minutes before showtime for the best seats, or invest in Signature Show Seating.** ✉ *Dolphin Theater* 🌐 *www.seaworldparks.com* ☞ *Duration: 20 mins. Crowds: Heavy. Audience: All Ages.*

Fodor's Choice ★ **Clyde and Seamore Take Pirate Island (Sea Lion & Otter Theater).** Along with presentations starring Shamu and the dolphins, the show here is one of the park's top crowd-pleasers. A multilevel pirate ship forms the set for this drama, in which otters, walruses, and California sea lions prevail over piratical treachery. During the performance, these animal thespians prove that they can outperform the human actors in a hilarious swashbuckling adventure that revolves around lost loot, pirate plunder, and misadventure on the high seas. Get ready for plenty of audience interaction, cheap laughs, and good-natured gags designed to please the kids as the animal actors waddle, dive, slide, dance, and scoot through this melodrama. Watching an otter swipe a treasure map, laughing at a seal in a staring contest with a sailor, and enjoying an entire range of silly slapstick are just a few of the priceless moments. ■**TIP→ Arrive at least 15 minutes early to catch the preshow—the mime is always**

HOW IT BEGAN

Hard to believe that four frat brothers intent on creating a restaurant would inadvertently build the foundation for one of the world's most popular theme parks. In the early 1960s UCLA grads Milton Shedd, David DeMott, Ken Norris, and George Millay (who's also credited with inventing Wet 'n Wild, the first water park) were ready to parlay their talent and ambition into an underwater restaurant, but as plans changed, they ended up building San Diego's SeaWorld, which opened in early 1964.

Within the first year the park welcomed more than 400,000 visitors. It took several more years before the second SeaWorld, in Ohio, opened. This was followed in 1973 by Orlando's SeaWorld and, in 1988—under the ownership of publishing firm Harcourt Brace Jovanovich—a fourth park in San Antonio.

a crowd favorite, and arrange Signature Show Seating if needed. Sit toward the center for the best view. **For people with disabilities:** Guests using wheelchairs enter on the lower level, where a team member leads them to a special seating area. ✉ *Sea Lion & Otter Theater* 🌐 *www.seaworldparks.com* ☞ *Duration: 40 mins. Crowds: Light. Audience: All Ages.*

Dolphin Cove. Dolphin Cove is a huge freeform pool where a few dozen Atlantic bottlenose dolphins skim around and nose up to the edge to be fed fish ($5 a tray) by generous guests. Once or twice a day, trainers will come out to host a scheduled feeding. Often a SeaWorld guide will offer a commentary about the dolphins' behaviors and remind everyone that the pool's residents enjoy having their sides rubbed and petted. Who doesn't? Be sure to walk to the far end of the lagoon where the walkway descends to a grotto to reveal an underwater view of the dolphins, providing an entirely new perspective that is both fascinating and entertaining—it's almost as if you're diving with the dolphins. **For people with disabilities:** This attraction is completely accessible to guests using wheelchairs. **■ TIP→ On your way to or from a show, come see the dolphins. If it's crowded, go shopping until the crowds disperse.** ✉ *Key West at SeaWorld* 🌐 *www.seaworldparks.com* ☞ *Duration: Up to You. Crowds: Light–Moderate. Audience: All Ages.*

Key West at SeaWorld. Dolphin Cove is within a laid-back area modeled after Key West, Florida's southernmost outpost (famous for spectacular sunsets and a festive mood). And although there are no distinct "lands" within SeaWorld, this Jimmy Buffett–style "island paradise" comes close. It contains individual tropical-style shows and attractions within its loosely defined borders. ✉ *Key West at SeaWorld* 🌐 *www.seaworldparks.com*

Dolphin Nursery. Although largely overshadowed by the more magnificent attractions, this large pool, which has been here since the park opened in 1973, continues to please guests by allowing them to watch dolphin moms and babies (with birth dates posted on signs) play and leap and splash. You can't get close enough to pet or feed them, so you'll have to be content peering from several feet away and asking the host questions during a regular Q&A session. Here's a popular answer: No, you can't take one home. Hint: if you just *have* to touch a dolphin, head over to Dolphin Cove in the Key West section. **For people with disabilities:** Fully wheelchair accessible. **■ TIP→ Get ready to lift up small kids so they can see into the pool.** *www.seaworldparks.com* ☞ *Duration: Up to You. Crowds: Light. Audience: All Ages.*

Journey to Atlantis. SeaWorld's coaster offering is a hybrid, combining the elements of a high-speed water ride and a roller coaster with lavish special effects and a story line. The lost continent of Atlantis has risen in the harbor of a quaint Greek fishing village, and you board a Greek fishing boat to explore it. An ominous current tugs at your vessel, and an old fisherman (actually Hermes, the messenger of the gods, in disguise) offers a golden sea horse to protect you from the evil Sirens. The LCD technology, lasers, and holographic illusions are really cranked up during a watery battle between Hermes and Allura, queen of the Sirens. Amid this story, you experience frequent twists, turns, and short, shallow dives as well as one hair-raising plunge that sends you nearly 60 feet into the main harbor (plan on getting soaked). This is followed by a final nosedive into S-shaped, bobsled-like curves. Although the ride is a little dated, it's still not for the faint of heart, anyone with back, neck, or heart problems; anyone who's pregnant; or anyone who dislikes the dark or enclosed spaces. **For people with disabilities:** You must transfer from your wheelchair to the ride vehicle. **■ TIP→ Come first thing in the morning or about an hour before closing. Going at night is awesome, and if there's a wait at all, it will be short. Last resort: Spring for a Quick Queue Pass.** *www.seaworldparks.com* ☞ *Duration: 6 mins. Crowds: Heavy. Audience: Not Small Kids. Height minimum: 42 inches with an adult; 48 inches without.*

Fodor's Choice ★ **Kraken.** As the park opens, many coaster lovers head straight for Kraken, and when you see its loops and dips you'll know why. Named after an angry sea monster, this wickedly fast coaster takes you underground three times, lifts you higher (up to 149 feet), drops you longer, and spirals you faster than you'd expect. Kraken also packs a serious punch thanks to its floorless seats (your legs dangle loosely), seven inversions, and moments of weightlessness. The line for it moves pretty quickly because of a high seating capacity. Note that bags aren't allowed past the turnstiles. It costs about 50¢ to leave them in a locker, but it's worth the investment. This is one cool coaster, though not for anyone with motion sickness or back, neck, or heart conditions. **For people with disabilities:** You must transfer from your wheelchair to the ride vehicle. **■ TIP→ Come as soon as the park opens—especially to snag front-row seats. Otherwise, use a Quick Queue pass (extra fee required) or come near closing or during a Blue Horizons show.** *www.seaworldparks.com* ☞ *Duration: 6 mins. Crowds: Heavy. Audience: Not Small Kids. Height minimum: 54 inches.*

Fodor's Choice ★ **Manta.** While waiting in line for this incredible coaster, you're ushered past 10 aquariums with more than 3,000 creatures, including 100 species of fish, graceful rays, sea dragons, and sea horses. This alone is fascinating, but the gentle encounter is followed by the sight of row after row of guests being locked down, strapped in, and firmly secured for. what's about to happen. You're suspended horizontally (face down!) beneath a 12-foot, stingray-shaped, roller-coaster car, which leaps out of the station, attaining speeds of up to 56 mph on a ½-mile race of loops as it spins around and above the aquarium. At times you are so close to the water that the coaster's wings skim the surface. There are four inversions and a drop of more than 10 stories. Halfway through, the ride slows down a bit, and you may think it's over—but it's not. There are more twists and spins ahead. Kids will love the aquarium entrance; daring older children and adults will love the thrill of the ride. Avoid this ride if you're pregnant; suffer from motion sickness; or have back, neck, or heart problems. **For people with disabilities:** You must transfer to the ride seat, properly use the ride restraint, and be able to grip harness with one hand. ■ **TIP→ Come first thing or late in the day, or use a Quick Queue pass (extra fee required).** *www.seaworldparks.com* *Duration: 6 mins. Crowds: You Bet! Audience: Not Small Kids. Height minimum: 54 inches.*

Fodor's Choice ★ **One Ocean (Shamu Stadium).** Within this stadium, SeaWorld's iconic mascot, Shamu, and other orcas star in a choreographed spectacle. For safety the trainers stay out of the water, which dilutes the thrills, but everything—not just the animals—still seems larger than life. A three-story whale-tail backdrop, enormous LED screens, a brilliant oceanic color palette, rhythmic music, and surround sound set the scene for the killer-whale performances. Celebrating how we and other creatures are all connected to the world we share, the show also incorporates fountains, an innovation inspired by regular interactions between whales and trainers, who have long used water hoses in play sessions. Perhaps you've heard tales of so-called splash zones? They exist. It takes only a wave of these creatures' massive flukes or a well-placed belly flop to throw gallons of water into the stands. Even in the upper reaches of the splash zones, you'll still get wet—fun at the time, but less so a few hours later if you didn't bring a change of clothes. If you've seen *Believe,* you may be disappointed; if not, this show may still be entertaining. **For people with disabilities:** If you're using a wheelchair, you and a companion can sit in a special area near the front-row splash zone, and others in your party can sit nearby. Assisted-listening devices are available. ■ **TIP→ The show itself lasts about 25 minutes, but there's also a 20-minute preshow, so plan accordingly. For an extra fee, reserve a seat through Signature Show Seating.** *Shamu Stadium* *www.seaworldparks.com* *Duration: 25 mins. Crowds: Moderate–Heavy. Audience: All Ages.*

Pacific Point Preserve. A nonstop chorus of "aarrrps" and "yawps" coming from behind Sea Lion & Otter Stadium leads you to the 2½-acre home of California sea lions and harbor and fur seals. This naturalistic expanse of beaches, waves, and huge outcroppings of upturned rock, designed to replicate the northern Pacific coast, has a calming effect. The area is roughly circular. Stroll around the edge of the surf zone, a favorite hangout for fun-loving pinnipeds, who swim up close for a share of the smelt you've just bought ($5) or flop over on their sides and laze in the Florida sun. On the far side of the complex you can

8

SEAWORLD ORLANDO AND DISCOVERY COVE

NAME	Height Req.	Type of Entertainment	Duration	Crowds	Audience	
SeaWorld						
Antarctica: Empire of the Penguins	48"	Tour/Thrill Ride	5 mins.	Heavy	All Ages	Come early.
A'Lure, the Call of the Ocean	n/a	Show	20 mins.	Heavy	All Ages	Plenty of seats, but arrive 15 mins. early for a wide selection.
Blue Horizons	n/a	Show	20 mins.	Heavy	All Ages	Arrive 20 mins. before showtime.
Dolphin Nursery	n/a	Aquarium	Up to you	Light	All Ages	Come during a Shamu show so the kids can be up front.
Journey to Atlantis	At least 42"	Thrill Ride with Water	6 mins.	Heavy	All but Young Kids	You can make a beeline here first thing or come about an hour before closing. But the best time for this is at night.
Key West at SeaWorld	n/a	Walk-Through/ Aquarium	Up to you	Light to Moderate	All Ages	If too crowded, wander until crowds disperse.
★ Kraken	At least 54"	Thrill Ride	6 mins.	Heavy	All but Young Kids	Get to the park when it opens and head straight to Kraken; otherwise, hit it near closing time or during a Blue Horizons show.
Manatees Rescue	n/a	Aquarium	Up to you	Light to Moderate	All Ages	Come during a Shamu show but *not* right after a dolphin show.
★ Manta	At least 54"	Thrill Ride with Water	6 mins.	You Bet!	All but Young Kids	Come first thing or late in the day, or purchase a Quick Queue pass for front-of-ride access.
Pacific Point Preserve	n/a	Aquarium	Up to you	Light	All Ages	Come anytime.
Pets Ahoy	n/a	Show	15–20 mins.	Moderate to Heavy	All Ages	Gauge the crowds, and come here early if necessary.
★ Sea Lion & Otter Stadium	n/a	Show	40 mins.	Heavy	All Ages	Sit toward the center for the best view, and don't miss the pre-show mime. Plenty of seats.

Shamu's Happy Harbor	n/a	Playground with Water	Up to you	Heavy	Young Kids	Don't come first thing in morning, or you'll never drag your child away. Bring a towel to dry them off.
★ Shamu Stadium (One Ocean)	n/a	Show	25 mins.	Moderate to Heavy	All Ages	Show itself lasts 25 minutes, but there's a 30-minute pre-show; plan accordingly.
Shark Encounter	n/a	Aquarium	Up to you	Light to Moderate	All Ages	Come during the sea lion show.
Sky Tower	48"	Tour/ Thrill Ride	6 mins.	Light	All Ages	Come whenever there's no line. Note the extra $4 charge, though.
Stingray Lagoon	n/a	Aquarium	Up to you	Moderate to Heavy	All Ages	Walk by if it's crowded, but return before dusk.
Turtle Point	n/a	Zoo	Up to you	Light	All Ages	Come anytime.
Wild Arctic	At least 42"	Simulator Exp./ Aquarium	5+ mins.	Moderate to Heavy	All Ages	Come during a Shamu show. You can skip the ride if you just want to see the mammals.
Discovery Cove						
Beaches	n/a	Beach Area	Up to you	Light	All Ages	Arrive early and head to the far side for a private spot.
★ Dolphin Lagoon	n/a	Pool	45–60 mins.	n/a	All but Young Kids	Be mindful of your appointment time.
Explorer's Aviary	n/a	Aviary	Up to you	Light to Moderate	All Ages	Come early, when the birds are most active.
Tropical Reef	n/a	Aquarium/ Pool Area	Up to you	Light to Moderate	All Ages	Monitor crowds and come when they're lightest. Popular with teens.
Wind-Away River	n/a	Aquarium	Up to you	Light to Moderate	All Ages	When it gets hot, slip into the water. Popular with teens.

★ **Fodor's** Choice

SEAWORLD GROWN-UP TOURS

Strolling through SeaWorld is comforting. Quiet sidewalks and landscaped lanes abound. Indeed, a number of local senior citizens who were part of mall-walking clubs have learned that an annual pass gives them access to a very pleasant walk in the park—as well as a day filled with wonderful attractions. Follow in their footsteps on a walk of up to a mile, from west to east.

WEST SIDE STORY

The west side has most of the attractions—and the most paths. From the entrance, walk around the information center and to the left toward **Pelican Preserve,** where a flock of rescued pelicans are shuffling about.

Turn left into **Key West at SeaWorld,** where you can enjoy nature—first by feeding and petting the slippery skates at Stingray Lagoon and then by spending time with the residents of Dolphin Cove; be sure to head to the far end of the cove and drop down into the grotto, where a wide window reveals their underwater world. A little farther along, take your pick of **Turtle Trek** (home of turtles and manatees) and/or the **Blue Horizons** show at the Dolphin Theater. Afterward, loop back toward the entrance before peeling off to your left toward the **Waterfront** area. When you reach the shores of the lagoon, stroll past the **Sky Tower**—unless you'd like a bird's-eye view of the entire park. In that case, head on up and see the sights. You may also want to spend a few minutes watching the action at **Pearl Dive** before catching the show at the **Sea Lion and Otter Theater.** And be sure to explore **Antarctica: Empire of the Penguin** (both the land and the ride).

EAST SIDE STORY

Start at the **Seafire Inn,** a great place to grab a bite to eat and cool off. Head to the boardwalk and take it across the lagoon. This pleasing, uncongested walk brings you to the rear of **Shamu Stadium,** and although you can circle it in either direction, go right to avoid crowds of kids gathered at Shamu's Happy Harbor. If there's a show at the stadium, perfect. If not, not too far down the lane are the Nautilus Theater and the Cirque-style show, **A'Lure: The Call of the Ocean.** If your timing's off, after crossing the boardwalk just walk over to **Wild Arctic** where an observation area affords a glimpse of polar bears and walrus. Spend some time in the frozen North before returning to the sidewalk, which winds its way behind the Atlantis Bayside Stadium and back toward the park entrance and, all too soon, the real world.

walk down into a grotto where a large Plexiglas wall allows you to see them darting and diving and playing underwater. Priceless. **For people with disabilities:** This attraction is completely accessible to guests using wheelchairs. ■ **TIP→ Come anytime. It shouldn't be too hard to find a place away from the crowds.** ⊕ *www.seaworldparks.com* ☞ *Duration: Up to You. Crowds: Light. Audience: All Ages.*

Pets Ahoy. About a dozen dogs, a dozen-plus cats, and an assortment of ducks, doves, parrots, and a pot-bellied pig (nearly all rescued from a local animal shelter) are the stars of this lively, hilarious show. The

There are bubbles but no toil and trouble with the Sea Witches of Sea World.

animals perform complex stunts on a stage that looks like a seaside village. From stealing a string of sausages to driving their "girlfriends" on a date, these cute-as-a-button actors perform feats that are each more incredible than the last. Look around and you'll notice that the show is just as appealing to foreign guests; you don't have to speak English to enjoy what is essentially a live version of a silent movie. Stick around and you'll have a chance to shake paws with the stars. **For people with disabilities:** Special seating for guests using wheelchairs and assisted-listening devices are available. **■ TIP→ Gauge the crowds, and arrive early if necessary.** *www.seaworldparks.com* ☞ *Duration: 15–20 mins. Crowds: Moderate–Heavy. Audience: All Ages.*

Shamu's Happy Harbor. Sprawling, towering, and (for kids) beyond incredible, this 3-acre playground has places to crawl, climb, explore, bounce, and get wet. There's an adjacent arcade with midway games; there are pipes to crawl through; a tent with an air-mattress floor; and "ball rooms"—one for toddlers and one for grade-schoolers—with thousands of plastic balls to wade through. Keep on looking and you'll discover miniaturized thrill rides— roller coasters and spinning rides and an assortment of other rides that inject a pint-sized dose of adrenalin. Then there are big sailing ships to explore and webbed ropes to climb and water to play in and around. For kids, this part of the park is worth the price of admission—they could be here for hours. **For people with disabilities:** Various areas offer different levels of clearance. Check with attendants about accessibility. **■ TIP→ Don't come first thing, or you'll never drag your child away; that said, it's busy here midafternoon or near dusk. Bring a towel to dry them off.** *www.seaworldparks.*

com ☞ Duration: Up to you. Crowds: Heavy. Audience: Small Kids. Minimum Height: 42 inches.

Shark Encounter. Within a large, innocuous, white structure are some thoroughly creepy critters: eels, barracuda, sharks, and poisonous fish. You may even spy a few creatures you've never seen (or even imagined) before, like the weedy sea dragon and his cousin, the leafy sea dragon, which look like branches of a tree. But the stars of the show are the sharks, and this attraction doesn't scrimp. The real fun comes when you enter large transparent corridors and see the fish, eels, and half-dozen species of sharks slice gracefully through the water all around you—even overhead—providing a sensational new sensation. Consider visiting the attraction in conjunction with a meal at the extraordinarily well-designed Sharks Underwater Grill, where you can order fresh fish and Floribbean cuisine while watching your entrée's cousins. **For people with disabilities:** Open spaces allow access to guests using wheelchairs. ■ **TIP→ Spend at least 20 minutes here. Crowds are biggest when the adjacent sea lion and otter show gets out; time your visit accordingly.** 🌐 *www.seaworldparks.com ☞ Duration: Up to You. Crowds: Light–Moderate. Audience: All Ages.*

Sky Tower. The focal point of the park is this 400-foot-tall tower, the main mast for a revolving double-decker platform. During the six-minute rotating up and down round-trip, you'll get the inside scoop on the park's history, its attractions, and surrounding sights. All in all, it's peaceful, relaxing, and gives you a new perspective on SeaWorld and Orlando. Adjacent to it is Pearl Dive, a small area where you can sit and watch pearl divers snag oysters. **For people with disabilities:** The tower can accommodate two wheelchairs per cycle. ■ **TIP→ Come whenever there's not a line, or use Quick Queue if necessary (extra fee required).** 🌐 *www.seaworldparks.com ☞ Duration: 6 mins. Crowds: Light. Audience: All Ages. Height minimum: 48 inches or accompanied by an adult for the tower trip.*

Stingray Lagoon. In this interactive hands-on exhibit (aka a shallow pool), dozens of circling stingrays are close enough to touch, as evidenced by the many outstretched hands surrounding the rim. Buy stingray delicacies (smelts, silversides, shrimp, and squid) available for $5 a tray, two for $9, three for $13 from the attendant. The best part is when the rays flap up for lunch, you can stroke their velvety skin. Even though they have stingers, they won't hurt you—they just want food (and they're obligingly hungry all day). Check out the nursery pool with its baby rays. **For people with disabilities:** This attraction is easily accessible to guests using wheelchairs. ■ **TIP→ Walk by if it's crowded, but return before dusk before the smelt concession stand closes.** 🌐 *www.seaworldparks.com ☞ Duration: Up to You. Crowds: Moderate–Heavy. Audience: All Ages.*

Turtle Trek. This walk-through attraction is a three-part experience that begins underground. Wide windows reveal a pool inhabited by surprisingly graceful manatees. SeaWorld, by the way, has rescued more manatees than anyone else in the world and has rescued an estimated 20,000 birds, fish, and animals since 1964. Part two moves you to a room where rescued sea turtles can be seen swimming past as a host discusses the life cycle of these docile creatures. The education leads to the final room, a domed 360-degree 3-D theater where you are introduced to Naia, a sea turtle who defies the 1 in 10 odds and makes it to the ocean after being hatched. You follow her through a series of near disasters until she returns to the beach to lay her own eggs. The predators attempting to get at Naia and her siblings may be too intense for kids, and the volume is cranked up to rock-concert levels. If you have a tinge of motion sickness, hang on to the support rails, because the film makes it seem as if the world's gone topsy-turvy. **■ TIP→ If you can't handle the virtual motion of the movie, skip the film and take a peek at the manatees and turtles from an outdoor observation area. If there's a long line, the fee-additional Quick Queue pass works here.** 🌐 *www.seaworldparks.com* ☞ *Duration: 30 mins for entire experience; 7 mins for movie: Crowds: Moderate: Audience: All Ages.*

Wild Arctic. At this pseudo ice station, you embark on a soaring and swooping virtual helicopter ride that takes you over the Arctic and through some dangerously close calls (if you're sensitive to the very real rolls and pitches, you can opt out for a stationary virtual helicopter). Then you exit onto a long walk through interactive, educational displays which leads to above- and below-water stations where you can watch Beluga whales, polar bears, and groaning tusked walruses (some weighing as much as 3,000 pounds) hoisting themselves onto a thick shelf of ice. This is a diverse and cute collection of animals you certainly don't see every day, which makes it vastly entertaining to simply eavesdrop on their day. Those who are pregnant or who suffer from neck, back, or heart conditions or motion sickness should opt out of the virtual-helicopter part of the attraction. **For people with disabilities:** You must transfer from your wheelchair to the ride vehicle. **■ TIP→ Come early, late, or during a Shamu show. You can skip the simulated helicopter ride if you just want to see the mammals. Should there be a line, spring for a Quick Queue pass (extra fee required).** 🌐 *www.seaworldparks.com* ☞ *Duration: Up to You. Crowds: Moderate–Heavy. Audience: All Ages. Height minimum: 42 inches.*

8

ANIMAL ENCOUNTERS AND TOURS

SeaWorld has several programs that put you closer to the animals. Up-Close and Behind-the-Scenes tours last 60 to 90 minutes and cost about $10 to $50. The six-hour VIP Tour starts at around $100 for adults and $80 for children.

You can book tours up to three months in advance. For a list, check the SeaWorld website (🌐 *www.seaworld.com*) or call the park (☎ *407/351–3600*).

Behind the Scenes Tour. On this 90-minute program, you'll have a chance to see how SeaWorld's animal experts care for rescued manatees and sea turtles. Where else can you touch a shark, step inside a hidden polar bear den, and play with a penguin? From $29 adults, $9 children. 🌐 *www.seaworldparks.com.*

The clear tunnel at Shark Encounter in Sea World takes you underwater and underneath the sharks.

Beluga Interaction Program. For this program (starting from $119 and up, depending on season) you don a wet suit and assist a trainer in feeding Beluga whales, which average about 15 feet and 2,000 pounds. They're good-natured and well trained enough to respond to hand signals you learn from the trainer. Must be 10 or older; 14 and younger must be accompanied by an adult. 🌐 *www.seaworldparks.com.*

Dolphins Up Close. They're amazing animals, of course, and on this 45-minute tour you'll be able to participate in a training session, touch a dolphin and use hand gestures to prompt behaviors. From $59 adults, $39 children. 🌐 *www.seaworldparks.com.*

Marine Mammal Keeper Experience. The daylong keeper experience (from $399) includes lunch, a T-shirt, seven consecutive days of park admission, and, perhaps, a lasting desire to become a SeaWorld trainer. Starting at 6:30 am, you work with trainers to care for, feed, and train dolphins, manatees, sea lions, and Beluga whales. An unforgettable experience that includes plenty of photo ops and lasting memories. 🌐 *www.seaworldparks.com.*

Sea Lions Up Close. If you'd like to spend some time with just about the cutest animals anywhere, this 60-minute tour focuses on the naturally funny sea lions. Snap a souvenir shot with a sea lion, and then make their day (and yours) by helping to feed buckets of fish to the sea lions and harbor seals at Pacific Point Preserve. From $39 adults, $19 children. 🌐 *www.seaworldparks.com.*

Sleepovers. These events are arranged primarily for kids, with special programs designed specifically for Boy Scouts, Girl Scouts, and students from grades 2 to 12. Summer sleepovers are geared to families with kids between kindergarten and fifth grade. The sleepovers are held indoors beside a habitat for sharks, manatees, dolphins, Beluga whales, polar bears, penguins, or manta rays. The evening begins at 6 and includes a pizza dinner, a walk around the exhibit with a trainer, and a continental breakfast. Expect to pay $95 for the experience (add $25 for next-day admission to the park). Call ahead to reserve a sleepover. ☎ *800/406–2244* 🌐 *www.seaworldparks.com.*

VIP Tours. The VIP Tour (from $100 adults, $80 children) provides instant access to Manta, Kraken, Journey to Atlantis, Turtle Trek, Antarctica: Empire of the Penguin, and Wild Arctic and reserved seating at the One Ocean, Blue Horizons, and Clyde and Seamore shows; a chance to feed sea lions, dolphins, and rays; and enjoy a meal at an All Day Dining Deal restaurant. Be aware you'll be traveling with a group of up to 12, but if you invest in the substantially more expensive Private VIP Tour (from $299 or, with park admission, from $349), it will be limited to you and your guests. The Private VIP Tour also adds preferred parking; reserved seating at shows; and replaces the buffet lunch with an upscale meal at Sharks Underwater Grill. 🌐 *www.seaworldparks.com.*

Wild Arctic Up Close Experience. On this hour-long program, you'll be able to interact with seals, walruses, and beluga whales. Trainers are there to take your questions—and you'll be delighted when you come face to snout with a whiskered walrus. From $59 adults and children. 🌐 *www.seaworldparks.com.*

DISCOVERY COVE

If you were pleasantly surprised by the pace at SeaWorld, believe it or not, you'll find it's even slower at Discovery Cove. Here your mission is to spend an entire day doing nothing but savoring a 32-acre tropical oasis. It's a task made easier by an all-inclusive admission that covers all meals, towels, a wet suit, masks, sunscreen, and the option of springing for the highlight of the day: a unique swimming experience with a bottlenose dolphin.

Even without a dolphin encounter, you can have a great time splashing around coral reefs, swimming into a spacious aviary, floating down a quiet river, and lazing on a sandy beach beneath lovely palms. New in 2012, Freshwater Oasis is a tropical rain-forest environment of sparkling clear springs offering face-to-face encounters with playful otters and curious marmoset monkeys, while thanks to a special diving helmet, SeaVenture lets you walk underwater through a reef filled with tropical fish and rays, which you can literally reach out and touch.

ORIENTATION AND PLANNING

GETTING ORIENTED

Thanks to Discovery Cove's daily cap on crowds, it may seem as if you have the park to yourself. Navigating the grounds is simple; signs point to swimming areas, cabanas, or the free-flight aviary—aflutter with exotic birds and accessible via walkway or (even better) by swimming to it beneath a waterfall.

TOURING TIP

In Discovery Cove make the aviary one of your first stops, since the 250-plus birds within will be more active in the morning. Remember that check-in starts at 7:30 am, and the waterways open around 9.

TOP DISCOVERY COVE ATTRACTIONS

Dolphin Lagoon. You can swim at several areas, but this is the only place where you can get the signature swimming experience—with an Atlantic bottlenose dolphin.

Snorkeling Pools. There are three spots to snorkel—Serenity Bay, Freshwater Oasis, and the Grand Reef—and they may well be Discovery Cove's most underhyped attractions. It's a real thrill to float lazily and silently amid tropical fish, to swim beneath a waterfall into an elaborate aviary, and to dive down a few feet to peer at sharks and barracuda through the porthole of a wrecked ship. There's also on-site snorkeling instruction.

DISCOVERY COVE PLANNER

PARK AMENITIES

Baby Care: There's no primary baby care center, but there are nursing and changing facilities in locker and changing rooms.

Cancellations: If your plans change and you can't make it to Discovery Cove, cancel more than 30 days out and you'll receive a full refund; within 30 days of your reservation, you'll receive a one-time complimentary date change, which you can schedule for up to a year away.

First Aid: First-aid station is near the Photo Area entrance.

Guest Services: You can get information on meals, cabanas, lockers, dolphin swims, merchandise, souvenir photos, and other aspects of the park at the **Discovery Cove Check-In Lobby** when you arrive, or at Guest Services (**aka Guest Relations**) just after you enter.

8

Lockers: Free lockers await you near the cabanas.

Lost People and Things: Lost kids and items are usually turned over to Discovery Cove attendants, who bring them to the attendants at the Check-In Lobby.

Package Pick-Up: If you buy something, allow two hours for delivery.

Pet Care Center: If you arrive at Discovery Cove with a pet, plan on boarding it for a day ($15) at the Pet Care Center at SeaWorld.

Services for People with Disabilities: There are free wheelchairs equipped with huge balloon-like tires to cross the sand. Reserve one in advance over the phone or online and it'll be waiting for you when you arrive. At both parks, aquariums, wading areas, theaters, and restaurants are wheelchair accessible. (Note that drinking straws aren't provided, out of concern for the safety of the animals.) Shops are level, but many are so packed with stuff that maneuvering in a wheelchair is a challenge.

EXPLORING DISCOVERY COVE

Beaches. Lined with swaying palms, tropical foliage, and quaint thatched huts, and speckled with shady umbrellas, hammocks, lounges, and beach chairs, this is where you claim your own private spot in the

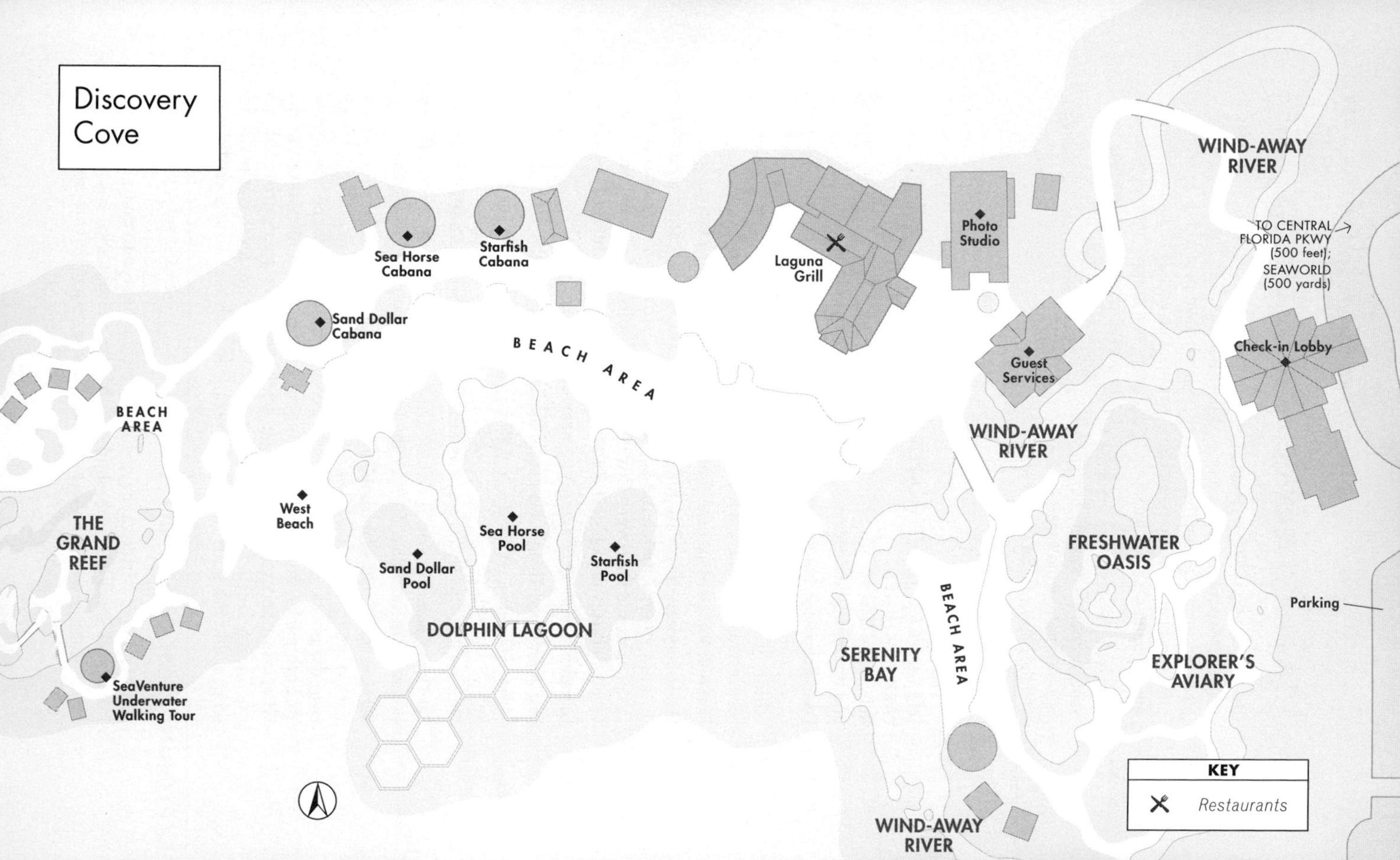
Discovery Cove
WIND-AWAY RIVER
TO CENTRAL FLORIDA PKWY (500 feet); SEAWORLD (500 yards)
Sea Horse Cabana
Starfish Cabana
Laguna Grill
Photo Studio
Check-in Lobby
Sand Dollar Cabana
BEACH AREA
Guest Services
BEACH AREA
WIND-AWAY RIVER
West Beach
THE GRAND REEF
Sea Horse Pool
Sand Dollar Pool
Starfish Pool
FRESHWATER OASIS
Parking
DOLPHIN LAGOON
SERENITY BAY
BEACH AREA
EXPLORER'S AVIARY
SeaVenture Underwater Walking Tour
KEY
Restaurants
WIND-AWAY RIVER

sand. Since the park's biggest selling point is its limited guest capacity, the most seductive aspect is lying in the sun and leaving the real world behind. For the most privacy, head to the far west end of Discovery Cove, where the beach chairs are more plentiful and private cabanas (from $60) are available. **For people with disabilities:** Modified beach wheelchairs are available. **■TIP→ With attendance limited to 1,000 guests, and plenty of sand to share, you should be fine. Just arrive early for the best spot.** ⊕ *www.discoverycove.com/* ☞ *Duration: Up to You. Crowds: Light. Audience: All Ages.*

Fodor's Choice ★ **Dolphin Lagoon (Dolphin Swim).** This is clearly the premier experience at Discovery Cove, but before you picture yourself frolicking alone with these playful creatures, remember that your "swim" is largely done alongside your fellow guests and is carefully supervised and restricted for the safety of both you and the dolphins. Despite the limitations, however, the attraction offers you the unique chance to touch, feed, play with, and even kiss a bottlenose dolphin, one of the most social and communicative marine animals. Before you can get into the lagoon, you must attend a 15-minute orientation, consisting of a film plus a few words from a dolphin trainer. Following the orientation, you and up to eight other guests will spend roughly 30 minutes interacting with one of a few dozen dolphins. Although you are only knee-deep in the water most of the time, it's surprisingly chilly, so you'll be grateful for the mandatory, Discovery Cove–provided wet suit.

In the water, trainers teach you hand signals used to communicate with the dolphins. Command your dolphin may roll over so you can touch its belly or signal it to leap into the air. Near the end of the session you have a chance to swim out to deeper water, catch hold of the dolphin's fin, and have it pull you back to shore. You even get a moment to pose for a picture with your newfound friend. Be prepared for the photo finish: after you leave the water and return to the orientation cabana, the skilled trainers quickly transform into a determined souvenir-photo sales team. **For people with disabilities:** Alert staffers to your hearing, vision, or mobility issues when you're making reservations, and they'll have someone there to offer special assistance—signing or having a modified wheelchair at the ready. Note that the pool here is "zero entry," so there are no steps to contend with. **■TIP→ Be mindful of the appointment time on your badge. You don't want to miss the experience of a lifetime.** ⊕ *www.discoverycove.com/* ☞ *Duration: 45–60 mins. Crowds: N/A. Audience: Not Young Kids. Age requirement: 6 yrs and up; 6–12 must be accompanied by an adult.*

Explorer's Aviary. There are several entrances to this 12,000-square-foot birdhouse—three of which access the aviary from beneath waterfalls falling beside the Wind-Away River (otherwise, you can walk in from the beach). However you arrive, you will enter a sanctuary populated with more than 250 small exotic birds, including darting hummingbirds, tiny finches, and honeycreepers. In the large-bird sanctuary, you get up close to perched and wandering toucans, peacocks, red-legged seriema, and other colorful winged creatures that stand as tall as 4 feet. Look for attendants who have carts filled with complimentary fruit and feed that you can use to attract the birds. It's a beautiful experience—especially when a bird hops onto your shoulder to say hello. Get the camera ready. **For people with disabilities:** A pathway through the aviary accommodates wheelchairs. ■**TIP→ Come early in the morning when the birds are most active.** 🌐 *www.discoverycove.com/* ☞ *Duration: Up to You. Crowds: Light–Moderate. Audience: All Ages.*

Freshwater Oasis. The oasis has a tropical theme with lush landscaping akin to a rain forest. Wade through a crystal-clear spring to reach an island with some outrageously cute marmosets (which are contained on the island thanks to convenient moat). Swim a little farther and come nose-to-nose with otters, which frolic behind a nearly invisible wall of acrylic. Beyond the menagerie and beneath a canopy of cooling vegetation, there are watery trails to explore. It truly is a seductive setting and effortlessly evokes that soothing Discovery Cove experience. 🌐 *www.discoverycove.com/* ☞ *Duration: Up to You. Crowds: Moderate. Audiences: All Ages.*

The Grand Reef. You can follow thousands of butterfly fish, angelfish, parrot fish, and a few dozen other species as you snorkel through this authentic-looking coral reef. Stingrays sail slowly and gracefully past, and fish come within touching distance, though when you reach out to them they scatter in nanoseconds. There's even an artificial shipwreck with panels of Plexiglas in its hull that reveal a separate pool filled with barracudas and sharks. (Thankfully, they're out of reach.) Even though you're hundreds of miles from the Caribbean, this is wonderful, accessible substitute. And remember: the brighter the day, the more brilliant the underwater colors. **For people with disabilities:** Guests with mobility issues who can readily maneuver themselves with limited assistance can experience the reef. ■**TIP→ It's easy to monitor crowds; come when they're light. It's suitable for all ages, but teens and adults enjoy it most.** 🌐 *www.discoverycove.com/* ☞ *Duration: Up to You. Crowds: Light–Moderate. Audience: All Ages.*

SeaVenture. If you've always wanted to experience the underwater world but don't have time for scuba lessons, SeaVenture is the solution. You don a dive helmet tethered to an air supply, which allows you to walk on the reef floor (about 15 feet deep), surrounded by schools of fish, sleek rays, and sharks. Even though the sharks are contained on the opposite side of lengthy panoramic panels of glass, you can't tell there's a partition, so the effect is chilling (so chilling, it makes a great souvenir photo). If you feel anxious, don't fret: guides float above you and beside you as you take your underwater stroll. The whole experience, including orientation, lasts about an hour, with about half the time spent on the underwater walk. At the end, you'll be handed a shaker filled with food. When you shake it and release its contents, you'll be instantly surrounded by a cluster of hungry fish. An unforgettable finish. The SeaVenture costs an extra $59. Some health restrictions apply. 🌐 *www.discoverycove.com/* ☞ *Duration: 60 mins. Crowds: N/A. Audience: Not Young Kids. Age requirement: 10 years old; under 14 must be accompanied by a paying adult.*

Serenity Bay. A key to Discovery Cove's popularity is that it gives you time to do absolutely nothing. So if doing nothing means something to you, Serenity Bay is your place. This large pool of refreshingly clear, 80-degree water is ready when you are—or not—because maybe you'd prefer to just find a spot on the beach and soak in the sun. Take your pick. It's your vacation, and this is your bay. *www.discoverycove.com/* *Duration: Up to You. Crowds: Light–Moderate. Audience: All Ages.*

Wind-Away River. As this river meanders through most of Discovery Cove, swimmers float lazily through different environments—a sunny beach; a dense, tropical rain forest; an Amazon-like river; a tropical fishing village; an underwater cave; and the aviary. The only drawbacks? The bottom of the river can feel like the bottom of a pool, and the too-often repeated scenery along the way can make it a little tedious. On the other hand, use this as a respite from the heat and a unique way to get around the park. **For people with disabilities:** Guests with mobility issues who can maneuver themselves with limited assistance can enjoy a tour of the river. **■ TIP→ Slip in when it gets hot. All are welcome, but it appeals most to teens and adults.** *www.discoverycove.com/* *Duration: Up to You. Crowds: Light–Moderate. Audience: All Ages.*

ANIMAL ENCOUNTERS

Trainer for a Day. This opportunity (from $428, but often $500-plus) rivals SeaWorld's Marine Mammal Keeper Experience. General admission includes meals, wet suits, and diving gear; this tour adds a gift bag, waterproof camera, trainer T-shirt, 30-minute dolphin swim, a private photo session with two dolphins, feeding fish in the Grand Reef, a meet and greet with tropical birds and small animals, and an almost exclusive (only eight guests in the entire lagoon) interaction that includes a "double-foot push" (two dolphins propel you across the lagoon by the soles of your feet). Ready for more? Shadow a trainer all day: head to the dolphin back area for a private tour and talk to trainers about how they teach and care for these amazing animals. Like other Discovery Cove admissions, this includes unlimited access to SeaWorld and Aquatica for 14 days. Call ahead to arrange a tour. *407/351–3600, 877/557–7404* *www.discoverycove.com.*

AQUATICA

Just across International Drive from SeaWorld, Aquatica is the 60-acre water park that does a wonderful job angling water-park lovers away from Disney's Typhoon Lagoon and Blizzard Beach and Universal's Wet 'n Wild. And, sure, Aquatica has all the slides you'd expect, but it also has plenty of whimsical SeaWorld touches.

Aquatica takes cues from SeaWorld and Discovery Cove in design and mood. The park also takes its cues from the tropics. Right after you clear the parking lot, you see a tropical pastiche of buildings that may convince you your ship just sailed into the Caribbean. So go with it. Get into a groove, relax, and enjoy yourself. In addition to super-slippery waterslides, there are quiet coves, phenomenally creative kids' play areas, lazy streams, and an atmosphere that is guaranteed to relieve your prevacation stress.

Ideally you'll have arrived with some snacks and drinks to combat the fatigue you'll feel after scaling to the tops of all those watery thrill rides. If not, fear not—there are plenty of places to find food and drink.

You should also be toting beach towels, sunscreen, and water shoes. Again, if not, fear not—there are a number of shops and kiosks where you can buy (or rent) all of this stuff and more.

Many of the rides have height restrictions, so if you're traveling with kids, have their heights checked at the Information Center, which you'll see right when you enter the park. Each child will be issued a colored wristband that alerts attendants to which rides are appropriate for him or her (or just look for the height requirement signposted at the entrance to each attraction—and check our reviews). If anyone in your group isn't comfortable in the water, this is also a good place to inquire about the swimming lessons that are offered.

After stashing excess supplies in a locker and generally settling in, it's time to explore. Unless it's peak season, several hours should be enough

DID YOU KNOW?

You can "swim" with the dolphins even if you didn't book a dolphin swim at Discovery Cove. Just take the Dolphin Plunge, a waterslide that jettisons you into a clear tube running through the pool inhabited by Commerson's dolphins.

TOP AQUATICA ATTRACTIONS

Big Surf Shores and Cutback Cove. The lagoons here aren't too deep and are perfect for cooling off. About every 10 minutes, a series of small waves move across the lagoon, and while they're not large enough for surfing, they're big enough so you can bob around like a cork.

Dolphin Plunge. Aquatica's commercials showcase this attraction, where you slip through a winding string of pitch-black tubes and then a stretch of clear tubes through the Commerson's dolphins' habitat.

Tassie's Twisters. After hopping into an inner tube and sloshing at a high speed through an enclosed tube, you're flung into a huge circular basin and spiraled into a drain and down a slide.

Taumata Racer. Eight colorful tubes are lined up waiting for you. After a countdown, you launch yourself into your chute and, after a twisting-and-turning ride, end up on a long and slippery slide into the splashdown pool.

to visit each ride and attraction once or twice, and will also allow for some downtime, lazing on the beach, or enjoying a leisurely meal.

ORIENTATION AND PLANNING

GETTING ORIENTED

Initially, you might find it hard to get your bearings amid the towering slides, Caribbean palms, winding sidewalks, and the seemingly random layout of restaurants, rides, slides, and facilities. And there are no paper maps, only posted diagrams throughout the park. But in reality, the park is fairly easy to navigate—its layout forms a simple circle. The services (restaurants, changing rooms, shops) form a core around which the attractions are situated.

At the entrance, turn right and you'll be at the premier attraction, Dolphin Plunge; but after that you may want to do an about-face and head straight to the shores of the beach at Cutback Cove. This way, you can set up a base and then work your way to other attractions around the circle while remaining conveniently close to meals at Waterstone Grill and the Banana Beach Cookout.

TOURING TIPS

Be aware of the sun. Avoid sunburn by reapplying sunscreen (they suggest SPF 30) often—even waterproof sunblock washes off. For even more sun protection, rent a standard cabana (about $60) or go all out and splurge on the "ultimate cabana" for eight, which includes an all-day locker, bottled water, towels, and discount coupons for merchandise.

Be aware of your feet. Wear sandals or water shoes (or even socks) to protect your feet from hot sand, sidewalks, and rough pool surfaces. At the major thrill rides, a "sneaker keeper" offers a place to stash your footwear while you experience the ride.

Buy tickets in advance. Prepurchased tickets get you early entrance, and this head start will enable you to hit the major flume and tube rides more than once.

Commune with nature. You can catch Commerson's dolphins at feeding times; spot macaws on tree limbs; or see small mammals in the Conservation Cabanas, where docents answer questions. A variety of animals are on display around the park.

AQUATICA PLANNER

PARK AMENITIES

Baby Care: One nursing area is near the center of the park, by the towel- and locker-rental area and the changing rooms; another is at the far north end of the park, near Kata's Kookaburra Cove and Big Surf Shores. The nursing areas and several restrooms—for men and women—have fold-down changing tables. (Keep in mind that children still in diapers must also be wearing waterproof protectors.)

First Aid: A medical attendant is on duty during regular business hours at the first-aid station at the far end of the park between Kata's Kookaburra Cove and Big Surf Shores.

Information: The Main Information Center is at the park entrance, just past the ticket kiosks. Also at the entrance are an ATM, telephones, and restrooms. This is where you check out the posted park map and plan your approach. On the walkways outside the information center and leading into the park, attendants are stationed to help you get your bearings and point out where to find strollers and wheelchairs, help you with lost-and-found inquiries, and describe combination-ticket packages.

Lockers: There are three areas with unlimited-access lockers to rent for a day. One is near the splashdown area at Walhalla Wave and HooRoo Run; two others are at the center and far end of the park, where there are also nursing facilities. You pay $15 for a small locker (enough for one backpack) and $30 for a large one (for about two backpacks); there's also a $5 deposit, which is refunded when you leave. The central locker area also rents towels for $4 ($1 of which is refunded upon return).

Lost People and Things: Lost items and people are taken to a small tent called the Concierge Cabana, which is right by the entrance to the beach area.

Services for People with Disabilities: Aquatica was designed to accommodate people with mobility concerns. Paved pathways lead around the entire park; none of the river or family attractions has steps to contend with; and floats, life vests, and inner tubes make it easy for anyone to enjoy the park. This isn't to say there aren't challenges: regular wheelchairs can't handle the sandy beach areas, and several attractions involve climbing to the top of a high tower (although the stairs for each are accessible by ADA guidelines). Basic wheelchairs rent for around $12 a day; the motorized versions cost $50.

EXPLORING AQUATICA

Antarctica: Empire of the Penguins. In mid-2013 SeaWorld opened this 4-acre "continent," which centers around an attraction that's a fun-filled Arctic trek. After walking through a realistic ice floe, you leave the preshow and board a circular vehicle that glides, track-free, on a polar journey. Choose mild (no extra motion) or wild (a low-grade virtual-reality ride) and then follow the life of Puck the penguin as he travels through blizzards, past hungry sea lions, and through an ice cave. Eventually, you arrive in a massive room where Puck's relations, a colony of 250-odd, always-entertaining Adélie, gentoo, king, and rock hopper penguins are diving, waddling, and swimming like darts. Unlike in the former attraction, where the penguins lived behind Plexiglas, now you can step up to a low wall and watch them cavort in their private empire.

For people with disabilities: Guests using wheelchairs must transfer into the ride vehicle; a separate line is available if you'd prefer to bypass the ride and just visit the exhibit. 🌐 *www.seaworldparks.com* ☞ *Duration: 5 mins. Crowds: Moderate. Audience: All Ages. Riders must be at least 42 inches tall; between 42 and 48 inches accompanied by a supervising companion at least 14 yrs old. Guests under 42 inches may ride the less intense Mild Expedition.*

Big Surf Shores and Cutback Cove. These two side-by-side lagoons (aka wave pools) are perhaps the centerpiece of the park. Although the names suggest waves that surfers would fear, the large pool has only modest swells, and the small pool may even be closed if crowds are light. Still, both edge the park's popular white-sand beach and both are exceedingly pleasant locations where you can laze the day away. If you plan on spending a lot of time in the park and need to keep an eye on the kids, the wave pools make great bases of operation. ■ **TIP→ If you're establishing base camp here, arrive as early as possible and stake your claim on the beach.** ✉ *Aquatica* 🌐 *www.aquaticabyseaworld.com* ☞ *Duration: Up to You. Crowds: Vary by Season. Audience: Tweens and Up.*

Fodor's Choice ★ **Dolphin Plunge.** Thanks to the presence of Commerson's dolphins in the broad bay near the base of this attraction, this has become Aquatica's signature experience. The beginning of the ride is similar to that of other slides within the park. You whiz swiftly through an enclosed tube for about 250 feet, a long stretch that immerses you in darkness before the tube suddenly turns crystal clear. This clear shot affords a fleeting glimpse at the water that surrounds you, which happens to be the very same pool where the dolphins (which look like mini-killer whales) swim. You have to look fast to see them, though, because a split second later you're making your splashdown at the end of the line. In fact the best view of the dolphins may be from the walkway outside the ride or through an underwater pane of acrylic glass at the grotto. ■ **TIP→ Keep an eye on the line, and step up when it's light—likely very early or late.** ✉ *Aquatica* 🌐 *www.aquaticabyseaworld.com* ☞ *Duration: 1 min. Crowds: Absolutely. Audience: Tweens and Up. Height minimum: 48 inches.*

HooRoo Run/Walhalla Wave. One tower leads to these two attractions, each of which banks on the fact that, after climbing about 10 stories,

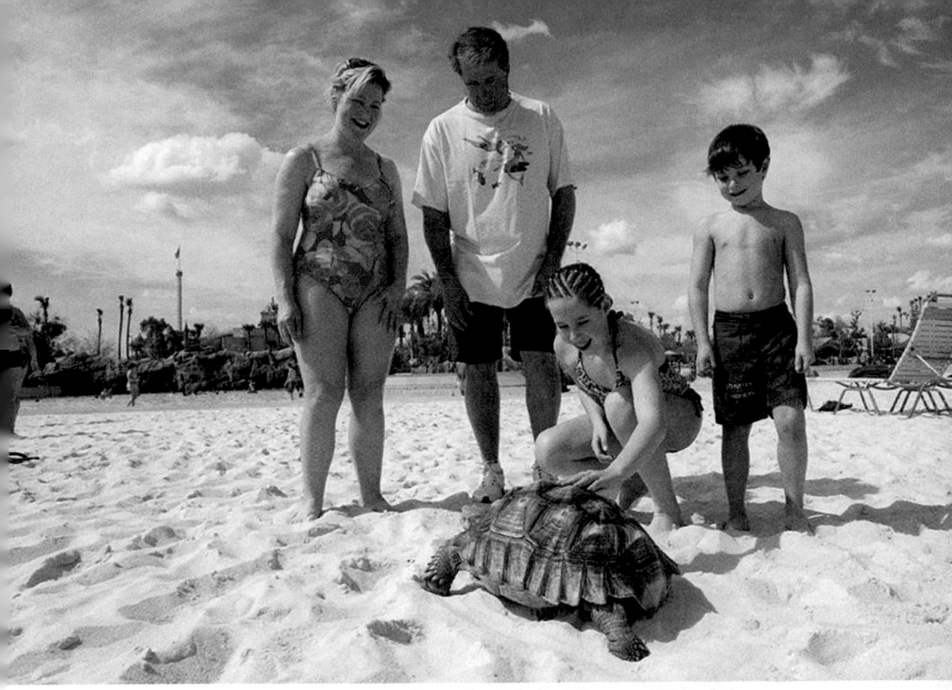

It's easy to make new friends—man or beast—on the sands of Big Surf Shores and Cutback Cove.

you'd rather face your fears and *slide* back down than have to *climb* back down. At the top is a string of yellow rafts that can hold two adults and a child, though some passengers go solo. Walhalla is on your right, HooRoo on your left. After selecting a side, you and your fellow passengers slip into a raft and are pushed into the current by an attendant. Walhalla sends you circling around corners and banking to the edges of tight curves before sliding you into an enclosed tunnel. HooRoo keeps you out in the open, bouncing you down, down, down over a series of mogul-like slides. Either way you go, you'll want to go again. ■ **TIP→ Come early or late—or be patient.** ✉ *Aquatica* 🌐 *www.aquaticabyseaworld.com* ☞ *Duration: 30 secs. Crowds: Heavy. Audience: Tweens and Up. Height minimum: 42 inches; under 48 inches requires a life vest.*

Kata's Kookaburra Cove. If the sight of cool slides and water features finds you wondering who Kata's is meant for, look at the height restrictions. To visit this area, between the beach and Walkabout Waters, you must be under 4 feet tall (or accompanied by someone who is). Yes, the entire area of special pint-sized slides, pools, and waterspouts is modified for the toddler set (the "deep end" is a modest two feet), but for them it's a big fun world. Clear, inflatable floats give them a chance to drift about, looking cool. Plus it gives adults a chance to take a break. Be aware the smallest participants will need to wear swim diapers, available at the gift shop, and the Baby Care center is conveniently close. ✉ *Aquatica* 🌐 *www.aquaticabyseaworld.com* ☞ *Duration: Up to You. Crowds: Moderate–Heavy. Audience: Small Kids. Height restrictions: Under 4 feet. Adults must be accompanied by a child no more than 48 inches.*

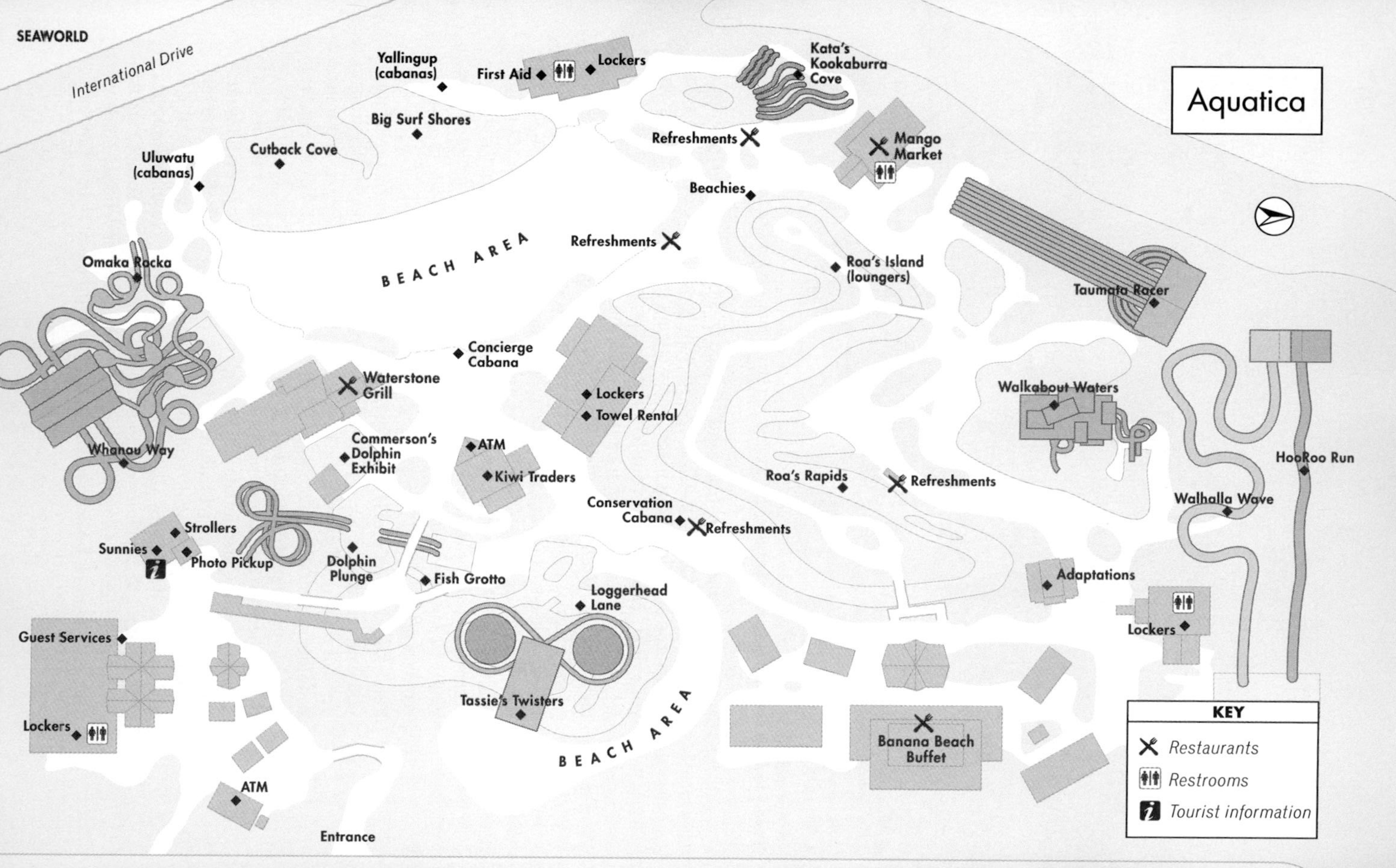
Aquatica
SEAWORLD
International Drive
Yallingup (cabanas)
First Aid
Lockers
Kata's Kookaburra Cove
Big Surf Shores
Refreshments
Mango Market
Uluwatu (cabanas)
Cutback Cove
Beachies
Refreshments
BEACH AREA
Roa's Island (loungers)
Omaka Rocka
Taumata Racer
Concierge Cabana
Waterstone Grill
Lockers
Towel Rental
Walkabout Waters
Commerson's Dolphin Exhibit
ATM
Kiwi Traders
Whanau Way
Roa's Rapids
Refreshments
HooRoo Run
Conservation Cabana
Refreshments
Walhalla Wave
Strollers
Sunnies
Photo Pickup
Dolphin Plunge
Fish Grotto
Adaptations
Loggerhead Lane
Lockers
Guest Services
Tassie's Twisters
Lockers
BEACH AREA
Banana Beach Buffet
ATM
Entrance
KEY
Restaurants
Restrooms
Tourist information

PACK A LUNCH

You'll be amazed at how much energy it takes to cover all the rides and attractions at Aquatica. You need to stay hydrated and well nourished, which can be a costly proposition. The park allows guests to bring in a small cooler of "serving-size" snacks, bottled water, and baby food in plastic containers. It's not so keen on "family-size" servings (think sandwiches, pizza, and 2-liter bottles of soft drinks).

Loggerhead Lane. For a wonderful way to relax, you simply go with the current of this gently flowing stream, bobbing along on a double or single tube that drifts down and around the bend. Along the way, there's a spot where you can exit the river and enter the line for Tassie's Twisters. A little farther, the calm stream flows into a 10,000-gallon grotto filled with thousands of colorful fish and a view of the Commerson's dolphins. This is indeed a lazy river: there's next to no pull so you might have to paddle a bit, especially if you choose the turn that leads into the fish grotto. Guests under 48 inches must wear a life vest. ■ **TIP→ Although there's plenty of river for everyone, try it when most people are at lunch.** ✉ *Aquatica* 🌐 *www.aquaticabyseaworld.com* ☞ *Duration: Up to You. Crowds: Light. Audience: Tweens and Up.*

Omaka Rocka. Like the tentacles on a huge plastic octopus, a series of tunnels and tubes snake off the platform to provide multiple options for different starting points. Regardless of where you start, once you climb into an innertube and slide into the slipstream you'll be riding and bouncing through some slick tubes, skimming past some half-pipe tunnels, and then sliding over some slippery moguls that splash you up on the side during some high-bank turns. Fast and furious. ■ **TIP→ Keep an eye on the line, and hop in when it's short.** ✉ *Aquatica* 🌐 *www.aquaticabyseaworld.com* ☞ *Duration: 1 min. Crowds: Heavy. Audience: Not Small Kids. Height minimum: 48 inches.*

Roa's Rapids. Even though it has "rapids" in its name, this attraction actually has a mild current that winds around numerous curves and "waterfalls" (really just sprays of water from the edge of the channel). Don a life vest and wade right in at either of two entrances (one red, the other blue, so you know where to exit). Then, whether you're traveling solo or hanging onto the kids, you simply go with the flow. Two advantages: there's no line, so you can always just drop right in, and you can go around and around for as long as you'd like. Guests less than 51 inches tall are required to wear a life vest. ■ **TIP→ Like Loggerhead Lane, there's plenty of river for everyone; still, come around lunchtime.** ✉ *Aquatica* 🌐 *www.aquaticabyseaworld.com* ☞ *Duration: Up to You. Crowds: Light. Audience: All Ages.*

Tassie's Twisters. This is one of the weirdest attractions at Aquatica. Reaching it from Loggerhead Lane's lazy river, you go ashore, climb a tower, settle into an inner tube, and launch yourself into currents that carry you away at an impressive speed. But that's not the weird part. After that, the enclosed pipe you've been in delivers you to a massive basin, where you and your inner tube circle around and around and around and around like a soap bubble circling a bathtub drain.

Eventually gravity takes over, and you slip through an opening in the side of the basin, straight into a short but thrilling slide into the splashdown pool. Strange and exciting. ■ **TIP→ Keep on eye on the line, and head upstairs when it's short.** ✉ *Aquatica* 🌐 *www.aquaticabyseaworld.com* ☞ *Duration: 1 min. Crowds: Heavy. Audience: Tweens and Up. Height minimum: Less than 48 inches requires a life vest, and you must be able to sit upright.*

Taumata Racer. In the aquatic equivalent of a bobsled run, you set yourself up on a blue mat at the opening of a large tube and, at the end of a countdown, you and the seven other racers beside you fling yourselves into the chutes. You then slide through 300 feet of enclosed twisting and turning tubes—but that's not the best part. Things really get going when you enter a stretch that's nearly pitch-black except for a small band of light beside you. After what seems like both an eternity and an instant, you reach the final drop and slide the last few yards into the splashdown pool. ■ **TIP→ If you can't see the end of the line, it's probably short—and it's time to head up. Eight lanes keep things moving along.** ✉ *Aquatica* 🌐 *www.aquaticabyseaworld.com* ☞ *Duration: 30 secs. Crowds: Light–Moderate. Audience: Not Small Kids. Height minimum: 42 inches.*

Walkabout Waters. A colorful 60-foot "rain fortress" anchors 15,000 square feet of family slides, pools, climb- and crawl-through trails, and two humongous buckets that are filling up constantly and, just as constantly, dumping their contents on frolickers far below. This is a fantastically creative play space comparable to Shamu's Happy Harbor at SeaWorld. Kids that are too big for Kata's Kookaburra Cove are at home here—they treat it as the most amazing aquatic playground they've ever experienced. The slides attached to the play structure flow slowly enough for beginners (note that kids aren't permitted to ride on grown-ups' laps on this one) and supercharged water cannons add another level of fun. ■ **TIP→ Save this area for later, when you're worn out but the kids want to play.** ✉ *Aquatica* 🌐 *www.aquaticabyseaworld.com* ☞ *Duration: Up to You. Crowds: Heavy. Audience: Young Kids. Height requirements: 36 to 42 inches for the main pool; over 42 inches for larger slides. Under 48 inches must wear a life vest on the larger slides.*

Whanau Way. Because waterpark guests can never get enough slipping and sliding, Aquatica offers this quadruple slide with an assortment of twists and turns. Depending on which tube you select, you enjoy a completely different experience. Like its partner slides, much of the attraction here is sliding straight into a darkened stretch; sure you know you're heading somewhere, but you're not exactly sure *where*. In the end, the answer reveals itself: you're heading down the final stretch on a long slide into the splashdown pool. Rinse and repeat. Riders must be at least 42" tall and able to retain an upright position unassisted; under 48" must wear a life vest. ■ **TIP→ Try it at lunchtime or near day's end.** ✉ *Aquatica* 🌐 *www.aquaticabyseaworld.com* ☞ *Duration: 1 min. Crowds: Heavy. Audience: Not Small Kids.*

9

ORLANDO AND ENVIRONS

WELCOME TO ORLANDO AND ENVIRONS

TOP REASONS TO GO

★ **Liberal Arts:** Orlando's theaters host symphony orchestras, Broadway road shows, and local thespians—from the Shakespearean to the progressive. Jazz, blues, world music, and rock are all part of the music scene. Area museums showcase folk art, Tiffany glass, and 14th- through 20th-century European and American paintings.

★ **The Sciences:** The Orlando Science Center has exhibits on human biology, technology, nature, and the stars. At WonderWorks, simulators let you survive an earthquake or pilot a jet. The Kennedy Space Center takes you to the final frontier.

★ **Cultivated Spaces:** Gardens devoted to historical blooms, camellias, azaleas, and roses are among the more refined outdoor offerings.

★ **Wild Places:** Go all gator at Gatorland or see rescued winged creatures at the Audubon Center for Birds of Prey. Fish, boat, canoe, or swim in Wekiwa Springs State Park or Ocala National Forest.

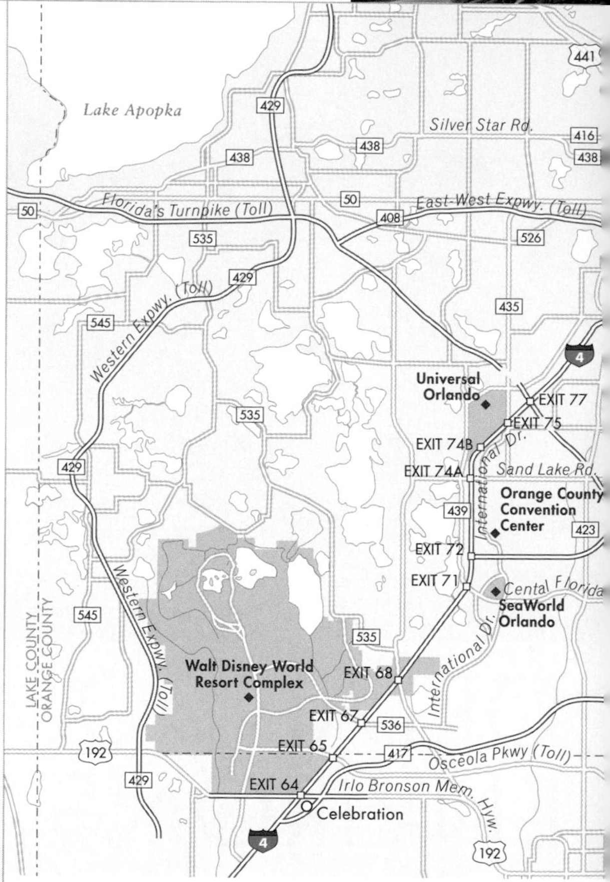

1 Orlando. There's more to Orlando than theme parks: a thriving Downtown with ample opportunity to stay, eat, and play. Internationally recognized cultural events, theater, and the evolving music scene make Downtown more than just a stopping point.

2 Orlando Environs. Natural Florida beckons with some of the most unspoiled land and amazing sportfishing in the state. Several towns—Kissimmee, Mount Dora, and Winter Park among them—recall Old Florida *and* have great shopping, world-class museums, or both.

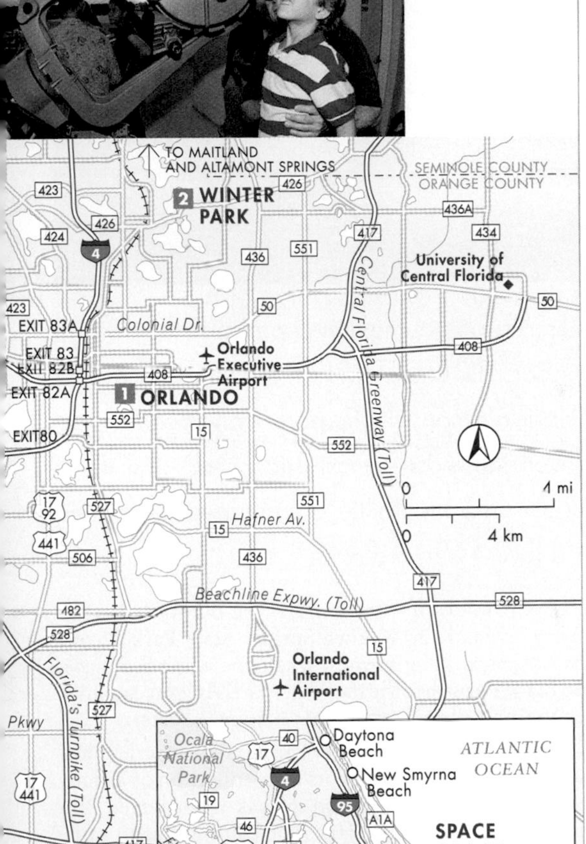

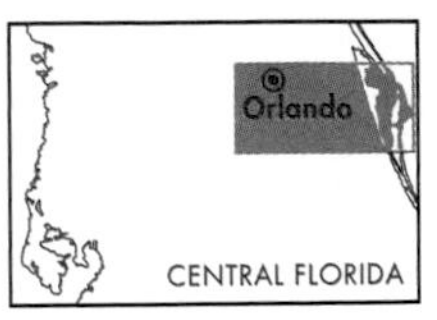

GETTING ORIENTED

Central Florida runs from Tampa/St. Petersburg in the west through Orlando to the coastal attractions of Daytona Beach and Cape Canaveral on the east coast. Orlando is more or less equidistant, about 90 minutes by car to the Gulf of Mexico. Walt Disney World is not, contrary to advertising, in Orlando, but lies about 25 miles southwest of the city.

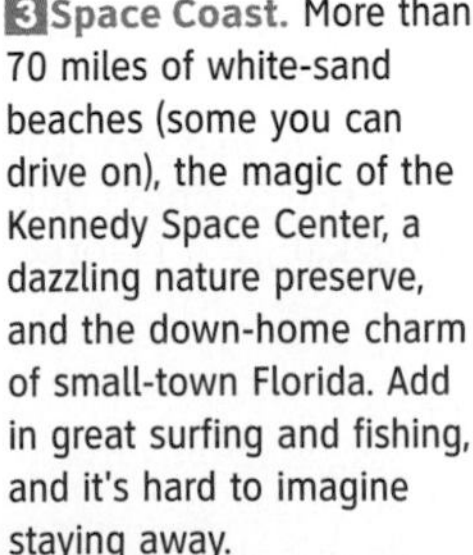

3 Space Coast. More than 70 miles of white-sand beaches (some you can drive on), the magic of the Kennedy Space Center, a dazzling nature preserve, and the down-home charm of small-town Florida. Add in great surfing and fishing, and it's hard to imagine staying away.

9

Updated by Jennie Hess

Most Orlando locals look at the theme parks as they would an unruly neighbor: it's big and loud, but it keeps a nice lawn. Central Florida's many theme parks can become overpowering for even the most enthusiastic visitor, and that's when an excursion into the "other" Orlando—the one the locals know and love—is in order.

There are ample opportunities for day trips. If the outdoors is your thing, you can swim or canoe at Wekiwa Springs State Park or one of the area's many other sparkling springs, where the water remains a refreshing 72°F no matter how hot the day. Alternatively, you can hike, horseback ride, canoe, and camp in the Ocala National Forest.

If museums are your thing, charming Winter Park has the Charles Hosmer Morse Museum of American Art with its huge collection of Tiffany glass, and the Cornell Fine Arts Museum on the oak-tree-covered Rollins College campus. While in Winter Park, you can indulge in some high-end shopping and dining on Park Avenue or take a leisurely boat tour of the lakefront homes.

Got kids to educate and entertain? Check out WonderWorks or the Orlando Science Center, where you can view live gators and turtles. Even more live gators (some as long as 14 feet) can be viewed or fed (or even eaten) at Gatorland, just south of Orlando.

Do the kids prefer rockets and astronauts? Don't miss a day trip to Kennedy Space Center, where you can tour a rocket forest, sit in a space capsule, or see a space shuttle up close.

Kissimmee is a 19th-century cattle town south of Orlando that proudly hangs on to its roots with a twice-yearly rodeo where real cowboys ride bulls and rope cattle. The town sits on Lake Tohopekaliga, a favorite spot for airboat rides or fishing trips.

ORLANDO

Orlando is a diverse town. The Downtown area, though small, is dynamic, thanks to an ever-changing skyline of high-rises, sports venues, museums, restaurants, nightspots, a history museum, and several annual cultural events—including film festivals and a world-renowned theater fest. Downtown also has a central green, Lake Eola Park, which offers a respite from otherwise frantic touring.

Neighborhoods such as Thornton Park (great for dining) and College Park (an outpost of great dining and live theater) are fun to wander. Not too far to the north, you can come in contact with natural Florida—its manatees, gators, and crystal clear waters in spring-fed lakes.

Closer to the theme-park action, International Drive, the hub of resort and conference hotels, offers big restaurants and even bigger outlet-mall bargains. Sand Lake Road, between the two, is Orlando's Restaurant Row, with plenty of exciting dining prospects.

GETTING HERE AND AROUND

Orlando is spread out. During rush hour, car traffic crawls along the often-crowded Interstate 4, which runs to both coasts. If you're heading east, you can also take Route 528 (aka the Beachline), a toll road that heads directly for Cape Canaveral and points along the Space Coast; no such option leads west.

If you avoid rush-hour traffic, traveling to points of interest shouldn't take too much time out of your vacation. Winter Park is no more than 20 minutes from Downtown; International Drive and the theme parks are about 30 minutes away in heavier traffic. Orlando International Airport is only 9 miles south of Downtown, but it will take about 30 minutes via a circuitous network of highways (Interstate 4 west to Florida's Turnpike south to Route 528 east).

ESSENTIALS

Hospitals Florida Hospital ✉ *601 E. Rollins St.* ☎ *407/303–5600* 🌐 *www.floridahospital.com.* **Orlando Regional Medical Center** ✉ *1414 Kuhl Ave., Downtown Orlando* ☎ *321/841–5111* 🌐 *www.orlandohealth.com.*

Tourist Information Orlando Visitors Bureau ☎ *407/363–5872, 800/972–3304* 🌐 *www.visitorlando.com.*

EXPLORING

CENTRAL ORLANDO

Fodor's Choice ★ **Harry P. Leu Gardens.** A few miles outside of downtown—on the former lakefront estate of a citrus entrepreneur—is this 50-acre garden. Among the highlights are a collection of historical blooms (many varieties of which were established before 1900), ancient oaks, a 50-foot floral clock, and one of the largest camellia collections in eastern North America (in bloom November–March). Mary Jane's Rose Garden, named after Leu's wife, is filled with more than 1,000 bushes; it's the largest formal rose garden south of Atlanta. The simple 19th-century Leu House Museum, once the Leu family home, preserves the furnishings and appointments of a well-to-do, turn-of-the-20th-century Florida

The 300-seat Dr. Phillips CineDome, a movie theater with an eight-story screen at the Orlando Science Center, offers large-format iWERKS films.

family. ✉ *1920 N. Forest Ave., Lake Ivanhoe* ☎ *407/246–2620* 🌐 *www.leugardens.org* 🎫 *$10, free 1st Mon. of month* ⏲ *Garden daily 9–5; guided house tours daily on hr and ½ hr 10–3:30; closed Dec. 25.*

FAMILY **Lake Eola Park.** This beautifully landscaped 43-acre park is the verdant heart of downtown Orlando, its mile-long walking path a gathering place for families, health enthusiasts out for a run, and culture mavens exploring area offerings. The well-lighted playground is alive with children, and ducks, swans, and native Florida birds call the lake home. A farmers' market takes up residence on Sunday afternoon.

The lakeside Walt Disney Amphitheater is a dramatic site for concerts, ethnic festivals, and spectacular July 4 fireworks. Don't resist the park's biggest draw: a ride in a swan-shaped pedal boat. Five adults can fit into each. (Children under 16 must be accompanied by an adult.)

The Relax Grill, by the swan-boat launch, is a great place for a snack. There are also several good restaurants in the upscale Thornton Park neighborhood along the park's eastern border. The ever-expanding skyline rings the lake with modern high-rises, making the peace of the park even more welcome. After a lightning strike in 2009, the landmark fountain was revamped and features an LED light and music show on summer evenings at 9:30 pm. ✉ *195 N. Rosalind Ave., Downtown Orlando* ☎ *407/246–4485 park, 407/246–4485 swan boats* 🎫 *Swan boat rental $15 per ½ hr* ⏲ *Park daily 6 am–midnight; swan boats Sun.–Tues. 10–7, Wed.–Sat. 10–10.*

Mennello Museum of American Folk Art. One of the few museums in the United States devoted to folk art has intimate galleries, some with lovely

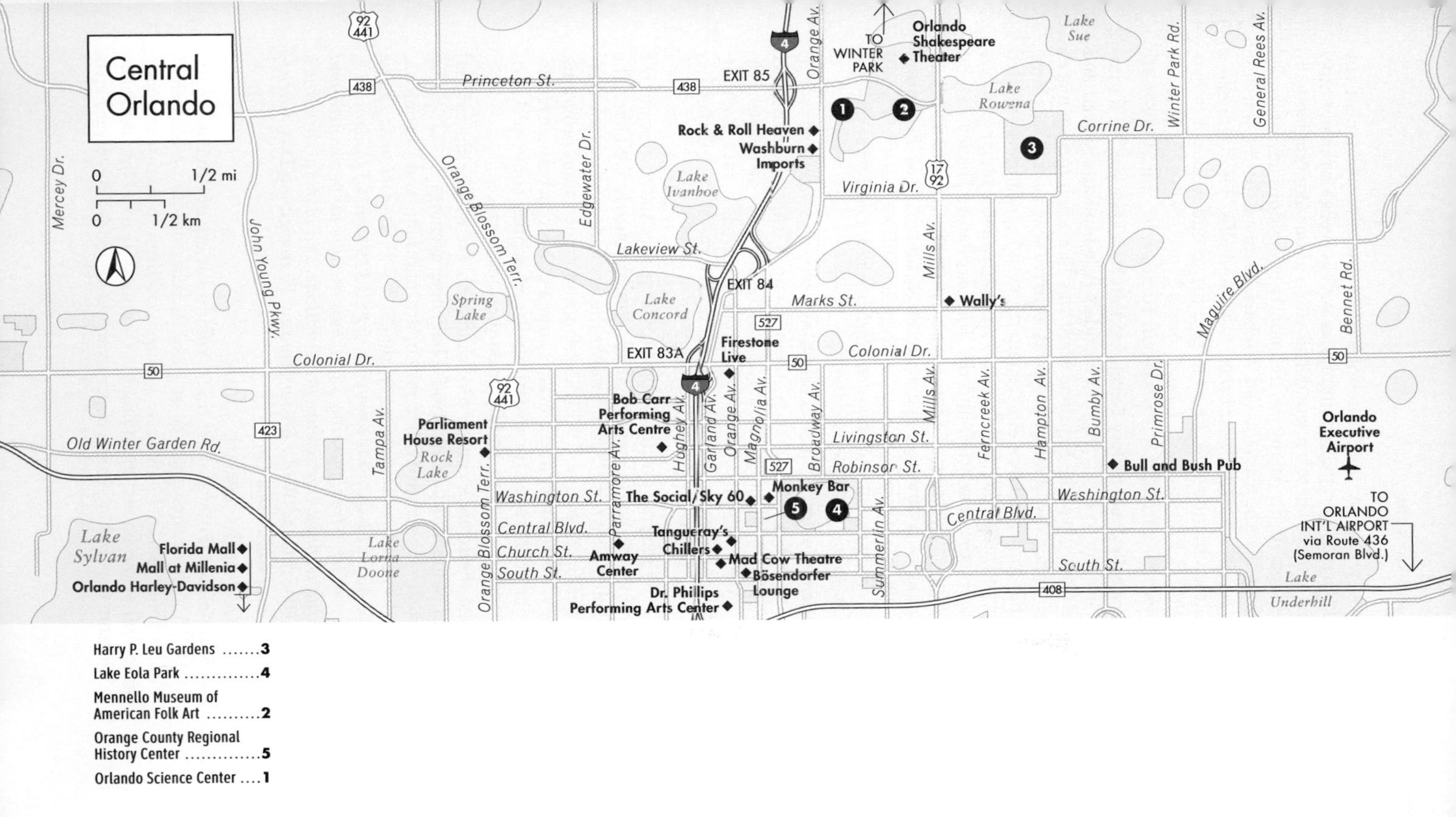
Central Orlando
0 1/2 mi
0 1/2 km
TO WINTER PARK
Orlando Shakespeare Theater
Lake Sue
Lake Rowena
Winter Park Rd.
General Rees Av.
Princeton St.
EXIT 85
Orange Av.
Corrine Dr.
Rock & Roll Heaven
Washburn Imports
Lake Ivanhoe
Virginia Dr.
Mercey Dr.
John Young Pkwy.
Orange Blossom Terr.
Edgewater Dr.
Lakeview St.
Mills Av.
EXIT 84
Maguire Blvd.
Bennet Rd.
Spring Lake
Lake Concord
Marks St.
Wally's
Firestone Live
EXIT 83A
Colonial Dr.
Bob Carr Performing Arts Centre
Hughey Av.
Garland Av.
Magnolia Av.
Broadway Av.
Ferncreek Av.
Hampton Av.
Bumby Av.
Primrose Dr.
Orlando Executive Airport
Parliament House Resort
Tampa Av.
Old Winter Garden Rd.
Rock Lake
Parramore Av.
Livingston St.
Robinson St.
Bull and Bush Pub
Washington St.
The Social/Sky 60
Monkey Bar
Central Blvd.
Summerlin Av.
TO ORLANDO INT'L AIRPORT via Route 436 (Semoran Blvd.)
Lake Sylvan
Florida Mall
Mall at Millenia
Orlando Harley-Davidson
Lake Lorna Doone
Church St.
Amway Center
Tanqueray's
Chillers
Mad Cow Theatre
Bösendorfer Lounge
South St.
Dr. Phillips Performing Arts Center
Lake Underhill
Harry P. Leu Gardens 3
Lake Eola Park 4
Mennello Museum of American Folk Art 2
Orange County Regional History Center 5
Orlando Science Center 1

lakefront views. Look for the nation's most extensive permanent collection of Earl Cunningham paintings as well as works by many other self-taught artists. There's a wonderful video about Cunningham and his "curio shop" in St. Augustine. Temporary exhibitions have included the works of Wyeth, Cassatt, and Michael Eastman. At the museum shop you can purchase folk-art books, toys, and gifts. The Mennello is the site of the Orlando Folk Festival, held the second weekend of February. ✉ *900 E. Princeton St., Lake Ivanhoe* ☎ *407/246–4278* 🌐 *www.mennellomuseum.org* 🎟 *$5* ⏲ *Tues.–Sat. 10:30–4:30, Sun. noon–4:30.*

FAMILY **Orange County Regional History Center.** Exhibits here take you on a journey back in time to discover how Florida's Paleo-Indians hunted and fished the land, what the Sunshine State was like when the Spaniards first arrived, and how life in Florida was different when citrus was king. Visit a cabin from the late 1800s, complete with Spanish moss–stuffed mattresses and mosquito netting over the beds. Seminole Indian displays include interactive activities, and the Tourism Before Disney exhibit previews Florida's destiny as a future vacation mecca. Traveling exhibits bring modern technology and art to the Museum. ✉ *65 E. Central Blvd., Downtown Orlando* ☎ *407/836–8500, 800/965–2030* 🌐 *www.thehistorycenter.org* 🎟 *$15; seniors, students $13; 5–12 $12; under 4 free* ⏲ *Mon.–Sat. 10–5, Sun. noon–5.*

FAMILY Fodor's Choice ★ **Orlando Science Center.** With all the high-tech glitz and imagined worlds of the theme parks, is it worth visiting Orlando's reality-based science center? If you're a kid crazy about science, the answer is an overwhelming "yes." With exhibits about the human body, mechanics, computers, math, nature, the solar system, and optics, the science center has something for every child's inner geek.

The four-story internal atrium is home to live gators and turtles and is a great spot for simply gazing at what Old Florida once looked like. The 300-seat Dr. Phillips CineDome, a movie theater with a giant eight-story screen, offers large-format iWERKS films and planetarium programs. The Crosby Observatory and Florida's largest publicly accessible refractor telescope are here, as are several smaller telescopes; some weekends you can safely view spots and flares on the sun's surface.

Adults like the science center, too, thanks to events like the annual Science of Wine and Cosmic Golf Challenge; evenings of stargazing in the Crosby Observatory, live music, art, and film; and Otronicon, the annual interactive technology expo. ✉ *777 E. Princeton St., Lake Ivanhoe* ☎ *407/514–2000* 🌐 *www.osc.org* 🎟 *$19; senior, student $17; 3–11 $13; under 2 free; parking $5; tickets include all permanent and special exhibits, films, live science presentations, and planetarium shows* ⏲ *Daily 10–5; closed Wed., Easter Sunday, Thanksgiving Day, Christmas Eve, and Christmas Day.*

INTERNATIONAL DRIVE AREA

FAMILY **Fun Spot America.** Four go-kart tracks offer a variety of driving experiences. Though drivers must be at least 10 years old and meet height requirements, parents can drive younger children in two-seater cars on several of the tracks, including the Conquest Track. Nineteen rides range from the dizzying Paratrooper to an old-fashioned Revolver Ferris

CLOSE UP

Central Florida Art

There are a surprising number of world-class art museums in Central Florida—from Orlando and Winter Park to St. Petersburg and Sarasota; from sublime stained glass to surrealist paintings and folk art to circus folk.

Mennello Museum of American Folk Art, Orlando. The Mennello holds the nation's most extensive permanent collection of Earl Cunningham paintings, as well as pieces by many other "outsider" artists. Works by Wyeth, Cassatt, Eastman, and others have made their Central Florida debuts here.

Charles Hosmer Morse Museum of American Art, Winter Park. Known as the "Tiffany museum," the galleries contain the largest and most comprehensive collection of art by Louis Comfort Tiffany, including stained-glass windows and lamps, blown-glass vases, and gem-studded jewelry.

Salvador Dalí Museum, St. Petersburg. Built upon the collection of an Ohio industrialist, this is the world's most comprehensive gathering of oils, watercolors, drawings, sculptures, photographs, and objets d'art by the Spanish surrealist. The museum moved into a new, Dalí-inspired building in 2011.

FSU Ringling Center for the Cultural Arts, Sarasota. This artistic compound stars the John and Mable Ringling Museum of Art and the Ringling Circus Museum. Classical masters of art share space with sideshow memorabilia. Don't miss the enchanting scale model of a 1920s Ringling Bros. and Barnum & Bailey Circus.

Wheel to the twirling toddler Teacups. Fun Spot recently expanded from five to 15 acres and now features Central Florida's only wooden roller coaster as well as the Freedom Flyer steel suspension family coaster, a kiddie coaster, and what's billed as the world's second-tallest (250 feet) SkyCoaster—part skydive, part hang-glide. The tallest, at 300 feet, is located at sister park Fun Spot USA, in Kissimmee. There's also an arcade. From Exit 75A, turn left onto International Drive, then left on Fun Spot Way. ✉ *5700 Fun Spot Way, I-Drive area* ☎ *407/363–3867* 🌐 *www.funspotattractions.com* 🎫 *$39.95 for all rides (online discounts available) or pay per ride; admission for nonriders free; arcade extra; parking free* 🕒 *Apr.–Oct., daily 10 am–midnight; Nov.–Mar., weekdays noon–11, weekends 10 am–midnight.*

Ripley's Believe It or Not! Odditorium. A 10-foot-square section of the Berlin Wall. A pain and torture chamber. Two African fertility statues that women swear have helped them conceive. These and almost 200 other oddities (shrunken heads included) speak for themselves in this museum-cum-attraction in the heart of tourist territory on International Drive. The building itself is designed to appear as if it's sliding into one of Florida's notorious sinkholes. Give yourself an hour or two to soak up the weirdness, but remember: this is a looking, not touching, experience; it might drive antsy youngsters—and their parents—crazy. ■ **TIP→ Buy tickets online ahead of time, and you can get discounts.**

✉ *8201 International Dr., I-Drive area* ☎ *407/351–5803* 🌐 *www.ripleysorlando.com* 🎟 *$19.99; 4–12 $12.99; parking free* ⏲ *Daily 9 am–midnight; last admission at 11 pm.*

NEED A BREAK?

Café Tu Tu Tango. Here's something unusual: good tapas in a tourist area. With a light, breezy atmosphere (painters work in the Spanish Artist's loft as you eat) and small, shareable dishes (including Tango Alligator Bites), it's a great place for a quick snack while on I-Drive. ✉ ***8625 International Dr., I-Drive area*** ☎ ***407/248–2222*** 🌐 ***www.cafetututango.com.***

FAMILY **WonderWorks.** The building seems to be sinking into the ground. Not only that, but it seems to be sinking into the ground at a precarious angle and upside down. Many people stop to take pictures in front of the topsy-turvy facade, complete with upended palm trees and broken skyward-facing sidewalks. Inside, the upside-down theme continues only as far as the lobby. After that, it's a playground of 100 interactive experiences—some incorporating virtual reality, others educational (similar to those at a science museum), and still others pure entertainment. You can experience an earthquake or a hurricane, land a space shuttle using simulator controls, make giant bubbles in the Bubble Lab, play laser tag in the enormous laser-tag arena and arcade, design and ride your own roller coaster, lie on a bed of real nails, and play baseball with a virtual Major League batter. ✉ *9067 International Dr., I-Drive area* ☎ *407/351–8800* 🌐 *www.wonderworksonline.com/orlando* 🎟 *$24.99; seniors, 4–12 $19.99; laser tag and Outta Control Magic Comedy Dinner Show extra (online discounts available); parking $3–$9* ⏲ *Daily 9 am–midnight.*

SPORTS AND THE OUTDOORS

There are many ways to enjoy the outdoors here. You can navigate the more than 2,000 lakes and waterways, perhaps on a sportfishing excursion—something to consider in what is one of the bass-fishing capitals of the world. You can also take to the air in a glider or hot-air balloon, or stay firmly planted hiking or biking a trail.

You can tee off at one of the more than six dozen area greens. Indeed, you'll probably be amazed by the country club–like golf courses (and tennis courts) run by the City of Orlando and accessible at bargain prices.

Orlando's sports arena and its three pro teams (basketball, hockey, and arena football) bring in the crowds. Throughout Central Florida, professional baseball comes down from the frozen North to warm up during spring training.

BALLOONING

Fodor's Choice ★ **Bob's Balloons.** Bob's offers one-hour rides over protected marshland and even flies over the Disney area if wind and weather conditions are right. You meet at Champions Gate, near Disney World, at dawn, where Bob and his assistant take you by van to the launch site. It takes about 15 minutes to get the balloon in the air, and then you're off on an adventure that definitely surpasses Peter Pan's Flight in the Magic Kingdom.

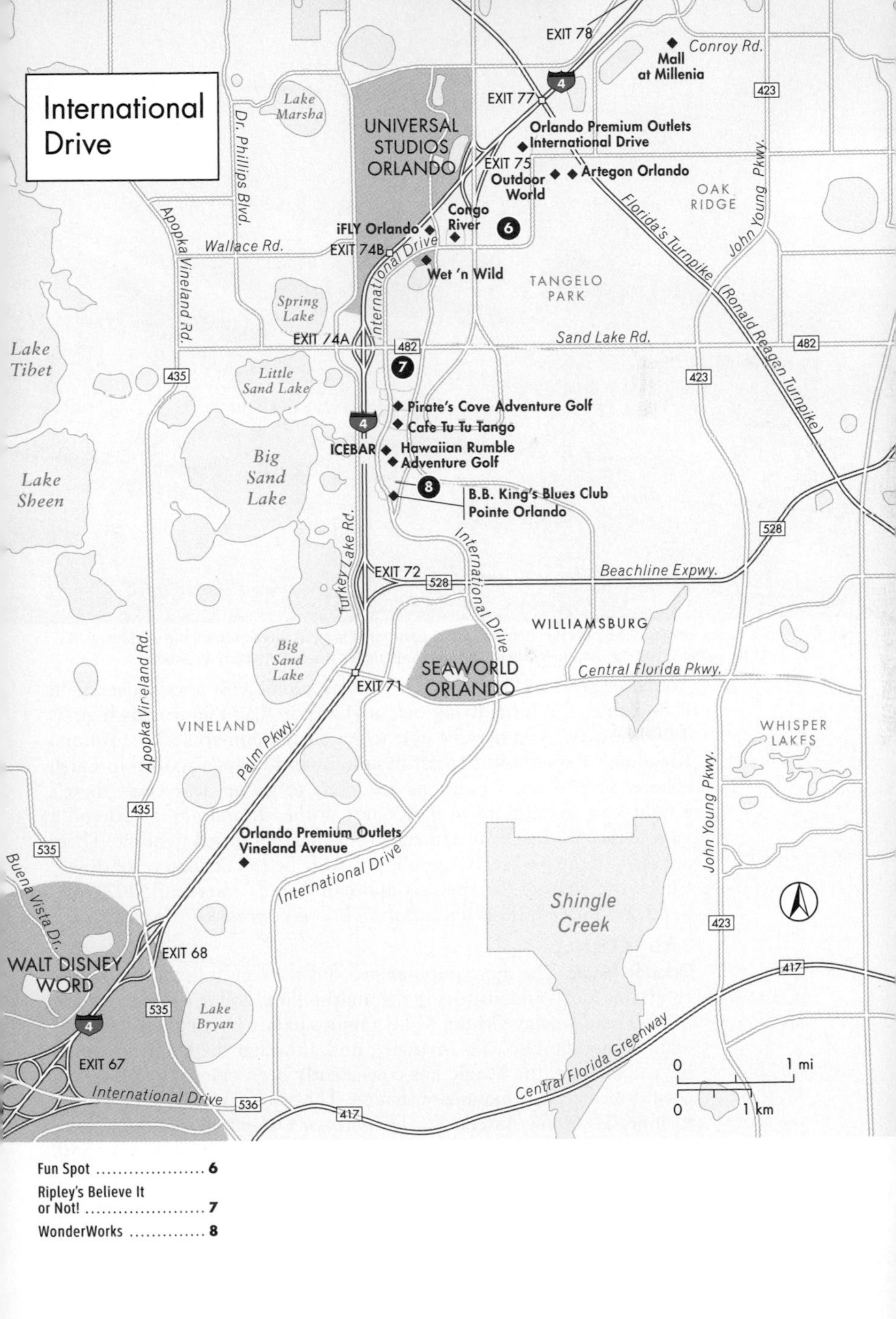

- Fun Spot **6**
- Ripley's Believe It or Not! **7**
- WonderWorks **8**

Kissimmee's Lake Tohopekaliga (affectionately known as Lake Toho) is famous with fishers the world over. It's also great for wildlife spotting—an especially exhilarating experience when done from an airboat.

You'll see farm and forest land for miles, along with horses, deer, wild boar, cattle, and birds flying *below* you. Bob may take you as high as 1,000 feet, and you may be able to see such landmarks as the Animal Kingdom's Expedition Everest mountain and Epcot's Spaceship Earth sphere. Several other balloons are likely to go up near you—there's a tight-knit community of ballooners in the Orlando area—so you'll view these colorful sky ornaments from an unparalleled sightline. There are seats in the basket, but you'll probably be too thrilled to sit down. Check the website for specials and call Bob to reserve. ☎ *407/466–6380, 877/824–4606* 🌐 *www.bobsballoons.com* 🎟 *$175 per person.*

BASKETBALL

Orlando Magic. The most popular pro sports team in town, the Magic entertains locals and visitors in the multimillion-dollar, state-of-the art, 20,000-seat Amway Center. Many famous names have come out of this team (Shaquille O'Neal, anyone?), and although the team's fortunes have fluctuated, the Magic has consistently been one of the most successful of the NBA expansion teams. The season runs from October to June. ✉ *600 W. Amelia St., Downtown Orlando* ☎ *407/896–2442* 🌐 *www.nba.com/magic* 🎟 *$30–$1,400; parking $10–$20, VIP lot $50.*

BIKING AND RUNNING

Thanks to the Orlando community's commitment to the nationwide Rails to Trails program, the city now has several biking, running, and in-line skating trails—converted from former railroad lines—in both rural and urban surroundings.

Orlando City Transportation Planning Division. You can get information about Orlando bike and running trails here. ✉ *Orlando City Hall, 400 S. Orange Ave.* ☎ *407/246–2821* 🌐 *www.cityoforlando.net.*

Bill Frederick Park at Turkey Lake. Renamed in honor of former Orlando Mayor Bill Frederick, this 178-acre park, about 4 miles from Universal Studios, has a 3-mile biking trail that's popular with runners, a pool, disc golf course and a lake that attracts the casual fisherman. Rental cabins and a 36-site Recreational Vehicle campground welcome visitors. Several wooded hiking trails also make for a good run. The park closes at 5 pm November–March and 7 pm April–October. ✉ *3401 S. Hiawassee Rd., West Orlando* ☎ *407/246–4486* 🌐 *www.cityoforlando.net/fpr/Html/Parks/BillFrederick.htm* 🎫 *$4 per car.*

Cady Way Trail. A favorite of local bikers, joggers, and skaters, the Cady Way connects eastern Orlando with the well-manicured enclave of Winter Park. The pleasant trail, open sunrise to sunset, is 6½ miles long, with water fountains and shaded seating along the route. The best access point is the parking lot on the east side of the Orlando Fashion Square Mall (✉ *3201 E. Colonial Dr., about 3 miles east of I–4 Exit 83B*). The northern access is at the Orange County Recreation Center (✉ *4863 N. Goldenrod Rd., Winter Park*). ✉ *1360 Truman Rd.* ☎ *407/836–6160* 🌐 *www.cityoforlando.net/fpr/html/Trails/CadyWay.htm.*

West Orange Trail. The trail runs some 22 miles from the Orange County–Lake County line, through the towns of Killarney and Oakland and the bustling center of the revived city of Winter Garden, and across U.S. 441 through downtown Apopka. Highlights are views of Lake Apopka and the butterfly garden at the Tildenville outpost. Among the trail's many access points is Chapin Station (✉ *501 Crown Point Cross Rd., Winter Garden*). There are some great places to rest and eat in Winter Garden. ✉ *501 Crown Point Cross Rd., Winter Garden* 🌐 *www.traillink.com/trail/west-orange-trail.aspx.*

West Orange Trail Bikes & Blades. Bicycles and in-line skates can be rented starting at $6 per hour and $30 per day. ✉ *17914 State Rd. 438, Winter Garden* ☎ *407/877–0600* 🌐 *www.orlandobikerental.com.*

9

FOOTBALL

Orlando Predators. With a new home in the CFE Arena on the University of Central Florida campus, this professional arena-football team plays from March through July. The team has been in Orlando since 1991 and has reached the league playoffs for 19 consecutive seasons. ✉ *12777 Gemini Blvd. N, UCF* ☎ *407/648–4444* 🌐 *www.orlandopredators.com* 🎫 *$12–$250; parking $10 and up.*

GOLF

If golf is your passion, you already know that Arnold Palmer and Gary Player—in fact, almost half of the PGA tour—make Orlando their off-road home. It's not by accident that the Golf Channel originates from here. The Bay Hill Invitational and several LPGA tourneys (the headquarters is in Daytona) come to Orlando every year. And with more than 80 public and private courses, there's ample opportunity for you to play on world-class courses such as Grand Cypress or Champions Gate.

MINIATURE GOLF

FAMILY **Congo River.** Here mini-putt meets theme park, with multilevel courses wandering amid waterfalls, rocky summits, caves, and rain forests. Kids love the live alligators (not loose on the course), the arcade room, and the treasure hunt. Congo River also has locations in Kissimmee and East Orlando. ✉ *5901 International Dr., I-Drive area* ☎ *407/248–9181* 🌐 *www.congoriver.com* 🎟 *$11.99; 10 and under $9.99* ⏲ *Sun.–Thurs. 10 am–11 pm, Fri. and Sat. 10 am–midnight.*

FAMILY Fodor's Choice ★ **Hawaiian Rumble Adventure Golf.** Who can resist golfing around an erupting volcano? Hawaiian Rumble combines a tropical setting with waterfalls, tunnels, tiki gods, and flame-belching mountains. There's also a location in the Lake Buena Vista area. ✉ *8969 International Dr., I-Drive area* ☎ *407/351–7733* 🌐 *www.hawaiianrumbleorlando.com* 🎟 *$9.95–$11.95* ⏲ *Sun.–Thurs. 9 am–11 pm, Fri. and Sat. 9 am–11:30 pm.*

FAMILY **Pirate's Cove Adventure Golf.** Two 18-hole courses wind around artificial mountains, through caves, and into lush foliage. The beginner's course is called Captain Kidd's Adventure; the more advanced course is Blackbeard's Challenge. There's another Pirate's Cove on International Drive. ✉ *12545 State Rd. 535, Lake Buena Vista* ☎ *407/827–1242* 🌐 *www.piratescove.net* 🎟 *$10.45–$14.95* ⏲ *Daily 9 am–11 pm.*

SKYDIVING

Fodor's Choice ★ **iFLY Orlando.** OK, you technically aren't skydiving, but you come pretty close in a 12-foot-high, 1,000-horsepower wind tunnel that lets you experience everything skydivers do, but closer to the ground. The experience starts with instruction, after which you suit up and hit the wind tunnel, where you soar like a bird under your instructor's watchful eye. It's all so realistic that skydiving clubs come to hone their skills. The attraction is safe for anyone under 250 pounds and older than 3. You can purchase a video of your "jump" for $24.95. ✉ *6805 Visitors Circle, I-Drive area* ☎ *407/903–1150* 🌐 *www.skyventureorlando.com* 🎟 *$59.95 and up, depending on package* ⏲ *Daily 10–10:30.*

TENNIS

Tennis awaits on well-tended public tennis courts and on courts in resort hotels. There are more than 50 courts run by City Parks & Recreation, some free and others reasonably priced.

Fort Gatlin Tennis Complex. Close to downtown Orlando, Fort Gatlin has the finest city-run courts open to the public. Ten hard courts equipped for day or night play, a pro shop that's open daily, and lessons are among this beautiful facility's offerings. ✉ *2009 Lake Margaret Dr., Downtown Orlando* ☎ *407/254–9878* 🌐 *www.mgtennis.com/fort-gatlin-tennis-center* 🎟 *$4–$6 per court per hr* ⏲ *Weekdays 8 am–10 pm, weekends 8–8.*

Orlando Tennis Center. Run by the City of Orlando, this fine facility offers adult tennis clinics (18 and up), private lessons, and youth tennis programs (6 and up). ✉ *649 W. Livingston St., Downtown Orlando* ☎ *407/246–4469* 🌐 *www.orlandotenniscenter.com* 🎟 *$5 soft court per hr, $4 hard court* ⏲ *Weekdays 8 am–9:30 pm, weekends 8–2:30.*

SHOPPING

Visitors from as far away as Britain and Brazil often arrive in Orlando with empty suitcases for their purchases. Although shopping has all but disappeared from Downtown, the metro area is filled with options. There really is something for everyone—from high-end fashion to outlet-mall chic, from the world's largest flea market to a boutique-filled town, from an antique treasure to a hand-hewn Florida find.

The College Park area, once an antiques-hunter's dream, still has some treasures to be found along North Orange Avenue and Edgewater Drive, including the largest vinyl-record shop in Florida.

The simultaneously glitzy and kitschy International Drive has almost 500 designer outlet stores and odd, off-brand electronics shops. The factory outlets on the north end of the Drive once consisted of shops with merchandise piled on tables; today the shops here are equal to their higher-priced first-run cousins. The strip also has plenty of restaurants and, for those in your group who don't feel like shopping, movie theaters.

CENTRAL ORLANDO AREA

MALLS

Florida Mall. With 250-plus stores and 1.8 million square feet of shopping, it's big enough for you to vacation here—in fact, there's even an attached hotel. Only 7 miles from the airport, the mall attracts crowds of international visitors eager for American bargains. Anchor stores include Sears, JCPenney, Dillard's, Macy's, and Nordstrom. An expanded food court adds a total of almost 50 casual eateries and sit-down restaurants to the shopping mix. Stroller and wheelchair rentals are available; there are even concierge services and a currency exchange. The mall is 4½ miles east of Interstate 4 and International Drive at the corner of Sand Lake Road and South Orange Blossom Trail. ✉ *8001 S. Orange Blossom Trail, South Orlando* ☎ *407/851–7234* 🌐 *www.simon.com* ⏲ *Mon.–Sat. 10–9, Sun. 11–7.*

Fodor's Choice ★ **Mall at Millenia.** "Deluxe" is the word for this mall, a high-end collection of designer shops, including Gucci, Burberry, Chanel, Jimmy Choo, Hugo Boss, Cartier, Tiffany, and Ferragamo. You'll also find Neiman Marcus, Bloomingdale's, and an Apple store, but the biggest attraction may be the adjacent IKEA. A few minutes northeast of Universal, the mall is easy to reach via Interstate 4 Exit 78. ✉ *4200 Conroy Rd., South Orlando* ☎ *407/363–3555* 🌐 *www.mallatmillenia.com* ⏲ *Mon.–Sat. 10–9, Sun. 11–7.*

SPECIALTY SHOPS

Orlando Harley-Davidson. During Daytona Beach Bike Week in March and Biktober Fest in October, this is Hog Central. Anything Harley is available, from chrome pipes, leather clothing, and cycle GPS units to actual motorcycles to buy or rent—yes, rent. The staff can teach you how to ride or paint flames on the side of your bike, and the calendar includes themed events with free food and live music. There are other locations in East Orlando and Kissimmee, as well as shops selling gear on International Drive, at Downtown Disney, and at the airport. ✉ *3770 37th St., South Orlando* ☎ *407/423–0346* 🌐 *www.orlandoharley.com* ⏲ *Mon.–Sat. 9–7, Sun. 10–6.*

Rock & Roll Heaven. Vinyl records are popular again, but according to R&R Heaven, they never left. Thousands upon thousands of LPs, 45s, CDs, and cassettes, in every conceivable (and a few unbelievable) music style can be found here, starting at as little as $1. The posters rock, too. ✉ *1814 N. Orange Ave., Lake Ivanhoe* ☎ *407/896–1952* 🌐 *www.rock-n-rollheaven.com* ⏲ *Mon.–Sat. 10–7:30, Sun. 11–4.*

Washburn Imports. Here you'll find an eclectic mix of antiques, commissioned furniture, and one-of-a-kind home furnishings made in India, Indonesia, and Thailand. There's a second location in Sanford. After hours, the back room turns into the Imperial Wine Bar, a popular haven of craft beers and local wine. ✉ *1800 N. Orange Ave., Lake Ivanhoe* ☎ *407/228–4403* 🌐 *www.washburnimports.com* ⏲ *Mon.–Sat. 10–6, Sun. 11–5; Imperial Mon.–Thurs. 5–midnight, Fri. and Sat. 5–2 am.*

INTERNATIONAL DRIVE AREA

CENTERS AND MALLS

Artegon/Festival Bay. A new artisanal-market approach to shopping malls, Artegon replaces much of Festival Bay with an indoor farmers' market and a collection of 250 to 300 stores, stands, and kiosks in which artisans will sell their work, and an indoor farmers' market for local produce. Shepler's Western Wear, Bass Pro Shops Outdoor World, and Ron Jon Surf Shop continue to attract customers, as does the 20-screen Cinemark Theater and several restaurants. ✉ *5250 International Dr.* ☎ *407/351–7718* 🌐 *www.artegonorlando.com* ⏲ *Mon.–Sat. 10–9, Sun. 11–7.*

Pointe Orlando. What was once an enclosed shopping center is now a dining, shopping, and entertainment hot spot—one that's within walking distance of five top hotels and the Orange County Convention Center. In addition to WonderWorks and the enormous Regal IMAX theater, the complex has specialty shops such as Armani Exchange, Tommy Bahama, Chico's, Tommy Hilfiger, Hollister, Charming Charlie, and Victoria's Secret. Restaurants have become a reason to visit, with the very high-end Capital Grille, the Oceanaire Seafood Room, Cuba Libre Restaurant and Rum Bar, The Pub, Marlow's Tavern, the popular Funky Monkey Wine Company, B.B. King's Blues Club, and Taverna Opa. Blue Martini and Minus5 Ice Bar provide after-hours adult beverages. Parking ($3 for 15 minutes–2 hours, $6 daily) can be validated by the movie theater and many of the restaurants. ✉ *9101 International Dr.* ☎ *407/248–2838* 🌐 *www.pointeorlando.com* ⏲ *Oct.–May, Mon.–Sat. noon–10, Sun. noon–8; June–Sept., Fri. and Sat. noon–9, Sun.–Thurs. noon–8.*

FACTORY OUTLETS

Orlando Premium Outlets International Drive. This is a prime destination for international shoppers who can find shoes, clothing, cosmetics, electronics, and household goods at a fraction of their home-country prices. The massive complex at the north tip of International Drive includes Saks Fifth Avenue OFF 5TH, Coach, Kate Spade New York, Victoria's Secret Outlet, and a Disney outlet. Searching for bargains works up an

DID YOU KNOW?

Old Town in Kissimmee—just one of many Orlando-area sights outside the theme parks—has several dozen shops, nine restaurants, 18 rides and attractions, and three or so antique-car shows a week.

appetite, and there are plenty of places to eat here, either in the well-lit food court or in one of several sit-down and highly regarded restaurants. ✉ *4951 International Dr.* ☎ *407/352–9600* 🌐 *www.premiumoutlets.com* ⏲ *Mon.–Sat. 10 am–11 pm, Sun. 10–9.*

Orlando Premium Outlets Vineland Avenue. This outlet capitalizes on its proximity to Disney (it's at the confluence of Interstate 4, State Road 535, and International Drive). It's easier to see from the highway than to enter, and parking is tedious and scarce, but smart shoppers have lunch on International Drive and take the I-Ride Trolley right to the front entrance (it runs every 15 minutes). The center's design makes this almost an open-air market, so walking can be pleasant on a nice day. You'll find Prada, Gap, Nike, Adidas, Tory Burch, Polo Ralph Lauren, Giorgio Armani, Burberry, Tommy Hilfiger, Reebok, and about 100 other stores. ✉ *8200 Vineland Ave.* ☎ *407/238–7787* 🌐 *www.premiumoutlets.com* ⏲ *Mon.–Sat. 10 am–11 pm, Sun. 10–9.*

SPECIALTY STORE

Bass Pro Shops Outdoor World. Inside a 150,000-square-foot Western-style lodge—and with fishing ponds, deer tracks in the concrete, and a massive stone fireplace—the store packs in countless boats, RVs, tents, rifles, deep-sea fishing gear, freshwater fishing tackle, scuba equipment, fly-tying materials (classes are offered, too), a pro shop, outdoor clothing, and Uncle Buck's Cabin (a snack bar). If you're an outdoors enthusiast, this is a must-visit. ✉ *5156 International Dr.* ☎ *407/563–5200* 🌐 *www.basspro.com* ⏲ *Mon.–Sat. 9 am–10 pm, Sun. 10–8.*

SPAS

SOUTH ORLANDO

Portofino Bay Mandara Spa. Adjacent to the bustling Italian-themed square at Universal's Portofino Bay resort, the doors to this Asian-themed sanctuary waft you into a more tranquil world, with bamboo screens, exotic statuary, and silk hangings. Warm blankets comfort you while you wait in the relaxation lounge for one of the 16 treatment rooms. Try the Ceremony of the Hands and Feet, an indulgence that scrubs, exfoliates, and massages your extremities, finishing with a mani-pedi. Separate men's and women's steam rooms and saunas add to the sense of serenity, but the men needn't worry about missing a game, as their lounge sports a plasma TV. Portofino's serene sand-bottomed pool is next door, as is the fitness center. Massage therapies include four hands, deep tissue, hot stone, Balinese, or Swedish. Facials and peels are available, as are full makeup, hair, and salon services. Massages from $89. Packages from $360. ✉ *5601 Universal Blvd., Universal Orlando area* ☎ *407/503–1244* 🌐 *www.mandaraspa.com.*

Ritz-Carlton Orlando, Grande Lakes Spa. Prepare to be wowed as you enter this lavish, grand spa, Orlando's largest with 40 treatment rooms, a fitness center, salon, private pool, and café. Get here in plenty of time to take a tour and get your bearings, shed your tourist togs, don a plush robe, and prepare to unwind. Unisex and co-ed waiting areas with couches and chairs are available, each on a different floor, with tea, water, fruits, and snacks. Treatments include massage, skin therapy,

ORLANDO-AREA DINNER SHOWS

Dinner shows are an immensely popular form of nighttime entertainment around Orlando, particularly in Kissimmee. What the shows lack in substance and depth they make up for in grandeur and enthusiasm. The result is an evening of light entertainment that youngsters, in particular, enjoy.

For a single price (which seems like an ever-increasing price), you get a theatrical production and a multicourse meal. Performances run the gamut from jousting matches to Jamborees, and meals tend to be about average. Unlimited beer, wine, and soda are usually included, but mixed drinks (and often *any* drinks before dinner) cost extra.

Seatings are usually between 7 and 9:30, with one or two performances a night and an extra show during peak periods. You might sit with strangers at tables for 10 or more, but that's part of the fun. Always reserve in advance, especially for weekend shows, and ask about discounts, although you can often find online coupons (sometimes for half off) that you can print out yourself. Since performance schedules can vary by season, it's always smart to call in advance to verify show times. When buying tickets, ask if the cost includes a gratuity.

and deep-cleaning HydraFacials that gently extract impurities from the skin. Massage techniques include traditional Swedish, neuromuscular, stone therapy, Ashiatsu, and even one in a hammock, under the stars. Special treatments for mothers to be. Massage from $145; 20% service charge is added. ✉ *Ritz-Carlton Orlando, 4024 Central Florida Pkwy.* ☎ *407/393–4200* 🌐 *www.ritzcarlton.com/orlando* ☞ *Parking: valet parking discounted with spa validation.*

9

The Spa at Shingle Creek. The romance of Old Florida surrounds the Rosen Shingle Creek resort, and most of the spa treatments feature Florida products such as citrus and cedar oils, aloe, and an Everglades sugar scrub. The Calusa Cocoon begins with an exfoliation using grapefruit, eucalyptus, and peppermint-infused clay and ends with a moisturizing wrap rich with citrus oils that relieves stress while feeding your skin. Types of massage include Swedish, aromatherapy, warm stone, and Ashiatsu barefoot massage, in which the therapist uses gravity to reach deep into your muscle tissue. A variety of facials and salon treatments are available, and you can add on a 25-minute siesta where you're wrapped in hot packs after your treatment, and awakened by gentle bells. Massages begin at $110. Packages begin at $215. Gratuity is included in the cost. Parking, either self or valet, is validated for day guests. ✉ *Rosen Shingle Creek, 9939 Universal Blvd.* ☎ *407/996–9939* 🌐 *www.spaatshinglecreek.com* ☞ *Parking: complimentary valet or self parking with spa validation.*

INTERNATIONAL DRIVE AREA

nèu lotus spa at Renaissance Orlando at Seaworld. Let the world's cares disappear as you recline in the candle-lit relaxation area, or make use of the steam room before your treatment at this bright, modern spa. An Asian-style barefoot massage can work the knots out of the most tense muscles, while the hot-and-cold-stone massage offers a more relaxing, restorative experience. Facials and skin treatments combine skin rejuvenation with shoulder relaxation and scalp massage. The spa also has a 2,600-square-foot fitness center with the latest equipment and a full-service salon. Massages include barefoot, aromatherapy, hot and cold stone, and bamboo shoot. Massage from $75. Packages from $239. Gratuity at guest's discretion. ✉ *6677 Sea Harbor Dr.* ☎ *407/248–7428* 🌐 *www.neulotusspa.com.*

The Spa at Hilton Orlando. From the deeply cushioned chaise longues in the waiting room, where guests relax in fleecy robes and blankets, to the complimentary infused water, juices, teas, and fruits, guests are made to feel cherished from the moment they enter this big (15 treatment rooms) resort spa. Orange blossom is the source of the oil for the signature Neroli massage, and essences of rosemary, pine, and lavender soothe the senses during aromatherapy treatments. Massages include Swedish, deep tissue, and heated stones, and guests are welcome to linger in the steam room, full-body showers, or to have a treatment in a cabana by the pool. Special services are available for youngsters and teens. Massages from $75. Packages from $335. An 18% service charge is added. Day pass available. Self-parking is free for nonhotel guests. ✉ *6001 Destination Pkwy.* ☎ *407/313–4300* 🌐 *www.thehiltonorlando.com.*

The Spa at Hyatt Regency Orlando. Getting to this 22,000-square-foot, full-service contemporary retreat, set at the heart of a huge convention resort (formerly the Peabody), can be quite a hike, so guests are happy to shed their clothes and cares, don fluffy robes and slippers, and settle in for some serious rejuvenation. The separate locker rooms offer whirlpools, steam room, and showers, and guests have access to a private serenity pool, where they can soak before and after their treatments. Massages include deep tissue, aromatherapy, and warm stone. A variety of facials and complete salon services are available. Massage from $125. Packages from $425. Gratuity added. ✉ *9801 International Dr.* ☎ *407/284–1234* 🌐 *www.orlando.regency.hyatt.com.*

The Spa at Rosen Centre. An intimate spa in a resort right across from the convention center, The Spa at Rosen Center caters to busy, stressed-out businesspeople as well as bridal parties, girlfriends' getaways, and more. Once clothes and cares are exchanged for luxurious robes and comfy slippers in the separate locker rooms, guests move to the serene, candle-lit, and aroma-enhanced separate relaxation rooms. The men's room has a TV for those who can't or won't miss a game or the news, but the sound is off, making sure that relaxation is the ultimate goal. If those muscles need a real workout, be sure to experience a traditional Ashiatsu massage, where the masseuse, supported by a wooden frame, uses gravity and her bare feet to reach deep into those knots. Massage techniques include Swedish, therapeutic, deep tissue, warm stone, Ashiatsu, and Asian-fusion barefoot. Massages from $125. Packages from $335. Day pass available for hotel guests and nonguests. Parking validated for nonguests. ✉ *9840 International Dr.* ☎ *407/996–1248* 🌐 *www.thespaatrosencentre.com.*

NIGHTLIFE

Outside of Downtown Disney and Universal's CityWalk, the focal point of adult Orlando nightlife is Downtown. If you stand on the corner of Orange Avenue and Church Street long enough, you can watch all types of gussied-up revelers walk by. The bars and music clubs here hop even after the 2 am last call.

CENTRAL ORLANDO

BARS

Bull and Bush Pub. After more than a quarter century in the same location, this is still one of the most atmospheric places in town, where you can get a hand-drawn pint, play a game of darts, and have a (still) smoky chat. The tap lineup covers 11 imported beers and ales. Darts leagues and weekly pub quizzes make it feel like a piece of old London. ✉ *2408 E. Robinson St., Downtown Orlando* ☎ *407/896–7546* 🌐 *www.bullandbushorlando.com* ⏱ *Closed Sun.*

Monkey Bar. You access this tiny pocket of sophistication amid the frenetic energy of the Wall Street entertainment area by walking through the WaiTiki Retro Tiki Lounge and finding the all-but-hidden elevator at the back. There's a relatively quiet room inside and an almost New Orleans–style balcony. Call ahead for happy hour times. ✉ *19 N. Orange Ave., Downtown Orlando* ☎ *407/481–1199* 🌐 *www.wallstplaza.net/venues/monkey-bar/* ⏱ *Wed.–Fri. 5 pm–2 am, Sat. 9–2.*

Sky Sixty. You have to head up to the roof using the side staircase of The Social nightclub to reach this breezy hot spot. The great view of busy Orange Avenue is accompanied by dance-friendly DJ beats and cool mojitos. Score a cozy cabana seat for prime people-watching. Sunday Funday features mimosa and other drink discounts. ✉ *60 N. Orange Ave., Downtown Orlando* ☎ *407/246–1599* 🌐 *www.skysixty.com/* ⏱ *Thurs.–Sat. 10 pm–2 am, Sun. 5–11.*

Wally's. One of Orlando's oldest bars (circa 1954), this longtime local favorite is a hangout for a cross section of cultures and ages. Some would say it's a dive, but that doesn't matter to the students, bikers, lawyers, and barflies who land here to drink surrounded by the go-go-dancer wallpaper and '60s-era interior. Just grab a stool at the bar to take in the scene and down a cold one. ✉ *1001 N. Mills Ave., Downtown Orlando* ☎ *407/896–6975* 🌐 *www.wallysonmills.com* ⏱ *Mon.–Sat. 7:30 am–2 am.*

MUSIC CLUBS

Bösendorfer Lounge. One of only two Imperial Grand Bösendorfer pianos takes center stage at this, perhaps the classiest gathering spot in Orlando. The highly civilized (but not stuffy) lounge attracts a cross section of trendy Orlandoans, especially the after-work crowd, among whom the conversation and camaraderie flow as smoothly as the champagne, beer, wine, and cocktails. Art on the walls, comfortable couches, rich fabrics, sleek black marble, and seductive lighting invite you to stay awhile. If music is what attracts you, call in advance for the schedule of jazz combos and solo pianists who perform in the lounge. Many are among the area's finest and most talented musicians.

✉ Grand Bohemian Hotel, 325 S. Orange Ave., Downtown Orlando ☎ 407/313–9000 ⊕ www.grandbohemianhotel.com ⏲ Fri. and Sat. 10 am–2 am, Sun.–Thurs. 10–1.

Firestone Live. Based in an old automotive repair shop, this multilevel, high-energy club draws international music acts. Something's always going on to make the crowd hop: DJ mixes, big band, jazz, hip-hop, rock. Often the dance floor is more like semicontrolled chaos than a place to just listen, so be prepared. Hours and prices vary by event; check the website. *✉ 578 N. Orange Ave., Downtown Orlando ☎ 407/872–0066 ⊕ www.firestonelive.net.*

Fodor's Choice ★ **The Social.** Beloved by locals, The Social is a great place to see touring and area musicians. Up to seven nights a week you can sip trademark martinis while listening to anything from indie rock to rockabilly to undiluted jazz. Several now-national acts got their start here, including Matchbox Twenty, Seven Mary Three, and other groups that don't have numbers in their names. Hours vary. *✉ 54 N. Orange Ave., Downtown Orlando ☎ 407/246–1419 ⊕ www.thesocial.org 🎫 $5–$30, depending on entertainment.*

Tanqueray's. Of all the entertainment possibilities in Downtown Orlando, the most interesting one may be the hardest to find. Housed in a former bank vault, Tanqueray's is a belowground hideaway featuring live music nightly and a full bar, including craft beers and nightly drink specials. If you don't mind the smoky atmosphere, you can enjoy a variety of entertainment from one night to the next, including reggae, funk, and high-energy blues. No food is served here. *✉ 100 S. Orange Ave., Downtown Orlando ☎ 407/649–8540.*

NIGHTCLUBS

Chillers. Known as Orlando's original party bar, Chillers features an entire wall of frozen daiquiri machines and sells craft beers and premium liquors as well. A DJ spins Top 40 dance music, and there's karaoke every Thursday. Drinks are $1 on Wednesday starting at 7:30. *✉ 33 W. Church St., Downtown Orlando ☎ 407/649–4270 ⊕ www.churchstreetbars.com/chillers.*

Parliament House Resort. For those enamored of gay, lesbian, and high-camp entertainment, Parliament House is legendary and welcoming to every kind of audience. The 250-seat art-deco performance space, which has been open since 1975, hosts live theater, musical acts, karaoke, cabaret, dance, and bawdy and hilarious drag shows. Le Club Disco and Dance bar, along with four other bars, draws thousands of partiers weekly. Unfortunately Orange Blossom Trail remains a sketchy area, so wandering around the neighborhood isn't advised. *✉ 410 N. Orange Blossom Trail, Downtown Orlando ☎ 407/425–7571 ⊕ www.parliamenthouse.com ⏲ Le Club: Mon.–Sat. 9 pm–2 am, Sun. 3 pm–when they decide to close. Hrs vary at other bars.*

THEATER

Mad Cow Theatre. Orlando's longest-standing professional theater company is where risks are taken. Regional premieres, new works, and thoughtful interpretations of classics such as *Death of a Salesman* make this a stage worth seeking. Local actors eager to show their talents line up to work here. ✉ *54 W. Church St., Downtown Orlando* ☎ *407/297–8788* 🌐 *www.madcowtheatre.com.*

Orlando Shakespeare Theater. "Orlando Shakes" has four stages, where a typical season includes 11 plays covering classics (including Shakespeare, of course), contemporary, and children's productions. The theater also hosts the very popular Orlando International Fringe Festival, the oldest in America. The season runs June through April, with the Fringe Festival in May. PlayFest! The Harriett Lake Festival of New Plays offers world-premiere and staged-reading opportunities for new playwrights. The theater is in Loch Haven Cultural Park, just a few minutes north of Downtown, where the Orlando Science Center and the Museum of Art also stand. ✉ *812 E. Rollins St., Lake Ivanhoe* ☎ *407/447–1700* 🌐 *www.orlandoshakes.org.*

INTERNATIONAL DRIVE AREA

DINNER SHOW

Fodor's Choice ★ **Sleuths Mystery Dinner Show.** If Sherlock Holmes has always intrigued you, head on over for a four-course meal served up with a healthy dose of conspiracy. Sleuths is a hotbed of local acting talent, with 13 rotating whodunnit performances staged throughout the year in three different theaters. The comedy-mystery show begins during your appetizer, and murder is the case by the time they clear your plates. You'll get to discuss clues and question still-living characters over dinner and solve the crime during dessert. Prizes go to top sleuths. Comedy and magic shows fill up the late-night lineup on weekends. ✉ *8267 International Dr., I-Drive area* ☎ *407/363–1985* 🌐 *www.sleuths.com* 🎫 *$57.95; 3–11 $23.95* ⏲ *Performances usually daily at 7:30 but call ahead.*

MUSIC CLUB

B.B. King's Blues Club. The blues great was doing quite well as a musician before becoming a successful entrepreneur, with blues clubs in Memphis, Nashville, Las Vegas, and West Palm Beach as well as Orlando. Like the others, this club has music at its heart. There's a dance floor and stage for live performances by the B.B. King All-Star Band or visiting musicians seven nights a week. You can't really experience Delta blues without Delta dining, so the club doubles as a restaurant with fried dill pickles, catfish bites, po'boys, ribs, and other comfort foods. Oh, yeah, and there's a full bar. ✉ *Pointe Orlando, 9101 International Dr., I-Drive area* ☎ *407/370–4550* 🌐 *www.bbkingclubs.com/?page=orlhome* ⏲ *Fri. and Sat. noon–2 am, Sun.–Thurs. noon–midnight.*

NIGHTCLUB

ICEBAR. Thanks to the miracle of refrigeration, this is Orlando's coolest bar—literally and figuratively. Fifty tons of pure ice is kept at a constant 27°F and has been cut and sculpted by world-class carvers into a cozy (or as cozy as ice can be) sanctuary of tables, sofas, chairs, and a bar. The staff loans you a thermal cape and gloves (upgrade to a fur coat for $10), and when you enter the frozen hall your drink is served in a glass made of crystal-clear ice. There's no cover charge if you just want to hang out in the Fire Lounge or outdoor Polar Patio, but you will pay $19.95 to spend as much time as you can handle in the subfreezing ICEBAR. There's no beer or wine inside; it's simply too cold.

✉ Pointe Orlando, 8967 International Dr., I-Drive area ☎ 407/426-7555 🌐 www.icebarorlando.com ⏲ Fri. and Sat. 7 pm–2 am, Sun.–Wed. 7–midnight, Thurs. 7–1.

ORLANDO ENVIRONS

Although the small towns around Orlando aren't historic in a European sense, they reflect the early settlers' desire to capitalize on the subtropical climate—much as you and other visitors do today.

To the south lies Kissimmee, a former cattle town on Lake Tohopekaliga, one of Florida's largest, and a good place to go fishing or take an airboat ride. Kissimmee retains its ranching roots, with a twice-annual rodeo that's worth a visit.

Winter Park, to the northeast, offers a more intellectual look at Florida's past. The town exudes charm, with brick streets and Spanish moss–draped oaks. Park Avenue, the main drag, is lined with unique shops edged by a landscaped park. You can take a leisurely boat tour on waterways that snake through town or visit the large collection of Tiffany glass and other artworks in the Morse Museum of American Art.

To the northwest of Orlando is Mount Dora, built with citrus money in the 19th century. It's on Lake Dora, and the shops and restaurants lining its charming streets often have a water view.

KISSIMMEE

18 miles south of Orlando, 10 miles southeast of Walt Disney World (WDW).

Although Kissimmee is primarily known as the gateway to Disney (technically, the vast Disney property of theme parks and resorts lies in both Osceola and Orange counties), its non-WDW attractions just might tickle your fancy. They range from throwbacks to old-time Florida to dinner shows for you and 2,000 of your closest friends. Orlando used to be prime cattle country, and the best sampling of what life was like is here during the Silver Springs Rodeo in February and June.

With at least 100,000 acres of freshwater lakes, the Kissimmee area brings anglers and boaters to national fishing tournaments and speedboat races. A 50-mile-long series of lakes, the Kissimmee Waterway, connects Lake Tohopekaliga—a Native American name that means "Sleeping Tiger"—with huge Lake Okeechobee in South Florida, and from there, to both the Atlantic Ocean and the Gulf of Mexico.

GETTING HERE AND AROUND

From Downtown Orlando it's easy to reach Kissimmee's main road, U.S. 192, from Interstate 4, Exit 64, just past the last Disney exit. Osceola Parkway (Toll Road 522) heads directly from Disney property, and Florida's Turnpike runs north–south through Kissimmee.

ESSENTIALS

Visitor Information Experience Kissimmee. Get a travel guide and discount coupons here, in person or online. *✉ 215 Celebration Pl., Suite 200 ☎ 407/742-8200 🌐 www.experiencekissimmee.com/.* **Florida Fish and Wildlife.** To be able to catch those big Lake Toho bass, you need a license. ☎ *850/488–4676* 🌐 *www.myfwc.com/recreation* 🎟 *Nonresident licenses: saltwater or freshwater $17 3-day, $30 7-day, $47 annual.*

⇨ *For information on Kissimmee hotels and restaurants, see "Where to Stay" and "Where to Eat."*

EXPLORING

FAMILY **Gatorland.** This campy attraction near the Orlando–Kissimmee border on U.S. 441 has endured since 1949 without much change, despite competition from the major parks. Over the years, the theme park and registered conservancy has gone through some changes while retaining its gator-rasslin' spirit. Kids get a kick out of this unmanufactured, old-timey thrill ride.

The Gator Gulley Splash Park is complete with giant "egrets" spilling water from their beaks, dueling water guns mounted atop giant gators, and other water-park splash areas. There's also a small petting zoo and an aviary. A free train ride is a high point, taking you through an alligator breeding marsh and a natural swamp setting where you can spot gators, birds, and turtles. A three-story observation tower overlooks the breeding marsh, swamped with gator grunts, especially come sundown during mating season.

For a glimpse of 37 giant, rare, and deadly crocodiles, check out the Jungle Crocs of the World exhibit. To see eager gators leaping out of the water to catch their food, come on cool days for the Gator Jumparoo Show (summer heat just puts them to sleep). The most thrilling is the first one in the morning, when the gators are hungriest. There's also a Gator Wrestlin' Show, and although there's no doubt who's going to win the match, it's still fun to see the handlers take on those tough guys with the beady eyes. In the educational Upclose Encounters show, the show's host handles a variety of snakes. Recent park additions include Panther Springs, featuring brother-and-sister endangered panthers, and the Screamin' Gator Zip Line (additional cost). This is a real Florida experience, and you leave knowing the difference between a gator and a croc. ✉ *14501 S. Orange Blossom Trail, between Orlando and Kissimmee* ☎ *407/855–5496, 800/393–5297* 🌐 *www.gatorland.com* 🎟 *$26.99; 3–12 $18.99; discount coupons online* 🕓 *Daily 10–5.*

FAMILY **Old Town USA.** A collection of shops, restaurants, and giant amusement-park rides, Old Town was literally the heart of tourist Kissimmee before Disney moved in. With a 1950s theme, it's made a good go at keeping families coming by maintaining a Ferris wheel; the 150-foot-tall Super Shot free-fall ride; the Windstorm steel roller coaster; go-karts; and classic car shows on Wednesday, Friday, and Saturday. ✉ *5770 W. Irlo Bronson Memorial Hwy.* ☎ *407/396–4888* 🌐 *www.myoldtownusa.com/* 🎟 *Free (admission and parking)* 🕓 *Daily 10 am–11 pm (bars open until 2 am).*

SPORTS AND THE OUTDOORS

FISHING

Fishers the world over congregate in Central Florida to catch bass, speckled perch, bream, stripers, and catfish. Top fishing waters include Lake Kissimmee, the Butler and Conway chains of lakes, and Lake Toho. Your best chance for trophy fish is between November and April on Toho or Kissimmee. For good creels, the best bet is usually the Butler area, which has the additional advantage of its scenery—lots of live oaks and cypresses, plus the occasional osprey or bald eagle.

Toho and Kissimmee are also good for record-setting largemouth bass. The Butler chain yields largemouth, some pickerel, and the occasional huge catfish. Services range from equipment and boat rental to full-day trips with guides and guarantees. Like virtually all lakes in Florida, these are teeming with alligators, which pose little threat unless you engage in the unwise practice of swimming at night.

To fish in Florida waters (though not those at Disney), anglers over 16 need a fishing license, available at bait-and-tackle shops, fishing camps, most sporting-goods stores, and Wal-Mart and Kmart. Some locations may not sell saltwater licenses, so call ahead if this matters. For non-residents of Florida, freshwater or saltwater licenses cost $17 for three consecutive days, $30 for seven consecutive days, and $47 for one year. **■ TIP→ Fishing on a private lake with the owner's permission—which is what anglers do at Disney—doesn't require a state fishing license.**

Guides fish out of the area's fishing camps, and you can usually make arrangements to hire them through the camp office. Rates vary, but for two people a good price is $250 for a half day and $350 for a full one. Many area guides are part-timers who fish on weekends or take a day off from their full-time job.

Bass Challenger Guide. With Captain Eddie at the helm, BCG takes you wherever the fishing is best that day. It might be Lake Toho or the St. Johns River—Florida's longest and one of the few that runs north—which is a prime bass site. Indeed, bass is the only quarry. Half-day trips for one or two people begin at $300, six-hour trips are $350, and full-day trips begin at $400. Each additional person pays $75 more. BCG also sells bait, arranges for transportation to and from your hotel, organizes multiday trips, and books area accommodations. ✉ *Sanford* ☎ *407/273–8045, 800/241–5314* 🌐 *www.basschallenger.com.*

East Lake Fish Camp. Eastern Lake Toho's camp has a restaurant and country store, sells live bait and propane, and rents boats. You can also take a ride on an airboat from here. The camp has 286 RV sites ($40–$45 per night, $180 a week, or $400 per month) and simple, rustic cabins ($65 per night). Try to reserve the 24 cabins at least two weeks in advance in winter and spring. ✉ *3705 Big Bass Rd.* ☎ *407/348–2040* 🌐 *www.eastlakefishcamp.com.*

Lake Charters. This outfitter conducts trips from November to May on Lake Toho (January through April is high season, so reserve accordingly), and has done so for more than 20 years. It's possible to catch a 14-pound bass here. Rods and reels are included in the costs, and transportation is available. Half-day freshwater trips are $250, six-hour trips

Go gator! After a visit to authentic, rustic Kissimmee's Gatorland, you'll truly know the difference between a gator and a croc (and you'll see both).

are $300, and full-day trips are $350. Prices are for one to two people. A third participant costs $50 more. You can also buy your licenses here. ✉ *1550 Scottys Rd.* ☎ *407/891–2275, 877/326–3575* 🌐 *www.lakecharter.com.*

Lake Toho Resort. Although some of the full hookups at the 200 RV sites here are booked year-round, electrical and water hookups are usually available, as are live bait, food, and drinks. Sites are $28 per night or $315–$365 per month, plus electricity and an initial $100 refundable deposit. Boat slips start at $45 a month, depending on the length of your boat. ✉ *4715 Kissimmee Park Rd., St. Cloud* ☎ *407/892–8795* 🌐 *www.laketohoresort.com.*

Richardson's Fish Camp. This camp on western Lake Toho has seven cabins with kitchenettes, 16 RV sites, and six tent sites as well as boat slips and a bait shop. The RV sites are $30 per night; tent sites are $24.50; and cabins run $44 for one bedroom, $68 for two bedrooms, and $79 for three bedrooms. ✉ *1550 Scottys Rd.* ☎ *407/846–6540.*

HORSEBACK RIDING

Horse World Riding Stables. Here's a way to get a taste of the days when the Orlando area had more horse and cattle farms than Texas. Horse World offers lessons and rides for groups or individuals on three unspoiled Florida woods trails. Trail rides take about an hour and cost $45.95–$74.95 per person (weeklong ride passes cost $229–$279). Call at least a week ahead for reservations in winter and spring. ✉ *3705 Poinciana Blvd.* ☎ *407/847–4343* 🌐 *www.horseworldstables.com.*

Silver Spurs Rodeo. Twice a year since the 1940s, bull riders and cowboys have been competing in the Silver Spurs Rodeo, the largest east of the

Mississippi. The event is held at Osceola Heritage Park each February and June and features bull and bronc riding, steer wrestling, and barrel racing. From Interstate 4 Exit 77, take Florida's Turnpike south to Exit 244 (Kissimmee–St. Cloud). ✉ *1875 Silver Spur La.* ☎ *321/697–3495* 🌐 *www.silverspursrodeo.com* 🎟 *$15; under 15 free* ⏲ *Hrs vary.*

ICE-SKATING

The Ice Factory. Ice-skating in Florida? Yup! This Olympic-class facility has two rinks. Teens are drawn to Friday's DJ Night, and there are family-night rates on Saturday. ✉ *2221 Partin Settlement Rd.* ☎ *407/933–4259* 🌐 *www.icefactory.com* 🎟 *$5–$10; $3 skate rental* ⏲ *Daily; hrs vary by rink and day.*

SHOPPING

Lake Buena Vista Factory Stores. Although it has scant curb appeal, it does have a good collection of standard outlet stores for Aeropostale, Converse, Eddie Bauer, Fossil, Gap, Izod, LOFT, Nike, Old Navy, and Tommy Hilfiger. Check out the coupons on the website, too. Take Exit 68 off Interstate 4, and go 2 miles south on State Road 535. ✉ *15657 S. Apopka Vineland Rd. (State Rd. 535), Lake Buena Vista* ☎ *407/238–9301* 🌐 *www.lbvfs.com* ⏲ *Mon.–Sat. 10–9, Sun. 10–7.*

192 Flea Market Outlet. With 400 booths, this market is about a fourth the size of Flea World in Sanford, but it's much more convenient if you're staying in the Disney World area, and it's open daily. The all-new merchandise includes toys, luggage, sunglasses, jewelry, clothes, beach towels, sneakers, electronics, and the obligatory T-shirts. ✉ *4301 W. Vine St. (U.S. 192)* ☎ *407/396–4555* 🌐 *www.192fleamarketprices.com* ⏲ *Daily 9–6.*

SPAS

Mokara Spa at Omni Orlando Resort. Golf courses surround the Omni Orlando Resort at Championsgate, and Mokara Spa offers special treatments to ease tension and soreness in those stressed shoulders and backs. The Sports Massage uses muscle-warming oil, massage, and stretching to make sure you are ready for another round. There are plenty of choices for the nongolfer in the group, which is good, since this resort is far, far away from anything. Separate locker rooms, steam rooms, and relaxation rooms ensure privacy and serenity while you wait for your treatment. A full-service salon offers hair and nail services, and massages include Swedish, hot stone, deep tissue, and mothers to be. Massages from $120. Packages from $205. A 20% gratuity is added to the bill. Parking is validated if you are a day-spa visitor. ✉ *1500 Masters Blvd., ChampionsGate* ☎ *407/390–6603* 🌐 *www.mokaraspas.com/orlando.*

Relâche Spa & Salon at Gaylord Palms Resort. The 20,000-square-foot spa is in the Everglades Atrium of this giant, Florida-themed resort, and guests may feel like explorers in a tropical wilderness as they make the trek toward tranquillity. Once inside the doors, cares and clothes shed, the soft pastels and generous chaise longues of the tearoom radiate serenity. Fresh fruit and beverages keep you hydrated while you wait, then it's on to serious relaxation. Try one of the signature Florida treatments, such as Islamorada Glow using coconut milk, pure cane sugar, and

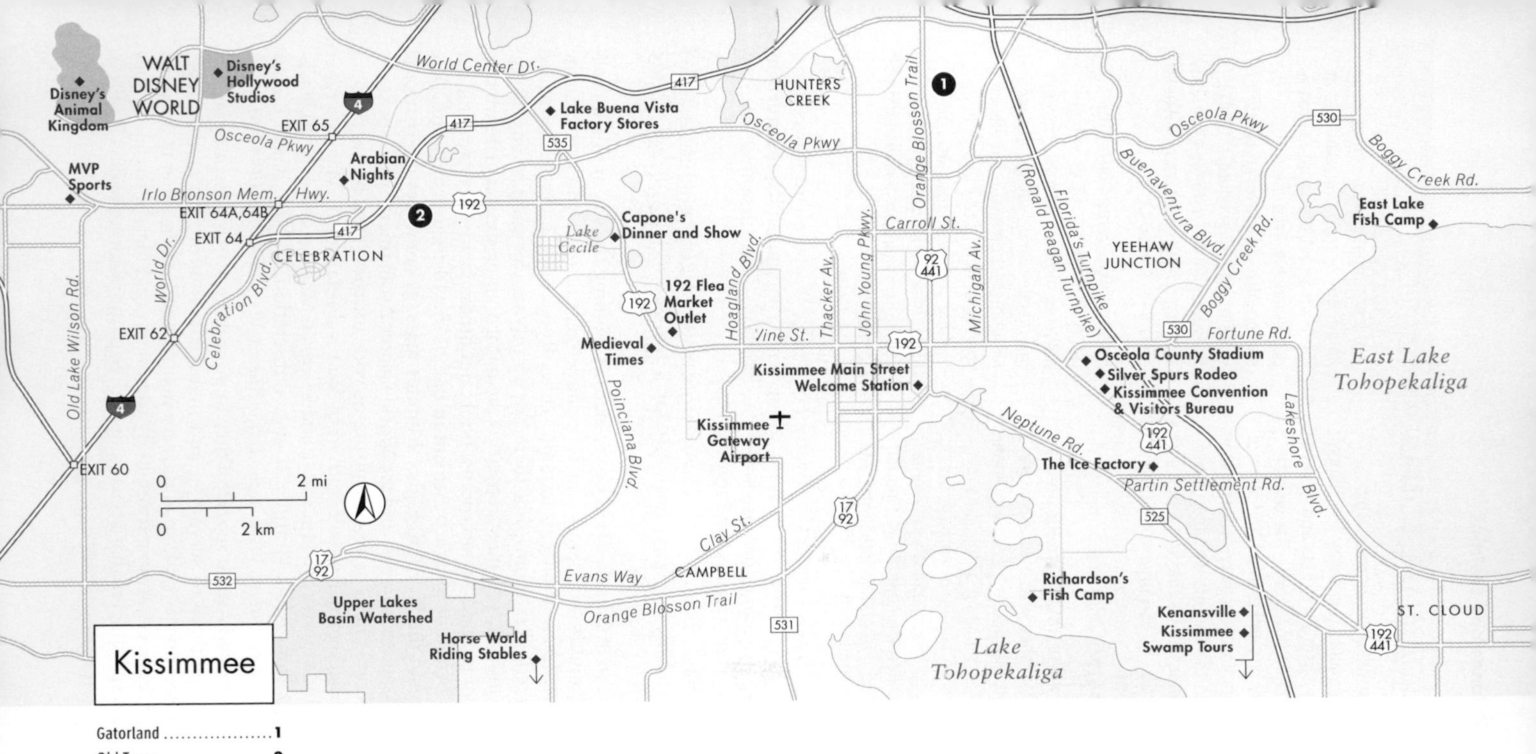

Gatorland 1
Old Town 2

KISSIMMEE TOURS

Haunted Kissimmee. This 90-minute tour takes you through the shadowy streets and alleys of historic downtown. The community has amassed a huge store of paranormal activity over the years, and the docents who lead these outings know where the bodies are buried. ✉ *804 Bryan St.* ☎ *321/251-5204* 🌐 *www.hauntedkissimmee.com* 🎟 *$19* 🕓 *Daily at 8:30 pm.*

Historic Downtown Kissimmee. Established well over a century ago, Kissimmee has a story rooted in the founding of the state. It was an important air base during World War II, and it was vital in the development of the Orlando cattle and orange industries. You can learn more on the self-guided audio tour or map tour available at the Main Street Welcome Station or downloadable from the website. The station plans to move, so check the website for a new address. ✉ *421 Broadway* ☎ *407/846-4643* 🌐 *www.kissimmeemainstreet.com* 🕓 *Weekdays 9–5, Sat. 10–2.*

Kissimmee Swamp Tours. The 60- or 90-minute cruises in high-powered airboats take you through the marshes and swamps of Lake Kissimmee—home to hundreds of species of birds and other critters. ✉ *4500 Joe Overstreet Rd., Lake Kissimmee, Kenansville* ☎ *407/436-1059* 🌐 *www.kissimmeeswamptours.com* 🎟 *$47–$61.*

tropical oils, or the Clearwater Hydrating Wrap, where warm stones are applied after exfoliation, along with a vitamin-filled moisturizing wrap. Massages include hot stone, bamboo, Thai stretching, deep tissue, aromatherapy, and more.

Massages from $75. Packages from $300. A 20% gratuity is added on to bill. Day pass available for a fee. ✉ *6000 W. Osceola Pkwy.* ☎ *407/586–4772.*

The Spa at Orlando World Center Marriott. Finding the spa in this sprawling, multitower resort can be a challenge, but once you arrive at the lower-level entrance, tranquillity rules. Robes and slippers are provided in the locker rooms, but there are no private changing rooms. If you are modest, you must retreat to the bathroom or shower. The waiting room is co-ed. Steam rooms, pool, and fitness facility are available for use before or after a treatment in one of the 14 treatment rooms. The Around the World in Eighty Minutes massage combines international massage techniques, and the World Center Aromatherapy Escape starts with tea and a deluxe cleansing of your tootsies, then proceeds to an aromatherapy massage and wrap for total relaxation. Massage types include pressure, warm stone, and Swedish. Massages from $120. Packages from $200. Gratuity at guests' discretion. ✉ *8701 World Center Dr., Lake Buena Vista area, Lake Buena Vista* ☎ *407/239–4200.*

The Waldorf Astoria Spa. Don't try to pour your own tea—your gracious valet is there to serve you and make you comfortable at this huge, 22-treatment-room spa in a very deluxe hotel. Everything is designed for the guest, from custom body treatments and facials, to plush robes and spa slippers that actually fit you. Separate waiting rooms lead to a eucalyptus steam room; experiential shower that surrounds you with water, sound, and light; and a tea lounge. Try the Diamond Body, an over-the-top decadent treatment that incorporates precious stones and gold-enriched creams. The full-service salon offers every service imaginable. Massages include warm stone, Swedish, and deep tissue. Massages from $149. Packages from $380. A 20% service charge is added, but parking is complementary. Day pass $30 for nonguests. ✉ *Waldorf Astoria, 14200 Bonnet Creek Resort La., Bonnet Creek, Orlando* ☎ *407/597–5360* 🌐 *www.waldorfastoriaorlando.com* ☞ *Parking: valet only, complimentary with spa validation, but please tip.*

NIGHTLIFE

Capone's Dinner and Show. This musical dramedy brings you back to gangland Chicago of the 1930s, when mobsters and their molls were the height of underworld society. You'll meet Al Capone and learn that you can become a member of the "family," but you've got to help take care of a rat in the organization. Flashy costumes and musical numbers are accompanied by an all-you-can-eat American and Italian buffet that includes beer, alcoholic mixed drinks, and cocktails for kids. Check the website for a 50%-off coupon. ✉ *4740 W. Irlo Bronson Memorial Hwy.* ☎ *407/397–2378, 800/220–8428* 🌐 *www.alcapones.com* 🎟 *$59.99; online discounts.*

FAMILY **Medieval Times.** In a huge, ersatz-medieval manor you'll see a tournament of sword fights, jousting matches, and other exciting games. More than a dozen charging horses and a cast of 75 knights, nobles, wizards, and maidens participate. Sound silly? It is. But it's also a true extravaganza. That the show takes precedence over the meat-and-potatoes fare is obvious: everyone sits facing forward at long, narrow banquet tables stepped auditorium-style above the tournament area. Kids love eating without forks; adults are swept away by the tremendous horse-riding artistry. Check the website for discounts. ✉ *4510 W. Vine St.* ☎ *407/396–1518, 888/935–6878* 🌐 *www.medievaltimes.com* 🎟 *$62.95–$82.95; 12-under $36.95* ⏲ *Castle daily 9–4, performances usually daily at 8.*

LEGOLAND

50 miles southwest of Orlando.

LEGOLAND Florida. The quiet town of Winter Haven is home to numerous lakes and a waterskiing school. From 1936 until 2009, it was also home to the Sunshine State's first theme park, Cypress Gardens. Today the spot holds the world's largest LEGOLAND, set on 150 acres and built using nearly 56 million LEGOs. In addition to its 1:20-scale miniature reproductions of U.S. cities, the park features more than 50 rides, shows, and attractions throughout 10 different zones, as well as the marvelous botanical gardens from the original park. Just opened mid-2013, the World of Chima presented by Cartoon Network invites guests into a fantastical world of animal tribal habitats anchored by an interactive water ride, the Quest for CHI. In Chima's new Speedorz Arena, participants compete to win a supply of the mystical CHI energy

CLOSE UP

History You Can See

A long history, from early Native American occupants through Spanish, French, and British settlers, has left indelible marks on Central Florida. Add to that the influx of wealthy vacationers from the North and hopeful immigrants from Europe, and history comes alive in these repositories of knowledge.

DeSoto National Memorial, Bradenton. Hernando de Soto came ashore with his men and 200 horses near what is now Bradenton in 1539; this federal park commemorates that landing. From mid-December to late April, park workers dress in period costumes at Camp Uzita and demonstrate how European explorers lived.

Ybor City, Tampa. One of only four National Historic Landmark districts in Florida, Tampa's rollicking Cuban quarter has antique-brick streets and wrought-iron balconies, hand-rolled cigars, and fresh-roasted coffee. The neighborhood has become one of Tampa's hot spots, as empty cigar factories and social clubs have been transformed into boutiques, art galleries, restaurants, and nightclubs.

Florida Holocaust Museum, St. Petersburg. A permanent History, Heritage, and Hope exhibit; an original boxcar; and an extensive collection of photographs, art, and artifacts give new perspective to one of the largest collections of its kind. Conceived as a learning center for children, many of the exhibits avoid overly graphic content.

Tarpon Springs. Tarpon Springs has been the home of Greek sponge divers for more than 120 years, and the combination of sun, great food, and history can't be beat. Take time to visit St. Nicholas Greek Orthodox Cathedral, a replica of St. Sophia Cathedral in Constantinople.

source. A 4-D movie and Chima-character meet and greets round out the experience.

The Danish toy company's philosophy is to help children "play well." And play they do, as LEGOLAND attractions are very hands-on. Kids can hoist themselves to the top of a tower, power a fire truck, or navigate a LEGO robot. Sights include huge LEGO dragons, wizards, knights, pirates, castles, roller coasters, racetracks, villages, and cities.

The cityscapes in Miniland USA fascinate children and adults, who delight in discovering what's possible when you have enough bricks. Miniland opens with Kennedy Space Center, where a 6-foot shuttle waits on the launch pad. Miami Beach features bikini-clad bathers and art deco hotels; St. Augustine and its ancient fort play into LEGO's pirate theme; Key West's Mallory Square is accurate right down to the trained cats leaping through rings of fire. The rest of the United States is not ignored: New York City, Las Vegas, San Francisco, and Washington D.C. appear in intricate detail. Visitors spend hours looking for amusing details hidden in each city, like New York's purse snatcher.

Among other highlights are LEGO Kingdoms, whose castle towers over a jousting area and a roller coaster where knights, damsels, dragons, and ogres are found; Land of Adventure, where you can explore hidden tombs and hunt for treasure; and the Imagination Zone, showcasing LEGO Mindstorms robots, where a giant head of Albert Einstein invites kids to explore and invent. Things get wild in LEGO Technic, the most active of the park's zones, where Test Track, Aquazone Wave Racers, and Technicycle let the family expend some energy. And Pirates' Cove provides a chance to sit in the shade and watch a full-sized pirate battle, with actors wearing LEGO suits defending the huge ship from attacking pirates on water skis.

LEGOLAND Water Park features a wave pool; Build-a-Raft, where families construct a LEGO vessel and float down a lazy river; a 375-foot pair of intertwined waterslides that plunge riders into a pool; and a DUPLO toddler water play area. Not to be forgotten, Cypress Gardens, at the heart of the park, preserves one of Florida's treasures. Families can wander the lush, tropical foliage and gasp at one of the world's largest banyan trees.

The trip to Winter Haven is worth it. The rides, interactive games, gardens, water park, and other attractions will amuse and engage. Round-trip transportation from Orlando Premium Outlets, on Vineland Avenue, leaves at 9 and costs $5. ✉ *1 Legoland Way, Winter Haven* ☎ *877/350–5346* ⊕ *www.legoland.com* 🎟 *$84; 3–12, seniors $77; parking $14* ⏲ *Hrs vary seasonally.*

BOK TOWER GARDENS

57 miles southwest of Orlando, 42 miles southwest of WDW.

Fodor's Choice ★ **Bok Tower Gardens.** You'll see citrus groves as you ride south along U.S. 27 to the small town of Lake Wales and the Bok Tower Gardens. This appealing sanctuary of plants, flowers, trees, and wildlife has been something of a local secret for years. Shady paths meander through pine forests with silvery moats, mockingbirds and swans, blooming thickets, and hidden sundials. The majestic, 200-foot Bok Tower is constructed of coquina—from seashells—and pink, white, and gray marble. The tower houses a carillon with 60 bronze bells that ring out each day at 1 and 3 pm during 30-minute recitals that might include early-American folk songs, Appalachian tunes, Irish ballads, or Latin hymns. The bells are also featured in recordings every half hour after 10 am, and sometimes even moonlight recitals.

The landscape was designed in 1928 by Frederick Law Olmsted Jr., son of the planner of New York's Central Park. The grounds include the 20-room, Mediterranean-style Pinewood Estate, built in 1930 and open for self-guided touring. January through April, guides lead you on a 60-minute tour of the gardens (included in the admission price); tours of the inside of the tower are a benefit of membership ($100 and up).

Take Interstate 4 to Exit 55 and head south on U.S. 27 for about 23 miles. Proceed past Eagle Ridge Mall, then turn left after two traffic lights onto Mountain Lake Cut Off Road, and follow the signs. ✉ *1151 Tower Blvd., Lake Wales* ☎ *863/676–1408* ⊕ *www.boktower.org* 🎟 *$12–$18; 5–12 $3–$8* ⏲ *Daily 8–6.*

NEED A BREAK?

Chalet Suzanne Country Inn. While at Bok Gardens, it's worth planning a stop at time-worn but charming Chalet Suzanne, where dinners, including the renowned soups (take a can home), are served in five quaint lakeside rooms. ✉ ***3800 Chalet Suzanne Dr., Lake Wales*** ☎ ***800/433–6011*** 🌐 ***www.chaletsuzanne.com.***

WEKIWA SPRINGS STATE PARK

13 miles northwest of Orlando, 28 miles north of WDW.

FAMILY Fodor's Choice ★

Wekiwa Springs State Park. "Wekiva" is a Creek Indian word meaning "flowing water"; *wekiwa* means "spring of water." The river, springs, and surrounding 6,400-acre Wekiwa Springs State Park are well suited to camping, hiking, picnicking, swimming, canoeing, and fishing. The area is also full of Florida wildlife: otters, raccoons, alligators, bobcats, deer, turtles, and birds.

Canoe trips can range from a simple hour-long paddle around the lagoon to observe a colony of water turtles to a full-day excursion through the less congested parts of the river, which haven't changed much since the area was inhabited by the Timacuan Indians. You can rent canoes ($17.98 for two hours and $3.20 per hour after that) in the town of Apopka, near the park's southern entrance.

The park has 60 campsites: some are "canoe sites" that you can reach only via the river, and others are "trail sites," meaning you must hike a good bit of the park's 13½-mile trail to reach them. Most, however, are for the less hardy—you can drive right up to them. Sites go for $24 a night with electric and water hookups.

To get here, take Interstate 4 Exit 94 (Longwood) and turn left on Route 434. Go 1¼ miles to Wekiwa Springs Road; turn right and go 4½ miles to the entrance, on the right. ✉ *1800 Wekiva Circle* ☎ *407/884–2008, 800/326–3521 campsites, 407/884–4311 canoe rentals* 🌐 *www.floridastateparks.org/wekiwasprings/default.cfm* 🎫 *$2 per pedestrian or bicycle; $6 per vehicle* 🕒 *Daily 8–dusk.*

MOUNT DORA

35 miles northwest of Orlando, 50 miles north of WDW.

The unspoiled Lake Harris chain surrounds remote Mount Dora, an artsy valley community with a slow and easy pace, a rich history, New England–style charm, and excellent antiquing. Although the town's population is only about 12,000, there's plenty of excitement here, especially in fall and winter. The first weekend in February is the annual Mount Dora Art Festival, which opens Central Florida's spring art-fair season. Attracting more than 250,000 people over a three-day period, it's one of the region's major outdoor events.

During the year there's also the annual Taste in Mount Dora event (April), a sailing regatta (April), a bicycle festival (October), a crafts fair (October), and many other happenings. Mount Dora draws large crowds during monthly antiques fairs (third weekend, except December)

Wildlife-rich Wekiwa Springs State Park is a great place to camp, hike, picnic, canoe, fish, swim, or snorkel.

and thrice-yearly antiques "extravaganzas" (third weekends of January, February, and November) at popular Renninger's Twin Markets, an antiques center plus farmers' and flea markets.

9

GETTING HERE AND AROUND

Take U.S. 441 (Orange Blossom Trail in Orlando) north or take Interstate 4 to Exit 92, then Route 436 west to U.S. 441, and follow the signs.

ESSENTIALS

Tourist Information Mount Dora Chamber of Commerce. A historic train depot serves as the chamber's offices. Stop in and pick up a self-guided tour map. Don't forget to ask about the trolley tour, during which a guide gives you the skinny on local historical spots and throws in a ghost story. ✉ *341 Alexander St., at 3rd Ave.* ☎ *352/383–2165* 🌐 *www.mountdora.com* 🕓 *Weekdays 9–5, Sat. 10–4, Sun. 10–2; after hrs, maps on display at kiosk.*

EXPLORING

Lakeside Inn. Listed on the National Register of Historic Places, this country inn, built in 1883, overlooks 4,500-acre Lake Dora. A stroll around the grounds makes you feel as if you've stepped out of the pages of *The Great Gatsby.* You can book cruises and seaplane tours that leave from the inn's large dock. ✉ *100 N. Alexander St.* ☎ *352/383–4101* 🌐 *www.lakeside-inn.com.*

FAMILY **Mount Dora Center for the Arts.** Local and national artists are highlighted in this lovely art center that grew out of the annual arts festival. The center is a focal point for the community, serving as headquarters of the arts festival, a gallery, a gift shop, and a place to take art lessons. ✉ *138*

E. 5th Ave. ☎ *352/383–0880* 🌐 *www.mountdoracenterforthearts.org* ⏲ *Gallery: weekdays 10–4, Sat. 10–2.*

SHOPPING

The Renaissance. Built in the 1920s, what was once known as the Dora Hotel is now the Renaissance, a Victorian-style shopping arcade with more than 20 shops and the Frog and the Monkey restaurant. ✉ *411 N. Donnelly St.* ☎ *352/735–2608.*

Renninger's Twin Markets. This may be Florida's largest gathering of antiques and collectibles dealers. Atop the hill, 700 flea-market dealers sell household goods, garage-sale surplus, produce, baked goods, pets, and anything else you can think of. Below, 200 antiques booths purvey old phonographs, art deco fixtures, antique furniture, and more. If you have the time, hit the flea market first, since that's where antiques dealers find many of their treasures. Both markets are open every weekend, but on the third weekend of the month the antiques market has a fair attracting about 300 dealers. The really big shows—drawing 800 booths—are three-day extravaganzas in November, January, and February. A Guitars, Cars, and Cycles Swap Meet is held the second Sunday of each month. You can spend a morning or all day at these events. Renninger's is busiest from October through May. From Interstate 4, take Florida's Turnpike north to Exit 267A to Route 429 east and, 8 miles later, U.S. 441 north to Mount Dora. ✉ *20651 U.S. 441* ☎ *352/383–8393* 🌐 *www.renningers.com* 🎫 *Markets and antiques fairs free; extravaganzas $10 Fri., $6 Sat., $4 Sun., $15 for 3 days* ⏲ *Antiques center: weekends 9–5; antiques fairs: Mar.–Oct., 3rd weekend of month 9–5; extravaganzas: Jan., Feb., and Nov., 3rd weekend of month 8–5.*

Uncle Al's Time Capsule. This is a great place to sift through some terrific Hollywood memorabilia and collectibles. Hottest sellers are autographed items featuring *The Wizard of Oz, Gone with the Wind,* Elvis, and Marilyn Monroe. ✉ *140 E. 4th Ave.* ☎ *352/383–1958* 🌐 *www.awautographs.com.*

NEED A BREAK?

Pisces Rising. This upscale, New Orleans–themed seafood and steak house overlooks Lake Dora. It's open for lunch and dinner and offers a jazz brunch on Sunday and live entertainment Thursday through Sunday on its deck. ✉ ***239 W. 4th Ave.*** ☎ ***352/385–2669*** 🌐 ***www.piscesrisingdining.com*** ⏲ ***Mon.–Thurs. 11:30–9, Fri. and Sat. 11:30–10, Sun. 11–9.***

WINTER PARK

6 miles northeast of Orlando, 20 miles northeast of WDW.

This peaceful, upscale community may be just outside the hustle and bustle of Orlando, but it feels like a different country. The town's name reflects its early role as a warm-weather haven for those escaping the frigid blasts of Northeast winters. From the late 1880s until the early 1930s, wealthy industrialists and their families would travel to Florida by rail on vacation, and many stayed, establishing grand homes and cultural institutions. The lovely, 8-square-mile village retains its charm with brick-paved streets, historic buildings, and well-maintained lakes and parkland. Even the town's bucolic 9-hole golf course is on the National Register of Historic Places.

On Park Avenue you can spend a few hours sightseeing, shopping, or both. The street is lined with small boutiques and fine restaurants and bookended by world-class museums: the Charles Hosmer Morse Museum of American Art, with the world's largest collection of artwork by Louis Comfort Tiffany, and the Cornell Fine Arts Museum, on the campus of Rollins College (the oldest college in Florida).

WORD OF MOUTH

"You could go to Winter Park, which is a very charming little town, and visit the Morse museum: loads of Louis Comfort Tiffany stained glass, which most people find pretty cool. You can also have lunch and browse boutiques. The Ravenous Pig is a gastropub that routinely gets national attention, including James Beard nominations, but is casual. . . ." –NewbE

GETTING HERE AND AROUND

From Downtown Orlando, take Interstate 4 for 4 miles to Exit 87, and head east on Fairbanks Avenue for 3 miles to Park Avenue. LYNX Bus Nos. 102 and 443 run from the main depot to Winter Park.

ESSENTIALS

Bus Information LYNX Bus ✉ *455 N. Garland Ave., Downtown Orlando* ☎ *407/841–5969* 🌐 *www.golynx.com.*

Hospital Winter Park Hospital ✉ *200 N. Lakemont Ave.* ☎ *407/646–7000* 🌐 *www.floridahospital.com/winter-park-memorial.*

Tour Scenic Boat Tour. Head east from Park Avenue and, at the end of Morse Boulevard, you'll find the launching point for this tour, a Winter Park tradition since 1938. The one-hour cruise takes in 12 miles of waterways, including three lakes and narrow, oak- and cypress-shaded canals built in the 1800s as a transportation system for the logging industry. A well-schooled skipper shares stories about the moguls who built their mansions along the shore and points out wildlife and remnants of natural Florida still surrounding the expensive houses. Cash or check only is accepted. ✉ *312 E. Morse Blvd.* ☎ *407/644–4056* 🌐 *www.scenicboattours.com* 🎟 *$12; 2–11 $6* ⏲ *Daily 10–4.*

Visitor Information City of Winter Park ✉ *401 Park Ave. S* ☎ *407/599–3399* 🌐 *www.cityofwinterpark.org.*

⇨ *For information on Winter Park hotels and restaurants, see "Where to Stay" and "Where to Eat."*

EXPLORING

Albin Polasek Museum and Sculpture Gardens. Stroll along on a guided tour through gardens showcasing the graceful sculptures created by internationally known Czech sculptor Albin Polasek (1879–1965). The late artist's home, studio, galleries, and private chapel are centered on 3 acres of exquisitely tended lawns, colorful flower beds, and tropical foliage on the edge of Lake Osceola. Paths and walkways lead past classical life-size, figurative sculptures and whimsical mythological pieces. Inside the museum are works by Hawthorne, Chase, and Mucha. The Capen

9

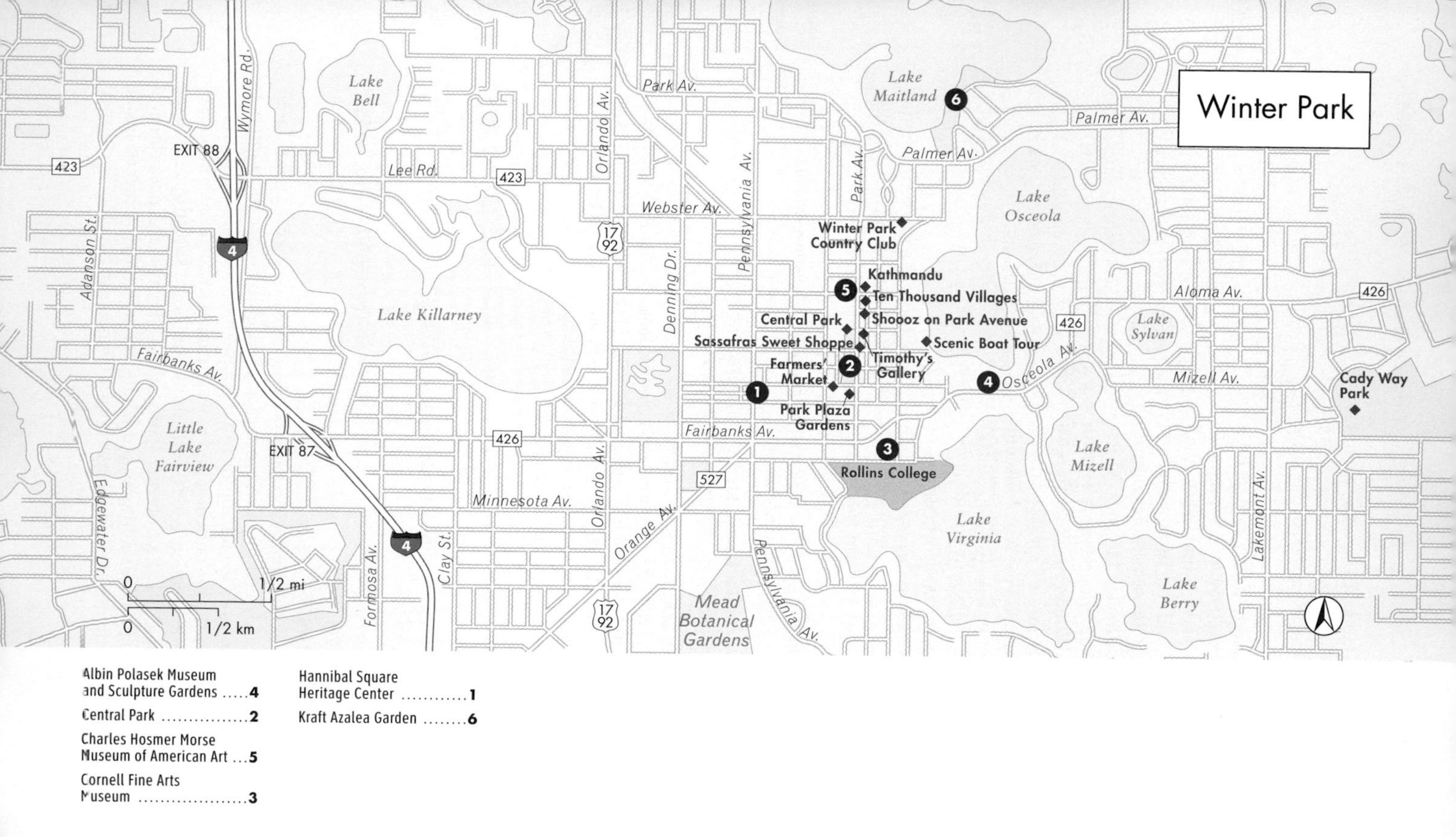

Winter Park
Lake Maitland
Lake Bell
Lake Killarney
Lake Osceola
Lake Sylvan
Lake Mizell
Lake Virginia
Lake Berry
Little Lake Fairview
Mead Botanical Gardens
Rollins College
Winter Park Country Club
Kathmandu
Ten Thousand Villages
Shoooz on Park Avenue
Central Park
Sassafras Sweet Shoppe
Scenic Boat Tour
Farmers' Market
Timothy's Gallery
Park Plaza Gardens
Cady Way Park
Park Av.
Palmer Av.
Wymore Rd.
Orlando Av.
Lee Rd.
Webster Av.
Pennsylvania Av.
Denning Dr.
Adanson St.
Aloma Av.
Fairbanks Av.
Osceola Av.
Mizell Av.
Minnesota Av.
Orange Av.
Formosa Av.
Clay St.
Edgewater Dr.
Lakemont Av.
EXIT 88
EXIT 87
423
426
527
17 92
4
0
1/2 mi
1/2 km
Albin Polasek Museum and Sculpture Gardens 4
Central Park 2
Charles Hosmer Morse Museum of American Art ...5
Cornell Fine Arts Museum 3
Hannibal Square Heritage Center 1
Kraft Azalea Garden 6

House, an historic 1885 building, has been moved to the grounds to be used for public events. ✉ *633 Osceola Ave.* ☎ *407/647–6294* 🌐 *www.polasek.org* 🎫 *$5* ⏲ *Tues.–Sat. 10–4, Sun. 1–4.*

Central Park. Given to the City of Winter Park by the Genius family (benefactors of the Morse Museum), this 11-acre green spot has manicured lawns, specimen plantings, a rose garden, a fountain, and a gazebo. If you take a seat and listen as the Amtrak passenger train rolls by the west end of the park, it's not hard to imagine how Winter Park looked and sounded in the late 19th century. The Winter Park Farmers' Market draws people to the southwest corner on Saturday morning. If you don't want to browse in the shops across the street, a walk through the park beneath the moss-covered trees is a delightful alternative. ✉ *251 Park Ave. S.*

Fodor's Choice ★

Charles Hosmer Morse Museum of American Art. The world's most comprehensive collection of work by Louis Comfort Tiffany—including immense stained-glass windows, lamps, watercolors, and desk sets—is in this museum, which also contains American decorative art and paintings from the mid-19th to the early 20th centuries.

Among the draws is the 1,082-square-foot Tiffany Chapel, originally built for the 1893 World's Fair in Chicago. It took craftsmen 2½ years to painstakingly reassemble the chapel here. Many of the works were rescued from Tiffany's Long Island estate, Laurelton Hall, after a 1957 fire destroyed much of the property. The 12,000-square-foot Laurelton Hall wing, opened in 2011, allows for much more of the estate's collection to be displayed at one time. Exhibits in the wing include architectural and decorative elements from Laurelton's dining room, living room, and Fountain Court reception hall. There's also a re-creation of the striking Daffodil Terrace, so named for the glass daffodils that serve as the capitals for the terrace's marble columns. ✉ *445 N. Park Ave.* ☎ *407/645–5311* 🌐 *www.morsemuseum.org* 🎫 *$5; free Nov.–Apr., Fri. 4–8* ⏲ *Tues.–Sat. 9:30–4, Sun. 1–4; Nov.–Apr., Fri. until 8.*

Cornell Fine Arts Museum. On the Rollins College campus, this museum houses Florida's oldest art collection (its first paintings acquired in 1896)—one with more than 5,000 works, from Italian Renaissance to 19th- and 20th-century American and European paintings. Special exhibitions feature everything from Native American artifacts to Soviet propaganda posters. Outside the museum, a small but charming garden overlooks Lake Virginia. The museum is free to visit; Free guided tours weekends at 1 pm. ✉ *Rollins College, 1000 Holt Ave.* ☎ *407/646–2526* 🌐 *www.rollins.edu/cfam* 🎫 *Free* ⏲ *Tues.–Fri. 10–4, weekends noon–5.*

Hannibal Square Heritage Center. Almost crowded out by the glitz of new shops, restaurants, and art galleries is the original, once-thriving town of Hannibal Square, one of the oldest African-American communities in the country and home to Pullman porter families to this day. The Heritage Center hosts a permanent photographs- and oral-history collection of the significant West Winter Park area. It's a touching and important memorial to a neighborhood that influenced American history. ✉ *642 W. New England Ave.* ☎ *407/539–2680* 🌐 *www.*

hannibalsquareheritagecenter.org 🎟 *Free* ⏲ *Tues.–Thurs. noon–4, Fri. noon–5, Sat. 10–2.*

Kraft Azalea Garden. Enormous cypress trees shade this 5-acre public park on the shores of Lake Maitland, which is alive with heady color from January through March. The thousands of blooming azaleas (hence the name) make a perfect backdrop for romantic strolls, and sunset weddings are common at the park's exedra monument overlooking the lake. ✉ *1365 Alabama Dr.* ☎ *407/599–3334* 🌐 *www.cityofwinterpark.org* ⏲ *Daily 8–dusk.*

NEED A BREAK?

Park Plaza Gardens. This elegant bistro at the Park Plaza Hotel has sidewalk tables and an atrium-style dining room. Though it specializes in seafood entrées, it also serves great sandwiches, beer on tap, an extensive wine selection, and offers great people-watching. ✉ ***319 Park Ave. S*** ☎ ***407/645–2475*** 🌐 ***www.parkplazagardens.com.***

SPORTS AND THE OUTDOORS

Winter Park Country Club. At the north end of Park Avenue this historic country club offers nonresidents access to its immaculate golf course. Opened in 1914, the 9-hole walking course was modeled after authentic Scottish links. ✉ *761 Old England Ave.* ☎ *407/599–3339* 🌐 *www.winterparkcountryclub.com* 🎟 *$10 weekdays, $17 weekends.*

SHOPPING

Park Avenue in downtown Winter Park is definitely a shopper's heaven. This inviting brick street has chic boutiques, sidewalk cafés, and hidden alleyways that lead to peaceful nooks and crannies with even more restaurants and shops. The last several years have seen a mass exodus of the chain stores that came to dominate shopping on Park Avenue, leaving the street open to the return of boutiques. Most of these stores are privately owned and offer merchandise that cannot be easily found elsewhere.

A stroll across the railroad tracks that run through Winter Park brings you to the gentrified Hannibal Square. Centered on the intersection of New England and Pennsylvania avenues, the upscale dining and shopping found here has revitalized the area.

Farmers' Market. Try to schedule your visit to Winter Park for a Saturday morning, so you can begin your day at the weekly farmers' market, which takes place from 7 am to 1 pm at the city's old train depot, two blocks west of Park Avenue. It's a bustling, vibrant market with vendors selling farm-fresh produce, dazzling flowers, and prepared foods. Pick up locally harvested honey, locally made cheese, and freshly baked croissants. ✉ *200 W. New England Ave.* ☎ *407/599–3397* 🌐 *www.cityofwinterpark.org.*

SPECIALTY SHOPS

Charles Hosmer Morse Museum Gift Shop. The obvious reasons to shop here are for the representations of Tiffany glass, silk scarves with stained-glass motifs, and fine-art glass that Louis Comfort himself would have treasured. There are also many objects from world museum gift collections and a wide assortment of books about the Arts

The Charles Hosmer Morse Museum of American Art is also known as the "Tiffany Museum" because of its extensive collection of art by Louis Comfort Tiffany.

and Crafts movement. ✉ *445 N. Park Ave.* ☎ *407/645–5316* 🌐 *www.morsemuseum.org* ⏲ *Tues.–Sat. 9:30–4, Sun. 1–4.*

Kathmandu. The unique items here come from exotic locales like India, Indonesia, Nepal, and Turkey. Hats, turquoise and crystal jewelry, and brass figures of Indian gods are among the merchandise. Follow your nose to the smell of patchouli and sandlewood. ✉ *352 N. Park Ave.* ☎ *407/647–7071* ⏲ *Mon.–Thurs. 9:30–6, Fri. and Sat. 9:30–9, Sun. 11–6.*

FAMILY **Sassafras Sweet Shoppe.** Around a corner from Park Avenue, this quaint, old-timey sweet shop is packed with goodies from yesterday and today, from vintage candy to popcorn balls. This is a perfect pit stop for kids (and adults) after a long day of shopping or touring. ✉ *115 E. Morse Blvd.* ☎ *407/388–0101* 🌐 *www.sassafrassweetshoppe.com.*

Shoooz on Park Avenue. Mephisto, Taryn Rose, Rieker, Naot, Salpy, and BeautiFeel just begin the list of designers in this cozy, shoe-only shop. ✉ *303 N. Park Ave.* ☎ *407/647–0110* ⏲ *Mon.–Sat. 10–6, Sun. noon–5.*

Ten Thousand Villages. This fascinating little store sells fair-trade, artisan-crafted home decor, jewelry, and gifts of all kinds from the smaller corners of the world. ✉ *346 N. Park Ave.* ☎ *407/644–8464* 🌐 *www.winterpark.tenthousandvillages.com* ⏲ *Mon.–Sat. 10–6, Sun. 11–5.*

Timothy's Gallery. It's not a museum gallery; rather, Timothy's sells wearable, sittable, usable art. Hand-carved exotic woods crafted by local artists become jewelry; blown, fused, and shaped glass turns into showcase vases and bowls; and carved furniture can turn a room into a masterpiece. ✉ *236 N. Park Ave.* ☎ *407/629–0707* 🌐 *www.timothysgallery.com* ⏲ *Mon.–Sat. 10–5:30, Sun. noon–5.*

NIGHTLIFE

Rollins College. The gorgeous Mediterranean-revival campus is home to cultural venues and a renowned festival. The Annie Russell Theatre produces student-acted classic and modern plays and dance programs in its beautiful (and, some say, haunted) building. The music department hosts local and international classical, jazz, and world-music artists in a multimillion-dollar performance hall. The annual Bach festival, in late February and early March, honors all things classical and is held at locations throughout Rollins College and Winter Park. ✉ *1000 Holt Ave.* ☎ *407/646–2000* 🌐 *www.rollins.edu.*

MAITLAND

10 miles northeast of Orlando, 25 miles northeast of WDW.

An Orlando suburb with an interesting mix, Maitland is home to both the Florida Save the Manatee Society and one of Central Florida's larger office parks. A number of spectacular homes grace the shores of this town's various lakes, and there's a bird sanctuary and an art center.

GETTING HERE AND AROUND

Take Interstate 4 Exit 90A, then Maitland Boulevard east, and turn right (south) on Maitland Avenue.

EXPLORING

FAMILY **Audubon Center for Birds of Prey.** More than 20 bird species, including hawks, eagles, owls, falcons, and vultures, make their home at this wildlife rehabilitation center on Lake Sybelia. You can take a self-guided conservation tour with interactive exhibits and walkways through the wetlands, or you can call ahead for a private tour ($100), which includes up-close interaction with different birds in the center. There's an earnestness to this working facility, which takes in more than 800 injured wild birds of prey each year. Fewer than half of the birds can return to the wild; some permanently injured birds continue to live at the center and can be seen in the aviaries along the pathways and sitting on outdoor perches. From U.S. 17–92 turn west on Lake Avenue, then north on East Street. ✉ *1101 Audubon Way* ☎ *407/644–0190* 🌐 *fl.audubon.org* 🎫 *$5* ⏲ *Tues.–Sun. 10–4.*

Maitland Arts Center. Hidden down a tree-lined side street is this collection of 23 buildings in the Mayan Revival style—with Mesoamerican motifs—that contain an art gallery and artists studios. Recognized by Florida as a historic site and on the National Register of Historic Places, the center was founded as an art colony in 1937 by American artist and architect André Smith (1880–1959). It continues his tradition of art instruction and contains a major collection of his works. Part of the Art & History Museums Maitland, including the Maitland Historical Museum and the quirky telephone Museum. ✉ *231 W. Packwood Ave.* ☎ *407/539–2181* 🌐 *www.artandhistory.org* 🎫 *$3* ⏲ *Tues.–Sun. 11–4.*

Zora Neale Hurston National Museum of Fine Arts. This museum is in Eatonville, just a few minutes west of Maitland, the first African-American town to be incorporated after the Civil War. It showcases works by artists of African descent during five six-week-long exhibits each year, with one reserved for up-and-comers. The museum is named after former resident Zora Neale Hurston (1891–1960), a writer, folklorist, and anthropologist best known for her novel *Their Eyes Were Watching God*. This is the home of Zora Fest, a street festival and cultural arts and music event celebrating Hurston's life, which is held each year in late January. ✉ *227 E. Kennedy Blvd., Eatonville* ☎ *407/647–3307* 🌐 *www.zoranealehurstonmuseum.com* 🎫 *Donations accepted* ⏲ *Weekdays 9–4, Sat. 11–1.*

NEED A BREAK?

Jeremiah's Italian Ice. There's always a long line in front of this little corner shop thanks to the fresh fruit ices and dozens of gelato flavors. It's also thanks to the pleasant staff, who give "pup cups" to well-behaved dogs. Bring your sweet tooth. ✉ ***111 S. Orlando Ave.*** ☎ ***407/599–9991*** 🌐 ***www.jeremiahsice.com.***

SANFORD

30 miles northeast of Orlando, 45 miles northeast of WDW.

At one time Sanford was the heart of Central Florida—a vital vacation spot and transportation hub on the St. Johns River. But that was before vacationers focused on Orlando and Walt Disney World. In an attempt to turn things around, Sanford has been slowly rebuilding its picturesque downtown overlooking Lake Monroe and increasing the size of its airport (Orlando–Sanford International), which is favored by flights from the United Kingdom. But the main reason most folks make the 30-mile haul northeast of Downtown Orlando (about 45 minutes) is Flea World, which claims to be America's largest flea market under one roof. The town also has the Orlando area's only traditional zoo.

9

EXPLORING

FAMILY **Central Florida Zoo and Botanical Gardens.** Sanford has had a zoo since 1923, and while there's nothing here to rival San Diego or New York, there's a certain charm about the place. In addition to 400-plus animals, including cheetahs, monkeys, and crocodiles, there's the ZOOm Air Adventure Park, with rope bridges and a zip-line through the treetops, and the Wharton-Smith Tropical Splash Ground, a mini water playground. The steam-powered 1/5-scale train that puffs around the zoo is as fun for adults as it is for kids. Take I–4 to Exit 104 and turn left on U.S. 17–92; the zoo is on the right. ✉ *3755 N.W. U.S. 17–92* ☎ *407/323–4450* 🌐 *www.centralfloridazoo.org* 🎫 *$14.95; 3–12 $10.95; ZOOm Air and train extra; parking free* ⏲ *Daily 9–5.*

SHOPPING

Flea World. Merchants at more than 1,700 booths sell predominately new merchandise—car tires, Ginsu knives, pet tarantulas, gourmet coffee, biker clothes, darts, NASCAR souvenirs, rugs, books, incense, leather lingerie, and beaded evening gowns. It's also a great place to buy cheap Florida and Mickey Mouse T-shirts. In one building 50 antiques and collectibles dealers cater to people who can pass up the combination digital ruler and egg timer for some good old junk and authentic collectibles. A free newspaper, distributed at the parking-lot entrance, provides a map and directory. Children are entertained at Fun World next door, but don't expect Disney's squeaky-clean veneer. This mildly gritty amusement park has two unusual miniature golf courses, arcade games, go-karts, bumper cars, bumper boats, children's rides, and batting cages. Flea World is 3 miles east of I–4. Take Exit 98 to Lake Mary Boulevard, and then go 1 mile south on U.S. 17–92. ✉ *4311 S. Orlando Dr. (U.S. 17–92)* ☎ *407/330–1792* 🌐 *www.fleaworld.com* 🎫 *Free* ⏲ *Fri.–Sun. 9–6.*

Jeanine Taylor Folk Art. Taylor's evolving collection of heartfelt, offbeat works is housed in a building with a collagelike facade. This gallery doubles as studio space, so you can meet and chat with the artists as they work. ✉ *211 E. 1st St.* ☎ *407/323–2774* 🌐 *www.jtfolkart.com* ⏲ *Mon. by appt., Tues.–Sat. 10–6, Sun. noon–5.*

Maya Books & Music. Relaxation prevails at proprietress Yvette Comeau's cozy used bookstore, where a dog stretches across the floor amid teetering stacks of books and records. The shop offers 100,000 gently used books, vinyl records and CDs. ✉ *201 E. 1st St.* ☎ *407/321–6504* ⏲ *Mon.–Wed. 10–5, Thurs. 10–6, Fri. and Sat. 10–7, Sun. noon–5.*

OCALA NATIONAL FOREST

Eastern entrance 40 miles west of Daytona Beach, northern entrance 52 miles south of Jacksonville.

This breathtaking 383,000-acre national forest off Route 40 has lakes, springs, rivers, hiking trails, campgrounds, and historic sites. It also has the largest off-highway vehicle trail system in the Southeast and three major recreational areas: Alexander Springs, Salt Springs, and Juniper Springs. To get here, take Interstate 4 east to Exit 92, and head west on Route 436 to U.S. 441, which you take north to Route 19 north.

Alexander Springs Recreation Area. In this recreation area you'll find a stream for swimming and a campground. ✉ *49525 Rte. 445 S, off Rte. 40, Altoona* 🌐 *www.recreation.gov* 🎫 *$5.50.*

Juniper Springs Recreation Area. Here you'll find a stone waterwheel house, a campground, a natural-spring swimming pool, and hiking trails. The 7-mile Juniper Springs run is a narrow, twisting, and winding canoe ride, which, although exhilarating, isn't for the novice. ✉ *14100 Rte. 40 N, Silver Springs* 🌐 *www.recreation.gov* 🎫 *$5.*

Oklawaha Visitor Center. The busiest of the three visitor centers for Ocala National Forest is just outside Silver Spring. Stop in to get information on recreation and trails in the forest as well as maps. This is the center that can give you information on recreation throughout the region. ✉ *Ocala National Forest, 3199 N.E. Rte. 315, and Gulf Dr., Silver Springs* ☎ *352/236–0288* 🌐 *www.fs.usda.gov/ocala.*

Salt Springs Recreation Area. The draw here is a natural saltwater spring where Atlantic blue crabs come to spawn each summer. The forest has a visitor center here as well. ✉ *Visitor Center, 14100 Rte. 19, Fort McCoy* ☎ *352/685–3070* 🎫 *$5.50.*

SPORTS AND THE OUTDOORS

CANOEING

Juniper Springs Canoe Rentals. This operator inside the national forest offers canoe rentals. ✉ *Juniper Springs Recreation Area, 26701 Florida 40, Silver Springs* ☎ *877/444–6777.*

FISHING

Captain Tom's Custom Charters. Charter fishing trips offered by this company range from two hours to a full day. You can arrange sightseeing cruises as well. Trips are by reservation only and are operated in a variety of areas within the national forest. ☎ *352/236–0872* 🌐 *www.captaintomscustomcharters.net/.*

HORSEBACK RIDING

Adopt a Horse Club. Located within the Ocala National Forest, this outfitter offers trail riding and lessons (walk, gait, and canter) for all ages. ✉ *22651 S.E. Rte. 42, Umatilla* ☎ *352/821–4756, 800/731–4756* 🌐 *www.adoptahorseclub.com.*

THE SPACE COAST

South of the Daytona Beach area and Canaveral National Seashore are Merritt Island National Wildlife Refuge and the John F. Kennedy Space Center. This area is also home to the laid-back town of Cocoa Beach, which attracts visitors on weekends year-round because it's the closest beach to Orlando, 50 miles to the east.

VISITOR INFORMATION

Contact Space Coast Office of Tourism ☎ *877/572–3224, 321/433–4470* 🌐 *www.visitspacecoast.com.*

TITUSVILLE

9

34 miles south of New Smyrna Beach, 67 miles east of Orlando.

It's unusual that such a small, easily overlooked community could accommodate what it does, namely the magnificent Merritt Island National Wildlife Refuge and the entrance to the Kennedy Space Center, the nerve center of the U.S. space program (⇨ *see In-Focus feature, "Soaring High at Kennedy Space Center"*).

EXPLORING

American Police Hall of Fame & Museum. You know police officers deserve your respect, and you'll be reminded why at this intriguing attraction. In addition to memorabilia like the Robocop costume and Blade Runner car from the films, informative displays offer insight into the dangers officers face every day: drugs, homicides, and criminals who can create knives from dental putty and guns from a bicycle spoke (really). Other exhibits spotlight the history of capital punishment (from hangings to the guillotine to the electric chair) and crime scene investigation, terrorism, and a rotunda where more than 9,000 names are etched in marble to honor police officers who have died in the line of duty. The 24-lane shooting range provides rental guns (Tuesday to Friday

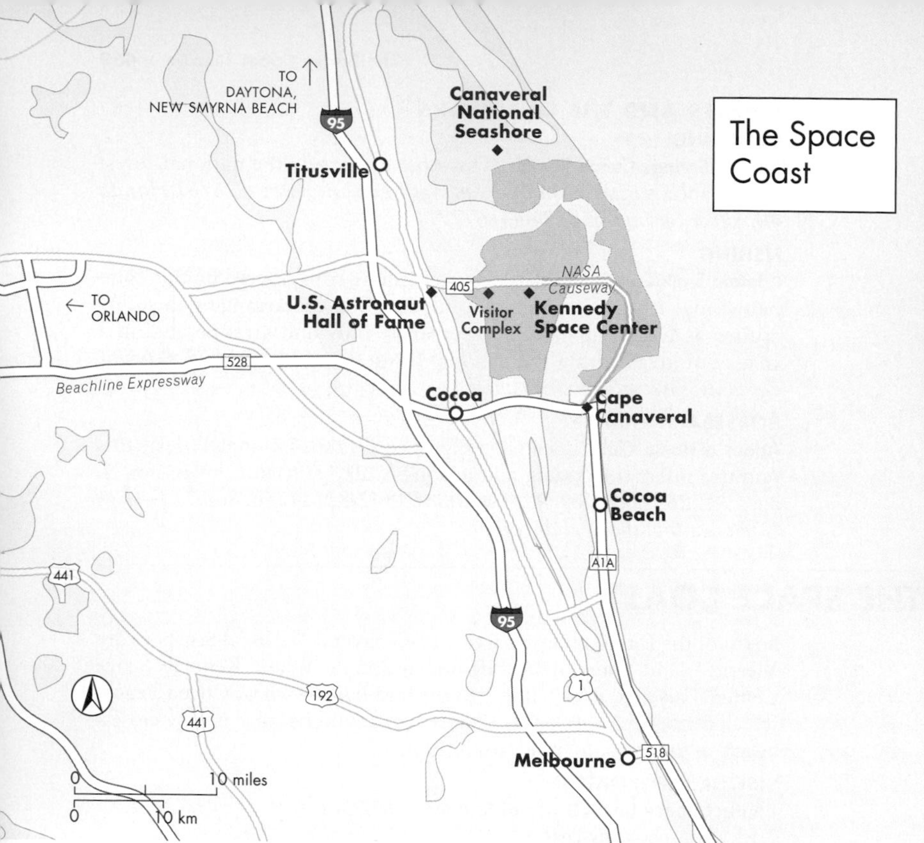

noon–8, weekends noon–6). ✉ *6350 Horizon Dr.* ☎ *321/264–0911* 🌐 *www.aphf.org* 🎟 *$13* ⏲ *Daily 10–6.*

Valiant Air Command Warbird Museum & Tico Airshow. Although its exterior looks sort of squirrelly, what's inside here is certainly impressive. Aviation buffs won't want to miss memorabilia from World Wars I and II, Korea, and Vietnam, as well as extensive displays of vintage military flying gear and uniforms. There are posters that were used to identify Japanese planes, plus there's a Huey helicopter and the cockpit of an F-106 that you can sit in. In the north hangar it looks like activity day at the senior center as a volunteer team of retirees busily restores old planes. It's an inspiring sight, and a good place to hear some war stories. The lobby gift shop sells real flight suits, old flight magazines, bomber jackets, books, models, and T-shirts. ✉ *6600 Tico Rd.* ☎ *321/268–1941* 🌐 *www.vacwarbirds.org* 🎟 *$18* ⏲ *Daily 9–5.*

BEACH

Playalinda Beach. The southern access for the Canaveral National Seashore, remote Playalinda Beach has pristine sands and is the longest stretch of undeveloped coast on Florida's Atlantic seaboard. Hundreds of giant sea turtles come ashore here from May through August to lay their eggs. Fourteen parking lots anchor the beach at 1-mile intervals. From Interstate 95, take Exit 249 and head east. Bring bug repellent in case of horseflies, and note that you may see some unauthorized clothing-optional activity. **Amenities:** lifeguards (seasonal); parking (fee); toilets. **Best for:** solitude; swimming; walking. ✉ *Rte. 402, at northern end of Beach Rd.* ☎ *321/867–4077* 🌐 *www.nps.gov/cana* 🎟 *$5 per vehicle for national seashore.*

WHERE TO EAT

$$$ SEAFOOD **Dixie Crossroads.** This sprawling restaurant is always crowded and festive, but it's not just the rustic setting that draws the throngs—it's the seafood. The specialty is the difficult-to-cook rock shrimp, which are served fried, broiled, or steamed. Diners with a hearty appetite can opt for the all-you-can-eat rock shrimp, small shrimp, tilapia, or catfish. You might have to wait (up to 90 minutes) for a table, but if you don't have time to wait, you can order takeout or use the call-ahead seating option. And a word to the wise: as tempting as those corn fritters dusted with powdered sugar are, don't fill up on them. $ *Average main: $23* ✉ *1475 Garden St., 2 miles east of I–95 Exit 220* ☎ *321/268–5000* 🌐 *www.dixiecrossroads.com* *Reservations not accepted.*

WHERE TO STAY

$$ HOTEL **Hampton Inn Titusville.** Proximity to the Kennedy Space Center and reasonable rates make this four-story hotel a top pick for an overnight near the center. **Pros:** free Internet; extra-comfy beds; convenient to I–95. **Cons:** thin walls; no restaurant on-site; no room service. $ *Rooms from: $96* ✉ *4760 Helen Hauser Blvd.* ☎ *321/383–9191* 🌐 *www.hamptoninn.com* *86 rooms, 4 suites* *Breakfast.*

SPORTS AND THE OUTDOORS

Fodor's Choice ★ **Merritt Island National Wildlife Refuge.** Owned by the National Aeronautics and Space Administration (NASA), this 140,000-acre refuge, which adjoins the Canaveral National Seashore, acts as a buffer around Kennedy Space Center while protecting 1,000 species of plants and 500 species of wildlife, including 15 considered federally threatened or endangered. It's an immense area dotted by brackish estuaries and marshes and patches of land consisting of coastal dunes, scrub oaks, pine forests and flatwoods, and palm and oak hammocks. You can borrow field guides and binoculars at the visitor center (5 miles east of U.S. 1 in Titusville on State Road 402) to track down falcons, ospreys, eagles, turkeys, doves, cuckoos, owls, and woodpeckers, as well as loggerhead turtles, alligators, wild boar and otters. A 20-minute video about refuge wildlife and accessibility—only 10,000 acres are developed—can help orient you.

You might take a self-guided tour along the 7-mile Black Point Wildlife Drive. On the Oak Hammock Foot Trail you can see wintering migratory waterfowl and learn about the plants of a hammock community. If you exit the north end of the refuge, look for the Manatee Observation Area just north of the Haulover Canal (maps are at the visitor center). They usually show up in spring and fall. There are also fishing camps, fishing boat ramps, and six hiking trails scattered throughout the area. Most of the refuge is closed 24 hours prior to a launch. ✉ *Visitor Center, Rte. 402, 5 miles east of U.S. 1 across Titusville Causeway* ☎ *321/861–0667, 321/861–0669 visitor center* 🌐 *www.fws.gov/*

merrittisland 🎟 *Free; $5 per vehicle on Black Point Wildlife Dr. only* ⏲ *Daily sunrise–sunset; visitor center weekdays 8–4:30, weekends 9–5.*

COCOA

17 miles south of Titusville.

Not to be confused with the seaside community of Cocoa Beach, the small town of Cocoa sits smack-dab on mainland Florida and faces the Intracoastal Waterway, known locally as Indian River. There's a planetarium and a museum, as well as a rustic fish camp along the St. Johns River, a few miles inland.

WORD OF MOUTH

"We have been to KSC several times. Keep to the basic tour. The Astronaut Hall of Fame is also nice. My children's only complaint was that they showed pretty much the same film at each stop." –cbr

Folks in a rush to get to the beach tend to overlook Cocoa's Victorian-style village, but it's worth a stop and is perhaps Cocoa's most interesting feature. Within the cluster of restored turn-of-the-20th-century buildings and cobblestone walkways you can enjoy several restaurants, indoor and outdoor cafés, snack and ice-cream shops, and more than 50 specialty shops and art galleries. The area hosts music performances in the gazebo, arts-and-crafts shows, and other family-friendly events throughout the year. To get to Cocoa Village, head east on Route 520—named King Street in Cocoa—and when the streets get narrow and the road curves, make a right onto Brevard Avenue; follow the signs for the free municipal parking lot.

EXPLORING

FAMILY **Brevard Museum of History & Natural Science.** This is the place to come to see what the lay of the local land looked like in other eras. Hands-on activities draw children, who especially migrate toward the Imagination Center, where they can act out history or reenact a space shuttle flight. Not to be missed are Ice Age era creatures such as a fully articulated mastadon, giant ground sloth, and saber-tooth cat. The Windover Archaeological Exhibit features 7,000-year-old artifacts indigenous to the region. In 1984, a shallow pond revealed the burial ground of more than 200 American Indians who lived in the area about 7,000 years ago. Preserved in the muck were bones and, to the archaeologists' surprise, the brains of these ancient people. Nature lovers appreciate the museum's butterfly garden and the nature center with 22 acres of trails encompassing three distinct ecosystems—sand pine hills, lake lands, and marshlands. ✉ *2201 Michigan Ave.* ☎ *321/632–1830* 🌐 *www.brevardmuseum.org* 🎟 *$6* ⏲ *Thurs.–Sat. 10–4.*

WHERE TO EAT

$$$ ECLECTIC Fodor's Choice ★ ✕ **Café Margaux.** Eclectic, creative, and international is the best way to describe the cuisine and decor at this charming Cocoa Village spot. The menu blends French, Italian, and Asian influences with dishes like lollipop pork chop over English pea & orzo risotto, sweet onion-crusted fresh red snapper, and braised veal scallopini, and also features more exotic fare such as duck and ostrich. Themed dining rooms

are elaborately decorated with dramatic but not necessarily coordinating window treatments, wallpaper, and artwork. *Average main: $26 ✉ 220 Brevard Ave. ☎ 321/639–8343 🌐 www.margaux.com ⏲ Closed Sun.*

$ ECLECTIC ✕ **Lone Cabbage Fish Camp.** The word "rustic" doesn't even begin to describe this down-home, no-nonsense restaurant (translation: you eat off paper plates with plastic forks) housed in a weathered, old, clapboard shack along with a bait shop and airboat-tour company. Set your calorie counter for plates of catfish, frogs' legs, turtle, and alligator (as well as burgers and hot dogs). Dine inside or on the outdoor deck overlooking the St. Johns River with live music every Sunday. Who knows, you might even see your dinner swimming by. *Average main: $10 ✉ 8199 Rte. 520, at St. Johns River ☎ 321/632–4199 Reservations not accepted.*

SHOPPING

Cocoa Flea Market. With more than 1,000 booths, this is, essentially, the largest outdoor shopping center in Brevard County. The market is open Friday, Saturday, and Sunday from 8 to 4. *✉ 5605 N. U.S. 1 ☎ 321/631–0241.*

Cocoa Village. You could spend hours browsing in the more than 50 boutiques here, along Brevard Avenue and Harrison Street (the latter has the densest concentration of shops). Although most stores are of the gift and clothing variety, the village is also home to antiques shops, art galleries, restaurants, a tattoo parlor, and a spa. *✉ Rte. 520 and Brevard Ave. ☎ 321/631–9075.*

Super Flea & Farmers' Market. You're sure to find a bargain at one of the 900 booths at this market, which is held every Friday, Saturday, and Sunday from 9 to 4. *✉ 4835 W. Eau Gallie Blvd., Melbourne ☎ 321/242–9124 🌐 www.superfleamarket.com.*

SPORTS AND THE OUTDOORS

BOATING

Twister Airboat Rides. If you haven't seen the swampy, alligator-ridden waters of Florida, then you haven't really seen Florida. This thrilling wildlife tour goes where eagles and wading birds coexist with water moccasins and gators. The Coast Guard–certified deluxe airboats hit speeds of up to 45 mph and offer unparalleled opportunities to photograph native species. The basic tour lasts 30 minutes, but 60- and 90-minute ecotours are also available at an additional cost by reservation only. Twister Airboat Rides is inside the Lone Cabbage Fish Camp, about 9 miles west of Cocoa's city limits, 4 miles west of Interstate 95. *✉ 8199 Rte. 520, at St. Johns River ☎ 321/632–4199 🌐 www.twisterairboatrides.com $22 ⏲ Daily 10–4:30.*

CAPE CANAVERAL

5 miles east of Cocoa via Rte. A1A.

The once-bustling commercial fishing area of Cape Canaveral is still home to a small shrimping fleet, charter boats, and party fishing boats,

Continued on page 482

The astronauts prepare for the launch of Endeavour STS-118 on Pad 39-A.

SOARING HIGH AT THE KENNEDY SPACE CENTER

by John Blodgett and Steve Master

Ever since the National Aeronautics and Space Administration (NASA) was founded in 1958, the United States has been working on missions that launch us heavenward. When these dreams were about to become reality, and until 2011, when it was time for blastoff, Kennedy Space Center in Cape Canaveral, Florida, was where the action could be found.

NASA FROM COAST TO COAST

The Vehicle Assembly Building housed the space shuttle before a launch.

You've heard the words: "Houston, the *Eagle* has landed." And *Apollo 13*'s "Houston, we have a problem." But have you wondered, "Why are they talking to Houston if they left from Florida?"

NASA actually has operations at centers scattered across the United States. Its major centers are in Florida, Texas, and California. NASA's Launch Operations Center, known as the Kennedy Space Center, in Cape Canaveral, Florida, is where the famous countdowns are heard as a mission prepares for launch. You could say this is like NASA's big airport for outbound flights.

Once a mission (with a crew inside) is airborne, Houston takes over. In addition to operating all manned space flights, the Lyndon B. Johnson Space Center in Houston, Texas, is home base for American astronauts. They train here in laboratories that simulate weightlessness and other space-related concepts.

Not to be left out, the West Coast also gets a piece of the space-action pie. At Moffet Field, in California's Silicon Valley, the Ames Research Center is research and development central for NASA technology. If a mission can't happen because the technology isn't there yet, it's the job of the Ames Research Center to figure it out. Also in California is the Dryden Flight Research Center, at Edwards Air Force Base in Southern California. The center is where a lot of smart people who know a lot about aerodynamics get to test out their ideas; it's also where space shuttle orbiters land.

So, in a nutshell, you could say California is the brains of NASA's operations, Texas is its heart, and Florida is its wings.

NASA TIMELINE

OCT. 1958: NASA begins operating with 8,000 employees and $100 million. Ten days later, *Pioneer* I takes off.

MAY 1961: Alan B. Shepard, Jr., becomes the first American in space.

FEB. 1962: John Glenn is the first American to orbit the Earth.

JUNE 1965: Edward H. White II is the first American to walk in space.

DEC. 1968: Three astronauts orbit the moon aboard *Apollo 8*.

JULY 1969: *Apollo 11* brings man to the moon.

JULY 1976: *Viking 1* lands on Mars.

APRIL 1981: First space shuttle orbiter launches two astronauts into space.

JAN. 1986: Space shuttle *Challenger* explodes 73 seconds after launch; seven onboard astronauts die.

APRIL 1990: Hubble telescope launches.

JULY 1997: Mars Pathfinder lands on the red planet.

JULY 1999: Eileen Collins is the first woman to command a space shuttle mission.

FEB. 2002: Mars Odyssey begins mapping the red planet.

FEB. 1, 2003: Space shuttle *Columbia* explodes over Texas 15 minutes before scheduled landing; seven astronauts on board die.

JULY 2004: Cassini–Huygens spacecraft begins orbiting Saturn.

MAY 2010: Shuttle *Atlantis* delivers new Russian module and critical spare parts to International Space Station.

DID YOU KNOW?

Known as the Moon Rockets, the Saturn Vs stood over 363 feet high. NASA sent more than a dozen of these expendable rockets skyward between 1967 and 1973. See one at the Apollo/Saturn V Center.

THE KENNEDY SPACE CENTER

The 140,000-acre Kennedy Space Center is one of central Florida's most popular sights. The must-see attraction gives you a hands-on opportunity to learn about the past, present, and future of America's space program. View old rockets and other artifacts from space flight operations, talk with astronauts during Q&As, experience a simulated launch, and become part of the awed crowd on launch days as you watch the blastoff from a viewing site on the grounds or nearby.

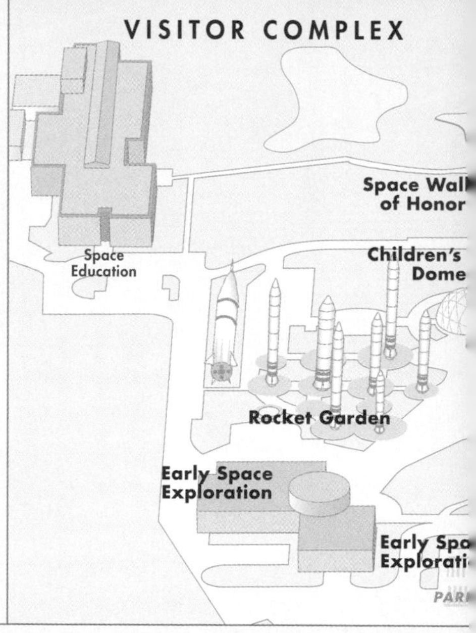

VISITOR COMPLEX

Kennedy Space Center Visitor Complex is the starting place for your visit. It's home to several attractions and is also where you can board the bus for tours of the center beyond the visitor complex.

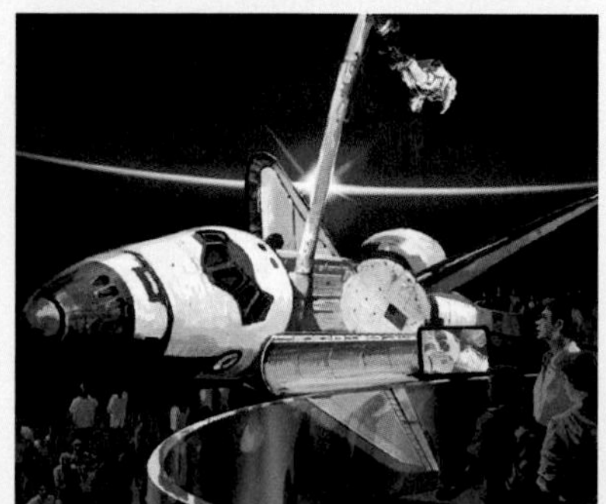

EXHIBITS

A **Space Shuttle Atlantis** exhibit puts visitors nose to nose with the historic spacecraft, which is tilted at a 43.21° angle with its payload door open and robot arm extended. The **Early Space Exploration** display highlights the Mercury and Gemini space programs; **Robot Scouts** is a walk-through exhibit of unmanned planetary probes; and the **Exploration Space: Explorers Wanted** exhibit immerses visitors in exploration beyond Earth. Don't miss the outdoor **Rocket Garden,** winding around rockets, from early Atlas spacecraft to a Saturn IB. The most moving exhibit is the **Astronaut Memorial,** the imposing black-granite tribute to astronauts who lost their lives in the name of space exploration.

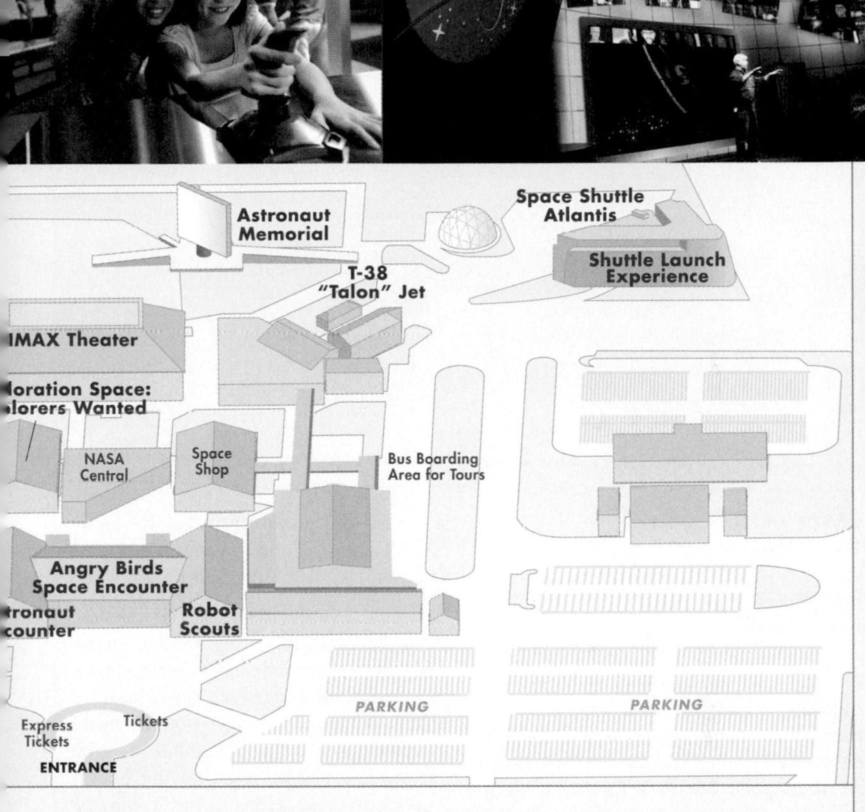

INTERACTIVE SHOWS AND RIDES

Astronaut Encounter Theater has two daily programs where NASA astronauts share their adventures in space travel and show a short film. More befitting Walt Disney World or Universal Studios (complete with the health warnings), the **Shuttle Launch Experience** is the center's spectacular attraction. Designed by a team of astronauts, NASA experts, and renowned attraction engineers, the 44,000-square-foot structure uses a sophisticated motion-based platform, special-effects seats, and high-fidelity visual and audio components to simulate the sensations experienced in an actual space-shuttle launch, including MaxQ, Solid Rocker Booster separation, main engine cutoff, and External Tank separation. The journey culminates with a breathtaking view of Earth from space. For those under 44 inches, **Children's Play Dome** enables kids to play among the next generation of spacecraft, climb a moon-rock wall, and crawl through rocket tunnels.

MOVIES

At the world's only back-to-back twin **IMAX Theater** the dream of space flight comes to life on a movie screen five stories tall with dramatic footage shot by NASA astronauts during missions. Realistic 3-D special effects will make you feel like you're in space with them. Films alternate throughout the year.

BEYOND THE VISITOR COMPLEX

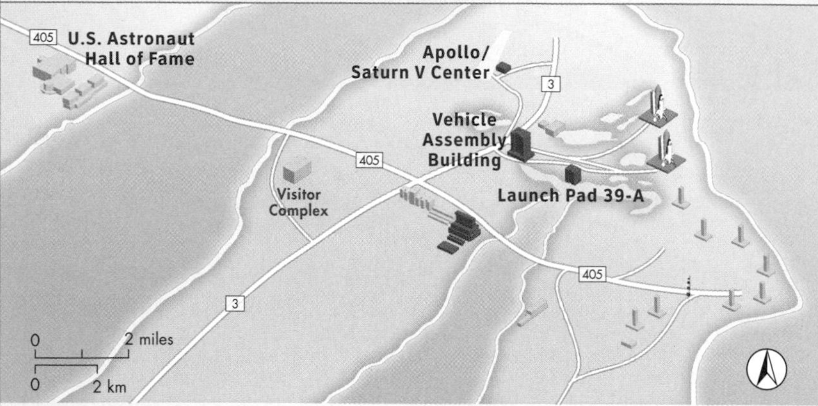

SPACE CENTER TOURS

To explore the remainder of the space center, you will need to take a tour by bus. Buses depart every 15 minutes from the Visitor Complex; the tour duration is two hours, but you can get off and back on again at will at various sites. The bus tour takes guests past such iconic spots as the **Vehicle Assembly Building** and **Launch Pad 39-A.** At the **Apollo/Saturn V Center,** with a don't-miss presentation at the Firing Room Theater, the launch of America's first lunar mission, 1968's *Apollo VIII*, is re-created with a ground-shaking, window-rattling liftoff. The **Apollo/Saturn V Center** features one of the three remaining Saturn V moon rockets. This bus tour is included with admission; four others are available for additional fees (*see Add-Ons*).

U.S. ASTRONAUT HALL OF FAME

The original Mercury 7 team and the later Gemini, Apollo, Skylab, and shuttle astronauts contributed to make the United States Astronaut Hall of Fame the world's premium archive of astronauts' personal stories. Authentic memorabilia and equipment from their collections tell the story of human space exploration. This stand-alone attraction is across the river from the Kennedy Space Center; admission to it is included with your Visitor Complex ticket.

You can see one-of-a-kind items like Wally Schirra's relatively archaic Sigma 7 Mercury space capsule, Gus Grissom's spacesuit (colored silver only because NASA thought silver looked more "spacey"), and a flag that made it to the moon. The exhibit First of the Moon focuses on crew selection for Apollo 11 and the Soviet Union's role in the space race. One of the more challenging activities at the hall of fame is a space-shuttle simulator that lets you try your hand at landing the craft—and afterward replays a side view of your rolling and pitching descent. Don't miss Simulation Station, an area with interactive exhibits about space travel. There are also videos of historic moments.

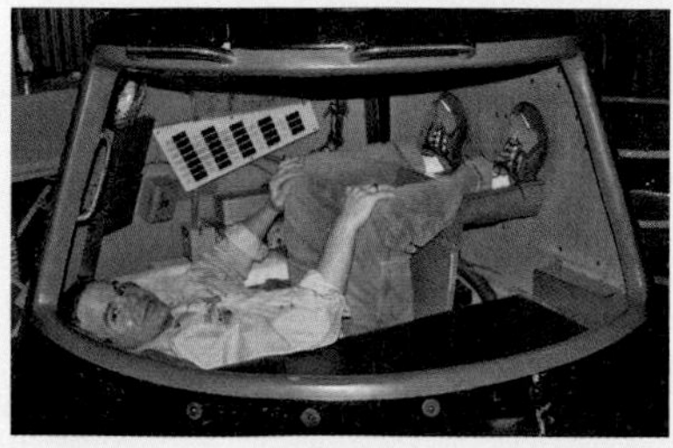

The life of an astronaut can mean a tight squeeze! See for yourself at the U.S. Astronaut Hall of Fame.

ADD-ONS

The following tours and programs are available for extra cost beyond admission and should be reserved in advance.

- A new **KSC Up-Close Tour** takes visitors past the launch pads, the Vehicle Assembly Building, and the Shuttle Landing Facility. This tour costs $25 and last 2 to 2½ hours.
- See how far the space program has come on the **Cape Canaveral: Then and Now Tour** ($21). It puts you up close to the original launch pads, brings you to the Air Force Space and Missile Museum, and lets you watch the active unmanned rocket program.
- During **Lunch With an Astronaut** ($24.99), astronauts talk about their experiences and engage in Q&A (kids often ask "How do you eat/sleep/relieve yourself in space?").
- If you want to live the life of an astronaut, you can enroll in the **Astronaut Training Experience** (ATX) at the U.S. Astronaut Hall of Fame. The half-day program combines hands-on training and preparation for the rigors of space flight. NASA astronauts helped design the program, and you'll hear first-hand from them as you progress through an exciting day at the busiest launch facility on Earth. The $145 cost includes flight training simulators, a full-scale space shuttle mission simulation, a meet-and-greet with a NASA astronaut, and ATX Gear. Age restrictions apply. Reserve your spot well in advance.

Cape Canaveral Then and Now Tour.

PLANNING YOUR TRIP

GETTING HERE

Kennedy Space Center Visitor Complex and the U.S. Astronaut Hall of Fame are near Titusville, about a 45-minute drive from Orlando. From Orlando International Airport, take the north exit to 528 East (the Beachline Expressway) and drive east to the exit marked "407, Titusville, Kennedy Space Center." Take 407 until you reach Rte. 405 (Columbia Boulevard/NASA Parkway) and then turn right. After approximately 1 mile you will see the U.S. Astronaut Hall of Fame on your right. Continue another 5 mi until you reach the visitor complex, your starting point for all tours.

BUDGETING YOUR TIME

Plan to spend a full day at the Visitor Complex and hall of fame, or at the very least, several hours.

ADMISSION

Your $50 (plus tax) admission ticket grants you one day's admission to Kennedy Space Center Visitor Complex and related tours as well as a second day's free admission to the U.S. Astronaut Hall of Fame, which is just across the causeway.

CONTACT INFORMATION

✉ Off Rte. 405

☎ 877/313–2610

🌐 www.kennedyspacecenter.com

🎫 $50

🕘 Daily 9 am; closing times vary. (Call ahead for restrictions if you're visiting on a launch day.)

but its main business these days is as a cruise-ship port. This isn't the spiffiest place around, but what is becoming quite clean and neat is the north end of the port, where the Carnival, Disney, and Royal Caribbean cruise lines set sail. Port Canaveral is now Florida's second-busiest cruise port for multiday cruises, which makes this a great place to catch a glimpse of these giant ships.

EXPLORING

FAMILY **Exploration Tower.** The best view at Port Canaveral is no longer from the top of your cruise ship. In fact, the view from atop this towering seven-story structure, which opened in late 2013, makes the cruise ships look—well, not so massive after all. The tower, a short walk from the cruise port, is equal parts museum and scenic overlook. The seventh-floor observation deck offers impressive views of the cruise port, the Atlantic Ocean, the Banana River, and even the Vehicle Assembly Building at Kennedy Space Center. Other floors house exhibits highlighting cultural history of the area, from space flight to surfing, bird and sea life to the rich maritime history. Kids will enjoy interactive exhibits, including a virtual ship bridge that allows you to pilot a boat through the Canaveral Channel and into the Atlantic. A theater shows a 20-minute film dedicated to the history of Brevard County, and a small café sells refreshments and baked goods. ✉ *670 Dave Nisbet Dr.* ☎ *321/394–3408* 🌐 *www.portcanaveral.com/welcomecenter/index.php* 🎫 *$6.50* ⏲ *Daily 9–6.*

BEACH

Jetty Park. A wonderful taste of the real Florida, this 4½-acre beach and oceanfront campground has picnic pavilions, bike paths, and a 1,200-foot-long fishing pier that doubles as a perfect vantage point from which to watch a lift-off from Cape Canaveral. Lifeguards are on duty all year, and beach wheelchairs are available for rent. A jetty constructed of giant boulders adds to the landscape, and a walkway that crosses it provides access to a less populated stretch of beach. Real and rustic, this is Florida without the theme-park varnish. **Amenities:** food and drink; lifeguards; parking (fee); showers; toilets; water sports. **Best for:** sunrise; surfing; swimming; walking. ✉ *400 Jetty Rd.* ☎ *321/783–7111* 🌐 *www.jettyparkbeachandcampground.com* 🎫 *$5–$10 cars, $7–$15 RVs.*

WHERE TO EAT

$ SEAFOOD ✕ **Seafood Atlantic.** Locals think of this casual waterfront seafood market/eatery as a well-kept secret, but more and more cruise patrons are making their way here for a pre- or postcruise treat. The market is connected to the restaurant, guaranteeing not only freshness but an array of choices. You don't just order a fish sandwich or plate of steamed shrimp; you choose from at least four varieties of fish (try the Golden Tile in season) and several varieties of shrimp (the Royal Reds may be the best you've ever tasted). Seating is alfresco, with views of the inland waterway and nearby cruise ships. Best for lunch or an early dinner, the restaurant closes at 8 on Friday and Saturday, earlier other nights. [$] *Average main: $12* ✉ *520 Glen Cheek Dr.* ☎ *321/784–1963* 🌐 *www.seafoodatlantic.net* ✍ *Reservations not accepted* ⏲ *Closed Tues.*

$$ THAI **Thai Thai III.** The mouthwatering photos on the menu aren't just a marketing ploy. The pictures don't do the real stuff justice. Locals and cruise-ship vacationers frequent this casual Thai/Japanese eatery within walking distance of cruise-port hotels. Seafood is an emphasis here, with specialties like lobster pad Thai and snapper with ginger and scallion. The Thai curries, noodles, and soups can be prepared "Thai hot," but "medium" packs a subtle punch, too. On the sushi side, try the Beauty and the Beast roll: half tuna, half eel, with avocado, asparagus, scallions, and roe. Decor is eclectic and relaxing, with brightly painted walls and low-hanging sconces. Don't fret if you see a crowd out front. The place does a brisk take-out business. *Average main: $16* *8660 Astronaut Blvd.* *321/784–1561* *www.thaithai3.com.*

WHERE TO STAY

$ HOTEL **Radisson Resort at the Port.** For cruise-ship passengers who can't wait to get under way, this splashy resort, done up in pink and turquoise, already feels like the Caribbean. **Pros:** cruise-ship convenience; pool area; free shuttle. **Cons:** rooms around the pool can be noisy; loud air-conditioning in some rooms; no complimentary breakfast. *Rooms from: $122* *8701 Astronaut Blvd.* *321/784–0000, 888/201–1718* *www.radisson.com/capecanaveralfl* *284 rooms, 72 suites* *No meals.*

$$ HOTEL **Residence Inn Cape Canaveral/Cocoa Beach.** Billing itself as the closest all-suites hotel to the Kennedy Space Center, this four-story Residence Inn, painted cheery yellow, is also convenient to other area attractions such as Port Canaveral, the Cocoa Beach Pier, the Brevard Zoo, and Cocoa Village, and is only an hour from the Magic Kingdom. **Pros:** helpful staff; free breakfast buffet; pet-friendly. **Cons:** less than picturesque views; street noise in some rooms. *Rooms from: $179* *8959 Astronaut Blvd.* *321/323–1100, 800/331–3131* *www.marriott.com* *150 suites* *Breakfast.*

SHOPPING

Cove Marketplace. Whether you're at Port Canaveral for a cruise or are just passing through, this retail marketplace on the south side of the harbor has enough shops, restaurants, and entertainment venues to keep you occupied. Since most of the bars and eateries are located on the public waterfront area, you'll have a view of the cruise ships—and their colorful passengers. *Glen Cheek Dr., at Scallop Dr., Port Canaveral* *www.portcanaveral.com/covemarketplace* *Free* *Hrs vary by business.*

9

COCOA BEACH

5 miles south of Cape Canaveral, 58 miles southeast of Orlando.

After crossing a long and high bridge just east of Cocoa Village, you drop down upon a barrier island. A few miles farther and you'll reach the Atlantic Ocean and picture-perfect Cocoa Beach at Route A1A.

In the early 1960s Cocoa Beach was a sleepy, little-known town. But in 1965 the sitcom *I Dream of Jeannie* premiered. The endearing show centered on an astronaut, played by Larry Hagman, and his "Jeannie" in a bottle, Barbara Eden, and was set in Cocoa Beach. Though the series was never shot in Florida, creator Sidney Sheldon paid homage to the town with local references to Cape Kennedy (now known as the Kennedy Space Center) and Bernard's Surf restaurant. Today the town and its lovely beach are mecca to Florida's surfing community.

ESSENTIALS

Visitor Information Cocoa Beach Convention and Visitors Bureau ☎ *321/454–2022, 877/321–8474* 🌐 *www.visitcocoabeach.com.*

EXPLORING

Cocoa Beach Pier. By day, it's a good place to stroll—if you don't mind weather-worn wood and sandy, watery paths. Although most of the pier is free to walk on, there's a $1 charge to enter the fishing area at the end of the 800-foot-long boardwalk, and a $5 fishing fee. You can rent rods and reels here for an additional $10. By night, visitors and locals—beach bums and surfers among them—head here to party. Come on Friday night for the Boardwalk Bash, with live acoustic and rock-and-roll music; Wednesday and Saturday also see live music. ■ **TIP→ The pier is a great place to watch launches from Kennedy Space Center.** ✉ *401 Meade Ave.* ☎ *321/783–7549* 🌐 *www.cocoabeachpier.com.*

BEACH

Cocoa Beach. This is one of the Space Coast's nicest beaches—and the place where the great professional surfer Kelly Slater got his start. The beach boasts one of the steadiest surf breaks on the East Coast and has wide stretches that are excellent for biking, jogging, and strolling. In some places there are dressing rooms, showers, playgrounds, picnic areas with grills, snack shops, and surfside parking lots. Beach vendors offer necessities, and lifeguards are on duty in the summer.

A popular entry road, Route 520 crosses the Banana River into Cocoa Beach. At its east end, 5-acre **Alan Shepard Park,** named for the famous astronaut, aptly provides excellent views of launches from Kennedy Space Center. Facilities here include 10 picnic pavilions, shower and restroom facilities, and more than 300 parking spaces. Beach vendors carry necessities for sunning and swimming. Parking is $7, $10 on weekends and holidays March through Labor Day. Shops and restaurants are within walking distance. Another enticing Cocoa Beach entry point is 10-acre **Sidney Fischer Park,** in the 2100 block of Route A1A in the central beach area. It has showers, playgrounds, changing areas, picnic areas with grills, snack shops, and plenty of well-maintained, inexpensive parking lots ($5 for cars). **Amenities:** food and drink; lifeguards (summer); parking (fee); showers; toilets; water sports. **Best for:** sunrise; surfing; swimming; walking. ✉ *Rte. A1A from Cape Canaveral to Patrick Air Force Base, 401 Meade Ave.*

WHERE TO EAT

$$$ GERMAN ✕ **Heidelberg.** As the name suggests, the cuisine here is definitely German, from the sauerbraten served with potato dumplings and red cabbage to the beef Stroganoff and spaetzle to the classically prepared Wiener schnitzel. All the soups and desserts are homemade; try the Viennese-style apple strudel and the rum-zapped almond-cream tortes. Elegant interior touches include crisp linens and fresh flowers. There's live

music Wednesday through Saturday evening. You can also dine inside the jazz club, Heidi's, next door. *Average main: $28 ✉ 7 N. Orlando Ave., opposite City Hall ☎ 321/783–6806 🌐 www.heidisjazzclub.com ⊗ Closed Mon. and Tues. No lunch Sun.*

$ SEAFOOD ✕ **Oh Shucks Seafood Bar.** At the only open-air seafood bar on the beach, at the entrance of the Cocoa Beach Pier, the main item is oysters, served on the half shell. You can also grab a burger here, crab legs by the pound, or Oh Shucks's most popular item, coconut beer shrimp. Some diners complain that the prices don't jibe with the ultracasual atmosphere (e.g., plastic chairs), but they're also paying for the "ex-Pierience." During high season, there's live entertainment on Wednesday, Friday, Saturday, and Sunday. *Average main: $12 ✉ 401 Meade Ave., Cocoa Beach Pier ☎ 321/783–7549 🌐 www.cocoabeachpier.com.*

WHERE TO STAY

$ HOTEL **Best Western Oceanfront Hotel & Suites.** Families love this Best Western for its affordable suites; everyone loves it for its location—a half block from the Cocoa Beach Pier—and great views of launches from Kennedy Space Center. **Pros:** free Internet; complimentary breakfast. **Cons:** not all rooms have an ocean view; small bathrooms; noise from the pier. *Rooms from: $95 ✉ 5600 N. Atlantic Ave. ☎ 321/784–4343, 800/367–1223 🌐 www.bestwesterncocoabeach.com 230 rooms Breakfast.*

$ HOTEL **DoubleTree by Hilton Cocoa Beach Oceanfront.** Proximity to the beach and comforts like in-room microwaves and refrigerators—and DoubleTree's famous chocolate-chip walnut cookies—make this six-story hotel a favorite of vacationing families, particularly Orlandoans on weekend getaways. **Pros:** private beach access; comfy beds; complimentary parking. **Cons:** extra charge for beach-chair rental; thin walls; slow elevators; no breakfast with standard room. *Rooms from: $164 ✉ 2080 N. Atlantic Ave. ☎ 321/783–9222 🌐 www.cocoabeachdoubletree.com 148 rooms, 12 suites No meals.*

$ HOTEL **Hilton Cocoa Beach Oceanfront.** You can't get any closer to the beach than this seven-story oceanfront hotel. **Pros:** beachfront; friendly staff; clean. **Cons:** small pool and bathrooms; no balconies; room windows don't open; breakfast not included with standard rate. *Rooms from: $124 ✉ 1550 N. Atlantic Ave. ☎ 321/799–0003 🌐 www.hiltoncocoabeach.com 285 rooms, 11 suites No meals.*

$ B&B/INN **Inn at Cocoa Beach.** This charming oceanfront inn has spacious, individually decorated rooms with four-poster beds, upholstered chairs, and balconies or patios; most have ocean views. **Pros:** quiet; romantic; honor bar. **Cons:** no on-site restaurant; "forced" socializing. *Rooms from: $155 ✉ 4300 Ocean Beach Blvd. ☎ 321/799–3460, 800/343–5307 outside Florida 🌐 www.theinnatcocoabeach.com 50 rooms Breakfast.*

$$ RESORT FAMILY Fodor's Choice ★ **The Resort on Cocoa Beach.** Even if the beach weren't in its backyard, this family-friendly, oceanfront property offers enough activities and amenities—from tennis and basketball courts to a game room and 50-seat movie theater—to keep everyone entertained. **Pros:** full kitchens; in-room washers and dryers; large balconies. **Cons:** check-in not until 4 and checkout at 10; not all rooms are oceanfront; slow elevators. *Rooms from: $180 ✉ 1600 N. Atlantic Ave. ☎ 321/783–4000 🌐 www.theresortoncocoabeach.com 124 suites No meals.*

9

The Cocoa Beach Pier is a magnet for nightlife in Cocoa Beach after dark.

NIGHTLIFE

The Cocoa Beach Pier has several nightspots as well as live-music sessions a couple of nights a week.

Heidi's Jazz Club. Local and nationally known jazz musicians (Boots Randolph and Mose Allison have taken the stage) play Tuesday through Sunday, with showcase acts appearing on weekends. ✉ *7 Orlando Ave. N* ☎ *321/783–4559.*

SHOPPING

Merritt Square Mall. The area's only major shopping mall is about a 20-minute ride from the beach. Stores include Macy's, Dillard's, JCPenney, Sears, Foot Locker, Island Surf and Skate, and roughly 100 others. There's a 16-screen multiplex, along with a food court and several restaurant chains. ✉ *777 E. Merritt Island Causeway, Merritt Island* ☎ *321/452–3270.*

SPORTS AND THE OUTDOORS

KAYAKING

Adventure Kayak of Cocoa Beach. Specializing in manatee encounters, this outfitter organizes one- and two-person kayak tours of mangroves, channels, and islands. Tours launch from various locations in the Cocoa Beach area. Rates run about $30 per person. ☎ *321/480–8632* 🌐 *www.kayakcocoabeach.com.*

SURFING

Cocoa Beach Surf Company. The world's largest surf complex has three floors of boards, apparel, sunglasses, and anything else a surfer, wannabe-surfer, or souvenir-seeker could need. Also on-site are a 5,600-gallon fish and shark tank and the Shark Pit Bar & Grill. Here you can also rent surfboards, bodyboards, and wet suits, as well as umbrellas, chairs, and bikes. And staffers teach grommets (dudes) and gidgets (chicks)—from kids to seniors—how to surf. There are group, semi-private, and private lessons available in one-, two-, and three-hour sessions. Prices range from $40 (for a one-hour group lesson) to $120 (three-hour private). All gear is provided. ✉ *4001 N. Atlantic Ave.* ☎ *321/799–9930.*

Fodor's Choice ★ **Ron Jon Surf Shop.** It's impossible to miss Ron Jon: it takes up nearly two blocks along Route A1A and has a giant surfboard and an art-deco facade painted orange, blue, yellow, and turquoise. What started in 1963 as a small T-shirt and bathing-suit shop has evolved into a 52,000-square-foot superstore that's open every day 'round the clock. The shop rents water-sports gear as well as chairs and umbrellas, and it sells every kind of beachwear, surf wax, plus the requisite T-shirts and flip-flops. ✉ *4151 N. Atlantic Ave., Rte. A1A* ☎ *321/799–8820* 🌐 *www.ronjonsurfshop.com.*

Ron Jon Surf School. If you can't tell a tri-skeg stick from a hodaddy shredding the lip on a gnarly tube, then you may want to avail yourself of the Ron Jon Surf School. Private lessons and clinics are offered for surfers of all levels. The most popular sessions last two hours ($65 clinics, $95 private). Boards are provided, but you should bring your own towels and sunscreen. ✉ *150 E. Columbia La.* ☎ *321/868–1980.*

MELBOURNE

20 miles south of Cocoa Beach.

Despite its dependence on the high-tech space industry, this town is decidedly laid-back. Most of the city is on the mainland, but a small portion trickles onto a barrier island, separated by the Indian River Lagoon and accessible by several inlets, including the Sebastian.

EXPLORING

FAMILY Fodor's Choice ★ **Brevard Zoo.** At the only Association of Zoo and Aquariums–accredited zoo built by a community, you can stroll along the shaded boardwalks and get a close-up look at rhinos, giraffes, cheetahs, alligators, crocodiles, giant anteaters, marmosets, jaguars, eagles, river otters, kangaroos, exotic birds, and kookaburras. Alligator, crocodile, and river-otter feedings are held on alternate afternoons—and no, the alligators don't dine on the otters. Stop by Paws-On, an interactive learning playground with a petting zone, wildlife detective training academy, and the Indian River Play Lagoon. Hand-feed a giraffe in Expedition Africa or a lorikeet in the Australian Free Flight Aviary, and step up to the Wetlands Outpost, an elevated pavilion that's a gateway to 22 acres of wetlands through which you can paddle kayaks and keep an eye open for the 4,000 species of wildlife that live in these waters and woods. Adventurers seeking a chimp's-eye view can zipline through the zoo on Treetop Trek. ✉ *8225 N. Wickham Rd.* ☎ *321/254–9453* 🌐 *www.brevardzoo.org* 🎫 *$16, including train and giraffe and lorikeet food $20.50, Treetop Trek $22–$57* 🕓 *Daily 9:30–5, last admission 4:15.*

9

BEACHES

Paradise Beach. Small and scenic, this 1,600-foot stretch of sand is part of a 10-acre park north of Indialantic, about 20 miles south of Cocoa Beach on Route A1A. It has a refreshment stand, volleyball courts, outdoor showers, a beachfront park with pavilions, grills, picnic tables, and lifeguards in summer. **Amenities:** food and drink; lifeguards (seasonal); parking; showers; toilets. **Best for:** sunrise; surfing; swimming; walking. ✉ *2301 N. Rte. A1A.*

Satellite Beach. The sands of this sleepy little community just south of Patrick Air Force Base, about 15 miles south of Cocoa Beach on Route A1A, are cradled between the balmy Atlantic Ocean and biologically diverse Indian River Lagoon. It's a popular spot for family vacations because of its slow pace and lack of crowds as well as its beachfront park with playground, five pavilions, and picnic facilities. **Amenities:** food and drink; lifeguards; parking; showers; toilets; water sports. **Best for:** sunrise; surfing; swimming; walking. ✉ *Rte. A1A, Satellite Beach.*

SPORTS AND THE OUTDOORS

BASEBALL

Space Coast Stadium. Even though they play in our nation's capital during the regular season, the Washington Nationals use this stadium for their spring training site. For the rest of the season, the facility is home to the Brevard County Manatees (☎ *321/633–9200*), one of the Milwaukee Brewers' minor-league teams. ✉ *5800 Stadium Pkwy., Viera* ☎ *321/633–4487* 🌐 *www.viera.com.*

GOLF

Baytree National Golf Links. "Challenging but fair" is how golfers describe this links-style course, designed by PGA legend Gary Player (aka "The Black Knight"). This semi-private course, built in 1992, is known for its unique red shale coquina waste areas. A round can be something of a rollercoaster ride, with an easy hole or two followed by a perplexingly challenging one. The 454-yard , par-4 18th, for instance, is rated among the toughest in Brevard County. It plays into the wind and requires an imposing carry over wetlands, followed by an approach into a green guarded by water on all sides. The club has a restaurant and full practice facility. ✉ *8207 National Dr.* ☎ *321/259–9060* 🌐 *www.baytreenational.com* 🎟 *$69 for 18 holes, $20 for 9 holes* 🏌 *18 holes, 7,043 yards, Par 72.*

Viera East Golf Club. Rated among the best public courses—and values—on the Space Coast, Viera East reflects course architect Joe Lee's credo that "golf should be enjoyable, not a chore." Novices appreciate the forgiving, open layout with generous landing areas; more advanced players embrace the challenge of Lee's strategically placed bunkers (there are 66), water hazards, and expansive, undulating greens. The coastal breezes can make club selection tricky at times. Opened in 1994, the course is framed by marshlands, lakes, ponds, pine and cypress trees. The par-5 14th is among the more picturesque and challenging holes, with a green surrounded by water. ✉ *2300 Clubhouse Dr., Viera* ☎ *321/639–6500* 🌐 *www.vieragolf.com* 🎟 *$60 for 18 holes* 🏌 *18 holes, 6,720 yards, par 72.*

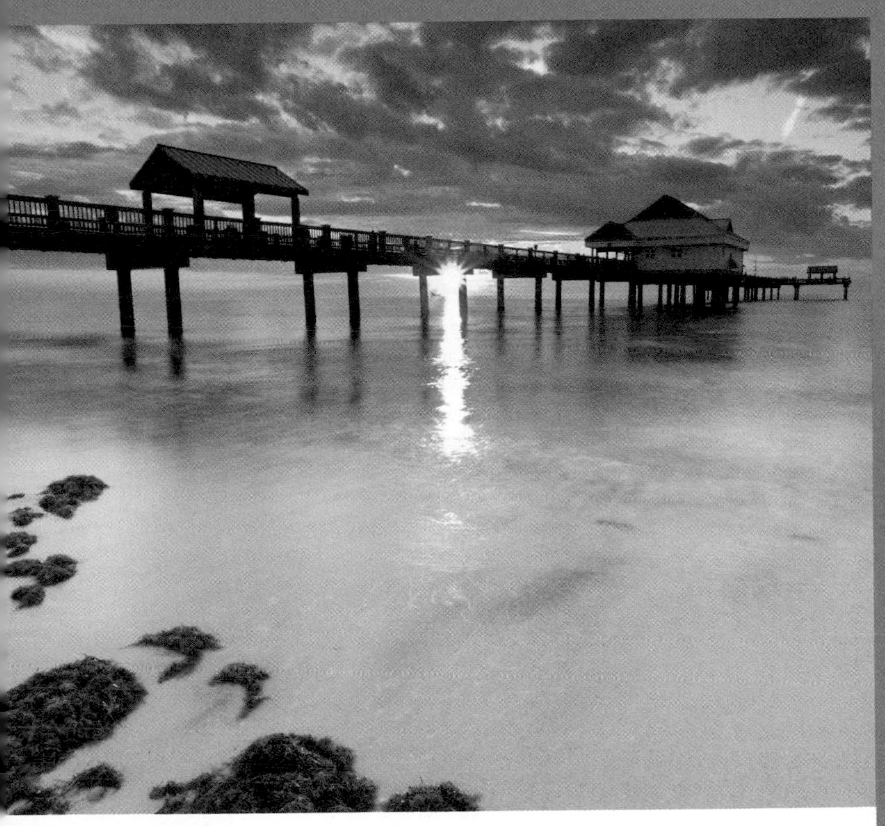

THE TAMPA BAY AREA

10

WELCOME TO THE TAMPA BAY AREA

TOP REASONS TO GO

★ **Art gone wild:** Whether you take the guided tour or chart your own course, experience the one-of-a-kind collection at the Salvador Dalí Museum, which has relocated to a gorgeous waterfront building in downtown St. Petersburg.

★ **Cuban roots:** You'll find great food and vibrant nightlife in historic Ybor City, just east of downtown Tampa.

★ **Beachcomber bonanza:** Caladesi Island State Park has some of the best shelling on the Gulf Coast, and its five-star sunsets are a great way to end the day.

★ **Culture fix:** If you love the arts, there's no finer offering in the Bay Area than at the Florida State University Ringling Center for the Cultural Arts in Sarasota.

1 Tampa. Situated on a large bay of the same name, Tampa is a growing waterfront metropolis that's packed with state-of-the-art zoos, plenty of museums, and inviting shopping districts. Among the main draws is Busch Gardens, which doubles as a theme park and a zoo.

2 St. Petersburg. Although downtown St. Petersburg can be rowdy, there are also pockets of culture. The mellow but pricey Pinellas County beach towns include St. Pete Beach and Treasure Island.

3 Clearwater and Vicinity. Quiet during the winter, the beach areas north of St. Petersburg buzz all spring and summer. In addition to Clearwater, the area includes Dunedin and Tarpon Springs.

4 Sarasota and Vicinity. Sarasota County's barrier islands lure travelers to a battery of white-sand beaches, but Sarasota's cultural treasures are the true draw for many of its visitors.

Cosme
Carrollwood
Oldsmar
Temple Terrace
Tampa International Airport
Courtney Campbell Causeway
Rocky Point
Old Tampa Bay
St Petersburg-Clearwater International Airport
Howard Frankland Bridge
TAMPA
Ybor City
Kennedy Blvd.
Adamo St.
Fletcher Ave.
Fowler Ave.
Busch Blvd.
Hillsborough Ave.
Gunn Hwy.
Waters Ave.
Sheldon Rd.
Dale Mabry Hwy.
Nebraska Ave.
South Crosstown Expwy.
West Shore Blvd.
BIG ISLAND
Gandy Bridge
Hillsborough Bay
MacDill Air Force Base
Gadsden Point
East Tampa
Gibsonton
Adamsville
WEEDON I.
ROSS I.
62nd Ave. N
ST. PETERSBURG
Tampa Bay
Boyd Hill Nature Park
COQUINA KEY
54th Ave. S
Pinellas Point
Mangrove Point
Apollo Beach
Tamiami Rd.
Ruskin
Gulf City
Little Manatee River
Sun City
Valroy
Piney Point
TO SARASOTA
Gillette
Parrish
Sunshine Skyway (toll)
75
275
41
598
597
586
580
583
60
92
574
BUS 41
19
301
1
2
4

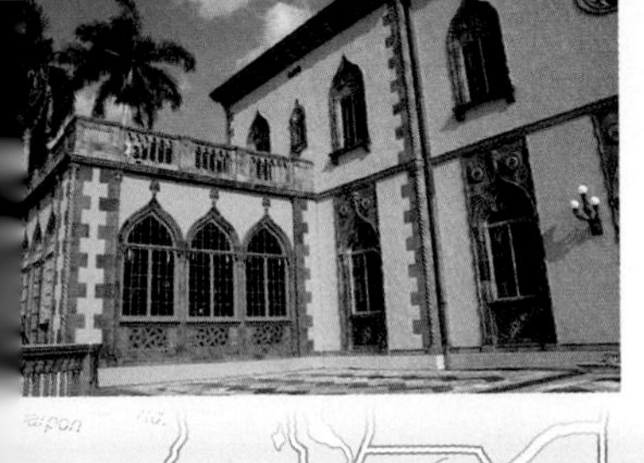

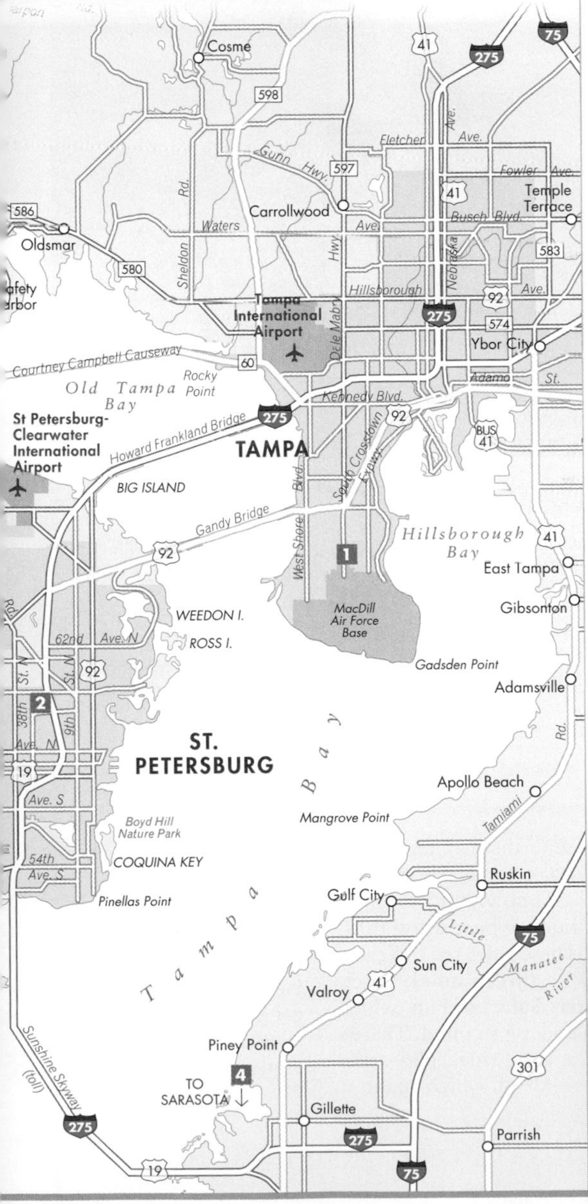

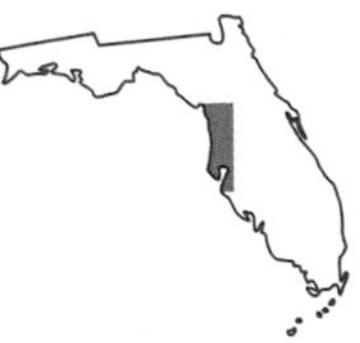

GETTING ORIENTED

On the east side of the bay, Tampa is a sprawling cosmopolitan city offering attractions like Busch Gardens and Ybor City. To the west, St. Petersburg and Clearwater boast lovely barrier island beaches. Moving to the south, Sarasota's arts scene is among the finest in Florida.

10

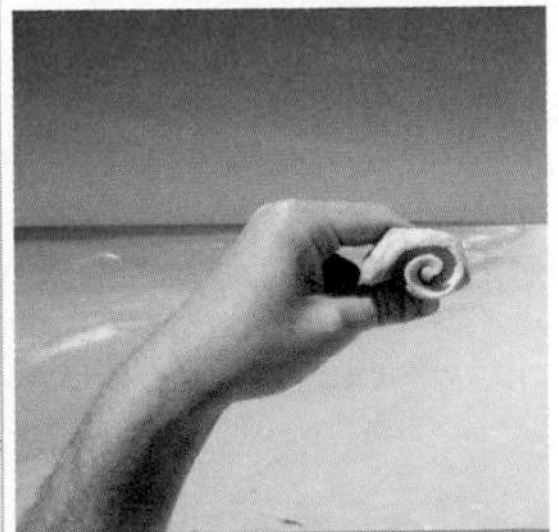

BUSCH GARDENS

Busch Gardens was opened in Tampa on March 31, 1959, by the Anheuser-Busch company. It was originally designed as an admission-free animal attraction to accompany the brewing plant, but it eventually was turned into a theme park, adding more exotic animals, tropical landscaping, and rides to entertain its guests.

Today the 335-acre park has nine distinct territories packed with roller coasters, rides, eateries, shops, and live entertainment. The park is best known for its incredible roller coasters and water rides, which draw thrill seekers from around the globe. These rides tend to cater to those over the age of 10. With this in mind, Busch Gardens created the **Sesame Street Safari of Fun,** which is designed solely with children under 5 in mind. There's a lot packed into this area: junior thrill rides, play areas (some with water), and shows—all of which make it exciting for the kids.

GETTING ORIENTED

The park is set up on a north–south axis, with Nairobi being in the center.

Your first encounter at the park is the Moroccan market (grab a map here). There are several small eateries and souvenir shops in this area. If you head west from Morocco, you'll get to the Sesame Street Safari of Fun, Stanleyville, and Jungala. Heading north you'll find Nairobi, Pantopia, and the Congo. Heading east takes you to Egypt and the Serengeti Plain. If you get lost, there are team members available almost everywhere to help you.

TOP ATTRACTIONS

FOR AGES 7 AND UP

Cheetah Hunt. Riders zoom over 4,000 feet of Serengeti-like landscape and down through a rocky cave.

Falcon's Fury. Facing down, riders plummet from the top of this 335-foot freestanding tower at speeds of up to 60 mph.

Gwazi. The largest, fastest wooden dueling roller coaster in the world boasts crossing speeds of 100 mph.

Kumba. Riders on this coaster experience weightlessness, cobra rolls, corkscrews, and inverted rolls.

Montu. This 150-foot-tall inverted coaster reaches speeds of 60 mph, and has a zero-G roll and seven inversions.

Rhino Rally. A Land Rover takes you on an off-road safari with up-close animal encounters and a raging river adventure.

SheiKra. This coaster is 200 feet tall with a 200-foot vertical descent, and isn't for the faint of heart.

Wild Surge. You're shot out of a mountain crater up 40 feet and then bounced up and down, creating a free-fall experience.

FOR AGES 6 AND UNDER

Air Grover. Take a ride on Grover's plane and soar through the Sahara on this junior coaster.

Bert and Ernie's Watering Hole. It's a water adventure filled with bubblers, geysers, jets, dumping buckets, and more.

Rosita's Djembe Fly-Away. Rosita takes you on a swing ride that sends you above the African canopy.

Walkabout Way. You don't have to be a kid to enjoy this Australian-theme attraction, which allows you and the little ones to hand-feed a bunch of cuddly kangaroos.

Zoe-Petra & the Hippos of the Nile. A kid-size flume ride with Zoe's hippo friends gives children a river glimpse of Africa.

VISITING TIPS

- The park is least crowded during the week, with weekends bringing in a lot of locals. Summer and the holidays also are crowded.
- Ride the thrill rides as early in the day as possible. Think about purchasing a Quick Queue pass for $14.95, which grants you no-wait access. It's good only once per ride but ensures you'll hit all the big rides quickly.
- Bring extra quarters for all the locker rentals at each of the coasters.
- You can pick up a map at the entrance, which lists showtimes, meet-the-keeper times, and special hours for attractions and restaurants.
- Vegetarians will enjoy the veggie burgers at **Zagora Café** or the **Colony House**'s delicious vegetable platter. A money saver is the All Day Dining Deal, which costs $32.99 per adult and $14.99 per child. It's accepted at most dining venues. If eating at the Colony House, you'll want to make your reservations immediately upon entering the park.

Updated by Kate Bradshaw

If you seek a destination that's no one-trick pony, the Tampa Bay region is a spot you can't miss. Encompassing an area from Tarpon Springs to Tampa proper and all the way south to Sarasota, it's one of those unsung places as dynamic as it is appealing—and word has definitely started to spread about its charms. With its long list of attractions—from pristine beaches to world-class museums—it's easy to see why.

First and foremost, Tampa Bay's beaches are some of the best in the country. Whether you want coarse or fine sand, and whether you seek a mellow day of shelling or a raucous romp on a crowded stretch of waterfront, this place has it all. Of course, you can choose from a range of water activities, including charter fishing, parasailing, sunset cruises, kayaking, and more.

The region has its share of boutique districts spotted with shops and sidewalk cafés. Tampa's Hyde Park Village and downtown St. Petersburg's Beach Drive are among the top picks if you're looking to check out some upscale shops and dine alfresco while getting the most of the area's pleasant climate. Vibrant nightlife tops off Tampa Bay's list of assets. Ybor City attracts the club set, and barrier islands like St. Pete Beach offer loads of live music and barefoot dancing into the wee hours.

Tampa Bay has lots of family-friendly attractions, too. You can check out Busch Gardens, Adventure Island, and the Clearwater Marine Aquarium, to name a few. And art fanatics will find an astonishing array of attractions, including Sarasota's Ringling Museum of Art, St. Petersburg's enrapturing Salvador Dalí and Dale Chihuly collections (both permanent and housed in exquisite new digs), and Tampa's Museum of Art. Come prepared to explore and see for yourself what a compelling, unforgettable place the Tampa Bay area really is.

PLANNING

WHEN TO GO

Winter and spring are high season, and the amount of activity during this time is double that of the off-season. Beaches do stay pretty packed throughout the sweltering summer, which is known for massive, almost-daily afternoon thunderstorms. Summer daytime temperatures hover around or above 90°F. Luckily the mercury drops to the mid-70s at night, and the beaches have a consistent onshore breeze that starts just before sundown, which enabled civilization to survive here before air-conditioning arrived.

GETTING HERE AND AROUND

AIR TRAVEL

Tampa International Airport, the area's largest and busiest airport, with 19 million passengers per year, is served by most major carriers and offers ground transportation to surrounding cities. Many of the large U.S. carriers also fly into and out of Sarasota–Bradenton International Airport. St. Petersburg–Clearwater International Airport, 9 miles west of downtown St. Petersburg, is much smaller than Tampa International and has limited service.

Airport Transfers: SuperShuttle is one of the easiest ways to get to and from the airport if you forgo a rental car. All you need to do is call or visit the SuperShuttle website to book travel—they'll pick you up and drop you off wherever you're staying at any hour. Basic service costs around $28.

Blue One Transportation provides service to and from Tampa International Airport for areas including Hillsborough (Tampa, Plant City), Pinellas (St. Petersburg, St. Pete Beach, Clearwater), and Polk (Lakeland) counties. Rates vary by pickup location, destination, and fuel costs.

Airport Sarasota–Bradenton International Airport ✉ *Sarasota* ☎ *941/359–2777* 🌐 *www.srq-airport.com.* **St. Petersburg–Clearwater International Airport** ✉ *Clearwater* ☎ *727/453–7800* 🌐 *www.fly2pie.com.* **Tampa International Airport** ✉ *Tampa* ☎ *813/870–8700* 🌐 *www.tampaairport.com.*

Airport Transfers Blue One Transportation ☎ *813/282–7351* 🌐 *www.blueonetransportation.com.* **SuperShuttle** ☎ *800/258–3826* 🌐 *www.supershuttle.com.*

BOAT TRAVEL

Dolphin Landings Charter Boat Center has daily four-hour cruises to unspoiled Egmont Key at the mouth of Tampa Bay. Hubbard's Marina also operates a ferry to Egmont Key on most days. Climb aboard the glass-bottom boats of St. Nicholas Boat Line to take a sightseeing cruise of Tarpon Springs' historic sponge docks and see a diver at work.

On Captain Memo's Pirate Cruise, crew members dressed as pirates take you on sightseeing and sunset cruises in a replica of a 19th-century sailing ship. Starlite Cruises operates two very different ships for lunch, sightseeing, and dinner cruises: the *Starlite Majesty*, a sleek, yacht-style vessel; and *Starlite Princess*, an old-fashioned paddle wheeler that sails out of St. Pete Beach.

Tour Operators **Captain Memo's Pirate Cruise** ✉ *Clearwater Beach Marina, 25 Causeway Blvd., at end of Rte. 60, Clearwater Beach* ☎ *727/446–2587* 🌐 *www.captainmemo.com.* **Dolphin Landings Charter Boat Center** ✉ *4737 Gulf Blvd., St. Pete Beach* ☎ *727/360–7411* 🌐 *www.dolphinlandings.com.* **Hubbard's Marina** ✉ *170 John's Pass, Madeira Beach* ☎ *727/393–1947* 🌐 *www.hubbardsmarina.com.* **St. Nicholas Boat Line** ✉ *693 Dodecanese Blvd., Tarpon Springs* ☎ *727/942–6425.* ***Starlite Cruises*** ✉ *Clearwater Beach Marina, 25 Causeway Blvd., at end of Rte. 60, Clearwater Beach* ☎ *727/462–2628* 🌐 *www.starlitecruises.com.*

BUS AND TROLLEY TRAVEL

Hillsborough Area Regional Transit and TECO Line Street Cars replicate Tampa's first electric streetcars, transporting cruise-ship passengers to Ybor City and downtown Tampa. Pinellas Suncoast Transit Authority offers bus service throughout Pinellas County, from the county's inland parts out to the beaches. PSTA also runs the Suncoast Beach Trolley, which takes passengers up and down the beaches—from Pass-A-Grille all the way up to Clearwater Beach and downtown Clearwater—for $2 each way.

Manatee County Area Transit (MCAT) has buses throughout Bradenton and the nearby towns of Palmetto and Ellenton, as well as connections to Sarasota attractions. Service is inexpensive, but it's really no substitute for a car.

St. Petersburg Trolley will get you to key destinations throughout downtown St. Pete, and even offers free service between the Chamber of Commerce Visitor's Bureau and certain destinations.

Contacts **Hillsborough Area Regional Transit** ☎ *813/254–4278* 🌐 *www.gohart.org.* **Pinellas Suncoast Transit Authority** ☎ *727/540–1900* 🌐 *www.psta.net.* **St. Petersburg Trolley** ☎ *727/821–5166* 🌐 *www.stpetetrolley.com.* **TECO Line Street Cars** ☎ *813/254–4278* 🌐 *www.tecolinestreetcar.org.*

CAR TRAVEL

Interstates 75 and 275 span the Bay Area from north to south. Coming from Orlando, you're likely to drive west into Tampa on Interstate 4. Along with Interstate 75, U.S. 41 (the Tamiami Trail) stretches the length of the region and links the business districts of many communities; avoid this route during rush hours (7–9 am and 4–6 pm).

TRAIN TRAVEL

Amtrak trains run from the Northeast, the Midwest, and much of the South into Tampa; the Tampa station is at 601 N. Nebraska Avenue.

Train Contacts **Amtrak** ☎ *800/872–7245* 🌐 *www.amtrak.com.*

HOTELS

Many convention hotels in the Tampa Bay area double as family-friendly resorts—taking advantage of nearby beaches, marinas, spas, tennis courts, and golf links. However, unlike Orlando and some other parts of Florida, the area has been bustling for more than a century, and its accommodations often reflect a sense of its history.

You'll find a turn-of-the-20th-century beachfront resort where Zelda and F. Scott Fitzgerald stayed, a massive all-wood building from the 1920s, plenty of art deco, and Spanish-style villas. But one thing they all have in common is a certain Gulf Coast charm.

For expanded reviews, facilities, and current deals, visit Fodors.com.

RESTAURANTS

Fresh gulf seafood is plentiful—raw bars serving oysters, clams, and mussels are everywhere. Tampa's many Cuban and Spanish restaurants serve paella with seafood and chicken, *boliche criollo* (sausage-stuffed eye-round roast) with black beans and rice, *ropa vieja* (shredded flank steak in tomato sauce), and other treats. Tarpon Springs adds classic Greek specialties. In Sarasota the emphasis is on ritzier dining, though many restaurants offer extra-cheap early-bird menus.

HOTEL AND RESTAURANT COSTS

Prices in the restaurant reviews are the average cost of a main course at dinner or, if dinner is not served, at lunch. Prices in the hotel reviews are the lowest cost of a standard double room in high season. Prices do not include taxes (6%, more in some counties, and 1%–5% tourist tax for hotel rooms).

WHAT IT COSTS

	$	$$	$$$	$$$$
Restaurants	under $15	$15–$20	$21–$30	over $30
Hotels	under $100	$101–$140	$141–$220	over $220

VISITOR INFORMATION

Contacts Bradenton Area Convention and Visitors Bureau. This organization has all you need to know about everything Bradenton, Anna Maria Island, Palmetto, and Ellenton have to offer. ☎ *941/729–9177* 🌐 *www.bradentongulfislands.com.* **Manatee County Area Transit** 🌐 *www.mymanatee.org.* **Sarasota Convention and Visitors Bureau.** This organization has the skinny on South Tampa Bay. ✉ *701 N. Tamiami Trail, Sarasota* ☎ *941/957–1877* 🌐 *www.sarasotafl.org.* **Tampa Bay & Company** ✉ *401 E. Jackson St., Suite 2100, Tampa* ☎ *800/448–2672, 813/223–1111* 🌐 *www.visittampabay.com.* **Tampa Bay Beaches Chamber of Commerce.** The staff here will give you the lowdown on the Pinellas County beaches. ✉ *6990 Gulf Blvd., St. Pete Beach* ☎ *727/360–6957* 🌐 *www.tampabaybeaches.com.*

TAMPA

84 miles southwest of Orlando via I–4.

Tampa, the west coast's business-and-commercial hub, has a sprinkling of high-rises and heavy traffic. A concentration of restaurants, nightlife, stores, and cultural events is amid the bustle. The city has really come into its own in recent years. The downtown Tampa waterfront features stunning views and excellent museums. Animal lovers flock here for attractions like Lowry Park Zoo, Busch Gardens, Big Cat Rescue, and Giraffe Ranch. Revelers will enjoy the strip of bars and clubs that constitutes Ybor City, a historic area with a heavy Cuban influence. The city also abounds with art museums, shops, and a wide array of restaurants. Downtown and Ybor City are both excellent spots to look for live music. Not too far out of town are some great golf courses and nature trails. Tampa is also a short drive from a long stretch of gorgeous Gulf Coast beaches.

GETTING AROUND

Downtown Tampa's Riverwalk, on Ashley Drive at the Hillsborough River, connects waterside entities such as the Florida Aquarium, the Channelside shopping-and-entertainment complex, and Marriott Waterside. The landscaped park is 6 acres and extends along the Garrison cruise-ship channel and along the Hillsborough River downtown. The walkway is being expanded as waterside development continues.

Although downtown Tampa, the Channelside District, and Ybor City are easy to navigate without a car, you'll want to rent one if you plan on hitting the beaches or heading to Busch Gardens, Hyde Park, International Plaza, or any of the zoos.

VISITOR INFORMATION

Contacts Tampa Bay & Company ✉ *401 E. Jackson St., Suite 2100* ☎ *800/448–2672, 813/223–1111* 🌐 *www.visittampabay.com.* **Tampa Bay Beaches Chamber of Commerce.** The staff here will give you the lowdown on the Pinellas County beaches. ✉ *6990 Gulf Blvd., St. Pete Beach* ☎ *727/360–6957* 🌐 *www.tampabaybeaches.com.* **Ybor City Chamber Visitor Bureau** ✉ *1800 E. 9th Ave.* ☎ *813/248–3712* 🌐 *www.ybor.org.*

EXPLORING

TOP ATTRACTIONS

Fodor's Choice ★ **Big Cat Rescue.** Suburban Citrus Park in North Tampa is probably the last place you'd expect to be able to get face-to-face with an 800-pound tiger. Yet at the end of a shaded road just yards off the Veterans' Expressway, you can do just that. This rescue center is home base for a nonprofit organization that serves as a sanctuary for tigers, ocelots, bobcats, cougars, and members of any other large cat species you can imagine. Each and every one of these marvelous creatures has a unique story. Some arrived here after narrowly avoiding becoming an expensive coat. Others were kept as pets until the owners realized how pricey 15 pounds of meat per day (what it takes to feed some of these creatures) can be. They're all kept in large enclosures. A volunteer guide will lead you around the property and tell you every cat's story. You'll also get an earful of little-known facts about these big cats, from the true origin of the white tiger to why some cats have white spots on the backs of their ears. Tours (no unescorted visits are allowed) are every day but Thursday, but kids under 10 are only allowed on a special kids' tour at 9 am on Saturday and Sunday. Night tours, feeding tours, and appointment-only private tours are also available. ✉ *12802 Easy St., Citrus Park* ☎ *813/920–4130* 🌐 *bigcatrescue.org* 🎫 *$29* 🕒 *Mon.–Wed. and Fri. at 3 pm; weekends at 10 am and 1 pm; kids' tour weekends at 9 am. Other special tours available by reservation only, at varying costs.*

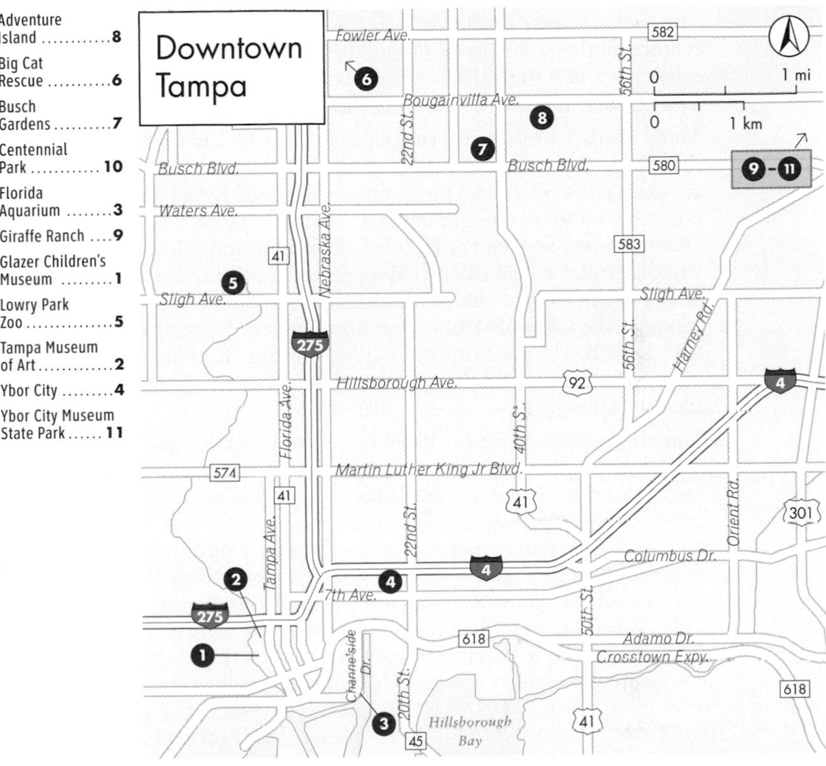

FAMILY **Fodor's Choice ★** **Busch Gardens.** The Jungala exhibit at Busch Gardens brings Bengal tigers to center stage and puts them at eye level—allowing you to view them from underground caves and underwater windows. The big cats are just one of the reasons the theme park attracts some 4.5 million visitors each year. This is a world-class zoo, with more than 2,000 animals, and a live-entertainment venue that provides a full day (or more) of fun for the whole family. If you want to beat the crowds, start in the back of the park and work your way around clockwise.

The 335-acre adventure park's habitats offer views of some of the world's most endangered and exotic animals. For the best animal sightings, go to their habitats early, when it's cooler. You can experience up-close animal encounters on the Serengeti Plain, a 65-acre free-roaming habitat, home to reticulated giraffes, Grevy's zebras, white rhinos, bongos, impalas, and more. Myombe Reserve allows you to view lowland gorillas and chimpanzees in a lush, tropical-rain-forest environment. Down Under–themed Walkabout Way offers those ages 5 and up an opportunity to hand-feed kangaroos and wallabies (a cup of vittles is $5).

Interested in watching a tiger get a dental checkup? Then head over to the Animal Care & Nutrition Center, where you can observe veterinary care for many of the park's animals.

The park's newest thrill ride is Falcon's Fury, a 335-foot drop that is reportedly the tallest freestanding drop ride on the continent. It's the centerpiece of a the park's newest "land," Pantopia, a colorful collection of rides, cafés, and retail space that replaces its Timbuktu section.

Many consider the seven roller coasters to be the biggest lure. On the wings of an African hawk, SheiKra—North America's first dive coaster—takes riders on a three-minute journey 200 feet up, then (gulp!) plunges 90 degrees straight down at 70 mph. The park's coaster lineup also includes steel giants Kumba, Scorpion, and Montu; a double, wooden roller coaster called Gwazi; and Sand Serpent, a five-story family coaster full of hairpin turns and breathtaking dips. When it's running, the Cheetah Hunt is an absolutely exhilarating 4,429-foot-high launch coaster. With three different launch points, this coaster takes you through the Serengeti and into a rocky gorge with a top speed of 60 mph.

The off-road-safari Rhino Rally brings you face-to-face with zebras, elephants, and white rhinos. Catering to the shorter set, the Sesame Street Safari of Fun is a 5-acre kids' playground with Sesame-themed rides, shows, and water adventures. The Air Grover Rollercoaster takes kids (and parents) on minidives and twisty turns over the Sahara, while Jungle Flyers gets them swinging and screeching. If you're looking to cool off, your best bets are Congo River Rapids, Tanganyika Tidal Wave, Stanleyville Falls (a flume ride), or Bert & Ernie's Water Hole—complete with bubblers, geysers, water jets, and dumping buckets. Character lunches are available (but you might want to wait until after your rides). ✉ *10165 N. Malcolm McKinley Dr., Central Tampa* ☎ *813/987–5000, 888/800–5447* 🌐 *www.buschgardens.com* 🎫 *$92; parking $15* ⏲ *Daily 9:30–6.*

FAMILY **Florida Aquarium.** Although eels, sharks, and stingrays are the headliners, the Florida Aquarium is much more than a giant fishbowl. This architectural landmark features an 83-foot-high, multitier, glass dome; 250,000 square feet of air-conditioned exhibit space; and more than 20,000 aquatic plants and animals representing species native to Florida and the rest of the world—from black-tip sharks to leafy sea dragons.

Floor-to-ceiling interactive displays, behind-the-scenes tours, and in-water adventures allow kids to really get hands-on—and even get their feet wet. Adventurous types (certified divers age 15 and up) can dive with mild-mannered sharks and sea turtles, participate in shark-feeding programs (age 12 and up), or shallow-water swim with reef fish such as eels and grouper (age 6 and up).

However, you don't have to get wet to have an interactive experience: the Ocean Commotion exhibit offers virtual dolphins and whales and multimedia displays and presentations. The Coral Reef Gallery is a 500,000-gallon tank with viewing windows, an awesome 43-foot-wide panoramic opening, and a walk-through tunnel that gives the illusion of venturing into underwater depths. There you see a thicket of elkhorn coral teeming with tropical fish, and a dark cave reveals sea life you would normally see only on night dives. The new Journey to Madagascar exhibit features ring-tailed lemurs, hissing cockroaches, and an

Indian Ocean coral reef to showcase the nation's vast diversity of creatures and ecosystems.

If you have an extra 90 minutes, try the Wild Dolphin Adventure Cruise, which takes up to 130 passengers onto Tampa Bay in a 72-foot catamaran for an up-close look at bottlenose dolphins and other wildlife. The outdoor Explore a Shore exhibit, which gives younger kids a chance to release some energy, is an aquatic playground with a waterslide, water-jet sprays, and a climbable replica pirate ship. Last but not least, two black-footed South African penguins make daily appearances in the Coral Reef Gallery. For an extra cost, you can get an up-close look at the daily lives of these penguins during the half-hour-long Penguins: Backstage Pass demonstration. ✉ *701 Channelside Dr., Downtown* ☎ *813/273–4000* 🌐 *www.flaquarium.org* 🎫 *Aquarium $21.95; Aquarium/Adventure Cruise combo $37.95; Penguins: Backstage Pass combo $48.95; Behind the Scenes Combo $29.95; Dive with the Sharks $175; Swim with the Fishes $75; parking $6* 🕒 *Daily 9:30–5.*

OFF THE BEATEN PATH

Giraffe Ranch. Rural Dade City is known mostly for its strawberries, but word is quickly spreading about something else that makes people flock here: giraffes. These graceful creatures are the headliners at this nearly 50-acre ranch. You can view them as part of a safari-style vehicle tour or from the back of a camel; on either tour, you can hand-feed them cabbage leaves. You'll also see tons of zebras, a pair of pygmy hippos, a couple of rhinos, ostriches, and many other animal species roaming the grounds. Near the ranch's welcome center and gift shop is a corral of enclosures where you can watch guinea pigs chomp on sweet-potato chunks, hold a baby goat, and, for a little extra cash, feed grapes to lemurs or bathe a rhino. The ranch's proprietors have encyclopedic knowledge of the animal kingdom, and the overall experience is meant to impart a sense of connection to the animal world—and the environment—on those who visit. Tours take about two hours, and reservations are required. Credit cards are not accepted. ✉ *38650 Mickler Rd., Dade City* ☎ *813/482–3400* 🌐 *www.girafferanch.com* 🎫 *$69 for tour in safari van; $150 for tour by camelback* 🕒 *Tours daily at 11 am and 2 pm, by reservation only.*

FAMILY **Glazer Children's Museum.** It's all about play here, and with 53,000-square-feet, more than a dozen themed areas, and 175 "interactives," there's plenty of opportunity for it. Areas designed to nurture imagination and strengthen confidence allow children and families to experience everything from flying an airplane to shopping for groceries. Kids can also create art, control the weather, navigate a mini–shipping channel, and "drive" a miniature (stationary) fire truck through Tampa. A Water's Journey Tree lets kids climb the tree to the second floor and mimics the water cycle. ✉ *110 W. Gasparilla Plaza, Downtown* ☎ *813/443–3861* 🌐 *wwww.glazermuseum.org* 🎫 *$15 adult; $9.50 children* 🕒 *Weekdays 10–5, Sat. 10–6, Sun. 1–6.*

FAMILY **Lowry Park Zoo.** Natural-habitat exhibits include Safari Africa, where a herd of African elephants (including two calves) is free to roam, make the 56-acre Lowry Park Zoo one of the best midsize zoos in the country. Asia gardens features two clouded snow leopards, and residents of the

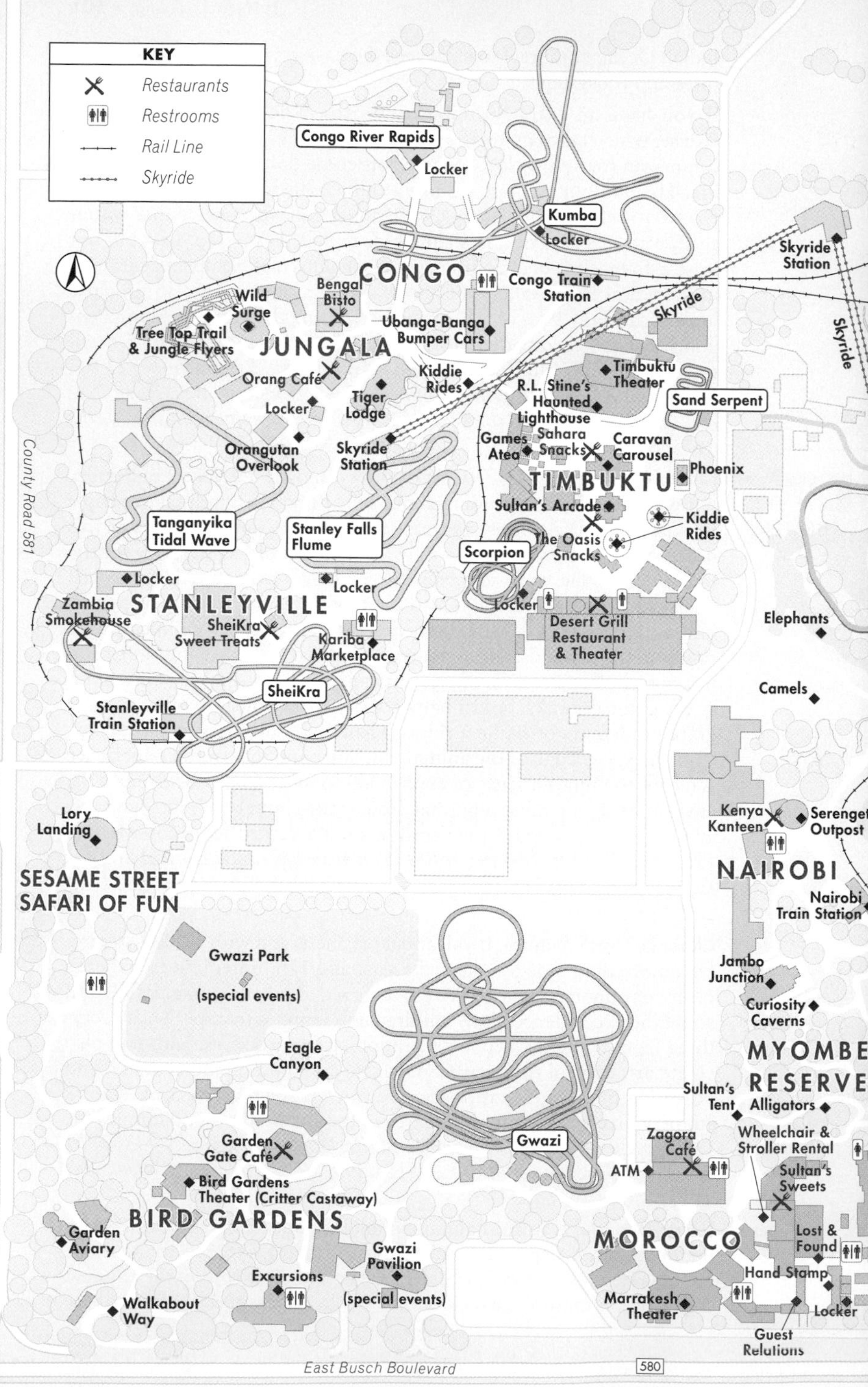
KEY
Restaurants
Restrooms
Rail Line
Skyride
Congo River Rapids
Locker
Kumba
Locker
Skyride Station
CONGO
Congo Train Station
Skyride
Skyride
Bengal Bisto
Wild Surge
Tree Top Trail & Jungle Flyers
JUNGALA
Ubanga-Banga Bumper Cars
Orang Café
Kiddie Rides
Timbuktu Theater
Tiger Lodge
R.L. Stine's Haunted Lighthouse
Sand Serpent
Locker
Orangutan Overlook
Skyride Station
Games Atea
Sahara Snacks
Caravan Carousel
Phoenix
TIMBUKTU
County Road 581
Sultan's Arcade
Kiddie Rides
Tanganyika Tidal Wave
Stanley Falls Flume
The Oasis Snacks
Scorpion
Locker
Locker
Zambia Smokehouse
STANLEYVILLE
Locker
Desert Grill Restaurant & Theater
Elephants
SheiKra Sweet Treats
Kariba Marketplace
SheiKra
Camels
Stanleyville Train Station
Lory Landing
Kenya Kanteen
Serengeti Outpost
SESAME STREET SAFARI OF FUN
NAIROBI
Nairobi Train Station
Gwazi Park
(special events)
Jambo Junction
Curiosity Caverns
Eagle Canyon
MYOMBE RESERVE
Sultan's Tent
Alligators
Garden Gate Café
Gwazi
Zagora Café
Wheelchair & Stroller Rental
ATM
Sultan's Sweets
Bird Gardens Theater (Critter Castaway)
BIRD GARDENS
Garden Aviary
MOROCCO
Lost & Found
Gwazi Pavilion
Excursions
Hand Stamp
(special events)
Walkabout Way
Marrakesh Theater
Locker
Guest Relations
East Busch Boulevard
580

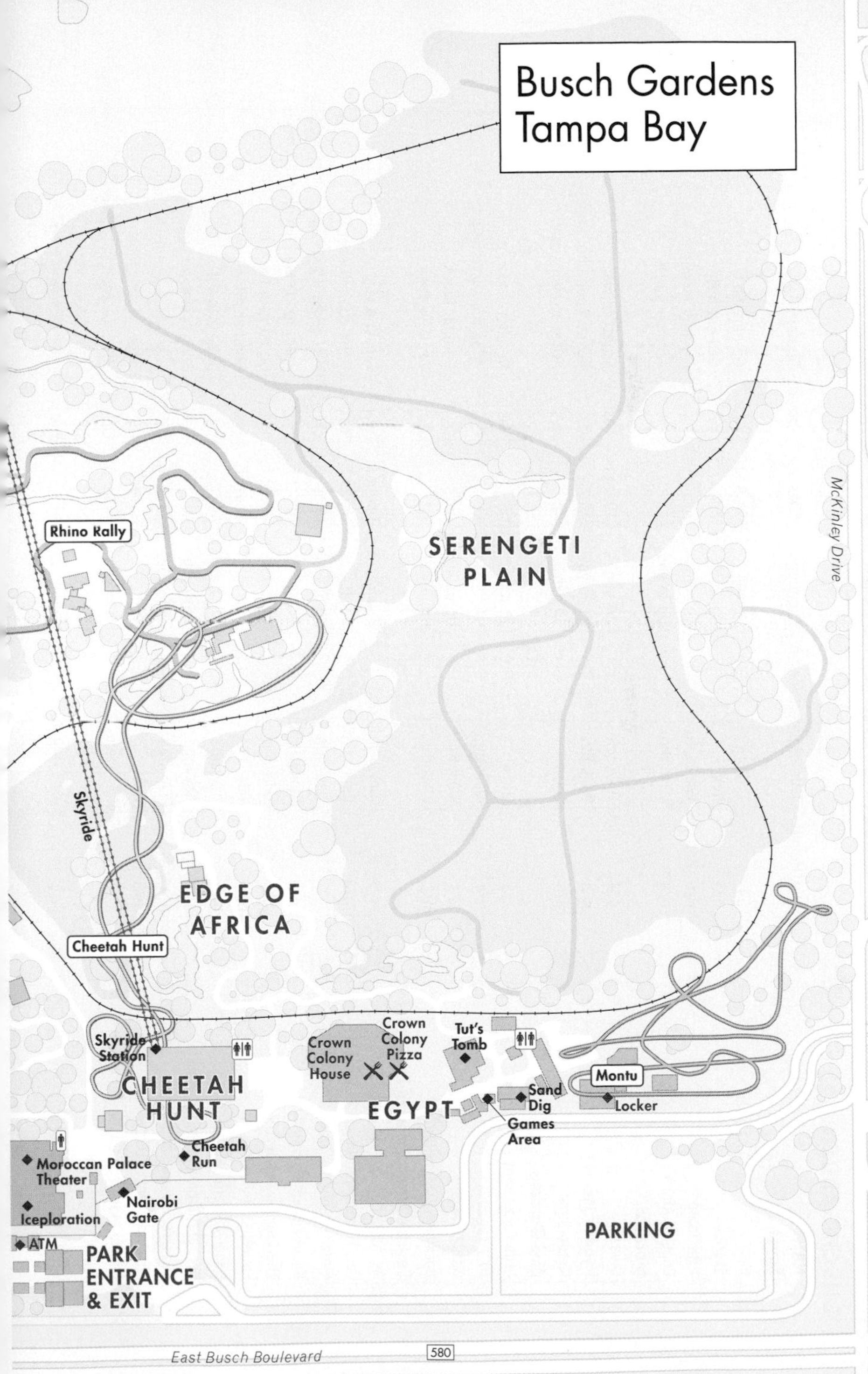
Busch Gardens
Tampa Bay
Rhino Rally
SERENGETI
PLAIN
McKinley Drive
Skyride
EDGE OF
AFRICA
Cheetah Hunt
Skyride
Station
CHEETAH
HUNT
Crown
Colony
House
Crown
Colony
Pizza
Tut's
Tomb
EGYPT
Sand
Dig
Games
Area
Montu
Locker
Cheetah
Run
Moroccan Palace
Theater
Nairobi
Gate
Iceploration
ATM
PARK
ENTRANCE
& EXIT
PARKING
East Busch Boulevard
580

BUSCH GARDENS

NAME	Min. Height	Type of Entertainment	Duration	Suits	Crowds	Strategy
Egypt						
Montu	54"	Thrill ride	3 min.	14 & up	Yes!	Go here first
Skyride	n/a	Ride	5 min.	All	Yes	Can get busy
Tut's Tomb	n/a	Walk thru	10 min.	All	OK	Go after Montu
Edge of Africa	n/a	Walk thru	Up to you	All	OK	Go after lunch
Morocco						
Gwazi	48"	Thrill ride	2.5 min.	10 & up	Yes!	Expect to wait
Myombe Reserve	n/a	Walk thru	Up to you	All	OK	Before noon photo op
Iceploration	n/a	Show	30 min.	All	Yes	Arrive 15 min. early
Bird Gardens						
Critter Castaway	n/a	Show	25 min.	All	Yes	Do after Gwazi
Lory Landing	n/a	Walk thru	Up to you	All	OK	Bring money to feed
Garden Aviary	n/a	Walk thru	Up to you	All	OK	Go after lunch
Backyard Wildlife Habitat	n/a	Walk thru	Up to you	All	Yes	Good anytime
Sesame Street Safari of Fun						
Air Grover	n/a	Junior thrill ride	2 min.	Under 6	Yes!	Expect a wait
Zoe-Petra & the Hippos of the Nile	n/a	Junior thrill ride	3 min.	Under 6	Yes	Good cool-off spot
Elmo's Treehouse Trek	n/a	Play area	Up to you	Under 6	OK	May be hard to keep track of toddlers
Rosita's Djembe Fly-Away	n/a	Junior thrill ride	2 min.	Under 6	Yes	Older toddlers may enjoy this more
The Count's Zambezi Rally	n/a	Ride	Up to you	Under 6	Yes	Go early in the day
Elmo's Safari Go-Round	n/a	Ride	3 min.	Under 6	Yes	Good anytime
Oscar's Swamp Stomp	n/a	Play area	Up to you	All	OK	Bring a towel
Bert and Ernie's Watering Hole	n/a	Play area	Up to you	All	OK	Bring a bathing suit
Slimey's Sawara Sand	n/a	Play area	Up to you	All	OK	Chance for parents to relax
Big Bird's Whirly Birdy	n/a	Ride	3 min.	Under 6	OK	Excellent for toddlers
Cookie Monster's Canopy Crawl	n/a	Play area	Up to you	Under 6	OK	Good for energetic children
Telly's Jungle Jam	n/a	Play area	Up to you	All	OK	Slow- paced area
Big Bird's 123-Smile With Me	n/a	Walk thru	Up to you	All	Yes	Photo/autograph op

Stanleyville						
SheiKra	54"	Thrill ride	2.5 min.	14 & up	Yes!	Use the lockers
Stanley Falls Flume	46"	Thrill ride	3 min.	10 & up	Yes	Lengthy lines
Tanganyika Tidal Wave	48"	Thrill ride	2 min.	10 & up	Yes	Bring a change of clothes or poncho
Jungala						
Jungle Flyers	48"	Junior thrill ride	3 min.	6 to 13	Yes	Skip for other rides
Wild Surge	38"	Thrill ride	2 min.	5 & up	Yes!	
Tree Top Trails	n/a	Walk thru	Up to you	All	Yes	Gets crowded
Tiger Lodge	n/a	Walk thru	Up to you	All	Yes	Close-up views
Orangutan Overlook	n/a	Walk thru	Up to you	All	Yes	Morning photo op
Jungala Stiltwalkers	n/a	Show	15 min.	All	OK	Very entertaining
Congo						
Congo River Rapids	42"	Thrill ride	6 min.	10 & up	Yes!	Bring extra clothes or poncho
Kumba	54"	Thrill ride	3 min.	14 & up	Yes!	Go early or before closing
Ubanga-Banga Bumper Cars	42"	Ride	2 min.	8 & up	Yes	Long wait times
Timbuktu						
Animal Care Center	n/a	Educational Exhibit	n/a	5 & up	No	
Carousel Caravan	n/a	Ride	3 min.	All	OK	Slow-paced ride
Cheetah Hunt		Thrill ride	3.5 min.	12 & up	Yes!	Newer ride, expect lines
Pirate 4-D Movie	n/a	Show	15 min.	All	OK	Arrive 15 min. early
Phoenix	48"	Thrill ride	2 min.	12 & up	Yes	Go after Scorpion
Sand Serpent	46"	Junior thrill ride	2 min.	All	Yes	Very popular
Scorpion	42"	Thrill ride	2 min.	14 & up	Yes	Go during Dance to the Music show
Dance to the Music	n/a	Seasonal show	20 min.	All	Yes	Arrive 15 min. before show
Sesame Street Presents Lights, Camera, Action!	n/a	Show	20 min.	All	OK	Good break from the sun
Nairobi						
Rhino Rally	39"	Vehicle ride	10 min.	10 & up	Yes	This ride is bumpy—hold on to your valuables
Serengeti Express	n/a	Vehicle ride	12–35 min.	All	No	Great way to relax and see the park
Curiosity Caverns	n/a	Walk thru	Up to you	All	No	Good to get out of the sun
Elephant Habitat	n/a	Walk thru	Up to you	All	OK	Go during Meet the Keeper
Rhino Habitat	n/a	Walk thru	Up to you	All	Yes	Earlier the better
Edge of Africa	n/a	Walk thru	Up to you	All	OK	Great break from the crowds

DID YOU KNOW?

One of six roller coasters at Busch Gardens, the steel, 60-foot-tall Scorpion twists and turns at speeds near 50 mph and then throws you into a 360-degree vertical loop. During the two-minute ride you'll experience a 3.5 g-force.

nearby Ituri Forest include a cheetah and lovably plump pygmy hippos. As you stroll through, keep an eye out for okapis, a rare forest giraffe from Central Africa. The stars at Primate World range from cat-size lemurs to a family of heavyweight Bornean orangutans that love to ham for the camera.

For hands-on experiences, Lowry has more options than most large parks, including chances to feed a giraffe, hold a colorful lorikeet, or touch a slippery stingray. Majestic red-tailed hawks and other raptors put on a show at the Birds of Prey Center, and a flock of majestic macaws soars through the zoo in a one-of-a-kind free-flight experience each day at 10 and 2. You can come face-to-face with Florida manatees at the Manatee Aquatic Center, the only nonprofit manatee hospital on the planet.

Dwindling native species like Florida panthers, black bears, and red wolves may be tough to find in the wild, but you can easily find them at the Florida Wildlife Center. Kookaburras, koala, emus, and wallabies populate the Wallaroo Station children's zoo. There are also water-play areas, rides (all of which are included with zoo admission), shows, and restaurants. ✉ *1101 W. Sligh Ave., Central Tampa* ☎ *813/935–8552* 🌐 *www.lowryparkzoo.com* 🎟 *$24.95* 🕓 *Daily 9:30–5.*

Fodor's Choice ★ **Ybor City.** Tampa's lively Latin quarter is one of only a few National Historic Landmark districts in Florida. Bordered by I–4 to the north, 22nd Street to the east, Adamo Drive to the south, and Nebraska Avenue to the West, it has antique-brick streets and wrought-iron balconies. Cubans brought their cigar-making industry to Ybor (pronounced *ee-bore*) City in 1886, and the smell of cigars—hand-rolled by Cuban immigrants—still wafts through the heart of this east Tampa area, along with the strong aroma of roasting coffee. These days the neighborhood is one of Tampa's hot spots, if at times a rowdy one, as empty cigar factories and historic social clubs have been transformed into trendy boutiques, art galleries, restaurants, and nightclubs. ✉ *Ybor City.*

WORTH NOTING

FAMILY **Adventure Island.** From spring until fall, rides named Everglides, Gulf Scream, and Key West Rapids promise heat relief at Busch Gardens' water park. Tampa's most popular "wet" park features waterslides and artificial wave pools, along with tranquil "beaches" in a 30-acre package. One of the attraction's headliners, Riptide, challenges you to race three other riders on a sliding mat through twisting tubes and hairpin turns. Planners of this park also took the younger kids into account, with offerings such as Fabian's Funport, which has a scaled-down pool and interactive water gym. Along with a volleyball complex and a rambling river, there are cafés, snack bars, picnic and sunbathing areas, changing rooms, and private cabanas. ✉ *10001 N. McKinley Dr., less than 1 mile north of Busch Gardens, Central Tampa* ☎ *813/987–5660, 888/800–5447* 🌐 *www.adventureisland.com* 🎟 *$47; parking $12* 🕓 *Mid-Mar.–Aug., daily 10–5; Sept. and Oct., weekends only 10–5.*

Centennial Park. You can step back into the past at Centennial Park, which re-creates a period streetscape and hosts a farmer's market called the "Fresh Market" every Saturday, among a host of other events like festivals and pottery classes. ✉ *1800 E. 8th Ave., Ybor City.*

Tampa Museum of Art. Housed in an exquisitely designed new building, the Tampa Museum of Art is emblematic of the city's efforts to revitalize the downtown riverfront. The facility overlooks Curtis Hixon Park, the towering minarets of the University of Tampa, and the Hillsborough River. The museum's 66,000 square feet of gallery space displays an impressive permanent collection of 20th- and 21st-century sculpture as well as Greek and Roman antiquities. Five additional galleries host traveling exhibits ranging from the classics to some of the most prominent artists working today. Also notable is Sono, the museum's café, which is operated by Mise en Place, one of Tampa's top restaurants. ✉ *120 W. Gasparilla Plaza, Downtown* ☎ *813/274–8130* 🌐 *www.tampamuseum.org* 🎫 *$10* ⏲ *Mon.–Thurs. 11–7, Fri. 11–8, weekends 11–5.*

Ybor City Museum State Park. This park provides a look at the history of the cigar industry. Admission includes a tour of La Casita, one of the shotgun houses occupied by cigar workers and their families in the late 1890s, held every half-hour between 10 am and 3 pm. ✉ *1818 E. 9th Ave., between Nuccio Pkwy. and 22nd St. from 7th to 9th Aves., Ybor City* ☎ *813/247–6323* 🌐 *www.ybormuseum.org* 🎫 *$4* ⏲ *Daily 9–5.*

WHERE TO EAT

$$$$ STEAKHOUSE Fodor'sChoice ★

Bern's Steak House. With the air of an exclusive club, this is one of Florida's finest steak houses. Rich mahogany paneling and ornate chandeliers define the legendary Bern's, where the chef ages his own beef, grows much of his own produce, and roasts his own coffee. There's also a Cave Du Fromage, housing a discriminating selection of artisanal cheeses from around the world. Cuts of topmost beef are sold by weight and thickness. There's a 60-ounce strip steak that's big enough to feed your pride (of lions), but for most appetites the veal loin chop or 8-ounce chateaubriand is more than enough. The wine list includes approximately 7,000 selections (with 1,000 dessert wines). After dinner, tour the kitchen and wine cellar before having dessert upstairs in a cozy booth. The dessert room is a hit. For a real jolt, try the Turkish coffee with an order of Mississippi mud pie. Casual business attire is recommended. Those looking for the Bern's touch but aren't up for donning a jacket and tie should opt for Side Bern's, the steak house's more low-key sister property a few blocks up the road. 💲 *Average main: $32* ✉ *1208 S. Howard Ave., Hyde Park* ☎ *813/251–2421* 🌐 *www.bernssteakhouse.com* ✍ *Reservations essential* 👔 *Jacket and tie.*

$$$ ASIAN FUSION

BT. Local restaurateur B. T. Nguyen has earned quite a following since opening her first eatery more than two decades ago. Her modern take on conscientiously sourced local ingredients fits well within its upscale South Tampa surroundings, and the high-style Vietnamese cuisine features fresh herbs grown on-site and a drink list that includes organic sake martinis—some flavored with herbs from that same garden. With a motto like "eat local, think global," the menu is inevitably sophisticated yet simple, with creative offerings like Shaken beef, a go-to dish for regulars, consisting of cubed filet mignon flavored with cognac and shallots. Vegetarians and vegans can rest easy here, with options such as Food Karma (braised tofu, edamame, eggplant, and ginger in coconut broth over black rice). Casual dress is acceptable, but patrons tend to dress up. *Average main: $28* *2507 S. MacDill Ave., Suite B, Hyde Park* *813/258–1916* *www.restaurantbt.com.*

$$ ECLECTIC **Café Dufrain.** Dogs can tag along if you dine on the front patio at pet-friendly Café Dufrain, an eatery right on the Hollsborough River across from the Tampa Bay Times Forum. Creative menu items, which vary by season, include fried chicken and waffles (a Southern classic) and ceviche with sweet potato and toasted macadamia nuts. The bar menu has a nice selection of craft beers. In mild weather, opt for the waterfront view of downtown Tampa. *Average main: $20* *707 Harbour Post Dr., Downtown* *813/275–9701* *www.cafedufrain.com.*

$ PIZZA **Cappy's Pizza.** Chicago may be the first place you think of when you hear the words "deep dish pizza," which is why the high-quality pies this local chain offers may surprise (and please) you. The menu at this family-friendly spot is pretty simple: choose either a Chicago- or New York–style crust, and select your toppings. The "Cappy" features a blend of pepperoni, ham, onions, green pepper, sausage, and mushrooms. You can also go with a calzone. There's no hostess here, so put your name on the (usually long) list you see when you first walk in. If it's not too packed, try to get garden seating. The feel inside is very nostalgic—vintage signs and an old toy train set adorn the walls. You'll find a lengthy list of craft brews, and the kids might enjoy an IBC root beer. This location is cash-only, but there is an ATM on-site. *Average main: $12* *4910 N. Florida Ave., Seminole Heights* *813/238–1516* *cappyspizzaonline.com* *Reservations not accepted* *No credit cards* *No lunch.*

$$ SPANISH Fodor's Choice ★ **Columbia.** Make a date for some of the best Latin cuisine in Tampa. A fixture since 1905, this magnificent structure with an old-world air and spacious dining rooms takes up an entire city block and seems to feed the entire city—locals as well as visitors—throughout the week, but especially on weekends. The paella, bursting with seafood, chicken, and pork, is arguably the best in Florida, and the 1905 salad—with ham, olives, cheese, and garlic—is legendary. The menu has Cuban classics such as *boliche criollo* (tender eye of round stuffed with chorizo), *ropa vieja* (shredded beef with onions, peppers, and tomatoes), and *arroz con pollo* (chicken with yellow rice). Don't miss the flamenco dancing show every night but Sunday. This place is also known for its sangria. If you can, walk around the building and check out the elaborate, antique decor along every inch of the interior. *Average main: $19* *2117 E. 7th Ave., Ybor City* *813/248–4961* *www.columbiarestaurant.com.*

$ SOUTHERN **Kojak's House of Ribs.** Few barbecue joints can boast the staying power of this family-owned and -operated pit stop. Located along a shaded stretch in South Tampa, it debuted in 1978 and has since earned a following of sticky-fingered regulars who have turned it into one of the most popular barbecue stops in central Florida. It's located in a 1927 house complete with veranda, pillars supporting the overhanging roof, and brick steps. Day and night, three indoor dining rooms and an outdoor dining porch have a steady stream of hungry patrons digging into tender pork spareribs that are dry-rubbed and tanned overnight before visiting the smoker for a couple of hours. Then they're bathed in the sauce of your choice. Kojak's also has a nice selection of sandwiches, including chopped barbecue chicken and country-style sausage. This is definitely not the kind of place you'd want to bring a vegan. *Average main: $14 ✉ 2808 Gandy Blvd., South Tampa ☎ 813/837–3774 🌐 kojaksbbq.net ⏲ Closed Mon.*

$ HOT DOG

✕ **Mel's Hot Dogs.** This is a must after a long day of riding roller coasters and scoping out zebras at Busch Gardens. Visitors as well as passersby usually are greeted by a red wiener-mobile parked on the north side of the highway near Busch Gardens. Venture inside to find walls dotted with photos from fans and a hot-diggity menu that's heaven for tube-steak fans. You can order a traditional dog, but try something with a little more pizzazz, such as a bacon-cheddar Reuben-style bowwow on a poppy-seed bun, or the Mighty Mel, a quarter-pounder decked out with relish, mustard, and pickles. Herbivores, fear not: there's a vegan option on the menu, and it's mighty tasty. To avoid lunch crowds, arrive before 11:30 or after 1:30. *Average main: $8 ✉ 4136 E. Busch Blvd., Central Tampa ☎ 813/985–8000 🌐 www.melshotdogs.com 💳 No credit cards ⏲ Closed Sun.*

$$$ MODERN AMERICAN

✕ **Mise en Place.** Known to locals as "Mise" (pronounced *meez*), this upscale, modern downtown space is a popular lunch spot for Tampa's political and social elite. At night, it transforms into an elegant, understated dining destination with a menu that offers adventurous yet meticulously crafted modern American cuisine. The menu changes every week, save for staples like the chicken liver pâté and the rack of lamb. Another thing that doesn't change is the intricacy of every item listed—whether it's tandoori-crusted tofu or pumpkin-spiced rubbed scallops. The long list of boutique wines and specialty cocktails further demonstrate the intelligence and imagination that go into the crafting of the menu. This place is on the western edge of downtown, just across the street from University of Tampa's shining minarets. Parking and entry are behind the building. *Average main: $29 ✉ 442 W. Kennedy Blvd., Suite 110, Downtown ☎ 813/254–5373 🌐 www.miseonline.com ⏲ Closed Sun. and Mon.*

OFF THE BEATEN PATH

✕ **Pearl in the Grove.** For those who need a break from the urban sprawl, or are just in search of a decent early dinner after a Giraffe Ranch excursion, this farm-to-table eatery will hit the spot. Situated in an old one-story farmhouse in the middle of a kumquat grove, this spot serves as a low-key escape for the most cultured of Tampa Bay residents (though casual dress is fine here). Popular dishes include, as one might expect, fried green tomatoes, shrimp creole, honey-chili-glazed quail, and rabbit confit, but keep in mind that the menu is ever-changing with the seasons. The beer menu features local brews, and the wine list is extensive. Brunch (11–2) is offered Sunday. *Average main: $20 ✉ 31916 St. Joe Rd., Dade City ☎ 352/588–0008 🌐 pearlinthegrove.com ✍ Reservations essential ⏲ Closed Mon. and Tues. No lunch. No dinner Sun.*

$ MEXICAN

✕ **Taco Bus.** It's a Mexican joint with a simple name in a less-than-magnificent location, but that matters not to anyone who's ever eaten to this legendary late-night establishment. Its popularity has turned what was little more than a food truck into a small local chain. You have a long list of meat, seafood, and vegetarian/vegan options, which employees will stuff into the casing of your choice and hand to you through the window of a stationary bus. Don't let the low-key nature of this establishment fool you—the menu features classier items like ceviche, butternut-squash tostadas, and chicken mole among the quesadillas and carne asada. There is also a downtown Tampa location (505 Franklin Street) as well as one in St. Petersburg's Grand Central District (2324 Central Avenue). *Average main: $9 ✉ 913 E. Hillsborough Ave., Central Tampa ☎ 813/232–5889.*

WHERE TO STAY

$$$ B&B/INN **Don Vicente de Ybor Historic Inn.** Built as a home in 1895 by town founder Don Vicente de Ybor, this inn shows that the working-class cigar city had an elegant side, too. **Pros:** elegant rooms; rich in history; walking distance to nightlife. **Cons:** rowdy neighborhood on weekend nights. *Rooms from: $150 ✉ 1915 Republica de Cuba, Ybor City ☎ 813/241–4545, 866/206–4545 🌐 www.donvicenteinn.com 14 rooms, 2 suites Breakfast.*

$$$$ HOTEL Fodor's Choice ★ **Epicurean.** Brought to you in part by the people at Bern's Steak House (which happens to be across the street), this vibrant, cuisine-centric installment of Marriott's Autograph Collection is an absolute must for foodies, but it doesn't make nonfoodies feel left out. **Pros:** excellent service; great location; tons of amenities. **Cons:** can get pricey; exclusive vibe. *Rooms from: $240 ✉ 1207 S. Howard Ave., SoHo ☎ 813/999–8701, 855/829–2536 🌐 epicureanhotel.com 142 rooms, 5 suites No meals.*

$$$ HOTEL **Floridan Palace Hotel.** This newly restored 1926 hotel at the northern end of downtown Tampa offers a well-manicured glimpse into a bygone era amid a bustling modern urban core. **Pros:** great downtown location; historic hotel. **Cons:** far from beaches. *Rooms from: $189 ✉ 905 Florida Ave., Downtown ☎ 813/225–1700 🌐 www.floridanpalace.com 195 rooms, 18 suites No meals.*

$$$ RESORT **Grand Hyatt Tampa Bay.** Situated on the western edge of Tampa, near the airport and overlooking the Courtney Campbell Causeway, the Grand Hyatt has a lot to offer—both in its guest rooms and on the property. **Pros:** extensive amenities; amazing views; world-class dining. **Cons:** far from beach; getting here can be tough due to traffic and awkward road layout. *Rooms from: $169 ✉ 2900 Bayport Dr., West Tampa ☎ 813/874–1234 🌐 www.grandtampabay.hyatt.com 442 rooms No meals.*

$$$ HOTEL **Hilton Garden Inn Tampa Ybor Historic District.** Although its modern architecture makes it seem out of place in this historic district, this chain hotel's location across from Centro Ybor is a plus. **Pros:** located in top cultural and nightlife district; reasonable rates. **Cons:** neighborhood can be rowdy on weekends; chain-hotel feel. *Rooms from: $179 ✉ 1700 E. 9th Ave., Ybor City ☎ 813/769–9267 🌐 www.hiltongardeninn.com 81 rooms, 14 suites No meals.*

$$$$ RESORT **Saddlebrook Resort Tampa.** If you can't get enough golf and tennis, here's your fix. **Pros:** away from urban sprawl; great choice for the

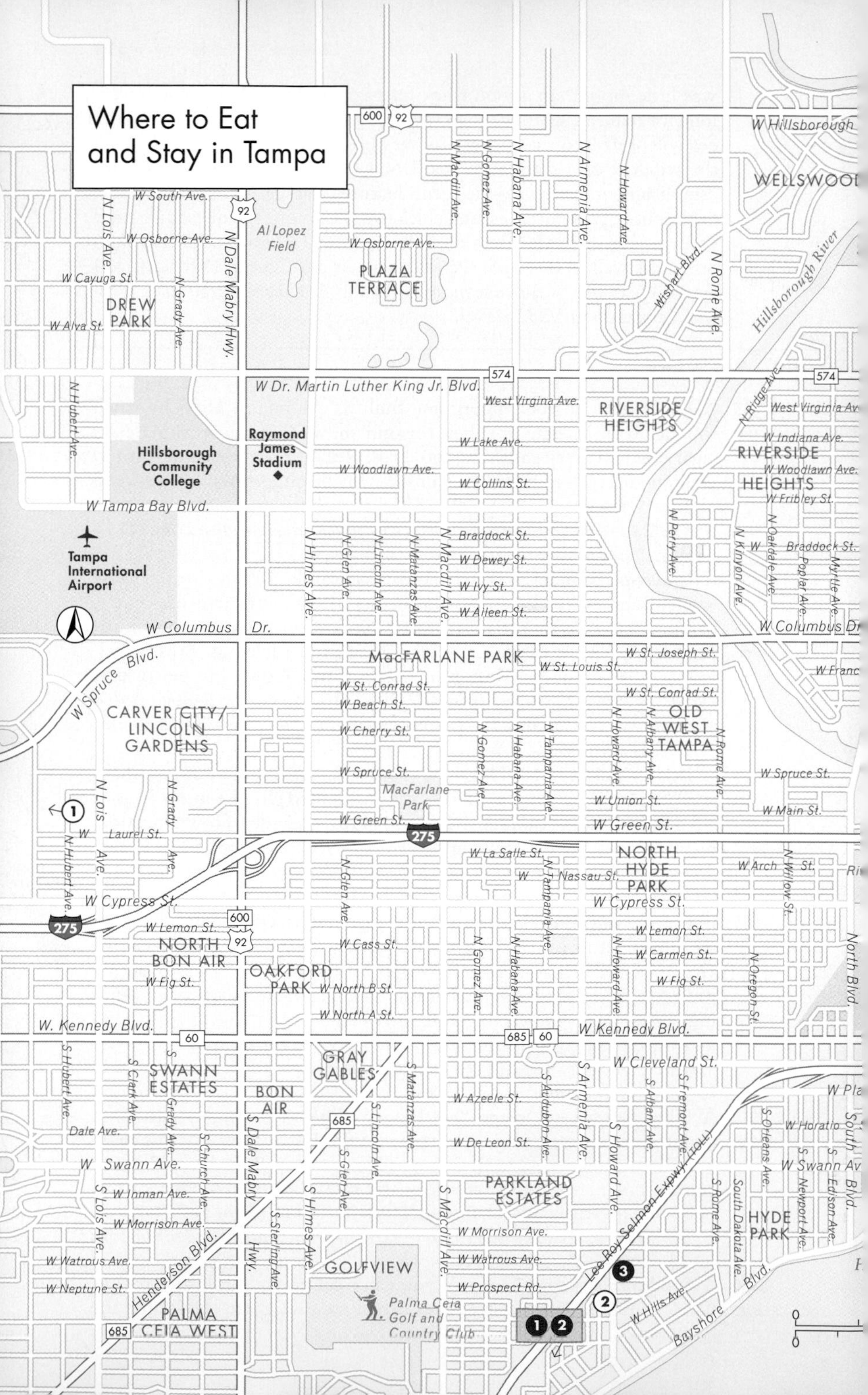
Where to Eat and Stay in Tampa
W Hillsborough
WELLSWOOD
DREW PARK
PLAZA TERRACE
Al Lopez Field
W Dr. Martin Luther King Jr. Blvd.
RIVERSIDE HEIGHTS
Raymond James Stadium
Hillsborough Community College
Tampa International Airport
W Tampa Bay Blvd.
W Columbus Dr.
MacFARLANE PARK
MacFarlane Park
CARVER CITY/ LINCOLN GARDENS
OLD WEST TAMPA
NORTH HYDE PARK
NORTH BON AIR
OAKFORD PARK
W Kennedy Blvd.
SWANN ESTATES
GRAY GABLES
BON AIR
PARKLAND ESTATES
HYDE PARK
GOLFVIEW
Palma Ceia Golf and Country Club
PALMA CEIA WEST
Hillsborough River
Lee Roy Selmon Expwy. (TOLL)
Bayshore Blvd.
Henderson Blvd.

Restaurants

Bern's Steak House 3
BT 1
Café Dufrain 5
Cappy's Pizza 7
Columbia 6
Kojak's House of Ribs 2
Mel's Hot Dogs 10
Mise en Place 4
Pearl in the Grove 9
Taco Bus 8

Hotels

Don Vicente de Ybor Historic Inn 6
Epicurean 2
Floridan Palace Hotel 5
Grand Hyatt Tampa Bay 1
Hilton Garden Inn Tampa Ybor Historic District 7
Saddlebrook Resort Tampa 8
Tampa Marriott Waterside Hotel & Marina 4
Westin Tampa Harbour Island 3

fitness minded. **Cons:** a bit isolated. *Rooms from: $249 ✉ 5700 Saddlebrook Way, Wesley Chapel ☎ 813/973–1111, 800/729–8383 ⊕ www.saddlebrookresort.com 540 rooms, 407 suites No meals.*

$$$ HOTEL **Tampa Marriott Waterside Hotel & Marina.** Across from the Tampa Convention Center, this downtown hotel was built for conventioneers but is also convenient to tourist spots such as the Florida Aquarium and the Ybor City and Hyde Park shopping and nightlife districts. **Pros:** great downtown location; near sights, dining, nightlife. **Cons:** gridlock during rush hour; streets tough to maneuver; area sketchy after dark. *Rooms from: $190 ✉ 700 S. Florida Ave., Downtown ☎ 888/268–1616, 813/221–4900 ⊕ www.marriott.com 683 rooms, 36 suites No meals.*

$$$$ HOTEL **Westin Tampa Harbour Island.** Few folks think of the islands when visiting Tampa, but this 12-story hotel on a 177-acre man-made islet is a short drive from downtown Tampa and even closer to the cruise terminal. **Pros:** close to downtown; nice views; on the TECO streetcar line. **Cons:** a bit far from the action; chain-hotel feel. *Rooms from: $169 ✉ 725 S. Harbour Island Blvd., Harbour Island ☎ 813/229–5000 ⊕ westintampaharbourisland.com 299 rooms, 19 suites No meals.*

NIGHTLIFE

When it comes to entertainment, there's never a dull moment in Tampa. Colorful Ybor City, a heavily Cuban-influenced area minutes from downtown, is a case in point. It has by far the biggest concentration of nightclubs (too many to list here), all situated along 7th and 8th avenues. Ybor comes alive at night and on weekends, when a diverse array of bars and clubs open their doors to throngs of partygoers. Whether it's bumping house music or some live rock and roll you seek, you'll find it here. Downtown Tampa is also becoming a formidable nightlife destination. When it comes to the arts—visual, musical, performing, or otherwise—Tampa is one of the South's leading spots.

BARS

Blue Martini Lounge. This spot in International Plaza has live entertainment nightly, except Sunday, and a menu of killer martinis. *✉ 2223 N. West Shore Blvd., West Tampa ☎ 813/873–2583 ⊕ bluemartini lounge.com.*

Centro Cantina. There are lots of draws here: a balcony overlooking the crowds on 7th Avenue, live music Thursday through Sunday nights, a large selection of margaritas, and more than 30 brands of tequila. Food is served until 2 am. *✉ 1600 E. 8th Ave., Ybor City ☎ 813/241–8588 ⊕ centrocantina.comm.*

Cigar City Brewing Tasting Room. Offering the fruits of the adjacent Cigar City brewery, the large tasting room here puts Tampa on the map for craft beer enthusiasts. On tap, it offers mainstay brews like Jai Alai IPA and Maduro Brown Ale as well as an interesting rotation of seasonal beers. It's a cozy spot with friendly staff and generally good music. But beware: happy hour can be packed. Brewery tours are available on the hour Wednesday through Saturday between 11 am and 2 pm for a nominal fee. ✉ *3924 W. Spruce St., Suite A, Central Tampa* ☎ *813/348–6363* ⏲ *Sun.–Thurs. 11–11, Fri. and Sat. 11 am–1 am.*

Fly Bar. A happy hour mecca for hip young professionals, Fly Bar and Restaurant offers an intriguing selection of creative cocktails. Consider the Huck Cinn, made from huckleberry vodka, cinnamon syrup, and fresh lemon. East of Eden is a cocktail consisting of bison grass vodka, Calvados, and chai syrup. The list goes on. If you're hungry, you'll find a food menu to match. There's live music on weekends and occasionally during the week. A huge draw is the rooftop deck, which offers views of surrounding downtown Tampa. ✉ *1202 N. Franklin St., Downtown* ☎ *813/275–5000* 🌐 *www.flybarandrestaurant.com.*

Gaspar's Grotto. Spanish pirate Jose Gaspar was known for swashbuckling up and down Florida's west coast in the late 18th and early 19th century. His legend has inspired a massive, raucous street festival each winter. This Ybor City drinkery has adopted his name, and rightly so. Decked out in tons of pirate memorabilia, it's the cornerstone to any night spent barhopping on the Ybor strip. The sangria is a good choice, but the aged rums may be a better fit here. You'll also find a food menu that goes well beyond standard bar fare. ✉ *1805 E. 7th Ave., Ybor City* ☎ *813/248–5900* 🌐 *www.gasparsgrotto.com.*

Hub. Considered something of a dive—but a lovable one—by a loyal and young local following that ranges from esteemed jurists to nose-ring-wearing night owls, the Hub is known for strong drinks and a jukebox that goes well beyond the usual. ✉ *719 N. Franklin St., Downtown* ☎ *813/229–1553* 🌐 *thehubbartampa.com.*

CASINO

Seminole Hard Rock Hotel & Casino. In addition to playing one of the hundreds of Vegas-style slot machines, gamers can get their kicks at the casino's poker tables and video-gaming machines. The lounge serves drinks 24 hours a day. Hard Rock Cafe, of course, has live music, dinner, and nightlife. There is a heavy smell of cigarette smoke here, as with most casinos. ✉ *5223 N. Orient Rd., off I–4 at N. Orient Rd. Exit, East Tampa* ☎ *866/502–7529* 🌐 *www.seminolehardrock.com* ⏲ *Daily 24 hrs.*

10

COMEDY CLUBS

Side Splitters. Comedians perform Thursday through Sunday nights (and other nights, sporadically, throughout the week). ✉ *12938 N. Dale Mabry Hwy., Central Tampa* ☎ *813/960–1197* 🌐 *www.sidesplitterscomedy.com.*

Tampa Improv. Top comedians perform here Wednesday through Sunday. ✉ *Centro Ybor, 1600 E. 8th Ave., Ybor City* ☎ *813/864–4000* 🌐 *www.improvtampa.com.*

MUSIC CLUB

Skippers Smokehouse. A junkyard-style restaurant and oyster bar, Skippers has live reggae on Wednesday, Uncle John's Band (a long-running Grateful Dead cover act) on Thursday, and great smoked fish every night. Check their calendar for exceptional musical lineups on the weekends. ✉ *910 Skipper Rd., Northeast Tampa* ☎ *813/971–0666* 🌐 *www.skipperssmokehouse.com.*

SHOPPING

MALLS

Centro Ybor. Ybor City's destination within a destination is this dining-and-entertainment palace. It has shops, trendy bars and restaurants, and a 20-screen movie theater. ✉ *1600 E. 8th Ave., Ybor City* 🌐 *www.centroybor.com.*

Channelside Bay Plaza. Right next to Tampa's cruise-ship terminal, this mall offers a vast array of shopping and dining options, as well as live music in a large courtyard. Look out for Qachbals Chocolatier, Tinatapa's (for a mojito), and Splitsville, a bowling alley and restaurant chain targeting a younger crowd. ✉ *615 Channelside Dr., Downtown* 🌐 *www.channelsidebayplaza.com.*

International Plaza. If you want to grab something at Neiman Marcus or Nordstrom, this is the place. You'll also find Juicy Couture, Burberry, Michael Kors, Louis Vuitton, and many other upscale shops. Stick around after hours, when watering holes in the mall's courtyard become a high-end club scene. ✉ *2223 N. West Shore Blvd., Airport Area* 🌐 *www.shopinternationalplaza.com.*

Old Hyde Park Village. It's a typical upscale shopping district in a quiet, shaded neighborhood near the water. Williams-Sonoma and Anthropologie are mixed in with bistros and sidewalk cafés. ✉ *1602 W. Swann Ave., Hyde Park* 🌐 *www.hydeparkvillage.net.*

SPECIALTY SHOPS

King Corona Cigar Factory. If you are shopping for hand-rolled cigars, head to Ybor City, where a few hand-rollers practice their craft in small shops. This is one of the more popular places thanks to its plentiful outdoor seating, perfect if you want to grab some nibbles and a Cuban coffee or a beer. ✉ *1523 E. 7th Ave., Ybor City* ☎ *813/251–9109* 🌐 *www.kingcoronacigars.com.*

La France. One of the landmark vintage shops in the Tampa Bay area, La France stocks such items as antique beaded wedding gowns, psychedelic mini-dresses, and period costumes that will make you a hit should you sport one at the Gasparilla Pirate Fleet parade. If you're in any way a vintage clothing buff, prepare to spend a solid couple of hours (and a good chunk of change) here. ✉ *1612 E. 7th Ave., Ybor City* ☎ *813/248–1381.*

Squaresville. From the mildly unusual to the downright bizarre this vintage store has it all—from the mid-20th century, that is. Among the finds are Cuban clothing, Elvis posters, and Bettie Page clocks. ✉ *3224 W. Bay to Bay Blvd., Hyde Park* ☎ *813/259–9944* 🌐 *www.squaresvilletampa.com* ⏲ *Weekdays 11–6, Sat. 11–5:30; closed Sun.*

SPORTS AND THE OUTDOORS

BASEBALL

George M. Steinbrenner Field. Locals and tourists flock each March to see the New York Yankees play about 17 spring training games at this 11,000-seat facility. (Call for tickets.) From April through September, the stadium belongs to a Yankee farm team, the Tampa Yankees, who play 70 games against the likes of the Daytona Cubs and the Sarasota Red Sox. ✉ *1 Steinbrenner Dr., near corner of Dale Mabry Hwy., off I-275 Exit 41B, Central Tampa* ☎ *813/879–2244* 🌐 *www.steinbrennerfield.com.*

FOOTBALL

Tampa Bay Buccaneers. Seeing the National Football League play isn't easy without connections, though catching a Bucs home game is a little easier than most. Tickets can be found for some games at the box office, though it's a safer bet when you buy them online in advance. ✉ *Raymond James Stadium, 4201 N. Dale Mabry Hwy., Central Tampa* ☎ *813/879–2827* 🌐 *www.buccaneers.com.*

GOLF

Bloomingdale Golfers Club. In addition to an 18-hole, par-72 course, this club has a two-tiered driving range, a 1-acre putting green, and a restaurant. Green fees are $30–$80. ✉ *4113 Great Golfers Pl., Valrico* ☎ *813/685–4105* 🌐 *www.bloomingdalegolf.com.*

The Claw at USF. Named for its many doglegged fairways, the 18-hole, par-71 course is on a preserve with moss-draped oaks and towering pines. Greens fees are $20–$45. ✉ *13801 N. 46th St., North Tampa* ☎ *813/632–6893* 🌐 *www.theclawatusfgolf.com.*

Saddlebrook Golf Club. There's a lot on offer at this resort, which is half an hour northeast of Tampa: 36 holes and 70- and 71-par courses, a driving range, a golf shop, on-site pros, and a resort spa. The greens fees range from $50 to $105, depending on the season. ✉ *Saddlebrook Resort, 5700 Saddlebrook Way, Wesley Chapel* ☎ *813/973–1111* 🌐 *www.saddlebrook.com.*

Tournament Players Club of Tampa Bay. This public 18-hole 71-par course 15 miles north of Tampa was designed by Bobby Weed and Chi Chi Rodriguez; greens fee $79/$159. ✉ *5300 W. Lutz Lake Fern Rd., Lutz* ☎ *813/949–0090* 🌐 *www.tpctampabay.com.*

ST. PETERSBURG

21 miles west of Tampa.

Nicknamed the Sunshine City, St. Pete is much more than a mass of land between the airport and the beaches. In recent years it's seen a fierce arts and cultural revival, which you can plainly see as you stroll through the city's lively downtown area. The new Salvador Dalí Museum building is a testament to the great pride residents of the 'Burg take in their waterfront city. But the city has other arts-oriented attractions, including the Dale Chihuly Collection, the Fine Arts Museum, and the burgeoning young artist hub known as the 600 Block, where eateries and bars

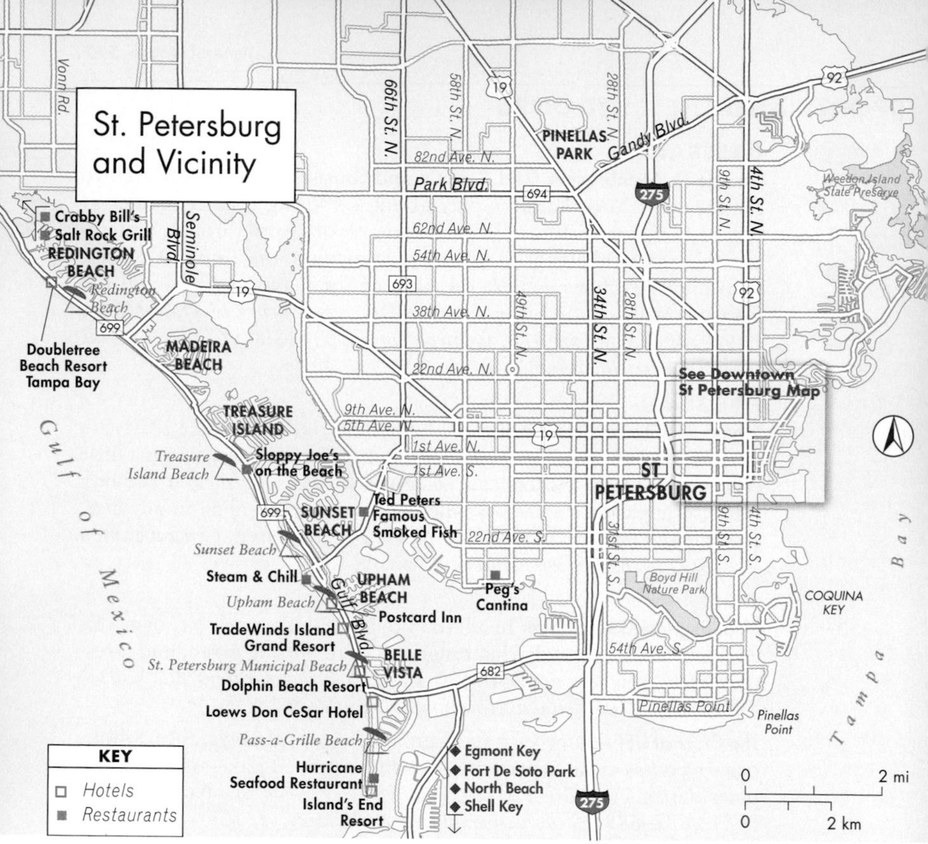

attract crowds in the evening. Beach Drive offers some upscale options, whereas Central Avenue appeals more to night owls. The Grand Central District offers some unique vintage and antiques shopping. Gulfport is a stylishly low-key suburb southwest of St. Petersburg. The long strip of barrier islands lining St. Pete's west coast offer miles of gorgeous white beaches as well as dining, nightlife, and phenomenal sunsets. Beach towns here include St. Pete Beach, Treasure Island, Madeira Beach, and Redington Shores. No trip to this area is complete without a visit to the remote, pristine beaches of Fort De Soto.

GETTING HERE AND AROUND

Interstate 275 heads west from Tampa across Tampa Bay to St. Petersburg, swings south, and crosses the bay again on its way to Terra Ceia, near Bradenton. U.S. 19 is St. Petersburg's major north–south artery; traffic can be heavy, and there are many lights, so try to avoid it. Alternatives include 66th and 4th streets. One key thing to remember about St. Pete is that the roads form an easy-to-navigate grid: streets run north to south; avenues run east to west. Central Avenue connects downtown to the beaches.

Around St. Petersburg, Pinellas Suncoast Transit Authority serves Pinellas County. Look for buses that cover the beaches and downtown exclusively.

Contacts Pinellas Suncoast Transit Authority ☎ *727/540–1800* 🌐 *www.psta.net.*

TOURS

All About Fun Tours. What sets this tour apart from others is you are not going by bus or boat—your self-guided chariot is a motorized Segway. Each tour starts with an easy 15- to 20-minute training session. Tours are 60 or 90 minutes and are offered up to three times daily. It's a carefree way to see downtown St. Petersburg, the park system, and the waterfront while learning about local history. Reservations are required. ✉ *335 N.E. 2nd Ave.* ☎ *727/896–3640* 🌐 *www.gyroglides.com* 🎫 *Tours $35–$50* 🕒 *Tues.–Sat. 10:30 and 2, Sun. 12:30 and 2:30, Mon. call for availability.*

Dolphin Landings Tours. This operation runs a four-hour shelling trip, a two-hour dolphin-sighting excursion powered mostly by sail, backbay or party-boat fishing, and other outings to Egmont Key and Shell Key. It's not easy to spot from the road: the boats are docked behind a strip mall. ✉ *4737 Gulf Blvd., St. Pete Beach* ☎ *727/360–7411* 🌐 *www.dolphinlandings.com.*

VISITOR INFORMATION

Contacts St. Petersburg Area Chamber of Commerce ☎ *727/821–4069* 🌐 *www.stpete.com.* **St. Petersburg/Clearwater Area Convention and Visitors Bureau** ☎ *727/464–7200, 877/352–3224* 🌐 *www.visitstpeteclearwater.com.*

EXPLORING

TOP ATTRACTIONS

Fodor's Choice ★ **Chihuly Collection.** For the uninitiated, those passing this collection's polished exterior may think it's a gallery like any other. Yet what's contained inside is an experience akin to *Alice in Wonderland*. This, the first permanent collection of world-renowned glass sculptor Dale Chihuly's work, has such impossibly vibrant, larger-than-life pieces as "Float Boat" and "Ruby Red Icicle." You can tour the museum independently or with one of its volunteer docents (no added cost; tours are given hourly on the half-hour during the week). Each display is perfectly lit, which adds to the drama of Chihuly's designs. After passing under a hallway with a semi-transparent ceiling through which a brilliant array of smaller glass pieces shine, you'll wind up at the breathtaking finale, "Mille Fiore" ("Thousand Flowers"), a spectacular, whimsical glass montage mimicking a wildflower patch, critters and all. Check out the gift shop at the end if you'd like to take some of the magic home with you. A combination ticket gets you a glimpse into Morean Arts Center's off-site glass-blowing studio, where you can watch resident artisans create a unique glass piece before your eyes. ✉ *400 Beach Dr., Downtown* ☎ *727/822–7872* 🌐 *www.moreanartscenter.com.* 🎫 *$15* 🕒 *Mon.–Sat. 10–5, Sun. noon–5.*

Fodor's Choice ★ **The Dalí Museum.** Inside and out, the waterfront Dalí Museum, which opened on 1/11/11 (Dalí is said to have been into numerology), is almost as remarkable as the Spanish surrealist's work. The state-of-the-art building has a surreal geodesic-like glass structure called the

Dalí Enigma, as well as an outdoor labyrinth and a DNA-inspired spiral staircase leading up to the collection. All this, before you've even seen the collection, which is one of the most comprehensive of its kind—courtesy of Ohio magnate A. Reynolds Morse, a friend of Dalí's.

Here, you can scope out his early impressionistic works and see how the painter evolved into the visionary he's now seen to be. The mind-expanding paintings in this downtown headliner include *Eggs on a Plate Without a Plate*, *The Hallucinogenic Toreador,* and more than 90 other oils. You'll also discover more than 2,000 additional works including watercolors, drawings, sculptures, photographs, and objets d'art. The museum also hosts temporary collections from the likes of Andy Warhol. Free hour-long tours are led by well-informed docents. ✉ *1 Dali Blvd.* ☎ *727/823–3767* 🌐 *www.thedali.org* 🎫 *$21* ⏲ *Mon.–Wed., Fri. and Sat. 10–5:30, Thurs. 10–8, Sun. noon–5:30.*

Egmont Key. In the middle of the mouth of Tampa Bay lies the small (350 acres), largely unspoiled but critically eroding island Egmont Key, now a state park, national wildlife refuge, national historic site, and bird sanctuary. On the island are the ruins of Fort De Soto's sister fortification, Fort Dade, built during the Spanish-American War to protect Tampa Bay. The primary inhabitants of the less-than-2-mile-long island are the threatened gopher tortoise and box turtles. The only way to get here is by boat—you can catch a ferry from Fort De Soto, among other places. Nature lovers will find the trip well worth it—the beach here is excellent for shelling, secluded beach bathing, wildlife viewing, and snorkeling. Hubbard's Marina operates a ferry to Egmont Key from Fort DeSoto most days. 🌐 *www.floridastateparks.org/egmontkey/.*

FAMILY **Sunken Gardens.** A cool oasis amid St. Pete's urban clutter, this lush 4-acre plot was created from a lake that was drained in 1903. Explore the cascading waterfalls and koi ponds, and walk through the butterfly house and exotic gardens where more than 50,000 tropical plants and flowers from across the globe thrive amid groves of some of the area's most spectacular palm trees. The on-site restaurant and hands-on kids' museum make this place a family favorite. ✉ *1825 4th St. N* ☎ *727/551–3102* 🌐 *www.sunkengardens.org* 🎫 *$8* ⏲ *Mon.–Sat. 10–4:30, Sun. noon–4:30.*

WORTH NOTING

Florida Holocaust Museum. The downtown Florida Holocaust Museum is one of the largest of its kind in the United States. It has the permanent History, Heritage, and Hope exhibit, an original boxcar, and an extensive collection of photographs, art, and artifacts. One compelling display includes portraits and biographies of Holocaust survivors. The museum, which also has a series of rotating exhibits, was conceived as a learning center for children, so many of the exhibits avoid overly graphic content; signs are posted outside galleries if the subject matter might be too intense for kids. ✉ *55 5th St. S* ☎ *727/820–0100* 🌐 *www.flholocaustmuseum.org* 🎫 *$16* ⏲ *Daily 10–5.*

FAMILY **Fort De Soto Park.** Spread over five small islands, 1,136-acre Fort De Soto Park lies at the mouth of Tampa Bay. It has 7 miles of waterfront (much of it beach), two fishing piers, a 4-mile hiking and skating trail,

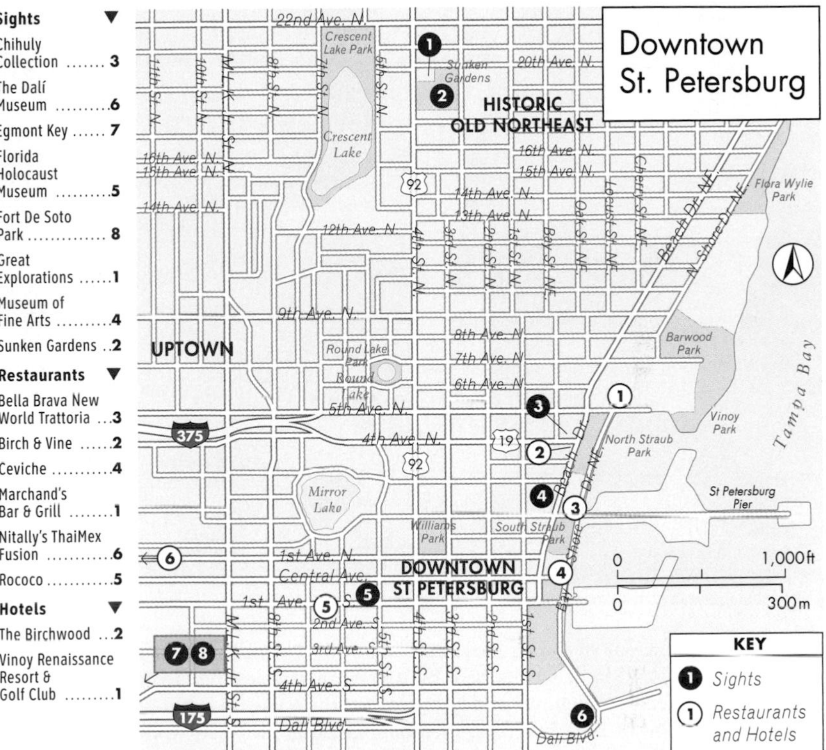

picnic-and-camping grounds, and a historic fort that kids of any age can explore. The fort for which it's named was built on the southern end of Mullet Key to protect sea lanes in the gulf during the Spanish-American War. Roam the fort or wander the beaches of any of the islands within the park. Kayaks and beach cruisers are available for rental. Although most of Tampa Bay's beaches don't allow dogs, Fort De Soto has a somewhat lengthy dog beach for those who can't bear to hit the sand without their best buddy. ✉ *3500 Pinellas Bayway St., Tierra Verde* ☎ *727/582–2267* 🌐 *www.pinellascounty.org/park/05_ft_desoto.htm* 🎟 *$5* ⏲ *Beaches, daily sunrise–sunset; fishing and boat ramp, 24 hrs.*

FAMILY **Great Explorations.** "Don't touch" are words never spoken here. The museum is hands-on through and through, with a Robot Lab, Climb Wall, Lie Detector, Fire House, Vet's Office, and other interactive play areas. Smart exhibits like the Tennis Ball Launcher, which uses compressed air to propel a ball through a series of tubes, and Sound Waves, where Styrofoam pellets in a clear tube show differences in sound frequencies, employ low-tech to teach high-tech principles. ✉ *1925 4th St. N* ☎ *727/821–8992* 🌐 *www.greatexplorations.org* 🎟 *$10* ⏲ *Mon.–Sat. 10–4:30, Sun. noon–4:30.*

Museum of Fine Arts. One of the city's cornerstones, this museum is a gorgeous Mediterranean-revival structure that houses outstanding

10

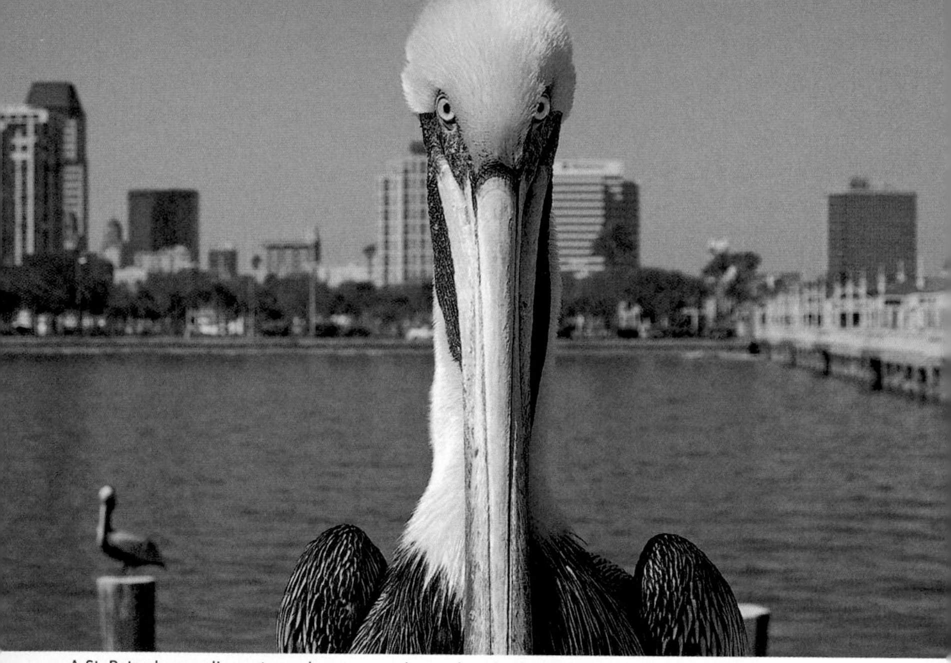

A St. Petersburg pelican stares down passersby on the wharf; photo by Seymour Levy, Fodors.com member.

collections of Asian, African, Native American, European, and American art. Major works here by American artists range from Hassam to O'Keeffe to Bellows and Morisot, but the museum is known for its collection of French artists, including Cézanne, Monet, Rodin, Gauguin, and Renoir. There are also photography exhibits that draw from a permanent collection of more than 14,000 works. The recent Hazel Hough Wing more than doubled the museum's exhibit space. A café offers visitors a lunch respite and a beautiful view of the bay. Docents give narrated gallery tours. ✉ *255 Beach Dr. NE* ☎ *727/896–2667* 🌐 *www.fine-arts.org* 🎫 *$17* 🕓 *Mon.–Wed., Fri. and Sat. 10–5, Sun. noon–5, Thurs. 10–8.*

BEACHES

Egmont Beach. An undeveloped island teeming with birds, shells, and native plants is a short ferry ride away. You'll find serene lengths of beach, abandoned former military buildings, and a lighthouse. You can grab a ferry here from Fort De Soto for as little as $15. **Amenities:** none. **Best for:** solitude; walking. ✉ *Accessible by boat only, Tierra Verde* ☎ *727/867–6569.*

Madeira Beach. Known to locals as "Mad Beach," this lively barrier island town occupies the southern tip of Shell Key. The beachfront consists of a long stretch of soft, shell-strewn sand, and it's often crowded with families as well as clusters of twentysomething beachgoers. You can get to the beach via numerous public access points, but your best bet is to park at the municipal beach parking lot and head to the sand from there. It's easily accessible from Treasure Island, northern St. Petersburg, and Clearwater Beach. **Amenities:** food and drink; parking; showers; toilets. **Best for:** partiers; swimming; walking. ✉ *14400 Gulf Blvd., Madeira Beach.*

North Beach, Fort De Soto. Pretty much anywhere you go in this county park can make you feel like you're hundreds of miles from civilization, but the beach on the northern tip of this island chain has perhaps the most remote feel. Sure, it gets pretty packed with weekend revelers and family reunions, but you can easily find your own space on this award-winning beach. It starts out wide at the entrance, and narrows as you go north, so it's perfect for those who enjoy a good stroll. There are some striking panoramic views of the park's undeveloped wetlands. Be warned that once you get past a certain point, the beach becomes clothing optional. **Amenities:** food and drink; parking; showers; toilets. **Best for:** solitude; sunset; swimming; walking. ✉ *3500 Pinellas Bayway, head right at flag, Tierra Verde.*

FAMILY Fodor's Choice ★ **Pass-a-Grille Beach.** At the southern tip of St. Pete Beach (past the Don Cesar), this is the epitome of Old Florida. One of the most popular beaches in the area, it skirts the west end of charming, historic Pass-a-Grille, a neighborhood that draws tourists and locals alike with its stylish yet low-key mom-and-pop motels and restaurants. On weekends, check out the Art Mart, an open-air market off the boulevard between 9th and 10th avenues that showcases the work of local artisans. **Amenities:** food and drink; parking; showers; toilets. **Best for:** sunset; windsurfing. ✉ *1000 Pass-a-Grille Way, St. Pete Beach.*

Redington Beach. Sand Key, the landmass that is home to Madeira Beach at the south end and Belleaire Beach in the north, is spotted with public beach access points. This particular spot has a bigger parking area than the others, though it's not free. It's also within walking distance of the Redington Pier, one of the most popular areas for fishing. **Amenities:** food and drink; parking; toilets. **Best for:** solitude; swimming; walking. ✉ *160th Ave. at Gulf Blvd., Redington Beach.*

Shell Key. If you want to find the most pristine beach possible without heading to some remote outpost, this is your best bet. The shuttle to this seemingly remote paradise runs out of Pass-A-Grille. You can catch it most days at 10 am, noon, and 2 pm. If you do, expect some amazing snorkeling, shelling, and bird-watching. You can also kayak or canoe here from a launch near Fort DeSoto. Overnight camping is allowed here in the part of the island not designated as a bird sanctuary. Watch for rip currents when swimming, as they can be pretty strong. **Amenities:** none. **Best for:** solitude; swimming; walking. ✉ *801 Pass-A-Grille Way, Pass-A-Grille, St. Pete Beach* ☎ *727/360–1348.*

St. Petersburg Municipal Beach. Though the beach is technically in the city of Treasure Island, the city of St. Pete Beach owns and maintains this stretch. Due in part to a concession stand and playground, it's excellent for families. The beach here is very, very wide, near hotels, and great for beach volleyball. **Amenities:** food and drink; parking; showers; toilets. **Best for:** solitude; partiers; sunset; swimming. ✉ *11260 Gulf Blvd., Treasure Island.*

FAMILY **Sunset Beach.** Technically part of Treasure Island, this 2-mile-long outcrop is one of Tampa Bay's best-kept secrets. The northern end has a mixed crowd—from bikers to spring breakers—the middle portion is good for families (there's a pavilion and playground at around 78th and West Gulf Boulevard), and the southern tip attracts the LGBT crowd. Surfers hit up Sunset Beach on the rare occasion that the gulf has some swells to offer. Once you turn onto West Gulf, you can find parking on the side streets, but make sure you park legally—it's all too easy to unwittingly get a barrage of parking tickets here. There are several pay lots starting to your right just south of 82nd Avenue. **Amenities:** parking; toilets. **Best for:** solitude; partiers; sunset. ✉ *West Gulf Blvd., Treasure Island.*

Treasure Island. Large, wide swaths of sand that are sans crowd abound, but you can also find some good crowds, especially on weekends. The Sunday-evening drum circle, which happens around sunset just southwest of the Bilmar, makes for some interesting people-watching, as do the many festivals occurring here each month. It's also the only beach that allows alcohol, as long as it's not contained in glass. Plus, getting here is super easy—just head west on St. Petersburg's Central Avenue, which dead-ends smack-dab in the middle of T.I. (that's what the locals call it), where the iconic Thunderbird Beach Resort sign towers over the boulevard. Hang a left at the light. There's a Publix right across the street if you're up for an impromptu picnic or don't want to pay beach-bar prices for a beer. **Amenities:** food and drink; parking; showers; toilets. **Best for:** solitude; partiers; sunsets. ✉ *10400 Gulf Blvd., Treasure Island.*

Upham Beach. One of the most notable things about this popular beach is the series of large objects that look like yellow school buses buried in the sand. These are actually designed to stabilize the shoreline (this beach is known for rapid erosion). The structures, called T-groins, may not please the eye, but that doesn't keep locals from flocking here. Upham is a wide beach with tons of natural landscaping, and it's near Postcard Inn and the TradeWinds. **Amenities:** food and drink; showers; toilets. **Best for:** partiers; sunset; swimming; walking. ✉ *900 Gulf Way, St. Pete Beach.*

WHERE TO EAT

$$ ITALIAN ✕ **Bella Brava New World Trattoria.** This trendy eatery is one of the more sought-after places on equally trendy Beach Drive. It offers a fresh, imaginative approach to Italian fare; a classic dish like ravioli Genovese is stuffed with fresh goat cheese and toasted pine nuts. Pork belly rigatone and the trattoria burger, which is loaded with Gorgonzola and garlic aioli, are some of the more decadent menu items, while a spate of colorful salads and flatbreads make up the lighter side of things. Specials often feature fresh, local seafood. There's almost always a lengthy wait for a table, even on a weeknight, so reservations are really a must. However, sitting at the bar, which has an equally creative beer, wine, and cocktail menu, is also an option. [$] *Average main: $18* ✉ *204 Beach*

Dr. NE, Downtown ☎ *727/895–5515* ⊕ *bellabrava.com* ⚠ *Reservations essential.*

$$$ MODERN AMERICAN ✕ **Birch & Vine.** Seasonal, locally sourced ingredients work equally well in both the surf and the turf columns at Birch & Vine, which has turned The Birchwood hotel lobby and patio into an evening dining destination for hunger diners in downtown St. Petersburg. Take particular note of the orange miso scallops, and the sous vide filet mignon, contemporary preparations that complement the reimagined 1920s property. Umbrella-covered patio tables face Beach Drive and North Straub Park to provide the best people watching. The lively weekend scene can create conversational challenges at the interior tables and banquettes; for a quiet dinner, reserve on Monday or Tuesday, or arrange to rent one of the private dining rooms for up to 12 guests. $ *Average main: $28* ✉ *The Birchwood, 340 Beach Dr., NE, Downtown* ☎ *727/896–1080* ⊕ *thebirchwood.com/birch-vine.html.*

$$$ TAPAS ✕ **Ceviche.** A choice romantic destination as well as an excellent launchpad for a night out, this tapas bar offers an astonishing spate of pleasant sensations for those with savvy taste buds. You can't go wrong with a huge order of seafood or chicken paella. The ceviche, *solomillo a la parilla* (prime fillet with wild mushrooms and brandy cream sauce), and super-garlicky spinach (sautéed with figs) are good bets for tapas. In the catacomb-like bar downstairs, there's jazz, salsa, and flamenco every night but Monday. While you're here, the sangria is a must. $ *Average main: $25* ✉ *10 Beach Dr., Downtown* ☎ *727/209–2299* ⊕ *www.ceviche.com.*

$$ SEAFOOD ✕ **Crabby Bill's.** Nothin' fancy about the crab-man's place—just some of the area's tastiest seafood served family-style (picture long picnic-style tables). Crustaceans are the house specialty, meaning your choice of blue or soft-shell, and, from October to May, delicious—though costly—stone crabs, among others. There's also a good selection of other treats, including scallops and oysters. Seafood aficionados will want to stick with items for which this place is best known, as the menu can be hit-or-miss. The views alone are a great reason to check it out. This restaurant sits on the beach front, something that turns the rooftop deck into prime real estate at sunset. Diners usually dress in the official uniform of the gulf coast beaches: shorts, T-shirts, and flip-flops. $ *Average main: $18* ✉ *5100 Gulf Blvd., St. Pete Beach* ☎ *727/360–8858* ⊕ *www.crabbybills.com.*

$$ SEAFOOD Fodor's Choice ★ ✕ **Hurricane Seafood Restaurant.** Sunsets and gulf views are the bait that hooks regulars as well as travelers who find their way to this somewhat hidden pit stop in historic Pass-A-Grille. Dating to 1977, it's mainly heralded as a watering hole where you can hoist a cold one while munching on one of the area's better grouper sandwiches. (Speaking of this sweet white fish, it's the real deal here, which—be warned—isn't always a guarantee in some restaurants.) There's also a range of seafood and steak entrées, and the crab cakes are legendary. The aforementioned sunsets are best seen from the rooftop sundeck. $ *Average main: $15* ✉ *809 Gulf Way, St. Pete Beach* ☎ *727/360–9558* ⊕ *www.thehurricane.com.*

$$$ ECLECTIC **Marchand's Bar & Grill.** Opened in 1925, this wonderful restaurant in the posh Renaissance Vinoy Resort has frescoed ceilings and a spectacular view of Tampa Bay. Upscale and special-occasion diners are drawn to Marchand's by an imaginative menu, which changes often and has recently embraced a farm-to-table approach. You'll always see salmon and cornish game hen on the menu. More recent additions include gluten-free and veggie options, such as a squash and corn taco. For early birds, the 1925 menu (named for the year the hotel originally opened) offers a four-course meal for just—as you may have guessed—$19.25. Sushi is available Thursday through Saturday. The wine list is extensive, including a number of by-the-glass selections. *Average main: $28 Renaissance Vinoy Resort, 501 5th Ave. NE 727/824–8072 www.marchandsbarandgrill.com.*

$$ ECLECTIC **Nitally's ThaiMex Fusion.** For those who take pride in their ability to handle the heat, this casual yet acclaimed fusion eatery is a must. It's run by a married couple, one of whom is from Thailand and the other from, as you may have guessed, Mexico. The resulting menu consists of many a match made in heaven by melding the spice and nuances of either cuisine into a spate of tasty options—think panang-mole curry or chorizo pad thai. (Some of these are even suitable for spice-phobes.) The bravest of souls can try the "inferno soup," which is less of a dish than a double dare, featuring a giant bowl of Thai chicken soup flavored with ghost peppers (finish it in a half hour and you win a cash prize). Regardless of what you order, go for a shade less spicy than you normally would: their idea of medium is what most restaurants consider hot. Portions are massive; if you order a burrito, you may actually receive two. Finally, keep in mind that this place can get packed at dinnertime, especially on weekends, so call ahead. *Average main: $18 2462 Central Ave. 727/321–8424 nitallys.com Closed Sun.*

$$ MODERN MEXICAN **Peg's Cantina.** A favorite watering hole for Tampa Bay's craft beer enthusiasts, Peg's also offers a variety of specialty pizzas and healthy Mexican options. Housed in an old bungalow along Gulfport's famed Beach Boulevard, it features excellent outdoor seating, and, in perfect Gulfport form, hospitable service for the canine set. Cyclists enjoy cruising here from the Pinellas Trail. Tap beers include house-brand brews as well as options from regional and national breweries. *Average main: $15 3038 Beach Blvd. S, Gulfport 727/328–2720 www.pegscantina.com Closed Mon. No lunch Tues.–Thurs.*

$$$ STEAKHOUSE **Rococo.** Yet another happening spot inspired by the St. Pete of yesteryear, this newly minted steak house sits in what was once a historic YWCA building. Possibly the only independent steak house in St. Petersburg, it gets its name from the late-baroque art movement and displays the work of local artists on its walls. Steak is obviously the main draw—corn-fed, aged, you name it—but the menu goes well beyond the normal steak-house bounds. On a given night, you can find elk, swordfish, or any number of less typical denizens of the land and sea, for those who are not enamored of beef. The chef is also attentive to special diets here, including the needs of gluten-free, vegetarian, and vegan diners. Craft cocktails have a local flair, and the beer and wine selection is expansive. It's really one of the best options in town

for a romantic night out in St. Pete. *Average main: $30 655 2nd Ave. S 727/822–0999 rococosteak.com Reservations essential No lunch.*

$$$ SEAFOOD **Salt Rock Grill.** This hot spot is where tourists and locals converge to enjoy a fun and lively waterfront atmosphere. The rock-solid (if slightly less than imaginative) menu is the best reason to come. Don't believe the Caribbean lobster is a "monster"—at 1¼ pounds it's on the small side, but it's twice cooked—including a finish on the grill—and quite tasty. Those more into the turf side of things might be interested in the "Chicken Rock'n Bleu," which adds fresh spinach and champagne-mushroom sauce into a classic chicken dish. In fair weather, dine on the dock; otherwise ask for a table with a view of the water. *Average main: $25 19325 Gulf Blvd., Indian Shores 727/593–7625 www.saltrockgrill.com.*

$$ SEAFOOD **Sloppy Joe's on the Beach.** A sister to the famous Hemingway haunt in Key West, this breezy spot is less gritty than the original and a little more focused on food than drink (although you will find a full menu of tasty tropical concoctions here as well). It's right on the beach, in the Bilmar Beach Resort, and the location affords diners amazing views. On particularly stunning beach days, you'll want to make reservations. Try to get seated on the sizable wooden deck that overlooks Treasure Island's massive beach. As you might imagine, seafood is big here, and the menu includes heaping portions of such favorites as lobster mac-and-cheese and gulf-caught shrimp. The salads are also a huge hit. If you come on a Sunday evening, look a little bit to the south, where a weekly drum circle turns into a huge beach bash come sunset. *Average main: $16 Bilmar Beach Resort, 10650 Gulf Blvd., Treasure Island 727/367–1600 www.sloppyjoesonthebeach.com.*

$ CAFÉ **Steam & Chill.** This eatery is a bit of a rare gem on St. Pete Beach, offering creative breakfast options that tend to be a bit healthier and more worldly than their greasy-spoon counterparts (think: vegan hash and berry-and-Brie crepes). It's also pretty much the only neighborhood spot where you'll find proper espresso drinks, not to mention formidable brunch and tapas menus. At night, the dining room transforms into a tapas bar with live music and flowing sangria. *Average main: $12 7400 Gulf Blvd., St. Pete Beach 727/360–8080 www.steamandchill.com.*

10

$ SEAFOOD Fodor's Choice ★ **Ted Peters Famous Smoked Fish.** Picture this: flip-flop-wearing anglers and beach-towel-clad bathers lolling on picnic benches, sipping a beer, and devouring oak-smoked salmon, mullet, mahimahi, and mackerel. Dinner comes to the table with heaped helpings of potato salad and coleslaw. If you're industrious enough to have hooked your own fish, the crew will smoke it for about $1.50 per pound. If not, there's always what many consider to be the best burger in the region. The popular smoked fish spread and Manhattan clam chowder are available to go. There's also indoor seating at Ted's, which has been a south-side fixture for more than six decades. Closing time is 7:30 pm, so dinner is only for early diners. *Average main: $13 1350 Pasadena Ave. S, South Pasadena 727/381–7931 tedpetersfish.com Reservations not accepted No credit cards Closed Tues.*

WHERE TO STAY

$$$ B&B/INN **The Birchwood.** Few things are as emblematic of Beach Drive's renaissance than this boutique hotel, which like many of downtown St. Pete's best attractions, seamlessly blends old and new. **Pros:** highly sought-after location; exquisite furnishings; close to downtown attractions. **Cons:** service seems more like a B&B than a hotel and is often MIA; not the best choice for families with kids; 20 minutes from the beach. *Rooms from: $220* *340 Beach Dr. NE, Downtown* *727/896–1080* *thebirchwood.com* *18 rooms.*

$$$ RESORT **Dolphin Beach Resort.** If you don't want to stay at a chain but can't afford a huge resort, this beachfront spot is probably a good choice. **Pros:** good bargain; on the beach. **Cons:** decor seems a little dated. *Rooms from: $159* *4900 Gulf Blvd., St. Pete Beach* *727/360–7011* *www.dolphinbeach.com* *173 rooms* *No meals.*

$$$ RESORT **Doubletree Beach Resort Tampa Bay.** This hotel from the Hilton family offers the chain's well-known luxury without diminishing the mellow charm of the surrounding area. **Pros:** lauded facility; quiet, beachfront location. **Cons:** few attractions nearby. *Rooms from: $179* *17120 Gulf Blvd., N. Redington Beach* *727/391–4000* *www.doubletreeresort.com* *126 rooms* *No meals.*

$$$$ HOTEL **Island's End Resort.** We love this converted 1950s-vintage motel because it has some of the area's best sunrise and sunset views and, like the rest of historic Pass-A-Grille, is totally friendly and totally Old Florida. **Pros:** good value; nice views; near restaurants and shops. **Cons:** access via a traffic-clogged road, parking can be tricky. *Rooms from: $229* *1 Pass-A-Grille Way, St. Pete Beach* *727/360–5023* *www.islandsend.com* *6 cottages* *Breakfast.*

$$$$ RESORT Fodor's Choice ★ **Loews Don CeSar Hotel.** Today the "Pink Palace," as it's called thanks to its paint job, is a storied resort and gulf-coast architectural landmark, with exterior and public areas oozing turn-of-the-20th-century elegance. **Pros:** romantic destination; great beach; tasty dining options. **Cons:** small rooms, can be quite pricey. *Rooms from: $269* *3400 Gulf Blvd., St. Pete Beach* *727/367–6952, 800/282–1116* *www.doncesar.com* *277 rooms, 40 suites, 70 condos* *No meals.*

$$$ HOTEL Fodor's Choice ★ **Postcard Inn.** Take a Waikiki surf shack from back in Duke's day, shake it up with a little Miami chic (circa 1955), and give it a clean modern twist—that's this ultrahip beachfront hotel to a T. **Pros:** lively fresh feel; on the beach; walking distance to restaurants and nightlife; friendly staff. **Cons:** can be crowded; not for squares. *Rooms from: $169* *6300 Gulf Blvd., St. Pete Beach* *727/367–2611, 800/237–8918* *www.postcardinn.com* *196 rooms* *Breakfast.*

$$$ RESORT FAMILY **TradeWinds Island Grand Resort.** The only resort on the beach offering up its own fireworks display, the island-chic TradeWinds is very popular with foreign travelers and the go-to place for beach weddings; it's also one of the few pet-friendly resorts in the area, with a play area and a room-service menu for dogs and cats. **Pros:** great beachfront location; close to restaurants. **Cons:** large, sprawling complex; lots of conventions; pesky resort fee. *Rooms from: $219* *5500 Gulf Blvd., St. Pete Beach* *727/363–2212* *www.tradewindsresort.com* *584 rooms, 103 suites* *No meals.*

$$$$ RESORT Fodor's Choice ★ **Vinoy Renaissance Resort & Golf Club.** Built in 1925, (making it roughly the same vintage as the Don CeSar), the Vinoy is a luxury resort in St. Petersburg's gorgeous Old Northeast. Thoughtful renovations keep its yesteryear glamour and spot on the National Register of Historic Places. **Pros:** charming property; friendly service; close to downtown museums. **Cons:** pricey; small rooms. *Rooms from: $269* ✉ *501 5th Ave. NE* ☎ *727/894–1000* 🌐 *www.vinoyrenaissanceresort.com* *346 rooms, 15 suites* *No meals.*

NIGHTLIFE

BARS AND PUBS

Ale and the Witch. Situated in the courtyard of an office building just off trendy Beach Drive, this establishment is a live-music hub—mostly jam bands—as well as the cornerstone of St. Petersburg's exploding craft-beer scene. Fans of IPAs, saisons, stouts, you name it, will find their beer of choice somewhere amid the lengthy list of brews on tap. There's some seating inside, but all the action happens outside in the courtyard, where there are plenty of tables and a makeshift band shell. Patrons are welcome to grab food from one of the complex's several restaurants to go along with their brews. Although it's a late-night draw, kids and dogs are welcome. ✉ *111 2nd Ave. NE, Downtown* ☎ *727/821–2533* 🌐 *thealeandthewitch.com.*

Daiquiri Shak. If frozen DayGlo concoctions spinning around in washing machine–like mechanisms are your thing, this place should certainly be on your list. If not, this is still a good go-to weekend watering hole on Madeira Beach (technically, it's across the street from the beach). In addition to selections like the Grape Ape and the Voodoo Loveshake, there's a respectable selection of beer on tap and a full bar. Entertainment ranges from a weekly pub quiz to full-on funk and rock bands on weekends. The menu includes loads of seafood, of course (oysters are a winner), and the late-night menu is served until 1:30 am. ✉ *14995 Gulf Blvd., Madeira Beach* ☎ *727/393–2706* 🌐 *www.daiquirishak.com.*

Green Bench Brewing Company. The name of this bar is a nod to the green benches that once lined Central Avenue, which retirees occupied in a bygone era. St. Pete has shaken its rap as a sleepy retirement town, and this brewery embodies the Sunshine City's recent revival as a craft-beer town. Barkeeps here serve up brews made on-site as well as a few guest batches. The interior has a lodgelike feel (as much as a bar can in Florida), but the real ambience lies outside, where Adirondack chairs and badminton sets are scattered across the lawn. It's also conveniently located a couple of blocks from Tropicana Field, so the place can get packed before and after the Rays play. ✉ *1133 Baum Ave., Downtown* ☎ *727/800–9836* 🌐 *greenbenchbrewing.com.*

Jimmy B's. The default beach bar for tourists and locals alike overlooks the vast dunes leading down to the beach. There's live music virtually every night. ✉ *6200 Gulf Blvd., behind Beachcomber Resort, St. Pete Beach* ☎ *727/367–1902.*

The Mandarin Hide. Perhaps the epitome of downtown St. Pete's bold transformation into a stylish nightlife destination, this place exudes a classy yet jubilant speakeasy vibe. A claw-foot bathtub is one of the first things you see when you walk in the door. Just as vintage as the decor is the drinks menu, which features numerous classic cocktails (made the old-fashioned way), tasty concoctions you'll find nowhere else, and craft beers. You'll find either live music or a DJ most nights. On Sunday they open early to serve up a mean bloody Mary. It's closed on Monday and Tuesday. ✉ *231 Central Ave., Downtown* ☎ *727/231–4007* 🌐 *www.mandarinhide.com.*

World of Beer. The name says it all. This local chain is less than a decade old, but it's caught on beyond Tampa Bay. There are now locations throughout the state, including outlets in Tampa and West Palm Beach, but this one fits right in with the downtown St. Pete vibe and locals' endless thirst for craft brew. A new and improved version of the neighborhood pub, WOB offers bottle and draft beers from as far away as New Zealand and as nearby as St. Pete or Tampa. There's live music on weekends. ✉ *100 4th St. S, Downtown* ☎ *727/823–2337* 🌐 *www.wobusa.com.*

LIVE MUSIC VENUES

Mahaffey Theater. This event spot sits on the south end of the downtown waterfront and is one of the only places in St. Petersburg to see big-ticket national acts as well as the Florida orchestra, which comes through often. ✉ *400 1st St. S* ☎ *727/892–5798* 🌐 *themahaffey.com.*

Ruby's Elixir. If you want to scope out some vintage jazz, blues, or swing, this is the place to do it. It has much better ventilation than most other bars downtown, and you can bring your beverages to one of the outdoor tables—if you can snag one. It's also a great place to find a unique cocktail. ✉ *15 3rd St. N, Downtown* ☎ *727/898–7829* 🌐 *www.rubyselixir.com.*

SHOPPING

There's no need for a trip to the mall here. Few places in the Tampa Bay area offer so many eclectic shopping options as the St. Petersburg area. Downtown St. Petersburg's Beach Drive is sprinkled with tons of smart yet pricey boutiques. The Grand Central district has plenty of antiques and vintage clothing shops. Beach shopping hubs John's Pass Village and 8th Avenue offer souvenir shopping that goes well beyond the norm. Each of these is also packed with a range of enticing eateries, many with outdoor seating and live entertainment.

Epitomizing St. Petersburg's cultural rebirth, the block-long stretch of Central Avenue between 6th and 7th streets has loads of art galleries and indie shops, as well as dive bars frequented by tattooed hipsters. The central point is Crislip Arcade, where you'll find a vintage clothing shop (Ramblin' Rose), local art galleries (eve-N-odd and Olio, to name a couple), and a unique jewelry shop (Kathryn Cole). Local businesses line the street, including one that specializes in Moroccan imports (Treasures of Morocco), one that hawks a colorful array of vintage clothing and campy memorabilia (Star Booty), and a smoky bar specializing in craft beer and punk rock (Fubar). Local 662 and the State Theater are two music venues on this block that attract national indie music acts.

Art Village. It's hard to believe that the low-key yet vibrant artist enclave of Gulfport was once a blighted fishing village. Now, it's a colorful waterfront community that's very welcoming to the LGBT community. It's pretty much in between St. Pete Beach and St. Petersburg proper, and Beach Boulevard's Art Village sports a high volume of locally owned boutiques, galleries and eclectic eateries. Highlights include Hula Hula, a shop dealing in vintage tropical attire and decor, and Domain, where you can find items—Floridiana or otherwise—you'll find nowhere else, given that much of it was forged at the hands of local artisans. An Art Walk occurs every first Friday and third Saturday of the month, and there's a farmer's market every Tuesday. Keep an eye out for cool local events, as there are many here. ✉ *Beach Blvd. at Shore Dr., Gulfport.*

Florida Craftsmen Galleries. Downtown St. Pete's bursting art revival is epitomized at Florida Craftsmen Galleries, a nonprofit that gives 125 local crafts people a chance to exhibit glassware, jewelry, furniture, and more. (Think: a vivid coral reef seascape made entirely out of yarn. Stuff like that.) While you're here, take a stroll along Central Avenue's 600 block for a real glimpse into downtown St. Pete's fresh, burgeoning art scene. The gallery is open Monday through Saturday, from 10 to 5:30. ✉ *501 Central Ave.* ☎ *727/821–7391* 🌐 *www.floridacraftsmen.net.*

Haslam's. One of the state's most notable bookstores, this family-owned emporium has been doing business in St. Petersburg's Grand Central District since the 1930s. Rumored to be haunted by the ghost of *On the Road* author Jack Kerouac (indeed the renowned Beat Generation author used to frequent Haslam's before he died in St. Pete in 1969), the store carries some 300,000 volumes, from cutting-edge best-sellers to ancient tomes. If you value a good book or simply like to browse, you could easily spend an afternoon here. ✉ *2025 Central Ave.* ☎ *727/822–8616* 🌐 *www.haslams.com.*

John's Pass Village and Boardwalk. This collection of shops and restaurants is in an old-style fishing village, where you can watch pelicans cavorting and dive-bombing for food or check out some mellow island music. This is also one of your bests bet for finding a place to rent a Jet Ski or catch a parasailing boat. There's even a live gator attraction here, where patrons can pay to feed the enormous Florida icons large slabs of meat. ✉ *12901 Gulf Blvd., Madeira Beach* 🌐 *www.johnspass.com.*

Pass-a-Grille 8th Avenue. Pass-A-Grille, the extremely laid-back portion of St. Pete Beach, is well known for its serene beaches, historic buildings, and small-town vibe. What many visitors—and locals—don't know is that eight blocks north of the island's southern tip lies a strip of upscale local shops and art galleries. Favorites include Evander Preston's (who also brews a beer sold locally), Paradiso (resortwear, etc.), and Mountcastle International Trading Company (featuring hand-crafted items from across the globe). An interesting variety of restaurants and bars, including a sweets shop, an all-vegan eatery, and Shadrack's, a quintessential beach dive, also line the street. ✉ *8th Ave., St. Pete Beach.*

SPORTS AND THE OUTDOORS

BASEBALL

Tampa Bay Rays. Major League Baseball's Tampa Bay Rays completed an improbable worst-to-first turnaround when they topped the American League Eastern Division in 2008, and again in 2010. Then there was that dramatic end-of-season comeback in 2011. Tickets are available at the box office for most games, but you may have to rely on the classifieds sections of the *Tampa Tribune* and *Tampa Bay Times* for popular games. Get here early; parking is often at a premium (pregaming at Ferg's is always a safe bet). ✉ *Tropicana Field, 1 Tropicana Dr., off I–175* ☎ *727/825–3137* 🌐 *www.tampabay.rays.mlb.com.*

CLEARWATER AND VICINITY

Clearwater is 12 miles north of St. Petersburg via U.S. 19.

In Clearwater itself, residential areas are a buffer between the commercial zone that centers on U.S. 19 and the beach, which is moderately quiet during winter but buzzing with life during spring break and in summer. There's a quaint downtown area on the mainland, just east of the beach. You'll find a nightly sunset celebration on the beach and tons of options for dining and entertainment. Among this area's celebrity residents is Winter, the young dolphin who was fitted with a prosthetic tail and depicted in the 2011 film Dolphin Tale; she's helping put this place and its renowned beaches on the map.

If you're up for a day trip, you have two good options if you head north on U.S. 19. One is Dunedin, a Scottish settlement that's packed with cute shops, restaurants, and craft beer bars. You'll find some gorgeous beaches to the west.

Farther north is charming Tarpon Springs, which has a highly Greek-influenced downtown. Here, you'll find historic sponge docks, a Greek restaurant or two, and some great beaches for watching the sunset.

GETTING HERE AND AROUND

Clearwater is due west from Tampa International Airport via State Road 60, and it's about 45 minutes north of St. Petersburg. If you want to fly directly to Clearwater instead of Tampa, though, St. Pete/Clearwater International Airport is another option. From St. Pete you can get here via U.S. 19, which is notorious for its congestion, Alternate U.S. 19, or County Road 1. If you're up for a scenic yet slower drive, Gulf Boulevard takes you all the way to Clearwater from St. Pete Beach—as does a beach trolley that runs along that route.

VISITOR INFORMATION

Contacts Clearwater Regional Chamber of Commerce ☎ *727/461–0011* 🌐 *www.clearwaterflorida.org.* **Greater Dunedin Chamber of Commerce** ☎ *727/733–3197* 🌐 *www.dunedin-fl.com.* **Tarpon Springs Chamber of Commerce** ☎ *727/937–6109* 🌐 *www.tarponspringschamber.com.*

Continued on page 538

SPRING TRAINING, FLORIDA-STYLE

by Jim Tunstall and Connie Sharpe

Sunshine, railroads, and land bargains were Florida's first tourist magnets, but baseball had a hand in things, too. The Chicago Cubs led the charge when they opened spring training in Tampa in 1913—the same year the Cleveland Indians set up camp in Pensacola.

Over the next couple of decades, World War I and the Great Depression interrupted normal lives, but the Sunshine State became a great fit for the national pastime. Soon, big-league teams were flocking south to work off the winter rust.

At one point, the Florida "Grapefruit League" held a monopoly on spring training, but in 1947 Arizona's "Cactus League" started cutting into the action.

Today, roughly half of Major League Baseball's 30 teams arrive in Florida in February for six weeks of calisthenics, tryouts, and practice games. The clubs range from the Detroit Tigers, who have been in the same city (Lakeland) longer than any other team (since 1934), to the Tampa Bay Rays, who moved to a new spring home (Port Charlotte) in 2009.

The Los Angeles Dodgers play the Washington Nationals in Viera during a spring training game.

HERE COME THE FANS

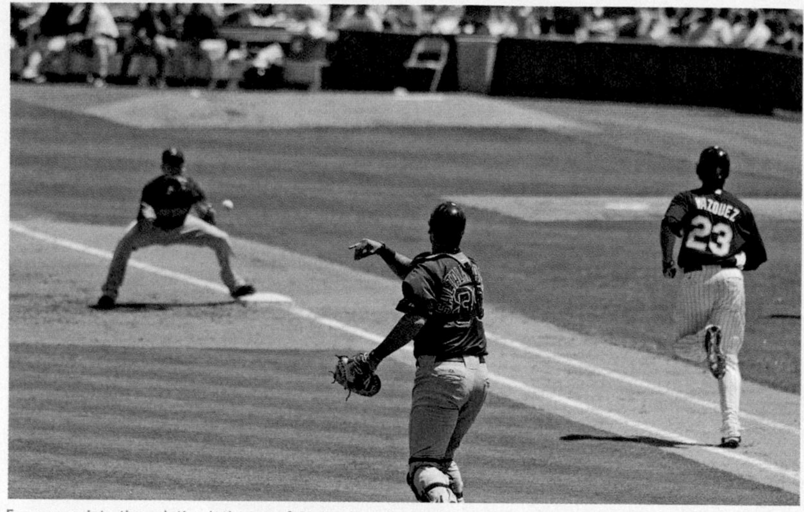

Fan appreciate the relative intimacy of Spring Training stadiums.

Florida's spring training teams play 25 or 30 home and away games, to the delight of 1.68 million annual ticker buyers. Diehards land as soon as the first troops—pitchers and catchers—come to practice around the third week of February. Intersquad games start in the fourth week, while the real training schedule begins by the end of February or first of March and lasts until the end of the month or early April. These games don't count in the regular season, but they give managers and fans a good idea of which players will be on the opening-day rosters, and who will be traded, sent to the teams' minor leagues, or told it's time to find a regular day job.

Spring training games provide a great excuse for local baseball fans to cut out of work early, while visitors from the North can leave ice, snow, and sleet behind. And who doesn't want a few chili dogs, brats, burgers, and brews on a March day? Spring training's draw is more than just a change of venue with an early sample of concession-stand staples. There is also the ample choice of game sites. Teams are scattered around most of the major tourist areas of central and southern Florida, so those coming to watch the games can try a different destination each spring—or even make a road trip to several. Baseball fans also like that it's a melting pot—teams from more than a dozen cities are represented here.

Finally, you can't beat the price—tickets are usually cheaper than during the regular season—nor the access you have to baseball celebrities. In fact, the relaxed atmosphere of spring training makes most players more willing to sign your ball, glove, or whatever. You can get autographs during pregame workouts (practice sessions), which are free, as well as after the game.

4 TIPS

■ **Have a game plan.** Don't just show up. Most teams only have about 15 home games, and those involving popular teams often sell out weeks in advance. Consider buying tickets ahead of time, and if needed, make hotel room reservations at the same time.

■ **Beat the crowds.** The best chance to do this is to go to a weekday game. You'll still encounter lots of fans, but weekday games generally aren't as well attended as weekenders. Also, each team only has a few night games.

■ **Pack a picnic.** Some stadiums let you bring coolers through the turnstiles. Many game attendees also gather for a tailgate party, grilling burgers and sipping a lemonade or beer while jawing with fellow fans (have a chair in tow).

■ West coast games get a lot of sun. Seats in the shade are premium.

(above) Hammond Stadium in Ft. Myers is where the Minnesota Twins practice.
(right) St. Louis Cardinals Chris Duncan is tagged out at Roger Dean Stadium in Jupiter.

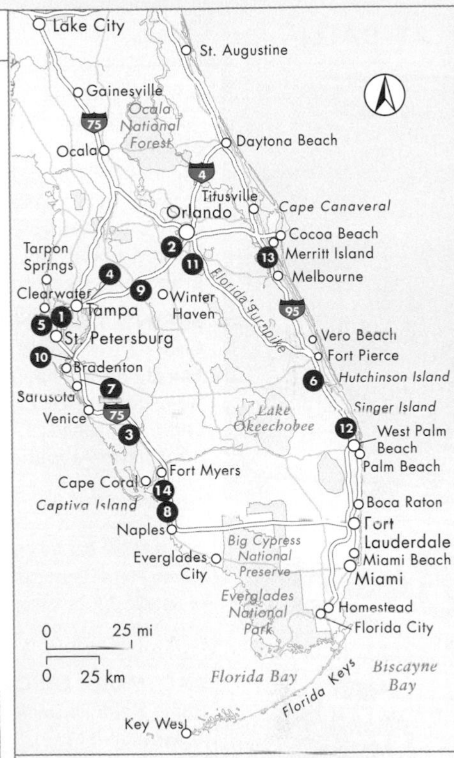

Atlanta Braves	2	New York Yankees	4
Baltimore Orioles	7	Philadelphia Phillies	1
Boston Red Sox	14	Pittsburgh Pirates	10
Detroit Tigers	9	St. Louis Cardinals/ Florida Marlins	12
Houston Astros	11	Tampa Bay Rays	3
Minnesota Twins	8	Toronto Blue Jays	5
New York Mets	6	Washington Nationals	13

PLAY BALL!

Spring training schedules are determined around Thanksgiving. Ticket prices change each year. For all of these teams, you also can order spring training tickets through Ticketmaster (☎ 866/448–7849 🌐 www.ticketmaster.com) or through the respective team's box office or team Web site. For more information about any of the teams, visit 🌐 www.floridagrapefruitleague.com.

SPRING TRAINING GUIDE

Order a free Guide to *Florida Spring Training* from the **Florida Sports Foundation** (✉ 2930 Kerry Forest Parkway, Tallahassee, FL ☎ 850/488–8347 🌐 www.flasports.com). Published in February each year, it's packed with information about teams, sites, tickets, and more.

New York Mets catcher Ramon Castro.

ATLANTA BRAVES

Home Field: Champion Stadium, Walt Disney World Wide World of Sports, 700 S. Victory Way, Lake Buena Vista. **Tickets:** $10–$49 ☎ 407/939–4263 🌐 www.braves.mlb.com

BALTIMORE ORIOLES

Home Field: Ed Smith Stadium, 2700 12th St., Sarasota. **Tickets:** $8–$32 ☎ 941/954–4101 🌐 www.orioles.mlb.com

BOSTON RED SOX

Home Field: JetBlue Park, 11500 Fenway South Dr., Fort Myers. **Tickets:** $10–$46 ☎ 239/334–4700, 888/733–7696 🌐 www.redsox.mlb.com

DETROIT TIGERS

Home Field: Joker Marchant Stadium, 2301 Lakeland Hills Blvd., Lakeland. **Tickets:** $10–$32 ☎ 863/686–8075 🌐 www.tigers.mlb.com

HOUSTON ASTROS

Home Field: Osceola County Stadium, 631 Heritage Parkway, Kissimmee. **Tickets:** $15–$27 ☎ 321/697–3200 🌐 www.astros.mlb.com

MIAMI MARLINS

Home Field: Roger Dean Stadium (shared with St. Louis Cardinals), 4751 Main St., Jupiter. **Tickets:** $15–$28 ☎ 561/775–1818 🌐 www.marlins.mlb.com

	**MINNESOTA TWINS** **Home Field:** Lee County Sports Complex, 14100 Six Mile Cypress Parkway, Fort Myers. **Tickets:** $13–$29 ☎ 800/338-9467 🌐 www.twins.mlb.com
	**NEW YORK METS** **Home Field:** Mets Field, 525 NW Peacock Blvd., Port St. Lucie. **Tickets:** $8–$25 ☎ 772/871-2115 🌐 www.mets.mlb.com
	**NEW YORK YANKEES** **Home Field:** George M. Steinbrenner Field, 1 Steinbrenner Dr., Tampa. **Tickets:** $17–$33 ☎ 813/879-2244 🌐 www.yankees.mlb.com
	**PHILADELPHIA PHILLIES** **Home Field:** Bright House Networks Field, 601 N. Old Coachman Rd., Clearwater. **Tickets:** $14–$39 ☎ 727/467-4457 🌐 www.phillies.mlb.com
	**PITTSBURGH PIRATES** **Home Field:** McKechnie Field, 1611 9th St. W, Bradenton. **Tickets:** $12–$22 ☎ 941/747-3031 🌐 www.pirates.mlb.com
	**ST. LOUIS CARDINALS** **Home Field:** Roger Dean Stadium (shared with Miami Marlins), 4751 Main St., Jupiter. **Tickets:** $15–$28 ☎ 561/630-1828 🌐 www.cardinals.mlb.com
	**TAMPA BAY RAYS** **Home Field:** Charlotte County Sports Park, 2300 El Jobean Rd., Port Charlotte. **Tickets:** $10–$27 ☎ 888/326-7297 🌐 www.rays.mlb.com
	**TORONTO BLUE JAYS** **Home Field:** Florida Auto Exchange Park, 373 Douglas Ave., Dunedin. **Tickets:** $15–$30 ☎ 727/733-0429 🌐 www.bluejays.mlb.com
	**WASHINGTON NATIONALS** **Home Field:** Space Coast Stadium, 5800 Stadium Parkway, Viera. **Tickets:** $12–$26 ☎ 321/633-4487 🌐 www.nationals.mlb.com

EXPLORING

Clearwater Marine Aquarium. This aquarium gives you the opportunity to participate in the work of saving and caring for endangered marine species. Many of the sea turtles, dolphins, and other animals living at the aquarium were brought here to be rehabilitated from an injury or saved from danger. The dolphin exhibit has an open-air arena giving the dolphins plenty of room to jump during their shows. This aquarium is also home to Winter, a dolphin fitted with a prosthetic tail that was the subject of the 2011 film *Dolphin Tale*. The aquarium conducts tours of the bays and islands around Clearwater, including a daily cruise on a pontoon boat (you might just see a wild dolphin or two), and kayak tours of Clearwater Harbor and St. Joseph Sound. ✉ *249 Windward Passage* ☎ *727/441–1790* 🌐 *www.seewinter.com* 🎫 *$20* 🕒 *Daily 9–6.*

Konger Tarpon Springs Aquarium. Although it's not on par with larger facilities in Tampa and Clearwater, this is certainly an entertaining attraction. There are some good exhibits, including a 120,000-gallon shark tank complete with a coral reef. (Divers feed the sharks several times daily.) Also look for tropical fish exhibits and a tank where you can touch baby sharks and stingrays. ✉ *850 Dodecanese Blvd., off U.S. 19, Tarpon Springs* ☎ *727/938–5378* 🌐 *www.tarponspringsaquarium.com* 🎫 *$7.75* 🕒 *Mon.–Sat. 10–5, Sun. noon–5.*

FAMILY **Pier 60.** This spot is the terminus of State Road 60 (hence the name), which runs under various names between Vero Beach on the east coast and Clearwater Beach on the west coast. Around 3:30 pm each day, weather permitting, the area surrounding the pier starts to liven up. Local artists and craftspeople populate their folding tables with beaded jewelry, handmade skin-care products, and beach landscape paintings. Jugglers, musicians, break-dancers, and fire breathers put on some lively shows for those in attendance. And the grand finale is the sun setting over the Gulf of Mexico. On weekends when the weather is mild, there are also free, family-friendly movie screenings. ✉ *10 Pier 60 Dr., Clearwater Beach* ☎ *727/449–1036* 🌐 *www.sunsetsatpier60.com.*

The Sponge Factory. This shop, museum, and cultural center reveals more than you ever imagined about how a lowly sea creature created the industry that built this village. See a film about these much-sought-after creatures from the phylum *porifera* and how they helped the town prosper in the early 1900s. You'll come away converted to (and loaded up with) natural sponges. ✉ *15 Dodecanese Blvd., off Alt. U.S. 19, Tarpon Springs* ☎ *727/938–5366* 🌐 *www.spongedocks.net* 🎫 *Free* 🕒 *Daily 9–6.*

BEACHES

Caladesi Island State Park. Quiet, secluded, and still wild, this 3½-mile-long barrier island is one of the best shelling beaches on the Gulf Coast, second only to Sanibel. The park also has plenty of sights for birders—from common sandpipers to majestic blue herons to rare black skimmers—and miles of trails through scrub oaks, saw palmettos, and cacti (with tenants such as armadillos, rabbits, and raccoons). The landscape also features mangroves and dunes, and the gradual slope of the sea

Clearwater's Bait House lures in those heading to the pier to fish; photo by watland, Fodors.com member.

bottom makes this a good spot for novice swimmers and kids. You have to get to Caladesi Island by private boat (there's a 108-slip marina) or through its sister park, Honeymoon Island State Recreation Area, where you take the hourly ferry ride across to Caladesi. Ferry rides cost $14 per person. **Amenities:** food and drink; showers; toilets. **Best for:** solitude; swimming. ✉ *Dunedin Causeway, Dunedin* ☎ *727/469–5918* 🌐 *floridastateparks.org/caladesiisland* 🎫 *$8 per boat; $2 per kayaker* 🕒 *Daily 8–sunset.*

Fodor's Choice ★ **Clearwater Beach.** On a narrow island between Clearwater Harbor and the gulf is a stretch of sand with a widespread reputation for beach volleyball. It's also the site of a nightly sunset celebration, complete with musicians and artisans. It's one of the area's nicest and busiest beaches, especially on weekends and during spring break, but it's also one of the costliest in terms of parking fees, which can reach $2 per hour. **Amenities:** food and drink; showers; toilets. **Best for:** partiers; sunset; walking. ✉ *Western end of Rte. 60, 2 miles west of downtown Clearwater.*

Honeymoon Island State Park. If you're seeking an almost completely undeveloped beach that's still easily accessible by car, this is one of your best bets. Northwest of Clearwater, this large state park offers some of the best shell hunting you'll find, as well as thousands of feet of serene beachfront. If you head north along the park road, you find extensive hiking trails, along which you'll see an astonishing array of birds. **Amenities:** food and drink; showers; toilets. **Best for:** solitude; swimming; walking. ✉ *1 Causeway Blvd., Dunedin* 🌐 *floridastateparks.org/honeymoonisland* 🎫 *Single occupant vehicle $8* 🕒 *Daily 8 am–sunset.*

Howard Park Beach. It comes in two parts: a shady mainland picnic area with barbecues and a white-sand beach island. The causeway is a popular hangout for windsurfers, and the entire area is great for birding. **Amenities:** showers; toilets. **Best for:** sunset; swimming; windsurfing. ✉ *1700 Sunset Dr., Tarpon Springs* 🎫 *$5.*

Indian Rocks Beach. This beach community is a mellow alternative to the oft-crowded shorelines of Clearwater and St. Pete Beach along the gulf coast. This is a town in which the road narrows to two lanes and is lined with upscale residential condos instead of busy hotels. There are quite a few beach access points, though your best bet is a landscaped facility offering ample parking, nearby food and drink, and an occasional event. **Amenities:** food and drink; parking; showers; toilets. **Best for:** solitude; swimming; walking. ✉ *Indian Rocks Beach Nature Preserve, 1700 Gulf Blvd., Indian Rocks Beach* 🌐 *www.indian-rocks-beach.com.*

Sand Key Park. This is a mellow counterpart to often-crowded Clearwater Beach to the north. It has a lovely beach, plenty of green space, a playground, and a picnic area in an otherwise congested area. **Amenities:** food and drink; lifeguards; showers; toilets. **Best for:** solitude; sunset; swimming. ✉ *1060 Gulf Blvd.* ☎ *727/588–4852.*

Sunset Beach. As the name suggests, this beach park is known as one of the best places in North Pinellas County to watch the sunset. It's a small beach but a great place to barbecue. From April through November there's a weekly concert. **Amenities:** toilets. **Best for:** sunset; swimming. ✉ *1800 Gulf Rd., Tarpon Springs.*

WHERE TO EAT

$$$ AMERICAN

✕ **Bob Heilman's Beachcomber.** The Heilman family has fed hungry diners since 1920. Although it's very popular with tourists, you'll also rub shoulders with devoted locals. Despite the frequent crowds, the service is fast and friendly. The sautéed chicken is an American classic—arriving with mashed spuds, gravy, veggie du jour, and fresh baked bread. Or try some Gulf shrimp prepared in nearly any way you can imagine, including lightly breaded and fried, tossed with pasta primavera and sautéed vegetables, or served Rockefeller-style. $ *Average main: $25* ✉ *447 Mandalay Ave., Clearwater Beach* ☎ *727/442–4144* 🌐 *www.bobheilmans.com.*

$$$ EUROPEAN

✕ **Bon Appétit.** Known for its creative fare, this waterfront restaurant has a menu that changes frequently, offering such entrées as broiled rack of lamb in herbed walnut crust, and red snapper on a bed of lobster hash. The creative grouper options, i.e. grouper gyros, get well-deserved plaudits from many patrons. Bon Appétit has staying power, having served at the same location for more than three decades. It's a great place to catch a sunset over the Gulf of Mexico. There's live music every night, and a pianist plays Wednesday through Sunday evenings and at Sunday brunch. $ *Average main: $25* ✉ *148 Marina Plaza, Dunedin* ☎ *727/733–2151* 🌐 *www.bonappetitrestaurant.com.*

$$ MEXICAN

✕ **Casa Tina.** At this colorful Dunedin institution, vegetarians can veg out on roasted chiles rellenos (cheese-stuffed peppers), enchiladas with vegetables, and a cactus salad that won't prick your tongue but will tickle your taste buds with the tantalizing flavors of tender pieces of cactus, cilantro, tomatoes, onions, lime, and *queso fresco* (a mild white cheese). The stuffed sapote squash also makes the grade. Tamales, tacos, and tortillas are prepared in dozens of ways. The place is often crowded, and service can be slow as a result, but there's a reason everyone's eating here. $ *Average main: $15* ✉ *365 Main St., Dunedin* ☎ *727/734–9226.*

$$ SEAFOOD ✕ **Frenchy's Rockaway Grill.** Quebec native Mike "Frenchy" Preston runs four eateries in the area, including the fabulous Rockaway Grill. Visitors and locals alike keep coming back for the grouper sandwiches that are moist and not battered into submission. (It's also real grouper, something that's not a given these days.) Frenchy also gets a big thumbs-up for the she-crab soup, and, on the march-to-a-different-drummer front, the grouper eggrolls. In mild weather, eat on the deck, though the screaming yellow awning can be nearly as blinding as the sun. $ *Average main: $15* ✉ *7 Rockaway St.* ☎ *727/446–4844* 🌐 *www.frenchysonline.com.*

$$ SEAFOOD ✕ **Palm Pavilion Beachside Grill & Bar.** Long heralded as one of the best spots for watching sunsets, this place also gets high marks for its fresh seafood offerings. The grouper sandwich in particular gets rave reviews. Healthier fare includes an array of wraps. The restaurant is casual but not too casual. It's got a bit of a Tommy Bahama feel to it, so you may want to ditch the beach attire if you plan to dine here. Be advised that it gets pretty packed around sunset, when a live band plays island music and the margaritas flow. $ *Average main: $15* ✉ *10 Bay Esplande, Clearwater Beach* ☎ *727/446–2642* 🌐 *www.palmpavilion.com.*

WHERE TO STAY

$$$ HOTEL **Hilton Clearwater Beach.** This marquee property has a look that is clean and modern without losing the Clearwater Beach vibe, and staying here may be a little less pricey than you might expect. **Pros:** on the beach; about as modern as you can get. **Cons:** chain hotel feel; lots of conventions; resort fee. $ *Rooms from: $219* ✉ *400 Mandalay Ave., Clearwater Beach* ☎ *727/461–3222* 🌐 *www.hiltonclearwaterbeach.com* *416 rooms, 12 suites* *No meals.*

$$$$ RESORT **Hyatt Regency Clearwater Beach.** One of the more recent additions to the Clearwater Beach skyline, this upscale resort towers above almost everything else in the immediate area, both in terms of height and luxury. **Pros:** gorgeous facility; plenty of amenities; near the action. **Cons:** beach is across busy street; some floors are residential; expensive. $ *Rooms from: $450* ✉ *301 S. Gulfview Blvd.* ☎ *727/373–1234* 🌐 *www.clearwaterbeach.hyatt.com* *250 suites* *No meals.*

$$$ RESORT **Innisbrook Resort & Golf Club.** A massive pool complex with a 15-foot waterfall, two winding waterslides, and a sandy waterfront are part of the allure of this sprawling resort, but it may be the 72 holes of golf, including the challenging Copperhead course, that are the real draw. **Pros:** great for serious golfers; varied dining options. **Cons:** far from attractions. $ *Rooms from: $179* ✉ *36750 U.S. 19 N, Palm Harbor* ☎ *727/942–2000, 888/794–8627* 🌐 *www.innisbrookgolfresort.com* *50 rooms, 550 suites* *No meals.*

DID YOU KNOW?

Sponging began in Tarpon Springs 120 years ago. At one time it was the state's leading industry. Divers harvest the sea sponges, and visitors can bid on some of them at the weekly auctions on the sponge docks.

$$$$ RESORT **Safety Harbor Resort & Spa.** Those who enjoy old-school pampering love this hotel's exceptional 50,000-square-foot spa, which has the latest in therapies and treatments. **Pros:** charm to spare; good choice for pampering. **Cons:** far from beach; not ideal for families with children. *Rooms from: $269* ✉ *105 N. Bayshore Dr., Safety Harbor* ☎ *727/726–1161, 877/784–6835* 🌐 *www.safetyharborspa.com* *175 rooms, 16 suites* *No meals.*

$$$$ RESORT **Sandpearl Resort.** Two things set this expansive, luxurious Clearwater Beach resort apart from other upscale accommodations in the vicinity: it's not part of a major chain, and the property has deep local ties. **Pros:** on the beach; tons of amenities and dining options. **Cons:** resort fee; lots of conventions. *Rooms from: $279* ✉ *500 Mandalay Ave.* ☎ *727/441–2425* 🌐 *sandpearl.com* *203 rooms, 50 suites* *No meals.*

$$$$ RESORT **Sheraton Sand Key Resort.** Expect something special when you stay here, including a modern property and one of the few uncluttered beaches in the area. **Pros:** private beach; great views; no resort fee and parking is also free. **Cons:** near crowded Clearwater Beach; views come with a high price tag. *Rooms from: $230* ✉ *1160 Gulf Blvd., Clearwater Beach* ☎ *727/595–1611* 🌐 *www.sheratonsandkey.com* *375 rooms, 15 suites* *No meals.*

NIGHTLIFE

Dunedin Brewery. Tampa Bay is seen by many as a flourishing craft-beer hub. If it weren't for Dunedin Brewery, that might not be the case. It was the first of its kind in the area and continues to offer delicious brews to throngs of patrons. It doesn't hurt that it offers live music many nights of the week, either. ✉ *937 Douglas Ave., Dunedin* ☎ *727/736–0606* 🌐 *dunedinbrewery.com.*

SPORTS AND THE OUTDOORS

BASEBALL

Philadelphia Phillies. The Phillies get ready for the season with spring training here (late February to early April). The stadium also hosts the Phillies' farm team. Check out their minor league team, the Clearwater Threshers, at Bright House Field during the summer months. ✉ *Bright House Networks Field, 601 N. Old Coachman Rd.* ☎ *727/467–4557* 🌐 *philadelphia.phillies.mlb.com.*

Toronto Blue Jays. The Jays play around 15 to 20 spring training games here, starting in February, which is why Dunedin is packed with Canadians this time of year. The team has trained here since its 1977 inception—and this consistency is not common for a major league team. A farm team plays here in the summer. The training fields are several miles away, at 1700 Solon Avenue. ✉ *Florida Auto Exchange Stadium, 373 Douglas Ave., north of Hwy. 580, Dunedin* ☎ *727/733–9302* 🌐 *toronto.bluejays.mlb.com/.*

BIKING

Pinellas Trail. This 42-mile paved route spans Pinellas County, from near the southernmost point all the way north to Tarpon Springs. Along a former railway line, the trail runs adjacent to major thoroughfares, no more than 10 feet from the roadway, so you can access it from almost any point. The trail, also popular with in-line skaters, has spawned trailside businesses such as repair shops and health-food cafés. There are also many lovely rural areas to bike through and plenty of places to rent bikes. Be wary of traffic in downtown Clearwater and on the congested areas of the Pinellas Trail, which still needs more bridges for crossing over busy streets, and avoid the trail at night. To start riding from the route's south end, park at Trailhead Park (37th Street South at 8th Avenue South) in St. Petersburg. To ride south from the north end, park your car in downtown Tarpon Springs (East Tarpon Avenue at North Stafford Avenue). ☎ *727/549–6099* 🌐 *www.pinellascounty.org/trailgd.*

GOLF

Dunedin Golf Club. Dunedin is Tampa Bay's little Scotland, the birthplace of golf, so it's only natural that one of the area's better courses is here. Designed by influential golf-course architect Donald Ross, this semi-private, recently restored facility also has a driving range, a pro shop, and clubhouse. The course itself offers numerous challenging holes with names like "It Isn't Easy," "Calamity Jane," and "Devil's Kick," with the twists and turns to match. Water hazards aren't too overwhelming here, except on the 14th hole, known as "Round the Lake." ✉ *1050 Palm Blvd., Dunedin* ☎ *727/733–7836* 🌐 *www.dunedingolfclub.com* 🎫 *$50 for 18 holes* ⛳ *18 holes, 6,625 yards, par 72.*

Innisbrook. Considered one of the top 100 golf destinations in Florida, this resort is home to Larry Packard-designed Copperhead Course, which hosts the annual PGA Tour Valspar Championship. Open to resort guests as well as the public, the four courses here take full advantage of the fact that they're on the coast, with plenty of ponds and sand traps adding to the scenery as well as the challenge. Fairways here on the Copperhead Course consist of rolling hills lined with trees, which are prime for spotting blue herons, squirrels, and even an alligator or two. The Island Course offers narrow fairways, some of which are lined by Lake Innisbrook, others by tall stands of pine and cypress trees. The North Course features tight fairways, numerous bunkers and 11 water hazards, while the South Course has more of a links courselike layout. The Fox Squirrel Course is a quick 9-hole course available to guests only. ✉ *36750 U.S. Hwy. 19, North, Palm Harbor* ☎ *888/794–8627, 727/942–2000* 🌐 *innisbrookgolfresort.com* 🎫 *Copperhead Course: $280. Island Course: $240. North and South Courses: $190.* ⛳ *Copperhead Course: 18 holes, 7,430 yards, par 72. Island Course: 18 holes, 7,310 yards, par 70. North Course: 18 holes, South Course, 18 holes, 6,620 yards, par 71; Fox Squirrel Course: 9 holes, 1,236 yards, par 36 (resort guests only, closed during high season).*

SURFING

FlowRider at Surf Style. Surf Style, in the towering Hyatt, is a chain store that sells beach essentials like sarongs, sunblock, and souvenirs. But what sets this particularly enormous store apart is the FlowRider, an indoor pool that generates artificial waves suitable for surfing; for $20 per half-hour, you and the kids can surf or learn to surf, something you can't usually do out in the gulf. An instructor is on hand to show you the ropes. ✉ *Hyatt Regency Clearwater Beach, 311 S. Gulfview Blvd.* ☎ *727/446–6566* 🌐 *www.surf-style.com.*

CITRUS COUNTY

The coastal and western inland areas of Citrus County north of Tampa and St. Petersburg are sometimes called the Nature Coast, and aptly so. Flora and fauna have been well preserved in this area, and West Indian manatees are showstoppers. These gentle vegetarian marine mammals, distantly related to elephants, remain an endangered species, though their numbers have grown to 3,500 or more today. Many manatees have massive scars on their backs from run-ins with boat propellers. Extensive nature preserves and parks have been created to protect them and other wildlife indigenous to the area, and these are among the best spots to view manatees in the wild. Although they're far from mythical beauties, it's believed that manatees inspired ancient mariners' tales of mermaids. This is one of the only spots in the world where you can legally swim with—and even touch—these gentle creatures.

GETTING HERE AND AROUND

U.S. 19 and the Suncoast Parkway, a toll road, are the prime north–south routes through this rural region, and traffic flows freely once you've left the congestion of St. Petersburg, Clearwater, and Port Richey. In most cases, the Suncoast Parkway is a far quicker drive than U.S. 19, though you'll have to pay several dollars in tolls. If you're planning a day trip from the Bay Area, pack a picnic lunch before leaving, since most of the sights are outdoors.

HOMOSASSA SPRINGS

65 miles north of St. Petersburg on U.S. 19.

A little more than an hour north of Clearwater, you'll come upon this small and friendly hub for water lovers. Along with a phenomenal manatee-centric state park, you'll find more than a handful of charming restaurants, some featuring live music in the evening. This and Crystal River provide you with the once-in-a-lifetime chance to swim with manatees, something best done in winter. Summer's scallop season is also a massive draw.

EXPLORING

FAMILY **Ellie Schiller Homosassa Springs Wildlife State Park.** Here you can see many manatees and several species of fish through a floating glass observatory known as the Fish Bowl—except in this case the fish are outside the bowl and you are inside it. The park's wildlife walk trails lead you to excellent manatee, alligator, and other animal programs. Among the species are bobcats, a western cougar, white-tailed deer, a black bear, pelicans, herons, snowy egrets, river otters, whooping cranes, and even a hippopotamus named Lu, a keepsake from the park's days as an exotic-animal attraction. Boat cruises on Pepper Creek lead you to the Homosassa wildlife park (which takes its name from a Creek Indian word meaning "place where wild peppers grow"). ✉ *4150 S. Suncoast Blvd., U.S. 19* ☎ *352/628–5343* 🌐 *loridastateparks.org/homosassasprings/* 🎫 *$13* 🕐 *Daily 9–5:30; last boat departs at 3:15.*

Yulee Sugar Mill Ruins Historic State Park. This state park has the remains of a circa-1851 sugar mill and other remnants of a 5,100-acre sugar plantation owned by Florida's first U.S. senator, David Levy Yulee. It makes for pleasant picnicking and dog-walking, although it is somewhat lacking visually. ✉ *Rte. 490(Yulee Dr.), 3 miles off U.S. 19/98* ☎ *352/795–3817* 🌐 *floridastateparks.org/yuleesugarmill* 🎫 *Free* 🕐 *Daily 8 am–sunset.*

WHERE TO EAT

$ SEAFOOD ✕ **Dan's Clam Stand.** Four reasons to go: the fried grouper sandwich, the clam "chowda," anything else seafood, and the beef burgers. The original location is about 2 miles east of Homosassa Springs State Wildlife Park. It's very popular among locals—just check out the packed parking lot at lunch and dinner. New England–style seafood is a house specialty, including whole-belly clams and lobster, but the grouper and mahimahi are fresh from local waters. Best of all, Dan's won't bust your budget. There's another branch in Crystal River. $ *Average main: $10* ✉ *7364 Grover Cleveland Blvd.* ☎ *352/628–9588* 💳 *No credit cards* 🕐 *Closed Sun.* $ *Average main: $10* ✉ *2315 N. Sunshine Path, off Rte. 44, Crystal River* ☎ *352/795–9081*

$ CUBAN ✕ **Museum Cafe.** A short trip west of Homosassa Springs State Wildlife Refuge, this tiny eatery housed in the Olde Mill House Printing Museum is known for its Cuban sandwiches. It's only open for lunch, but it's well worth making room for a visit here in your itinerary. You can sit at a table within the museum itself or one of the tables in the very casual main dining room. Another option is to get your lunch to go and picnic at nearby Yulee Sugar Mill Ruins State Park. $ *Average main: $10* ✉ *10466 W. Yulee Dr.* ☎ *352/628–1081* 🕐 *No dinner.*

$$ SEAFOOD ✕ **Neon Leon's Zydeco Steakhouse.** If you couldn't already tell, the Nature Coast is about as Southern as you can get. This place is a case in point. This roadhouse-style eatery is co-owned by family members of former Lynyrd Skynyrd bassist Leon Wilkeson. Legend has it that Wilkeson had long dreamed of opening a restaurant serving Southern and Cajun food like fried okra and gator tail, with music to match. You'll hear nightly live zydeco here, and the menu offers Dixieland staples like jambalaya (a favorite here), frog legs, and catfish. It may have a roadhouse feel and plenty of musical memorabilia, but it's also smoke-free and pretty family-friendly. A word of caution: the music can get loud. $ *Average main: $15* ✉ *10350 Yulee Dr.* ☎ *352/621–3663* 🌐 *www.neonleonszydecosteakhouse.com* 🕐 *Closed Mon.*

CRYSTAL RIVER

6 miles north of Homosassa Springs on U.S. 19.

Situated along the peaceful Nature Coast, this area is *the* low-key getaway spot in one of the most pristine and beautiful areas in the state.

It's also one of the only places on the planet where you can legally swim with manatees. The river's fed by a spring that's a constant 72°F, which is why manatees enjoy spending their winters here. Boating and snorkeling are popular, as is scalloping in the summer. This is a true paradise for nature lovers, and absolutely worth making room for in your vacation itinerary.

EXPLORING

Crystal River National Wildlife Refuge. This is a U.S. Fish and Wildlife Service sanctuary for the endangered manatee. Kings Bay, around which manatees congregate in winter (generally from November to March), feeds crystal-clear water into the river at 72°F year-round. This is one of the sure-bet places to see manatees in winter since hundreds congregate near this 90-acre refuge. The small visitor center has displays about the manatee and other refuge inhabitants. If you want to get an even closer look at these gentle giants, several dive companies provide opportunities for you to swim among them—if you don't mind shelling out some extra cash, donning a wetsuit, and adhering to some strict interaction guidelines. In warmer months, when most manatees scatter, the main spring is fun for a swim or scuba diving. ✉ *1502 S.E. Kings Bay Dr.* ☎ *352/563–2088* 🌐 *www.fws.gov/crystalriver* *Free* *Daily 7:30–4.*

BEACH

Fort Island Gulf Beach. This is one of the most remote beaches you will find north of Fort De Soto, the isolated beach south of St. Petersburg. One of the best parts of coming here is the drive. The beach sits as the terminus of Fort Island Trail, the same road where you'll find the Plantation Inn & Golf Resort. A 9-mile drive through the wetlands gets you here, offering sweeping views along the way (though the Crystal River nuclear plant looms to the north). The beach itself is raw and subdued, though there are picnic shelters, barbecues and a fishing pier. Don't expect many frills, but if you need to relax after a long day of playing in the water, this is your place. **Amenities:** showers; toilets. **Best for:** solitude; sunset. ✉ *16000 W. Fort Island Trail.*

WHERE TO STAY

$$ RESORT **Plantation on Crystal River.** On the shore of Kings Bay, this two-story plantation-style resort is on 232 acres near nature preserves and rivers. **Pros:** good location; perfect for nature lovers. **Cons:** lots of conventions; basic rooms. *Rooms from: $130* ✉ *9301 W. Fort Island Trail* ☎ *352/795–4211* 🌐 *www.plantationinn.com* *196 rooms, 12 villas* *No meals.*

10

GOLF

Plantation On Crystal River. Located across the street from the resort of the same name, this public course consists of long, peaceful, live oak–lined fairways and a spate of water hazards. Designed by Mark Mahannah in the late 1960s, the Championship Course boasts of challenges for golfers at every level. The Lagoon Course is a speedier option for golfers who want to get a quick game in between manatee swims or scalloping trips. Players can choose their nines here. ✉ *9301 W. Fort Island Trail* ☎ *352/795–7211* 🌐 *plantationoncrystalriver.com* *$17 for 9 holes; $50 for 18 holes* *Championship Course: 18 holes, 6,472 yards, par 72; Lagoons Course: 9 holes, 2,036 yards, par 31.*

MANATEE DIVES

American Pro Diving Center. This is one of several local operators in the area conducting manatee tours of Crystal River National Wildlife Refuge or Homosassa River, something you can't legally do pretty much anywhere else in the country. Tours start at around $30. ✉ *821 S.E. U.S. 19* ☎ *352/563–0041* 🌐 *www.americanprodiving.com.*

Crystal Lodge Dive Center. This dive center is one of the more popular operators offering dives, swims, and snorkel trips to see manatees, with rates starting as low as $25. ✉ *525 N.W. 7th Ave.* ☎ *352/795–6798* 🌐 *www.manatee-central.com.*

Plantation Dive Shop. An obvious choice if you're staying at the Plantation on Crystal River, this dive tour company stands on its own as a manatee tour operator. The guides bring you out to various spots along the river to interact with manatees, and tend to be long-time residents who know their subject well. If the weather is warm, that means no manatees, so opt for a sunset cruise instead. ✉ *Plantation on Crystal River, 9301 Fort Island Trail* ☎ *352/795–5797* 🌐 *www.crystalriverdivers.com* 🎫 *$30 plus equipment.*

SARASOTA AND VICINITY

Widely thought of as one of the best places in Florida to live, Sarasota County anchors the southern end of Tampa Bay. A string of barrier islands borders it with 35 miles of gulf and bay beaches. Sarasota County has something for anyone, from the athletic to the artistic. Thirteen public beaches, two state parks, 22 municipal parks, plus more than 60 public and private golf courses will help keep the active in motion. Spring training was an original destination attraction that now shares the stage with international rowing, swimming, and sailing events. Add to that a plentiful cultural scene dating to the era of circus magnate John Ringling, who chose this area for the winter home of his circus and his family.

BRADENTON

49 miles south of Tampa.

In 1539 Hernando de Soto landed near this Manatee River city, which has some 20 miles of beaches. Bradenton is well situated for access to fishing, both fresh- and saltwater, and it also has its share of golf courses and historic sites dating to the mid-1800s. Orange groves and cattle ranches mix with farmlands between Bradenton's beaches and Interstate 75.

GETTING HERE AND AROUND

You can get to Bradenton via Interstate 75, Interstate 275, and U.S. 41/301. West Manatee Avenue gets you out to the beaches. Manatee County Area Transit (MCAT) has buses throughout Bradenton and the nearby towns of Palmetto and Ellenton, as well as connections to Sarasota attractions. Fares for local bus service range from $1.25 to $3 (for an all-day pass); exact change is required. A $30 monthly "M-Card" is available for unlimited rides on all MCAT routes. However, if you want to get around efficiently—and want access to more places—you're best off renting a car.

Contacts Manatee County Area Transit *www.mymanatee.org.*

VISITOR INFORMATION

Contacts Bradenton Area Convention and Visitors Bureau. This organization has all you need to know about everything Bradenton, Anna Maria Island, Palmetto, and Ellenton have to offer. *941/729–9177* *www.bradentongulfislands.com.*

EXPLORING

Fodor's Choice ★

De Soto National Memorial. One of the first Spanish explorers to land in North America, Hernando de Soto came ashore with his men and 200 horses near what is now Bradenton in 1539; this federal park commemorates De Soto's expedition and the Native Americans he and his crew encountered. During the height of tourist season, from mid-December to late April, park staff and volunteers dress in period costumes at Camp Uzita, demonstrate the use of 16th-century weapons, and show how European explorers prepared and preserved food for their overland journeys. The season ends with a reenactment of the explorer's landing. The site also offers a film and short nature trail through the mangroves. *8300 De Soto Memorial Hwy.* *941/792–0458* *www.nps.gov/deso* *Free (donations accepted)* *Visitor center daily 9–5, grounds daily dawn–dusk.*

OFF THE BEATEN PATH

Gamble Plantation Historic State Park. Built in the 1840s, this antebellum mansion five miles northeast of Bradenton was home to Major Robert Gamble and is the headquarters of an extensive sugar plantation. It is the only surviving plantation house in South Florida. The Confederate secretary of state took refuge here when the Confederacy fell to Union forces. Picnic tables are available. Guided tours of the house are available six times a day. *3708 Patten Ave., Ellenton* *941/723–4536* *floridastateparks.org/gambleplantation* *Free, tours $6* *Weekends 8–sunset. Tours Thurs.–Mon. 8–5:40.*

Pine Avenue. Anna Maria Island's newly restored "Main Street" features numerous pricey mom-and-pop boutiques, including upscale yet beach-appropriate clothiers, beach-inspired home decor stores, and antique furniture shops. You can also find shops offering items such as quality vintage clothing and infused olive oil. The Anna Maria City Pier, which overlooks the southern end of Tampa Bay, sits at the end of the street. *Pine Ave., Anna Maria* *941/592–6642* *www.pineavenueinfo.com.*

OFF THE BEATEN PATH

Solomon's Castle. For a visit to the wild and weird side, particularly fun for children, head to this castle about 45 minutes east of Bradenton through orange groves and cattle farms. Artist and Renaissance man Howard Solomon began building the 12,000-square-foot always-in-progress work out of thousands of aluminum offset printing plates. Inside, you'll find tons of intrigues—everything from a knight assembled with Volkswagen parts to a chair fashioned out of 86 beer cans to an elephant made from seven oil drums. A restaurant serves sit-down lunches in a full-scale model of a Spanish galleon. It is also open Friday and

Saturday nights in season. ✉ *4585 Solomon Rd., Ona* ☎ *863/494–6077* 🌐 *www.solomonscastle.org* 🎫 *$10* 🕓 *Tues.–Sun 11–4; closed July–Sept.*

FAMILY **South Florida Museum and Parker Manatee Aquarium.** Snooty, the oldest manatee in captivity, is the headliner here. Programs about the endangered marine mammals run four times daily. View changing exhibits such as digital images of water and other natural resources in the East Gallery; glass cases and roll-out drawers on the second floor allow you to look at exhibits normally out of public view. At the Bishop Planetarium (with a domed theater screen), programs presented range from black holes to Jimi Hendrix, Pink Floyd, and other rockers. ✉ *201 10th St. W* ☎ *941/746–4131* 🌐 *www.southfloridamuseum.org* 🎫 *$18* 🕓 *Mon.–Sat. 10–5, Sun. noon–5. May, June, and Aug.–Dec., closed Mon.*

BEACHES

Anna Maria Island, Bradenton's 7-mile barrier island to the west, has a number of worthwhile beaches, as does Longboat Key. Manatee Avenue connects the mainland to the island via the Palma Sola Causeway, adjacent to which is a long, sandy beach fronting Palma Sola Bay. There are boat ramps, a dock, and picnic tables.

Anna Maria Bayfront Park. This narrow yet secluded beach fronts Tampa Bay at Passage Key Inlet and the Gulf of Mexico. It's also situated between two fishing piers. Don't forget to bring the picnic gear to this unforgettably scenic stretch of shoreline. **Amenities:** lifeguards; showers; toilets. **Best for:** solitude; sunset. ✉ *310 North Bay Blvd., adjacent to a municipal pier, Anna Maria Island.*

Coquina Beach. Singles and families flock to Coquina Beach, a wider swath of sand is at the southern end of Anna Maria Island. Beach walkers love this stretch since it's Anna Maria's longest beach, and it also attracts crowds of young revelers. **Amenities:** food and drink; lifeguards; showers; toilets. **Best for:** solitude; swimming; walking. ✉ *1800 Gulf Dr. S, Anna Maria Island.*

Cortez Beach. Towering Australian pines greet you at the entrance of this popular beach park, a favorite among locals and visitors alike. **Amenities:** lifeguards; showers; toilets. **Best for:** solitude; swimming; walking. ✉ *Gulf Blvd., between 5th and 13th Aves., Bradenton Beach.*

Greer Island Beach. Just across the inlet on the northern tip of Longboat Key, Greer Island Beach is accessible by boat or by car via North Shore Boulevard. You'll also hear this place referred to as Beer Can Island. The secluded peninsula has a wide beach and excellent shelling, but no facilities. **Amenities:** None. **Best for:** solitude; walking. ✉ *7500 Gulf of Mexico Dr., Longboat Key.*

Manatee Beach Park. In the middle of Anna Maria Island, Manatee County Beach is popular with beachgoers of all ages. Paid parking is in the gravel lot next to the beach. **Amenities:** food and drink; parking; showers; toilets. **Best for:** solitude; swimming; walking. ✉ *4000 S.R. 64, at Gulf Dr., Holmes Beach.*

DID YOU KNOW?

Sometimes called "sea cows," manatees are aquatic relatives of elephants. They can weigh more than 1,500 pounds and live 50-plus years. There are more than 3,000 in Florida's coastal waters.

WHERE TO EAT

$$$$ STEAKHOUSE Fodor's Choice ★ **Euphemia Haye.** A lush tropical setting on the barrier island of Longboat Key, this is one of the most romantic restaurants around. The staff is friendly and gracious, the food delightful, and the atmosphere contagious. Its popular dessert display is a sweet ending to the pricey menu items that feature signature dishes such as crisp roast duckling with bread stuffing, and flambéed prime peppered steak. The upstairs Haye Loft, once the home of the original owner's grandson, has been converted into a more casual bistro and lounge. *Average main: $40 ✉ 5540 Gulf of Mexico Dr., Longboat Key ☎ 941/383–3633 www.euphemiahaye.com Reservations essential No lunch.*

$ AMERICAN **Gulf Drive Café & Tiki.** Especially popular for breakfast (served all day), this unassuming landmark squats on the beach and serves cheap sit-down eats: mostly sandwiches, but also a sampling of entrées after 4 pm. *Average main: $14 ✉ 900 N. Gulf Dr. N, Bradenton Beach ☎ 941/778–1919.*

$$$ AMERICAN **Sandbar Seafood & Spirits.** If the grouper is not fresh, it is not on the menu at this beachfront restaurant. Ordered blackened, it can hold its own against the Island Salad made with mangoes, Gorgonzola, passion fruit, and pralines. The popular fish also goes over well here in taco form. Other fresh seafood options include a spicy Szechuan tilapia sandwich, and crab cakes and crab-crusted sea scallops, a blend of the Chesapeake and the Gulf. The outside deck sits on the beach—the view is spectacular and a great place to watch the sunset. *Average main: $22 ✉ 100 Spring Ave., Anna Maria Island ☎ 941/778–0444 www.groupersandwich.com.*

WHERE TO STAY

$$$ RENTAL **BridgeWalk.** This circa-1947 Caribbean colonial-style property is across from the beach and a community within itself. **Pros:** great location; variety of lodging and dining experiences. **Cons:** can be pricey. *Rooms from: $210 ✉ 100 Bridge St., Bradenton Beach ☎ 941/779–2545, 866/779–2545 www.silverresorts.com 28 apartments No meals.*

$$$$ RESORT **Longboat Key Club & Resort.** This spectacularly landscaped property is one of the best places to play golf in the state, and among the top tennis resorts in the country. **Pros:** upscale vibe; lovely grounds; most rooms have private balcony. **Cons:** service can feel snooty. *Rooms from: $379 ✉ 220 Sands Point Rd., Longboat Key ☎ 941/383–8821, 888/237–5545 www.longboatkeyclub.com 218 rooms and suites No meals.*

$$$ RESORT **Silver Surf Gulf Beach Resort.** A sister to BridgeWalk, the Silver Surf has the air of a well-maintained 1960s motel with a modern twist, thanks to recent renovations to all of the studios and full apartments. **Pros:** location; freshly renovated rooms and exterior; good value for your money. **Cons:** while nice, the rooms are still pretty basic (this is not luxury). *Rooms from: $160 ✉ 1301 Gulf Dr. N, Anna Maria Island, Bradenton Beach ☎ 941/778–6626, 800/441–7873 www.silverresorts.com 50 rooms No meals.*

Ringling Mansion Sarasota

GOLF

Buffalo Creek Golf Course. The excellent county-owned course was designed by Ron Garl to resemble a Scottish links course, making it among the more challenging courses in the area. Still, novice golfers have a shot here. There are water hazards on several holes (not to mention a gator or two), and the terrain varies throughout. Some consider it to be the best public golf course in the Tampa Bay area. All greens were renovated in 2014. Players can choose to play the whole course or just a quick 9-hole game. The clubhouse offers cold beer at the end of the course. ✉ *8100 Erie Rd., Palmetto* ☎ *941/776–2611* 🌐 *www.golfmanatee.com* 🎫 *$54 for 18 holes, $26 for 9 holes* ⛳ *18 holes, 7,005 yards, par 72.*

SARASOTA

30 miles south of Tampa and St. Petersburg.

Sarasota is a year-round destination and home to some of Florida's most affluent residents. Circus magnate John Ringling and his wife, Mable, started the city on the road to becoming one of the state's hotbeds for the arts. Today sporting and cultural events can be enjoyed anytime of the year, and there's a higher concentration of upscale shops, restaurants, and hotels here than in other parts of the Tampa Bay area. Across the water from Sarasota lie the barrier islands of Siesta Key and Lido Key, with myriad beaches, shops, hotels, condominiums, and houses.

GETTING HERE AND AROUND

Sarasota is accessible from Interstate 75, Interstate 275, and U.S. 41. The town's public transit company is Sarasota County Area Transit (SCAT). Fares for local bus service range from 75¢ to $3 (for an all-day pass); exact change is required. A $60 monthly "R-Card" is available for unlimited rides on all SCAT and Manatee County Area Transit (MCAT) routes. If you want to make it to the farther reaches of the area, though, renting a car is probably your best bet.

Contacts Sarasota County Area Transit (SCAT) ☎ *941/861–1234* 🌐 *www.scgov.net/scat.*

VISITOR INFORMATION

Contacts Sarasota Convention and Visitors Bureau. This organization has the skinny on South Tampa Bay. ✉ *701 N. Tamiami Trail* ☎ *941/957–1877* 🌐 *www.sarasotafl.org.*

EXPLORING

TOP ATTRACTIONS

FAMILY Fodor's Choice ★ **John and Mable Ringling Museum of Art.** Administered by Florida State University, the museum encompasses the entire Ringling estate, far more than just the art museum; there's also the Tibbals Learning Center and Circus Museums as well as Ca' d'Zan Mansion, the original Ringling home, and its expansive gardens. The entire compound covers 20 waterfront acres and also has the Historic Asolo Theater, restaurants, and a research library.

The **Art Museum** was a dream long in the making for John Ringling (of Ringling Brothers fame). Finally finished in 1931 after setbacks including a land bust and the death of his wife Mable, this enormous museum was originally built to house Ringling's mindblowingly expansive art collection. You'll find works ranging from Indian doorways elaborately carved with Jain deities to opulescent Baroque paintings from the likes of Rubens. There seems to be an endless number of rooms, themselves decorated in an appropriately gorgeous manner, housing these masterpieces. A wing that features traveling exhibits serves as a temporary home to many thought-provoking pieces throughout the year. The museum's exit opens out into an enormous courtyard, over which a towering statue of David replica presides, flanked by royal palms.

Circus magnate John Ringling's grand home, **Ca' d'Zan,** which was built along Sarasota Bay, was patterned after Doge's Palace in Venice. This exquisite mansion of 32 rooms, 15 bathrooms, and a 61-foot Belvedere Tower was completed in 1925, and today is the crowning jewel at the site of the Ringling Estate. Its 8,000-square-foot terrace overlooks the dock where Ringling's wife, Mable, moored her gondola. Mansion tours occur on the hour, and last half an hour. If you don't want a guided tour, show up on the half-hour for a self-guided tour.

Allot some extra time to wander around in the Mable Ringling's **Rose Garden,** a lush labyrinth surrounded by towering banyans and full of rare roses and haunting statues.

Don't let the name **Tibbals Learning Center** fool you. This Ringling estate attraction offers a colorful glimpse into a most wondrous element

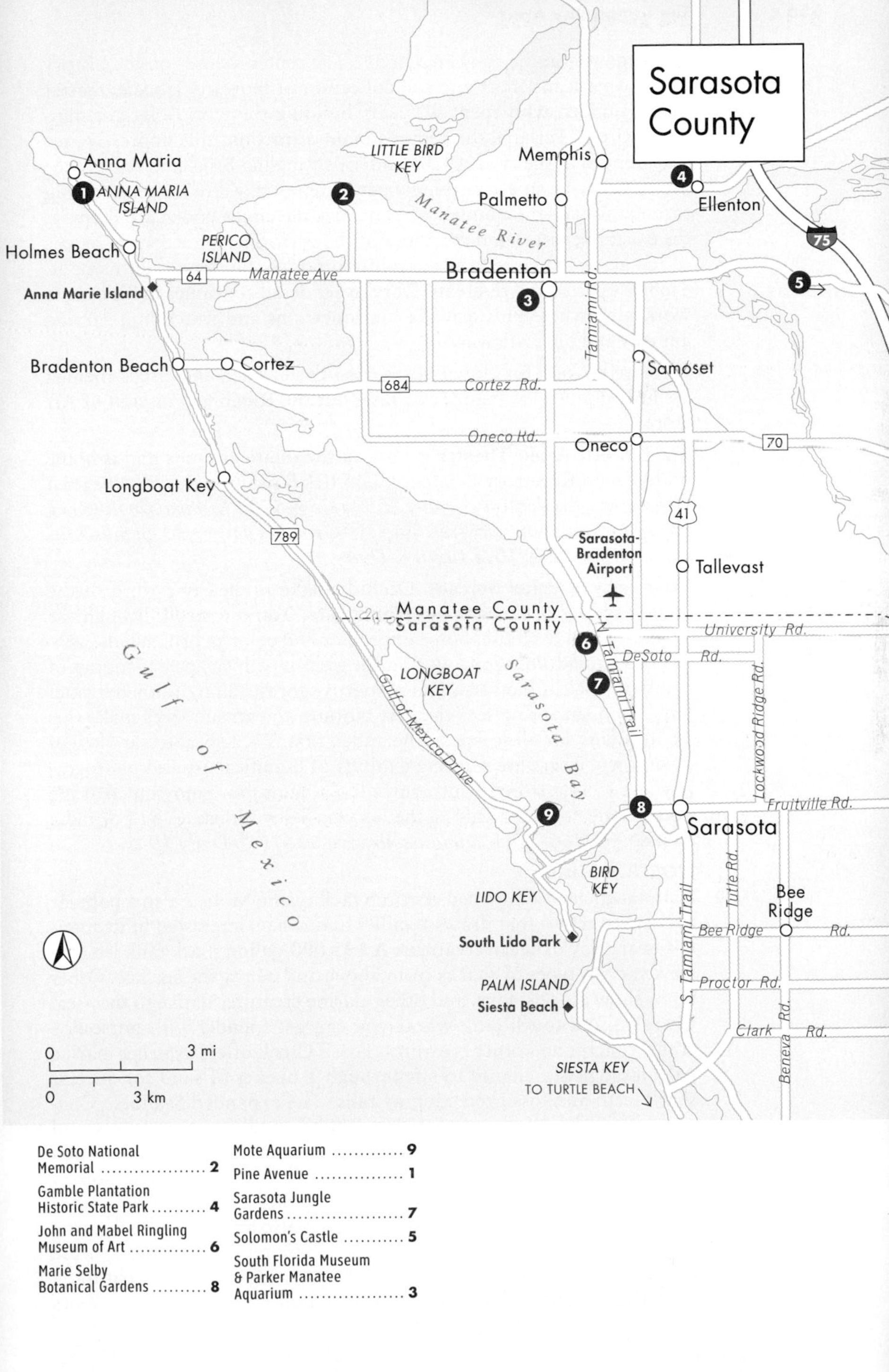
Sarasota County
Anna Maria
ANNA MARIA ISLAND
LITTLE BIRD KEY
Memphis
Palmetto
Ellenton
Manatee River
75
Holmes Beach
PERICO ISLAND
64
Manatee Ave
Bradenton
Anna Marie Island
Tamiami Rd.
Bradenton Beach
Cortez
Samoset
684
Cortez Rd.
Oneco Rd.
Oneco
70
Longboat Key
41
789
Sarasota-Bradenton Airport
Tallevast
Manatee County
Sarasota County
University Rd.
N Tamiami Trail
DeSoto Rd.
LONGBOAT KEY
Sarasota Bay
Gulf of Mexico
Gulf of Mexico Drive
Lockwood Ridge Rd.
Fruitville Rd.
Sarasota
BIRD KEY
LIDO KEY
S. Tamiami Trail
Tuttle Rd.
Bee Ridge
Bee Ridge Rd.
South Lido Park
PALM ISLAND
Proctor Rd.
Siesta Beach
Clark Rd.
Beneva Rd.
0
3 mi
0
3 km
SIESTA KEY
TO TURTLE BEACH
De Soto National Memorial 2
Gamble Plantation Historic State Park 4
John and Mabel Ringling Museum of Art 6
Marie Selby Botanical Gardens 8
Mote Aquarium 9
Pine Avenue 1
Sarasota Jungle Gardens 7
Solomon's Castle 5
South Florida Museum & Parker Manatee Aquarium 3

of a bygone era: the traveling circus. The center focuses on the history of the American circus and the collection of Howard Tibbals, master model builder, who spent 40 years building the world's largest miniature circus. Perhaps the center's main attraction, this impressive to-scale replica of the circa 1920s and '30s Ringling Bros. and Barnum & Bailey Circus is an astonishingly accurate portrayal of a circus coming through town—the number of pancakes the circus cooks are flipping, the exact likenesses and costumes of the performers, the correct names of the animals marked on the miniature mess buckets—you name it. Tibbals's passion to re-create every exact detail continues in his on-site workshop, where kids can ask him questions and watch him carving animals and intricate wagons.

If you're looking for clown noses, ringmaster hats, and circus-themed T-shirts, don't leave before checking out the **Ringling Museum of Art Store.**

The **Historic Asolo Theater** is also on the estate grounds and is home to the Asolo Repertory Company. ✉ *5401 Bay Shore Rd., ½ mile west of Sarasota-Bradenton Airport* ☎ *941/359–5700* 🌐 *www.ringling.org* 🎫 *$25 (art museum only free Mon.)* ⏲ *Grounds daily 9:30–6; museums and mansion daily 10–5 (until 8 Thurs.).*

Marie Selby Botanical Gardens. Orchids make up nearly a third of the 20,000 species of flowers and plants here. You can stroll through the Tropical Display House, home of orchids and colorful bromeliads gathered from rain forests, and wander the garden pathway past plantings of bamboo, ancient banyans, and mangrove forests along Little Sarasota Bay. Although spring sees the best blooms, the greenhouses make this an attraction for all seasons. The added bonus is a spectacular view of downtown. There are rotating exhibits of botanical art and photography in a 1934 restored Southern Colonial mansion. Enjoy lunch at the Local Coffee + Tea, a café in the historic Selby House. ✉ *811 S. Palm Ave.* ☎ *941/366–5731* 🌐 *www.selby.org* 🎫 *$19* ⏲ *Daily 10–5.*

WORTH NOTING

FAMILY **Mote Aquarium.** A renowned research facility, the Mote is also a popular tourist attraction that draws families and others interested in its international array of ocean creatures. A 135,000-gallon shark tank lets you view various types of sharks from above and below the surface. Other tanks show off eels, rays, and other marine creatures native to the area. There's also a touch tank where you can get friendly with horseshoe crabs, conchs, and other creatures. Fossil Creek offers aspiring marine paleontologists a chance to sift through a bucket of sand for ancient shark teeth and fossilized stingray tails. The expanded Seahorse Conservation Lab offers a glimpse into the unusual creatures' lives and how the aquarium is working to help them survive and thrive. Hugh and Buffett are the resident manatees and, though not as venerable as Snooty at the Parker Manatee Aquarium, they have lived here since 1996 as part of a research program. There's also a permanent sea-turtle exhibit. For an extra fee, Sarasota Bay Explorers (⇨ *see the separate listing under Boat Tours in Sports and the Outdoors*) offers boat tours from the museum's dock (reservations required), guided kayak tours through the mangroves, private tours and a "Nature Safari." ✉ *1600 Ken Thompson Pkwy., City Island* ☎ *941/388–4441* 🌐 *www.mote.org* 🎟 *Aquarium $19.75* ⏲ *Aquarium daily 10–5; boat tours daily at varying times.*

FAMILY **Sarasota Jungle Gardens.** One of Old Florida's charming, family-owned and -operated attractions, Sarasota Jungle Gardens fills 10 acres with native and exotic animals as well as tropical plants. The lush gardens date to 1939, and still have the small-world feel of yesterday's Florida. You'll find red-tailed hawks and great horned owls in the birds of prey show, American alligators and a variety of snakes in the reptile encounter, and bugs of many varieties in a show called Critters and Things. You can talk to trainers and get to know such plants as the rare Australian nut tree and the Peruvian apple cactus in the gardens. Also onsite are flocks of flamingos that guests can hand-feed, plus reptiles and a butterfly garden. ✉ *3701 Bay Shore Rd.* ☎ *941/355–5305* 🌐 *www.sarasotajunglegardens.com* 🎟 *$15* ⏲ *Daily 10–5.*

BEACHES

Fodor's Choice ★ **Siesta Beach.** With 40 acres of nature trails, this park is popular; you'll find tons of amenities. This beach has fine, powdery quartz sand that squeaks under your feet, very much like the sand along the state's northwestern coast. Don't forget to bring a volleyball—or a tennis racket. **Amenities:** food and drink; lifeguards; toilets. **Best for:** partiers; sunset; swimming; walking. ✉ *948 Beach Rd., Siesta Key.*

South Lido Park. At the southern tip of the island, South Lido Park has one of the best beaches in the region, but there are no lifeguards. The 100-acre park interacts with four significant bodies of water: the Gulf of Mexico, Big Pass, Sarasota Bay, and Brushy Bayou. The sugar-sand beach has plenty of early morning sand dollars and is a popular place to fish. Picnic as the sun sets through the Australian pines into the water. Facilities include nature trails, canoe and kayak trails, restrooms, and picnic grounds. This park was purchased by John Ringling in 1920 as part of his ambitious plan to develop island properties. His plan collapsed with the great Florida Land bust of 1926. Because of swift rip currents, swimming here is not recommended. **Amenities:** showers; toilets. **Best for:** solitude; walking. ✉ *2201 Ben Franklin Dr., Lido Key.*

Turtle Beach. A 14-acre beach-park that's popular with families, Turtle has 2,600 linear feet of beach frontage and is more secluded than most gulf beaches. Though narrower than most of the region's beaches, it's also much less crowded, so it doesn't feel so narrow. It's known for abundant sea turtles. It has covered picnic shelters, grills, and a volleyball court. Locals like the 40-site campground that is also open to visitors with advance reservations. Fittingly enough, this beach is near the über-mellow Turtle Beach Resort. **Amenities:** toilets. **Best for:** solitude; sunset; swimming; walking. ✉ *8918 Midnight Pass Rd., Siesta Key* ☎ *941/349–3839.*

WHERE TO EAT

$$$ CAFÉ Fodor's Choice ★ **Bijou Café.** Once a 50-seat 1920 gas station–turned-restaurant, the Bijou is now a 140-seat restaurant with the type of enchanting decor you might expect in a quaint, modern European café—think French windows and doors, sparkling glassware, bouquets of freshly picked flowers, and the soft glow of candlelight. Lunches begin with an inspired soup, salads, or sandwiches such as the pesto chicken salad croissant. Dinners emphasize fresh local produce and sustainable seafood. Opera season—typically February and March—is the only time Sunday dinner is served. *Average main: $30 1287 1st St. 941/366–8111 www.bijoucafe.net Apr.–Jan., closed Sun. No lunch weekends.*

$$ ITALIAN **Café Baci.** Specializing in Tuscan and Roman cuisine, Café Baci appeals to loyal locals and savvy travelers alike. Its menu highlights original family recipes; specialties range from fresh, succulent seafood dishes and homemade pastas to traditional veal recipes such as *piccata de vitella* simmered with white wine, lemon, and capers or grilled salmon served on spinach pesto risotto. From the moment you walk through the door, you'll enjoy the peaceful, elegant, Italian-inspired atmosphere. *Average main: $20 4001 S. Tamiami Trail 941/921–4848 www.cafebacisarasota.com No lunch weekends*

$$$$ CAFÉ **Café L'Europe.** Located in St. Armand's Circle, this sidewalk and indoor café has a spectacular menu featuring tableside specialties such as chateaubriand for two. Other popular entrées range from potato-crusted grouper and brandied duckling to rack of lamb. There's also a nice choice of wines by the glass. Veranda tables are a great place to watch shoppers and strollers. *Average main: $33 431 St. Armands Circle, Lido Key 941/388–4415 www.cafeleurope.net.*

$$$ AMERICAN **Michael's on East.** Not only do the lounge and piano bar, with their extensive wines and vintage cocktails, lure the after-theater set, but inspired cuisine and superior service also entice. Inside its Midtown Plaza shopping center location, you'll find a decor similar to New York's better bistros of the 1930s and '40s, but there is plenty of veranda seating for enjoying Sarasota's balmy weather. The fare ranges from bow-tie pasta with grilled chicken and sun-dried tomatoes to porcini-rubbed rack of lamb to roasted swordfish with red potatoes. The pecan-graham-crusted key lime tart served under a cloud of baked meringue is only one of the creative combinations for concluding your cuisine adventure. *Average main: $26 1212 East Ave. S 941/366–0007 www.michaelsoneast.com Closed Sun. No lunch Sat.*

$$ AMERICAN **The Old Salty Dog.** A menu of steamer and raw-bar options has been added to the much-enjoyed old favorites, including quarter-pound hot dogs, fish-and-chips, wings, and burgers. With views of New Pass between Longboat and Lido Keys, this is a popular stop for locals and visitors en route from Mote Aquarium and the adjoining bayfront park. Open-air dining area is comfortable even in summer, thanks to a pleasant breeze. Its bar is shaped from the hull of an old boat. There's another branch on Siesta Key (5023 Ocean Blvd., 941/349–0158). *Average main: $15 1601 Ken Thompson Pkwy., City Island 941/388–4311 www.theoldsaltydog.com Reservations not accepted.*

$$$$ AMERICAN **Ophelia's on the Bay.** Florida the way it should be: you can watch as dolphins swim past while blue herons lounge on the dock. Enjoy the flowering gardens while dining alfresco on the outdoor patio on its dock at Market #48 or in one of two casually elegant dining rooms. An ever-evolving menu highlights the Florida surroundings with selections such as Gulf of Mexico hog snapper with cracked pepper and orange honey, and Chilean salmon with blueberry lavender sauce. The tuna (bigeye, yellowfin, and more) is flown in from Hawaii thanks to owner Jane Ferro, who is also the grandniece of the restaurant's namesake. *Average main: $32 9105 Midnight Pass Rd., Siesta Key 941/349–2212 www.opheliasonthebay.net No lunch.*

$$ SOUTHERN **Owen's Fish Camp.** Nestled in a banyan-shaded corner of the hip Burns Court district of downtown Sarasota, this spot dishes out quintessentially Southern fare (though the menu is not geographically limited) that is particularly heavy on the seafood options—everything from an oyster po' boy with bacon to grilled giant prawns with chili, a popular appetizer. The restaurant is a converted cottage built in 1923, and the setting gives an additional layer of charm to a casual eatery that's already won the hearts of tourists and locals alike. Takeaway "jars" offered include shrimp and avocado cocktail, fried pickles, and boiled peanuts. Note: there can often be a wait, so get here early because you can't reserve a table. *Average main: $16 526 Burns Ct. 941/951–6936 owensfishcamp.com Reservations not accepted No lunch.*

$ AMERICAN **Yoder's.** Lines for meals stretch well beyond the hostess podium here. Pies—key lime, egg custard, banana cream, peanut butter, strawberry rhubarb, and others—are the main event at this family restaurant in the heart of Sarasota's Amish community. Daily specials typically include zesty goulash, chicken and dumplings, and pulled smoked pork. For breakfast, choose from French toast stuffed with cream cheese or perhaps a hearty stack of pancakes. Sandwiches include Manhattans (roast beef, turkey, or meat loaf on homemade bread with mashed potatoes and gravy). The entire village is always crowded, but there's plenty of waitstaff who keep tables clean and cleared, so the flow is steady. The decor retains its Old Florida efficiency appearance. *Average main: $10 3434 Bahia Vista 941/955–7771 www.yodersrestaurant.com Reservations not accepted Closed Sun.*

10

WHERE TO STAY

$$$$ B&B/INN **The Cypress, a Bed & Breakfast Inn.** The only bed-and-breakfast in downtown Sarasota, the inn has a delightful assortment of themed rooms. **Pros:** friendly staff; convenient to downtown; a five-minute drive (or a pleasant walk) from the beaches at Lido Key. **Cons:** no in-room phones. *Rooms from: $279 621 Gulfstream Ave. S 941/955–4683 www.cypressbb.com 2 rooms, 3 suites Multiple meal plans.*

$$ RENTAL **Gulf Beach Resort.** Lido Key's first motel, this beachfront condo complex has been designated a historic property. **Pros:** near shopping; well maintained; lots of beach; free Wi-Fi. **Cons:** basic rooms; motel feel. *Rooms from: $140 930 Ben Franklin Dr., Lido Key 941/388–2127, 800/232–2489 www.gulfbeachsarasota.com 8 rooms, 41 suites No meals.*

$$$$ HOTEL **Hyatt Regency Sarasota.** Popular among business travelers, the Hyatt Regency is contemporary in design and sits in the heart of the city across from the Van Wezel Performing Arts Hall. **Pros:** great location; stellar views. **Cons:** chain-hotel feel. *Rooms from: $250 ✉ 1000 Blvd. of the Arts ☎ 941/953–1234, 800/233–1234 🌐 www.sarasota.hyatt.com ⇨ 294 rooms, 12 suites 🍴 Multiple meal plans.*

$$$ RENTAL **Lido Beach Resort.** Superb gulf views can be found at this stylish beachfront resort. **Pros:** beachfront location; many rooms have kitchens. **Cons:** bland, somewhat dated furnishings. *Rooms from: $210 ✉ 700 Ben Franklin Dr., Lido Key ☎ 941/388–2161, 800/441–2113 🌐 www.lidobeachresort.com ⇨ 158 rooms, 64 suites 🍴 No meals.*

$$$$ HOTEL **Ritz-Carlton, Sarasota.** With a style that developers like to say is circus magnate John Ringling's realized dream, the Ritz is appointed with fine artwork and fresh-cut flowers. **Pros:** Ritz-style glitz; lots of amenities; attentive staff. **Cons:** long distance to golf course; not on the beach. *Rooms from: $450 ✉ 1111 Ritz-Carlton Dr. ☎ 941/309–2000, 800/241–3333 🌐 www.ritzcarlton.com/sarasota ⇨ 266 rooms, 30 suites 🍴 No meals.*

$$$$ HOTEL Fodor's Choice ★ **Turtle Beach Resort.** Reminiscent of a quieter time, many of the cottages at this friendly, affordable, family- and pet-friendly resort date to the 1940s, a romantic plus for yesteryear lovers. **Pros:** nice location; romantic setting; self-serve laundry and Wi-Fi included. **Cons:** far from the area's cultural attractions. *Rooms from: $299 ✉ 9049 Midnight Pass Rd., Siesta Key ☎ 941/349–4554 🌐 www.turtlebeachresort.com ⇨ 7 rooms, 3 suites, 10 cottages 🍴 No meals.*

NIGHTLIFE AND THE ARTS

NIGHTLIFE

Blase Cafe and Lounge. Siesta Key Village doesn't shut down after the dinner crowd vacates its eateries. To the contrary, there are quite a few places to grab a beverage or two. Blase is a good pick if you're in a martini mood. Although the café has some pretty sophisticated fare, you can be dressed casual if you want to belly up to the circular bar. *✉ 5263 Ocean Blvd., Siesta Key ☎ 941/349–9822 🌐 www.theblasecafe.com.*

5 O'clock Club. If you find yourself in Southside Village after dinner and are looking for a watering hole that offers live music, look no further. This spot has been one of Sarasota's key music venues for years. Musical offerings differ by night, but you can expect to hear blues, jazz, or rock covers on a given night. If you're looking for a more upscale club, look elsewhere; this is a no-frills kind of place. *✉ 1930 Hillview St. ☎ 941/366–5555 🌐 www.5oclockclub.net.*

Gator Club. A famous nightclub located in a beautifully restored, brick historic cornerstone building downtown, the Gator Club has live music and dancing 365 days a year. *✉ 1490 Main St. ☎ 941/366–5969 🌐 www.thegatorclub.com.*

Straight Up Night Club @ 15 South. St. Armand's Circle is a pretty bustling place in the daytime, but the action continues into the wee hours—if you know where to find it. This bar, which is upstairs from an upscale restaurant of the same name, has an excellent martini list and plenty of live music, especially salsa. ✉ *15 S. Blvd. of the Presidents, Lido Key* ☎ *941/388–1555* 🌐 *www.15southristorante.com.*

THE ARTS

Asolo Repertory Theatre. One of the best theaters in Sarasota stages productions from November to June in varying venues, which include the Historic Asolo Theater in the Ringling Estate. ✉ *5555 Tamiami Trail* ☎ *941/351–8000* 🌐 *www.asolorep.org.*

The Players Theatre. A long-established community theater, having launched such actors as Montgomery Clift and Paul Reubens, this troupe performs comedies, special events, live concerts, and musicals. ✉ *838 N. Tamiami Trail, U.S. 41 and 9th St.* ☎ *941/365–2494* 🌐 *www.theplayers.org.*

Sarasota Opera. Performing in a historic 1,122-seat downtown theater, the Sarasota Opera features internationally known artists singing the principal roles, supported by a professional chorus of young apprentices. ✉ *The Edwards Theater, 61 N. Pineapple Ave.* ☎ *941/328–1300* 🌐 *sarasotaopera.org.*

SHOPPING

St. Armand's Circle has a cluster of oh-so-exclusive shops and laid-back restaurants. It's just east of Lido Beach.

SHOPPING AREAS

Siesta Key Village. Not too far from Siesta Key's wildly popular beaches is a cluster of shops, restaurants, and watering holes you won't want to miss. This is a great place to shop and grab a bite after a the beach—or earlier if it's not a beach day. Park in the municipal lot at the end of Avenida Madera, then stroll down Ocean Boulevard, where you'll find clusters of upscale shops and a range of restaurants and bars. ✉ *Ocean Blvd., between Beach Rd. and Av. Madera, Siesta Key* 🌐 *www.siestakeyvillage.org.*

Southside Village. This is one of Sarasota's newer spots, with tons of sidewalk cafes, hip boutiques, jewelry stores, and an excellent gourmet market. This place hasn't gotten as much attention as St. Armand's Circle, but it's also got a much shorter history. It's popular among locals and is now starting to get on the radar for visitors. ✉ *Osprey Ave. at Hillview St.* ☎ *941/366–0771.*

St. Armand's Circle. No visit to Sarasota is complete without a visit to this busy yet laid-back shopping and dining hub. One can literally refer to it as a hub because it's arranged around a large traffic circle in the middle of Lido Key. You'll find a sprinkling of upscale retail chains, including White House Black Market, but the area's small, imaginative boutiques are the real draw. Among them is Foxy Lady, which sells trendy women's clothing. The Met is also a good option for women's fashion. St. Armand's Circle also offers plenty of dining/desert (especially ice cream) options, nightlife, and just plain people watching. Some days you can even spot a busker or two performing on one of the area's many street corners. ✉ *300 Madison Dr.* ☎ *941/388–1554* 🌐 *www.starmandscircleassoc.com.*

SPORTS AND THE OUTDOORS

BOAT TOURS

Sarasota Bay Explorers. Many visitors to the Mote Aquarium take the 105-minute boat trip onto Sarasota Bay. Conducted by Sarasota Bay Explorers, all boat trips are done in conjunction with the aquarium and leave from the aquarium's dock. The crew brings marine life on board, explains what it is, and throws it back to swim away. You are almost guaranteed to see bottlenose dolphins. Reservations are recommended. You can also charter the *Miss Explorer,* a 24-foot Sea Ray Sundeck, or take a guided kayak or nature tour. ⊠ *Mote Aquarium, 1600 Ken Thompson Pkwy.* ☎ *941/388–4200* 🌐 *www.sarasotabayexplorers.com* 🎫 *Boat tour $27, kayak tour $55, nature tour $45, charters $295–$445* ⏲ *Tours daily at 11, 1:30, and 4 (reservations required).*

FISHING

Flying Fish Fleet. Several boats can be chartered for deep-sea fishing, and there are daily group trips on a "party" fishing boat. ⊠ *2 Marina Plaza, U.S. 41, on the bay front at Marina Jack* ☎ *941/366–3373* 🌐 *www.flyingfishfleet.com.*

GOLF

Bobby Jones Golf Course. This public 45-hole course is over a century old and caters to a range of golfers. The setting is lush and green, with plenty of live oak trees and water. The grounds here are so pleasant that many choose to walk their chosen course, of which there are three. The American Course is best for less experienced golfers or those who want to practice their short shot, and features a range of lakes and varied terrain. The British Course is slightly more challenging, offering longer fairways dotted with water hazards and sand bunkers. The Gillespie Executive Course is recommended for beginners or those lacking the time needed for a full 18 holes. A large ravine divides much of the course from several of its greens approaches. ⊠ *1000 Circus Blvd.* ☎ *941/365–2200* 🌐 *www.bobbyjonesgolfclub.com* 🎫 *$25 for 9 holes, $35 for 18 holes* 🏌 *American Course: 18 holes, 6,031 yards, par 71; British Course: 18 holes, 6,710 yards, par 72; Gillespie Executive Course: 9 holes, 1,716 yards, par 30.*

KAYAKING

Sarasota Bay Explorers, which operates from the Mote Aquarium, also offers guided kayaking trips *(see ⇨ Boating)*.

Siesta Sports Rentals. Up for rent here are kayaks, bikes, beach chairs, scooters, and beach wheelchairs and strollers. Guided kayaking trips are also available. ⊠ *6551 Midnight Pass Rd., Siesta Key* ☎ *941/346–1797* 🌐 *www.siestasportsrentals.com.*

INDEX

I

J

K

N

O

P

Q

R

S

T

U

V

W

Y

Z

PHOTO CREDITS

Front cover: Vidler Steve/age fotostock [Description: Cinderella Castle, Magic Kingdom].1-2,˝ Disney. 5, SeaWorld Parks & Entertainment. Chapter 1: Experience Orlando and the Parks: 8-9, Universal Orlando Resort. 11, Universal Orlando. 12, Busch Entertainment Corporation. 13 (left), Universal Orlando Resort. 13 (right), PrincessAshley/Flickr. 14 (left), versageek/Flickr. 14 (top center), tom. arthur/Flickr. 14 (top right and bottom), Thomas_Jung/Flickr. 15 (top right), Universal Orlando Resort. 15 (top center), Troy House. 15 (bottom), Universal Orlando Resort. 15 (right), Busch Entertainment Corporation. 16, SeaWorld Parks & Entertainment. 17 (left), Stig Nygaard/Flickr. 17 (right), liangjinjian/Flickr. 18 (left), lrargerich/Flickr. 18 (right), Sky Hotels & Resort. 19 (left), The School House/ Flickr. 19 (right), sanctumsolitude/Flickr. 20, PrincessAshley/Flickr. 21 (left). Universal Orlando Resort. 21 (right), PrincessAshley/ Flickr. 22, VISIT FLORIDA. 25-26,˝ Disney. 27, Rennett Stowe/Flickr. 28 (left), Cruise News Weekly/Flickr. 28 (right), sanctumsolitude/Flickr. 29, Richard Cummins / age fotostock. 30 (left), flickrized/Flickr. 30 (right), flickrized/Flickr. 31, Cruise News Weekly/Flickr. 32,˝ Disney. 33, VISIT FLORIDA. 36 (left),˝ Disney. 36(right)-37, Orlando CVB. 38,˝ Disney. 39, Torres, Leora.l from Orlando, FL, USA/Wikimedia Commons. 40, Nick Traveller/Flickr. 41 (left), Jeff Kern/Flickr. 41 (right), 2Eklectik/Flickr. 42, coconut wireless/Flickr. 43, SeaWorld Parks & Entertainment. 44 (left), Stig Nygaard/Flickr. 44 (right), liangjinjian/Flickr. 45(left), lrargerich/Flickr. 45 (right), Sky Hotels & Resort. 46 (left), The School House/Flickr. 46 (right), sanctumsolitude/Flickr. Chapter 2: Planning An Orlando Vacation: 47, LimeBye/ Flickr. 52, ˝ Disney. 53, @ LaRsNoW @/Flickr. 54, Orlando CVS. 57, whiteafrican/Flickr. 61,Caza No 7/Flickr. 71, Walt Disney World Resort. Chapter 3: Where To Stay: 73, Daniels & Roberts INC/The Waldorf Astoria Orlando. 74, Greencolander/Flickr. 79, coconut wireless/ Flickr. 80, Troy House. 93. Disney's Animal Kingdom Lodge. 102, Universal Orlando Resort. 108. Dan Forer. Chapter 4: Where To Eat: 115, Emeril's. 116, ˝ Disney. 117 (bottom left), ckramer/Flickr. 117 (top right), meshmar2/Flickr. 118, Orlando CVB. 139, ˝ Disney. 140, Karen L/ Flickr (CC BYNC-SA 2.0). 141, Thomas_Jung/Flickr. 142 (top), JeffChristiansen/Flickr. 142 (bottom), Loren Javier/Flickr. 143 (left and top right), PrincessAshley/Flickr. 143 (bottom right), marada/Flickr. 144 (top),Thomas_Jung/Flickr. 144 (bottom), PrincessAshley/Flickr. 145 (left), jason tinder/Flickr. 145 (right), JeffChristiansen/Flickr. 146, Thomas_Jung/Flickr. Chapter 5: Walt Disney World: 171, hyku/ Flickr. 172, d4rr3ll/Flickr. 173, vanguardist/Flickr. 174, Paul Beattie/Flickr. 179, 185, 189, and 192, JoshMcConnell/Flickr. 194, SteamFan/Wikimedia Commons. 196, Photos 12 / Alamy. 197 and 198 (left and top right), Everett Collection. 198 (bottom right), WALT DISNEY PICTURES / Ronald Grant Archive / Mary Evans/Everett Collection. 198 (bottom), Dashu Pagla/Flickr. 199 (top left),˝Walt Disney Co./ Everett Collection. 199 (bottom left and right), Everett Collection. 199 (bottom), daryl_mitchell/ Flickr. 200 (top left), Sleeping Beauty Castle - Disneyland Paris by David Jafra www.flickr.com/photos/bartworldv6/4965387310/Attribution License. 200 (bottom left), Bob B. Brown/Flickr. 200 (right), seanosh/Flickr. 200 (bottom),Buena Vista Pictures/Courtesy Everett Collection. 201 (top left), Walt Disney Co./Courtesy Everett Collection. 201 (top right), Prosthetic Lips/Flickr. 201 (bottom), Walt Disney Co./Courtesy Everett Collection. 203, Orlando CVB. 204, Sam Howzit/ Flickr (CC BY 2.0). 211, ckramer/Flickr. 214, Growl Roar/Flickr. 220, ckramer/Flickr. 231,˝ Disney. 238, yeowatzup/Flickr. 243, ckramer/Flickr. 246, yeowatzup/Flickr. 251, CCRcreations/Flickr. 263, daryl_mitchell/Flickr. 272, Paul Beattie/Flickr. 281, tom.arthur/Flickr. 283, marada/ Flickr. 284, Jason Pratt/Flickr. 290, PrincessAshley/ Flickr. 296, PrincessAshley/Flickr. 298,˝ Disney. 305, Orlando CVB. 310,˝ Disney. Chapter 6: Universal Orlando: 315, Universal Orlando Resort. 316, Universal Orlando Resort. 317, (top), bea&txm/ Flickr. 317 (bottom), 318, and 321, Universal Orlando Resort. 329, Universal Orlando. 335, Universal Orlando Resort. 342, divemasterking2000/ Flickr. 354, Jessica Walsh. 357, Universal Orlando Resort. 360, PCL/Alamy. 363, Sam Hawzit/Flickr (CC BY 2.0). 366-371, Universal Orlando Resort. Chapter 7: Wet N Wild: 373-376, 378, and 383, Wet 'n Wild. Chapter 8: Seaworld, Discovery Cove, And Aquatica: 385, Jason Collier. 386, Cybjorg/Wikimedia Commons. 387 (top), Fantaz/Flickr. 387 (bottom), Wendy Piersall (@eMom)/Flickr. 388-416, SeaWorld Parks & Entertainment. 417, Jason Collier. 421, SeaWorld Parks & Entertainment. Chapter 9: Orlando And Environs: 425-426, VISIT FLORIDA. 427 (top and bottom), Orlando CVB. 428, Kissimmee - The Heart of Florida/Flickr. 430, Orlando CVB. 436. Kissimmee- The Heart of Florida/Flickr. 441, Orlando CVB. 451, Orlando CVB. 459, spakattacks/Flickr. 465, Courtesy of The Charles Hosmer Morse Museum of American Art. 474-75, jurvetson/Flickr. 476, thelastminute/Flickr. 477, yeowatzup/Flickr. 478 (all) and 479 (right), Kennedy Space Center. 480, by jonworth/Flickr. 481, bnhsu/Flickr. 486, (c) Louishenault/ Dreamstime.com. Chapter 10: The Tampa Bay Area: 489, (c) Sayran/ Dreamstime.com. 490 (bottom), CREDIT:VISIT FLORIDA. 490 (top), The TECO Line. 491 (top), Marje Cannon/istockphoto. 491 (bottom), gracious_tiger/Shutterstock. 492-493, Busch Entertainment Corporation. 494, istockphoto. 506, Martin Bennett/ Alamy. 522, Seymour Levy, Fodors.com member. 533, Ed Wolfstein/Icon SMI. 534 (top), Mtrommer |

Dreamstime.com. 534 (bottom), Asklar | Dreamstime.com. 535 (top), Evan Meyer/Shutterstock. 535 (bottom), 536 (bottom background photo), Mtrommer | Dreamstime.com, 536 (top), GARY IROTHSTEIN/Icon SMI. 536-37 (logos), wikipedia.org. 537 (background photo), Bokdavid | Dreamstime.com. 539, watland, Fodors.com member. 542, Richard T. Nowitz/age fotostock. 551, TIPTON DONALD/ age fotostock. 553, Elizabeth Shevloff, Fodors.com member. Back cover (from left to right): © Disney; LimeBye/Flickr (CC BY 2.0); Douglas Nesbitt. Spine: © Disney.

ABOUT OUR WRITERS

Tampa Bay and Naples updater and beach lover **Kate Bradshaw** lives in the Gulf Coast town of St. Pete Beach and writes for various Tampa Bay news, environmental, and entertainment outlets. On weekends, you may spot her strumming her guitar at a local beach haunt. Born in the Chicago area, Kate has lived in Hawaii, New Zealand, and New Mexico, among other places. She is proud to now be a Florida resident, and with her coverage for Fodor's, hopes to convey to visitors all the beauty and wonder of her adopted home.

Rona Gindin, who worked on the Where to Eat chapter, is a freelance writer, editor, and TV personality specializing in restaurants and travel. She is the dining editor of *Orlando Life Magazine*; the author of *The Little Black Book of Walt Disney World*, and regularly talks about area restaurants on local TV shows. She also contributes to *Zagat*, *Go*, Epicurious.com, and other print and online publications.

Where to Stay writer **Jennifer Greenhill-Taylor** has been a journalist for more than two decades—working as a travel editor, theater and film critic, wire editor, and freelance writer/editor. She was born in Edinburgh, Scotland, has lived in four countries and a dozen states, and travels widely for pleasure and profit. She lives in Orlando with her partner, playwright and freelance writer Joseph Reed Hayes, and enjoys sharing her extensive research on the area's hospitality with friends and family.

Freelance writer **Jennie Hess** covered what's new at Walt Disney World and across Orlando and its environs for this edition. When she's not trekking through theme parks or exploring Orlando's many treasures, Jennie keeps us up to date on the city's growth and the evolving Disney kingdom. Born in York, Pennsylvania, she has lived in Florida since 1979 and was a newspaper journalist before enlisting as a Disney publicist during the 1990s when Walt's world experienced a decade of rapid growth. A Fodor's contributor for more than a decade, Jennie lives in Orlando with her attorney husband, Walter. Sons Nathan and Sam, now in college, are Disney water park experts and help her update all rides involving high-speed splashdowns.

Orlando updater **Steve Master** can hear the engines roar, literally, from his Port Orange, Florida, home, 10 miles south of famed Daytona International Speedway. Steve spent 20 years as a sports writer for the *Daytona Beach News Journal,* where he won many awards, including a 2007 national honor from the Associated Press Sports Editors. He has written commentary for *NASCAR Illustrated* and covered travel for Orbitz Worldwide. Currently, he's an assistant professor of communication at Embry-Riddle Aeronautical University in Daytona Beach.

Gary McKechnie, who covered all of Universal and SeaWorld, knows a lot about Florida—his native state. During his student days, he worked as a Walt Disney World ferryboat pilot, Jungle Cruise skipper, steam train conductor, doubledecker bus driver, and was also an improv comedian at Epcot. He wrote the award-winning *Great American Motorcycle Tours*, the nation's best-selling motorcycle guidebook, and, following years of travel and research, National Geographic's *USA 101*, which highlights 101 iconic American places, events, and festivals. Gary also speaks on America's cultural heritage aboard the Cunard Line ships *Queen Mary 2* and *Queen Victoria* and at business and tourism meetings across America.